2013 Edition

Exclusive Profiles of America's Top Colleges

The Only College Rankings Based on ALUMNI SUCCESS

alumnifactor.com

ISBN#: 978-0-9859765-0-7

School photo attributions are listed on page 490.

Published by *The Alumni Factor*
PO Box 2744
Atlanta, GA 30301
404-889-8477
www.alumnifactor.com

First edition

Please visit *The Alumni Factor* website at www.alumnifactor.com.

Your comments and corrections are welcome. Please send them to:
The Alumni Factor
PO Box 2744
Atlanta, GA 30301
help@alumnifactor.com

Printed and bound in the United States

For parents,
who want the best for their children

For high school students,
who hope, dream and strive

For alumni,
who understand the impact of their college experience

The Alumni Factor
Table of Contents

Acknowledgements i

Introduction iii

CHAPTER 1 **Methodology** 1
- How We Determine the Rankings 2
- Frequently Asked Questions 3

CHAPTER 2 **Exclusive Rankings of Top Colleges and Universities** 5
- Liberal Arts Colleges 7
- National Universities 7
- Regional Universities 8
- All Schools Combined 9

CHAPTER 3 **Alumni Rate Their College Experience** 13
- Intellectual Development 17
- Social and Communication Skills Development 26
- Spiritual Development 29
- Friendship Development 32
- Preparation for Career Success 37
- Immediate Job Opportunities 40

CHAPTER 4 **Alumni Provide an Overall Assessment of Their College Today** 43
- Would Graduates Personally Choose Their College Again? 45
- Was College a Good Value for the Money? 48
- Would Graduates Recommend Their College to a Prospective Student Today? 51

CHAPTER 5 **Financial Success of Graduates** 55

CHAPTER 6 **Overall Happiness of Graduates** 67

CHAPTER 7 **Alumni Giving by College** 71

CHAPTER 8 **Graduation Rate by College** 79

CHAPTER 9 **Ultimate Outcomes℠ – Our Exclusive Measures of a School's Effectiveness** 83

CHAPTER 10 **Beliefs, Views & Politics of Graduates by College** 93

CHAPTER 11 **Overviews of Top Colleges and Universities** 133

CHAPTER 12 **Statistical Reliability of Our Methodology** 491
- Dr. David M. Goldsman, Ph.D., – Georgia Institute of Technology 492

Index 494

The Alumni Factor
Acknowledgments

A project of this magnitude could not have been completed without the help and collaboration of a uniquely talented group of dedicated friends, all interested in improving our colleges and universities – a challenging task, given that America's portfolio of colleges is broadly considered to be the finest in the world.

Dr. David Goldsman has played a unique and integral role in the development of *The Alumni Factor*. As an independent advisor, he was critical in shaping our methodology to ensure rigor, removal of bias and statistical reliability. His objectivity and expertise has been at the foundation of our ranking system, and without it our end product would not be nearly as sound as it is today. The fact that he has agreed to formally join our Advisory Board to continue in this capacity on an ongoing basis is something for which we are grateful.

We are extraordinarily fortunate to have had more than our fair share of the skills and passions of program manager and overall get-it-done champion Amanda Atkins, Jill Pullen and Jason Wade from Excelovation, Inc. and graphic designer Elaine Callahan. Each of these professionals has been with us from the start and added immense value to this work. At its core, this is a book of numbers, and we owe a tremendous debt of gratitude to Ana Lawless for wading into those numbers, making sure what we said in our prose and in our charts matched our data – at every revision. We also wish to thank Michael Goldsman and Paul Goldsman, who were very helpful in research and editing throughout the entire process of writing this book.

Gathering, analyzing and drawing accurate conclusions from the more than 2.2 million pieces of data we gathered in our research also required the wisdom, insight and counsel of a number of academics and administrators who have deep experience in post-secondary education. Here again, we are indeed fortunate that many talented professionals in college education today gave us their insight and ideas to improve our work. We are indebted to them for their ideas, their questions and their challenging candor. We are equally indebted to many high school advisors, guidance counselors, principals and heads of schools for their feedback. Creating a new methodology for assessing and ranking colleges is serious work and needs to be vetted with a variety of experts to ensure objectivity and credibility. The extent to which credibility is evident in this work is due largely to the input and expertise of these professionals. The blame for any lack thereof rests solely with *The Alumni Factor* team.

It would also have been impossible to write this book without the insights of tens of thousands of alumni from across the country who gave generously of their time to provide the responses and information we needed to determine actual outcomes for graduates, by college. As we further explain in the book, this group of US college graduates comprises some of the smartest, most powerful, most influential group of Americans alive today. They are at the forefront of the latest thinking and on the leading edge of the most innovative ideas in virtually every field in America today, from business and law, to medicine and the arts, to entertainment and government, to science and technology. We needed to thoroughly understand the role their college played in their overall lives and capture their insights about their college today. What began to emerge was a very clear picture of the unique capabilities of each college with regard to the development of their graduates. Needless to say, we are deeply grateful for the investment of time they made in our study, without which our work would have been impossible.

In the course of conducting formal consumer research, countless current college students, high school students and their parents shared their hopes and fears, as well as their experiences and frustrations with the college application process. We were humbled by their openness and honesty and hope our efforts do them justice.

We simply would not be writing this book, nor would we have begun the laborious process of conducting the necessary research, without a deep and abiding admiration and respect for the spectacular portfolio of US colleges and universities. They have educated our best and brightest for generations, demonstrating to the world the irreplaceable value of post-secondary education in human and societal progress over the last two centuries. Our US colleges serve as one of the world's brightest beacons of hope for continued human progress. It is our hope that this work can make even a small contribution towards helping each school move closer to the critically important and wonderfully ambitious mission statements that define their purpose and vision.

We would also like to salute those pioneers who have been working so diligently to refocus our K-12 system with outcomes-based measurements and accountability. No system is perfect, and the attempts in K-12 have certainly not been without controversy. Yet the fervent desire to focus on results to improve the lives of millions of children is admirable – and provides us with daily inspiration.

We would like to acknowledge the love, support, inspiration and forbearance from our families. What started as a spark of curiosity grew to a project beyond our imaginings. Without their patience and understanding, none of this would have been possible.

The Alumni Factor Team

The Alumni Factor
Introduction

This book began with a simple premise – that there is a better way to assess and rank colleges and universities in America than those currently being offered. The primary outcomes of most of today's rankings are:

1. To provide readers a view of what life is like as an undergraduate, and
2. To give insight into ***who comes into*** the college.

We, on the other hand, are more interested in ***who comes out***.

Our aim is to understand how well a college or university actually develops and shapes its students, and what becomes of them after they graduate. To accomplish this, we knew we would have to listen carefully to what has been the missing voice in college rankings – the voice of the alumni themselves – the only people who truly understand the role their college played in their personal development and in their overall lives. We are interested in the actual ***outcomes*** experienced by college graduates and the role their college played in creating those outcomes. We believe this information regarding graduate outcomes is truly essential to understanding and assessing our colleges and universities today.

The Alumni Factor has three primary goals as part of its overall mission:

1. To give prospective students and their parents a more empowering, performance-based method of measuring and choosing colleges.

2. To give colleges and universities an objective assessment of their performance, based on the actual results of and input from their own alumni, which can be compared to other relevant colleges and universities. This is often difficult for an individual school to achieve on its own, but is essential to its improvement.

3. To give college alumni themselves a better perspective on the role their college played in their personal development and in the development of others, and how it compares to other colleges. We've learned that not only is this interesting and entertaining for alumni, but that it also helps improve colleges, since alumni are often active and influential voices as colleges set their improvement agendas.

In line with these goals, *The Alumni Factor* provides a detailed, in-depth profile of graduates from 177 of our nation's top colleges. The profiles were constructed almost entirely with data and insights from the actual college alumni themselves. With four years of data collection, statistical research and analysis behind us, tens of thousands of graduates from America's best known colleges and universities have let us into their lives (at least statistically), to share their views of their college, their financial and career success, their happiness in life and their views on some of the most relevant social and political issues of the day. By understanding these real-world results, we can compare the responses of one group of graduates versus any other group, and use that information as the basis for understanding a school's actual performance versus its mission, its competition and its "reputation." Unfortunately, a school's "reputation" is the basis of much of the current thinking and ranking information being offered today. While a school's reputation is relevant, it has been given far too much weight in prominent college rankings. This has driven colleges to compete in a race for esteem that can take their focus off the main purpose of the institution and to implement changes that improve their rankings without helping students.

Most college rankings offered today measure virtually everything BUT the actual performance of the schools or their graduates. There are rankings of campus beauty, reputation, location, weather, the attractiveness of the student body, the supply and demand for the college (selectivity), class size, percent of faculty who are PhDs and a recent favorite – "hottest" – an interesting dynamic in itself. While each of these, at some point, may be important to understand when choosing a college, they are rarely sufficient, and often stand as a poor proxy for that which most rankings purport to measure: actual educational quality. Many of today's rankings seem intent on reducing colleges to mere caricatures – through oversimplified summaries that randomly emphasize one aspect over others in order to make a point. Like a celebrity who is famous because he is famous, or a political candidate who is elected because of name recognition, having your school fall high (or low) on any of these lists is the single largest determining factor of whether it will be ranked high (or low) on said list next year. And if it does change slightly from year to year, it certainly is not clear that the reason for the change had anything, even remotely, to do with a change in the school's delivery of real learning and development to its students. Yet these rankings are the focus of many college officials as they attempt to steer their brand's reputation toward higher rankings and greater esteem.

America's "elite" four-year colleges and universities, unlike community colleges and other less celebrated four-year programs, have been engaged in a fierce "esteem contest" to collect every positive endorsement available from every imaginable source. This creates a cycle wherein the more positive buzz around a college, the more students apply; the fewer applicants the college can actually accept (remember that "buzz" can be built faster than new dorm rooms); the lower their "acceptance rate" (a sign of selectivity which in turn drives esteem); the better the applicant pool becomes, the higher the price they can command; and, the colleges hope, the greater the donations from alumni and others to fund a larger endowment and increased investment toward the college's vision and mission. At the end of this *brand-building cycle*, administrators hope they can provide a better education.

This is the *brand-building cycle* that occupies the time and attention of virtually all college administrators, and it has worked quite well for those colleges that have mastered the art. Although many academic purists cringe at such a commercial concept, brand-building is being practiced regularly and is heavily used as a tool to market institutions of higher education. It is the rare prominent college or university that is not resolutely engaged in this process. The marketing of colleges and universities not only occupies the attention of the faculty and administrators, it increases expectations for a college and raises the bar for the institution to provide a better product for its students.

In today's world, we have every right to set high expectations for our post-secondary schools. We expect our colleges and universities to thoroughly teach and develop our youth – to enhance them intellectually, socially, politically, from a values or morals standpoint, and to prepare them for a meaningful life of contribution and fulfillment along whatever path a student chooses. We created *The Alumni Factor* because we are interested in knowing which colleges excel in fully developing students. **We want to pierce the bubble of reputation to understand how graduates actually perform post- graduation – and hear what they have to say about the job their college did to prepare them.** While there may be a number of legitimate means to assess this, listening to and analyzing the graduate is rarely used as a method. As the "output" of these schools, we believe graduates are the most authoritative source of this information. And while we may never know with statistical certainty the role their particular college played among the many factors impacting their life's path, we believe our methodology is a significant step toward that end and finally puts the "customer" – the graduate – at the center of the rankings debate.

What do we learn when we place the voice of "the customer" – actual college graduates – at the center of the college rankings debate? And what might prospective college students and their parents take away to inform their own application processes?

1. **Any definition of success is complex, personal and multi-faceted. Yet the obsession with attending "prestigious schools" overlooks this complexity, reducing one's very unique quest for lifelong success down to something ill-defined and generic.**
   Defining success is a tricky proposition – so we did not attempt to do it lightly, or on our own. We studied the current research regarding the objectives students have when attending colleges. We also asked students,

parents and graduates themselves what their most important goals were in choosing a college. From those insights we structured our research to understand how well colleges actually performed in developing students against the desired benefits identified. The 15 factors we measure and report upon in our ranking were ultimately those we deemed most important based on student, graduate and parental input. Anyone going through the college application process would be well advised to consider which of these are important in one's own life – along with other factors such as cost, size, location, and program offerings – and should be wary of ranking systems that assert a subjective view of what one's objectives should be, with a "one size fits all" methodology. This is particularly important in light of our learning that

2. **There are real and fundamental differences between colleges in terms of the actual outcomes of their graduates.**

For those lucky enough to experience them, the four years spent in undergraduate education are likely the most significant period of intellectual, social, emotional and political development experienced by a young adult. Values and beliefs are challenged, faiths are tested, visions are expanded, ambitions are hardened and characters are forged – raw carbon to rough diamond to brilliant gem. This transformation is, with minor variation in words, the mission of virtually all of America's leading colleges and universities. What we now know – thanks to the data provided by tens of thousand of college graduates – is that virtually all colleges and universities transform their students, but they each do it uniquely. ***A very select few produce graduates who experience equally strong outcomes across the diversity of things people might expect from a college education.*** Most, instead, seem to be very, very good at a handful of things, and the variability between schools across different metrics is striking. Indeed, the attribute with the smallest difference in rating between the lowest and highest rated school in our ranking shows a spread of 24.6 points on a scale from one to one hundred. The attribute with the largest spread shows 87.3 points of difference. Prospective students can think of this as a demonstration of each school's strengths and weaknesses, but it might be more rightly viewed as a reflection of the distinctive way each university fulfills its mission. Rather than reducing each institution down to some vague notion of reputation, it is worthwhile absorbing the more nuanced and realistic picture that the real-world experiences of alumni can provide. This is particularly important because, as the outcomes of college graduates show us,

3. **A college's reputation does not always translate into actual results for its alumni.**

In fact, our data suggest that about one-third of colleges we have studied have reputations that exceed actual graduate results (they are overrated); one-third have graduates whose outcomes are better than the college's reputation would suggest (they are underrated) and the remaining one-third have reputations that are matched by the actual results of their graduates. By studying actual outcomes we now know there are many graduates from less prestigious schools whose results across almost any dimension of success actually exceed those of graduates from the most sought-after schools. Yet, the "reputation game" and the intense marketing of selective colleges have obscured this basic reality. You do not need a degree from an Ivy League school to be financially successful or happy. Nor does a degree from a prestigious school assure that you will be financially successful or happy. ***It is important that prospective students are able to pierce the bubble of reputation*** to understand what a college can actually do for them and which colleges would provide them the best return on their (or their parent's) investment, whatever their individual goals may be.

4. **Your choice of college is not your destiny; that said, your odds of success do increase at some schools – assuming you find the right fit.**

Students enter into their college experience with an accumulated set of advantages brought about by parental education, family upbringing, socioeconomic status, individual traits and character, and prior educational experiences. Those don't magically disappear when one walks through ivy-clad gates. Ambitious, smart students can be found on every campus and indeed, one can find success stories from any and every college campus. In fact, our data on graduate outcomes bears this out. However, our results also show that the odds of becoming successful (again, as defined by the individual) are greater for graduates of certain colleges than others. Parents and prospective students should know these results when determining where all that hard work and ambition might be best placed. And one of the best ways to learn about results is through the feedback from the graduates who were essentially customers of their own collegiate experience.

One of the best illustrations of the power of customer feedback regarding actual, real-world performance comes to us from the US auto industry. Following a career as a researcher inside both Ford and General Motors, David Power knew there was a better way to give consumers a more objective way of determining who built the best cars. The US auto industry, long controlled by industry insiders arrogant enough to believe the consumer would fall in love with whatever came out of their behemoth plants, was very good at "inhaling its own exhaust," as the saying goes. When James David (J.D.) Power began his own research company in 1968, he began simply by asking consumers what they thought of the cars they had purchased. In the early days, when he would show his research to auto company executives, they would often scoff at any negative feedback from the consumers and dismiss it as either confused consumers or faulty research. Fortunately, through the persistence of his very good idea, J.D. Power changed the way we purchase cars – and changed the way auto companies build them. Auto companies began to listen to the people who know their cars best – the drivers. Imagine today if, instead of asking buyers about the quality and performance of their vehicle, a car was judged by, among other things, asking General Motors what they thought of Ford cars, and asking Chrysler what they thought of General Motors vehicles and so on; ranking how much money each auto maker had in its bank account; or counting how many people came to different branded auto dealerships to take a test drive. Yet, we have long accepted that sort of methodology in post-secondary education as the basis for determining the quality of our colleges and universities.

Today, more than at any time in our recent history, it is important to understand the real value of higher education, and the value of an education at one school versus another. As you already know and will see confirmed later in this book, a college degree is one of the keys to opening a life of personal development, fulfillment, success and happiness. However, the cost of obtaining that key has risen disproportionately to virtually every other sector in America save one – healthcare. Over the past generation, the cost of attending college has increased at about twice the rate of inflation. While the laws of supply and demand apply to colleges as they do to all enterprises, US colleges are a complex mix of private enterprise and public utility. The increasing economic and social need for a student to attain a college education in today's world has led to dramatic increases in the percentage of high school students who pursue a college degree. Add to that the growing number of foreign students who are applying to US colleges and it explains the dramatic acceleration of demand being placed upon our US collegiate system. Yet, supply has risen more slowly among the very best of colleges, putting upward pressure on the cost of a college education at the most highly regarded schools. This has led to a very select group of "luxury," high-end "brands" among the 2,400 four-year colleges and universities. Is the premium price for these high-end schools worth the money? You will see ahead that in some cases the answer is yes, while in other cases some are not worth the incremental money. And you will also find hidden gems that transform students' lives with very little fanfare and relatively low cost. ***The Alumni Factor* provides a detailed profile of graduates from the Top 177 colleges across the US**. Our research has shown that each institution, with its longstanding traditions and hallowed history, leaves a distinct and lasting impression on its graduates. We've learned that these unique impressions, like genetic DNA markers, can distinguish graduates of one college from those of another.

We certainly are not proposing that all differences between college graduates are the result of college choice. The diverse views and differentiated results of graduates are certainly a reflection of each individual graduate – their total education, their family upbringing and social environment – and are a reflection of thousands of other factors that resolutely make each of us unique individuals. Yet you will likely notice, as you view the results, that there are substantive differences in the beliefs and views of graduates across many of the colleges. Those differences are also noticeable in the financial success of graduates, in their levels of happiness and in their career pursuits. We do not conclude, however, that one's college is the sole driver of these differences. We know better. We know that it is unlikely any study will be able to isolate all variables well enough to determine the exact impact a college plays in that personal formation. All colleges produce successful and unsuccessful graduates – conservative and liberal graduates, happy and unhappy graduates, graduates who love their college and graduates who do not.

However, there is no debate that our US colleges and universities have long been a competitive advantage for our country – and that advantage continues today. Our nation's portfolio of colleges and universities is celebrated the world over for its excellence and leadership. The broad array of choices and the breadth of academic, social, intellectual and cultural options among them, allows each student the chance to find a near perfect fit. While historically it has been considered the finest collection of college brands in the world, our nation's leadership is being seriously challenged around the globe as other countries dramatically improve their post-secondary education offerings. It is our hope that this work will, in some way, contribute to maintaining and widening the competitive advantage currently enjoyed by the US in the post-secondary education market.

Ongoing work will broaden our list significantly to the point where we will be able to deeply probe well beyond the 177 colleges included in this edition to many more of the country's 2,400 under-graduate schools. You can already find information on over 1,300 additional unranked schools on our website. Please join us on our website at **www.alumnifactor.com**, where we share even more analyses and are continually updating our information.

If you are a college alumnus, come to our site to share your own perspectives on your educational experience. If you are a prospective college student, we encourage you to join us on our website to compare colleges and universities and to use our exclusive tool, *MatchMe2U*℠, to find the best fit for you by customizing our rankings to your individual goals and priorities.

We hope you will find *The Alumni Factor* to be a fascinating look at the incredibly diverse academic, social and cultural choices available to capable students today. If nothing else, you will be much better informed about each college by its alumni who have actually lived, studied and played on the campuses you are considering. Above all, we wish you the best in selecting your college and in making the most of the wonderful experience upon which you are about to embark.

The Editor

CHAPTER 1

Methodology

The Alumni Factor
Methodology

Data Collection

Our rankings are based on our proprietary research conducted among graduates of US colleges and universities aged 24 and above. Surveys were distributed to these college graduates via multiple approaches. All research was conducted independently, without the involvement of any college or university. Each respondent answered more than 30 questions about their college experience, their record of academic and extra-curricular achievement, their view of their college and its impact on their lives today, their household situation, their level of employment, their financial situation, their overall happiness and their demographic details. We also asked them to respond to 20 statements regarding relevant political and social issues. By the time the survey data were compiled, tens of thousands of graduates from over 450 colleges and universities had completed the survey. Ultimately, we narrowed the list of colleges to rank the 177 Top Colleges and Universities included in our report. We are continually expanding the number of colleges we rank and will report on them in future work.

Ranking Methodology

Our Overall Rankings are based on 15 attributes for each college – each is equally weighted. Data for 13 of the 15 attributes came from actual graduates. Only 2 of the 15 attributes – the Graduation Rate and the Alumni Giving percentage – are gained from a source other than graduates. The 15 attributes included in the overall ranking are:

- Intellectual Development
- Social And Communication Skill Development
- Friendship Development
- Preparation for Career Success
- Immediate Job Opportunities
- Willingness to Recommend the College to a Prospective Student
- Value for the Money
- Would You Choose the College Again for Yourself?
- Average Income of Graduate Households
- Percentage of High Income (>$150K annually) Graduate Households
- Average Net Worth of Graduate Households
- Percentage of High Net Worth (>$1 million) Graduate Households
- Overall Happiness of Graduates
- The Percentage of Alumni Who Annually Donate to the College or University (from 2008 to 2011)
- The College's Graduation Rate (from 2010)

We include and rank a number of other attributes for each college, but they are not included in our overall ranking. Only the 15 factors listed above are included in the rankings. For instance, we have a Spiritual Development score for each school and Ultimate Outcome℠ scores for each school, but we do not include these items in the rankings.

Data were scrubbed of statistical outliers and cross-checked against external sources for validation. In addition, we ensured variances in age distribution of respondents across schools did not skew results.

We kept it simple and transparent. We did not let our subjective judgment of what is important in an education lead to values-based weightings that might favor some schools more than others. After all, that is for you, the reader, to ultimately decide.

Results for any given school are included in this publication only if they were proven to be of a sufficient sample size to be statistically reliable at the 95% confidence level. If you are interested in learning more about the statistics, please see the commentary from our advisor, David M. Goldsman, Ph.D., at the end of this book.

Frequently Asked Questions

Are survey-based opinions from alumni valid? Won't alums actually inflate their responses to make their schools look good?

Opinion-based surveys have a long and proven history and are well-known as a valid research approach, so long as certain conditions are in place. The first of these is, of course, anonymity. Without anonymity, survey respondents may be induced to alter their responses out of fear of reprisal. *The Alumni Factor* does not have any way of identifying who our respondents are (other than to verify the college from which they graduated) and ensures respondents know their survey information will be aggregated with other responses to preserve anonymity. The second condition is that the research be conducted by a disinterested third party. Were the colleges and universities themselves conducting the survey, graduates might be tempted to "soften" their feedback out of a misguided sense of loyalty, or, on the other hand, sharpen it to "send a message" to the administration. *The Alumni Factor*, as an independent researcher, takes these emotional responses out of the equation and thereby gets a more accurate view. The third, which is just good research "hygiene," is that any unusual outliers in the data are identified and removed. *The Alumni Factor* does this as a matter of course.

Furthermore, we can and do validate the accuracy of responses by cross-referencing independent data where possible. For example, we ask alumni to indicate the range into which their SAT scores fall. Since colleges and universities report SAT data as well, we can cross-check that the ranges alumni report are consistent with those reported by schools. And, indeed, they are.

Finally, if alumni were systematically and regularly inflating their scores to make their schools look good, you would expect this to show up in the data as virtually no difference in ratings across the colleges and universities we examined, as well as virtually no difference across the ratings of different outcomes within an individual school. As you delve into the book, you will see this is not the case. Differences across colleges and across individual outcomes within schools are significant.

If you are still concerned that alumni respondents inflated their ratings, keep in mind that there would be no reason to believe that graduates of one school would inflate at a higher or lower rate than those of other schools, so the **relative** comparison between schools – or the **ranking** – would still be a valid measure, even if inflation of responses were to occur.

Why do you have only 177 schools featured in the book? How did you choose which 177 to feature?

We started our data collection effort with over 450 universities and colleges popularly considered among the ranks of the "elite." Schools that are not included in our ranking either did not have enough responses to be statistically valid at the time we went to press or did not rank highly enough to make our list. You can find information about these unranked schools on our website, www.alumnifactor.com.

What does it mean to be ranked #1 versus #15 or #70 on a list?

Rankings are a way to simplify lots of data into easily understandable terms. They also appeal to the inherent competitive spirit many people possess. We would encourage readers to look beyond a simple rank to understand the nuances of any individual school. Broadly speaking, groups of 25 might be considered roughly comparable. And remember, all 177 schools on our list are very elite and high performing. The key is to find the one best for *you*.

A Note on Reading the Chapters

The next few chapters of *The Alumni Factor* provide an in-depth view of our findings on every measured element that make up our rankings. Throughout the chapters, we refer to a few terms that may be helpful to define here.

All Graduates or Composite of All Graduates: refers to the average rating or percent agreement with a statement of all the alumni in our sample.

Correlation: refers to the observation of two variables that seem to be related to one another and move together (for example, the observation that people who attain a college degree also tend to have higher incomes). Things can be inversely correlated, or move in opposite directions in an observable relationship (for example, graduates with post-graduate degrees tend to have lower levels of reported friendships). Correlation does not necessarily imply causation – because two things seem to be related does not necessarily mean that one causes the other or vice versa.

Mean: refers to the arithmetic mean or simple average of any data set in question. Mathematically, it is the sum of a set of values, divided by the number of values.

Median: refers to the numerical value in a set of numbers that separates the upper half of the set from the lower half of the set.

Median Household Income: refers to the amount which divides the income distribution into two equal groups, half with household income above and half below. Many consider this to be a better indicator of average household income as it will be less dramatically skewed by extremely high or low outliers.

Net Worth: refers to a household's total assets (cash, property, equity, etc.) minus its liabilities or debts (credit card debt, unpaid portion of mortgages, etc.)

Other Ranked Colleges: refers to any school, regardless of type, which does not fall into the Top 50 or 100 on *The Alumni Factor* respective rankings, but does make our list of 177.

All "Other" Colleges: refers to unnamed colleges for which *The Alumni Factor* has alumni feedback in numbers too small to be statisically significant. Therefore, they are not included in our rankings.

Percent Agreed: refers to the percentage of graduates who agreed with the statement in question.

Top Box, Top 2 Box Scores: Top Box refers to the percent of alumni who responded *Strongly Agree*, which is the highest rating (or "box") on our survey scale. Top 2 Box refers to the combination of alumni responses *Strongly Agree* and *Agree*.

Top 50 Liberal Arts Colleges: refers to the Top 50 liberal arts colleges on *The Alumni Factor* Liberal Arts Colleges Ranking.

Top 50 National Universities: refers to the Top 50 national universities on *The Alumni Factor* National Universities Ranking.

Top 100 Colleges: refers to the Top 100 schools, regardless of type, on *The Alumni Factor* Overall Ranking.

Weighted Average: refers to an average in which the quantities to be averaged are assigned a weight to reflect their relative importance or to force a desired distribution of types of respondents.

CHAPTER 2

Exclusive Rankings of Top Colleges and Universities

The Alumni Factor
Exclusive Overall College Rankings

By most counts, there are roughly 2,475 accredited four-year colleges and universities in the US. To be among the Top 177 on *The Alumni Factor* list puts each of these schools in the rarified top 7% of all four-year colleges. Correspondingly, less than 5% of all college-bound US high school seniors will spend their undergraduate years at one of these institutions. Therefore, do not draw the tempting conclusion that a school rated 177th overall or in any one attribute does "poorly." It is likely better than 93% of all colleges across the country!

To develop our lists, we have evaluated these schools based on their performance against 15 attributes, across six broad criteria, as rated by their alumni:

- Quality of the College Experience (5 measures)
- Assessments of Value for Money and Willingness to Recommend (3 measures)
- Financial Success of graduates (4 measures).
- Overall Happiness of graduates (1 measure)
- The percent of alumni who donate to each college annually (1 measure)
- The graduation rate of each college (1 measure)

Overall, there are 15 individual measures for each school used to determine its overall ranking. Each measure is weighted equally. Graduate input is the direct source for 13 of the 15 attributes. The only attributes not taken directly from alumni input are the alumni giving percentage and the college's graduation rate.

A key point about our ranking is that, unlike most other lists, we combine data from all schools – national universities, liberal arts colleges and regional universities – when providing our overall *Alumni Factor* ranking. We do this to allow for comparisons across all colleges, since this is the way prospective students actually evaluate schools. Therefore, when comparing our comprehensive *Alumni Factor* ranking to other rankings, readers may notice that many schools achieve a different ranking than has typically been seen for that school (for example, a school that is ranked 10th on other lists may be 30th in *The Alumni Factor* ranking because the pool of comparison is larger). We do, however, additionally show rankings by college type to allow for that direct comparison.

In this chapter readers will find the ranking for each type of school (national universities, liberal arts colleges and regional universities). This allows readers to compare schools of like size and purpose. We also provide our overall *Alumni Factor* ranking, in which we put all the schools together and rank them as one group from 1 to 177. This list is the best way to compare some of the larger national universities to the smaller liberal arts schools and the regional schools. Individual school profiles will show where a school falls on both types of rankings.

Throughout the report we include other data for each college that, while not used to calculate the ranking, is helpful in understanding the overall performance of a college as judged by its graduates. These include: Spiritual Development, political and social views, and other insights that may be helpful in fully understanding the type of graduate each college produces. Most importantly, we provide the complete ranking of the 177 colleges for every one of the attributes we measure. This way, readers can judge colleges on whichever attribute or attributes they individually deem most important.

The Alumni Factor Rankings

Top Liberal Arts Colleges	Top National Universities
1. Washington and Lee University	1. Yale University
2. College of the Holy Cross	2. Princeton University
3. Middlebury College	3. Rice University
4. United States Naval Academy	4. University of Notre Dame
5. United States Military Academy	5. Stanford University
6. Claremont McKenna College	6. University of Virginia
7. Amherst College	7. Dartmouth College
8. Wellesley College	8. Virginia Polytechnic Institute and State University
9. Pomona College	9. Georgia Institute of Technology
10. Harvey Mudd College	10. Duke University
11. Centre College	11. Georgetown University
12. Wesleyan University	12. Cornell University
13. Davidson College	12. University of North Carolina at Chapel Hill
14. Swarthmore College	14. Brown University
15. University of Richmond	15. Massachusetts Institute of Technology
16. Bucknell University	16. The College of William & Mary
17. Mount Holyoke College	17. University of Michigan
18. Sewanee: The University of the South	18. Harvard University
19. Carleton College	19. Vanderbilt University
20. Colorado College	20. California Institute of Technology
21. Bowdoin College	21. Wake Forest University
22. Williams College	22. Auburn University
23. Gettysburg College	23. University of Wisconsin-Madison
24. Morehouse College	24. University of Southern California
25. Grinnell College	25. University of Pennsylvania
26. Scripps College	26. University of California, Berkeley
27. Smith College	27. University of Alabama
28. Spelman College	28. Texas A&M University
29. Vassar College	29. University of Texas at Austin
30. Whitman College	30. Washington University in St. Louis
31. Kenyon College	31. Lehigh University
32. Colby College	32. Boston College
33. Furman University	33. University of California, Los Angeles
34. Bates College	33. Purdue University
35. Pitzer College	35. Brigham Young University
36. Trinity College	36. University of Florida
37. St. Olaf College	37. Northwestern University
38. Colgate University	38. Clemson University
39. Oberlin College	39. Howard University
40. Lafayette College	39. University of Illinois at Urbana-Champaign
41. Haverford College	41. University of Kansas
42. Connecticut College	42. Columbia University
43. Hamilton College	42. Kansas State University
44. Occidental College	44. North Carolina State University
45. Bryn Mawr College	45. Johns Hopkins University
46. Franklin & Marshall College	46. Pennsylvania State University
47. Reed College	47. Miami University (OH)
48. Macalester College	48. University of Wyoming
49. Denison University	49. Michigan State University
50. Depauw University	50. Tufts University

The Alumni Factor Rankings

Top Regional Universities

1. Santa Clara University
2. United States Air Force Academy
3. Villanova University
4. Gonzaga University
5. Creighton University
6. Marquette University
7. Xavier University
8. Elon University
9. James Madison University
10. Loyola University New Orleans
11. Loyola Marymount University
12. Trinity University
13. The College of New Jersey
14. Valparaiso University
15. Rollins College
16. Loyola University Maryland
17. College of Charleston
18. Ohio Northern University
19. Bradley University
20. Loyola University Chicago

The Alumni Factor Ranking of Top Colleges & Universities

1. Washington and Lee University
2. Yale University
3. Princeton University
4. Rice University
5. College of the Holy Cross
6. University of Notre Dame
7. Middlebury College
8. United States Naval Academy
9. United States Military Academy
10. Stanford University
11. Claremont McKenna College
12. University of Virginia
13. Amherst College
14. Dartmouth College
15. Wellesley College
16. Pomona College
17. Harvey Mudd College
18. Centre College
19. Wesleyan University
20. Davidson College
21. Swarthmore College
22. University of Richmond
23. Bucknell University
24. Virginia Polytechnic Institute and State University
25. Georgia Institute of Technology
26. Mount Holyoke College
27. Duke University
28. Georgetown University
29. Cornell University
30. University of North Carolina at Chapel Hill
31. Brown University
32. Massachusetts Institute of Technology
33. The College of William & Mary
34. University of Michigan
35. Sewanee: The University of the South
36. Carleton College
37. Harvard University
38. Vanderbilt University
39. Colorado College
40. Bowdoin College
41. California Institute of Technology
42. Wake Forest University
43. Santa Clara University
44. Auburn University
45. United States Air Force Academy
46. University of Wisconsin-Madison
47. Williams College
48. University of Southern California
49. Villanova University
50. Gettysburg College
51. University of Pennsylvania
52. Gonzaga University
53. Morehouse College
54. Grinnell College
55. Scripps College
56. Smith College
57. Spelman College
58. Vassar College
59. University of California, Berkeley
60. Whitman College
61. University of Alabama
62. Kenyon College
63. Colby College
64. Furman University
65. Texas A&M University
66. Bates College
67. Pitzer College
68. Trinity College
69. Creighton University
70. St. Olaf College
71. University of Texas at Austin
72. Colgate University
73. Oberlin College
74. Washington University in St. Louis
75. Lehigh University
76. Boston College
77. Lafayette College
78. Purdue University
79. University of California, Los Angeles
80. Brigham Young University
81. University of Florida
82. Marquette University
83. Northwestern University
84. Clemson University
85. Howard University
86. University of Illinois at Urbana-Champaign
87. Haverford College
88. University of Kansas
89. Connecticut College
90. Xavier University
91. Columbia University
92. Kansas State University
93. Hamilton College
94. Occidental College
95. Bryn Mawr College
96. North Carolina State University
97. Elon University
98. Franklin & Marshall College
99. Reed College
100. Johns Hopkins University

The Alumni Factor Ranking of Top Colleges & Universities

101. James Madison University
102. Pennsylvania State University
103. Macalester College
104. Miami University
105. Loyola University New Orleans
106. University of Wyoming
107. Denison University
108. Loyola Marymount University
109. Trinity University
110. Michigan State University
111. Tufts University
112. The College of New Jersey
113. University of Mississippi
114. University of Chicago
115. Depauw University
116. Carnegie Mellon University
117. Pepperdine University
118. Worcester Polytechnic Institute
119. Skidmore College
120. Rensselaer Polytechnic Institute
121. Valparaiso University
122. University of Tennessee
123. University of California, Santa Barbara
124. Emory University
125. Ohio State University
126. University of Iowa
127. Oregon State University
128. University of Georgia
129. Indiana University Bloomington
130. Washington State University
131. University of California, Davis
132. University of Rochester
133. Rutgers University
134. Drexel University
135. University of California, San Diego
136. Rollins College
137. Loyola University Maryland
138. Clark University
139. University of California, Irvine
140. Baylor University
141. Florida State University
142. College of Charleston
143. Southern Methodist University
144. Syracuse University
145. Tulane University
146. University of Delaware
147. Northeastern University
148. University of Miami
149. University of Colorado Boulder
150. Dickinson College
151. University of Connecticut
152. Brandeis University
153. Iowa State University
154. Ohio Northern University
155. Bard College
156. Boston University
157. University of Arizona
158. Case Western Reserve University
159. American University
160. San Diego State University
161. University of Washington
162. Bradley University
163. University of Massachusetts Amherst
164. University of Utah
165. New York University
166. University of Nebraska-Lincoln
167. University of Pittsburgh
168. Loyola University Chicago
169. University of Vermont
170. Colorado State University
171. University of Oregon
172. University of Kentucky
173. University of California, Riverside
174. George Washington University
175. Arizona State University
176. University of Minnesota
177. DePaul University

How Different From One Another Are Colleges and Universities?

Measured Attribute (n=>42,000)	Highest Scoring College % Strongly Agree	All College Graduates % Strongly Agree	Lowest Scoring College % Strongly Agree
The Overall College Experience			
Intellectual Development	89.3%	49.6%	27.6%
Social/Communication Skills Development	67.7%	38.6%	16.3%
Spiritual Development	62.7%	12.8%	2.6%
Developed Deep Friendships	68.0%	37.4%	17.9%
Sustain Undergrad Friendships	50.0%	20.4%	5.8%
Preparation for Career Success	76.3%	31.9%	14.0%
Immediate Job Opportunities	93.6%	23.8%	6.3%
Alumni Assessment Today			
Would Choose Different College	0%	10.4%	24.6%
Would Recommend to Student	82.2%	55.0%	31.3%
Worth the Money Paid	77.3%	46.1%	19.2%
Happiness of Graduates	48.2%	32.8%	19.9%
Financial Success of Graduates			
% Households with Income Above US Median	95.7%	76.5%	65.8%
% Households with Income >$150K	50.0%	27.8%	12.0%
% Households with Net Worth >$200K	71.6%	51.0%	31.0%
% Households with Net Worth >$1MM	29.4%	14.6%	2.3%
Other Analyzed Attributes			
% Grads with GPA Above 3.5	47.6%	28.0%	7.3%
% Who Get Post-Graduate Degree	75.7%	58.8%	32.5%
% Who Teach at Any Level	28.6%	14.1%	2.9%
% Who Are College Professors	16.7%	6.6%	1.0%
% Who Are Very Liberal	39.2%	9.7%	1.2%
% Who Are Very Conservative	16.9%	4.9%	0.9%

How Different Are Grads in Their Political & Social Views by College?

Social or Political Issue (n=>39,000)	Highest Scoring College % Strongly Agree	All College Graduates % Strongly Agree	Lowest Scoring College % Strongly Agree
We need stronger controls on immigration	49%	19.8%	0%
Affirmative Action is fair	36%	7.9%	1%
Affirmative Action is unfair	27%	11.5%	0%
Abortion should be illegal	29%	9.0%	0%
Abortion should be legal	81%	41.7%	6%
Government-funded universal healthcare would be good for America	62%	26.3%	7%
Homosexuals should be allowed to marry	82%	45.1%	8%
The media leans to the liberal side	47%	19.1%	0%
The media leans to the conservative side	15%	3.8%	0%
The media basically tells the truth	4%	0.6%	0%
Guns should be more controlled than they are today	55%	30.8%	8%
Children should be allowed to pray in schools	47%	20.7%	3%
Political correctness has gone too far in America today	63%	27.8%	5%
Immigrants should be required to learn English	52%	25.3%	3%
Capitalism is a destructive force in our world today	17%	3.1%	0%
Capitalism is a positive force in our world today	45%	18.9%	2%
We should reinstate the military draft in America	9%	3.0%	0%
America is the best country in the world	63%	28.4%	6%
Police should be allowed to profile when searching for a criminal	19%	7.5%	0%
Capital punishment is immoral	41%	15.1%	4%

What Correlates to a High Ranking?

The chart below shows the level to which each of the attributes we measure correlates to overall ranking. To determine our rankings, remember that we give equal weighting to the 15 attributes marked below with an asterisk (*). As the chart indicates, even though all are equally weighted in our ranking, attributes such as Preparation for Career Success, Intellectual Development and Friendship Development are the best indicators of overall success – and, therefore, are most correlated to a higher ranking. Note that the three lowest attributes for correlation to ranking are cost of school, size of school and the average SAT score of incoming students.

	Alumni Outcomes	R-squared Factor	Rank
*	Preparation For Career Success	0.6154	1
*	Intellectual Development	0.5694	2
*	Friendship Development	0.559	3
*	Loyalty – Alumni Giving %	0.4826	4
*	Would Recommend Today	0.4077	6
*	Household Net Worth	0.4028	7
*	Social & Communication Skills Development	0.396	8
*	A Good Value for $	0.3799	9
*	Mean Household Income	0.3639	10
*	% High (>$150K) Household Income	0.3536	11
	Spiritual Development	0.3268	12
*	% Millionaire Households	0.318	13
*	Would Personally Choose Again	0.3151	14
*	Overall Happiness	0.2808	15
*	Provided Immediate Job Opportunities	0.2625	16
	School Indicators	**R-squared Factor**	
*	Graduation Rate Rank	0.4737	5
	SAT Score Rank	0.2486	17
	Size of Student Body	0.1793	18
	Cost of School	0.0801	19

Performance Versus Reputation

One would expect that, over time, the reputation of a product or service would closely track its actual performance in the market, assuming there is adequate transparency about that product's performance and some basis for comparison against similar products. The analysis below plots all 177 colleges we have included here in an attempt to broadly compare each college's actual results (e.g., alumni performance in the real world) versus the college's reputation. The "Results" ranking is simply the overall *Alumni Factor* ranking for each college, based on alumni reported success. The "Reputation" ranking is based on the "Peer Assessment" rank from the *US News and World Report's* college rankings. The *USN&WR* calculates this by surveying various college personnel, asking them to rank their peer schools on a scale of one to five. These "Peer Assessments" historically account for 22.5% of a college's overall *USN&WR* ranking, which can enhance or detract from a school's image in the market. The statistical challenge with these peer assessments is, first, that data points are often based on a limited number of observations and, second, that an administrator or faculty member at a college may be ranking schools they do not know, other than by reputation. Certainly, different raters have different views of which schools are peers, and each may have a different way of rating a school. Finally, consistency of raters by role across participating schools is very difficult to control and may introduce non-comparable points of view into the data. Given these methodological issues, we expected to find significant differences in a school's reputation as compared to the actual success and happiness of its graduates – and we did.

Each of the squares on the following graph represents one of the 177 colleges in our study. The x-axis plots the school's overall rank by *The Alumni Factor*, and the y-axis is the school's peer assessment rank from the *USN&WR* survey. As you can see, there is a modest correlation between the two (r-squared equals 0.4256), indicating that they are somewhat connected, as we expected. The colleges colored red are those where the graduates' real-world outcomes exceed the college's reputation. The colleges colored blue are those where the school's reputation is higher than the graduate performance in the market. The schools colored light blue have performance rankings in line with their reputations.

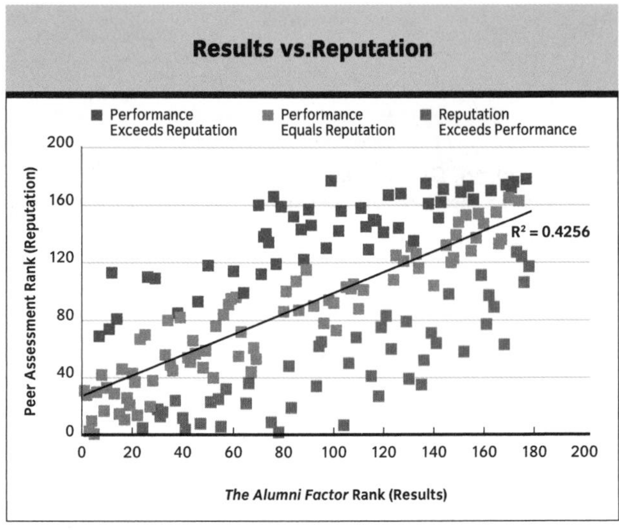

This information clearly demonstrates that, in many cases, a college's alumni actually do better or worse than the college's reputation would suggest. We believe that actual performance by alumni is a more credible indicator of the effectiveness of a college's performance. By piercing the bubble of reputation and looking at actual alumni outcomes, prospective students, parents, alumni, potential benefactors and others get a sharper tool by which to evaluate colleges. Most importantly, colleges get a more clear-eyed view of how they perform against their missions – something which may actually help them improve.

Now, for a final note: we are looking only at the reputation of the undergraduate programs of each college. A college or university may have graduate programs that would significantly change the reputation of the school. We are looking strictly at the reputation of a college's undergraduate programs, because we are only looking at the performance of undergraduates from each college.

CHAPTER 3

Alumni Rate Their College Experience

The Alumni Factor
The College Experience
Alumni Rate Their Colleges in Key Areas

Colleges and universities that earn the top spots in the overall College Experience rankings have been shown to deliver a transformative, life-altering undergraduate experience to their students who, in turn, leverage its value for a lifetime. Actual graduates, having lived in the real world following their undergraduate experience, are better able than current undergraduates to make an objective, informed assessment of their college's true impact. Their holistic and retrospective feedback, from the vantage point of their current life stage, is thus invaluable.

Therefore, alumni were asked to comment on areas that were defining elements of their undergraduate experience:

Key Components of the College Experience

- Intellectual development
- Social and communication skills development
- Spiritual development
- Deep friendship development
- Friendship retention – staying close to undergraduate friends
- Preparation for career success
- Ability to get a job after graduation

Take a close look at these ratings to see which college experiences stand the test of time with alumni in the real world.

Intellectual Development

Sharpening the Mind

Developing the mental capabilities of our nation's undergraduates is important business. We entrust many of our best young minds to our colleges and universities with the expectation that they will be rigorously exercised and strengthened. Of the seven attributes we measure in assessing the *college experience* for graduates, *intellectual development*, fortunately, scores the highest when looking across all graduates. Overall, graduates are pleased with the level of intellectual development being provided by our schools. Of all college graduates, nearly 50% *Strongly Agree* that their college developed them intellectually. That number climbs to 85% when you combine both *Strongly Agree* and *Agree* responses. Roughly 13% of all college graduates have mixed feelings (*Somewhat Agree* or *Somewhat Disagree* responses) about the strength of their intellectual development, and less than 2% of graduates *Disagree* or *Strongly Disagree* that they were developed intellectually. This is excellent news, indeed.

That said, it is clear that graduates of the top-ranked schools believe they've been intellectually developed more than graduates of unranked schools. As you read, you will notice a wide disparity among individual schools on this metric.

There are many factors across colleges and universities that can impact a graduate's perception of intellectual development, and we explore many of them in this chapter. Let's take a closer look at how well our colleges and universities are performing this important task and which colleges are particularly strong in this area.

Intellectual Development

Intellectual development is one of the highest purposes of any educational institution. This is particularly true for colleges and universities. Most parents, students and teachers cite this as one of the major objectives of any undergraduate education. Therefore, any assessment of colleges needs to begin with a view of how well a college develops its students intellectually. So to begin, we looked at intellectual development across all graduates to provide an overall view, as judged by alumni themselves, of how well US colleges develop intellectual muscle in their undergraduates. As the data in **Figure 3.1** indicate, more than 85% of all college and university graduates *Strongly Agree* or *Agree* that their college developed them intellectually.

Figure 3.1

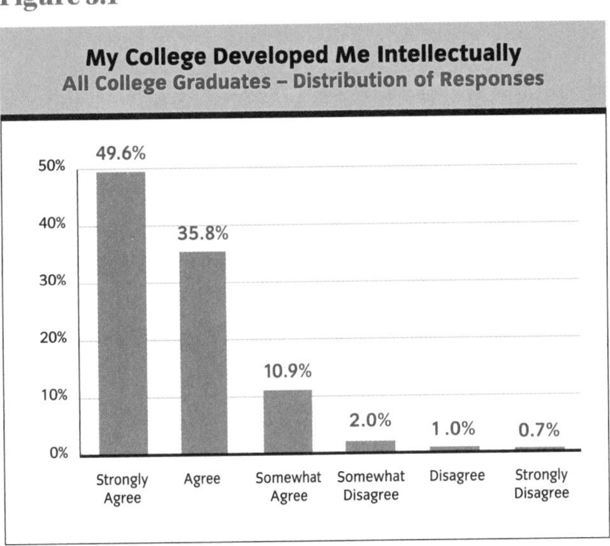

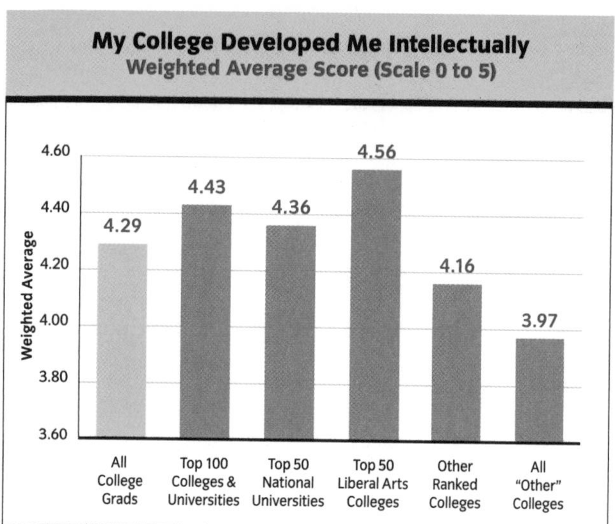

Figure 3.2

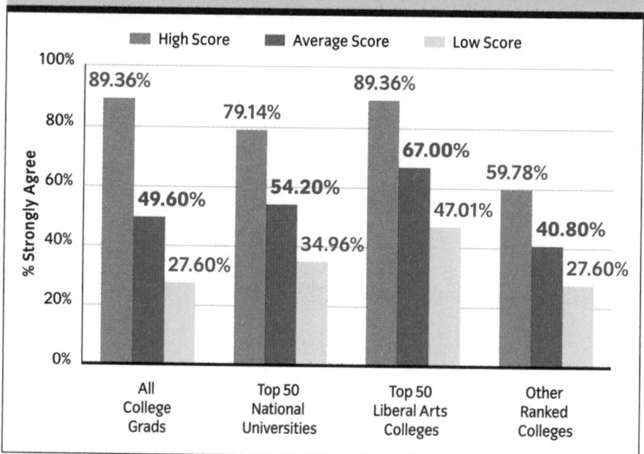

Figure 3.3

This is good news for academic institutions in general, although we will see there is a wide disparity between types of institution, and across individual colleges and universities. In fact, top box scores among the 177 colleges we analyzed ranged from a high of 89% (Sewanee) to a low of 28% (Northeastern and Arizona State University). Clearly, graduates have distinctly different views of the extent to which their college developed their intellectual capabilities. By more deeply analyzing these results, we can begin to see substantial differences between colleges.

To illustrate this point, **Figure 3.2** shows the difference in the weighted average score for intellectual development across six different ranking tiers of colleges and universities. Comparing the weighted average score of *All College Grads* to graduates of the *Top 100 Colleges & Universities, Top 50 National Universities, Top 50 Liberal Arts Colleges, Other Ranked Colleges* and *All "Other" Colleges,* we begin to see that there are significant differences across types of schools.

The *Top 50 National Universities* score significantly higher than *Other Ranked Colleges* and *All "Other" Colleges,* and there is a smaller gap (0.07 points) between the *Top 50 National Universities* score and the score across *All College Grads.* However, it is the *Top 50 Liberal Arts Colleges* that are rated significantly higher than any other group by their graduates for developing intellectual capability.

Further to this point, 21 of the Top 25 colleges in intellectual development are liberal arts colleges. Among the Top 25, the only 3 national universities are University of Chicago (4th), Rice University (14th) and Yale University (18th). Further still, 27 among the Top 40 colleges for intellectual development are liberal arts colleges.

While **Figure 3.2** shows the weighted average score for each group of colleges, it is important to understand that there is significant variation not only between groups of colleges, but also within each group itself. **Figure 3.3** shows the spread of top box % scores within each ranked group. It is clear from this data that graduates' perceptions of how well their college developed them intellectually differs greatly, even among the top national universities and the top liberal arts colleges across the country.

Figure 3.3 also shows that there are *Other Ranked Colleges* where intellectual development is higher than the development in some of the Top 100 schools. For example, Creighton University in Omaha, Nebraska, with a 59.8% top box score for intellectual development, scores higher than 30 of the Top 100 rated schools. Therefore, it is important to look at each school individually to see the job it is doing in developing its students intellectually. We show the results for each of our 177 schools at the end of this chapter, ranked in order of performance in intellectual development, as rated by their alumni.

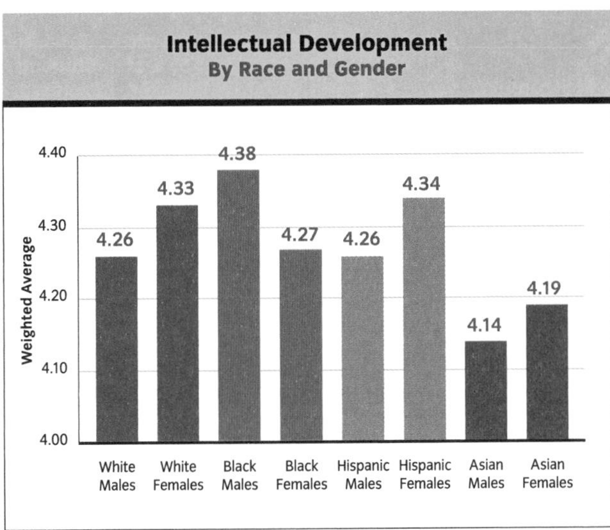

Figure 3.4

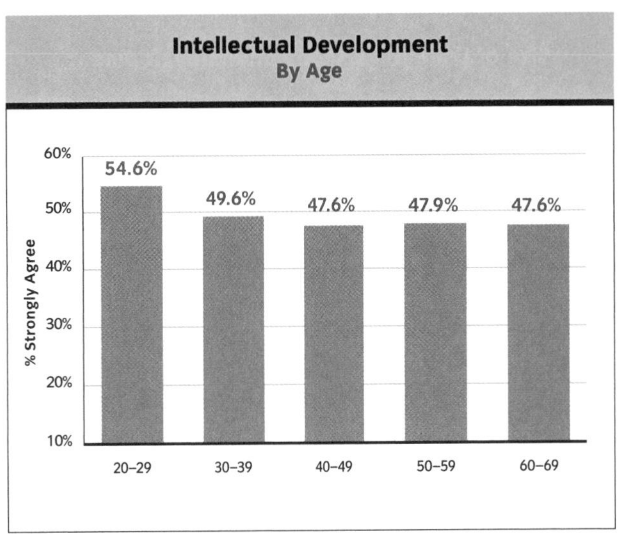

Figure 3.5

There are a number of factors that could potentially drive differences in scores for intellectual development. Among them are gender, race, age, size of enrollment, typical class size, professor quality, curriculum, major, the type of graduate and even the intellectual caliber of the graduate doing the rating (the theory being that the higher the intellect, the tougher the assessment of intellectual development). We've taken a look at some of these to see if they help explain some of the differences in intellectual development scores.

Do intellectual development assessments differ by gender or race?

Yes. Race and gender clearly do correlate with differences in intellectual development scores. In general, females rate their school's delivery of intellectual development higher than males; Asian males and females give the lowest scores overall; and Black males give the highest scores overall. White and Hispanic men and women are nearly identical in their scores. **Figure 3.4** graphs the differences by race and gender for intellectual development.

Does age affect intellectual development scores?

College graduates' views of their intellectual development appears to be highest in the first decade after graduation, after which it drops to a fairly consistent level throughout the rest of a graduate's life. Nearly 55% of graduates in their twenties *Strongly Agree* that they were developed intellectually by their college. By the time they reach their forties, that percentage drops to almost 48% and stays constant through their sixties. This generally applies equally to men and women. While starting at roughly the same intellectual development score in their twenties (54.4% for males, 54.2% for females), male scores decline more quickly and end lower than female scores.

Some might argue that lower scores among older alumni mean that the schools are now doing a better job of developing students. We do not believe that is the case, in general, for colleges and universities. We believe it has more to do with the differences between 25-year-olds and 50-year-olds. The nearness of the college experience and their relative inexperience in the real world positively distorts the twenty-something's view. Graduates in their forties and fifties likely have a broader and more rigorous definition of intellectual development; have a more realistic sense of their development versus others, given their successes and failures in life; and are, therefore, more objective regarding their college's prowess in this area. **Figure 3.5** provides a graphic depiction of this shift by age group.

However, not all colleges see a decline over time in their graduates' views of intellectual development. Schools with very strong ratings in intellectual development, such as Swarthmore, Sewanee, University of Chicago, Davidson and Yale, see no decline in their graduates' views by age. At all ages, graduates of these schools give credit to their colleges for deep intellectual development.

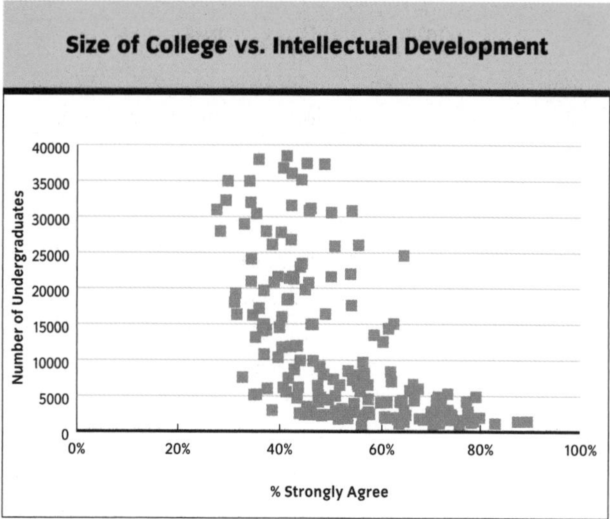

Figure 3.6

% Strongly Agree Score	Total % of Schools	% Schools Below 5000 Students	% with >55% of Classes under 20	% with Student: Professor Ratio <12
80% or higher	2%	100%	100%	100%
70%-79%	15%	96%	100%	100%
60%-69%	14%	64%	80%	84%
50%-59%	20%	43%	69%	71%
40%-49%	30%	23%	34%	30%
30%-39%	16%	3%	10%	7%
20%-29%	2%	0%	0%	0%

Figure 3.7

Does college size (number of undergrads) make a difference?

While the size of the college or university doesn't explain all the differences in graduate perception of intellectual development, **Figure 3.6** shows that smaller tends to be better. It is definitely easier to provide a powerful intellectual experience for fewer students than it is to create that same experience for large numbers.

The results shown in **Figure 3.6** indicate that there are only four schools with a score of 80% or better, all of which are small liberal arts colleges. There are 30 schools with a score of 70% or better, and 54 schools where 60% or more graduates *Strongly Agree* that their school developed them intellectually. There is only one school in the entire database that scores above 70% and has more than 5,000 undergraduates: Yale (73.5% strongly agree). Of the 54 schools above 60%, 45 of them (83%) have less than 5,000 undergraduates, and 9 have more than 5,000 students. Again, size alone does not dictate intellectual development, since there are many small schools (with less than 5,000 students) who do not score as well in this area, and also large schools who do score well. However, it is instructive to see who these top-performing schools are, and how size does play a role.

Size can be quantified in a number of ways, but there are three measurements that are typically used: 1) the number of undergraduates in a school, 2) the percent of classes with less than 20 students, and 3) the student to professor ratio. **Figure 3.7** lays out the importance of each element of size as a driver of intellectual development.

From the data shown in **Figure 3.7**, it is evident that when a college creates an intimate learning environment with small classes and a ratio of students to professors where they can connect personally, it is more likely that graduates will perceive they were fully developed intellectually. Virtually every college understands this, but not all of them execute it as well as others – and for some, the task is more difficult. Financial challenges, sheer number of students, the physical campus, building constraints and well-entrenched traditions that are important to the school can each make it more difficult to make smaller class sizes a reality.

It is important to remember that a small student body, small class sizes and a low student-to-professor ratio alone do not guarantee a college will deliver strong intellectual development. There are colleges that have all three of these characteristics but fail to achieve top scores relative to other colleges. That is because there are a number of other factors that can contribute, some of which are very hard to measure.

Does a high level of intelligence create a higher expectation for intellectual development?

What if we were to see a number of schools whose graduates each rated their college equally in intellectual

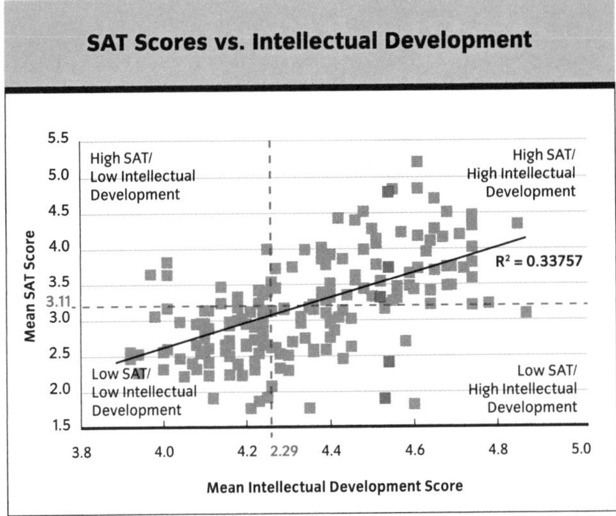

Figure 3.8

development, yet the intellectual caliber of students attending each school differed? Could that mean the schools with the smarter students (higher SAT scores) were held to a higher standard of intellectual development than the schools with students who had lower SAT scores? In other words, is intellectual development an absolute standard or is it relative to the individual?

As an actual example, **Figure 3.8** plots 185 schools against both intellectual development and SAT scores. Highlighted in red are five schools (Harvard, Macalester, Hamilton, Pitzer and Spelman) with nearly identical intellectual development scores, but significantly different SAT profiles among their students. While graduates of all five schools have SAT scores higher than the national average, three of them fall below the mean SAT score for the Top 177 colleges. We know for certain that graduates of each of these schools have similar perceptions of the intellectual development they received (they all rate their schools equally). However, a graduate can only provide a score for the college they experienced – their own. How should we think about these similar scores when they come from students with such seemingly different intellectual capability? Should we assume each of these schools offer, in the absolute, the same level of intellectual development? Or should we adjust scores based on other meaningful factors, like student SATs?

There is no simple way to answer these questions with any certainty across all colleges, but our hypothesis is that intellectual development is in the eye of the graduate who was developed, so understanding that graduate is critical to understanding the absolute development being provided. It is quite possible that if a graduate from Harvard were to instead attend Pitzer, the graduate may well score intellectual development differently, because they would have had a different experience. But we also know, factually, that the weighted average score for intellectual development across these schools is nearly identical. In other words, graduates of Macalester, Pitzer, Spelman and Hamilton feel they were as intellectually developed as do the graduates of Harvard. Until we can look at other objective measures that would tell us that one graduate's view of intellectual development is more correct than another's (and we don't have any at this point), we can confidently say the mean scores we have for intellectual development reflect each graduate's perception of the job their college did in developing them intellectually, and can be compared as such.

But we are as dissatisfied with that answer as you likely are. So, we've come up with a simple and clean way to attempt to factor in intellectual capability as a means of further differentiating colleges in intellectual development. The dotted lines in **Figure 3.8** intersect at the mean intellectual development score and the mean SAT score for the 400+ colleges in our database. We note the ongoing debate on the validity of SAT scores as a measure of intellectual capability. Because they are one of the only metrics available consistently across all schools, we rely upon them here. We believe schools in the upper-right box of **Figure 3.8** do a particularly good job of intellectual development, given that they are receiving high scores from high-caliber graduates who set, ostensibly, a high bar for intellectual development. Schools in the lower-right quadrant get relatively high intellectual development scores, but from graduates with lower SAT scores. Schools in the upper-left quadrant have graduates with high SAT scores but were rated lower than average by these alumni in intellectual development. Finally, schools in the lower-left quadrant are rated below average by their graduates in intellectual development and have a lower than average SAT profile. (Note that the "lower than average SAT profile" is relative only to the colleges on which we have focused in this analysis. In fact, the SAT profile for all 177 colleges, including those in the lower-left portion of **Figure 3.8**, is quite high relative to all college students). On the following page we list the schools which have both high SAT profiles and high intellectual development (those schools in the upper-right box of **Figure 3.8**).

Top 75 Colleges with High Intellectual Development and High SAT Scores

1.	California Institute of Technology	39.	Washington University in St. Louis
2.	Princeton University	40.	Mount Holyoke College
3.	Mass Institute of Technology	41.	Northwestern University
4.	Yale University	42.	United States Military Academy
5.	Harvard University	43.	Claremont McKenna College
6.	Swarthmore College	44.	University of Notre Dame
7.	Reed College	45.	St. Olaf College
8.	Rice University	46.	United States Air Force Academy
9.	University of Chicago	47.	Tufts University
10.	Harvey Mudd College	48.	Colorado College
11.	Pomona College	49.	The College of William & Mary
12.	Carleton College	50.	Smith College
13.	Williams College	51.	Georgetown University
14.	Stanford University	52.	Centre College
15.	Haverford College	53.	Sewanee: The University of the South
16.	Brown University	54.	Scripps College
17.	Amherst College	55.	University of Virginia
18.	Dartmouth College	56.	Carnegie Mellon University
19.	Wesleyan University	57.	Bates College
20.	Oberlin College	58.	College of the Holy Cross
21.	Barnard College	59.	Hamilton College
22.	Wellesley College	60.	University of California, Berkeley
23.	Bowdoin College	61.	Bard College
24.	Whitman College	62.	Franklin & Marshall College
25.	Columbia University	63.	Vanderbilt University
26.	Bryn Mawr College	64.	University of Michigan
27.	Grinnell College	65.	Colgate University
28.	Davidson College	66.	Wake Forest University
29.	Duke University	67.	Brigham Young University
30.	Vassar College	68.	Occidental College
31.	Middlebury College	69.	Colby College
32.	University of Pennsylvania	70.	University of California, Los Angeles
33.	Kenyon College	71.	Georgia Institute of Technology
34.	Johns Hopkins University	72.	Creighton University
35.	Macalester College	73.	University of Wisconsin
36.	Cornell University	74.	University of California, San Diego
37.	Washington and Lee University	75.	Connecticut College
38.	United States Naval Academy		

These are the 75 colleges and universities in the upper-right quadrant of **Figure 3.8** on the previous page, which are the nation's best colleges for intellectually developing highly talented students. Each of these 75 schools exceeds the mean of the 177 colleges measured (it is important to remember the mean for these 177 schools is significantly above the mean for all colleges and universities) for both the alumni rating of intellectual development and the mean SAT scores of its graduates. Therefore, each of these 75 excellent schools is highly capable of providing a strong intellectual challenge for the very brightest of students. Not surprisingly, this list is populated with many of the top-ranked schools in *The Alumni Factor* Overall Ranking, since fundamental intellectual development is a key driver of success and happiness in life.

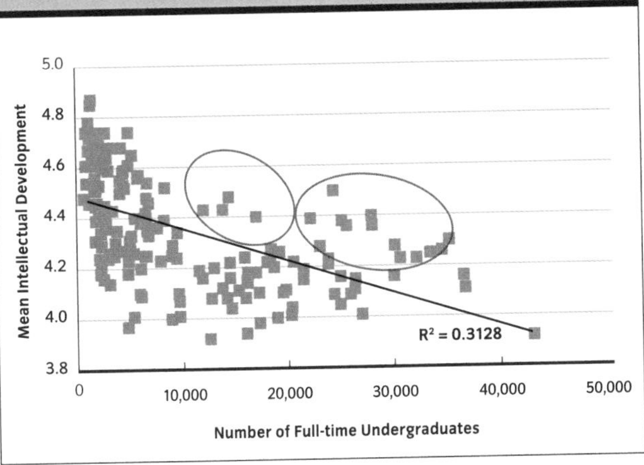

Figure 3.9

Which large schools do the best job of intellectual development?

There are 17 schools (circled in red in **Figure 3.9**) that, despite their large number of undergraduates, provide strong intellectual development to their students. While it certainly is not a given that small school size yields high intellectual development, schools that can deliver significant intellectual development with 10,000 undergraduates or more deserve special praise. These 17 schools have consistently managed to deliver high quality for the masses – a challenge that is rarely achieved in education. These are the schools, listed in alphabetical order:

Brigham Young University
Cornell University
Georgia Institute of Technology
Indiana University Bloomington
Michigan State University
Purdue University
Texas A&M University
University of California, Berkeley
University of California, Los Angeles
University of California, San Diego
University of Florida
University of Illinois at Urbana-Champaign
University of Michigan
University of North Carolina at Chapel Hill
University of Texas at Austin
University of Virginia
University of Wisconsin

Universities of >10,000 undergraduates with High Intellectual Development & High SATs

School	Under-graduate Population	Intellectual Develop-ment Average Score*	Average SAT Score**
UC Berkeley	24,385	4.50	3.33
University of VA	14,427	4.48	3.44
Cornell University	13,846	4.43	3.86
Georgia Tech	12,004	4.43	3.14
UC San Diego	22,205	4.39	3.10
University of Michigan	25,168	4.38	3.39
UCLA	25,629	4.36	3.22
University of WI (Mad)	28,043	4.36	3.15

Figure 3.10

** Scale = 5 Strongly Agree was Intellectually Developed to 0 = Strongly Disagree*

*** Mean SAT Score on a scale where 1 is a score less than 1100 and 6 is between 1500 and 1600. A score in the 3 range is between 1200 and 1299.*

However, the graduates of eight of these seventeen schools not only receive excellent intellectual development, but are also of consistently high intellectual capability (as measured by SAT scores that exceed the mean of the colleges in our database). This means the challenge of developing students is even higher at these eight colleges than it is for the average college or university. Listed in **Figure 3.10** are the eight large schools that do an excellent job of developing the intellect of their highly capable students. We believe these schools deserve special recognition for delivering excellence on a large scale to very bright students over a number of decades.

To best understand the truly unique accomplishment of these eight schools, it is instructive to make a few comparisons. Each of these eight schools exceeds the average intellectual development and the average SAT scores of the colleges in our database. Yet remarkably, they equal the intellectual development scores of much smaller schools that also have excellent reputations. For example, **Figure 3.11** shows two excellent smaller schools, the third is University of Michigan which is large, with intellectual development and SAT scores in the same range as these top eight large schools. When you consider the fact that the large schools are 10 to 20 times larger than these small schools, your admiration for their

School	Under-graduate Population	Intellectual Develop-ment Average Score*	Average SAT Score**
Colby College	1,867	4.39	3.28
Colgate	2,780	4.38	3.38
University of Michigan	25,168	4.38	3.39

* *Scale = 5 Strongly Agree was Intellectually Developed to 0 = Strongly Disagree*

** *Mean SAT Score on a scale where 1 is a score less than 1100 and 6 is between 1500 and 1600. A score in the 3 range is between 1200 and 1299.*

Figure 3.11

Factor	R-Squared Result	Correlation Coefficient
Student/Faculty Ratio	.41	-.64
% of Classes with <20	.39	.62
% w/ Post-grad Degree	.38	.61
% Students Graduate in 4 yrs	.36	.60
# of Undergrads Enrolled	.31	-.56

Figure 3.12

accomplishment rises. To put it in the proper perspective via an example: Over the last decade, Colgate has provided an excellent education to roughly 28,000 students, while the University of Michigan has provided an equally excellent education to more than 250,000 students – approximately nine times more.

What are the key drivers of intellectual development, as measured by graduates?

So, what is it that makes certain schools excel in the intellectual development of their graduates while other schools languish? We have analyzed our alumni responses in order to isolate some of the key drivers of intellectual development. Listed in **Figure 3.12** are the key elements that we have identified, along with a measure of their strength in driving intellectual development.

While none of these results are strong enough to be definitive, they give us an indication that, in general, small wins over large. Obviously, the many other factors that are driving graduate perception can be further studied and we intend to do that.

Summary

Intellectual development is one of the most desired outcomes by graduates of any college or university. While a majority of alumni believe their college did a good job in this area, there are clear differences among the Top 177 schools we have analyzed. Top box scores (*% Strongly Agree*) in intellectual development range from 27.6% to over 89%, indicating wide variation in how graduates view their college's prowess in this area. Small liberal arts colleges tend to excel at intellectual development, but there are 17 large schools that also do an excellent job of creating the environment required to fully develop their students. A graduate's perception of intellectual development at their college is most strongly correlated with: the student-faculty ratio, the percentage of classes with less than 20 students, the percentage of graduates with a post-graduate degree, and the percentage of students graduating in four years.

Top 50 Ranked Schools for: Intellectual Development

Rank	School	Rank	School
1.	Sewanee: The University of the South	25.	Middlebury College
2.	Reed College	25.	Princeton University
3.	Centre College	29.	Morehouse College
4.	Kenyon College	29.	Smith College
4.	Scripps College	31.	St. Olaf College
4.	Swarthmore College	31.	United States Naval Academy
4.	University of Chicago	33.	Gonzaga University
4.	Wesleyan University	34.	Brown University
4.	Whitman College	35.	Bates College
10.	Bryn Mawr College	35.	The College of William & Mary
11.	Carleton College	37.	Bard College
12.	Grinnell College	37.	Massachusetts Institute of Technology
12.	Mount Holyoke College	39.	Harvard University
14.	Davidson College	39.	Pitzer College
14.	Rice University	39.	Washington and Lee University
14.	United States Military Academy	42.	Occidental College
17.	Haverford College	42.	Spelman College
18.	Pomona College	42.	Wake Forest University
18.	Vassar College	45.	Hamilton College
18.	Yale University	45.	United States Air Force Academy
21.	College of the Holy Cross	45.	University of Notre Dame
21.	Colorado College	48.	Bowdoin College
21.	Oberlin College	48.	Macalester College
24.	Wellesley College	50.	Dartmouth College
25.	Amherst College	50.	University of California, Berkeley
25.	California Institute of Technology		

The schools with the best rankings are those with the highest weighted average level of agreement among six possible responses.

"My College Developed Me Intellectually."

	Highest School*	All College Grads**	Lowest School*
% Strongly Agree	89.0%	49.6%	28.0%

** Among 177 colleges and universities*

*** >42,000 college graduates from >400 colleges and universities*

Social and Communication Skills Development

Making Your Point

We expect our colleges and universities to provide not only rigorous intellectual development, but also to strengthen the social and communication skills of students. The traditions, culture and overall campus life can make four undergraduate years a positive growth experience, or something quite different. When we asked graduates, now with the benefit of hindsight, to tell us how well their college developed their social and communication skills, we got a wide variety of responses, reflecting the diversity of campus cultures across the US. So, here are *The Alumni Factor* colleges and universities rated by their ability to develop social and communication skills for their graduates. According to alumni, some schools excel at providing opportunities for students to interact socially in the classroom, to participate in a broad range of campus clubs and activities, and to have fun and enjoy their friends. There are other schools where these are simply not a priority.

The four top-ranked schools (and five of the Top 10) are all Southern schools where social graces, manners and polite conversation still hold sway. At most of these schools, boys still ask girls out on dates (believe it or not) and the fraternities and sororities have a major influence on the social scene. You will also notice that the Top 50 schools in this attribute are anything but a list of the "party" schools. Graduates have rated their colleges based on the development of social and communication skills that have proven to be valuable later in life.

Sewanee: The University of the South

#1 in Social & Communication Skill Development

Centre College

#2 in Social & Communication Skill Development

Small, Intimate Schools Tend Toward Higher Scores on This Attribute

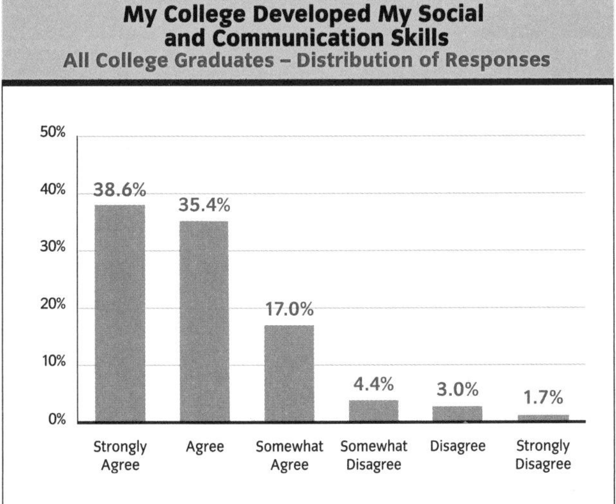

- The top-rated school in this attribute is Sewanee (68% *Strongly Agree*), and the lowest-rated school is RPI (16% *Strongly Agree*).
- Twelve of the 13 lowest-rated schools are technical or heavily quantitative schools.
- Virginia Tech (49th with 41% who *Strongly Agree*) is the highest-rated tech school.

Liberal Arts Schools Do the Best Job of Developing These Skills

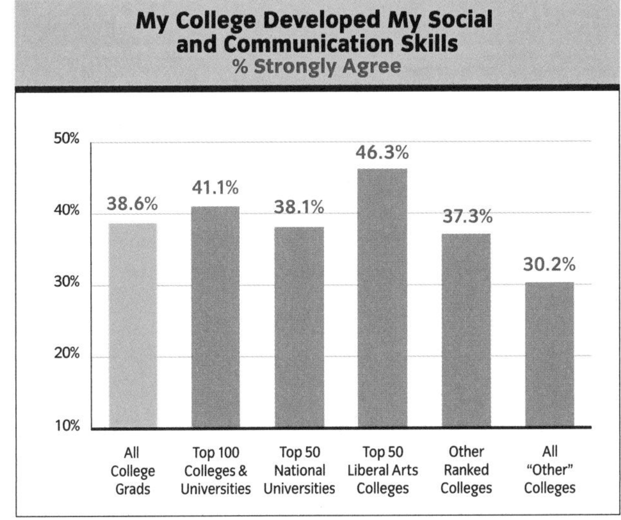

- The liberal arts colleges tend to do best in this measure – 15 of the Top 20 schools are liberal arts colleges.
- *All "Other" Colleges* underperform ranked colleges on this attribute.
- *Top 50 National Universities* perform at about the level of *All College Grads* on this attribute.

Overall Social and Communication Development Is Rated Highly by Graduates

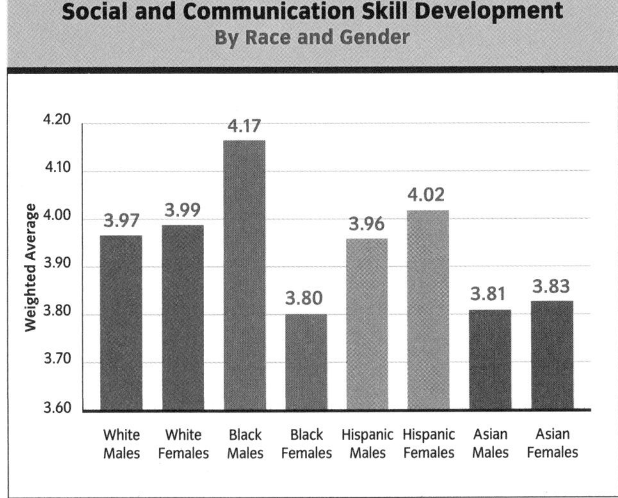

- Women rate their colleges slightly higher than men on this attribute, in all races except for Black.
- *Black Males* give the highest ratings to their colleges on this attribute.
- *Black Females* give the lowest rating to their colleges, with *Asian Males* only slightly above that low rating.
- White and Hispanic males and females provide roughly the same rating.

Grads Credit Their Colleges for These Skills at a Decreasing Rate with Age

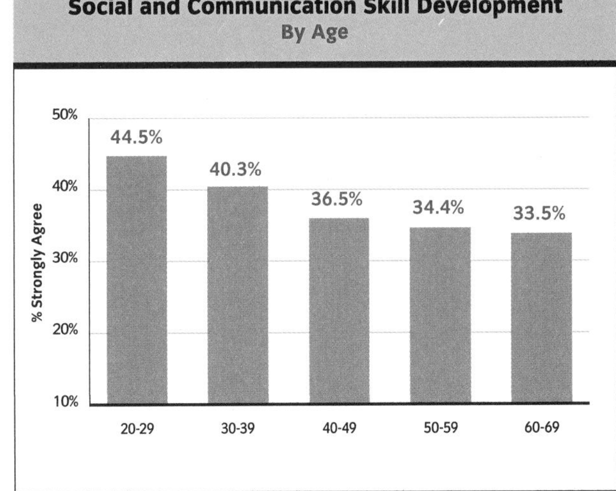

- Graduates lower their rating of their college's performance as they age.
- As graduates age they also realize the importance of this skill and give credit to environs beyond their college experience (work life, family) for development.
- Even 40 years after graduation, one-third of the graduates still *Strongly Agree* their college developed their social and communication skills.

Top 50 Ranked Schools for: Social & Communication Skills Development

1.	Sewanee: The University of the South	27.	Brigham Young University
2.	Centre College	27.	Elon University
3.	Spelman College	27.	Texas A&M University
3.	Washington and Lee University	30.	Davidson College
5.	Morehouse College	30.	James Madison University
6.	Gonzaga University	30.	Oberlin College
7.	Wake Forest University	30.	St. Olaf College
7.	Yale University	34.	Auburn University
8.	Colorado College	34.	Brown University
8.	Hamilton College	36.	Depauw University
11.	College of the Holy Cross	36.	Loyola University New Orleans
12.	University of North Carolina at Chapel Hill	36.	Mount Holyoke College
13.	Amherst College	36.	Princeton University
13.	Howard University	36.	Smith College
13.	United States Military Academy	41.	Dartmouth College
16.	Bucknell University	41.	University of Mississippi
16.	Pomona College	41.	Whitman College
16.	Scripps College	44.	Claremont McKenna College
19.	Bowdoin College	44.	Furman University
19.	Grinnell College	44.	Gettysburg College
19.	University of Virginia	44.	Pitzer College
22.	Middlebury College	44.	University of Kansas
22.	University of Alabama	49.	Rice University
24.	Colby College	49.	Trinity University
24.	Wesleyan University	49.	Vassar College
24.	Xavier University	49.	Virginia Polytechnic Institute and State University

The schools with the best rankings are those with the highest weighted average level of agreement among six possible responses.

"My College Developed My Social and Commuication Skills."

	Highest School*	All College Grads**	Lowest School*
% Strongly Agree	68.0%	38.6%	16.0%

** Among 177 colleges and universities*

*** >42,000 college graduates from >400 colleges and universities*

Spiritual Development

A Higher Purpose

What role should a college or university play in the spiritual development of a student? That actually depends on the college or university being asked the question. Some colleges consider spiritual development a fundamental mission of the institution, and build the community and curriculum around it. Other schools view spiritual development as an optional pursuit for each student; they offer a wide variety of courses for spiritual education and exploration, as well as the opportunity to openly practice many faiths. A few, though not many, are more culturally resistant and discourage religious pursuits on campus, but offer a range of academic options for study.

Of all the developmental attributes we measure, spiritual development gets the lowest ratings overall among graduates. Asian and Black graduates give their colleges the highest ratings on this attribute, while White grads give the lowest ratings. Females give lower ratings than males in all races except among Hispanics. Not surprisingly, most of the top-rated schools in this attribute are religiously affiliated. However, there are a few colleges in the Top 25 that may prompt a second glance. Remember, this attribute is not included in the overall ranking of colleges, since it is not a stated goal of many schools.

Brigham Young University

#1 in Spiritual Development

University of Notre Dame

#2 in Spiritual Development

46% of Grads Do Not Believe They Were Spiritually Developed

My College Developed Me Spiritually
All College Graduates – Distribution of Responses

Strongly Agree	Agree	Somewhat Agree	Somewhat Disagree	Disagree	Strongly Disagree
12.8%	16.5%	24.9%	15.3%	17.0%	13.6%

- Only 12.8% of graduates *Strongly Agree* they were spiritually developed – the lowest-rated of all attributes measured.
- Of the Top 10 colleges on this attribute, eight are religiously affiliated. The two schools in the Top 10 that are not religiously affiliated (Morehouse and Spelman) are historically Black colleges with a rich history of multi-faith practices.

Liberal Arts Graduates Are Most Spiritually Developed

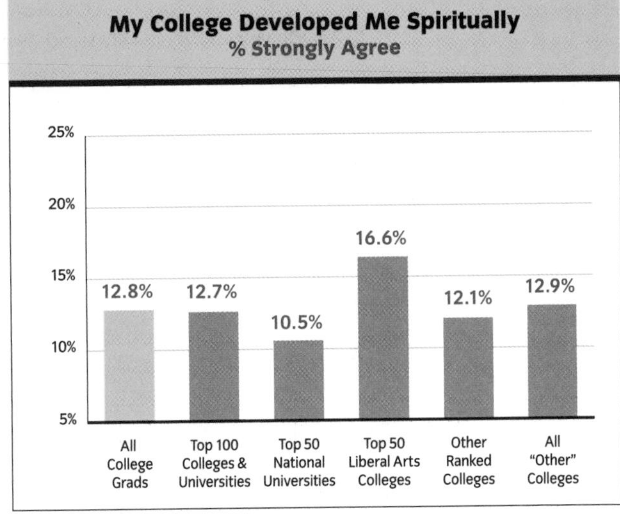

- Graduates of liberal arts colleges are more likely to agree they were developed spiritually.
- The *Top 50 National Universities* (mostly larger schools) are the lowest-rated on spiritual development.

Spiritual Development is Strongest Among Black and Asian Graduates

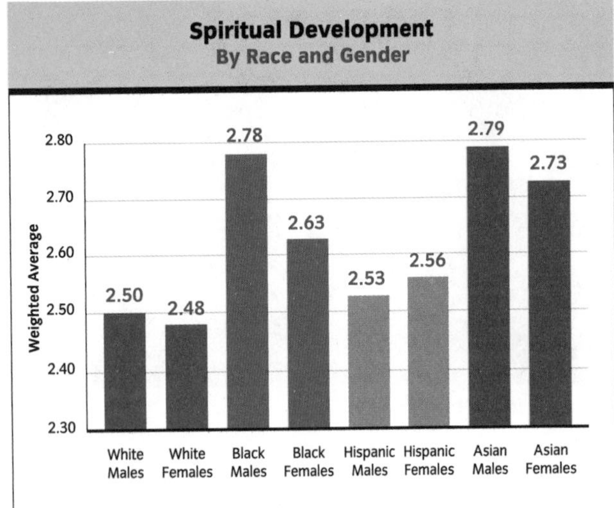

- *Asian Males* and *Black Males* give their colleges the highest ratings for spiritual development.
- White graduates score lower than Hispanic grads and significantly lower than Black and Asian alumni on this attribute.

The Belief that College Developed Grads Spiritually Declines Until Middle Age

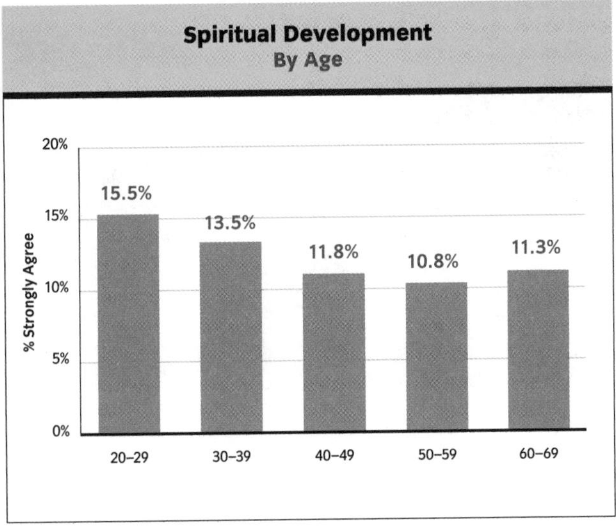

- By middle age, only 11% of graduates believe their college developed them spiritually.

Top 50 Ranked Schools for: Spiritual Development

1. Brigham Young University	26. United States Air Force Academy
2. University of Notre Dame	27. Grinnell College
3. College of the Holy Cross	28. Elon University
4. Spelman College	29. Loyola University Maryland
5. Gonzaga University	30. Furman University
6. Loyola University New Orleans	31. United States Naval Academy
7. Creighton University	32. Wesleyan University
8. Sewanee: The University of the South	33. Swarthmore College
9. Xavier University	34. Centre College
10. Morehouse College	35. Mount Holyoke College
11. St. Olaf College	36. Carleton College
12. Marquette University	37. Washington and Lee University
13. United States Military Academy	38. Yale University
14. Valparaiso University	39. Oberlin College
15. Loyola Marymount University	40. Trinity University
16. Santa Clara University	41. Pitzer College
17. Villanova University	42. Brown University
18. Baylor University	43. Ohio Northern University
19. Davidson College	44. Auburn University
20. Loyola University Chicago	45. Bryn Mawr College
21. Haverford College	46. Harvey Mudd College
22. Georgetown University	47. Kenyon College
23. Boston College	48. Middlebury College
24. Howard University	49. Reed College
25. Pepperdine University	50. Wake Forest University

The schools with the best rankings are those with the highest weighted average level of agreement among six possible responses.

"My College Developed Me Spiritually."

	Highest School*	All College Grads**	Lowest School*
% Strongly Agree	63.0%	12.8%	3.0%

** Among 177 colleges and universities*

*** >42,000 college graduates from >400 colleges and universities*

Developing Deep Friendships

Bonding Through Common Interests – The Best Time of Your Life?

A popular conception of one's college years is that it is not only a time of great personal growth and maturation, but also a period in which deep, personal bonds form between classmates, roommates, and teammates. It is natural, after all, since everyone is embarking on an intense journey of personal growth. It would be natural, indeed, to develop intense friendships in these circumstances, but our data show that there is a wide variation in friendship development across colleges and universities.

One of the most surprising findings in *The Alumni Factor* is that only 37.4% of alumni *Strongly Agree* that they developed deep friendships during their undergraduate years. In fact, slightly more than 20% of alumni disagree to some extent that they developed such friendships. What makes the difference in these unexpected outcomes?

Bonding Through Common Interests

Small, close-knit college communities with a relatively homogeneous student body tend to create the deepest friendships. Of the Top 25 ranked schools in this measure, only two (Notre Dame and Howard University) have more than 5,000 students. Not one college in the Top 25 has more than 8,500 students. In fact, 17 of the Top 25 have less than 3,000 students. The size of the undergraduate population clearly plays an important role in friendship development during the undergraduate years.

Another characteristic of the top colleges in this measure is having a concentrated student body of one gender, race or religion. Of the Top 25, three are considered the best historically Black colleges in the country (Morehouse, Spelman, Howard); eight colleges have males constituting more than 66% of the alumni (Navy, West Point, Air Force, Morehouse, Harvey Mudd) or females (Wellesley, Spelman, Howard); and in 15 of the Top 25, White men and women account for more than 70% of the alumni. This does not mean, however, that diverse schools cannot develop deep friendships. There are five schools in the Top 25 that are diverse in gender, race and religion (Grinnell, Swarthmore, Pomona, Wesleyan and Amherst). Note that these are all smaller liberal arts schools. Homogeneity does not act as a "silver bullet," guaranteeing close friendships, as both BYU (with a student body that is nearly 90% White, and over 98% members of the Church of the Latter Day Saints) and the University of Utah (84% in-state and 77% White), show fairly low scores for Friendship Development.

College Is a Key Time for Developing Close Friendships

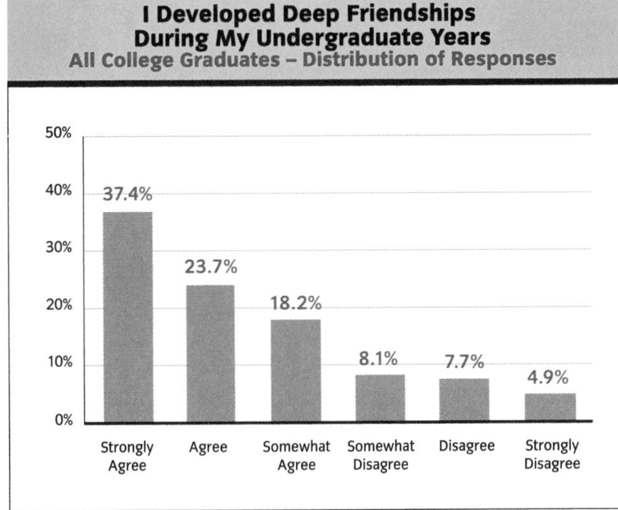

- Roughly 21% of graduates do not agree they made close friends in college.
- This Top 2 Box score (61.1%) is in the lower middle of all attributes in graduate agreement.

Liberal Arts Colleges Stand Out in Friendship Development

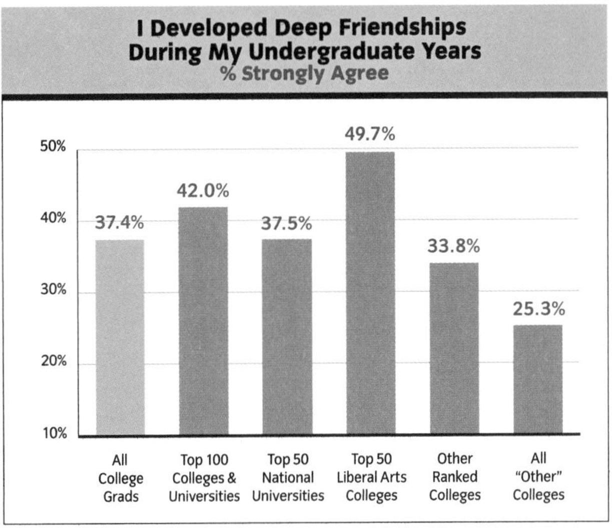

- Nineteen of the Top 20 schools and 23 of Top 25 schools on this attribute are small liberal arts colleges.
- Top box (*Strongly Agree*) scores range from 67% (Sewanee) to 19% (University of Utah).

Black Graduates Are Most Likely to Agree They Developed Close Friendships

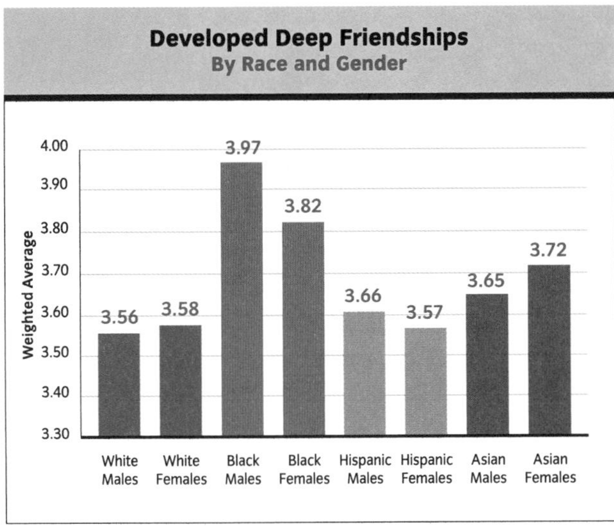

- Asian grads are significantly more likely to agree they developed deep friendships than White alumni.
- *White Males* give the lowest scores in friendship development.

The Recognition of Deep College Friendships Reduces with Age

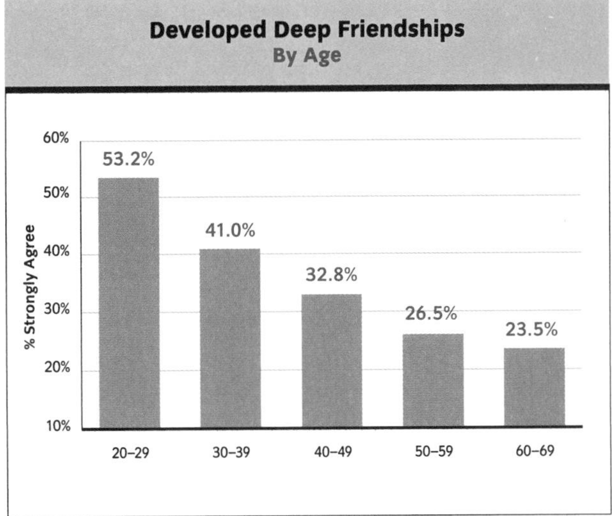

- As graduates age, they are less likely to agree they developed close friends as undergrads.
- Even in their sixties, nearly one-quarter of graduates still agree they developed close friendships in college.

Staying Close to Undergraduate Friends

Lifetime Connections

Strong, sustainable friendships can come from sharing deep life experiences. The extent to which an individual college provides the opportunities for moments that create lasting bonds between students determines its position on this list. The Top 25 schools in this category each provide unique life experiences that create friendships strong enough to survive life's ups and downs. Each of these schools finds a way to bring in a group of talented high school seniors, initially strangers, and unite them for life behind an intellectual pursuit, a social cause, a historic college tradition, a winning team, an inspired idea, a rich social community, or in the case of many of these colleges, all of the above. Schools such as West Point, Notre Dame, Morehouse, Wellesley, Princeton, Harvey Mudd and Davidson all have their very own cultures that help bring these special experiences to life.

Once again, smaller schools dominate the top positions on this list. Quite simply, it is easier to create these experiences in smaller communities. This section shows you the colleges that excel at doing so.

Morehouse College

#1 in Friendship Development

Sewanee: The University of the South

#2 in Friendship Development

Developing Friendships is Much Easier than Maintaining Them

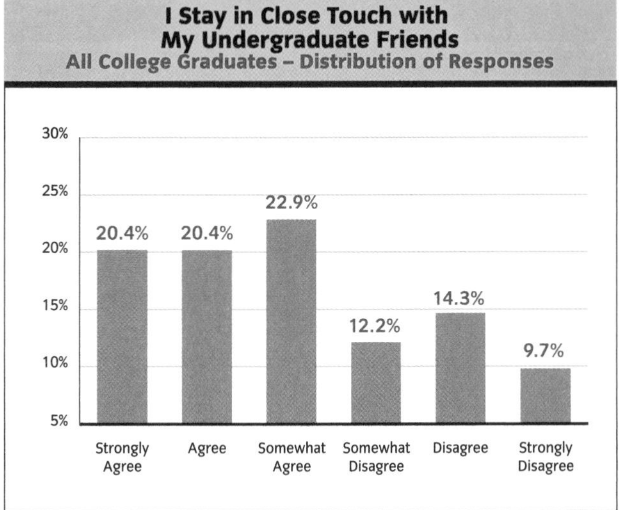

- Over a third (37%) of graduates *Strongly Agree* that they developed strong friendships, but only 20% stay in touch.
- Top box scores range from a high of 50% (Morehouse and Spelman) to a low of 6% (University of Wyoming).

Graduates of Liberal Arts Schools Do the Best Job of Sustaining Friendships

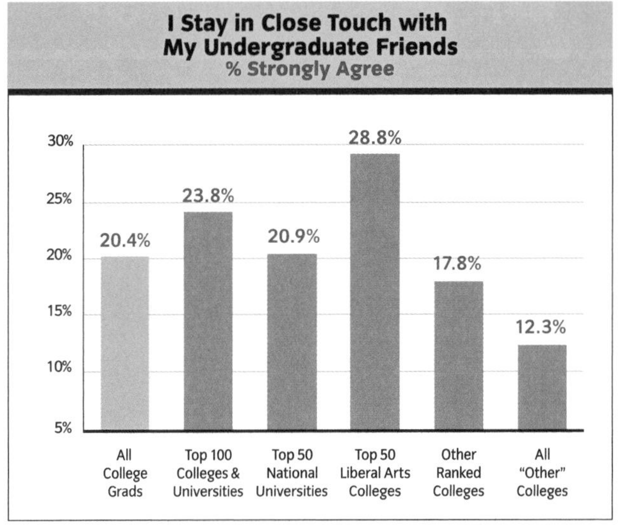

- The *Top 50 National Universities* do as well as *All Colleges* on the sustaining friendships attribute.
- *All "Other" Colleges* significantly underperform on sustaining friendships.

Black and Asian Graduates Maintain Friendships Better than White Alumni

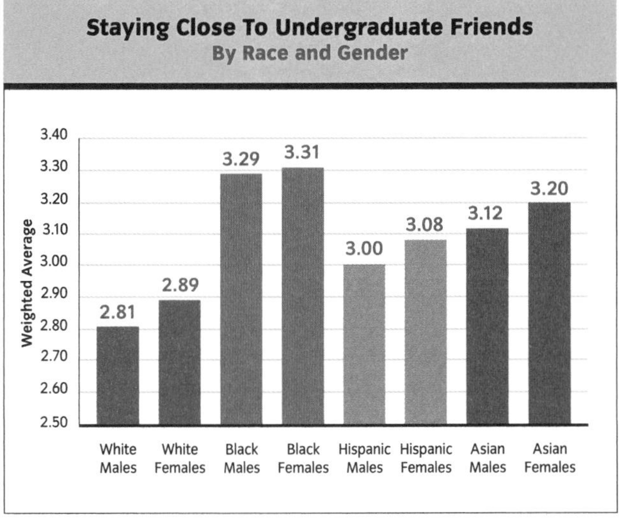

- Females outperform males on sustaining friendships across races.
- *White Males* significantly underperform every other race/gender breakout on this attribute.
- Some colleges have *White Male* top box scores over two times the average (West Point, Naval Academy, Centre, Washington & Lee).

Ability to Sustain College Friendships Lessens with Age

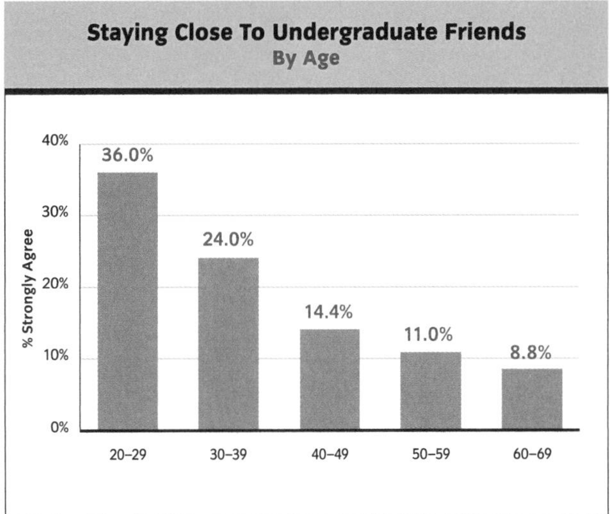

- On this attribute, most colleges and universities experience falloff with age; however, the best colleges experience significantly less. For example, Yale and Morehouse see no falloff with age.

Top 50 Ranked Schools for: Friendship Development

1.	Morehouse College	24.	Elon University
2.	Sewanee: The University of the South	24.	Franklin & Marshall College
3.	United States Military Academy	28.	University of Alabama
4.	Spelman College	29.	Bowdoin College
5.	United States Naval Academy	29.	Furman University
6.	Washington and Lee University	29.	Gettysburg College
7.	Kenyon College	29.	Princeton University
8.	St. Olaf College	29.	Yale University
9.	Harvey Mudd College	34.	Hamilton College
10.	Grinnell College	35.	Reed College
11.	Centre College	36.	Middlebury College
12.	Bucknell University	37.	Brown University
12.	College of the Holy Cross	37.	Mount Holyoke College
14.	Swarthmore College	37.	Smith College
15.	United States Air Force Academy	40.	Bryn Mawr College
15.	University of Notre Dame	40.	Whitman College
17.	Pomona College	42.	Williams College
17.	Wellesley College	43.	Dartmouth College
19.	Davidson College	43.	Wake Forest University
20.	Wesleyan University	45.	Cornell University
21.	Carleton College	46.	Colby College
21.	Howard University	47.	Colgate University
23.	Oberlin College	48.	Bard College
24.	Amherst College	48.	Duke University
24.	California Institute of Technology	48.	Rice University

The schools with the best rankings are those with the highest weighted average level of agreement among possible responses.

"I Developed Deep Friendships During My Undergraduate Years."

	Highest School*	All College Grads**	Lowest School*
% Strongly Agree	68.0%	37.4%	18.0%

** Among 177 colleges and universities*

*** >42,000 college graduates from >400 colleges and universities*

Preparation For Career Success

Integrity, Hard Work, Collaboration, Perseverance

While there are some students who enter college with a clear idea of what they want to do with their lives, most do not have detailed plans as freshmen. However, by the time they finish college, most graduates feel they have been well prepared for their careers. Nearly 66% of all college graduates feel their college armed them for success in their chosen field. As with virtually every attribute we analyzed, there is a wide disparity between colleges on this measure. The schools that perform the best, as rated by their graduates, are the military academies (West Point, Naval Academy, Air Force Academy) and two of the top technical schools (Georgia Tech, Caltech). Perhaps more surprising is that the Top 10 schools in this measure are rounded out by four Southern liberal arts schools (Centre College, Sewanee, Washington & Lee, Davidson) and one strong Southern university (Rice). According to graduates, preparation for success means being ready to work hard, with integrity, alongside others, over a sustained period. The schools that best instill these values get the highest marks from their graduates.

United States Military Academy

#1 in Preparation for Career Success

United States Naval Academy

#2 in Preparation for Career Success

Colleges Do a Good Job Overall Preparing Graduates for Career Success

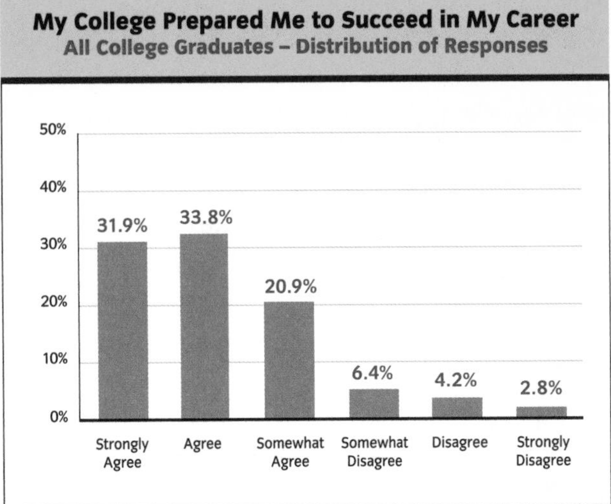

- Nearly 66% of college graduates *Strongly Agree* or *Agree* that they were prepared for career success; 27% of graduates are not quite sure (*Somewhat Agree* or *Somewhat Disagree*); and only 7% of graduates *Disagree* or *Strongly Disagree.*
- West Point, Naval Academy and Air Force are ranked 1st, 2nd and 4th respectively.

Liberal Arts Colleges Better Prepare Grads for Career Success

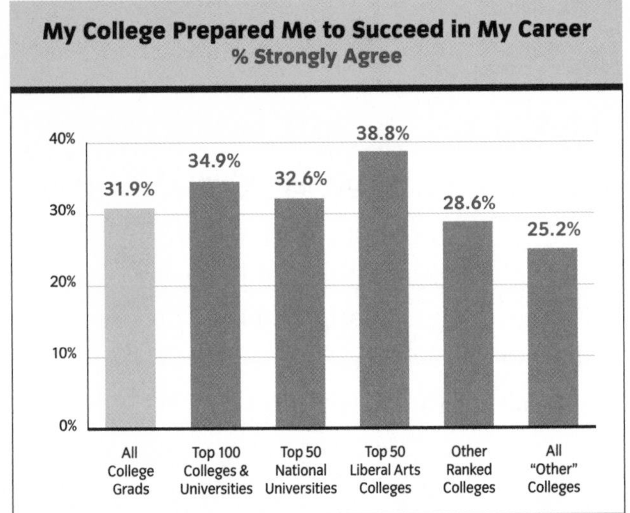

- Graduates of the *Top 50 Liberal Arts Colleges* are most likely to *Strongly Agree* that their college prepared them for Career Success.
- Graduates of *All "Other" Colleges* are least likely to *Strongly Agree* with this statement.
- Graduates of the *Top 50 National Universities* rate their schools in line with graduates of all colleges.

Black Male Graduates Rate Their Colleges Highest for Career Preparation

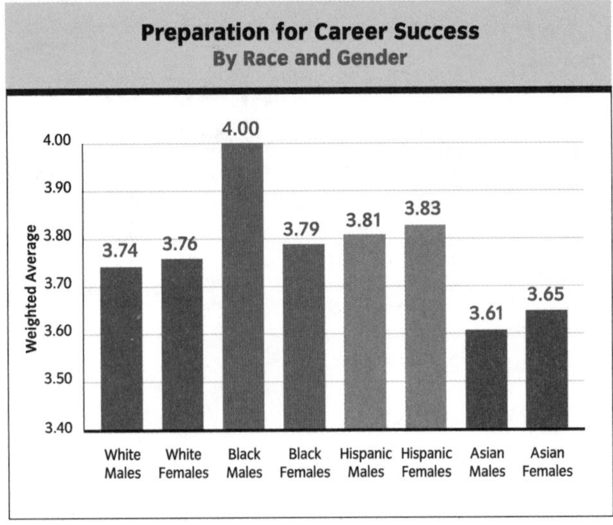

- Except for Black graduates, females rate their colleges higher than males across races.
- Asian grads rate their colleges lowest on this attribute.

Belief in Their Colleges' Prowess Holds Steady for Grads Over Time

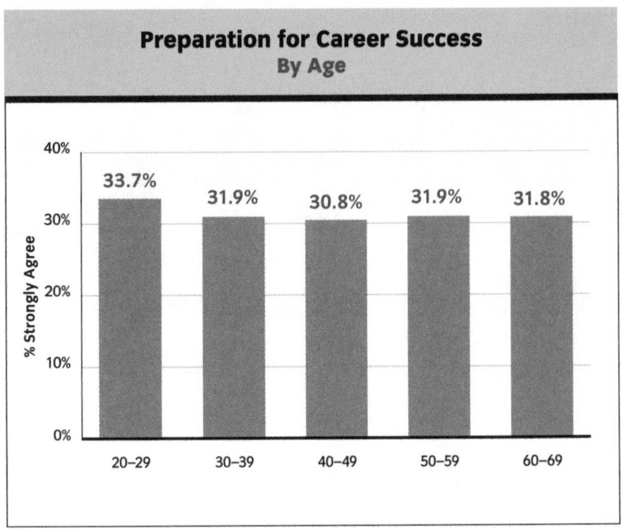

- There is little difference in a graduate's view of their college's performance on this attribute from their thirties onward.

Top 50 Ranked Schools for: Preparation for Career Success

1.	United States Military Academy	26.	Worcester Polytechnic Institute
2.	United States Naval Academy	27.	Creighton University
3.	Centre College	27.	Hamilton College
4.	United States Air Force Academy	29.	Grinnell College
5.	Morehouse College	29.	Princeton University
5.	Spelman College	29.	Virginia Polytechnic Institute and State University
7.	Georgia Institute of Technology	32.	Furman University
8.	Sewanee: The University of the South	32.	Massachusetts Institute of Technology
9.	Washington and Lee University	34.	Colorado College
10.	Rice University	34.	Dartmouth College
11.	California Institute of Technology	36.	Bucknell University
12.	Davidson College	36.	Claremont McKenna College
13.	Mount Holyoke College	36.	Wake Forest University
14.	Wellesley College	39.	Amherst College
15.	Yale University	39.	The College of William & Mary
16.	Gonzaga University	39.	St. Olaf College
16.	Texas A&M University	39.	University of Virginia
18.	Auburn University	43.	Purdue University
18.	Harvey Mudd College	43.	Smith College
18.	University of Notre Dame	45.	University of Wyoming
21.	Carleton College	46.	Georgetown University
22.	College of the Holy Cross	46.	Marquette University
22.	Xavier University	46.	University of Richmond
24.	Brigham Young University	49.	Elon University
24.	Howard University	49.	University of Florida

The schools with the best rankings are those with the highest weighted average level of agreement among six possible responses.

"My College Prepared Me to Succeed in My Career."

	Highest School*	All College Grads**	Lowest School*
% Strongly Agree	76.0%	31.9%	14.0%

** Among 177 colleges and universities*

*** >42,000 college graduates from >400 colleges and universities*

Immediate Job Opportunities

Getting on the Payroll

While finding a job immediately after graduation is not the only reason to get a good education, it is certainly a top consideration. Roughly two-thirds of all graduates feel their college helped them land a job after graduation; the remaining one-third do not. As is the case for the attribute Preparation for Career Success, the schools that perform the best on the measure of Immediate Job Opportunites, as rated by their graduates, are the military academies (West Point, Naval Academy, Air Force Academy) and the top technical schools (Georgia Tech, MIT, Caltech, Harvey Mudd, RPI). Across all schools, however, there is little correlation between success in getting a job immediately after graduation and preparation for overall career success. Liberal arts schools do not perform as well on this measure, although there are some exceptions. Schools that focus on this as a competency are recognized for it by their graduates.

United States Naval Academy

#1 in Providing Job Opportunities

United States Air Force Academy

#2 in Providing Job Opportunities

44% of Graduates *Strongly Agree* or *Agree* that Their College Helped Them Land a Job

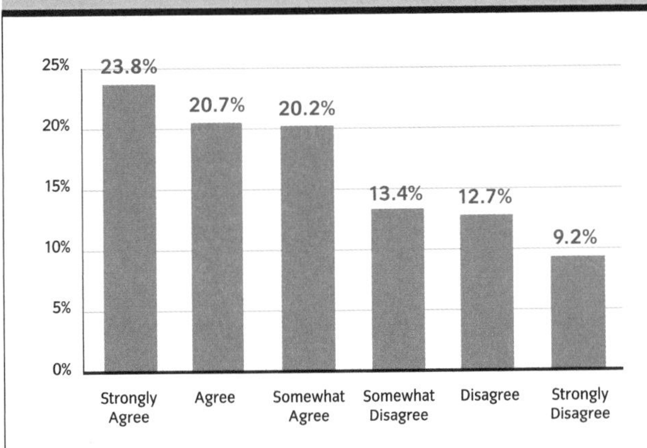

- Nearly 65% of college graduates *Strongly Agree*, *Agree* or *Somewhat Agree* with this statement.
- Over a third (35%) of college graduates disagree to some extent with this statement.
- Nine of the Top 10 schools on this attribute are military academies or technical schools.

Liberal Arts Colleges Do Not Get High Marks Overall on this Attribute

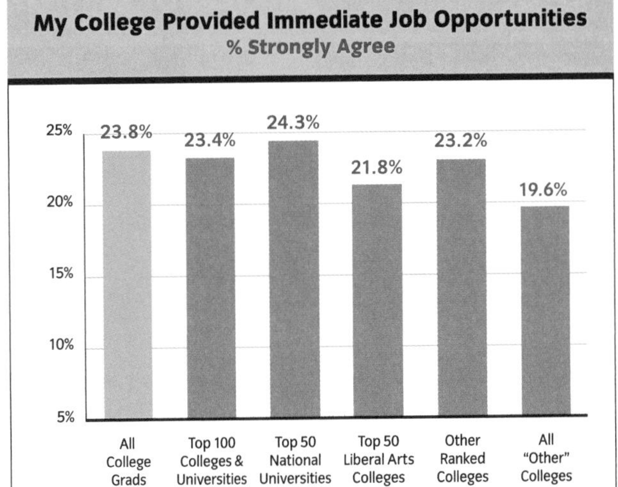

- There are only slight differences across the broad groupings of colleges measured.
- The *Top 50 Liberal Arts Colleges* and *All "Other" Colleges* rank slightly lower than the other groups.

Black and Hispanic Males Are Most Likely to See College as a Key to a Job

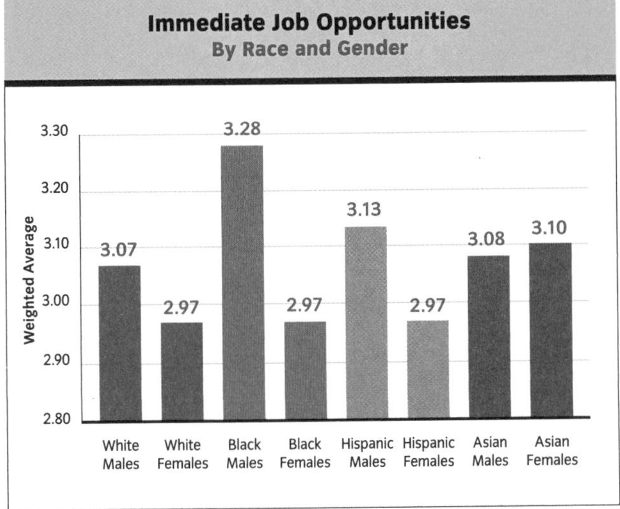

- *Asian Females* are more likely to credit their college with generating job opportunities, than White, Hispanic and Black females, who are least likely.

Graduate Appreciation for College as an Employment Advantage Grows with Age

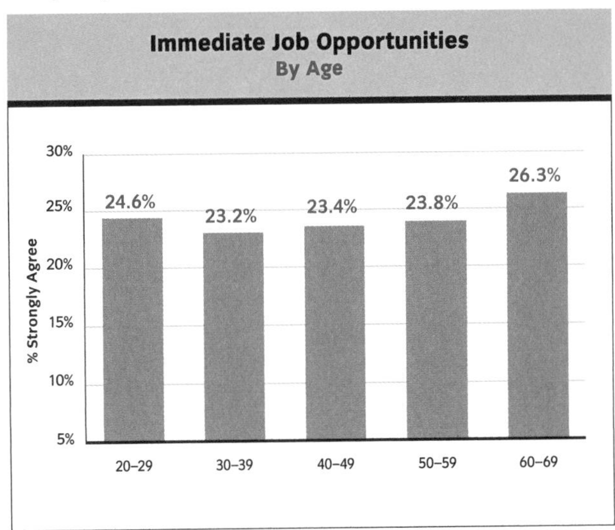

- Although quite low versus other attributes, graduate perception on this attribute initially drops and then rises through a graduate's thirties, forties, fifties and sixties.

Top 50 Ranked Schools for: Immediate Job Opportunities

1.	United States Naval Academy	26.	Stanford University
2.	United States Air Force Academy	28.	University of Wyoming
2.	United States Military Academy	29.	Xavier University
4.	Georgia Institute of Technology	30.	Bucknell University
5.	Massachusetts Institute of Technology	30.	Dartmouth College
6.	California Institute of Technology	30.	Ohio Northern University
7.	Harvey Mudd College	30.	Washington and Lee University
8.	Rensselaer Polytechnic Institute	34.	Claremont McKenna College
9.	Texas A&M University	34.	University of Richmond
10.	Northeastern University	34.	University of Southern California
11.	Auburn University	37.	University of Virginia
12.	University of Notre Dame	38.	Brigham Young University
13.	Drexel University	38.	Kansas State University
13.	Virginia Polytechnic Institute and State University	38.	Villanova University
13.	Worcester Polytechnic Institute	41.	Lehigh University
16.	Purdue University	41.	Santa Clara University
16.	Spelman College	43.	University of Alabama
18.	Creighton University	44.	Baylor University
18.	Princeton University	44.	North Carolina State University
20.	Rice University	46.	University of Tennessee
21.	Harvard University	47.	Cornell University
22.	University of Pennsylvania	47.	Davidson College
23.	Howard University	47.	Duke University
23.	Morehouse College	47.	Marquette University
23.	Yale University	47.	University of Michigan
26.	James Madison University	47.	Vanderbilt University

The schools with the best rankings are those with the highest weighted average level of agreement among six possible responses.

"My College Provided Immediate Job Opportunities."

	Highest School*	All College Grads**	Lowest School*
% Strongly Agree	94.0%	23.8%	6.0%

** Among 177 colleges and universities*

*** >42,000 college graduates from >400 colleges and universities*

CHAPTER 4

Overall Assessment by Alumni

The Alumni Factor
Overall College Assessment

Alumni were given three statements regarding their current view of their college and were asked the extent to which they agreed or disagreed with each statement.

Current College Assessment

1. Would they choose to attend their college again?
2. Was their education worth the money they paid?
3. Would they recommend their school to a prospective student today?

In giving alumni a chance to grade their college, it is necessary to put some distance between a graduate and their school to get a true sense of the overall value they assign to their undergraduate experience. As was the case when rating elements of their College Experience, alumni are more objective arbiters because they have more life experiences upon which to draw than do undergraduates.

These assessments hold significant value for the colleges themselves, as they indicate whether or not their alumni think they are on the right track today. Often, a college and its alumni begin to drift apart as one party changes its views on educational or social issues – or as alumni come to disagree with a school's policies and priorities. Over time, colleges shift their positions or emphasis on academic issues, athletic priorities, social issues, admissions standards or other critical operating elements. This can cause a rift in the relationship between the school and its alumni. This chapter details which colleges are best at maintaining strong alignment with their graduates on these and other critical issues.

Would Graduates Personally Choose Their College Again?

No Regrets

When a graduate reflects upon their alma mater and determines that they made a mistake in choosing their college, it is typically the result of a few key factors. This chapter discusses these factors and highlights the dramatic differences between those graduates with regrets and those who would do it all over again.

It is inevitable that there will be graduates from every school who wish they had gone to another college. As in every other factor we measure, there is a major difference from school to school. University of Michigan, Virginia Tech and Yale rank highest among the national universities, while Harvey Mudd, Reed and Amherst are tops among the liberal arts colleges. On the low end of the spectrum there are 39 schools where 10% to 25% of graduates *Strongly Agree* or *Agree* they should have gone to another college. For perspective, that same measurement is only 4% at Michigan and Yale.

Graduates who wish they had gone elsewhere tend to be older, male, not White, lower income, lower net worth and significantly less happy in their overall lives. They are, consequently, much less generous in their assessment of their college and their undergraduate experience.

Harvey Mudd College

#1 in Would Choose My College Again

Reed College

#2 in Would Choose My College Again

Most Graduates Would Choose Their College Again

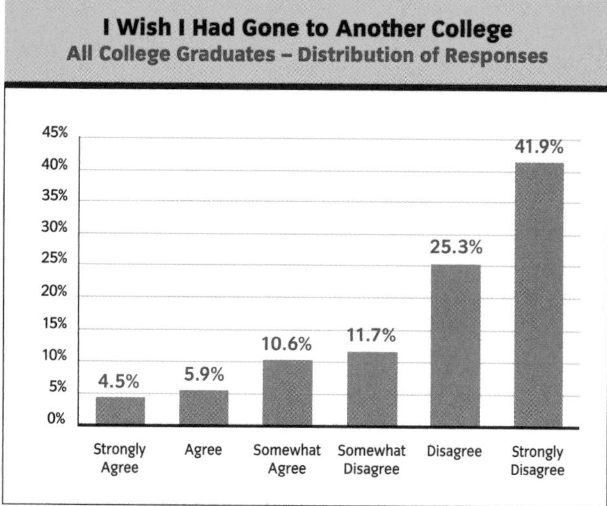

- A fifth (21%) of graduates wish to some extent they had gone to another college.
- However, two-thirds of the graduates would make the same choice again.
- The 10.4% of graduates who *Strongly Agree* or *Agree* they should have chosen differently are 59% more likely to be unemployed, 9% more likely to be male and 20% less likely to vote Republican.

Graduating From a Top 100 College or University Is the Best Way to Avoid Regret

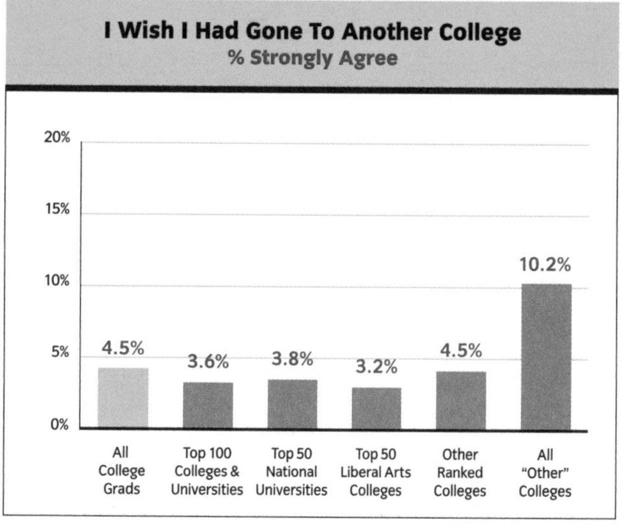

- The *Top 50 Liberal Arts Colleges* and *Top 50 National Colleges* have the lowest regret.
- The highest percentage of regret is among graduates of *All "Other" Colleges.*

Asian Grads Have the Highest Level of Regret

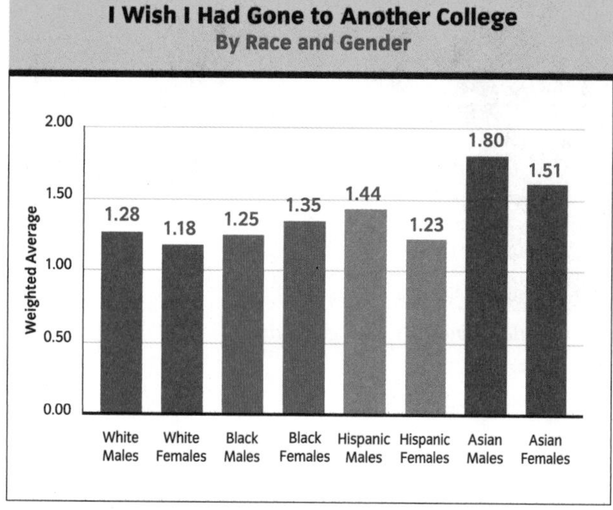

- *White* and *Hispanic Females* appear to be most satisfied with their college choice (the lowest score indicates highest satisfaction).

Although Regret Grows Slightly with Age, It is Still Very Low

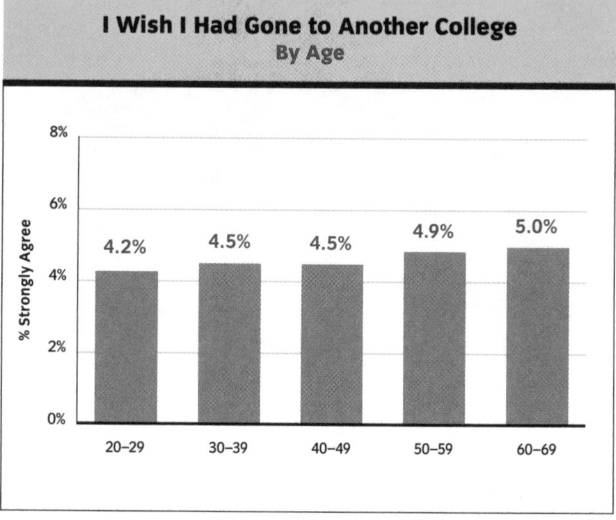

- Regret level never exceeds 5% *(% Strongly Agree)* over the life of graduates.

Top 50 Ranked Schools for: Would Choose My College Again

1. Harvey Mudd College	26. Centre College
2. Reed College	27. Pomona College
3. Amherst College	28. Kansas State University
4. Virginia Polytechnic Institute and State University	29. Haverford College
5. University of Michigan	30. Rice University
6. Yale University	31. Colorado College
7. College of Charleston	31. Stanford University
8. University of North Carolina at Chapel Hill	33. Pepperdine University
9. Morehouse College	33. Xavier University
10. Spelman College	35. University of Richmond
11. College of the Holy Cross	36. Sewanee: The University of the South
12. University of Kansas	37. North Carolina State University
13. Auburn University	38. Trinity University
13. Middlebury College	39. University of Iowa
15. University of Texas at Austin	40. University of California, Berkeley
15. University of Virginia	41. Furman University
17. Grinnell College	41. Howard University
18. Oregon State University	41. Princeton University
19. Washington and Lee University	41. University of California, Los Angeles
20. Gonzaga University	45. Michigan State University
20. Wesleyan University	46. Bradley University
22. Bucknell University	47. Valparaiso University
22. Rollins College	48. University of Notre Dame
24. Carleton College	49. Cornell University
25. Santa Clara University	50. University of Florida

The schools with the best rankings are those with the highest weighted average level of agreement among six possible responses.

"I Wish I Had Gone to Another College."

	Highest School*	All College Grads**	Lowest School*
% Strongly Agree	0.0%	4.5%	12.0%

** Among 177 colleges and universities*

*** >42,000 college graduates from >400 colleges and universities*

Was College a Good Value For the Money?

Graduates Get Their Money's Worth

It has never been more important to understand the real value of a college education. With discretionary incomes under extreme pressure and prices for higher education escalating with seemingly no end in sight, it is crucial for students and parents to hear how graduates feel about the true value of their undergraduate years. Roughly 25% of all graduates believe their college was not a good value for the money, yet we know there are some schools that truly stand out as excellent values. As you likely already know, and will see confirmed later in this book, a college degree is one of the keys to a life of personal development, fulfillment, success and happiness.

The reason most alumni (roughly 75%) rate their college as a good value is because it truly was – a college education is a high return investment in today's market. Whether you attend a college that charges $15,000 or $50,000 per year, the typical graduate more than offsets that expense with incremental earnings over their lifetime. After factoring in financial aid from schools and parents, the amount the typical student actually pays to attend college is significantly lower than the incremental earning potential they receive from their college degree. In addition, a school's "list price" is much higher than the actual price the typical student pays to attend. You will see this estimated "Net Price" for each college on the College Profile Overviews in Chapter 11. The Net Price of a college consists of the total annual expenses required to attend, less the value of grants and aid given to the student.

Regardless of the Net Price of a college, you will see in Chapter 5 the large economic advantage bestowed upon college graduates versus non-graduates. However, the economic advantage gained by graduates over those with no college degree has little or no correlation to the price of the college. There is no clear indication that a higher-priced school necessarily brings greater benefits to the graduates. Lower-priced schools often yield graduates who are just as successful and equally as happy.

Most Graduates Agree Their College Was Well Worth the Money Paid

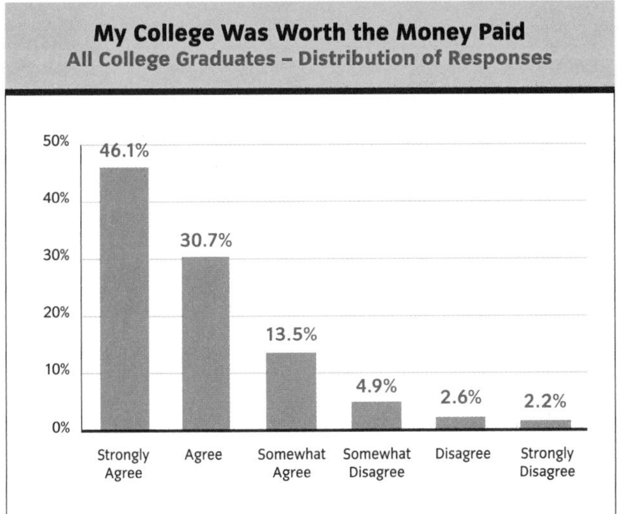

- Across all graduates, 76.8% *Strongly Agree* or *Agree* their school was a good value.
- Georgia Tech graduates rate their school highest on value (94% *Strongly Agree* or *Agree*).
- NYU graduates rate their school the lowest on value (44% *Strongly Agree* or *Agree*).

Top-Rated Schools Have Slightly Higher Value Rankings

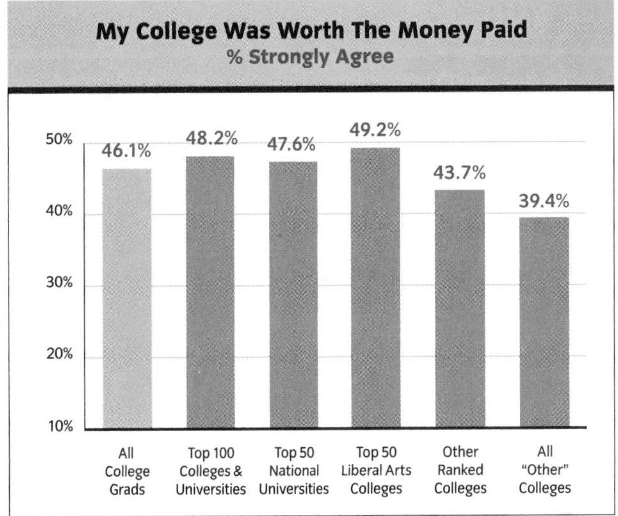

- *All "Other" Colleges* are rated significantly lower in value by graduates.
- Only 6 of the Top 20 schools in value are liberal arts schools.
- 74% of Georgia Tech alumni *Strongly Agree* it was a good value.

Females Generally Assign More Value to Their College Education than Do Males

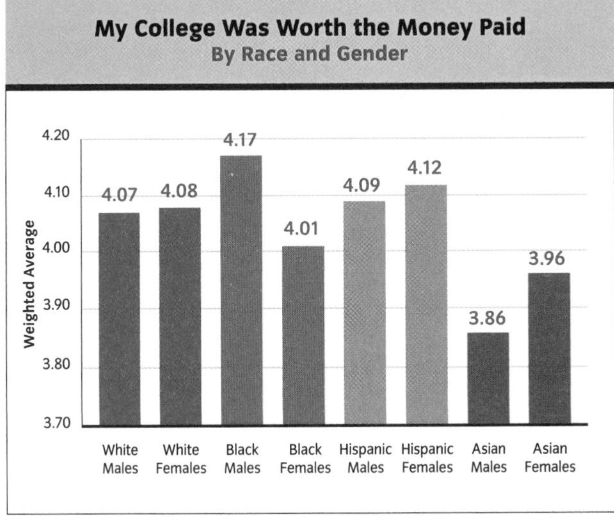

- *Black Females*, however, assign a lower value to their education than do *Black Males*.
- Asian graduates (particularly *Asian Males*) appear to ascribe a lower value to their college education than others.

The Perceived Value of a College Education Increases with Age

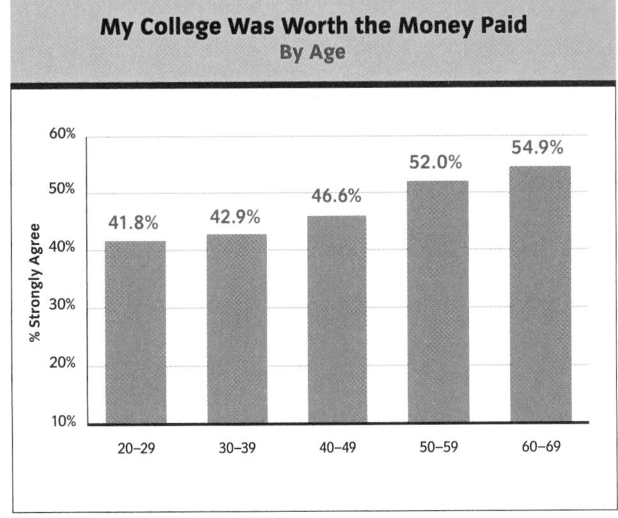

- Over time, a graduate's perspective on the value of their college education more closely matches the value we perceive in the real world.

Top 50 Ranked Schools for: Value For the Money

1.	United States Military Academy	27.	Claremont McKenna College
2.	United States Naval Academy	27.	Sewanee: The University of the South
3.	United States Air Force Academy	27.	Virginia Polytechnic Institute and State University
4.	Georgia Institute of Technology	30.	University of Texas at Austin
5.	Rice University	31.	Grinnell College
6.	Brigham Young University	32.	University of Florida
7.	University of Virginia	33.	Auburn University
8.	Centre College	34.	University of Georgia
8.	University of North Carolina at Chapel Hill	35.	University of Kansas
10.	University of California, Berkeley	35.	University of Notre Dame
11.	The College of William & Mary	37.	Davidson College
12.	Morehouse College	38.	Harvey Mudd College
12.	Spelman College	38.	Oberlin College
14.	University of California, Los Angeles	38.	University of Michigan
15.	Washington and Lee University	41.	Pomona College
16.	Texas A&M University	42.	Amherst College
17.	California Institute of Technology	42.	Florida State University
17.	Princeton University	44.	Swarthmore College
17.	University of Wyoming	45.	Bryn Mawr College
17.	Wellesley College	45.	Carleton College
21.	University of Wisconsin-Madison	45.	Colorado College
21.	Yale University	45.	Howard University
23.	Mount Holyoke College	45.	University of Illinois at Urbana-Champaign
23.	Reed College	50.	Clemson University
25.	The College of New Jersey	50.	Gonzaga University
25.	Loyola University New Orleans	50.	University of Tennessee

The schools with the best rankings are those with the highest weighted average level of agreement among six possible responses.

"My College was Worth the Money Paid."

	Highest School*	All College Grads**	Lowest School*
% Strongly Agree	74.0%	46.1%	19.0%

** Among 177 colleges and universities*

*** >42,000 college graduates from >400 colleges and universities*

Would Graduates Recommend Their College to a Prospective Student Today?

High Praise Indeed

This turned out to be a complex question for graduates to answer, although we never intended it to be. When we analyzed the responses from graduates, we saw that there were many dynamics at play in considering how to respond. The strongest correlation with recommending one's college is the degree to which graduates believe they were prepared to succeed in their careers. The second strongest correlation was with the rating they gave their college on social and communication skill development. This is why the highest-rated colleges in this measure do not necessarily line up with the best-rated schools overall. Schools that did well in these two slightly correlating factors did well in this attribute. In essence, schools that prepare you to deal with others, are enjoyable and fun, and help you succeed in your chosen field will be the most recommended by graduates. This seems very straightforward.

Interestingly, some graduates are less likely to recommend their schools for reasons that actually turn out to be strengths of the school: "it is very difficult to get high grades"; "the academics are very difficult, and most students would not do well there." These are often thinly veiled compliments to their school or boasting about themselves. Therefore, some of the most highly selective schools (and those rated highest overall and rated highest on intellectual development) are not necessarily the most recommended.

Regardless of the rationale behind the graduates' ratings, the list of the most recommended schools is a very good list for all prospective students to consider. A number of studies have shown that the highest praise possible for a consumer product is one person's recommendation to another. Someone places their personal reputation on the line by telling the other person that this would be a very good choice for them. If imitation is the sincerest form of flattery, recommendation may be the strongest form of persuasion.

This section analyzes the extent to which graduates are willing to recommend their college to a prospective student today. As with each attribute we have studied, there is a significant difference in the willingness of graduates to recommend their school. The Top 10 schools for this attribute are small schools (Spelman, Sewanee, Morehouse, Centre, Rice), large schools (Texas A&M, UNC-Chapel Hill, Auburn), an Ivy League school (Yale) and a technical school (Virginia Tech). Large or small, liberal arts or technical, the schools that are most recommended are certain to have a large pool of applicants well into the future.

55% of Graduates Would Strongly Recommend Their School to a Prospect

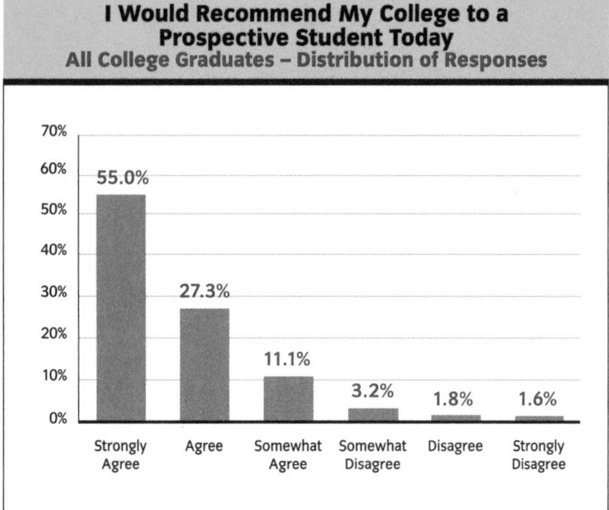

- There is a large difference between the most recommended college (Spelman, with 82% of graduates willing to recommend) and the least recommended (Case Western, with only 36% willing to recommend).

Higher Ranked Schools Tend to Have a Larger % of Graduates Who Would Recommend

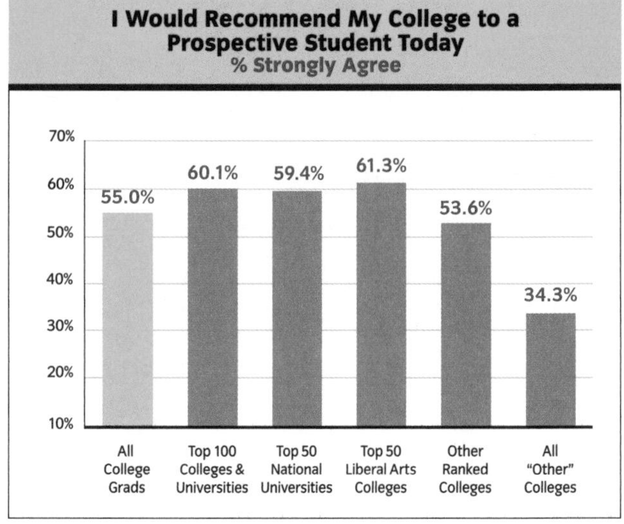

- *Top 50 Liberal Arts Colleges* are slightly more likely to be recommended by their graduates than *Top 50 National Universities.*
- *All "Other" Colleges* get recommended at much lower rates.

Females (Other than Black Females) Are More Likely to Recommend Their College than Males

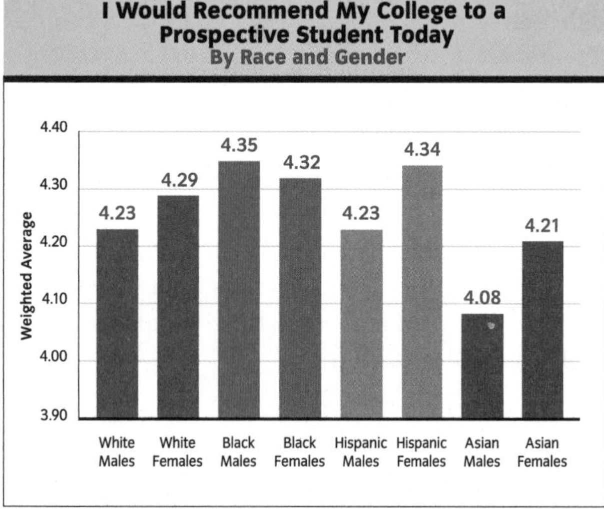

- *Asian Males* are the least likely to recommend their college.
- *Black Males* and *Hispanic Females* are the most likely to recommend their college.

The Likelihood of Recommending One's College Decreases Slightly with Age

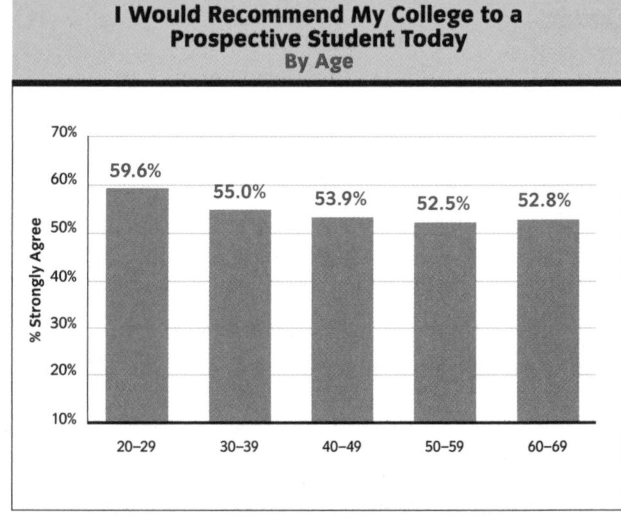

- Roughly 60% of graduates would recommend their college while in their twenties; that number falls only slightly to 53% by the time graduates reach their sixties.
- College love and loyalty appear to be quite sustainable!

Top 50 Ranked Schools for: I Would Recommend My College to a Prospective Student Today

1.	Spelman College	26.	North Carolina State University
2.	Sewanee: The University of the South	26.	University of Michigan
3.	Texas A&M University	26.	University of Texas at Austin
4.	University of North Carolina at Chapel Hill	30.	Loyola University New Orleans
4.	Yale University	31.	Gonzaga University
6.	Auburn University	31.	Pitzer College
6.	Virginia Polytechnic Institute and State University	31.	Pomona College
8.	Morehouse College	34.	Elon University
9.	Centre College	35.	Brown University
10.	Rice University	35.	Princeton University
11.	College of Charleston	35.	Santa Clara University
11.	University of Georgia	35.	University of California, Berkeley
13.	Clemson University	39.	Amherst College
14.	Grinnell College	39.	The College of William & Mary
14.	Stanford University	39.	United States Naval Academy
14.	University of Florida	42.	Carleton College
14.	University of Virginia	42.	Macalester College
18.	Georgia Institute of Technology	42.	University of Richmond
18.	Howard University	45.	Harvey Mudd College
18.	University of Kansas	45.	James Madison University
18.	University of Wisconsin-Madison	45.	Kenyon College
22.	Davidson College	45.	Purdue University
22.	Wesleyan University	45.	Trinity University
22.	Xavier University	45.	University of Alabama
25.	Wellesley College	45.	University of Notre Dame
26.	Colorado College		

The schools with the best rankings are those with the highest weighted average level of agreement among six possible responses.

"I Would Recommend My College to a Prospective Student Today."

	Highest School*	All College Grads**	Lowest School*
% Strongly Agree	82.0%	55.0%	32.0%

** Among 177 colleges and universities*

*** >42,000 college graduates from >400 colleges and universities*

Notes

CHAPTER 5

Financial Success of Graduates

The Alumni Factor
Financial Success

A college degree has long been the ticket to higher income, greater wealth and future economic success. That continues to be the case today. When compared to the average US household, college graduate households are significantly better off financially. According to the 2010 US census, roughly 20% of all US households have income in excess of $100,000. That number soars to 50% for college graduate households in our study. The statistics are similar for net worth – the median household net worth of a college graduate is more than three times that of a high school graduate. It is clear that college graduates are representative of the most influential, best educated and wealthiest segment of the US population. While there are significant differences between graduates of individual colleges, as you will see in this chapter, graduates as a whole are financially fortunate.

Of all the data we have collected and analyzed, the financial data typically generates the most interest. Everyone loves to see what others earn and how they stack up versus their contemporaries. However, financial success is not the primary goal of every graduate. For example, a school that develops excellent teachers and promotes a high proportion of its graduates to the teaching professions will not do as well in this measure. Keep that in mind when reading this chapter.

Also remember that household income and net worth differ by region of the country, gender, number of workers in a household, chosen field and a number of other factors. We've chosen not to equalize for those factors since they are, in fundamental ways, part of the very difference between the colleges themselves and should be understood as such.

We use four key financial measures for our rankings:

1. Weighted average income of graduate households
2. Percent of graduates with "high income" households (above $150K annually)
3. Weighted average net worth of graduate households
4. Percent of graduates with "high net worth" households (above $1 million)

Each of the four measures is given equal weight in our ranking process. You will also notice many other interesting facts about the financial benefits of being a college graduate, as well as which colleges produce the most financially successful graduates.

Graduate From College ... *It Pays!*

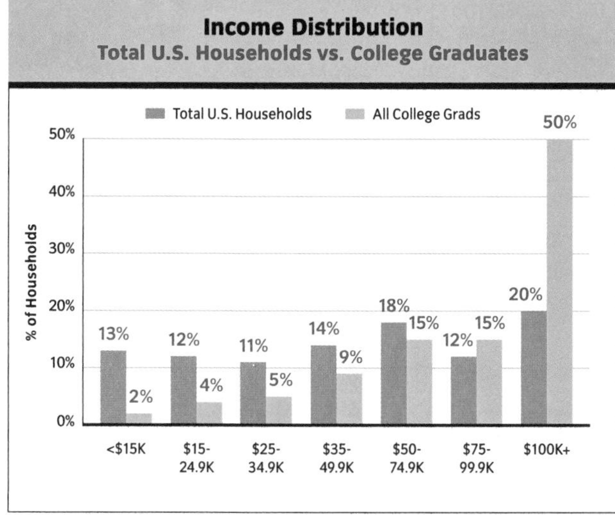

- College graduates are 2.5 times more likely to have a household income above $100K.
- College graduates are 2.5 times less likely to have a household income under $50K.
- An incredible 80% of college graduate households have income over $50K versus 50% for non-graduates.

Net Worth Soars for College Graduates

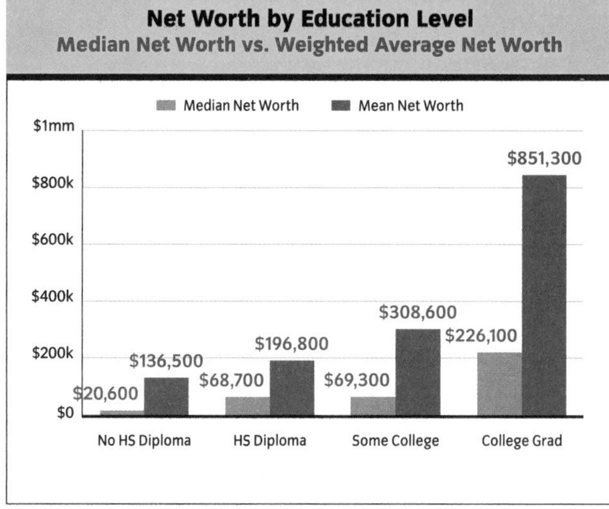

- The weighted average net worth of a college graduate is 4.3 times that of a high school graduate; the median is 3.3 times higher.
- There is only a minor difference in median net worth between attending some college and getting a high school diploma – so finishing college is a good investment.

Differences in Income Exist Across School Types

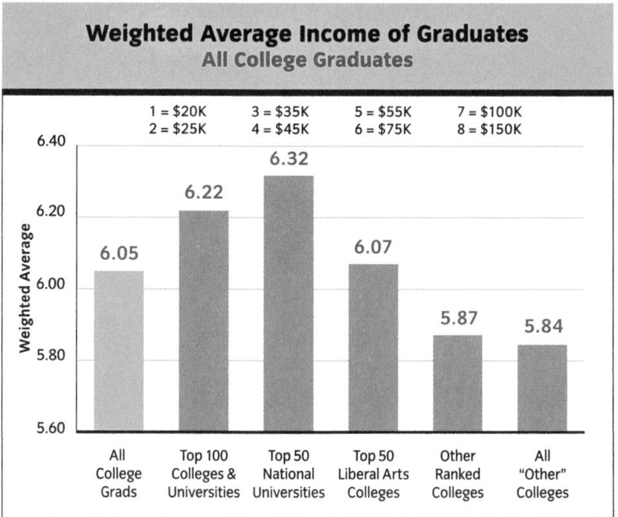

- Graduates of the *Top 50 National Universities* have the highest average household income at $85K.
- Graduates of the *Top 50 Liberal Arts Colleges* earn at about the average of *All College Graduates* ($77K).
- *Other Ranked Colleges* and *All "Other" Colleges* earn on average about $72K, below the average of *All College Grads.*

There is Wide Variation in Income Across Graduate Households

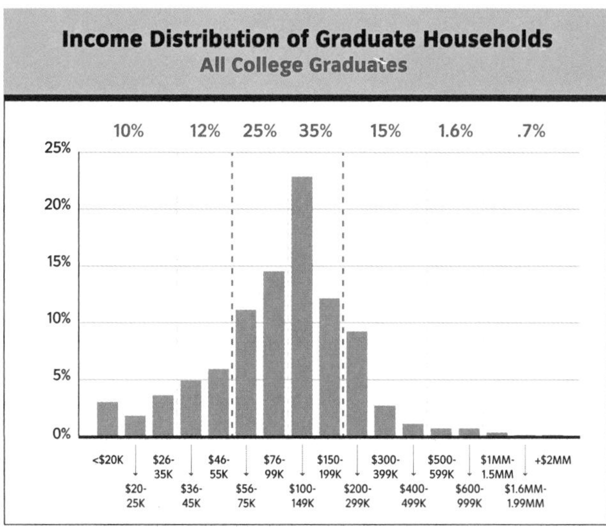

- 60% of all college graduates have household incomes in the $56k–$199K range.
- Roughly 10% of all college graduates live in households earning less than $35K.
- Less than 1% of all college graduate households have an income in excess of $1 million.

A College Degree Is a Good Bet for Rising Above the Median

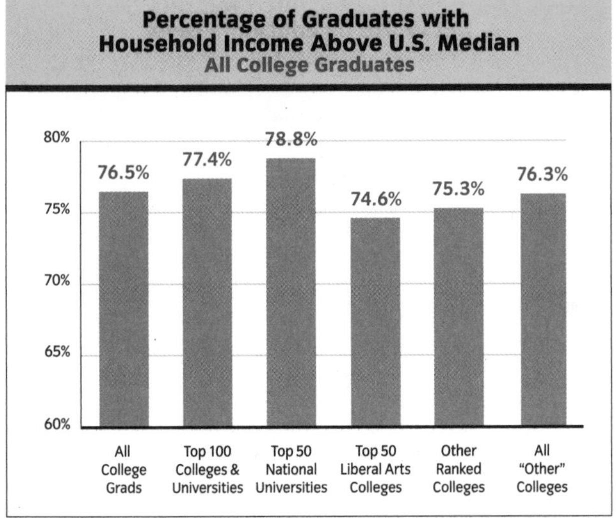

- About three-quarters of all graduate households earn above the median income of $55K.
- *Top 50 National Universities* have the highest percentage of graduates above the median.

Top 100 Colleges & Universities Are the Best Path to High Income

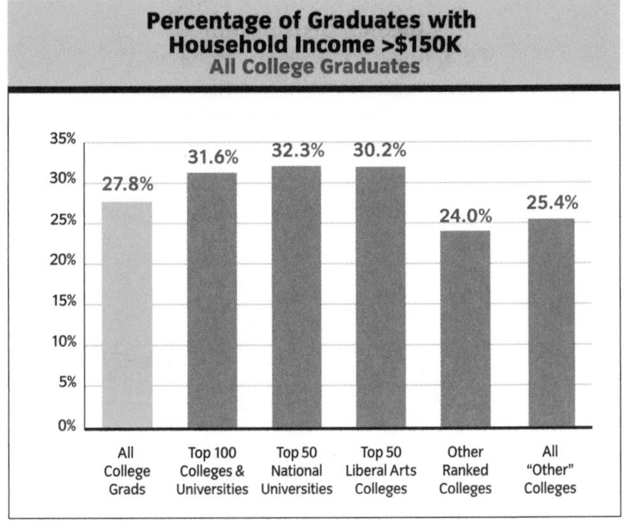

- You have a 24% better chance to have an income over $150K in the Top 100 versus *All "Other" Colleges.*

Household Income Peaks for Graduates in Their 40s and 50s

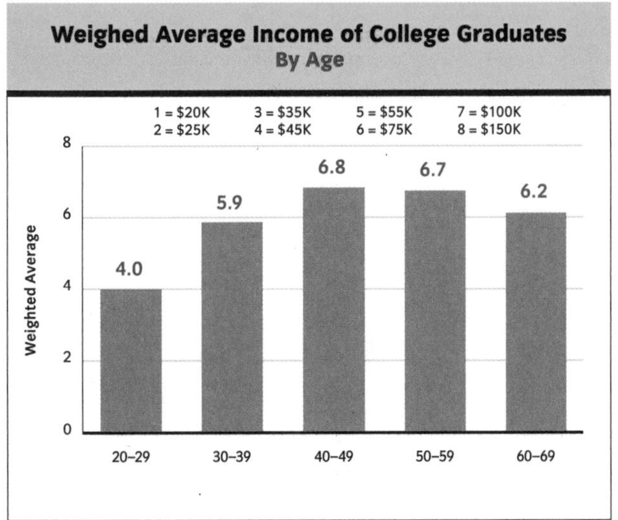

- Income in graduates' sixties exceeds income in their thirties.

Be Patient – Best Chance for Over a $150K Income Is Post-40

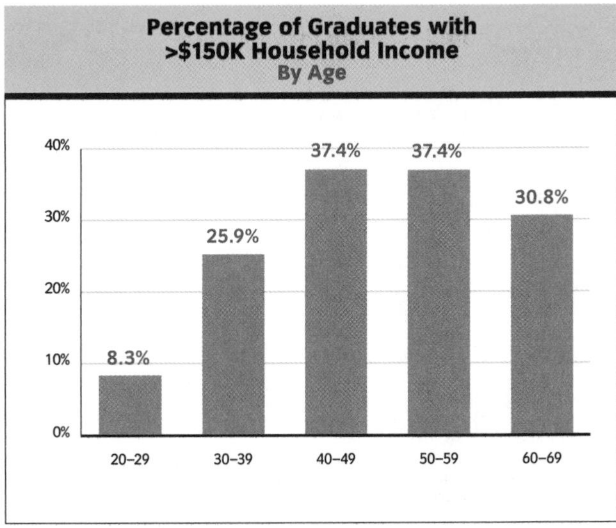

- Becoming a high income household is most likely in one's forties and fifties.

Top 50 Ranked Schools for: Overall Financial Success

1.	Princeton University	26.	Vanderbilt University
2.	Claremont McKenna College	27.	University of Southern California
3.	Washington and Lee University	28.	Colgate University
4.	Trinity College	29.	Wellesley College
5.	Middlebury College	30.	Gettysburg College
6.	Harvey Mudd College	31.	Wesleyan University
7.	Massachusetts Institute of Technology	32.	University of Notre Dame
8.	University of Pennsylvania	33.	Virginia Polytechnic Institute and State University
9.	Swarthmore College	34.	University of Virginia
10.	Stanford University	35.	Santa Clara University
11.	Villanova University	36.	Bucknell University
12.	Harvard University	37.	Denison University
13.	University of Richmond	38.	California Institute of Technology
14.	Georgia Institute of Technology	39.	University of California, Los Angeles
15.	Lehigh University	40.	Northwestern University
16.	Duke University	41.	University of Michigan
17.	Georgetown University	42.	Brown University
18.	Lafayette College	43.	Pomona College
19.	Dartmouth College	44.	Boston College
20.	Yale University	45.	Williams College
21.	Cornell University	46.	Columbia University
22.	College of the Holy Cross	47.	United States Military Academy
23.	Rice University	48.	University of Wisconsin-Madison
24.	Johns Hopkins University	49.	Bowdoin College
25.	United States Naval Academy	50.	Amherst College

The schools with the best rankings had the best composite ranking across the four financial metrics we measure.

Top 50 Ranked Schools for: Weighted Average Household Income

1. Claremont McKenna College
2. Washington and Lee University
3. Princeton University
4. Massachusetts Institute of Technology
5. Trinity College
6. Harvey Mudd College
7. University of Pennsylvania
8. Georgetown University
9. Swarthmore College
10. Yale University
11. University of Richmond
12. Duke University
12. Georgia Institute of Technology
14. Middlebury College
15. Cornell University
16. United States Military Academy
16. United States Naval Academy
18. Johns Hopkins University
18. Villanova University
20. Stanford University
21. Harvard University
22. Virginia Polytechnic Institute and State University
23. Dartmouth College
23. Lafayette College
25. Lehigh University
26. United States Air Force Academy
27. Bucknell University
27. University of Michigan
29. Rice University
30. College of the Holy Cross
31. Santa Clara University
32. Bates College
32. Colgate University
34. Columbia University
35. Northwestern University
36. University of Southern California
37. California Institute of Technology
38. Tufts University
38. University of California, Los Angeles
38. Wesleyan University
41. University of Virginia
42. University of Connecticut
43. Carnegie Mellon University
43. Rensselaer Polytechnic Institute
45. Boston College
45. Rutgers University
47. Brown University
48. University of Illinois at Urbana-Champaign
49. Denison University
49. University of Chicago
49. University of Wisconsin-Madison

The schools with the best rankings are those with the highest weighted average household income among eight possible responses.

Top 50 Ranked Schools for: Percent of High Income Households (>$150K)

1.	Princeton University	26.	Dartmouth College
2.	Claremont McKenna College	27.	Amherst College
3.	Swarthmore College	28.	Colgate University
4.	Harvey Mudd College	29.	Williams College
5.	Washington and Lee University	30.	Lafayette College
6.	University of Pennsylvania	31.	University of Michigan
7.	Georgetown University	32.	Bowdoin College
8.	Massachusetts Institute of Technology	33.	United States Naval Academy
9.	Villanova University	34.	Wesleyan University
10.	University of Richmond	35.	University of Southern California
11.	Bucknell University	36.	Lehigh University
12.	Middlebury College	37.	Bates College
13.	Harvard University	38.	University of Virginia
14.	Stanford University	39.	Denison University
15.	Trinity College	40.	University of California, Irvine
16.	Yale University	41.	Washington University in St. Louis
17.	Georgia Institute of Technology	42.	Columbia University
18.	College of the Holy Cross	43.	Northwestern University
19.	Johns Hopkins University	44.	Emory University
20.	United States Military Academy	45.	Brown University
21.	Cornell University	46.	United States Air Force Academy
22.	Duke University	47.	Wake Forest University
23.	Rice University	48.	Wellesley College
24.	Vanderbilt University	49.	Virginia Polytechnic Institute and State University
25.	University of Notre Dame	50.	Loyola College Maryland

The schools with the best rankings are those with the highest percentage of graduates with a household income above $150K.

Top Colleges Generate a Higher Household Net Worth

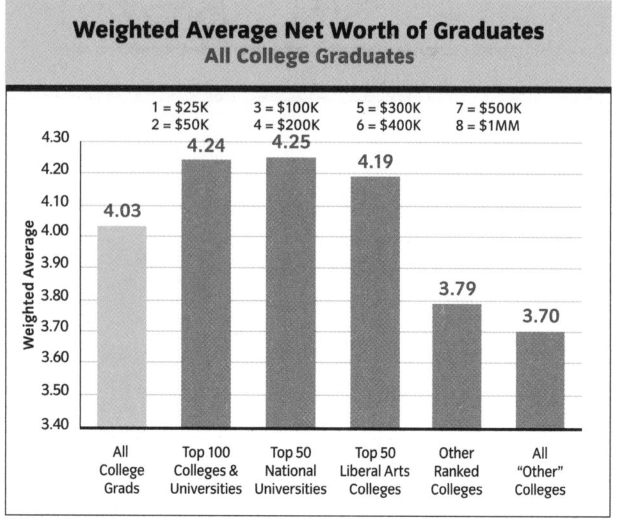

- Graduates of the *Top 50 National Universities* generate the highest household net worth ($200-299K).
- Graduates of the *Other Ranked* and *All "Other" Colleges* build less net worth ($100-199K).

45% of College Grads Have a Household Net Worth between $200K and $2MM

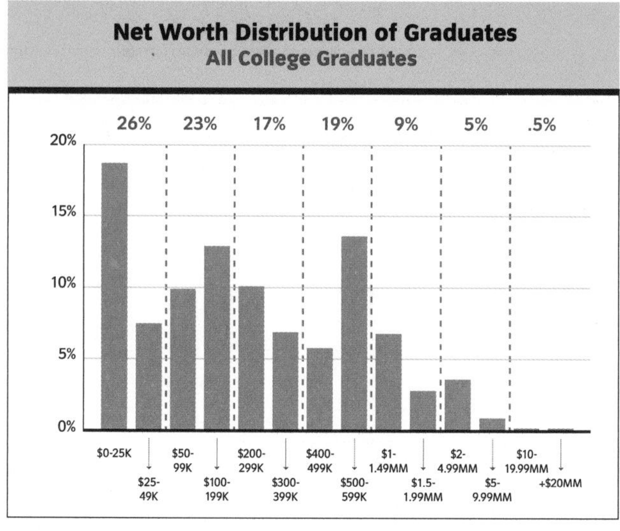

- About 14.5% of all college graduates are millionaires – more than twice the rate of non-college graduates.
- Roughly 50% of college grads have a household net worth below $200K.

Graduating From a Top 100 College Increases the Chance for High Net Worth

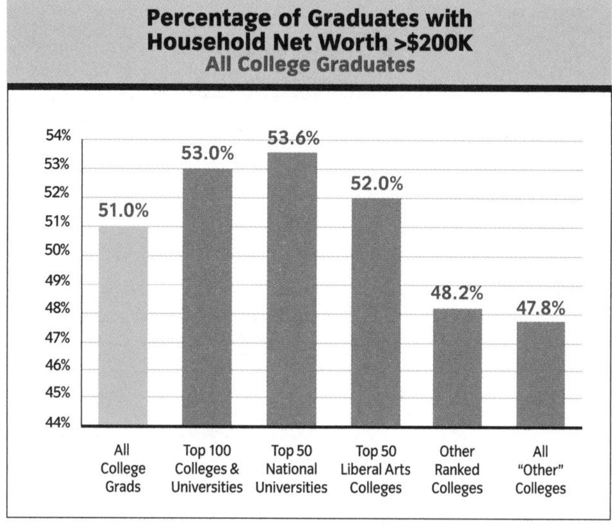

- *Top 50 National Universities* have the highest percent of over $200K net worth graduates.

Top 100 Grads Have a 50% Greater Chance of Becoming Millionaires

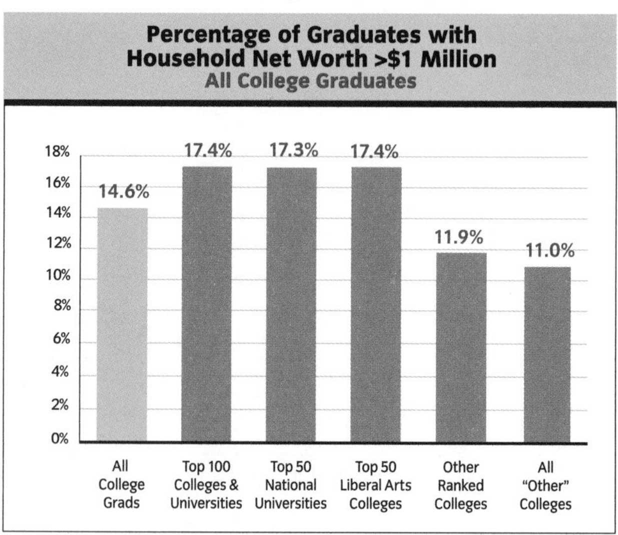

- Middlebury College has the highest percent of graduates in millionaire households at 29%.

Net Worth Increases with Age

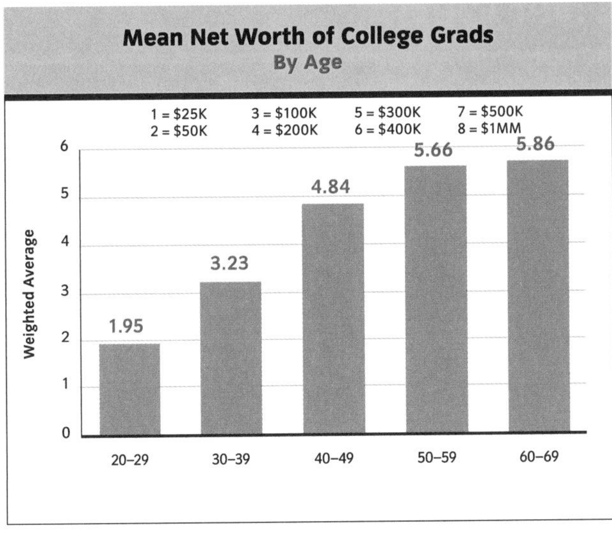

• The Net Worth of a typical graduate household increases three times between their twenties and their sixties.

Graduates Are Nearly 10x More Likely to Be Millionaires in Their 60s than in Their 20s

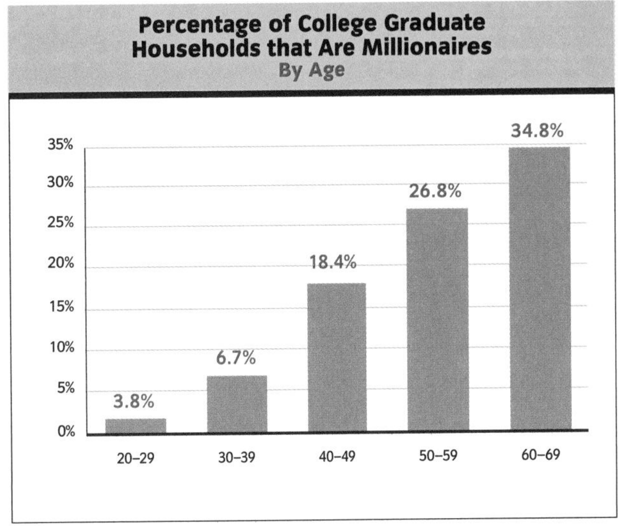

• More than one-third of all college graduates in their sixties are millionaires.

White and Asian Graduates Are More Likely to Have High Income

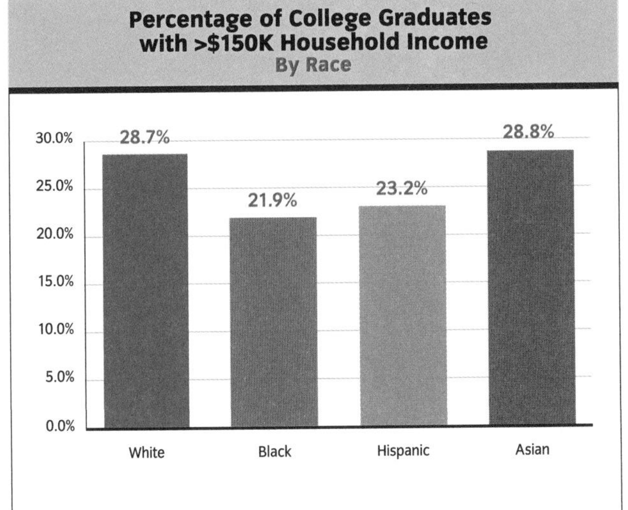

• One out of every 4.6 Black graduate households earns more than $150K (versus one of every 3.5 White/Asian households).

White and Asian Graduates Are More Likely to Be Millionaires

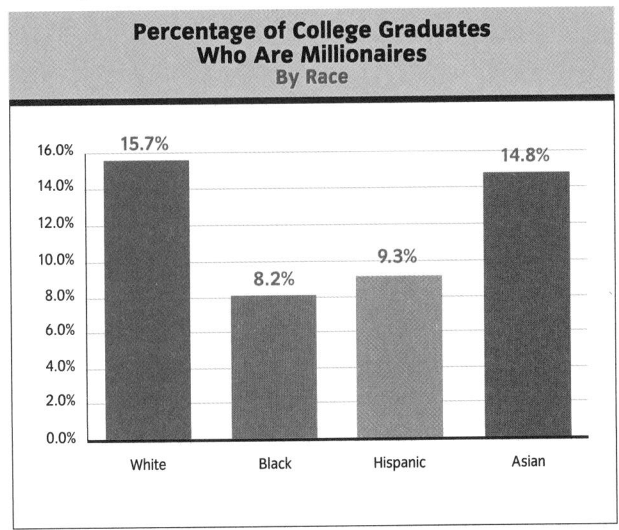

• One out of every twelve Black graduate households achieves a net worth over $1 million (versus one out of every seven for White graduates).

Top 50 Ranked Schools for: Weighted Average Household Net Worth

1.	Lafayette College	26.	Wellesley College
2.	Princeton University	27.	Georgetown University
2.	Villanova University	28.	Dartmouth College
4.	Claremont McKenna College	29.	Denison University
5.	Middlebury College	30.	Colgate University
6.	Trinity College	30.	Santa Clara University
7.	Stanford University	32.	Johns Hopkins University
8.	Georgia Institute of Technology	33.	United States Air Force Academy
9.	Harvey Mudd College	34.	Cornell University
10.	University of Richmond	35.	University of California, Los Angeles
11.	Gettysburg College	36.	Mount Holyoke College
12.	University of Pennsylvania	37.	University of Virginia
13.	Washington and Lee University	38.	Boston College
14.	Massachusetts Institute of Technology	38.	Wesleyan University
15.	Lehigh University	40.	California Institute of Technology
16.	United States Naval Academy	41.	Northwestern University
17.	Harvard University	41.	University of Notre Dame
17.	Rice University	43.	Brown University
19.	Swarthmore College	43.	United States Military Academy
20.	Skidmore College	45.	Loyola College Maryland
21.	Virginia Polytechnic Institute and State University	45.	University of Wisconsin-Madison
22.	Vanderbilt University	47.	Yale University
23.	College of the Holy Cross	48.	Rutgers University
23.	Duke University	49.	Pomona College
23.	University of Southern California	49.	Williams College

The schools with the best rankings are those with the highest weighted average household net worth among possible responses.

Top 50 Ranked Schools for: Percent of Millionaire Households

1. Middlebury College	26. Lafayette College
2. Wellesley College	27. Villanova University
3. Lehigh University	28. College of the Holy Cross
4. Trinity College	29. Cornell University
5. Washington and Lee University	30. University of Richmond
6. Princeton University	31. Rice University
7. Harvard University	32. Wesleyan University
8. Stanford University	33. University of Southern California
9. Dartmouth College	34. Johns Hopkins University
10. Claremont McKenna College	35. Georgia Institute of Technology
11. Clark University	36. Santa Clara University
12. Massachusetts Institute of Technology	37. University of California, Los Angeles
13. Colby College	38. Georgetown University
14. Swarthmore College	39. University of Virginia
15. Vanderbilt University	40. Amherst College
16. Harvey Mudd College	41. Colgate University
17. Pomona College	42. Mount Holyoke College
18. Creighton University	43. Emory University
19. University of Pennsylvania	44. Denison University
20. Duke University	45. Brown University
21. Skidmore College	46. Pepperdine University
22. Gettysburg College	47. United States Naval Academy
23. University of Notre Dame	48. University of Wisconsin-Madison
24. California Institute of Technology	49. Clemson University
25. Yale University	50. University of California, Berkeley

The schools with the best rankings are those with the highest percentage of graduates with a household net worth above $1 million.

Notes

CHAPTER 6

Overall Happiness of Graduates

The Alumni Factor
Overall Happiness

Picasso said that everything exists in limited quantity – especially happiness. While many search for wisdom, and some search for virtue, virtually everyone searches for happiness. There have been countless scientific studies attempting to determine the exact drivers of happiness. Genetics, health, life circumstances, relationships and social attachments, faith, income, wealth, success and achievement, art and entertainment, nature, food and drink, and physical activity are some of the factors that have been correlated to happiness. What causes happiness is extraordinarily complex – too complex to thoroughly examine here. However, we have a fairly good indication of which colleges produce the happiest graduates. We can't explain exactly why these graduates are more or less happy, but we can show you the rankings by college and let you theorize on your own as to the underlying causes.

33% of all college graduates claim to be *Very Happy.* The results range from a high of 48.2% among US Military Academy graduates to a low of 19.9% among Wesleyan University graduates. While we don't know exactly what role one's college plays in directly impacting happiness, we do know that college choice certainly does affect many of the key causes of happiness. After analyzing our data, we can say that happiness among graduates skews toward White and Hispanic Southern females who tend to be conservative and choose smaller colleges. Let's take a look at which colleges produce the happiest graduates.

Liberal Arts Grads Are Happiest

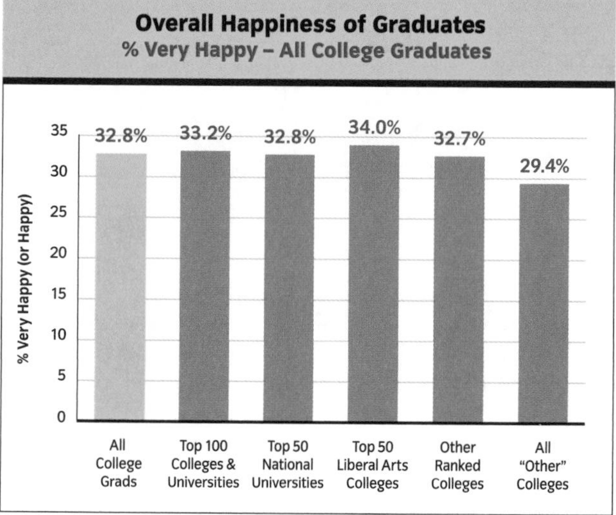

Happy Grads Are Good Ambassadors for Their College
Comparing the Happiest Grads to All College Grads

Question	Happiest Graduates (All Graduates Who Strongly Agreed)	All Graduates	Points +/-
Developed Intellectually (Top Box)	58.6%	49.6%	+9.0
Developed Social/Comm Skills (Top Box)	48.0%	38.6%	+9.4
Developed Spiritually (Top Box)	18.3%	12.8%	+5.5
Enabled Career Success (Top Box)	44.1%	31.9%	+12.2
Provided Immediate Job Opportunities (Top Box)	32.3%	23.8%	+8.5
Developed Deep Friendships (Top Box)	44.0%	37.4%	+6.6
Stay Close to Undergrad Friends (Top Box)	25.3%	20.4%	+4.9
Wish Had Gone to Other College (Top 2 Box)	7.8%	10.6%	-2.8
Worth the $ Paid (Top Box)	58.0%	46.1%	+11.9
Would Recommend College (Top Box)	64.8%	55.0%	+9.8

White and Hispanic Graduates Are Happiest

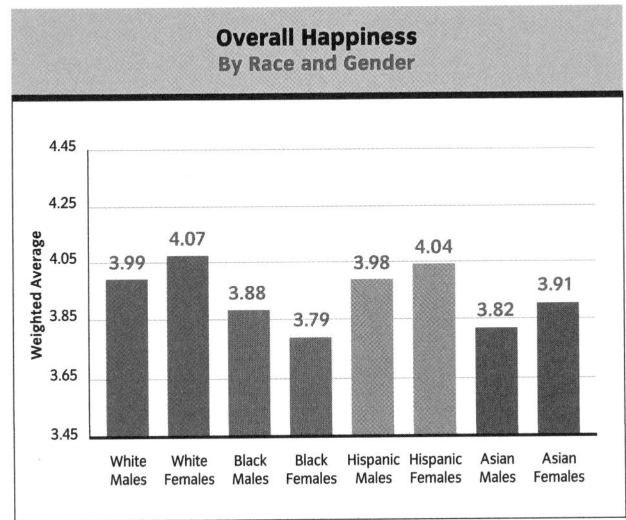

- *White Females* claim to be the happiest among race/gender groups.
- *Black Females* claim to be least happy.
- *Asian Males* are the least happy among males.

Happiness Increases with Age

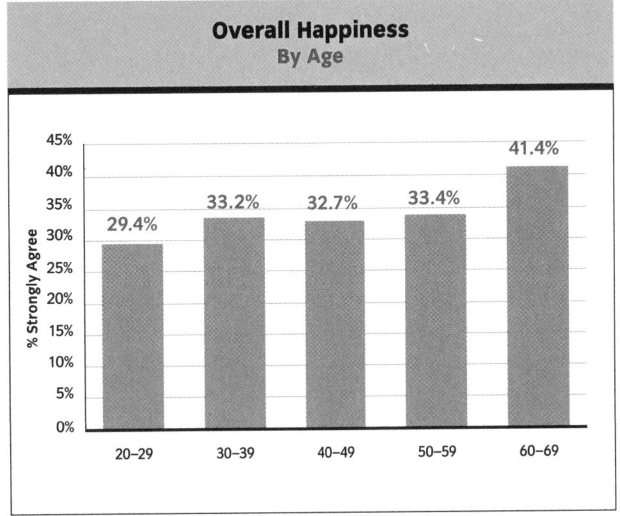

- Happiness is lowest in the early years, rises to a stable level in the middle years and increases in the sixties.

Top 50 Ranked Schools for: Overall Happiness

1.	Centre College	25.	The College of William & Mary
2.	United States Military Academy	25.	Colorado College
2.	United States Naval Academy	25.	Georgetown University
4.	Furman University	29.	College of the Holy Cross
5.	Auburn University	29.	University of Notre Dame
6.	Gonzaga University	31.	University of Utah
7.	United States Air Force Academy	32.	Gettysburg College
8.	Colby College	32.	Purdue University
9.	Pitzer College	34.	Bucknell University
10.	Brigham Young University	34.	Grinnell College
10.	St. Olaf College	34.	University of Kansas
12.	Washington and Lee University	37.	Virginia Polytechnic Institute and State University
13.	Claremont McKenna College	38.	University of Colorado Boulder
13.	Yale University	39.	Elon University
15.	Georgia Institute of Technology	39.	University of Alabama
15.	Sewanee: The University of the South	39.	Villanova University
17.	Kansas State University	42.	Miami University
17.	Middlebury College	43.	Scripps College
17.	Occidental College	44.	University of Texas at Austin
17.	University of North Carolina at Chapel Hill	45.	University of Virginia
17.	Wake Forest University	46.	Washington State University
22.	Carleton College	47.	Worcester Polytechnic Institute
22.	Mount Holyoke College	48.	Dartmouth College
22.	Rice University	49.	Marquette University
25.	Baylor University	50.	University of Tennessee

The schools with the best rankings are those with the highest weighted average level of agreement among six possible responses.

"How Happy Are You in Your Life Right Now?"

	Highest School*	All College Grads**	Lowest School*
% Very Happy	45.5%	32.8%	16.6%

** Among 177 colleges and universities*

*** >45,000 college graduates from >400 colleges and universities*

CHAPTER 7

Alumni Giving by College

The Alumni Factor
Alumni Giving

At many colleges, it starts even before graduation day. It may begin as a request for a "Senior Gift," or as a gathering to enlighten each senior about the importance of alumni giving to the school. Regardless of how it is first introduced, the immediate goal for a college is to quickly get graduates into the habit of giving back to the school. The ultimate goal is to sustain that generosity for a lifetime. A true indicator of the love for and loyalty to one's alma mater is the extent to which one is willing to support it financially. It also happens to be a reliable indicator of excellence. As it turns out, graduate giving is a very good barometer of how alumni view their colleges. Those schools with high levels of alumni giving also tend to do quite well on most of the attributes we measure.

This chapter examines the few causal factors that can help explain why alumni give (or do not give) to their schools. As virtually every college struggles through today's difficult economic environment, knowing what can be done to increase the level of alumni giving is valuable learning. And, since the annual percentage of alumni giving ranges from a high of 60% (Princeton) to the low single digits at many schools, it is clear that some college understand this better than others. Let's take a look at what can drive such wide disparities.

What prompts alumni to donate to their colleges?

When colleges get it right, they produce graduates who are successful in their chosen path and have an affinity to and love for their alma mater. One of the best ways graduates can demonstrate that loyalty is by donating to their school. **There are many reasons alumni give back to their college: to show appreciation for the education and development the school provided them; to provide others with a similar experience; to stay connected to the college community; and even to reap the social and emotional benefits associated with being a donor.** Regardless of the reason for giving, a large number of alumni participate in their college's annual fund drive and colleges track very closely the level of giving each year. For a host of reasons, it is a very important measure to many colleges. Not only does alumni giving help increase financial support for the college by virtue of the actual donations themselves, it is also a signal to other charitable institutions that this particular college is well loved and supported by its graduates. Some education-focused charitable organizations even match a portion of alumni donations. The percentage of living alumni who donate to a college can also serve as a good indication of alumni satisfaction with the direction their college has charted for the future. Thus, many colleges keep a close eye on this number as it changes (upward, hopefully) year to year.

As you might expect, there is wide variation among schools in the percentage of graduates who provide donations each year. Before getting into some of the key drivers of alumni giving, it is worthwhile to note a few important dynamics within the numbers. First, you will notice that most of the schools with very high percentages of alumni giving are private institutions. Often, graduates from large universities that are funded publicly are less likely to give to their university because it already receives governmental funding. It is actually quite interesting to see those public institutions that are still able to achieve a relatively high percentage of alumni donations. Something is going on in these unique universities that is worth understanding. Another dynamic you will notice is that small, private colleges dominate the Top 50 list for alumni donations. This can be partially attributed to the fact that small, private institutions (as we have seen throughout the analyses in *The Alumni Factor*) engender a very high level of alumni loyalty and affinity – it's simply easier to generate this goodwill when you are dealing with a smaller number of students in a highly selective institution. A separate but related point is that many smaller, private institutions (unlike publicly funded ones) truly rely on the money received from alumni donations to fund operations and to increase their endowment. Given that necessity is often the mother of invention, many of these smaller, private schools have become very effective at raising money from alumni. In fact, fundraising has become a top priority for the presidents of virtually every small and medium-sized college and for some large school presidents as well. To gain a better understanding of alumni giving, the chart below shows the Top 50 schools according to the percent of alumni who donated during the period 2008 to 2011.

Top 50 Ranked Schools for: Percent of Alumni Donating from 2008 to 2011

Rank	School	Rank	School
1.	Princeton University	26.	Claremont McKenna College
2.	Carleton College	26.	Colgate University
3.	Centre College	26.	Macalester College
4.	Williams College	30.	Kenyon College
5.	Amherst College	30.	Smith College
5.	Middlebury College	32.	Colby College
7.	Davidson College	32.	Duke University
8.	College of the Holy Cross	32.	Spelman College
9.	Trinity College	32.	University of Southern California
9.	Wesleyan University	36.	Brown University
11.	Hamilton College	36.	Connecticut College
11.	Washington and Lee University	36.	Mount Holyoke College
13.	Dartmouth College	36.	Stanford University
14.	Wellesley College	40.	Occidental College
15.	Scripps College	41.	Bucknell University
15.	Swarthmore College	41.	University of Pennsylvania
17.	Bard College	43.	Dickinson College
18.	Bowdoin College	43.	Franklin and Marshall College
18.	Pomona College	43.	Furman University
18.	University of Notre Dame	43.	Harvey Mudd College
21.	Bates College	43.	Lafayette College
21.	Haverford College	43.	Massachusetts Institute of Technology
23.	Grinnell College	49.	California Institute of Technology
24.	Sewanee University of the South	50.	Gettysburg College
24.	Whitman College	50.	Rice University
26.	Bryn Mawr College		

A quick glance at the Top 50 schools in alumni donations shows those with high alumni donation rates are also well loved by their alumni and rank high on the lists of many other key attributes we've analyzed. The Top 50 schools in alumni giving, nearly all of them among the finest colleges in the US, have long-standing traditions of alumni support based on the college's historic reputation for excellence and a campus life that binds students to the institution and to one another. Alumni financial contributions are one of the best indicators of a graduate's esteem for their school. As is often the case, money follows the heart.

The Top 10 schools in alumni donations are a uniquely accomplished group. While each of these schools has a long history of loyal and passionate alumni support, the tough economy of the last few years challenged the fundraising effectiveness of every institution in America, including these Top 10. Despite the difficult economic times, these ten schools continue to distinguish themselves for having graduates who demonstrate enduring alumni love and financial support:

Top 10 Schools	Average Alumni Giving % 2008–2011	Rank in Alumni Giving %	Number Under-grads
Princeton University	60%	1	5,142
Carleton College	59%	2	2,020
Centre College	57%	3	1,242
Williams College	56%	4	2,048
Amherst College	55%	5	1,794
Middlebury College	55%	5	2,532
Davidson College	54%	7	1,742
College of the Holy Cross	51%	8	2,899
Trinity College	49%	9	2,292
Wesleyan University	49%	9	2,854

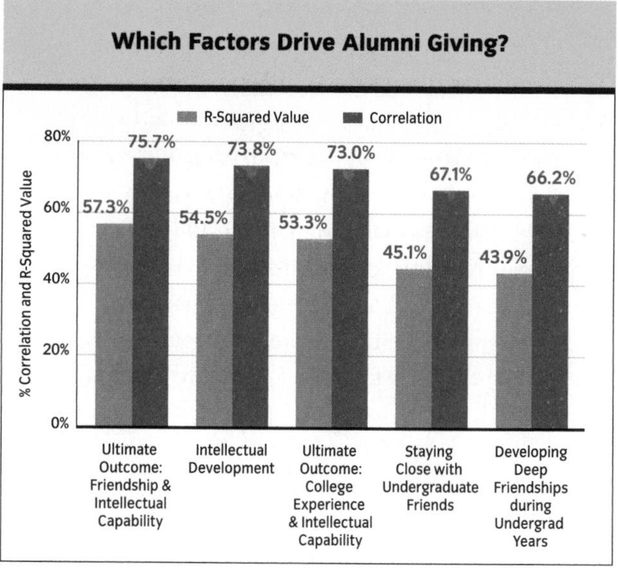

Figure 7.1

But what are the driving factors that make these schools and the other leaders so successful at generating alumni support for their school, while others watch as alumni deny their request for money? By carefully analyzing data from tens of thousands of college graduates and comparing it to the donation rates by college, we are able to develop a few hypotheses as to the key factors driving alumni donations.

In **Figure 7.1**, we list the top five factors in our database that are correlated to alumni giving. After looking at many combinations of alumni giving and other data, from happiness and political leaning to gender and financial success, we were able to pinpoint five measures that are the most highly correlated to alumni giving. This is not the complete answer, as none of them can fully explain the difference in giving rates among colleges. However, we're excited to uncover these relationships, and we're sure colleges will be as well. In short, colleges that provide strong intellectual development and allow for the development of deep friendships are most likely to have higher percentages of alumni donations.

The Ultimate Outcome℠ of Friendship & Intellectual Capability

Being fully developed intellectually, making deep friendships during one's undergraduate years and staying in close touch with those friends are the largest correlating factors in alumni giving, according to our research. The schools that rank highest in alumni giving are able to create campus environments where students are academically challenged while developing deep bonds with each other and ties to their college community. These ties bind them for what appears to be a long-term, consistent level of financial support for their college. Smaller schools, with smaller class sizes and communities where students get to know other students, faculty and administrators, are best positioned to deliver these benefits to students – and likely a reason that the list of the Top 50 schools is dominated by small, private institutions. In fact, 40 of the Top 50 schools in alumni giving have fewer than 3,000 undergraduate students, and 48 of the Top 50 schools have less than 10,000 students (University of Southern California and University of Pennsylvania being the exceptions).

To create this kind of close, collegial environment on a larger scale, across a larger campus with more students and a less personal touch, takes a unique effort, and only a handful of select schools are able to do it. Let's take a look at these successful larger schools and the special touches they use to defy the "law of large numbers" when it comes to alumni giving.

Which large schools create environments that encourage alumni financial support?

To begin, there are only three schools within the Top 25 for alumni giving percentage that have more than 3,000 students – each of these three schools hurdled the very difficult bar of having 40% or more of their alumni donate:

Alumni Giving 3 Large Schools >4,000 Students (>50% Alumni Giving)	Average Alumni Giving % 2008–2011	Rank in Alumni Giving %	Number Under-grads
Princeton University	60%	1	5,142
Dartmouth College	47%	13	4,248
University of Notre Dame	43%	18	8,442

This is an extraordinary accomplishment for these three schools, and a good indication that they develop and shape their graduates in ways that create a strong, long-term bond. There are eight other schools in the Top 50 with more than 3,000 undergraduates. These schools are listed in the chart below, and each one has had an alumni giving rate above 30% in the 2008 to 2011 period. This is an indication of the long tradition of alumni financial support for these schools, and of the high regard in which alumni hold these colleges.

8 Large Schools >3,000 Students Top 50 in Alumni Giving	Average Alumni Giving % 2008–2011	Rank in Alumni Giving %	Number Under-grads
Duke University	37%	32	6,697
University of Southern California	37%	32	17,380
Brown University	36%	36	6,318
Stanford University	36%	36	6,940
Bucknell University	34%	41	3,508
University of Pennsylvania	34%	41	11,940
Massachusetts Institute of Technology	33%	43	4,299
Rice University	31%	50	3,529

Finally, of the 71 schools in our database with more than 10,000 undergraduates, there are only nine schools among the Top 100 for alumni giving that achieve an alumni giving rate of 15% or greater. These schools are well known, popular universities that, despite being very large, generate high levels of alumni support and correspondingly high revenue from alumni giving. These nine schools each have a unique advantage that allows them to counter the penalty of size. Three of them are Ivy League schools (Cornell, Penn and Harvard) whose gold-plated reputations help them offset large student body size. The rest all share another trait – that magic combination of a strong academic reputation and a high-profile athletic program. Even the Ivy League schools have relatively strong and well-followed athletics (Cornell's strong showing in the 2010 NCAA men's basketball tournament serves as an example). And some, such as Harvard may be helped on the margin by the fact that their full-time, residential undergraduate populations are substantially smaller than their total undergraduate populations, helping them replicate that smaller school feel.

9 Schools with Over 10,000 Students and >15% Giving Rate	Average Alumni Giving % 2008–2011	Rank in Alumni Giving %	Number Under-grads
University of Southern California	37%	32	17,380
University of Pennsylvania	34%	41	11,940
Georgia Institute of Technology	24%	68	13,750
University of North Carolina at Chapel Hill	22%	72	18,579
Cornell University	21%	75	13,935
Clemson University	20%	79	15,459
Harvard University	19%	81	10,265
Kansas State University	19%	81	19,205
University of Virginia	19%	81	15,595

Having taken a broad look at some of the many factors that are correlated to alumni giving, and having examined the schools that excel in it versus all others, it is clear that the path to a high percent of alumni givers is easier to explain than it is to accomplish. Simply put, for many graduates their college experience is an important part of their identity, and the higher the regard they have for their college, the more likely they are to donate to it. The best path to that high regard is through strong intellectual development and deep friendships. For larger schools, intellectual development and deep friendships are also critical. However, where sheer numbers make delivering consistent intellectual excellence, deep friendships and a close tie to the community a tougher task, activities that unify the college community and their alumni (like strong athletic programs) can significantly increase the level of alumni support. There are, of course, many other ways large universities galvanize and unify their communities beyond athletics, but very few can do it like athletics can. The magic combination of high academic reputation and a strong athletic program is sure to increase alumni support at larger schools (in fact, it does so at smaller schools as well.)

In many ways, alumni donations are the definitive test of a graduate's love for their alma mater. Schools with high levels of alumni participation in annual fundraising tend to be schools that have served their graduates well by delivering on their promise of excellence in virtually all areas. The chart below compares the graduates of the Top 10 schools in giving percentage versus all college graduates on the key attributes of college experience, success and happiness. This data further confirms the link between alumni giving and a graduate's overall view of their school. Intellectual Development and the two Friendship Development attributes stand-out as the attributes in which these Top 10 shools put the most distance between themselves and others.

Attribute *% Strongly Agree or Agree*	Top 10 Schools: Alumni Giving	All Schools	+/- Points
Intellectual Development	71.2%	49.6%	+21.6
Social/Communication Skills Development	48.5%	38.6%	+9.9
Spiritual Development	20.3%	12.8%	+7.5
Preparation for Career Success	41.5%	31.9%	+9.6
Immediate Job Opportunities	20.2%	23.8%	-3.6
Developed Deep Friendships	51.6%	37.4%	+14.2
Sustain Undergraduate Friendships	32.0%	20.4%	+11.6
Worth the Money Paid	52.0%	46.1%	+5.9
Would Recommend	66.4%	55.0%	+11.4
% >$150K Household Income	35.5%	27.8%	+7.7
% >$200K Net Worth	55.7%	51.0%	+4.7
% Millionaires	20.4%	14.6%	+5.8
Top 2 Box Happiness	79.1%	77.0%	+2.1
% Post Grad Degree	66.6%	58.8%	+7.8

Summary

The percent of alumni who annually donate to their college is a measure closely watched by college administrators and other observers of higher education. Smaller, private colleges tend to excel in this measure versus other larger, publicly funded colleges for a number of reasons.

Small schools with high academic standards and a close-knit community do a better job than larger schools in creating an environment where intellectual development can occur and deep friendships can develop – these two factors appear to have the strongest correlation to alumni giving. Graduates of large, publicly funded schools are less likely to donate, since they feel that government already supports their schools. Smaller, private schools more heavily rely upon the donations of alumni, and hence have become skilled at convincing alumni to support them.

However, there are small, private schools that do not fare well, relative to others, in alumni giving. There are also large schools that do relatively well on this measure because they have managed to provide strong intellectual development to their graduates while creating a bond to the university through athletics or some other means. The schools that excel in alumni giving also tend to be schools with excellent reputations that rank highly on virtually every list we've generated in this study. Therefore, the percent of alumni who give to a school is a very good measure of a school's excellence. In fact, if prospective students had to limit themselves to one or two data points upon which to compare a list of schools, or finally choose their school, we believe this criterion would be an excellent choice, along with the results on our Ultimate Outcomes.

Notes

CHAPTER 8

Graduation Rate by College

The Alumni Factor
Graduation Rate

The degree to which a student completes their college or university education within six years says a great deal about both the college itself and the students they recruit and admit. For this reason, it is one of the attributes we measure. Graduating on time is certainly a goal of most college students – and a goal of the paying party – which is typically the parents.

It turns out that a school's six-year graduation rate ranking is a fairly good indicator of alumni success – it ranks 5th among 19 attributes in the strength of its correlation to overall ranking (behind Preparation for Career Success, Intellectual Development, Friendship Development and Alumni Giving Percent). We also know that the higher a student's SAT scores are, the more likely they are to graduate within six years. Therefore, it follows that schools with the highest SAT scores are the highest ranked in graduation rate.

However, there are other factors beyond academic readiness that could lead a school to a higher (or lower) graduation rate than SAT score alone would predict:

- The ease with which students can get into classes required for graduation.
- A student's financial capability (either through family funding, financial aid or work).
- Other family and societal pressures that encourage (or discourage) students to complete their studies.

For these and other reasons, a school with a strong graduation rate is highly likely to recruit and admit students who have been well prepared educationally, are on solid financial footing (financial aid can substitute for family wealth) and have family and societal influences that encourage staying in school until graduation. In many ways, the accumulated advantages a student receives in their life prior to entering college can predict their likelihood of graduating. You will see that the highest ranked schools in graduation rate are also those with very high selectivity and, consequently, very strong reputations.

Many of these top schools also do well in generating alumni success for similar reasons. In fact, of the Top 25 schools in graduation rate, 21 rank in the Top 50 overall in *The Alumni Factor* ranking for graduate outcomes, and 13 rank in the Top 25. Interestingly, there are 12 schools in the Top 25 of *The Alumni Factor* overall ranking that are NOT among the Top 25 in graduation rate. These are excellent schools such as Washington & Lee, US Military Academy, US Naval Academy, Wellesley, Harvey Mudd, Virginia Tech and others who are quite rigorous and produce students who are extremely successful on a broad basis.

Top Ranked Schools for: Graduation Rate

1.	Harvard University	16.	Vassar College
2.	Brown University	16.	Washington and Lee University
2.	Princeton University	29.	Bucknell University
2.	University of Notre Dame	29.	Haverford College
2.	University of Pennsylvania	29.	Rice University
2.	Yale University	32.	Boston College
7.	Amherst College	32.	Brandeis University
7.	Dartmouth College	32.	Davidson College
7.	Stanford University	32.	Middlebury College
7.	Williams College	32.	Tufts University
11.	Duke University	32.	University of California, Berkeley
11.	Northwestern University	32.	Vanderbilt University
11.	Pomona College	39.	California Institute of Technology
11.	Washington University in St. Louis	39.	Colby College
11.	Wesleyan University	39.	College of William and Mary
16.	Bowdoin College	39.	Johns Hopkins University
16.	Carleton College	39.	University of California, Los Angeles
16.	Claremont McKenna College	39.	University of Michigan
16.	College of the Holy Cross	39.	Villanova University
16.	Columbia University	39.	Wellesley College
16.	Cornell University	47.	Emory University
16.	Georgetown University	47.	Lafayette College
16.	Massachusetts Institute of Technology	47.	United States Naval Academy
16.	Swarthmore College	47.	University of Southern California
16.	University of Chicago	47.	Wake Forest University
16.	University of Virginia		

Notes

CHAPTER 9

Ultimate Outcomes℠

Our Exclusive Measures of a School's Effectiveness

The Alumni Factor
What are Ultimate Outcomes℠?

Look no further than the following six Ultimate Outcomes to best understand the type of graduate each college produces. We take four key goals of a college education: Intellectual Development, Financial Success, Friendship Development and Overall Happiness. We then pair them and measure which colleges do the best job of delivering on each combination of benefits. Here are the detailed definitions of each Ultimate Outcome and the 50 schools that are best at delivering them.

Ultimate Outcome Definitions

All Ways Wealthy: Financial Success & Happiness

Schools that excel in this Ultimate Outcome produce a large percentage of graduates who experience significant financial success and are very happy in their lives. We measure financial success by the mean household income and mean household net worth of the graduates from each school.

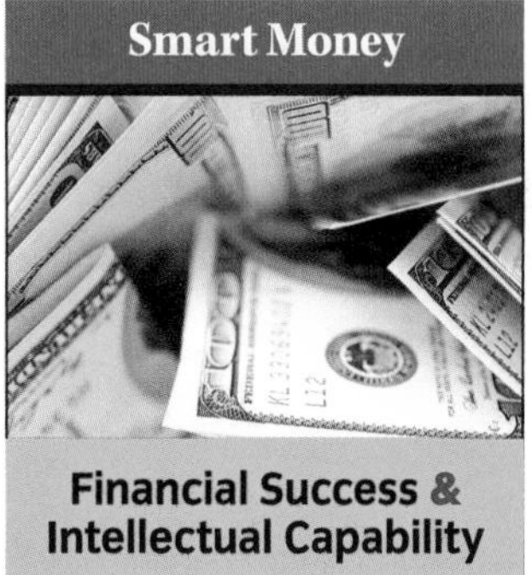

Smart Money: Financial Success & Intellectual Capability

This Ultimate Outcome measures the track record of each college in producing financially successful graduates who were thoroughly developed intellectually. For intellectual capability, we give equal weight to the following three measures: the percent of classes with fewer than 20 students, the six-year graduation rate of each college, and the level of agreement by the graduates of each school to the statement, "I was developed intellectually during my undergraduate years." Our analysis has shown class size and graduation rate to be the two biggest correlating factors with a high Intellectual Development rating by alumni.

Pursue Your Passions: Happiness & Intellectual Capability

For this Ultimate Outcome, we analyze a college's ability to consistently produce graduates who have high intellectual capability and who are happy. This is a rare and valuable combination in today's world.

Big Ideas: Friendships & Intellectual Capability

This Ultimate Outcome tells us which schools are best at producing graduates who build and maintain close ties to their undergraduate friends and who have deep intellectual capability. We measure Friendship Development through alumni responses regarding the depth of friendships they developed during their undergraduate years and the sustainability of those friendships.

Life to the Brim: Happiness & Friendships

This Ultimate Outcome gauges a school's ability to consistently produce happy graduates who are deeply connected to their undergraduate friends.

The Good Life: Financial Success & Friendships

If a college provides its graduates the means to create strong financial success and develop strong undergraduate friendships that enrich their lives, the school will do well in this Ultimate Outcome.

We believe these pairs are the single most effective means of understanding the type of graduate a college is likely to develop, relative to the other colleges we have measured. Parents and prospective students take note – here is a glimpse into your potential future. Use these pairs to narrow your selection of colleges and ultimately choose the best one for yourself.

Ultimate Outcome: Financial Success & Happiness

Strong Earning Potential and Overall Happiness in Life

Top 50 Schools

1.	Claremont McKenna College	26.	Gettysburg College
2.	Princeton University	27.	Cornell University
3.	Washington and Lee University	28.	Harvard University
4.	Middlebury College	29.	Johns Hopkins University
5.	Villanova University	30.	Auburn University
6.	Georgia Institute of Technology	31.	Bucknell University
7.	United States Naval Academy	32.	Santa Clara University
8.	Lafayette College	33.	University of Southern California
9.	Trinity College	34.	Vanderbilt University
10.	United States Military Academy	35.	University of Virginia
11.	University of Richmond	36.	University of Notre Dame
12.	Georgetown University	37.	University of North Carolina at Chapel Hill
13.	Yale University	38.	Colby College
14.	Stanford University	39.	University of Michigan
15.	Massachusetts Institute of Technology	40.	Colgate University
16.	United States Air Force Academy	41.	The College of William & Mary
17.	University of Pennsylvania	42.	Wellesley College
18.	Swarthmore College	43.	Boston College
19.	Rice University	44.	California Institute of Technology
20.	Virginia Polytechnic Institute and State University	45.	Denison University
21.	Duke University	46.	University of Illinois at Urbana-Champaign
22.	Lehigh University	47.	University of Wisconsin-Madison
23.	Harvey Mudd College	48.	Northwestern University
24.	College of the Holy Cross	49.	Pomona College
25.	Dartmouth College	50.	Brown University

Ultimate Outcome: Financial Success & Intellectual Capability

High Earning Potential and Unique Brainpower

Top 50 Schools

1. Claremont McKenna College
2. Princeton University
3. Middlebury College
4. Washington and Lee University
5. Swarthmore College
6. University of Pennsylvania
7. Yale University
8. Harvard University
9. Massachusetts Institute of Technology
10. University of Richmond
11. Stanford University
12. Duke University
13. Lafayette College
14. Trinity College
15. Harvey Mudd College
16. Georgetown University
17. Columbia University
18. United States Naval Academy
19. Northwestern University
20. Brown University
21. Dartmouth College
22. Johns Hopkins University
23. Williams College
24. Rice University
25. Vanderbilt University
26. Wellesley College
27. Colgate University
28. Pomona College
29. College of the Holy Cross
30. Cornell University
31. Villanova University
32. California Institute of Technology
33. Gettysburg College
34. Bates College
35. Wesleyan University
36. Davidson College
37. Tufts University
38. University of Notre Dame
39. Washington University in St. Louis
40. United States Air Force Academy
41. University of Chicago
42. Denison University
43. Bowdoin College
44. Skidmore College
45. Scripps College
46. Amherst College
47. Bucknell University
48. Emory University
49. Vassar College
50. University of Virginia

Ultimate Outcome: Happiness & Intellectual Capability

Overall Happiness in Life and Serious Brainpower

Top 50 Schools

1.	Claremont McKenna College	26.	University of Pennsylvania
2.	Yale University	27.	Wellesley College
3.	Middlebury College	28.	Grinnell College
4.	Washington and Lee University	29.	Bowdoin College
5.	Swarthmore College	30.	Vanderbilt University
6.	Princeton University	31.	Furman University
7.	Davidson College	32.	Dartmouth College
8.	Washington University in St. Louis	33.	Georgetown University
9.	Harvard University	34.	Rice University
10.	United States Naval Academy	35.	Northwestern University
11.	Haverford College	36.	University of Richmond
12.	Williams College	37.	Stanford University
13.	Scripps College	38.	Tufts University
14.	Whitman College	39.	Mount Holyoke College
15.	Vassar College	40.	Gettysburg College
16.	Brown University	41.	Connecticut College
17.	Sewanee: The University of the South	42.	College of the Holy Cross
18.	Pomona College	43.	Smith College
19.	University of Notre Dame	44.	United States Air Force Academy
20.	Duke University	45.	Depauw University
21.	Carleton College	46.	Emory University
22.	Amherst College	47.	California Institute of Technology
23.	St. Olaf College	48.	Bryn Mawr College
24.	Colby College	49.	Centre College
25.	Occidental College	50.	Skidmore College

Ultimate Outcome: Friendships & Intellectual Capability

Close Friends for Life and Considerable Brainpower

Top 50 Schools

1. Washington and Lee University
2. Sewanee: The University of the South
3. Swarthmore College
4. Davidson College
5. Kenyon College
6. Yale University
7. Wellesley College
8. Princeton University
9. United States Naval Academy
10. Spelman College
11. Middlebury College
12. Williams College
13. Hamilton College
14. Brown University
15. Pomona College
16. Harvey Mudd College
17. College of the Holy Cross
18. Bowdoin College
19. Carleton College
20. University of Notre Dame
21. Vassar College
22. California Institute of Technology
23. Haverford College
24. Claremont McKenna College
25. Wesleyan University
26. Smith College
27. Amherst College
28. Grinnell College
29. St. Olaf College
30. Whitman College
31. Duke University
32. Harvard University
33. Bryn Mawr College
34. Gettysburg College
35. Bucknell University
36. Centre College
37. Colby College
38. Dartmouth College
39. Mount Holyoke College
40. United States Air Force Academy
41. Franklin & Marshall College
42. Stanford University
43. Colgate University
44. Scripps College
45. Tufts University
46. Bates College
47. Vanderbilt University
48. Massachusetts Institute of Technology
49. Washington University in St. Louis
50. Furman University

Ultimate Outcome: Happiness & Friendships

A Lifetime of Happiness and Close Friends

Top 50 Schools

1.	United States Military Academy	26.	Gettysburg College
2.	Sewanee: The University of the South	27.	Harvey Mudd College
3.	Morehouse College	28.	Princeton University
4.	United States Naval Academy	29.	Franklin & Marshall College
5.	Washington and Lee University	30.	Mount Holyoke College
6.	Centre College	31.	Pomona College
7.	Spelman College	32.	Gonzaga University
8.	College of the Holy Cross	33.	California Institute of Technology
9.	St. Olaf College	34.	Amherst College
10.	United States Air Force Academy	35.	Howard University
11.	Carleton College	36.	Smith College
12.	Colby College	37.	University of Alabama
13.	Furman University	38.	Whitman College
14.	University of Notre Dame	39.	Claremont McKenna College
15.	Wellesley College	40.	Vassar College
16.	Yale University	41.	Dartmouth College
17.	Bucknell University	42.	Brown University
18.	Davidson College	43.	Wesleyan University
19.	Kenyon College	44.	Oberlin College
20.	Grinnell College	45.	Duke University
21.	Elon University	46.	Rice University
22.	Middlebury College	47.	Georgetown University
23.	Wake Forest University	48.	Occidental College
24.	Bowdoin College	49.	The College of William & Mary
25.	Swarthmore College	50.	Pitzer College

Ultimate Outcome: Financial Success & Friendships

High Earning Potential, Wealth and Close Friends for Life

Top 50 Schools

1.	Washington and Lee University	26.	Cornell University
2.	Harvey Mudd College	27.	University of Richmond
3.	Princeton University	28.	Pomona College
4.	United States Military Academy	29.	Kenyon College
5.	United States Naval Academy	30.	Trinity College
6.	Claremont McKenna College	31.	Colgate University
7.	Middlebury College	32.	Rice University
8.	Swarthmore College	33.	Brown University
9.	College of the Holy Cross	34.	Harvard University
10.	Yale University	35.	Bowdoin College
11.	Wellesley College	36.	Davidson College
12.	Massachusetts Institute of Technology	37.	Sewanee: The University of the South
13.	United States Air Force Academy	38.	Georgia Institute of Technology
14.	Stanford University	39.	Colby College
15.	Gettysburg College	40.	Virginia Polytechnic Institute and State University
16.	Bucknell University	41.	Franklin & Marshall College
17.	Duke University	42.	Vanderbilt University
18.	Wesleyan University	43.	University of Pennsylvania
19.	Lafayette College	44.	Williams College
20.	California Institute of Technology	45.	Bates College
21.	University of Notre Dame	46.	Lehigh University
22.	Dartmouth College	47.	Mount Holyoke College
23.	Georgetown University	48.	Amherst College
24.	Morehouse College	49.	Wake Forest University
25.	Villanova University	50.	Denison University

The Ultimate Outcomes Champions
17 schools that rank in the Top 50 for each Ultimate Outcome
(In alphabetical order)

Brown University	Princeton University
California Institute of Technology	Swarthmore College
Claremont McKenna College	United States Air Force Academy
College of the Holy Cross	United States Naval Academy
Dartmouth College	University of Notre Dame
Duke University	Washington and Lee University
Gettysburg College	Wellesley College
Middlebury College	Yale University
Pomona College	

There are 17 colleges and universities that stand above the rest in providing a comprehensive undergraduate experience that consistently produces Financial Success, Intellectual Capability, Friendships and Overall Happiness for its graduates. These 17 excellent colleges and universities are diverse in their approach, their size, their focus and in the experience they offer – but each can be relied upon to consistently deliver transformational undergraduate experiences that generate real results for graduates. Importantly, they best deliver on the critical goals that are foundational to the mission of any undergraduate education. Therefore, it is not surprising that eight of the Top Ten ranked *Alumni Factor* schools are on this list. These 17 schools also represent 12 of the Top 25 schools for *The Alumni Factor*. In fact, all 17 of them are in *The Alumni Factor* Top 50.

There are 12 other excellent schools deserving praise as the runners-up in Ultimate Outcomes performance. These 12 schools rank in the Top 50 in five of six Ultimate Outcomes:

Amherst College
Bowdoin College
Bucknell University
Colby College
Davidson College
Georgetown University
Harvard University
Harvey Mudd College
Rice University
Stanford University
Vanderbilt University
Williams College

All Ways Wealthy

Financial Success & Happiness

Smart Money

Financial Success & Intellectual Capability

Pursue Your Passions

Happiness & Intellectual Capability

Big Ideas

Friendships & Intellectual Capability

Life to the Brim

Happiness & Friendships

The Good Life

Financial Success & Friendships

CHAPTER 10

Social & Political Views by College

The Alumni Factor

Where Is Each College Positioned on The Alumni Factor Collegiate Political Spectrum?

We asked college graduates to give us their views on 15 of the hottest and most controversial social and political issues of the day. We have compiled the results and charted them in a variety of ways to give you insight into the way graduates think, and how graduates of each college differ. You will see distinct differences across the colleges we have analyzed and will begin to get a sense of the views that emanate from each college – reflected in their graduates.

From the responses of each graduate, we are able to place each college or university on *The Alumni Factor* Collegiate Political Spectrum. This exclusive spectrum shows where each college falls on the continuum of *Liberal* to *Conservative*, based on the responses of its graduates. In most cases, you will begin to see a clear pattern in each school's answers, and you will understand its placement on our spectrum relative to other colleges. One point to note is that a school's position on *The Alumni Factor* Collegiate Political Spectrum is relative only to the other colleges in our analysis. It is not an indicator of how liberal or conservative a college is versus the total population. Also note that, in general, a college-educated group tends to be more politically liberal and progressive than the overall US population.

Collegiate Political Spectrum Colleges & Universities

Very Liberal	Liberal	Somewhat Liberal	Somewhat Conservative	Conservative	Very Conservative

Very Liberal	Liberal	Somewhat Liberal	Somewhat Conservative	Conservative	Very Conservative

30 Very Liberal Colleges & Universities

1.	Reed College	16.	Bowdoin College
2.	Oberlin College	17.	Williams College
3.	Macalester College	18.	Brandeis University
4.	Grinnell College	19.	Yale University
5.	Bard College	20.	Kenyon College
6.	Swarthmore College	21.	Mount Holyoke College
7.	Haverford College	22.	Brown University
8.	Bryn Mawr College	23.	Harvard University
9.	Wesleyan University	24.	Wellesley College
10.	Smith College	25.	Colorado College
11.	Carleton College	26.	Hamilton College
12.	Vassar College	27.	University of California, Berkeley
13.	Scripps College	28.	University of California, Santa Barbara
14.	Amherst College	29.	Connecticut College
15.	Pomona College	30.	Spelman College

The lower the number the more liberal the alumni are, within this group.

Very Liberal	Liberal	Somewhat Liberal	Somewhat Conservative	Conservative	Very Conservative

30 Liberal Colleges & Universities

1.	Middlebury College	16.	Northwestern University
2.	Clark University	17.	Howard University
3.	Colby College	18.	Trinity College
4.	Stanford University	19.	University of Vermont
5.	Dartmouth College	20.	University of Massachusetts Amherst
6.	Whitman College	21.	Washington University in St. Louis
7.	Tufts University	22.	St. Olaf College
8.	Princeton University	23.	Syracuse University
9.	Occidental College	24.	Boston University
10.	Colgate University	25.	Massachusetts Institute of Technology
11.	Pitzer College	26.	University of Rochester
12.	University of Oregon	27.	Cornell University
13.	American University	28.	Rice University
14.	University of Chicago	29.	Skidmore College
15.	Bates College	30.	Morehouse College

The lower the number the more liberal the alumni are, within this group.

Very Liberal	Liberal	**Somewhat Liberal**	Somewhat Conservative	Conservative	Very Conservative

30 Colleges & Universities that Lean Liberal

1.	Duke University	16.	Loyola University Chicago
2.	Harvey Mudd College	17.	Denison University
3.	New York University	18.	Davidson College
4.	University of Pennsylvania	19.	University of California, Riverside
5.	California Institute of Technology	20.	Rutgers University
6.	Georgetown University	21.	University of Colorado Boulder
7.	George Washington University	22.	Sewanee: The University of the South
8.	Carnegie Mellon University	23.	Case Western Reserve University
9.	University of California, San Diego	24.	University of Washington
10.	University of Wisconsin-Madison	25.	Depauw University
11.	Columbia University	26.	Franklin & Marshall College
12.	Johns Hopkins University	27.	University of Virginia
13.	University of California, Los Angeles	28.	University of Minnesota
14.	Dickinson College	29.	Claremont McKenna College
15.	University of California, Davis	30.	DePaul University

The lower the number the more liberal the alumni are, within this group.

Very Liberal	Liberal	Somewhat Liberal	**Somewhat Conservative**	Conservative	Very Conservative

28 Colleges & Universities that Lean Conservative

1.	Lafayette College	15.	University of Delaware
2.	University of Southern California	16.	University of Connecticut
3.	Miami University	17.	Gettysburg College
4.	Gonzaga University	18.	Emory University
5.	The College of New Jersey	19.	Indiana University Bloomington
6.	Loyola Marymount University	20.	University of Michigan
7.	University of North Carolina at Chapel Hill	21.	Bucknell University
8.	College of the Holy Cross	22.	Worcester Polytechnic Institute
9.	University of Pittsburgh	23.	University of Iowa
10.	Michigan State University	24.	Trinity University
11.	Boston College	25.	Northeastern University
12.	San Diego State University	26.	The College of William & Mary
13.	University of Notre Dame	27.	Tulane University
14.	University of Illinois at Urbana-Champaign	28.	University of California, Irvine

The lower the number the more conservative the alumni are, within this group.

Very Liberal	Liberal	Somewhat Liberal	Somewhat Conservative	**Conservative**	Very Conservative

30 Conservative Colleges & Universities

1.	Iowa State University	16.	Loyola University Maryland
2.	Southern Methodist University	17.	Creighton University
3.	University of Richmond	18.	Loyola University New Orleans
4.	James Madison University	19.	Rensselaer Polytechnic Institute
5.	Drexel University	20.	Marquette University
6.	Valparaiso University	21.	Wake Forest University
7.	Elon University	22.	Centre College
8.	Xavier University	23.	University of Nebraska-Lincoln
9.	Arizona State University	24.	Vanderbilt University
10.	University of Florida	25.	University of Miami
11.	University of Kentucky	26.	Ohio State University
12.	University of Texas at Austin	27.	Santa Clara University
13.	University of Arizona	28.	Bradley University
14.	Oregon State University	29.	University of Kansas
15.	Pennsylvania State University	30.	Lehigh University

The lower the number the more conservative the alumni are, within this group.

Very Liberal	Liberal	Somewhat Liberal	Somewhat Conservative	Conservative	**Very Conservative**

29 Very Conservative Colleges & Universities

1.	United States Air Force Academy	16.	Villanova University
2.	Brigham Young University	17.	Ohio Northern University
3.	Auburn University	18.	North Carolina State University
4.	United States Naval Academy	19.	Kansas State University
5.	United States Military Academy	20.	Furman University
6.	Texas A&M University	21.	Colorado State University
7.	University of Mississippi	22.	University of Tennessee
8.	Georgia Institute of Technology	23.	University of Utah
9.	Baylor University	24.	University of Georgia
10.	University of Alabama	25.	College of Charleston
11.	Clemson University	26.	Washington State University
12.	University of Wyoming	27.	Pepperdine University
13.	Washington and Lee University	28.	Rollins College
14.	Purdue University	29.	Florida State University
15.	Virginia Polytechnic Institute and State University		

The lower the number the more conservative the alumni are, within this group.

Alumni Views on 15 of the Most Divisive Social Issues in America Today

Our Graduates Give Us Their Views

The graduates who come to life in these pages have been intellectually forged and sharpened in a post-secondary educational system celebrated the world over for its excellence and leadership. These alumni are part of the most influential, powerful, wealthy and educated segment of the US population. They lead our corporations, run our governments, craft our laws, teach our students, mobilize our communities, power our think-tanks, battle in our courtrooms, experiment in our labs, oversee our charitable institutions, cure our diseases, write our books, guide our religions and shape our culture. They are the fortunate graduates of America's most prestigious colleges and universities, and they have a profound impact on our world today and its direction in the future. Never has it been more important to know them, as they are presently at work creating the very trends that will define tomorrow. It has also never been more important to know their views about the key issues that will define our future.

We took the opportunity to ask these well-informed opinion-makers about their views on some of the most vexing political and social issues we face today in the US, with the hope that we could perhaps find some common ground from which we could begin to move forward to solve some of these persistent challenges.

While many would like to see clear consensus among these graduates on each of the issues put to them, the simple truth is that consensus is quite rare. Our graduates' views are as diverse as their backgrounds and are as varied as the colleges where they were educated. You will see this fact demonstrated in this chapter as you view the responses our graduates provided on each of these difficult issues.

15 of the Hottest Political and Social Issues

1. Immigration Control
2. Affirmative Action
3. Abortion
4. Government-Funded Healthcare
5. Homosexual Marriage
6. Media Bias
7. Gun Control Versus Right to Bear Arms
8. School Prayer
9. Political Correctness
10. Immigrants Learning English
11. Capitalism
12. The Military Draft
13. American Patriotism
14. Law Enforcement Profiling
15. Capital Punishment

Methodology:

For each topic, graduates were given statements and asked to indicate their level of agreement or disagreement with those statements. The choice of answers included: *Strongly Agree* (5), *Agree* (4), *Somewhat Agree* (3), *Somewhat Disagree* (2), *Disagree* (1), and *Strongly Disagree* (0). For each of the statements, we show the distribution of responses, as well as the mean response (the average of all graduate responses). A mean score of 2.5 is exactly in the middle. The spread of answers is also important to note when viewing the mean.

Political and Social Views of All College Graduates

Political/Social Viewpoint (In Order of Agreement – from Strong Agreement to Strong Disagreement)	Number of Graduate Responses (n=)	Average Score Scale: 5–0 (5=Strongly Agree)	Top Box Score % (% Strongly Agree)	Range Of Top Box % Scores For All Colleges	Standard Deviation	Level of Consensus
Abortion should be legal	39,500	3.56	41.7%	81%-6%	.536	Strong
Homosexuals should be allowed to marry	39,600	3.53	45.1%	82%-8%	.588	↑
America is the best country in the world today	39,494	3.45	28.4%	63%-6%	.397	
"Political Correctness" has gone too far in America	39,546	3.41	27.8%	63%-5%	.400	
Capitalism is a positive force in our world today	39,455	3.35	18.9%	45%-2%	.297	Consensus Agreement
Immigrants in America should be required to learn English	39,698	3.31	25.3%	52%-3%	.377	
Guns should be more controlled than they are today	39,670	3.30	30.8%	55%-8%	.494	
We need stronger controls on immigration	39,577	3.03	19.8%	49%-0%	.489	↓
Children should be allowed to pray in schools	39,569	3.00	20.7%	47%-3%	.490	Less Strong
The media leans to the liberal side	39,389	2.91	19.1%	47%-0%	.414	↑
Government-funded healthcare would be good for America	39,632	2.88	26.3%	62%-7%	.614	
Affirmative Action is fair	39,243	2.50	7.9%	36%-1%	.402	No Consensus
Affirmative Action is unfair	39,240	2.46	11.5%	27%-0%	.448	
Capital punishment is immoral	39,407	2.41	15.1%	41%-4%	.473	
Police should be able to profile when searching for criminals	39,528	2.35	7.5%	19%-0%	.349	↓
The media leans to the conservative side	39,386	1.90	3.8%	15%-0%	.343	↑
The media basically tells the truth	39,524	1.69	0.6%	4%-0%	.184	
Capitalism is a destructive force in our world today	39,364	1.68	3.1%	17%-0%	.323	Consensus Disagreement
We should reinstitute the military draft	39,534	1.39	3.0%	9%-0%	.192	
Abortion should be illegal	39,439	1.32	9.0%	29%-0%	.531	↓

Immigration Control

We asked each graduate to indicate their level of agreement with the following statement:

"We Need Stronger Controls on Immigration"

Graduates generally **agree** with this statement, with a **mean overall score of 3.03**. While geographic differences can explain some of the variation in the responses (points of entry for illegal immigrants tend to have a higher desire for immigration control), when analyzing responses by college it shows clear differences that are less driven by geography and more by a point of view or ideology.

Those most likely to agree with this statement tend to come from more conservative schools (the University of Mississippi scores highest with an average score of 4.04). Those most inclined to disagree come from the more liberal leaning schools (Reed College has the lowest average score at 1.59).

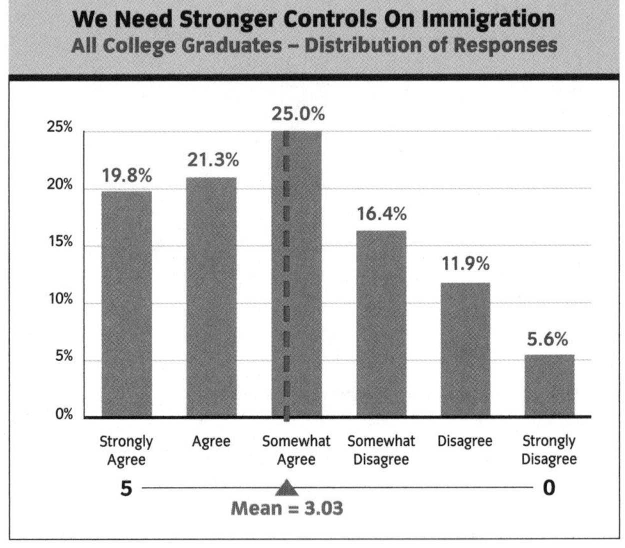

"We Need Stronger Controls on Immigration"

Top 25 Colleges to Agree	Top 25 Colleges to Disagree
1. University of Mississippi	1. Reed College
2. Auburn University	2. Swarthmore College
3. University of Wyoming	3. Carleton College
4. Ohio Northern University	4. Williams College
5. Elon University	5. Haverford College
6. University of Alabama	6. Oberlin College
7. United States Naval Academy	7. Grinnell College
8. Texas A&M University	8. Amherst College
9. Clemson University	9. Bard College
10. Kansas State University	10. Wesleyan University
11. North Carolina State University	11. Yale University
12. Rollins College	12. University of Chicago
13. Purdue University	13. Harvard University
14. Villanova University	14. Macalester College
15. Colorado State University	15. Pomona College
16. University of Tennessee	16. Vassar College
17. Florida State University	17. Bowdoin College
18. Furman University	18. Bryn Mawr College
19. United States Military Academy	19. Princeton University
20. Virginia Polytechnic Institute and State University	20. California Institute of Technology
21. United States Air Force Academy	21. Smith College
22. College of Charleston	22. Massachusetts Institute of Technology
23. Iowa State University	23. Brown University
24. San Diego State University	24. Mount Holyoke College
25. Baylor University	25. Brandeis University

Affirmative Action

We asked each graduate to indicate their level of agreement with the following statement:

"Affirmative Action Is Fair"

Graduates are more **broadly in the middle** on the issue of affirmative action than on any other issue we probed. With **mean scores of 2.50**, graduates are truly in the middle when it comes to deciding whether or not affirmative action is fair. Nearly 50% of all graduates either *Somewhat Agreed* or *Somewhat Disagreed* with this statement, and the remaining 50% are split nearly equally between agreement and disagreement.

Those most likely to favor affirmative action are graduates of the historically Black colleges (Morehouse, Spelman and Howard), the all-women colleges (Smith, Scripps, Bryn Mawr, Mount Holyoke) and the liberal colleges. Those most likely to oppose affirmative action are from the military academies, the technical schools and other conservative schools.

This subject also has the widest variation across colleges.

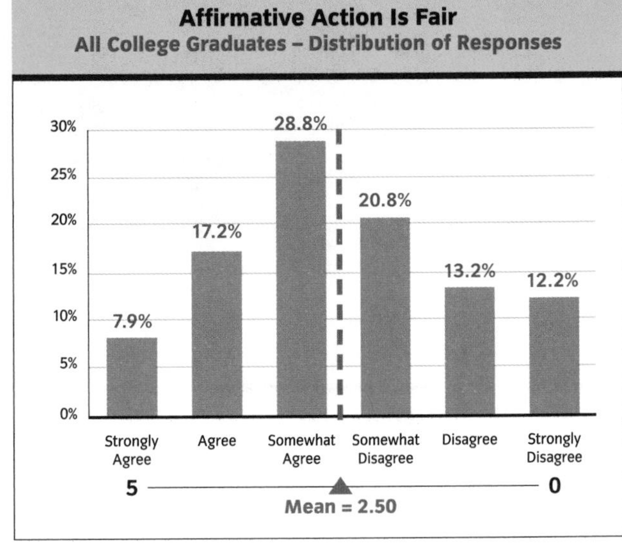

"Affirmative Action Is Fair"

Top 25 Colleges to Agree	Top 25 Colleges to Disagree
1. Morehouse College	1. United States Air Force Academy
2. Spelman College	2. Brigham Young University
3. Howard University	3. Georgia Institute of Technology
4. Reed College	4. Texas A&M University
5. Oberlin College	5. United States Naval Academy
6. Macalester College	6. University of Mississippi
7. Swarthmore College	7. Auburn University
8. Amherst College	8. University of Alabama
9. Haverford College	9. Washington and Lee University
10. Smith College	10. Clemson University
11. Bard College	11. Villanova University
12. Wesleyan University	12. United States Military Academy
13. Scripps College	13. Baylor University
14. Bryn Mawr College	14. College of Charleston
15. Grinnell College	15. University of Wyoming
16. Brown University	16. Rensselaer Polytechnic Institute
17. Carleton College	17. Purdue University
18. Colorado College	18. Virginia Polytechnic Institute and State University
19. Connecticut College	19. University of Georgia
20. Yale University	20. Ohio Northern University
21. Pomona College	21. Drexel University
22. Stanford University	22. Pepperdine University
23. Mount Holyoke College	23. Colorado State University
24. Williams College	24. University of Texas at Austin
25. Dartmouth College	25. Centre College

Abortion

We asked each graduate to indicate their level of agreement with the following statement:

"Abortion Should Be Legal"

Graduates are **broadly in favor of legal abortion** with almost 78% agreeing to some extent that abortion should be legal. Of course, this issue is much more complex than the answers to this question could ever indicate. The important subtleties of timing and reason for the procedure also tend to modify the acceptance or intolerance of abortion. There is a substantial 22% of graduates who disagree that abortion should be legal.

Those most strongly in favor of legal abortion are graduates of the liberal schools, while graduates of the conservative schools and some of the Catholic/Jesuit Schools are most strongly against legal abortion. There is also a significant difference between male and female graduates on this issue; 70% of female graduates *Strongly Agree* or *Agree* that abortion should be legal versus 56% of male graduates.

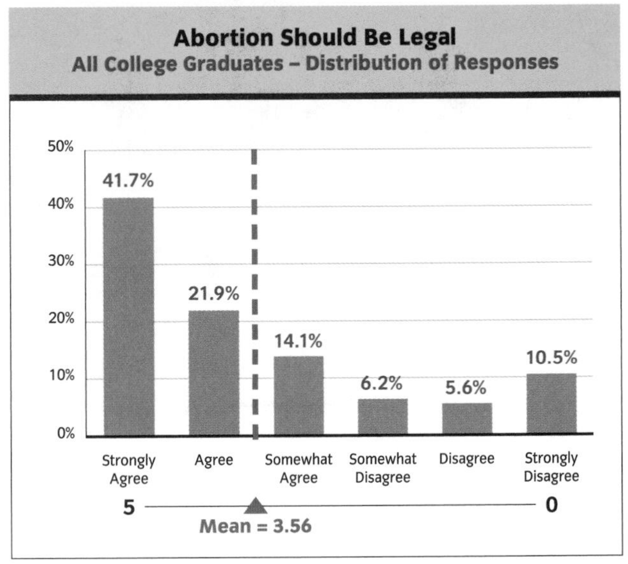

"Abortion Should Be Legal"

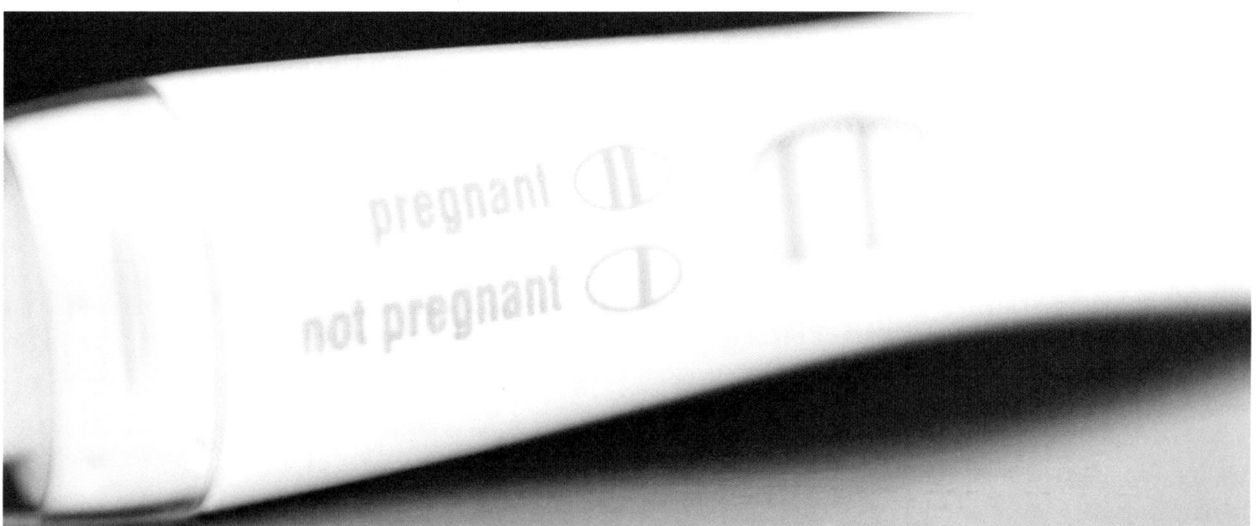

Top 25 Colleges to Agree	Top 25 Colleges to Disagree
1. Reed College	1. Brigham Young University
2. Smith College	2. United States Air Force Academy
3. Vassar College	3. Baylor University
4. Bryn Mawr College	4. Auburn University
5. Swarthmore College	5. United States Military Academy
6. Kenyon College	6. Xavier University
7. Brandeis University	7. Texas A&M University
8. Wesleyan University	8. Furman University
9. Connecticut College	9. University of Utah
10. Pomona College	10. University of Mississippi
11. Clark University	11. University of Notre Dame
12. Bard College	12. Kansas State University
13. Macalester College	13. Villanova University
14. Tufts University	14. Georgia Institute of Technology
15. Mount Holyoke College	15. United States Naval Academy
16. Grinnell College	16. University of Alabama
17. Skidmore College	17. Creighton University
18. Wellesley College	18. Gonzaga University
19. Colby College	19. University of Tennessee
20. University of California, Santa Barbara	20. Loyola University New Orleans
21. Carleton College	21. Ohio Northern University
22. Oberlin College	22. Loyola College Maryland
23. Haverford College	23. Purdue University
24. American University	24. University of Nebraska
25. Middlebury College	25. Pepperdine University

Government-Funded Healthcare

We asked each graduate to indicate their level of agreement with the following statement:

"Government-Funded Universal Healthcare Would Be Good for America"

Overall, graduates **lean slightly toward agreement** with this statement, with a **mean score of 2.88**. The split among all graduates is 63% agree and 37% disagree. However, there is significant polarization, as the two most frequent responses are *Strongly Agree* (26.3%) and *Strongly Disagree* (19.7%).

This is one of the issues where graduates define themselves clearly as liberal or conservative. Those most likely to agree with this statement tend to come from more liberal schools (Reed College scores highest with an average score of 4.39). Those most inclined to disagree are graduates of more conservative schools (the Air Force Academy has the lowest average score at 1.27).

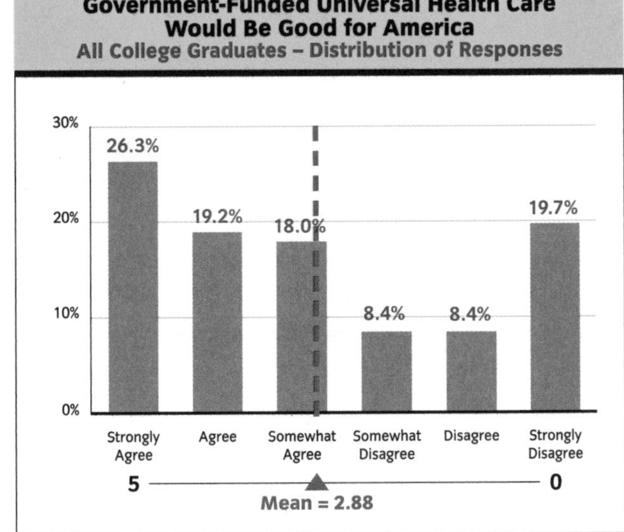

"Government-Funded Universal Healthcare Would Be Good for America"

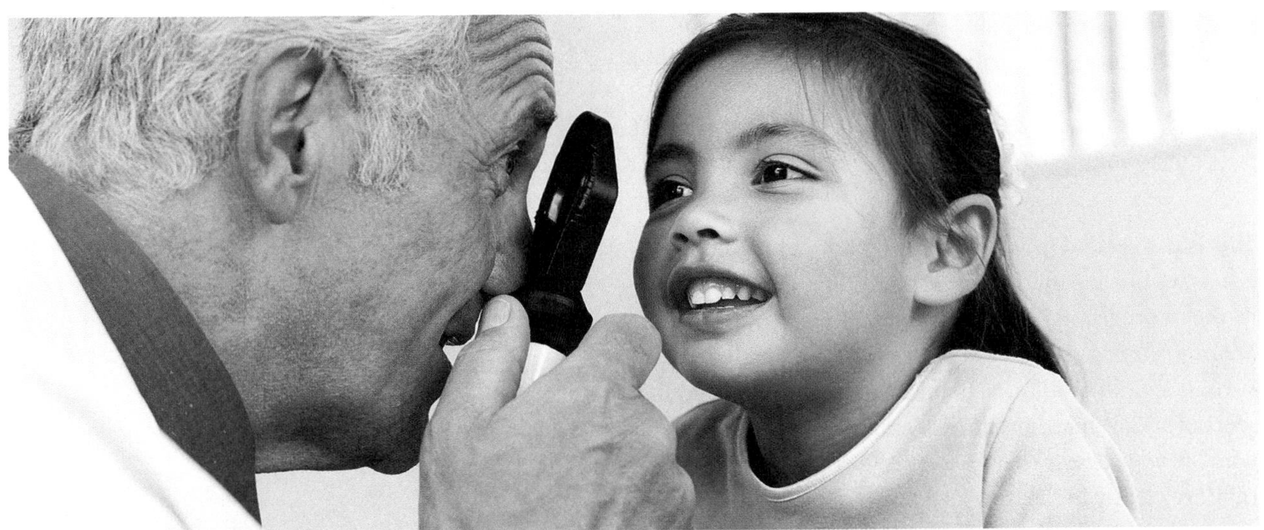

Top 25 Colleges to Agree	Top 25 Colleges to Disagree
1. Reed College	1. United States Air Force Academy
2. Bard College	2. Brigham Young University
3. Oberlin College	3. Auburn University
4. Macalester College	4. Texas A&M University
5. Bryn Mawr College	5. University of Mississippi
6. Scripps College	6. United States Naval Academy
7. Morehouse College	7. Georgia Institute of Technology
8. Haverford College	8. University of Alabama
9. Carleton College	9. United States Military Academy
10. Spelman College	10. Baylor University
11. Howard University	11. Washington and Lee University
12. Swarthmore College	12. Clemson University
13. Grinnell College	13. Villanova University
14. Smith College	14. Purdue University
15. University of California, Santa Barbara	15. Virginia Polytechnic Institute and State University
16. Vassar College	16. Furman University
17. Wesleyan University	17. Elon University
18. Amherst College	18. University of Georgia
19. Mount Holyoke College	19. Kansas State University
20. Hamilton College	20. Centre College
21. University of California, Berkeley	21. College of Charleston
22. Williams College	22. University of Richmond
23. Pomona College	23. University of Tennessee
24. Brandeis University	24. North Carolina State University
25. Kenyon College	25. Colorado State University

Homosexual Marriage

We asked each graduate to indicate their level of agreement with the following statement:

"Homosexuals Should Be Allowed to Marry"

This is the second most agreed to statement of all the issues we posed, and has the highest top box (Strongly Agree) score of any statement. **Over 74% of graduates *Strongly Agree, Agree* or *Somewhat Agree*** that homosexuals should be allowed to marry, with a mean overall score of 3.53. While there are still almost 19% of graduates who *Strongly Disagree* or *Disagree* with this statement, they are clearly in the minority.

The one group that is uniquely conservative on this issue is Black graduates; 28% of Black graduates *Disagree* or *Strongly Disagree* with this statement versus only 19% of all college graduates. This is why you will find Morehouse College and Howard University, both historically Black colleges, among the Top 25 colleges that disagree with this statement. Conversely, these same graduates are among the more liberal in the country on most other issues.

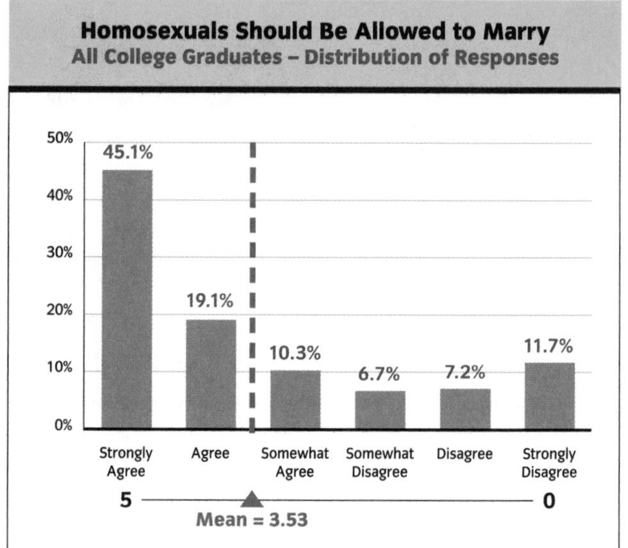

"Homosexuals Should Be Allowed to Marry"

Top 25 Colleges to Agree	Top 25 Colleges to Disagree
1. Reed College	1. Brigham Young University
2. Vassar College	2. United States Air Force Academy
3. Macalester College	3. Auburn University
4. Smith College	4. Baylor University
5. Bryn Mawr College	5. University of Utah
6. Grinnell College	6. United States Military Academy
7. Wesleyan University	7. United States Naval Academy
8. Oberlin College	8. University of Mississippi
9. Haverford College	9. Georgia Institute of Technology
10. Kenyon College	10. Texas A&M University
11. Bard College	11. Clemson University
12. Swarthmore College	12. University of Alabama
13. Carleton College	13. Morehouse College
14. Connecticut College	14. Kansas State University
15. Pomona College	15. Drexel University
16. Bowdoin College	16. North Carolina State University
17. Hamilton College	17. Howard University
18. Clark University	18. University of Tennessee
19. Brandeis University	19. Furman University
20. Williams College	20. Washington State University
21. Colby College	21. Pepperdine University
22. Mount Holyoke College	22. Ohio Northern University
23. Amherst College	23. Purdue University
24. Wellesley College	24. Florida State University
25. University of California, Santa Barbara	25. University of Wyoming

Media Bias

We asked each graduate to indicate their level of agreement with three statements:

"The Media Leans to the Liberal Side"

"The Media Leans to the Conservative Side"

"The Media Basically Tells the Truth"

A majority (60%) of graduates agree that the media leans to the liberal side, and 66% disagree that the media leans conservatively; so, the general view of graduates is that the media is somewhat liberally slanted. However, there is clear disagreement on this issue among graduates of certain colleges. Less than 20% of the graduates at some of the most liberal colleges (Reed, Oberlin, Bard, Carleton, Grinnell) agree that the media leans to the liberal side. When compared to results from the three military academies (West Point, Annapolis, Air Force) or other conservative schools, where more than 80% of graduates agree that the media leans left, it becomes apparent that there is a broad diversity of opinion and perspective among graduates on this issue today. Bias appears to be in the eye of the beholder.

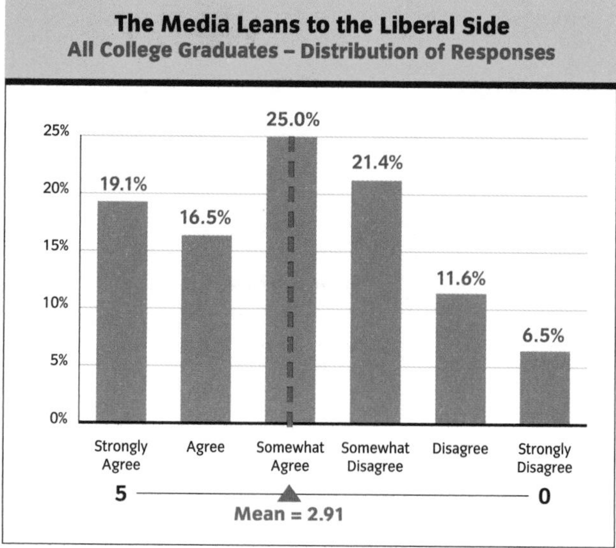

One of the most surprising responses on this issue is that **72% of graduates disagree that the media basically tells the truth.** This is a shocking statistic and partially helps explain consumers' rapid flights from traditional media to alternative sources of information that are more trusted. It is the content, the source and the format by which the content is delivered that will determine American perception of media veracity in the future. When nearly 72% of the nation's brightest minds do not trust the media, change is certain to follow.

"The Media Leans to the Liberal Side"

Top 25 Colleges to Agree	Top 25 Colleges to Disagree
1. United States Air Force Academy	1. Reed College
2. Brigham Young University	2. Oberlin College
3. United States Naval Academy	3. Carleton College
4. Auburn University	4. Grinnell College
5. United States Military Academy	5. Bard College
6. Texas A&M University	6. Hamilton College
7. Georgia Institute of Technology	7. Morehouse College
8. University of Mississippi	8. Macalester College
9. Furman University	9. Spelman College
10. Baylor University	10. Bryn Mawr College
11. Clemson University	11. Wesleyan University
12. Washington and Lee University	12. Howard University
13. University of Alabama	13. Pomona College
14. Virginia Polytechnic Institute and State University	14. Swarthmore College
15. Villanova University	15. Smith College
16. Kansas State University	16. Whitman College
17. Lafayette College	17. Colorado College
18. Purdue University	18. Haverford College
19. University of Richmond	19. University of California, Santa Barbara
20. College of Charleston	20. Vassar College
21. Southern Methodist University	21. Kenyon College
22. North Carolina State University	22. Amherst College
23. Elon University	23. Harvard University
24. Pepperdine University	24. Clark University
25. Loyola College Maryland	25. University of California, Berkeley

"The Media Leans to the Conservative Side"

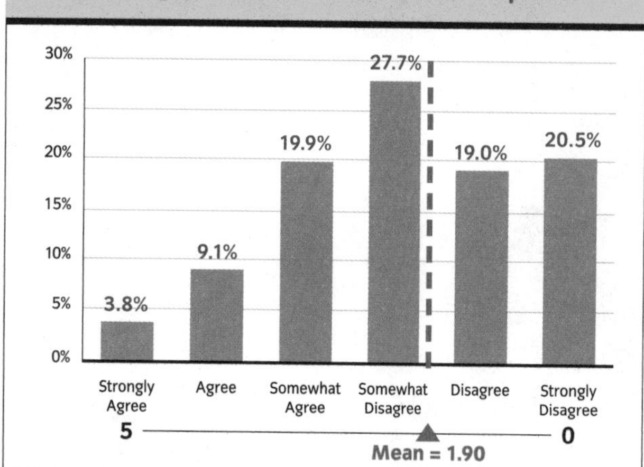

Top 25 Colleges to Agree	Top 25 Colleges to Disagree
1. Reed College	1. United States Air Force Academy
2. Bard College	2. Brigham Young University
3. Morehouse College	3. United States Naval Academy
4. Grinnell College	4. Texas A&M University
5. Oberlin College	5. Auburn University
6. Spelman College	6. United States Military Academy
7. Hamilton College	7. Washington and Lee University
8. Macalester College	8. Clemson University
9. Howard University	9. Georgia Institute of Technology
10. Carleton College	10. Baylor University
11. Bryn Mawr College	10. Furman University
12. Pomona College	12. Virginia Polytechnic Institute and State University
13. Smith College	13. University of Mississippi
14. Scripps College	14. Southern Methodist University
15. University of California, Santa Barbara	15. University of Alabama
16. Wesleyan University	16. Washington State University
17. Haverford College	17. University of Richmond
18. University of Massachusetts Amherst	18. Purdue University
19. Swarthmore College	19. University of Georgia
20. Vassar College	20. College of Charleston
21. Occidental College	21. Villanova University
22. Colorado College	22. Lafayette College
23. University of Oregon	23. Pepperdine University
24. Colby College	24. University of Wyoming
25. University of California, Berkeley	25. University of Tennessee

"The Media Basically Tells the Truth"

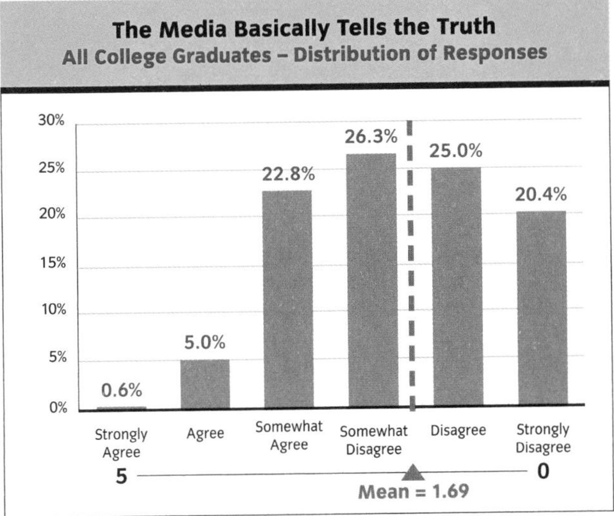

Top 25 Colleges to Agree	Top 25 Colleges to Disagree
1. Haverford College	1. Villanova University
2. Dartmouth College	2. Drexel University
3. Claremont McKenna College	3. Rollins College
4. Princeton University	4. Auburn University
5. Williams College	5. Texas A&M University
6. Davidson College	6. University of Mississippi
7. Duke University	7. Spelman College
8. Trinity College	8. University of California, Irvine
9. Georgetown University	9. University of California, Riverside
10. Swarthmore College	10. University of Wyoming
11. American University	11. Loyola Marymount University
12. Bates College	12. Pepperdine University
13. University of Virginia	13. DePaul University
14. Amherst College	14. University of Tennessee
15. Carleton College	15. Creighton University
16. California Institute of Technology	16. United States Air Force Academy
17. Syracuse University	17. Loyola University New Orleans
18. Harvard University	18. Occidental College
19. University of Notre Dame	19. Georgia Institute of Technology
20. Kenyon College	20. Colorado State University
21. Northwestern University	21. Skidmore College
22. Massachusetts Institute of Technology	22. Bradley University
23. Bowdoin College	23. Orgeon State University
24. Middlebury College	24. Baylor University
25. Cornell University	25. Loyola University Maryland

Gun Control versus Right to Bear Arms

We asked each graduate to respond to the following statement:

"Guns Should Be More Controlled Than They Are Today"

Graduates tend toward **agreement** with this statement, with a **mean overall score of 3.30**. Not surprisingly, graduates of military and conservative schools located in the South or West tend to have the highest disagreement with this statement. While agreement or disagreement does tend to follow liberal and conservative lines, there are some graduates who feel more strongly about this issue than others.

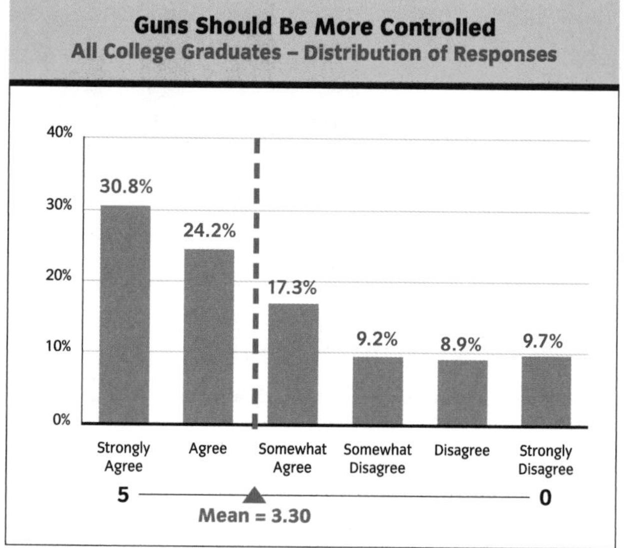

Much of the difference on the issue of gun control is driven by gender. Males are nearly two times more likely to *Disagree* or *Strongly Disagree* with this statement than are females; 61% of females are in the top two boxes of agreement on this statement versus only 47% of males.

Those graduates most likely to agree with this statement tend to come from more liberal schools (Scripps College scores highest with an average score of 4.19) and schools with a high proportion of females. Those inclined to disagree come from more conservative schools (Air Force Academy has the lowest average score at 1.70) and schools heavily weighted toward males.

"Guns Should Be More Controlled Than They Are Today"

Top 25 Colleges to Agree	Top 25 Colleges to Disagree
1. Scripps College	1. United States Air Force Academy
2. Haverford College	2. University of Wyoming
3. Spelman College	3. Brigham Young University
4. Wesleyan University	4. United States Military Academy
5. Macalester College	5. Texas A&M University
6. Swarthmore College	6. Auburn University
7. Skidmore College	7. Colorado State University
8. Oberlin College	8. United States Naval Academy
9. Connecticut College	9. Georgia Institute of Technology
10. Bryn Mawr College	10. University of Mississippi
11. Smith College	11. University of Alabama
12. Amherst College	12. Washington and Lee University
13. Howard University	13. Rensselaer Polytechnic Institute
14. Kenyon College	14. Kansas State University
15. Bowdoin College	15. Clemson University
16. Wellesley College	16. University of Georgia
17. Vassar College	17. Baylor University
18. Brown University	18. Oregon State University
19. Grinnell College	19. Ohio Northern University
20. Middlebury College	20. Washington State University
21. Brandeis University	21. University of Utah
22. Carleton College	22. Worcester Polytechnic Institute
23. Bard College	23. University of Tennessee
24. Reed College	24. Purdue University
25. Williams College	25. Iowa State University

School Prayer

We asked each graduate to respond to the following statement:

"Children Should Be Allowed to Pray in School"

Graduates are in general **agreement** with this statement, as two-thirds agree to some extent with allowing prayer in school. The mean overall score is 2.99. However, 20% of graduates *Strongly Disagree* or *Disagree* with prayer in school. These graduates tend to be skewed female, older, White, less happy, liberal, with a higher income and net worth, and are more likely to have a graduate degree.

This is an issue where Black graduates skew uniquely to the conservative side. Only 11% of Black graduates *Strongly Disagree* or *Disagree* with this statement versus 20% of all graduates. Therefore, you will see Spelman, Morehouse and Howard in the Top 10 schools who most agree with this statement.

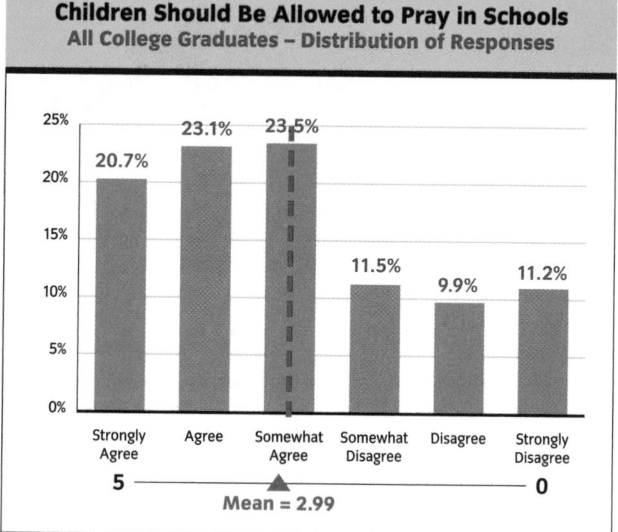

"Children Should Be Allowed to Pray in School"

Top 25 Colleges to Agree	Top 25 Colleges to Disagree
1. Auburn University	1. Brandeis University
2. Spelman College	2. Bryn Mawr College
3. Morehouse College	3. Reed College
4. United States Air Force Academy	4. Pomona College
5. University of Alabama	4. Swarthmore College
6. Howard University	6. Oberlin College
7. Texas A&M University	7. Vassar College
8. Baylor University	8. Wesleyan University
9. Xavier University	9. Tufts University
10. North Carolina State University	10. Haverford College
11. University of Mississippi	11. Grinnell College
12. Furman University	12. University of California, Berkeley
13. Brigham Young University	13. Hamilton College
14. Clemson University	14. Colby College
15. Valparaiso University	15. University of California, Santa Barbara
16. United States Military Academy	16. Brown University
17. James Madison University	17. Smith College
18. United States Naval Academy	18. Harvard University
19. Villanova University	19. Colorado College
20. Ohio Northern University	20. Connecticut College
21. University of Tennessee	21. New York University
22. University of Kentucky	22. University of Pennsylvania
23. Kansas State University	23. Mount Holyoke College
24. Purdue University	24. University of Rochester
25. Virginia Polytechnic Institute and State University	25. Carleton College

Political Correctness

We asked each graduate to indicate their level of agreement with the following statement:

"Political Correctness Has Gone Too Far in America Today"

It is actually quite hard to find many people who agree that more "political correctness" would be a good thing, since the term itself has such a negative connotation for most people in America. It has been defined, mostly derisively, as "language, behavior or policy that minimizes social offense due to age, race, gender, religion or a host of other differences between people." So, when we presented our statement about political correctness to graduates, 76% of them agreeed to some extent versus almost 23% who disagreed. This is the fourth most agreed-to statement among those we posed.

The almost 12% of graduates who *Disagree* or *Strongly Disagree* with this statement most likely define the meaning of "politically correct" as respect, dignity and equality for all. They tend to be women with lower incomes and net worth. They are twice as likely to be college professors and significantly more likely to call themselves liberal. "Has political correctness gone too far?" Our graduate responses suggest they think it has. Today's Americans often feel like they are walking a verbal tight-rope, careful to not offend any person or group lest they fall into the "PC" pit. The problem is that defining offense is extraordinarily easy in today's super-sensitive society, where grievance groups can be formed overnight. On the other hand, it is hard to disagree with respect, dignity and equality for all. That's what makes this particular issue so complex and why this debate has staying power.

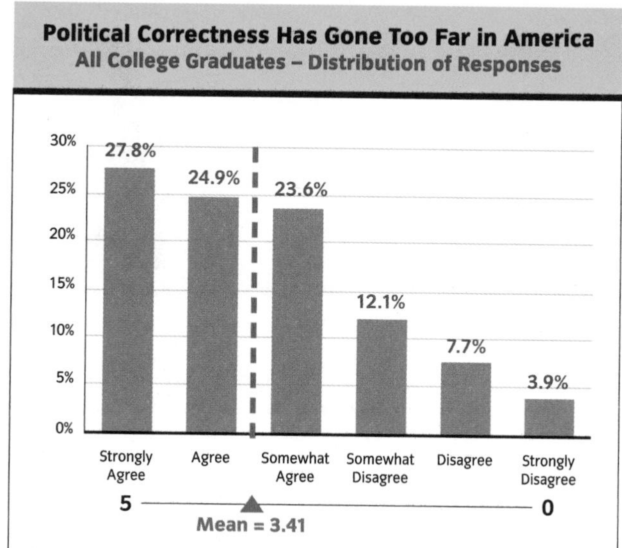

"Political Correctness Has Gone Too Far in America Today"

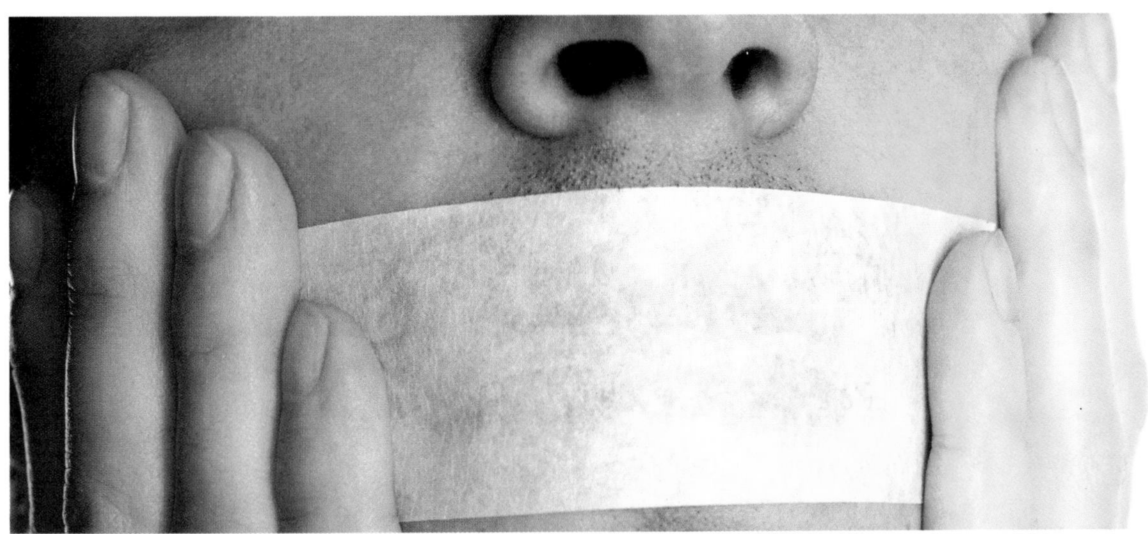

Top 25 Colleges to Agree	Top 25 Colleges to Disagree
1. Auburn University	1. Oberlin College
2. United States Naval Academy	2. Carleton College
3. United States Air Force Academy	3. Swarthmore College
4. Texas A&M University	4. Macalester College
5. Clemson University	5. Bryn Mawr College
6. United States Military Academy	6. Wesleyan University
7. University of Mississippi	7. Haverford College
8. Georgia Institute of Technology	8. Reed College
9. Brigham Young University	9. Grinnell College
10. Villanova University	10. Amherst College
11. University of Alabama	11. Williams College
12. Purdue University	12. Bard College
13. University of Wyoming	13. Yale University
14. Washington State University	14. Pomona College
15. Iowa State University	15. Harvard University
16. Ohio Northern University	16. Smith College
17. Colorado State University	17. Princeton University
18. Virginia Polytechnic Institute and State University	18. Wellesley College
19. North Carolina State University	19. Brown University
20. Baylor University	20. Bowdoin College
21. Kansas State University	21. Mount Holyoke College
22. Washington and Lee University	22. Hamilton College
23. Oregon State University	23. Spelman College
24. Furman University	24. Pitzer College
25. University of Georgia	25. Brandeis University

Immigrants Learning English

We asked each graduate to indicate their level of agreement with the following statement:

"Immigrants Should Be Required to Learn English"

Graduates **somewhat agree** with this statement, with a **mean overall score of 3.03**. As with the immigration control subject, geographic differences can explain some of the variation. However, analyzing responses by college shows clear differences.

Those most likely to agree with this statement tend to come from more conservative schools (the University of Mississippi scores highest with an average score of 4.08). Those most inclined to disagree come from the more liberal leaning schools (Reed College has the lowest average score at 2.10).

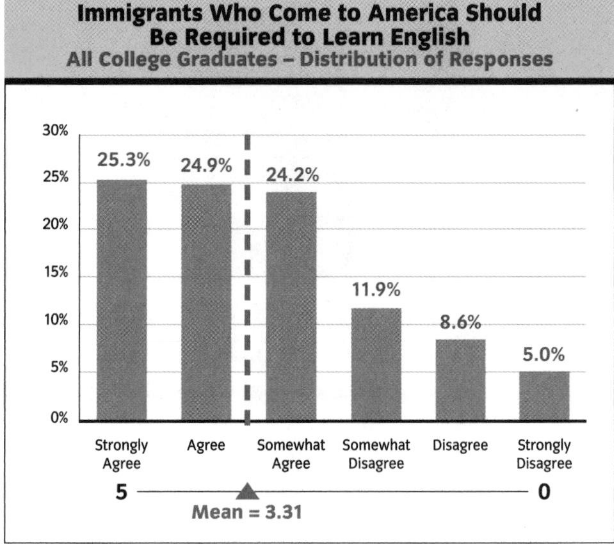

"Immigrants Should Be Required to Learn English"

	Top 25 Colleges to Agree		Top 25 Colleges to Disagree
1.	University of Mississippi	1.	Reed College
2.	Auburn University	2.	Grinnell College
3.	University of Wyoming	3.	Williams College
4.	Ohio Northern University	4.	Carleton College
5.	Elon University	5.	Macalester College
6.	Florida State University	6.	Yale University
7.	United States Naval Academy	7.	Amherst College
8.	Texas A&M University	8.	Oberlin College
9.	Purdue University	9.	Swarthmore College
10.	Villanova University	10.	Wesleyan University
11.	Rollins College	11.	Bowdoin College
12.	North Carolina State University	12.	Haverford College
13.	Clemson University	13.	Vassar College
14.	University of Tennessee	14.	Pomona College
15.	Howard University	15.	Kenyon College
16.	University of Miami	16.	Scripps College
17.	College of Charleston	17.	Rice University
18.	Kansas State University	18.	Bryn Mawr College
19.	Colorado State University	19.	Princeton University
19.	University of Alabama	20.	Whitman College
21.	Loyola University New Orleans	21.	Bard College
22.	United States Air Force Academy	22.	Harvard University
23.	Pennsylvania State University	23.	Brown University
24.	Iowa State University	24.	University of Chicago
25.	University of Florida	25.	Claremont McKenna College

Capitalism

We asked each graduate to indicate their level of agreement with the following statement:

"Capitalism Is a Positive Force in Our World Today"

Capitalism is **strongly viewed as a positive force** in society today by the majority of graduates. Only 8.4% *Strongly Disagree* or *Disagree* that capitalism is a positive force today. The statement on capitalism as a positive force is the fifth most agreed-to statement, with a mean of 3.35.

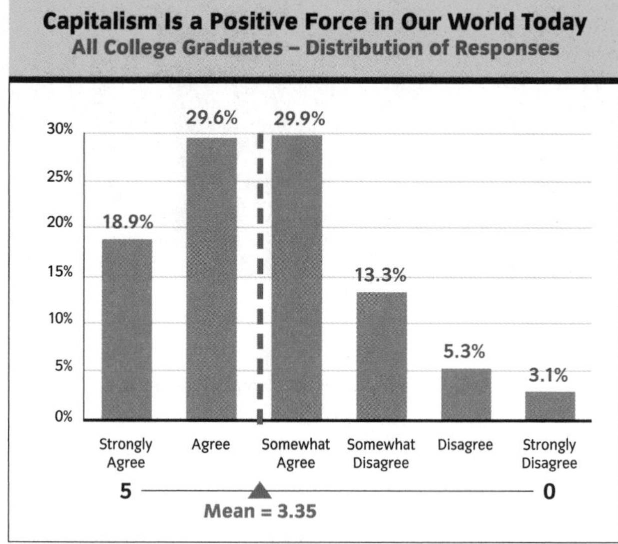

Not surprisingly, those most likely to see capitalism as a positive force are the military academies, the technical schools and other conservative schools. The two strongest supporters of capitalism (US Air Force Academy and Washington and Lee University) have top two box scores of 81% and 76% respectively. Conversely, the two colleges whose graduates disagreed most (Reed College and Bard College) have top two box scores of 14% and 26% respectively. It is illustrative of the "two Americas" that exist among our graduates when it comes to the role and impact of capitalism in America today.

"Capitalism Is a Positive Force in Our World Today"

Top 25 Colleges to Agree	Top 25 Colleges to Disagree
1. United States Air Force Academy	1. Reed College
2. United States Military Academy	2. Bard College
3. United States Naval Academy	3. Spelman College
4. Washington and Lee University	4. Howard University
5. Georgia Institute of Technology	5. Oberlin College
6. Brigham Young University	6. Macalester College
7. Auburn University	7. Grinnell College
8. Texas A&M University	8. Bryn Mawr College
9. University of Richmond	9. Scripps College
10. Virginia Polytechnic Institute and State University	10. Smith College
11. Claremont McKenna College	11. University of Massachusetts Amherst
12. Wake Forest University	12. University of California, Santa Barbara
13. University of Mississippi	13. Colby College
14. North Carolina State University	14. Morehouse College
15. Baylor University	15. University of Oregon
16. Lafayette College	16. University of California, Riverside
17. Villanova University	17. University of California, Berkeley
18. University of Utah	18. Swarthmore College
19. University of Alabama	19. Vassar College
20. Vanderbilt University	20. Colorado College
21. Lehigh University	21. Hamilton College
22. University of Georgia	22. Occidental College
23. Purdue University	23. St. Olaf College
24. Centre College	24. Wesleyan University
25. Bucknell University	25. Brandeis University

The Military Draft

We asked each graduate to indicate their level of agreement with the following statement:

"We Should Reinstate the Military Draft in America"

This is the **single most disagreed-to statement** among all the statements we fielded with graduates. With a **mean overall score of 1.39**, it is clear that graduates broadly disagree that the military draft should be restored in America. Even among the schools most likely to agree that a draft should be reinstated, the graduates' views would more accurately be described as "disagreeing with the statement to a lesser extent than other graduates." As an example, the highest-scoring school (the one with the highest agreement that a draft should be reinstated) was the US Naval Academy, where only 15.4% of graduates *Strongly Agreed* or *Agreed* with this statement. In fact, 47% of Naval Academy graduates actually *Strongly Disagree* or *Disagree* that the draft should be reinstated.

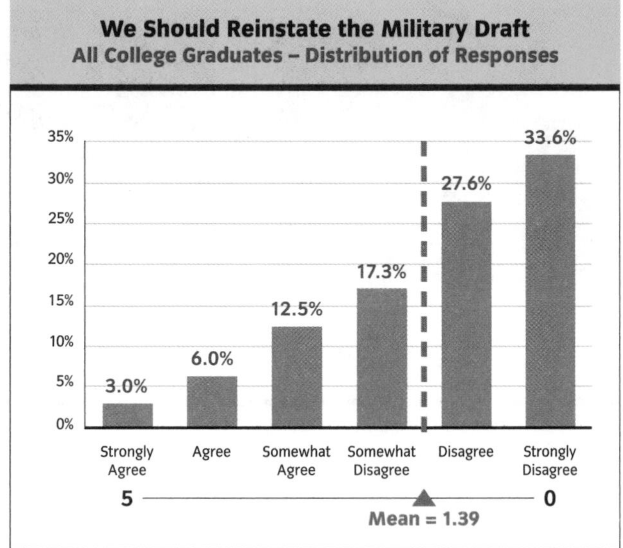

"We Should Reinstate the Military Draft in America"

Top 25 Colleges to Agree	Top 25 Colleges to Disagree
1. United States Naval Academy	1. Spelman College
2. University of Utah	2. Scripps College
3. Texas A&M University	3. Haverford College
4. United States Military Academy	4. Connecticut College
5. Grinnell College	5. Clark University
6. Virginia Polytechnic Institute and State University	6. University of California, San Diego
7. Columbia University	7. University of Rochester
8. University of Wyoming	8. Occidental College
9. Massachusetts Institute of Technology	9. Bard College
10. University of Tennessee	10. Mount Holyoke College
11. Harvey Mudd College	11. University of California, Santa Barbara
12. University of Mississippi	12. Howard University
13. North Carolina State University	13. Stanford University
14. Washington and Lee University	14. Smith College
15. Rollins College	15. Tufts University
16. Georgia Institute of Technology	16. Whitman College
17. Auburn University	17. Vassar College
18. Washington State University	18. University of Pennsylvania
19. Baylor University	19. Oberlin College
20. Kansas State University	20. University of Delaware
21. Sewanee: The University of the South	21. Loyola Marymount University
22. Swarthmore College	22. Hamilton College
23. Colorado State University	23. Bryn Mawr College
24. United States Air Force Academy	24. Reed College
25. Pepperdine University	25. Pitzer College

American Patriotism

We asked each graduate to indicate their level of agreement with the following statement:

"America Is the Best Country in the World"

As the **third most agreed-to statement** among graduates, **with a mean score of 3.45**, it is evident that most graduates patriotically agree that America is the best country in the world. The graduates with the highest level of agreement with this statement are from schools that skew military and Southern. Small liberal arts colleges tend to be the ones on the other end of the scale. This is another issue that tends to differ across gender lines, as 58% of males are in the top two boxes of agreement with this statement versus only 46% of females.

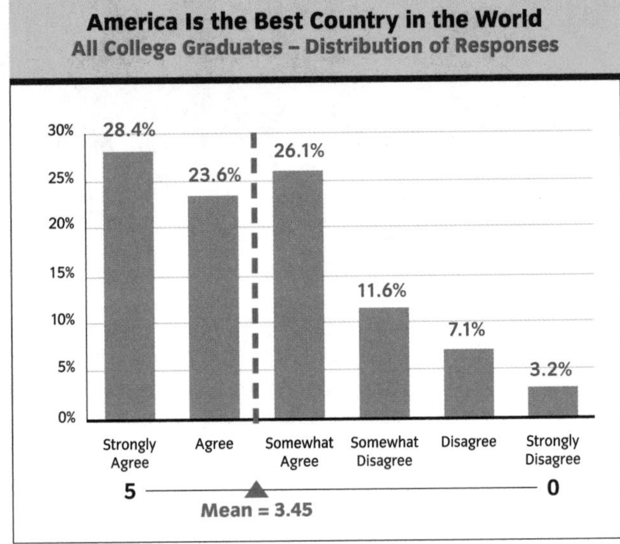

Those who are in disagreement (bottom two boxes) on this issue skew female; younger and lower income versus all graduates; are significantly less likely to recommend their college or consider it a good value; are nearly three times more likely to wish they had gone to another college; are 40% more likely to be a college professor; and are significantly less happy. Two-thirds of these graduates consider themselves *Very Liberal* or *Liberal* in their political views versus only 34% for all graduates.

"America Is the Best Country in the World"

Top 25 Colleges to Agree	Top 25 Colleges to Disagree
1. United States Air Force Academy	1. Reed College
2. United States Naval Academy	2. Bard College
3. United States Military Academy	3. Grinnell College
4. Auburn University	4. Haverford College
5. University of Mississippi	5. Bryn Mawr College
6. University of Alabama	6. Macalester College
7. University of Wyoming	7. Oberlin College
8. Clemson University	8. Bowdoin College
9. Texas A&M University	9. Vassar College
10. Kansas State University	10. Scripps College
11. Purdue University	11. Smith College
12. University of Tennessee	12. Whitman College
13. Brigham Young University	13. Carleton College
14. Georgia Institute of Technology	14. Swarthmore College
15. Colorado State University	15. Pomona College
16. Villanova University	16. Wesleyan University
17. North Carolina State University	17. Brandeis University
18. Baylor University	18. Amherst College
19. Virginia Polytechnic Institute and State University	19. University of Oregon
20. Washington and Lee University	20. Harvey Mudd College
21. University of Georgia	21. Brown University
22. University of Florida	22. St. Olaf College
23. Southern Methodist University	23. Kenyon College
24. Ohio Northern University	24. Williams College
25. James Madison University	25. University of California, Berkeley

Law Enforcement Profiling

We asked each graduate to indicate their level of agreement with the following statement:

"Police Should Be Allowed to Profile When Searching for a Criminal"

With a **mean score of 2.35, graduates tend toward disagreement** with this statement. However, the most frequent response was *Somewhat Agree*, with nearly 27% of graduates choosing that option. We believe they want law enforcement to have the ability to do what is needed, but do not want people's rights trampled in the process. The top three schools in disagreement with this statement are Morehouse, Spelman and Howard University.

Those most likely to agree with this statement come from schools which align with order, code and discipline (West Point, Naval Academy, Air Force), the technical schools (Georgia Tech, Virginia Tech) and some of the schools that lean conservative on many of the issues (Georgia, Mississippi, Baylor).

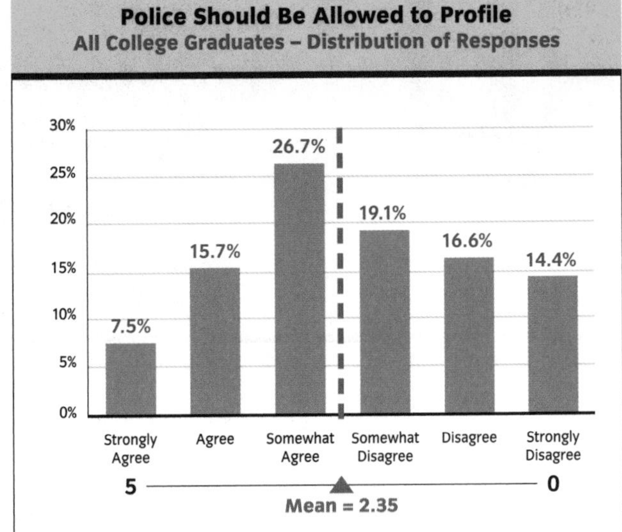

"Police Should Be Allowed to Profile When Searching for a Criminal"

	Top 25 Colleges to Agree		Top 25 Colleges to Disagree
1.	United States Naval Academy	1.	Morehouse College
2.	United States Military Academy	2.	Spelman College
3.	Auburn University	3.	Howard University
4.	United States Air Force Academy	4.	Reed College
5.	Washington and Lee University	5.	Oberlin College
6.	Georgia Institute of Technology	6.	Scripps College
7.	Villanova University	7.	Macalester College
8.	Texas A&M University	8.	Wesleyan University
9.	University of Richmond	9.	Bard College
10.	College of Charleston	10.	Vassar College
11.	University of Georgia	11.	Smith College
12.	University of Mississippi	12.	Amherst College
13.	Brigham Young University	13.	Yale University
14.	Washington State University	14.	Colorado College
15.	Furman University	15.	Swarthmore College
16.	Colorado State University	16.	Bowdoin College
17.	Purdue University	17.	Haverford College
18.	University of Wyoming	18.	Bates College
19.	Clemson University	19.	Bryn Mawr College
20.	Kansas State University	20.	Carleton College
21.	Virginia Polytechnic Institute and State University	21.	Brandeis University
22.	Oregon State University	22.	University of California, Berkeley
23.	Baylor University	23.	University of Chicago
24.	North Carolina State University	24.	Grinnell College
25.	Elon University	25.	Brown University

Capital Punishment

We asked each graduate to indicate their level of agreement with the following statement:

"Capital Punishment Is Immoral"

Graduates **slightly tend toward disagreeing** with this statement, **with a mean score of 2.41**. However, that doesn't mean everyone is undecided in the middle. Only 36% of graduates are in the middle two boxes with this issue. Roughly 45% of graduates are on the "agreement" side, while the other 55% are on the "disagreement" side. As with many difficult social and political issues, the answer is rarely black or white – it depends on the specific circumstances. That is certainly the case with the issue of capital punishment.

Those most likely to agree with this statement tend to come from the more liberal schools. Reed College is highest in agreement with a mean score of 3.77. Whereas, on the other side, the US Naval Academy is highest in disagreement with a mean score of 1.31.

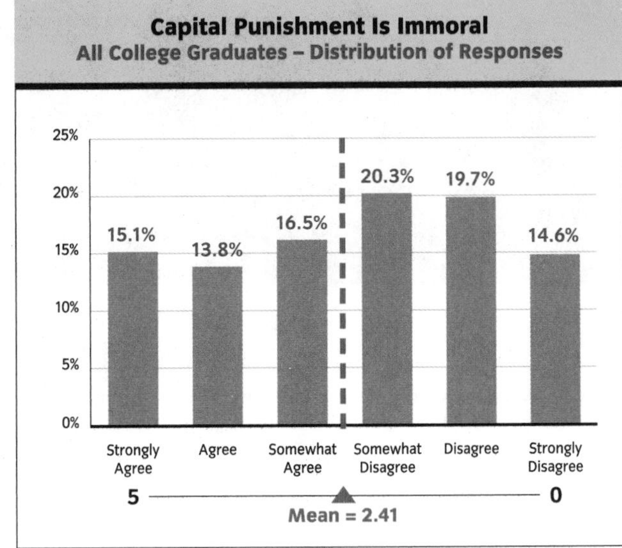

"Capital Punishment Is Immoral"

Top 25 Colleges to Agree	Top 25 Colleges to Disagree
1. Reed College	1. United States Naval Academy
2. Macalester College	2. Texas A&M University
3. Swarthmore College	3. United States Air Force Academy
4. Haverford College	4. Brigham Young University
5. Grinnell College	5. Auburn University
6. Bard College	6. Georgia Institute of Technology
7. Wesleyan University	7. United States Military Academy
8. Carleton College	8. University of Alabama
9. Oberlin College	9. University of Wyoming
10. Wellesley College	10. Clemson University
11. Bowdoin College	11. University of Mississippi
12. Scripps College	12. Washington State University
13. Bryn Mawr College	13. Oregon State University
14. Amherst College	14. Purdue University
15. Smith College	15. Virginia Polytechnic Institute and State University
16. Vassar College	16. Colorado State University
17. Kenyon College	17. College of Charleston
18. Williams College	18. Drexel University
19. Brandeis University	19. Washington and Lee University
20. Harvard University	20. North Carolina State University
21. Middlebury College	21. Elon University
22. University of Notre Dame	22. University of Florida
23. Mount Holyoke College	23. University of Utah
24. Yale University	24. Ohio Northern University
25. St. Olaf College	25. University of Miami

Notes

CHAPTER 11

Overviews of Top Colleges and Universities

The Alumni Factor
Understanding the School Summaries

This chapter of *The Alumni Factor* provides in-depth summaries of each of the 177 schools. Use this handy key to understand the components. Unless otherwise indicated, data other than the rankings themselves (indicated by *) are based on numbers reported to the National Center for Education Statistics.

Ⓐ Campus Setting
This describes the general geographic area in which the college is located, ranging from rural to large city.

Ⓑ 2011–2012 Total Expenses
The sum of tuition, fees, books, supplies, room, board and other expenses for an in-state student.

Ⓒ Estimated Average Discount
The 2011–2012 average amount of federal, state, local government or institutional grant, or scholarship aid received per in-state student. It is calculated by subtracting the Estimated Average Net Price from the Total Expenses for a college. We provide both the dollar amount and the percentage that dollar amount represents of the Total Expenses for an in-state student.

Ⓓ Estimated Average Net Price (In-State)
This is the average price students actually paid to attend this school in 2011–2012.

Ⓔ Type of Institution
These generally follow the Carnegie Foundation categories. We have used three designations: National Universities, Liberal Arts Colleges and Regional Universities.

Ⓕ Number of Undergraduates
The latest undergraduate enrollment data. Includes full-time and part-time students.

Ⓖ SAT Scores
The 2011 Reading and Math SAT scores for incoming freshmen. The range shown indicates the 25th and 75th percentile, meaning 50% of students scored within this range, while 25% scored above it, and 25% scored below.

Ⓗ Student/Faculty Ratio
Number of students per faculty member in 2010.

Ⓘ Transfer Out Rate
Percent of first-time, full-time students who transferred out of the college or university.

Ⓙ Institutional Type Rank
This is the school's rank among all schools of its type of the 177 schools we measure. We classify each school as one of the following three types: National Universities, Liberal Arts Colleges and Regional Universities.

American University

Location: Washington, D.C.
Ⓐ **Campus Setting:** City: Large
Ⓑ **Total Expenses:** $53,653
Ⓒ **Estimated Average Discount:** $22,206 (41%)
Ⓓ **Estimated Net Price:** $31,447

Ⓔ **Type of Institution:** National University
Ⓕ **Number of Undergraduates:** 7,070
Ⓖ **SAT Score:** Reading: 600–700, Math: 570–670
Ⓗ **Student/Faculty Ratio:** 13 to 1
Ⓘ **Transfer Out Rate:** Not Reported

Ⓙ **Rank Among 104 National Universities** 88

Ⓚ **Overall Rank Among 177 *Alumni Factor* Schools** 159

Ⓛ Overview

American University's dynamic Washington, D.C. location provides intimate access to the political buzz of our nation's capital and a vibrant campus life – the combination of which is a real differentiator for American. AU produces politically engaged grads, close friendships (ranked 42nd) and a roster of alumni who would choose AU all over again if given the choice (ranked 35th in Would Choose Again).

Graduates of American University perform at about the median in Financial Success versus all college graduates (85th) and are a happy lot (64th). The strongest outcome of this unique Washington, D.C.-based university is a politically aware and engaged graduate who understands and cares about world issues. Graduates often go on to become reporters, diplomats and engaged participants in the Washington political scene.

AU's strongest Ultimate Outcome is Happiness & Friendships (33rd). Financial Success may not be a top priority for many of its politically minded graduates. Ultimate Outcomes that include it tend to rank slightly lower. The American experience is very much about being in the center of the political world – and AU grads thrive in that environment.

Notable Alumni
Film producer and screenwriter Nancy Meyers, TV host Clark Howard and Fox anchor Alisyn Camerota.

The Alumni Factor Rankings Summary

Attribute	Ⓜ University Rank	Ⓝ Overall Rank
College Experience	**84**	**157**
Intellectual Development	86	157
Social Development	74	142
Spiritual Development	89	161
Friendship Development	42	105
Preparation for Career Success	81	150
Immediate Job Opportunities	72	115
Overall Assessment	**72**	**132**
Would Personally Choose Again	35	68
Would Recommend to Student	79	145
Value for the Money	98	169
Financial Success	**85**	**140**
Income per Household	76	117
% Households with Income >$150K	60	103
Household Net Worth	102	172
% Households Net Worth >$1MM	88	151
Overall Happiness	**64**	**111**
Alumni Giving	**67**	**131**
Graduation Rate	**60**	**118**
Overall Rank	**88**	**159**

Ⓞ **Other Key Alumni Outcomes**
2.0% Are college professors
7.4% Teach at any level
55.1% Have post-graduate degrees
43.2% Live in dual-income homes
89.4% Are currently employed

136 American University 2013 | alumnifactor.com

Ⓚ *The Alumni Factor* Overall Rank
This is the college's rank among all *Alumni Factor* schools regardless of the type of institution.

Ⓛ Overview*
This provides a summary of the school across all aspects of performance. Much of the data referred to in the summary is visible on this 2-page summary itself. When we refer to Ultimate Outcomes – the six benefit combinations most desired by students – you will find details in Chapter 9.

Ⓜ Rank of Attributes by Institution Type*
The college's ranking in each attribute versus its peer schools in its institution type.

Ⓟ Alumni Activities During College

38.4% Community Service
21.2% Intramural Sports
62.3% Internships
28.5% Media Programs
10.6% Music Programs
58.9% Part-Time Jobs

Ⓠ

Prepared Me for Career Success % Strongly Agree	Was A Good Value for the Money % Strongly Agree	Percent of Alumni Worth >$1MM

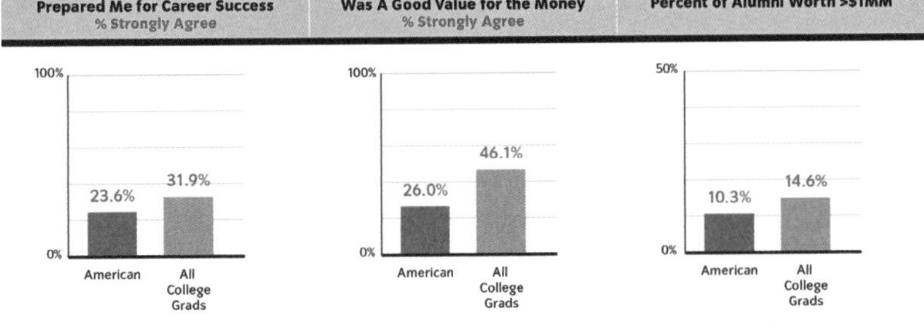

Ⓡ Alumni Employment

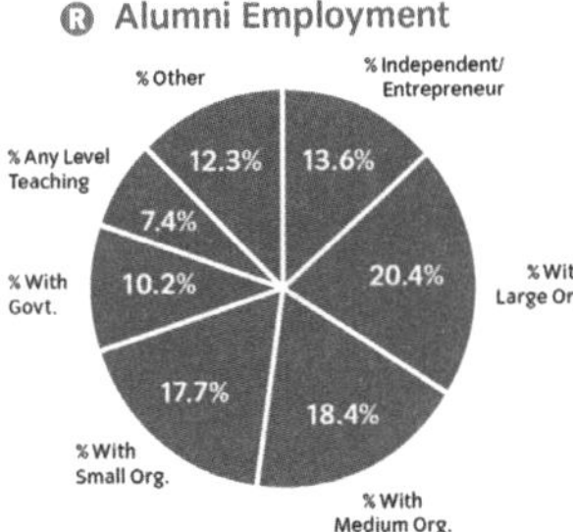

Ⓢ Income Distribution of Graduates

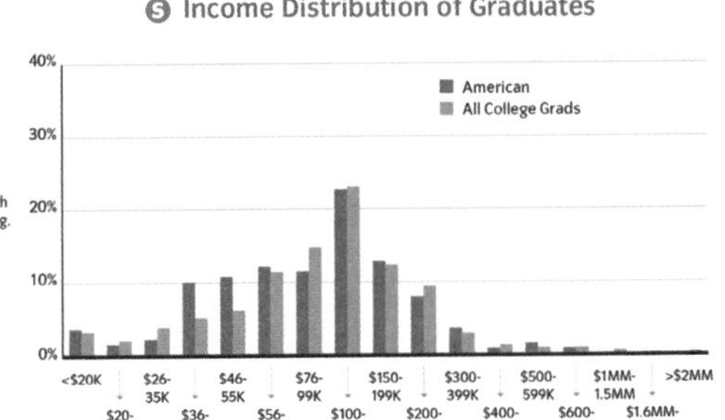

Current Selectivity & Demand Analysis for American University

Attribute	Ⓣ % Accepted	Ⓤ % Accepted Who Enroll	Ⓥ Freshman Retention Rate	Ⓦ Graduation Rate	Ⓧ Demand Index	Ⓨ Reputation Index
Score	42.0%	20.0%	91.0%	79.0%	12.14	0.48
Rank	85	161	102	118	43	127

Ⓩ Where are the Graduates of American University on the Political Spectrum?

Very Liberal	Liberal	Somewhat Liberal	Somewhat Conservative	Conservative	Very Conservative
	⇧				

alumnifactor.com | 2013 American University 137

Ⓝ Overall Rank of Attributes*

The college's ranking in each attribute among all measured colleges, regardless of institution type.

Ⓞ Other Key Alumni Outcomes*

This reports key graduate outcomes by percentage, based on alumni responses.

Ⓟ Alumni College Activities*

These show the percent of alumni who reported participation in specific activities during their undergraduate years.

Ⓠ Performance Charts*

These graphs depict a college's performance on Career Preparation, Value for the Money and Alumni Net Worth compared to all college grads, based on alumni responses.

Ⓡ Alumni Employment*

This provides a simple break-out of how graduates of the college are employed, based on responses. Those who are not employed, either because they cannot find work or because they have removed themselves from the labor force (through disability, retirement or the choice to stay at home), are noted as "other."

Ⓢ Income Distribution*

This shows the household income distribution of a college's graduates compared to the income distribution of all college graduates, based on responses.

Ⓣ % Accepted

The number of students accepted in 2011 as a percentage of the total applicants, and the rank among all 177 *Alumni Factor* schools.

Ⓤ % Accepted Who Enroll

The percent of students who were accepted that enrolled, and the rank among all 177 schools.

Ⓥ Freshman Retention Rate

Percent of full-time freshmen who successfully move on to their second year, and the corresponding rank among all 177 schools.

Ⓦ Graduation Rate

The percent of full-time, first-time students who complete their program "within 150% of the normal time to completion", as required by the Student Right-To-Know Act (typically 6 years).

Ⓧ Demand Index*

This index shows how many students apply to the college for every one who enrolls as a freshman. It is the ratio of the number of applicants to the number of freshmen enrollees.

Ⓨ Reputation Index*

Compares the percentage of students who enroll in the school (U) to the percent of students who are accepted (T). A school whose Reputation Index is strong will have a low percentage of students who are accepted and a high percentage of accepted students who enroll. Using Harvard University as an example, a mere 6% of applicants are accepted and of those, 76% enroll – yielding a 12.67 Reputation Index (ranks #1). **In our view, this index is the best way to judge a school's reputation in the market.**

Ⓩ Political Spectrum*

A visual representation of the political views of alumni from this school based on their responses to specific questions about current social and political issues.

See pages 134–135 for detailed explanations and definitions.

American University

Location: Washington, D.C.
Campus Setting: City: Large
Total Expenses: $53,653
Estimated Average Discount: $22,206 (41%)
Estimated Net Price: $31,447

Type of Institution: National University
Number of Undergraduates: 7,070
SAT Score: Reading: 600–700, Math: 570–670
Student/Faculty Ratio: 13 to 1
Transfer Out Rate: Not Reported

Rank Among 104 National Universities	**88**
Overall Rank Among 177 *Alumni Factor* Schools	**159**

Overview

American University's dynamic Washington, D.C. location provides intimate access to the political buzz of our nation's capital and a vibrant campus life – the combination of which is a real differentiator for American. AU produces politically engaged grads, close friendships (ranked 42nd) and a roster of alumni who would choose AU all over again if given the choice (ranked 35th in Would Choose Again).

Graduates of American University perform at about the median in Financial Success versus all college graduates (85th) and are a happy lot (64th). The strongest outcome of this unique Washington, D.C.-based university is a politically aware and engaged graduate who understands and cares about world issues. Graduates often go on to become reporters, diplomats and engaged participants in the Washington political scene.

AU's strongest Ultimate Outcome is Happiness & Friendships (33rd). Financial Success may not be a top priority for many of its politically minded graduates. Ultimate Outcomes that include it tend to rank slightly lower. The American experience is very much about being in the center of the political world – and AU grads thrive in that environment.

Notable Alumni

Film producer and screenwriter Nancy Meyers, TV host Clark Howard and Fox anchor Alisyn Camerota.

The Alumni Factor Rankings Summary

Attribute	University Rank	Overall Rank
College Experience	**84**	**157**
Intellectual Development	86	157
Social Development	74	142
Spiritual Development	89	161
Friendship Development	42	105
Preparation for Career Success	81	150
Immediate Job Opportunities	72	115
Overall Assessment	**72**	**132**
Would Personally Choose Again	35	68
Would Recommend to Student	79	145
Value for the Money	98	169
Financial Success	**85**	**140**
Income per Household	76	117
% Households with Income >$150K	60	103
Household Net Worth	102	172
% Households Net Worth >$1MM	88	151
Overall Happiness	**64**	**111**
Alumni Giving	**67**	**131**
Graduation Rate	**60**	**118**
Overall Rank	**88**	**159**

Other Key Alumni Outcomes

2.0% Are college professors
7.4% Teach at any level
55.1% Have post-graduate degrees
43.2% Live in dual-income homes
89.4% Are currently employed

See pages 134–135 for detailed explanations and definitions.

Alumni Activities During College

38.4% Community Service
21.2% Intramural Sports
62.3% Internships
28.5% Media Programs
10.6% Music Programs
58.9% Part-Time Jobs

Prepared Me for Career Success % Strongly Agree	Was A Good Value for the Money % Strongly Agree	Percent of Alumni Worth >$1MM
American 23.6%; All College Grads 31.9%	American 26.0%; All College Grads 46.1%	American 10.3%; All College Grads 14.6%

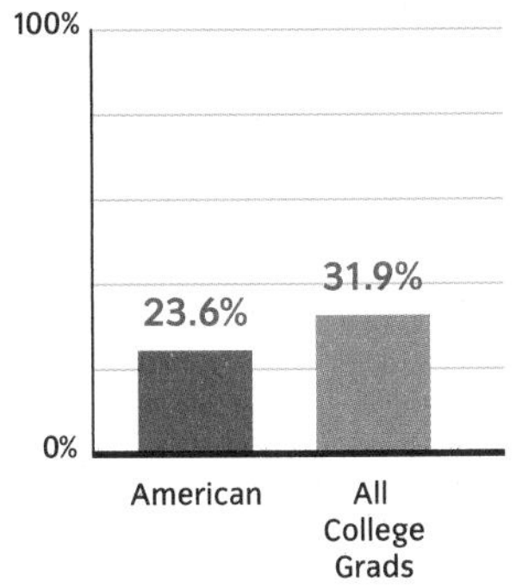

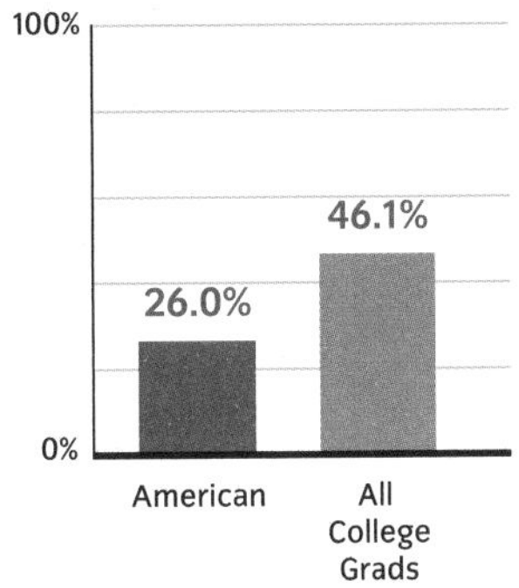

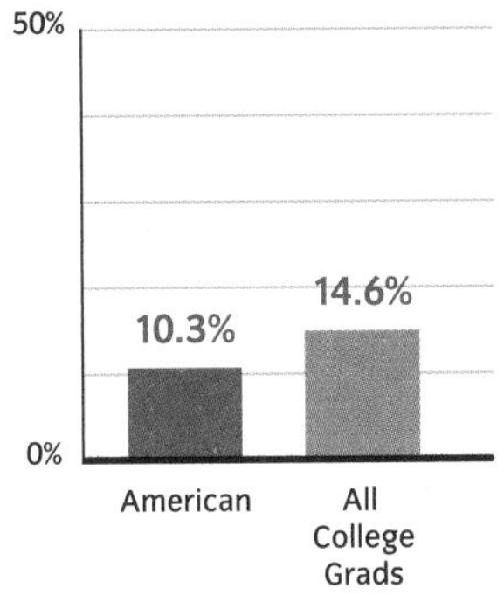

Alumni Employment

- % Independent/Entrepreneur: 13.6%
- % With Large Org.: 20.4%
- % With Medium Org.: 18.4%
- % With Small Org.: 17.7%
- % With Govt.: 10.2%
- % Any Level Teaching: 7.4%
- % Other: 12.3%

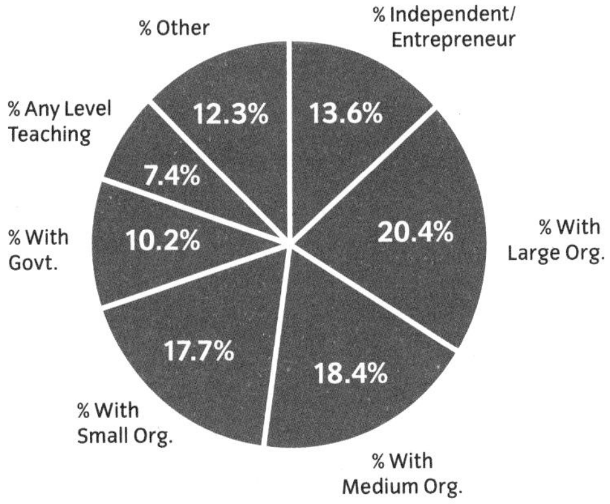

Income Distribution of Graduates

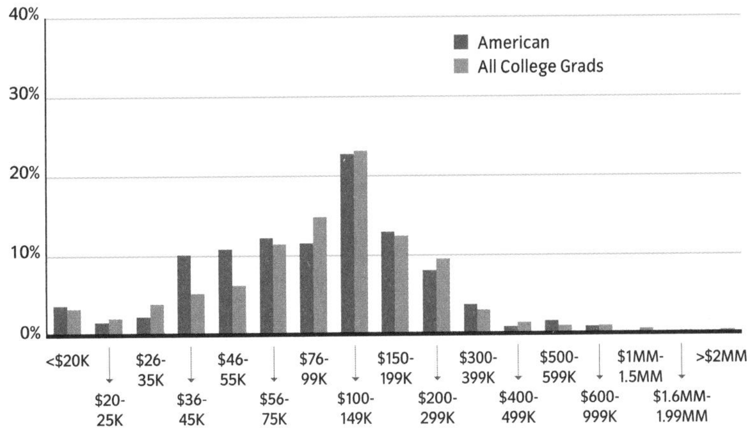

American / All College Grads

0% 10% 20% 30% 40%

<$20K, $20-25K, $26-35K, $36-45K, $46-55K, $56-75K, $76-99K, $100-149K, $150-199K, $200-299K, $300-399K, $400-499K, $500-599K, $600-999K, $1MM-1.5MM, $1.6MM-1.99MM, >$2MM

Current Selectivity & Demand Analysis for American University

Attribute	% Accepted	% Accepted Who Enroll	Freshman Retention Rate	Graduation Rate	Demand Index	Reputation Index
Score	42.0%	20.0%	91.0%	79.0%	12.14	0.48
Rank	85	161	102	118	43	127

Where are the Graduates of American University on the Political Spectrum?

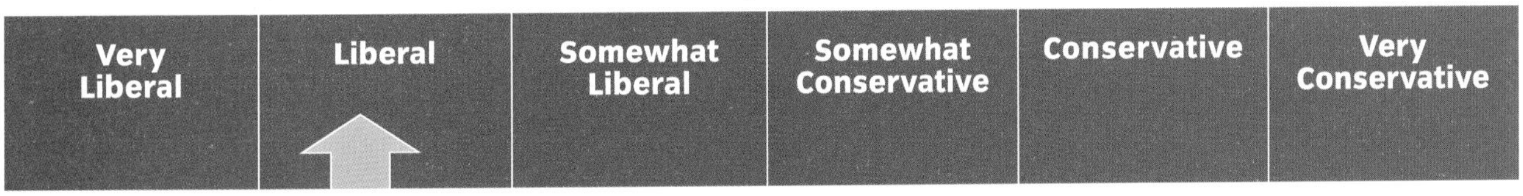

Very Liberal	Liberal	Somewhat Liberal	Somewhat Conservative	Conservative	Very Conservative
	↑				

See pages 134–135 for detailed explanations and definitions.

Amherst College

Location: Amherst, MA
Campus Setting: Town: Fringe
Total Expenses: $56,898
Estimated Average Discount: $39,324 (69%)
Estimated Net Price: $17,574

Type of Institution: Liberal Arts College
Number of Undergraduates: 1,794
SAT Score: Reading: 660–760, Math: 660–770
Student/Faculty Ratio: 9 to 1
Transfer Out Rate: 3%

Rank Among 53 Liberal Arts Colleges	**7**
Overall Rank Among 177 *Alumni Factor* Schools	**13**

Overview

Broadly considered one of the finest liberal arts colleges in the country, Amherst consistently graduates successful alumni who deeply admire their school and would do it all over again if they had the chance. Amherst ranks 3rd among all colleges in the percentage of grads who would choose the school again. Ranked 4th among all liberal arts colleges in the percent of alumni who financially support their school, graduates of Amherst truly value their undergraduate experience (ranked 13th in the College Experience). The small, challenging, connected community unites students with a strong bond that endures. It boasts the highest Graduation Rate among all liberal arts schools.

Despite its high price tag, Amherst grads consider the investment a wise one (ranked 17th in value) and are among the top in recommending their college to prospective students (12th). Among all schools, Amherst is one of only 21 schools that ranks in the top third in at least 6 of the 7 major categories we measure. Widely successful and loyal, Amherst graduates are walking endorsements for this world-class liberal arts college.

Notable Alumni

Calvin Coolidge; former Supreme Court chief justice Harlan Fiske Stone; novelist Scott Turow; Prince Albert II of Monaco; George Papandreou (former prime minister of Greece); co-founder of Bain Capital Eric Kriss and a long list of business leaders, elected officials, academic luminaries and notable scholars.

The Alumni Factor Rankings Summary

Attribute	Liberal Arts Rank	Overall Rank
College Experience	**13**	**21**
Intellectual Development	22	25
Social Development	9	13
Spiritual Development	39	71
Friendship Development	21	24
Preparation for Career Success	20	39
Immediate Job Opportunities	19	77
Overall Assessment	**6**	**16**
Would Personally Choose Again	3	3
Would Recommend to Student	12	39
Value for the Money	17	42
Financial Success	**21**	**50**
Income per Household	24	75
% Households with Income >$150K	11	27
Household Net Worth	29	80
% Households Net Worth >$1MM	16	40
Overall Happiness	**26**	**66**
Alumni Giving	**4**	**5**
Graduation Rate	**1**	**7**
Overall Rank	**7**	**13**

Other Key Alumni Outcomes

10.6% Are college professors
20.5% Teach at any level
67.7% Have post-graduate degrees
48.7% Live in dual-income homes
92.9% Are currently employed

See pages 134–135 for detailed explanations and definitions.

Alumni Activities During College

35.7% Community Service
26.6% Intramural Sports
19.5% Internships
44.8% Media Programs
42.8% Music Programs
13.0% Part-Time Jobs

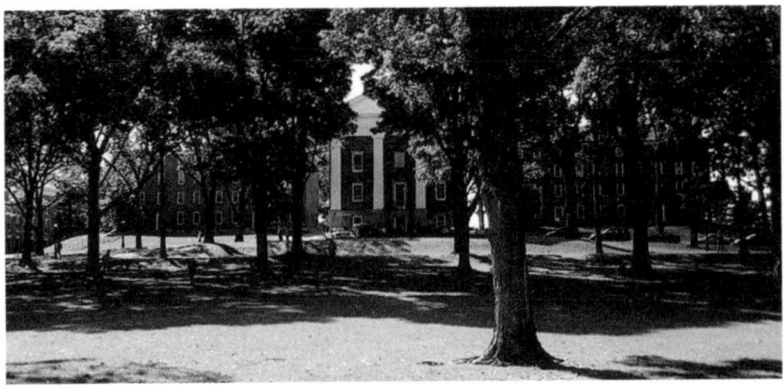

Prepared Me for Career Success % Strongly Agree	Was A Good Value for the Money % Strongly Agree	Percent of Alumni Worth >$1MM

100%
0%
40.8%
31.9%
Amherst
All College Grads

100%
0%
52.3%
46.1%
Amherst
All College Grads

50%
0%
19.7%
14.6%
Amherst
All College Grads

Alumni Employment

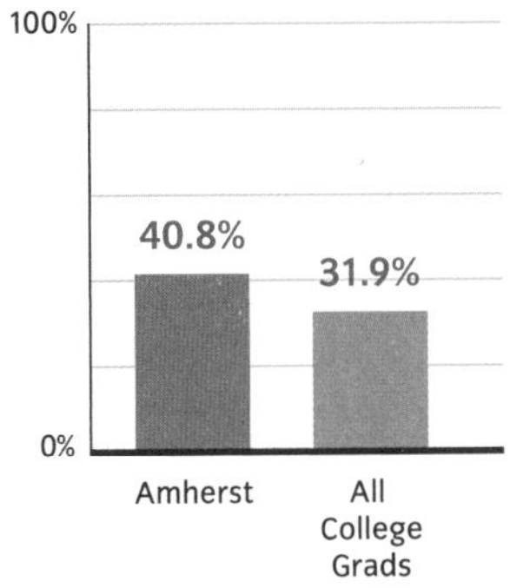

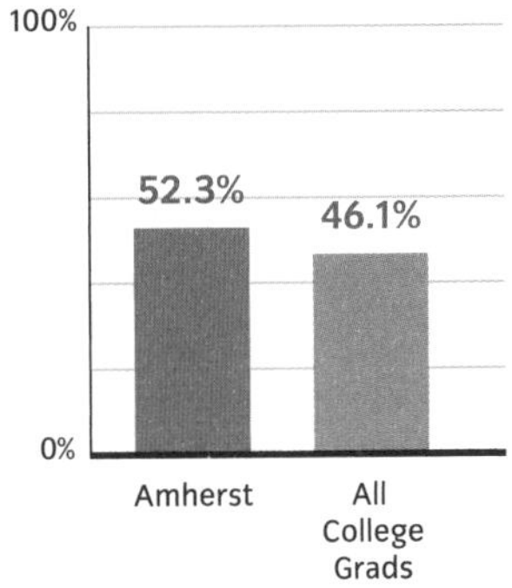

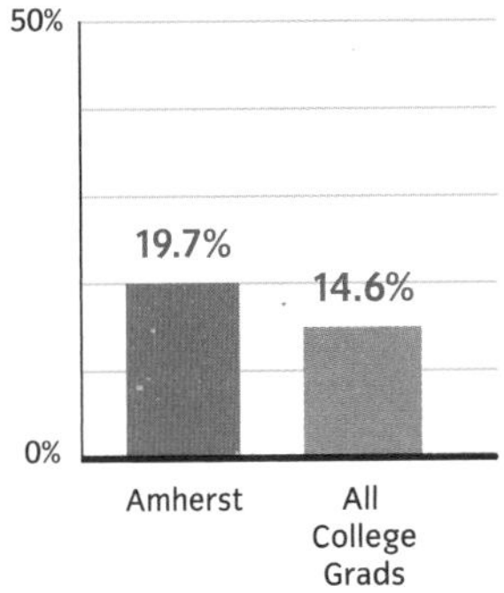

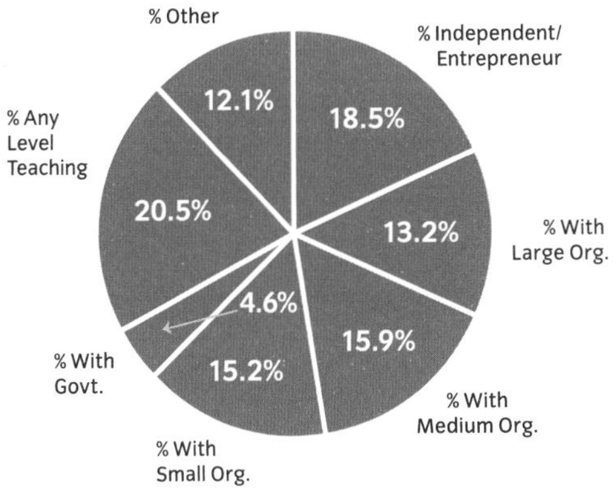

% Other
12.1%
% Independent/ Entrepreneur
18.5%
% With Large Org.
13.2%
% With Medium Org.
15.9%
% With Small Org.
15.2%
% With Govt.
4.6%
% Any Level Teaching
20.5%

Income Distribution of Graduates

40%
30%
20%
10%
0%
Amherst
All College Grads
<$20K
$20-25K
$26-35K
$36-45K
$46-55K
$56-75K
$76-99K
$100-149K
$150-199K
$200-299K
$300-399K
$400-499K
$500-599K
$600-999K
$1MM-1.5MM
$1.6MM-1.99MM
>$2MM

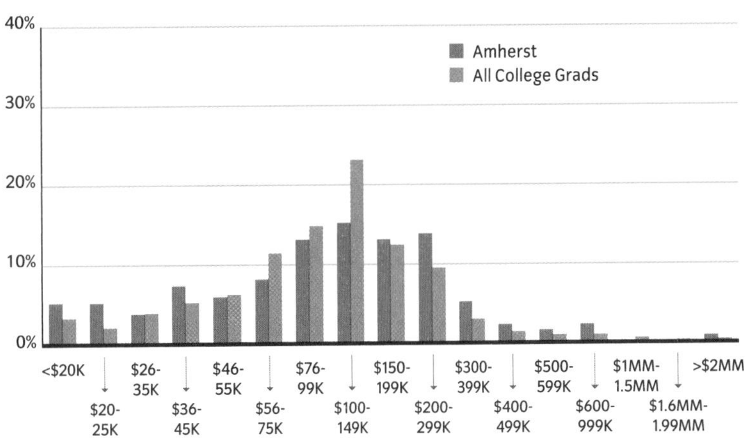

Current Selectivity & Demand Analysis for Amhest College

Attribute	% Accepted	% Accepted Who Enroll	Freshman Retention Rate	Graduation Rate	Demand Index	Reputation Index
Score	13.0%	41.0%	96.0%	95.0%	18.35	3.15
Rank	13	39	27	7	10	14

Where are the Graduates of Amherst College on the Political Spectrum?

Very Liberal	Liberal	Somewhat Liberal	Somewhat Conservative	Conservative	Very Conservative
↑					

See pages 134–135 for detailed explanations and definitions.

Arizona State University

Location: Tempe, AZ
Campus Setting: City: Midsize
Total Expenses: $25,548
Estimated Average Discount: $14,949 (59%)
Estimated Net Price: $10,599

Type of Institution: National University
Number of Undergraduates: 56,562
SAT Score: Reading: 480–600, Math: 490–620
Student/Faculty Ratio: 23 to 1
Transfer Out Rate: Not Reported

Rank Among 104 National Universities	**102**
Overall Rank Among 177 *Alumni Factor* Schools	**175**

Overview

Arizona State University epitomizes the challenge faced by very large universities across the country: how to provide academic excellence on a campus with tens of thousands of diverse students and an admissions policy that promotes broad access. ASU is working to find the right blend that makes this goal achievable and, like many large public universities, is making real progress in finding it.

The ratings for ASU reflect the reality that it is more difficult for larger institutions to consistently deliver strong results than it is for smaller, more selective institutions. ASU rankings fall in the bottom third of the Top 177 colleges and universities featured here. Its four strongest attributes are Job Opportunities, Overall Happiness, Value for the Money and the Percentage of Grads with a High Net Worth. To make it into the Top 177 colleges with this large a population is quite an accomplishment for ASU.

Notable Alumni

Designer Kate Spade; filmmaker John Hughes and political legend Barry Goldwater.

The Alumni Factor Rankings Summary

Attribute	University Rank	Overall Rank
College Experience	**100**	**173**
Intellectual Development	103	176
Social Development	90	161
Spiritual Development	97	169
Friendship Development	97	169
Preparation for Career Success	85	155
Immediate Job Opportunities	75	119
Overall Assessment	**96**	**167**
Would Personally Choose Again	100	169
Would Recommend to Student	96	165
Value for the Money	77	139
Financial Success	**91**	**152**
Income per Household	91	146
% Households with Income >$150K	91	148
Household Net Worth	95	162
% Households Net Worth >$1MM	74	125
Overall Happiness	**82**	**135**
Alumni Giving	**102**	**175**
Graduation Rate	**100**	**171**
Overall Rank	**102**	**175**

Other Key Alumni Outcomes

4.9% Are college professors
14.3% Teach at any level
41.7% Have post-graduate degrees
48.4% Live in dual-income homes
89.1% Are currently employed

See pages 134–135 for detailed explanations and definitions.

Alumni Activities During College

23.6% Community Service
18.8% Intramural Sports
27.2% Internships
9.0% Media Programs
10.2% Music Programs
48.9% Part-Time Jobs

Prepared Me for Career Success % Strongly Agree	Was A Good Value for the Money % Strongly Agree	Percent of Alumni Worth >$1MM
ASU 20.9%; All College Grads 31.9%	ASU 35.5%; All College Grads 46.1%	ASU 12.1%; All College Grads 14.6%

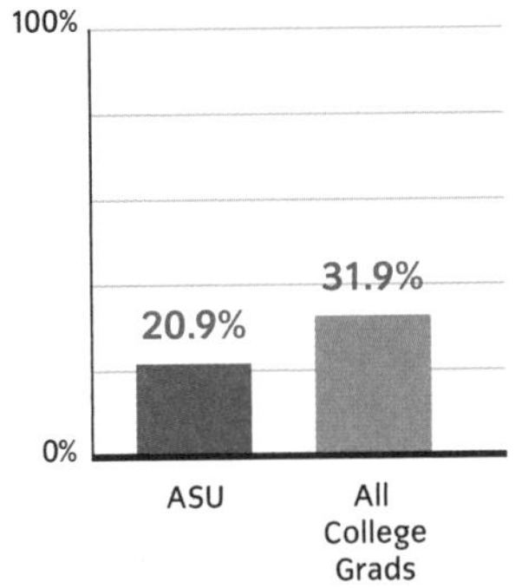

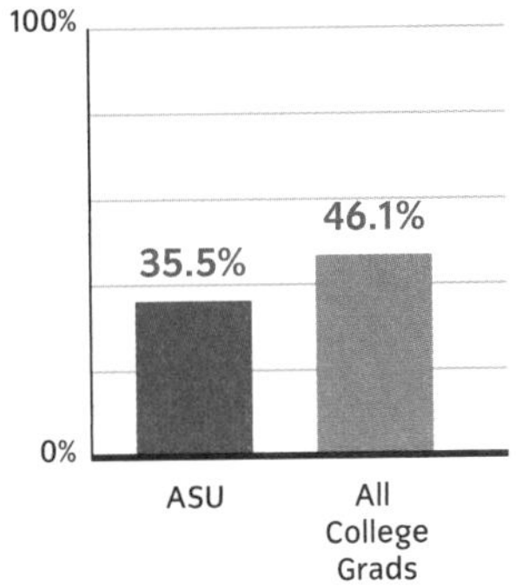

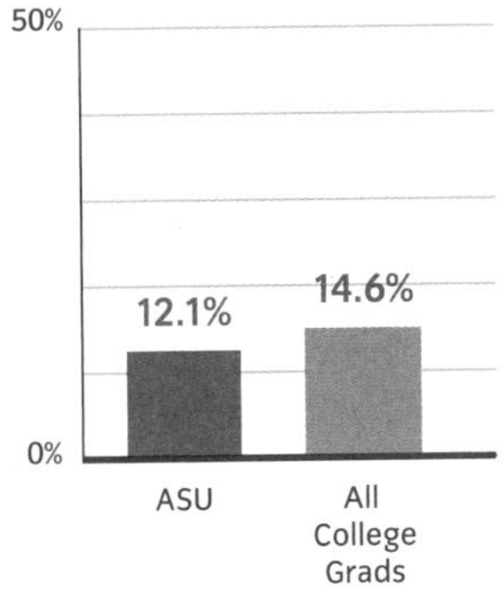

100%
0%
ASU 20.9%
All College Grads 31.9%

100%
0%
ASU 35.5%
All College Grads 46.1%

50%
0%
ASU 12.1%
All College Grads 14.6%

Alumni Employment

% Independent/ Entrepreneur 13.0%
% With Large Org. 23.4%
% With Medium Org. 11.7%
% With Small Org. 11.4%
% With Govt. 10.0%
% Any Level Teaching 14.3%
% Other 16.2%

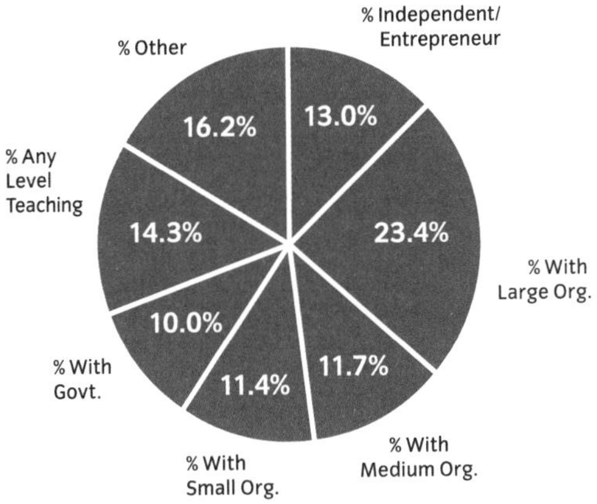

Income Distribution of Graduates

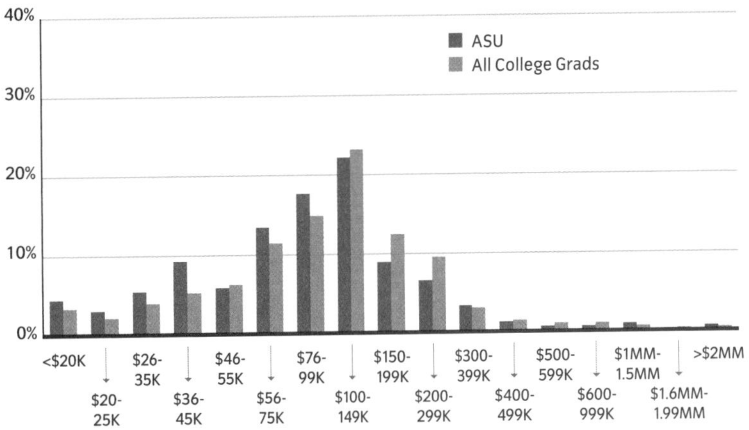

ASU
All College Grads

40%
30%
20%
10%
0%

<$20K
$20-25K
$26-35K
$36-45K
$46-55K
$56-75K
$76-99K
$100-149K
$150-199K
$200-299K
$300-399K
$400-499K
$500-599K
$600-999K
$1MM-1.5MM
$1.6MM-1.99MM
>$2MM

Current Selectivity & Demand Analysis for Arizona State University

Attribute	% Accepted	% Accepted Who Enroll	Freshman Retention Rate	Graduation Rate	Demand Index	Reputation Index
Score	87.0%	37.0%	84.0%	59.0%	3.22	0.43
Rank	173	60	158	171	167	142

Where are the Graduates of Arizona State University on the Political Spectrum?

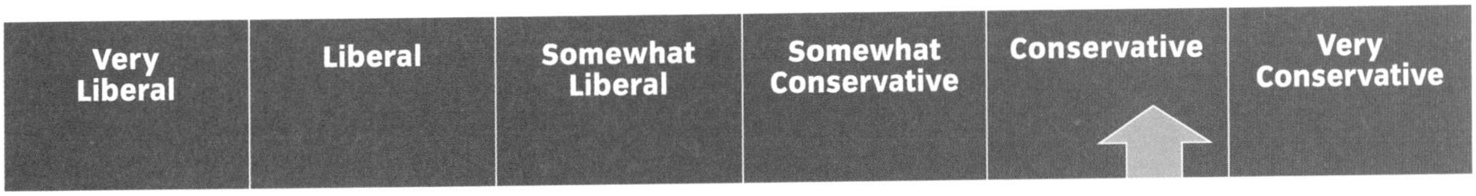

Very Liberal	Liberal	Somewhat Liberal	Somewhat Conservative	Conservative	Very Conservative

See pages 134–135 for detailed explanations and definitions.

Auburn University

Location: Auburn, AL
Campus Setting: City: Small
Total Expenses: $22,352
Estimated Average Discount: $8,265 (37%)
Estimated Net Price: $14,087

Type of Institution: National University
Number of Undergraduates: 20,221
SAT Score: Reading: 500–600, Math: 520–620
Student/Faculty Ratio: 18 to 1
Transfer Out Rate: 22%

Rank Among 104 National Universities	**22**
Overall Rank Among 177 *Alumni Factor* Schools	**44**

Overview

Some of the happiest alumni in America come from Auburn – with good reason. Auburn grads are deeply loyal, well-prepared for their careers, do very well financially and are ranked 6th in Would Personally Choose Again among national universities. They are also ranked 4th in willingness to recommend their college to prospective students.

Auburn ranks an impressive 16th in the Ultimate Outcome of Financial Success & Happiness. While graduates rate Auburn lower for Intellectual Development than for other elements of the undergraduate experience, Auburn compensates with excellent career development and job opportunities. In fact, Auburn grads achieve income and net worth values well above the typical college graduate (ranked 27th in Household Net Worth) and have the 6th lowest unemployment rate among the Top 177.

With these stats, it follows that Auburn grads rank 6th among all colleges and universities in their willingness to recommend Auburn.

Notable Alumni

Millard Fuller, founder of Habitat for Humanity; Timothy Cook, CEO of Apple; and athlete Bo Jackson.

The Alumni Factor Rankings Summary

Attribute	University Rank	Overall Rank
College Experience	**11**	**36**
Intellectual Development	56	122
Social Development	9	34
Spiritual Development	10	44
Friendship Development	25	81
Preparation for Career Success	6	18
Immediate Job Opportunities	7	11
Overall Assessment	**6**	**9**
Would Personally Choose Again	6	13
Would Recommend to Student	4	6
Value for the Money	18	33
Financial Success	**51**	**86**
Income per Household	42	68
% Households with Income >$150K	72	120
Household Net Worth	27	51
% Households Net Worth >$1MM	69	119
Overall Happiness	**1**	**5**
Alumni Giving	**62**	**125**
Graduation Rate	**91**	**160**
Overall Rank	**22**	**44**

Other Key Alumni Outcomes

4.4%	Are college professors
15.5%	Teach at any level
47.1%	Have post-graduate degrees
55.6%	Live in dual-income homes
96.9%	Are currently employed

See pages 134–135 for detailed explanations and definitions.

Alumni Activities During College

20.4% Community Service
32.8% Intramural Sports
20.6% Internships
12.7% Media Programs
20.1% Music Programs
45.3% Part-Time Jobs

Prepared Me for Career Success % Strongly Agree	Was A Good Value for the Money % Strongly Agree	Percent of Alumni Worth >$1MM
Auburn: 40.3% All College Grads: 31.9%	Auburn: 53.5% All College Grads: 46.1%	Auburn: 12.7% All College Grads: 14.6%

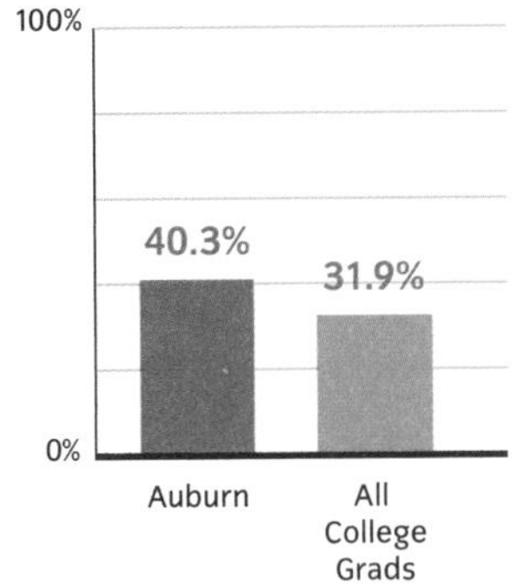

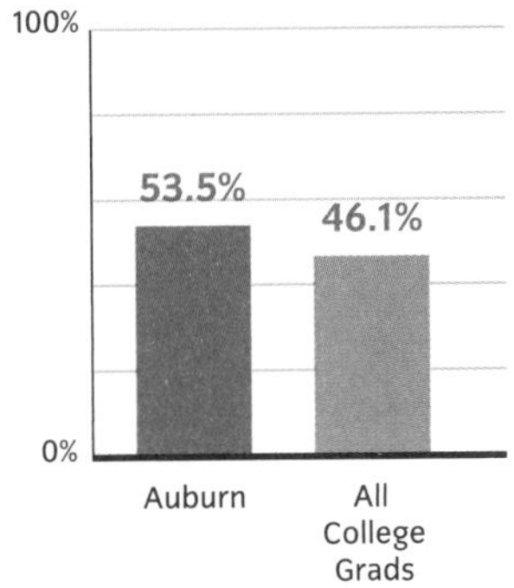

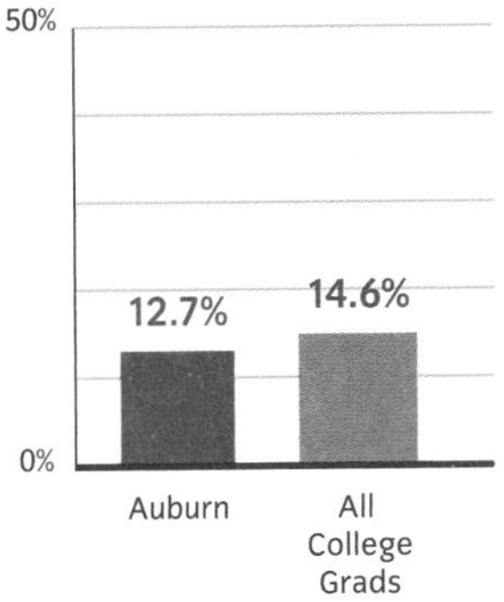

Alumni Employment

- % Independent/Entrepreneur: 13.7%
- % With Large Org.: 20.4%
- % With Medium Org.: 12.6%
- % With Small Org.: 14.4%
- % With Govt.: 12.1%
- % Any Level Teaching: 15.5%
- % Other: 11.3%

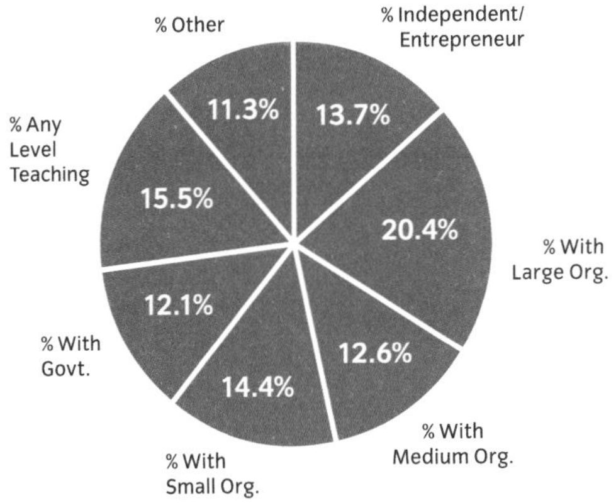

Income Distribution of Graduates

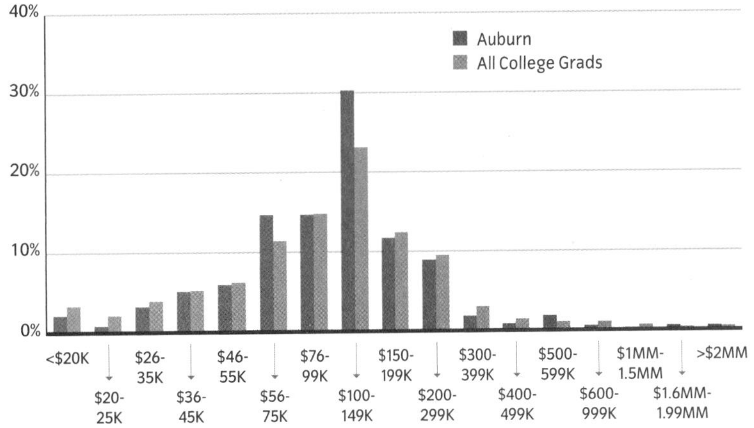

■ Auburn
■ All College Grads

40%, 30%, 20%, 10%, 0%

<$20K, $20-25K, $26-35K, $36-45K, $46-55K, $56-75K, $76-99K, $100-149K, $150-199K, $200-299K, $300-399K, $400-499K, $500-599K, $600-999K, $1MM-1.5MM, $1.6MM-1.99MM, >$2MM

Current Selectivity & Demand Analysis for Auburn University

Attribute	% Accepted	% Accepted Who Enroll	Freshman Retention Rate	Graduation Rate	Demand Index	Reputation Index
Score	70.0%	33.0%	87.0%	66.0%	4.36	0.47
Rank	149	83	140	160	148	130

Where are the Graduates of Auburn University on the Political Spectrum?

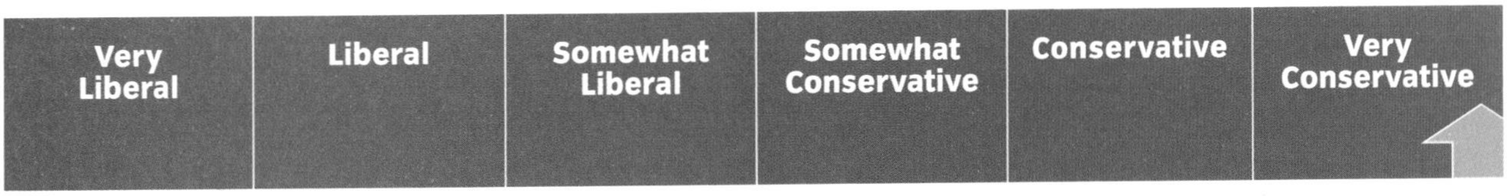

Very Liberal	Liberal	Somewhat Liberal	Somewhat Conservative	Conservative	Very Conservative
					↑

See pages 134–135 for detailed explanations and definitions.

Bard College

Location: Annandale-on-Hudson, NY
Campus Setting: Town: Fringe
Total Expenses: $58,292
Estimated Average Discount: $32,817 (56%)
Estimated Net Price: $25,475

Type of Institution: Liberal Arts College
Number of Undergraduates: 1,968
SAT Score: Not Reported
Student/Faculty Ratio: 10 to 1
Transfer Out Rate: Not Reported

Rank Among 53 Liberal Arts Colleges	**53**
Overall Rank Among 177 *Alumni Factor* Schools	**155**

Overview

Eccentric and curious, Bard graduates tend to pursue an individual and unique path. Poets, screenwriters, actors, journalists, musicians (and the occasional investment banker) are among the wide variety of Bard graduates. Bard defies simple categorization when compared to the 177 colleges and universities in our sample:

- Bard grads are among the Top 5 most liberal in their political beliefs and views
- Bard grads are among the Top 15 in Alumni Giving and rank among the Top 40 in Intellectual Development
- Bard grads are 21% more likely to become college professors than all college grads

One would expect these high ratings to be well correlated with other hallmarks of success. Yet:

- Bard ranks last in both Preparation for Career Development and Immediate Job Opportunities
- Bard grads are among the bottom 10 in overall Financial Success
- Bard grads claim to be the least happy among all liberal arts college graduates
- Bard grads pursue post-graduate degrees at a rate 11 points lower than all college graduates

Intellectually deep, socially progressive and creatively driven, Bard grads reflect the rigors and bent of a true liberal arts education – emphasis on the "arts." That may be why, despite what may seem like a mixed record, 70% of Bard grads would choose it again.

Notable Alumni

Chevy Chase, comedian; Blythe Danner, actress; Larry Hagman, actor; and the co-founders of Steely Dan, Walter Becker and Donald Fagen.

The Alumni Factor Rankings Summary

Attribute	Liberal Arts Rank	Overall Rank
College Experience	**48**	**111**
Intellectual Development	29	37
Social Development	47	130
Spiritual Development	26	52
Friendship Development	37	48
Preparation for Career Success	53	177
Immediate Job Opportunities	53	177
Overall Assessment	**42**	**126**
Would Personally Choose Again	28	79
Would Recommend to Student	46	138
Value for the Money	51	158
Financial Success	**50**	**168**
Income per Household	52	174
% Households with Income >$150K	51	171
Household Net Worth	49	160
% Households Net Worth >$1MM	46	136
Overall Happiness	**53**	**170**
Alumni Giving	**15**	**17**
Graduation Rate	**51**	**134**
Overall Rank	**53**	**155**

Other Key Alumni Outcomes

8.0% Are college professors
11.6% Teach at any level
47.7% Have post-graduate degrees
50.5% Live in dual-income homes
88.5% Are currently employed

See pages 134–135 for detailed explanations and definitions.

Alumni Activities During College

20.7% Community Service
20.7% Intramural Sports
23.4% Internships
36.0% Media Programs
34.2% Music Programs
35.1% Part-Time Jobs

Prepared Me for Career Success % Strongly Agree	Was A Good Value for the Money % Strongly Agree	Percent of Alumni Worth >$1MM
Bard 20.7%; All College Grads 31.9%	Bard 34.8%; All College Grads 46.1%	Bard 11.2%; All College Grads 14.6%

Alumni Employment

% Other 15.2%
% Independent/ Entrepreneur 28.5%
% With Large Org. 16.1%
% With Medium Org. 10.7%
% With Small Org. 14.3%
% With Govt. 3.6%
% Any Level Teaching 11.6%

Income Distribution of Graduates

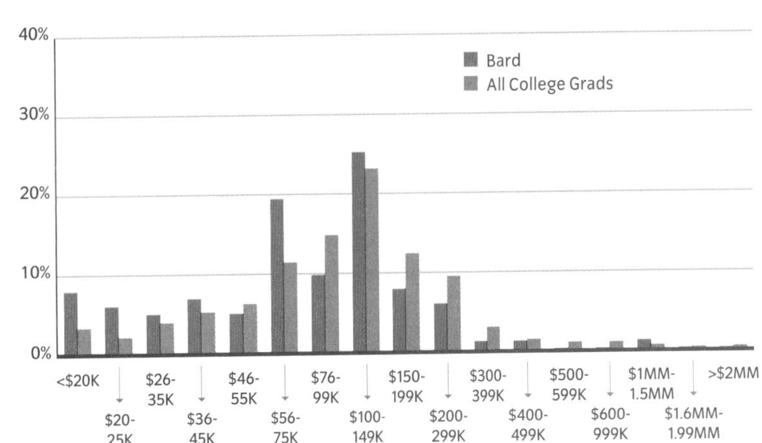

Current Selectivity & Demand Analysis for Bard College

Attribute	% Accepted	% Accepted Who Enroll	Freshman Retention Rate	Graduation Rate	Demand Index	Reputation Index
Score	35.0%	25.0%	90.0%	76.0%	11.67	0.71
Rank	67	130	113	134	48	84

Where are the Graduates of Bard College on the Political Spectrum?

Very Liberal	Liberal	Somewhat Liberal	Somewhat Conservative	Conservative	Very Conservative

See pages 134–135 for detailed explanations and definitions.

Bates College

Location: Lewiston, ME
Campus Setting: City: Small
Total Expenses: $57,350
Estimated Average Discount: $35,948 (63%)
Estimated Net Price: $21,402

Type of Institution: Liberal Arts College
Number of Undergraduates: 1,725
SAT Score: Not Reported
Student/Faculty Ratio: 10 to 1
Transfer Out Rate: 9%

Rank Among 53 Liberal Arts Colleges	**34**
Overall Rank Among 177 *Alumni Factor* Schools	**66**

Overview

A small, liberal arts college in the Quaker tradition, Bates has long been one of the finest liberal arts colleges in the country, in steep competition with its two Maine neighbors – Bowdoin and Colby. The College Experience at Bates is unifying and bond-building for undergrads (ranked 40th among all liberal arts schools). While liberal in their political views relative to all college graduates, Bates grads are less liberal than Bowdoin or Colby grads. Bates grads, in many ways, reflect the Quaker history of practicing a caring entrepreneurialism. Notably, Bates was the first racially integrated, co-ed college in the East.

Bates separates itself from its in-state rivals in two key elements of the college experience: Intellectual Development (28th) and Preparation for Career Success (31st). It outranks its two Maine competitors in each of these attributes. It is also 1st among the three Maine schools in graduate income (13th) and in net worth (21st).

Bates' strongest Ultimate Outcome is the combination of Financial Success & Intellectual Capability, where it ranks 16th among liberal arts schools. However, its 18th ranking for Alumni Giving is the best indication of the love and loyalty graduates have for Bates.

Notable Alumni

Journalist Bryant Gumbel; CEO of Medco David Snow; Pulitzer Prize-winning author Elizabeth Strout ; former General Mills CEO Robert Kinney; and former governor and US secretary of state Edmund Muskie.

The Alumni Factor Rankings Summary

Attribute	Liberal Arts Rank	Overall Rank
College Experience	**40**	**76**
Intellectual Development	28	35
Social Development	35	59
Spiritual Development	44	87
Friendship Development	38	54
Preparation for Career Success	31	70
Immediate Job Opportunities	40	147
Overall Assessment	**38**	**107**
Would Personally Choose Again	38	98
Would Recommend to Student	39	101
Value for the Money	39	111
Financial Success	**24**	**59**
Income per Household	13	32
% Households with Income >$150K	18	37
Household Net Worth	21	54
% Households Net Worth >$1MM	45	132
Overall Happiness	**43**	**148**
Alumni Giving	**18**	**21**
Graduation Rate	**20**	**52**
Overall Rank	**34**	**66**

Other Key Alumni Outcomes

7.0% Are college professors
17.4% Teach at any level
66.1% Have post-graduate degrees
62.7% Live in dual-income homes
90.8% Are currently employed

See pages 134–135 for detailed explanations and definitions.

Alumni Activities During College

33.1% Community Service
40.7% Intramural Sports
22.0% Internships
40.7% Media Programs
29.6% Music Programs
16.1% Part-Time Jobs

Prepared Me for Career Success — % Strongly Agree

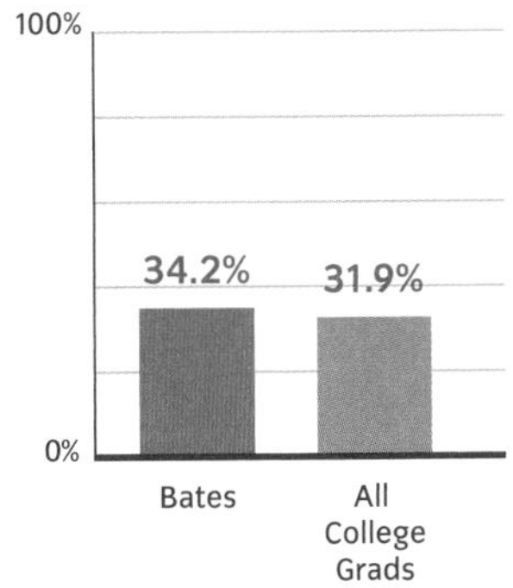

	Bates	All College Grads
% Strongly Agree	34.2%	31.9%

Was A Good Value for the Money — % Strongly Agree

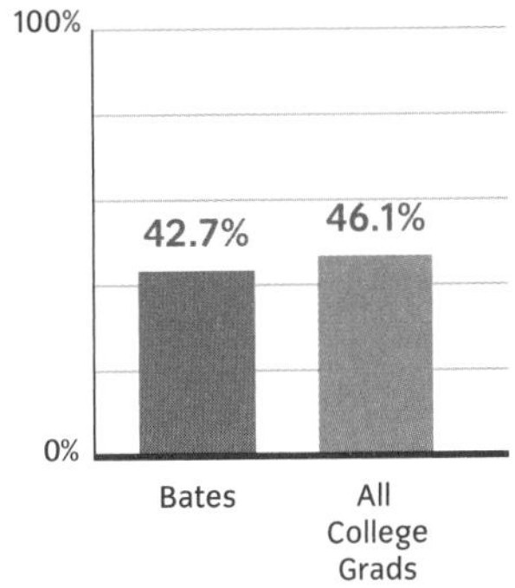

	Bates	All College Grads
% Strongly Agree	42.7%	46.1%

Percent of Alumni Worth >$1MM

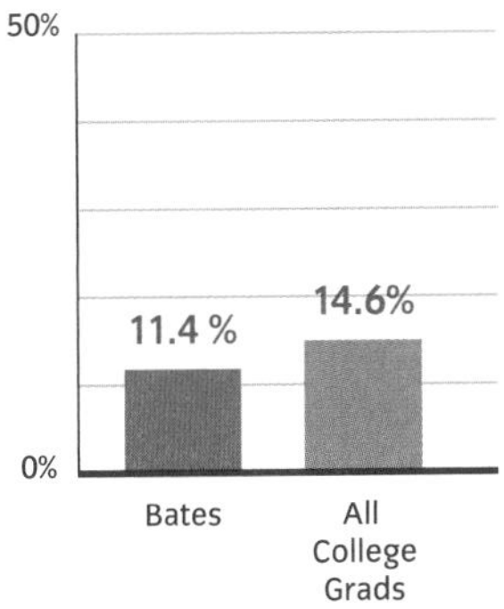

	Bates	All College Grads
%	11.4 %	14.6%

Alumni Employment

Category	%
% Independent/ Entrepreneur	12.1%
% With Large Org.	23.5%
% With Medium Org.	13.0%
% With Small Org.	20.0%
% With Govt.	5.3%
% Any Level Teaching	17.4%
% Other	8.7%

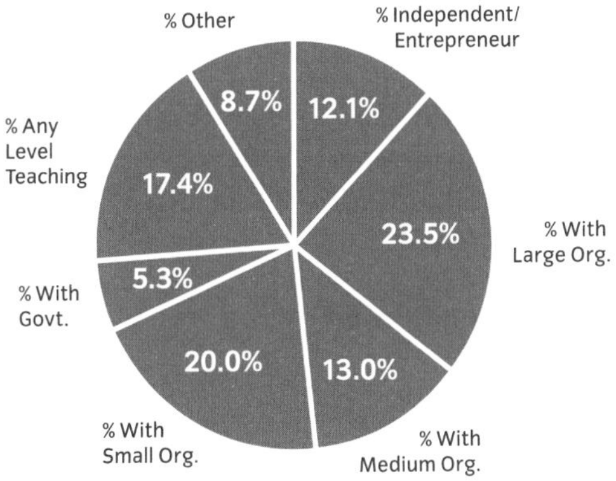

Income Distribution of Graduates

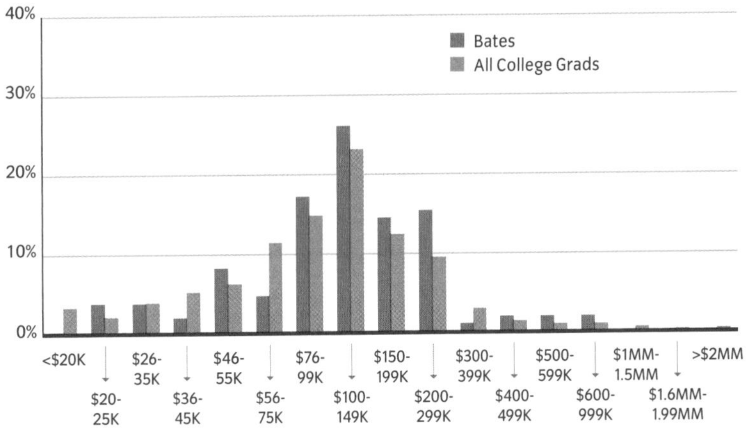

Current Selectivity & Demand Analysis for Bates College

Attribute	% Accepted	% Accepted Who Enroll	Freshman Retention Rate	Graduation Rate	Demand Index	Reputation Index
Score	27.0%	36.0%	92.0%	88.0%	10.35	1.33
Rank	44	68	86	52	66	45

Where are the Graduates of Bates College on the Political Spectrum?

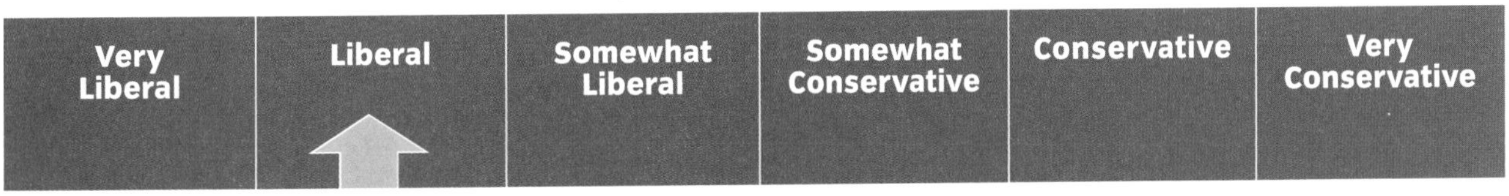

Very Liberal	Liberal	Somewhat Liberal	Somewhat Conservative	Conservative	Very Conservative
	⇧				

See pages 134–135 for detailed explanations and definitions.

Baylor University

Location: Waco, TX
Campus Setting: City: Midsize
Total Expenses: $45,011
Estimated Average Discount: $18,141 (40%)
Estimated Net Price: $26,870

Rank Among 104 National Universities **73**

Overall Rank Among 177 *Alumni Factor* Schools **140**

Overview

A Christian university in the Baptist tradition, Baylor grads are among the happiest (ranked 9th among national universities) and most conservative (ranked 9th among all schools) in the country. Baylor offers a practical, values-based intellectualism. Referred to as a "Baptist Notre Dame," Baylor grads have strong job opportunities and rank 55th in household income. The strongest Ultimate Outcome for Baylor graduates is the combination of Happiness & Friendships (36th). The Baylor community creates bonds through common beliefs and values.

The Baylor undergraduate experience is a unique one. Spiritual Development (3rd) is a major part of the Baylor experience, and its highest ranking attribute. When strong Spiritual Development is coupled with excellent career preparation and significant job opportunities, the result is a graduate who chooses careers with a purpose beyond financial reward. That is certainly the case for Baylor graduates.

Truly happy, values-based and well-prepared for their role in the world, Baylor graduates often follow a higher call and thoroughly enjoy the journey.

Notable Alumni

Olympic gold medalist Michael Johnson and former Texas governor Ann Richards.

Type of Institution: National University
Number of Undergraduates: 12,438
SAT Score: Reading: 560–660, Math: 570–680
Student/Faculty Ratio: 14 to 1
Transfer Out Rate: Not Reported

The Alumni Factor Rankings Summary

Attribute	University Rank	Overall Rank
College Experience	**29**	**83**
Intellectual Development	67	137
Social Development	44	101
Spiritual Development	3	18
Friendship Development	42	105
Preparation for Career Success	33	77
Immediate Job Opportunities	28	44
Overall Assessment	**82**	**147**
Would Personally Choose Again	74	132
Would Recommend to Student	92	161
Value for the Money	73	133
Financial Success	**82**	**133**
Income per Household	55	88
% Households with Income >$150K	79	129
Household Net Worth	87	148
% Households Net Worth >$1MM	89	152
Overall Happiness	**9**	**25**
Alumni Giving	**83**	**152**
Graduation Rate	**75**	**141**
Overall Rank	**73**	**140**

Other Key Alumni Outcomes

5.4% Are college professors
20.5% Teach at any level
55.0% Have post-graduate degrees
53.3% Live in dual-income homes
95.4% Are currently employed

See pages 134–135 for detailed explanations and definitions.

Alumni Activities During College

41.8% Community Service
32.6% Intramural Sports
20.7% Internships
12.7% Media Programs
23.3% Music Programs
35.2% Part-Time Jobs

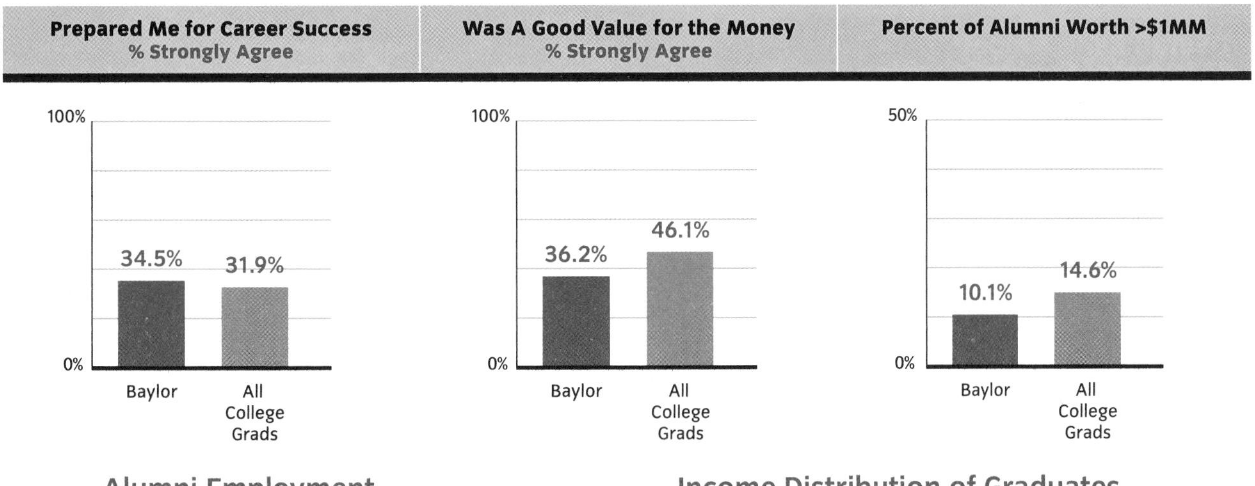

Alumni Employment

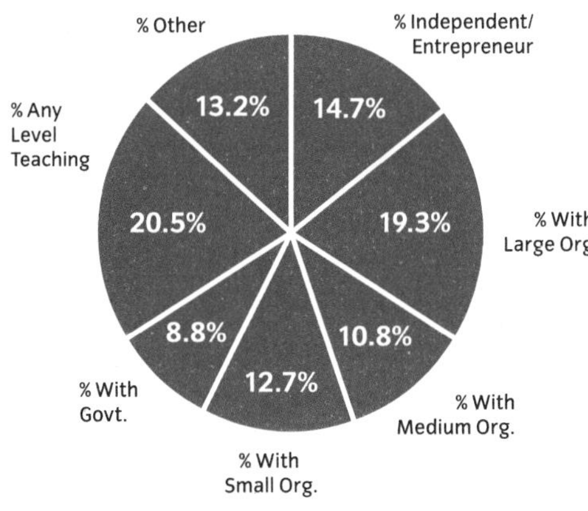

Income Distribution of Graduates

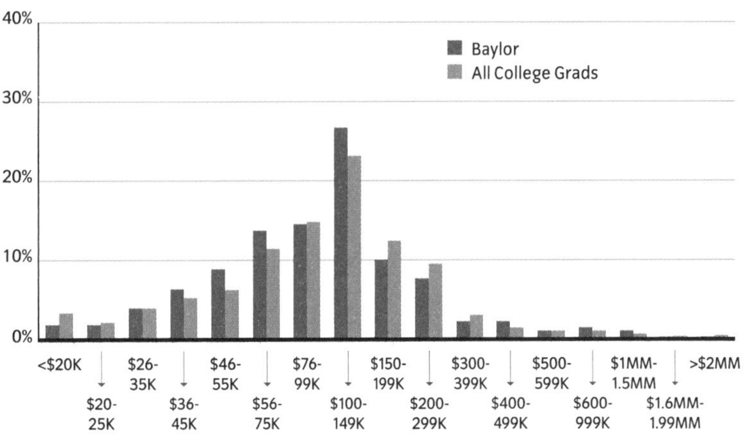

Current Selectivity & Demand Analysis for Baylor University

Attribute	% Accepted	% Accepted Who Enroll	Freshman Retention Rate	Graduation Rate	Demand Index	Reputation Index
Score	40.0%	20.0%	82.0%	71.0%	12.85	0.50
Rank	77	161	167	141	37	121

Where are the Graduates of Baylor University on the Political Spectrum?

Very Liberal	Liberal	Somewhat Liberal	Somewhat Conservative	Conservative	Very Conservative
					↑

Boston College

Location: Chestnut Hill, MA
Campus Setting: City: Small
Total Expenses: $56,728
Estimated Average Discount: $32,986 (58%)
Estimated Net Price: $23,742

Type of Institution: National University
Number of Undergraduates: 9,895
SAT Score: Reading: 620–710, Math: 640–730
Student/Faculty Ratio: 16 to 1
Transfer Out Rate: 5%

Rank Among 104 National Universities	**32**
Overall Rank Among 177 *Alumni Factor* Schools	**76**

Overview

Boston College graduates are financially successful (ranked 25th); well-developed intellectually (38th) and spiritually (5th); and have a positive view of their undergraduate experience (30th). Their scores in Would Personally Choose Again (75th) and in Would Recommend to a Prospective Student (60th) are only low in comparison to the other overwhelming strengths BC possesses as the 32nd ranked national university. These slightly lower ratings may be a reflection of the rapid growth BC has undergone over the last two decades and its escalating cost as the 7th most expensive school on our list. The two highest Ultimate Outcomes for BC are Financial Success & Happiness (24th) and Financial Success & Intellectual Capability (25th).

A top national university, Boston College has long been one of the top Jesuit colleges in the country. Of the 12 Jesuit colleges among the Top 177, its strongest point of distinction is Financial Success, where it ranks 4th (behind Georgetown, Holy Cross and Santa Clara). Well-prepared intellectually, slightly conservative and powered by a strong and connected network of alumni, BC grads excel in their fields and enjoy a level of financial success that is in the Top 50 among all colleges and universities.

Notable Alumni

Tip O'Neill; investor extraordinaire Peter Lynch; Heisman trophy winner Doug Flutie; CEO of Campbell's Denise Morrison; personalities Ed McMahon and Elisabeth Hasselbeck; actor Chris O'Donnell and sportscaster Lesley Visser.

The Alumni Factor Rankings Summary

Attribute	University Rank	Overall Rank
College Experience	**30**	**85**
Intellectual Development	38	95
Social Development	44	101
Spiritual Development	5	23
Friendship Development	51	114
Preparation for Career Success	36	83
Immediate Job Opportunities	48	77
Overall Assessment	**73**	**134**
Would Personally Choose Again	75	133
Would Recommend to Student	60	115
Value for the Money	76	138
Financial Success	**25**	**44**
Income per Household	27	45
% Households with Income >$150K	34	58
Household Net Worth	19	38
% Households Net Worth >$1MM	29	53
Overall Happiness	**57**	**102**
Alumni Giving	**17**	**67**
Graduation Rate	**19**	**32**
Overall Rank	**32**	**76**

Other Key Alumni Outcomes

4.3%	Are college professors
13.4%	Teach at any level
55.4%	Have post-graduate degrees
50.3%	Live in dual-income homes
92.2%	Are currently employed

See pages 134–135 for detailed explanations and definitions.

Alumni Activities During College

32.1% Community Service
29.1% Intramural Sports
21.2% Internships
17.0% Media Programs
23.0% Music Programs
42.4% Part-Time Jobs

Prepared Me for Career Success % Strongly Agree	Was A Good Value for the Money % Strongly Agree	Percent of Alumni Worth >$1MM
BC 31.7%; All College Grads 31.9%	BC 38.0%; All College Grads 46.1%	BC 17.6%; All College Grads 14.6%

Alumni Employment

- % Independent/ Entrepreneur: 11.5%
- % With Large Org.: 23.2%
- % With Medium Org.: 11.0%
- % With Small Org.: 18.9%
- % With Govt.: 5.6%
- % Any Level Teaching: 13.4%
- % Other: 16.4%

Income Distribution of Graduates

Current Selectivity & Demand Analysis for Boston College

Attribute	% Accepted	% Accepted Who Enroll	Freshman Retention Rate	Graduation Rate	Demand Index	Reputation Index
Score	28.0%	25.0%	96.0%	91.0%	14.64	0.89
Rank	46	130	27	32	24	70

Where are the Graduates of Boston College on the Political Spectrum?

Very Liberal	Liberal	Somewhat Liberal	Somewhat Conservative	Conservative	Very Conservative
			⇧		

Boston University

Location: Boston, MA
Campus Setting: City: Large
Total Expenses: $56,842
Estimated Average Discount: $26,943 (47%)
Estimated Net Price: $29,899

Type of Institution: National University
Number of Undergraduates: 18,714
SAT Score: Reading: 580–670, Math: 600–700
Student/Faculty Ratio: 13 to 1
Transfer Out Rate: Not Reported

Rank Among 104 National Universities	**85**
Overall Rank Among 177 *Alumni Factor* Schools	**156**

Overview

A well-respected, private university located in the heart of Boston's Back Bay, BU is the nation's 4th largest private university. In a city with many colleges, BU is an excellent choice. While there is little campus in the traditional sense (the city of Boston is difficult to separate from the campus), the College Experience is still one of the better available at a large metropolitan university (ranked 76th). BU grads are above average in household income (64th) and rank 43rd in the Ultimate Outcome of Financial Success & Intellectual Capability. BU grads rank a strong 54th in the Ultimate Outcomes and are 96th in overall Happiness among national universities. The relatively low rate of happiness is common among grads of large Eastern big city universities such as NYU, Syracuse, Columbia, and GWU. Still, it is worth remembering that nearly 72% of BU grads consider themselves Very Happy or Happy.

One of BU's distinguishing traits is the stellar job it does educating high-performing students, despite its large size. BU grads with an SAT score over 1300 outperform college grads with similar SAT scores in both Income per Household and Household Net Worth. Very few large universities can make that claim.

Notable Alumni

Actresses Geena Davis, Julianne Moore and Olympia Dukakis; J. Crew and GAP founder Mickey Drexler; and a long list of former and current senators, congressmen and governors.

The Alumni Factor Rankings Summary

Attribute	University Rank	Overall Rank
College Experience	**76**	**147**
Intellectual Development	64	133
Social Development	78	146
Spiritual Development	48	114
Friendship Development	57	123
Preparation for Career Success	78	146
Immediate Job Opportunities	74	118
Overall Assessment	**90**	**159**
Would Personally Choose Again	72	128
Would Recommend to Student	85	154
Value for the Money	97	168
Financial Success	**64**	**105**
Income per Household	64	99
% Households with Income >$150K	55	96
Household Net Worth	69	117
% Households Net Worth >$1MM	61	104
Overall Happiness	**96**	**163**
Alumni Giving	**83**	**152**
Graduation Rate	**41**	**86**
Overall Rank	**85**	**156**

Other Key Alumni Outcomes

5.7% Are college professors
14.4% Teach at any level
58.8% Have post-graduate degrees
49.2% Live in dual-income homes
89.4% Are currently employed

See pages 134–135 for detailed explanations and definitions.

Alumni Activities During College

27.9% Community Service
23.3% Intramural Sports
31.7% Internships
16.8% Media Programs
11.4% Music Programs
53.1% Part-Time Jobs

Prepared Me for Career Success % Strongly Agree	Was A Good Value for the Money % Strongly Agree	Percent of Alumni Worth >$1MM
BU 23.6%; All College Grads 31.9%	BU 28.1%; All College Grads 46.1%	BU 13.6%; All College Grads 14.6%

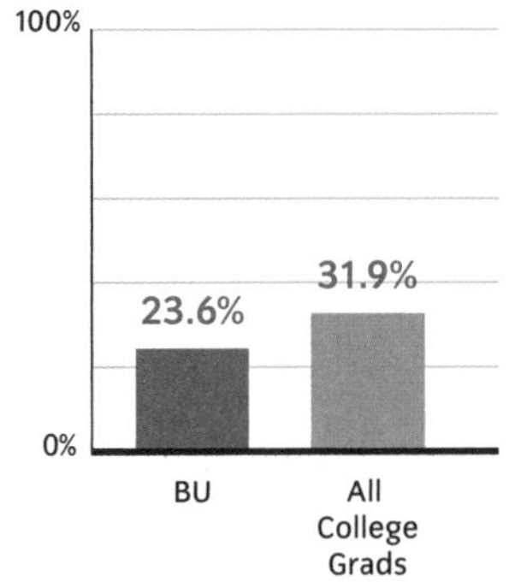

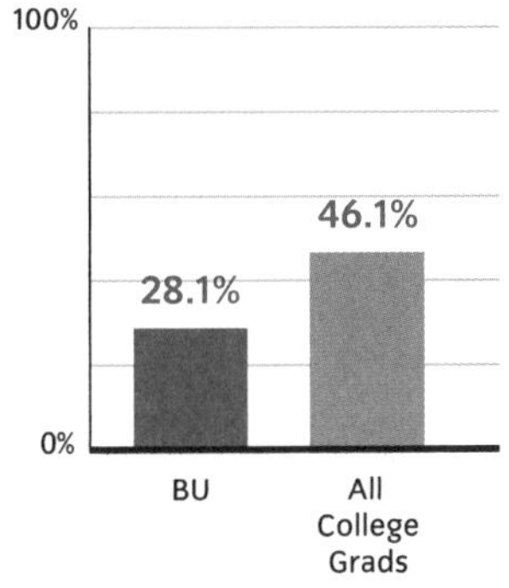

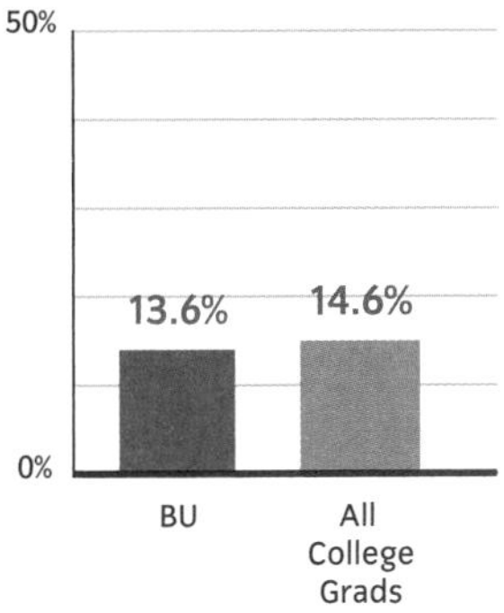

Alumni Employment

% Other 12.3%
% Independent/ Entrepreneur 14.0%
% With Large Org. 21.6%
% With Medium Org. 12.9%
% With Small Org. 20.5%
% With Govt. 4.3%
% Any Level Teaching 14.4%

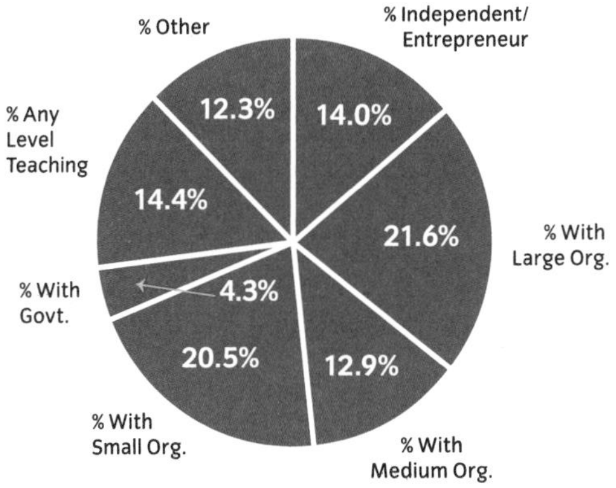

Income Distribution of Graduates

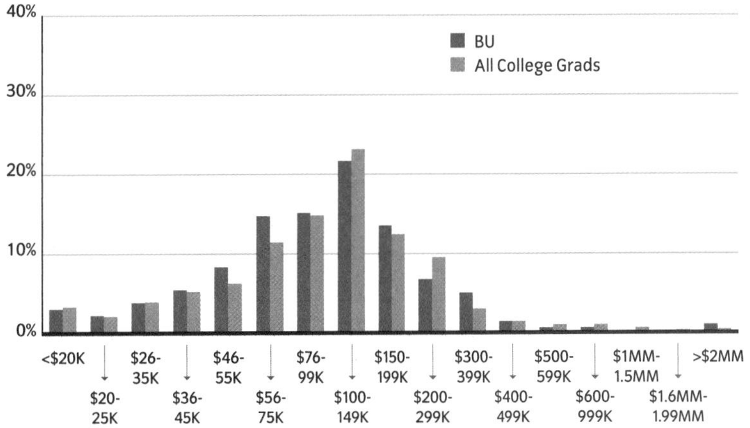

BU / All College Grads

<$20K, $20-25K, $26-35K, $36-45K, $46-55K, $56-75K, $76-99K, $100-149K, $150-199K, $200-299K, $300-399K, $400-499K, $500-599K, $600-999K, $1MM-1.5MM, $1.6MM-1.99MM, >$2MM

0%, 10%, 20%, 30%, 40%

Current Selectivity & Demand Analysis for Boston University

Attribute	% Accepted	% Accepted Who Enroll	Freshman Retention Rate	Graduation Rate	Demand Index	Reputation Index
Score	58.0%	20.0%	91.0%	83.0%	9.51	0.34
Rank	119	161	102	86	76	160

Where are the Graduates of Boston University on the Political Spectrum?

Very Liberal	Liberal	Somewhat Liberal	Somewhat Conservative	Conservative	Very Conservative

See pages 134–135 for detailed explanations and definitions.

Bowdoin College

Location: Brunswick, ME
Campus Setting: Town: Distant
Total Expenses: $56,540
Estimated Average Discount: $34,015 (60%)
Estimated Net Price: $22,525

Type of Institution: Liberal Arts College
Number of Undergraduates: 1,762
SAT Score: Reading: 670–750, Math: 660–740
Student/Faculty Ratio: 9 to 1
Transfer Out Rate: Not Reported

Rank Among 53 Liberal Arts Colleges	**21**
Overall Rank Among 177 *Alumni Factor* Schools	**40**

Overview

Consistently viewed as one of the finest liberal arts colleges in the country, Bowdoin's stellar reputation is well deserved. Ranked in the Top 25 in all Ultimate Outcomes and in the Top 35 in the four developmental aspects of the College Experience, Bowdoin grads are very successful in their chosen fields and are extremely loyal to Bowdoin. This small, intimate community is bound by a healthy intellectual environment that allows big ideas to bloom and deep friendships to take root (ranked 23rd in Friendship Development).

Bowdoin has the highest overall ranking (21st) among the three excellent Maine liberal arts colleges (Colby is 32nd and Bates is 34th). Bowdoin grads have slightly higher Financial Success than graduates of in-state rivals Bates and Colby, ranking a strong 20th overall.

In fact, it is hard to find a flaw in the Bowdoin proposition. Bowdoin is properly respected and envied by colleges and universities across the nation and around the world. Its overall excellence is apparent in every aspect of the Bowdoin education.

Notable Alumni

Franklin Pierce (14th US President), Henry Wadsworth Longfellow, Nathaniel Hawthorne, Ken Chenault, George Mitchell, Stanley Druckenmiller, and Joan Benoit Samuelson.

The Alumni Factor Rankings Summary

Attribute	Liberal Arts Rank	Overall Rank
College Experience	**30**	**54**
Intellectual Development	35	48
Social Development	14	19
Spiritual Development	27	53
Friendship Development	23	29
Preparation for Career Success	42	115
Immediate Job Opportunities	25	107
Overall Assessment	**36**	**100**
Would Personally Choose Again	40	123
Would Recommend to Student	26	72
Value for the Money	35	93
Financial Success	**20**	**49**
Income per Household	18	55
% Households with Income >$150K	15	32
Household Net Worth	28	78
% Households Net Worth >$1MM	23	55
Overall Happiness	**26**	**66**
Alumni Giving	**16**	**18**
Graduation Rate	**5**	**16**
Overall Rank	**21**	**40**

Other Key Alumni Outcomes

8.2%	Are college professors
15.6%	Teach at any level
64.8%	Have post-graduate degrees
56.7%	Live in dual-income homes
96.7%	Are currently employed

See pages 134–135 for detailed explanations and definitions.

Alumni Activities During College

39.3% Community Service
32.8% Intramural Sports
13.9% Internships
35.3% Media Programs
42.7% Music Programs
26.2% Part-Time Jobs

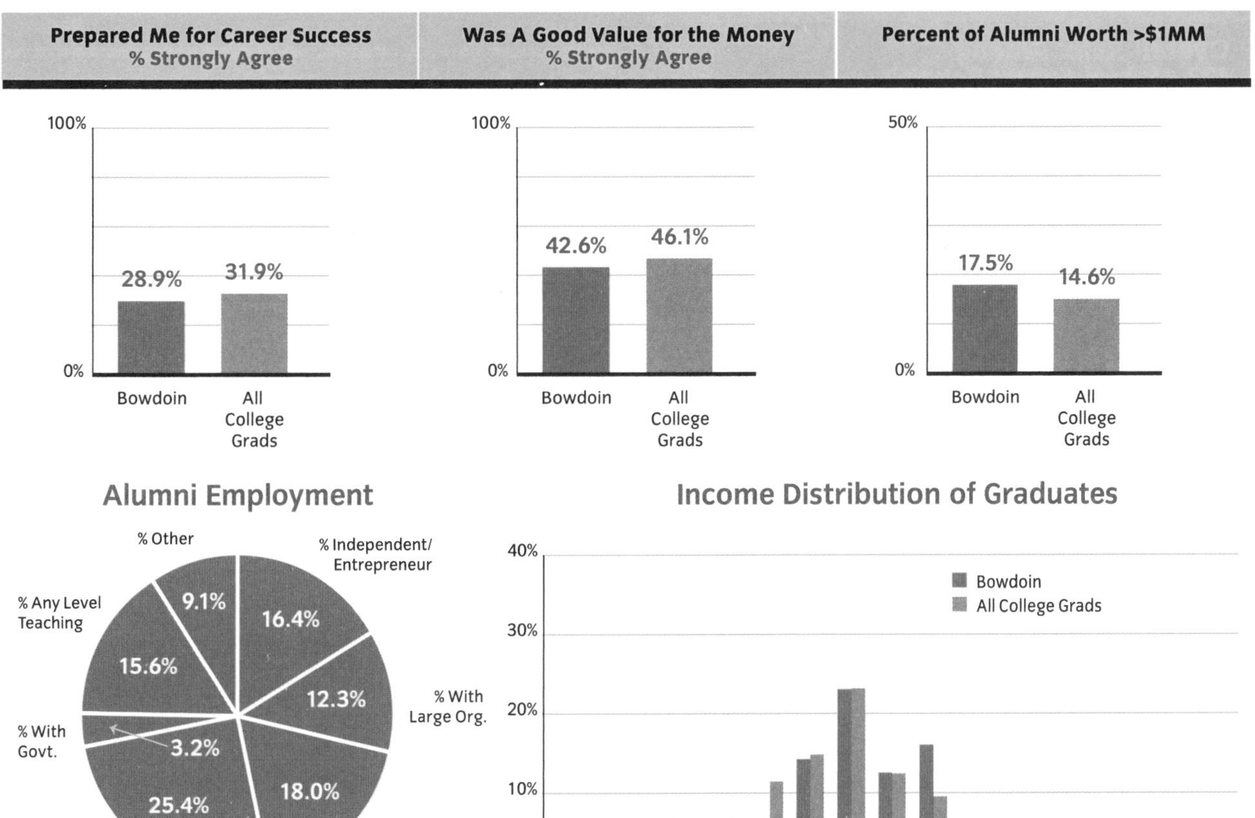

Current Selectivity & Demand Analysis for Bowdoin College

Attribute	% Accepted	% Accepted Who Enroll	Freshman Retention Rate	Graduation Rate	Demand Index	Reputation Index
Score	16.0%	46.0%	94.0%	93.0%	13.57	2.88
Rank	18	24	58	16	29	15

Where are the Graduates of Bowdoin College on the Political Spectrum?

Very Liberal ↑	**Liberal**	**Somewhat Liberal**	**Somewhat Conservative**	**Conservative**	**Very Conservative**

See pages 134–135 for detailed explanations and definitions.

Bradley University

Location: Peoria, IL
Campus Setting: City: Midsize
Total Expenses: $38,230
Estimated Average Discount: $15,310 (40%)
Estimated Net Price: $22,920

Type of Institution: Regional University
Number of Undergraduates: 5,067
SAT Score: Reading: 510–620, Math: 540–660
Student/Faculty Ratio: 13 to 1
Transfer Out Rate: Not Reported

Rank Among 20 Regional Universities	**19**
Overall Rank Among 177 *Alumni Factor* Schools	**162**

Overview

A friendly, upbeat, Midwestern university that has the resources of a large school and the intimacy of a small liberal arts college, Bradley produces graduates that are a reflection of itself. Conservative (in the top one-third among all colleges), connected via deep friendships (ranked 96th among 177 schools), and well prepared for their career, Bradley graduates would overwhelmingly choose the school again (ranked 46th).

Bradley grads achieve Financial Success (143rd) beyond what the school's overall ranking would suggest. Bradley's relatively strong performance in Friendship Development, Immediate Job Opportunities and the two Net Worth rankings indicate it is a friendly environment with a practical bent towards preparing its graduates for success. Grads are less likely to pursue post-grad degrees than other colleges (44% versus 58% for all colleges).

Conservative, friendly and smart, with a practical Midwestern sensibility, the Bradley graduate reflects values born of its location. With a record of success, Bradley graduates are people who can be relied upon in today's world.

Notable Alumni

Business leader George Shaheen; former Minnesota Twin Kirby Puckett; and former NATO chief general John Shalikashvili.

The Alumni Factor Rankings Summary

Attribute	Overall Rank
College Experience	**156**
Intellectual Development	174
Social Development	130
Spiritual Development	174
Friendship Development	96
Preparation for Career Success	157
Immediate Job Opportunities	98
Overall Assessment	**131**
Would Personally Choose Again	46
Would Recommend to Student	165
Value for the Money	171
Financial Success	**143**
Income per Household	163
% Households with Income >$150K	154
Household Net Worth	113
% Households Net Worth >$1MM	118
Overall Happiness	**153**
Alumni Giving	**125**
Graduation Rate	**138**
Overall Rank	**162**

Other Key Alumni Outcomes

3.5% Are college professors
15.9% Teach at any level
44.2% Have post-graduate degrees
51.8% Live in dual-income homes
93.6% Are currently employed

See pages 134–135 for detailed explanations and definitions.

Alumni Activities During College

31.9% Community Service
28.3% Intramural Sports
23.0% Internships
29.1% Media Programs
23.9% Music Programs
52.2% Part-Time Jobs

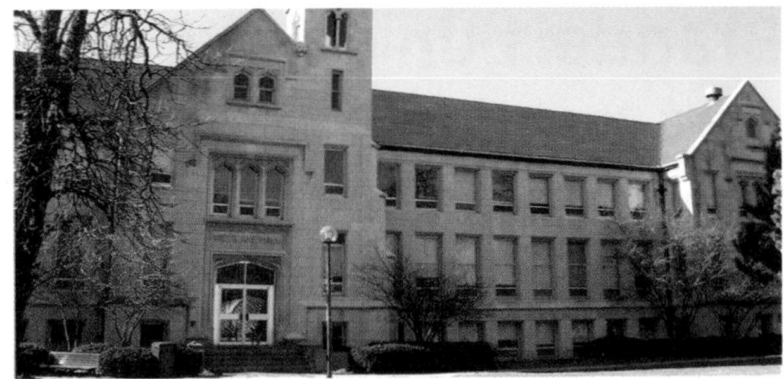

Prepared Me for Career Success % Strongly Agree	Was A Good Value for the Money % Strongly Agree	Percent of Alumni Worth >$1MM

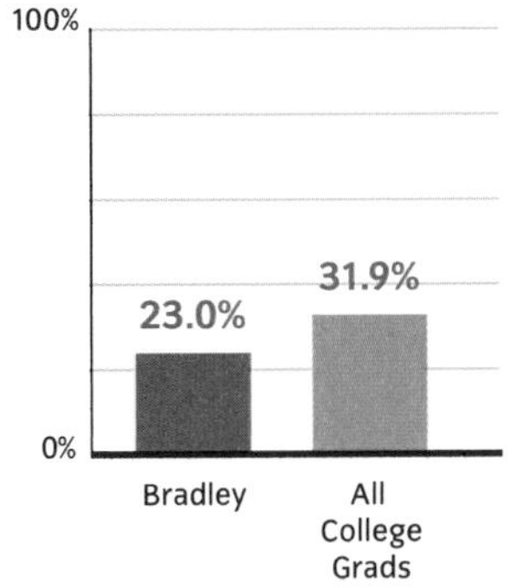
100%
0%
23.0%
31.9%
Bradley
All College Grads

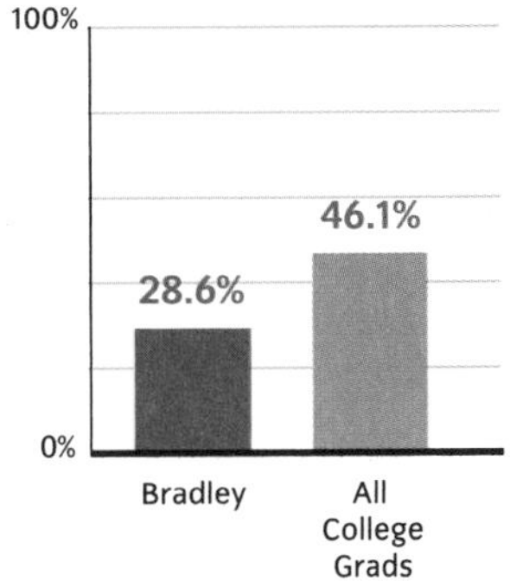
100%
0%
28.6%
46.1%
Bradley
All College Grads

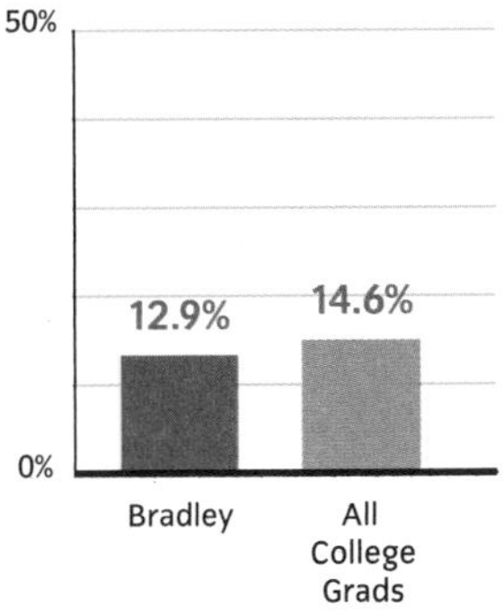
50%
0%
12.9%
14.6%
Bradley
All College Grads

Alumni Employment

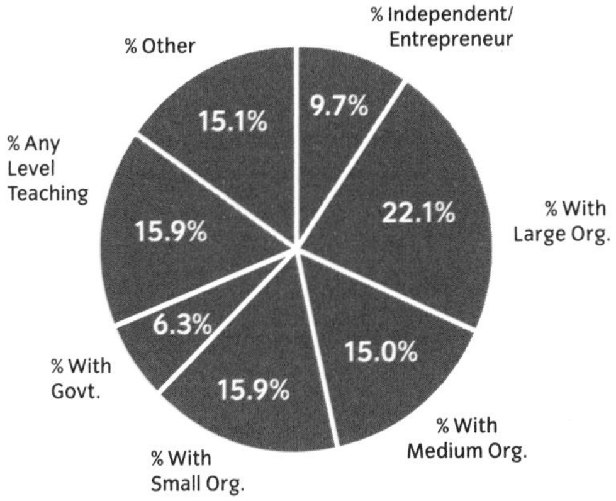
% Independent/ Entrepreneur
9.7%
% With Large Org.
22.1%
% With Medium Org.
15.0%
% With Small Org.
15.9%
% With Govt.
6.3%
% Any Level Teaching
15.9%
% Other
15.1%

Income Distribution of Graduates

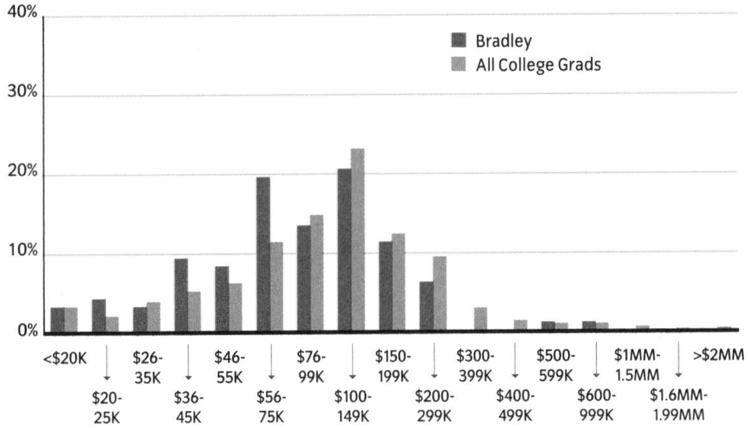
Bradley
All College Grads
40%
30%
20%
10%
0%
<$20K
$20-25K
$26-35K
$36-45K
$46-55K
$56-75K
$76-99K
$100-149K
$150-199K
$200-299K
$300-399K
$400-499K
$500-599K
$600-999K
$1MM-1.5MM
$1.6MM-1.99MM
>$2MM

Current Selectivity & Demand Analysis for Bradley University

Attribute	% Accepted	% Accepted Who Enroll	Freshman Retention Rate	Graduation Rate	Demand Index	Reputation Index
Score	70.0%	22.0%	87.0%	73.0%	6.34	0.31
Rank	149	149	140	138	123	166

Where are the Graduates of Bradley University on the Political Spectrum?

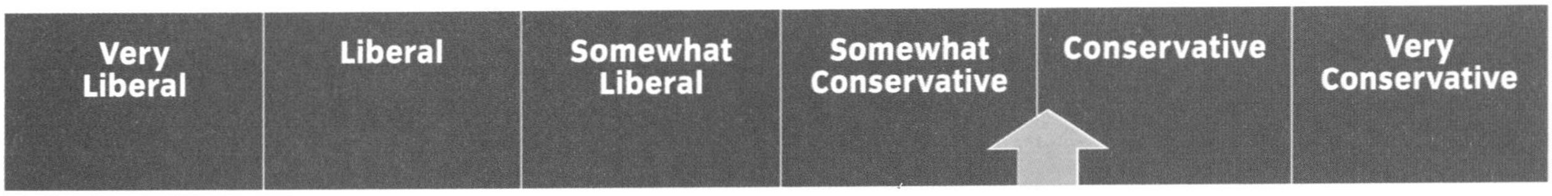
Very Liberal
Liberal
Somewhat Liberal
Somewhat Conservative
Conservative
Very Conservative

Brandeis University

Location: Waltham, MA
Campus Setting: City: Small
Total Expenses: $56,416
Estimated Average Discount: $30,138 (53%)
Estimated Net Price: $26,278

Type of Institution: National University
Number of Undergraduates: 3,341
SAT Score: Reading: 600–710, Math: 630–740
Student/Faculty Ratio: 9 to 1
Transfer Out Rate: Not Reported

Rank Among 104 National Universities	**83**
Overall Rank Among 177 *Alumni Factor* Schools	**152**

Overview

A Brandeis graduate is a passionate, globally aware, progressive thinker who is committed to a cause. Trained to think deeply and freely, Brandeis graduates pursue a variety of diverse fields from the arts and entertainment to academia and the non-profit world.

Twenty percent of all Brandeis grads become educators (versus 14% among all college graduates). This ratio climbs to nearly 24% for female graduates. It is, therefore, not surprising that over 72% of Brandeis graduates go on to get an advanced degree (versus 58% for all college grads).

Brandeis' two strongest Ultimate Outcomes are Financial Success & Intellectual Capability (26th) and Happiness & Intellectual Capability (18th). These two ratings, combined with a high Alumni Giving ranking (15th), indicate Brandeis grads are a force to be reckoned with in today's world. Interestingly, the three Overall Assessment attributes do not reflect the relatively high Alumni Giving rate as it does for many other colleges. Deeply trained and serious in their pursuit of excellence, Brandeis grads enjoy success in all fields and give back both to their college and to the communities in which they live.

Notable Alumni

Mitch Albom, Abbie Hoffman, Debra Messing and Thomas Friedman.

The Alumni Factor Rankings Summary

Attribute	University Rank	Overall Rank
College Experience	**78**	**150**
Intellectual Development	44	102
Social Development	100	173
Spiritual Development	18	74
Friendship Development	47	110
Preparation for Career Success	92	163
Immediate Job Opportunities	103	174
Overall Assessment	**102**	**174**
Would Personally Choose Again	95	162
Would Recommend to Student	102	175
Value for the Money	98	169
Financial Success	**66**	**108**
Income per Household	84	126
% Households with Income >$150K	51	85
Household Net Worth	60	103
% Households Net Worth >$1MM	64	108
Overall Happiness	**86**	**142**
Alumni Giving	**15**	**62**
Graduation Rate	**19**	**32**
Overall Rank	**83**	**152**

Other Key Alumni Outcomes

8.2% Are college professors
19.6% Teach at any level
72.2% Have post-graduate degrees
58.3% Live in dual-income homes
93.7% Are currently employed

See pages 134–135 for detailed explanations and definitions.

Alumni Activities During College

38.4% Community Service
18.2% Intramural Sports
23.3% Internships
26.4% Media Programs
18.8% Music Programs
36.5% Part-Time Jobs

	Prepared Me for Career Success % Strongly Agree	Was A Good Value for the Money % Strongly Agree	Percent of Alumni Worth >$1MM
Brandeis	24.0%	28.3%	13.3%
All College Grads	31.9%	46.1%	14.6%

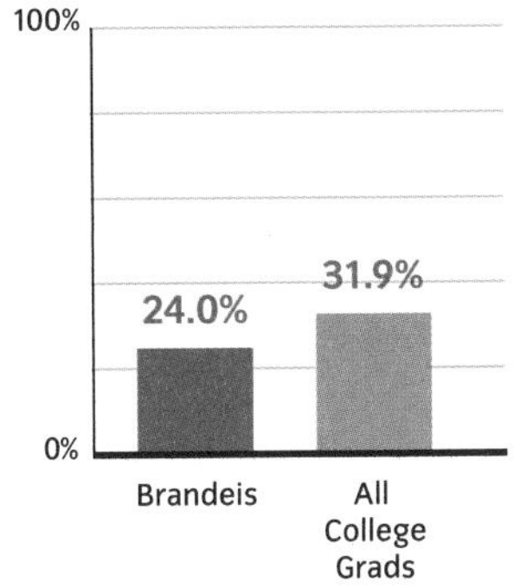

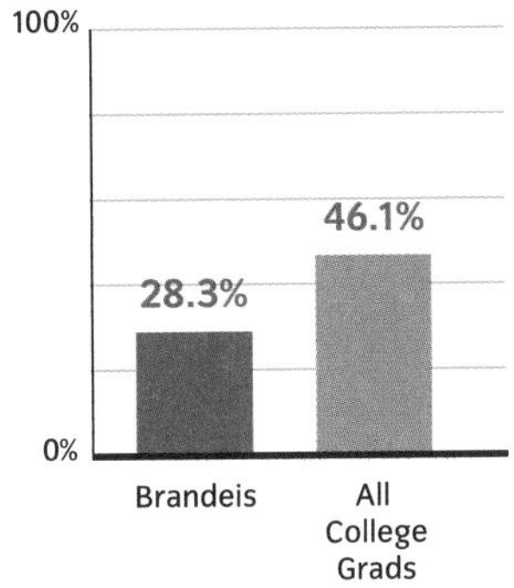

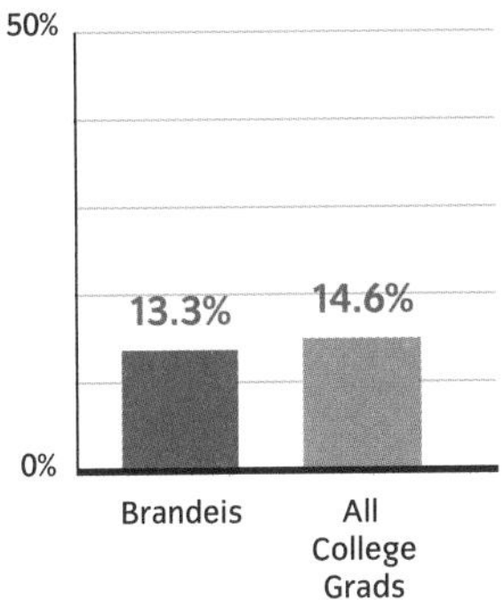

Alumni Employment

Category	%
% Other	10.1%
% Independent/ Entrepreneur	15.8%
% With Large Org.	15.2%
% With Medium Org.	8.2%
% With Small Org.	20.9%
% With Govt.	8.9%
% In Farm/ Agr.	1.3%
% Any Level Teaching	19.6%

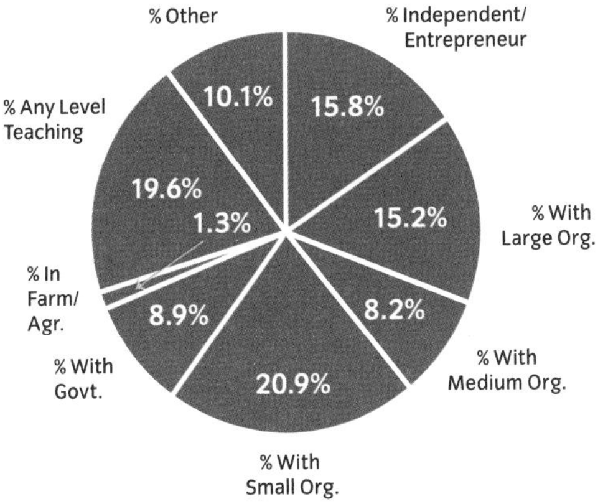

Income Distribution of Graduates

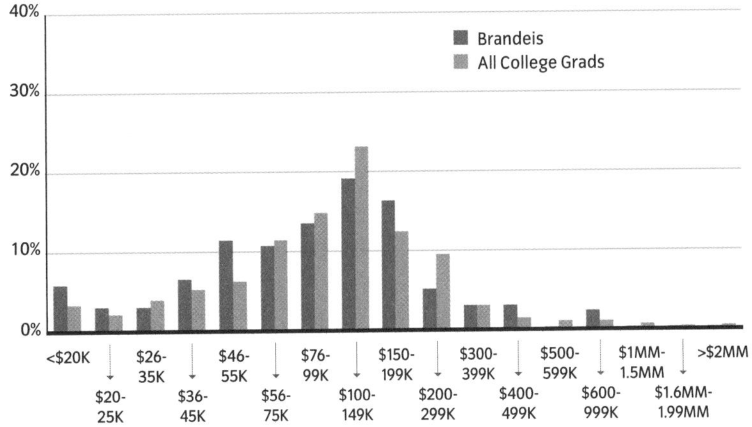

Current Selectivity & Demand Analysis for Brandeis University

Attribute	% Accepted	% Accepted Who Enroll	Freshman Retention Rate	Graduation Rate	Demand Index	Reputation Index
Score	40.0%	24.0%	92.0%	91.0%	10.39	0.60
Rank	77	138	86	32	64	103

Where are the Graduates of Brandeis University on the Political Spectrum?

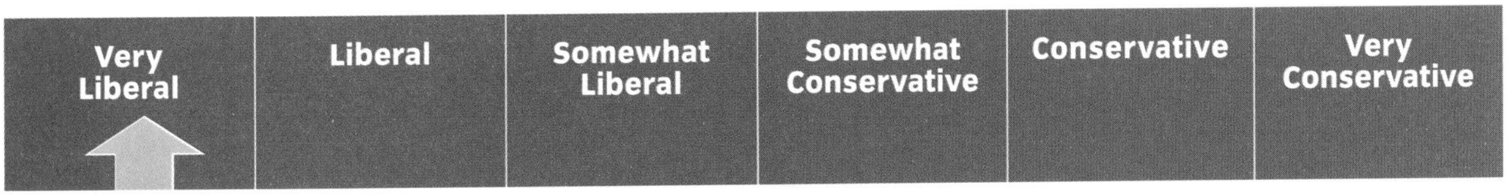

Very Liberal ↑	Liberal	Somewhat Liberal	Somewhat Conservative	Conservative	Very Conservative

See pages 134–135 for detailed explanations and definitions.

Brigham Young University

Location: Provo, UT
Campus Setting: City: Midsize
Total Expenses: $16,588
Estimated Average Discount: $4,971 (30%)
Estimated Net Price: $11,617

Type of Institution: National University
Number of Undergraduates: 30,409
SAT Score: Reading: 570–680, Math: 580–680
Student/Faculty Ratio: 21 to 1
Transfer Out Rate: Not Reported

Rank Among 104 National Universities	**35**
Overall Rank Among 177 *Alumni Factor* Schools	**80**

Overview

Brigham Young University graduates are truly unique. Graduates rank BYU 1st in Spiritual Development; 2nd in Overall Happiness, and among the top 35 in every element of the College Experience. Grads rank their overall college experience 7th among national universities, and 3rd in Value for the Money. As to Financial Success, BYU is ranked 104th among 104 national universities. BYU ranks at or near the bottom in each of the four measures of Financial Success. Given these lower ratings are a clear departure from the high marks grads give BYU for Job Opportunities and Preparation for Career Success, this may be a reflection of the typical BYU grad's priorities more than anything else.

BYU grads are products of a university with a distinctly rigorous honor code – very little smoking, drinking, swearing or dishonesty exists on campus. Not surprisingly, BYU graduates are the second most conservative group of any college we measured – only the US Air Force Academy graduates are more conservative.

BYU grads are morally and spiritually resolute, guided by the Mormon Church. Grads are very pleased with their college and the job it did in developing them. They are also among the happiest graduates in the nation as they follow their higher calling – their quest for perfection and eternal life.

Notable Alumni

Mitt Romney, Johnny Miller, Danny Ainge, Steve Young and numerous other religious and business leaders.

The Alumni Factor Rankings Summary

Attribute	University Rank	Overall Rank
College Experience	**7**	**22**
Intellectual Development	24	67
Social Development	7	27
Spiritual Development	1	1
Friendship Development	33	90
Preparation for Career Success	8	24
Immediate Job Opportunities	24	38
Overall Assessment	**17**	**33**
Would Personally Choose Again	28	59
Would Recommend to Student	26	52
Value for the Money	3	6
Financial Success	**104**	**173**
Income per Household	97	156
% Households with Income >$150K	99	164
Household Net Worth	104	176
% Households Net Worth >$1MM	103	171
Overall Happiness	**2**	**10**
Alumni Giving	**35**	**93**
Graduation Rate	**62**	**123**
Overall Rank	**35**	**80**

Other Key Alumni Outcomes

6.1% Are college professors
11.2% Teach at any level
54.1% Have post-graduate degrees
35.5% Live in dual-income homes
90.9% Are currently employed

See pages 134–135 for detailed explanations and definitions.

Alumni Activities During College

38.7% Community Service
36.3% Intramural Sports
24.8% Internships
8.5% Media Programs
25.5% Music Programs
51.2% Part-Time Jobs

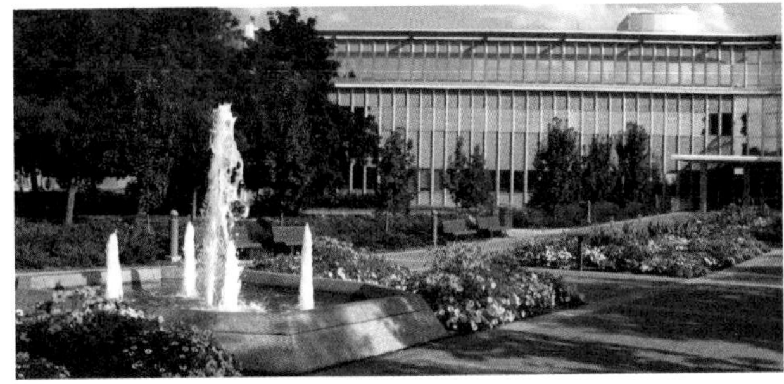

Prepared Me for Career Success
% Strongly Agree

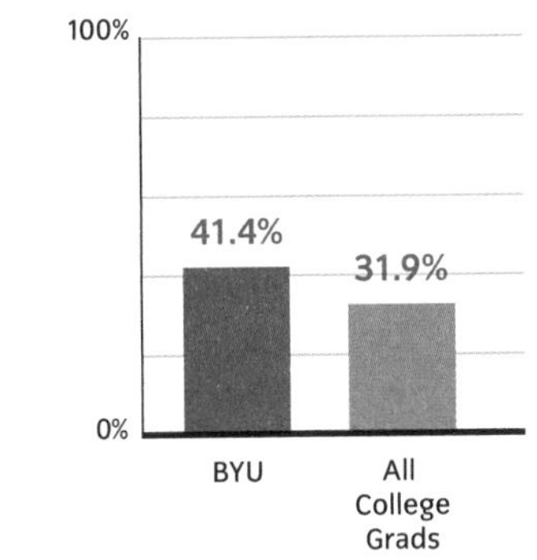
100%
0%
41.4%
31.9%
BYU
All College Grads

Was A Good Value for the Money
% Strongly Agree

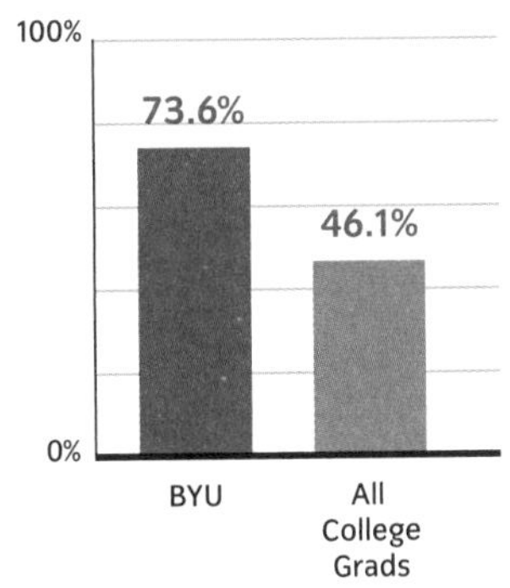
100%
0%
73.6%
46.1%
BYU
All College Grads

Percent of Alumni Worth >$1MM

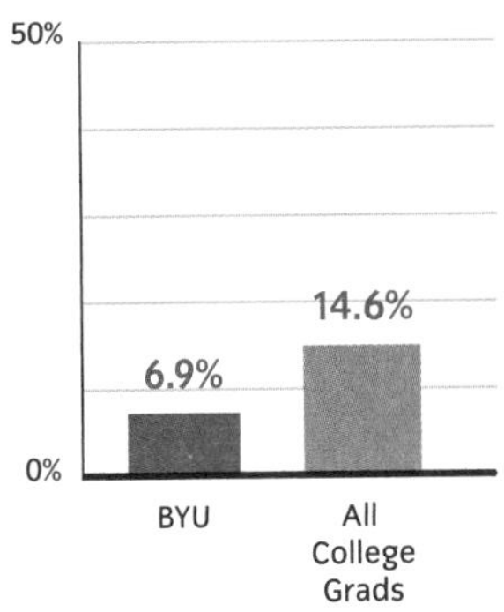
50%
0%
6.9%
14.6%
BYU
All College Grads

Alumni Employment

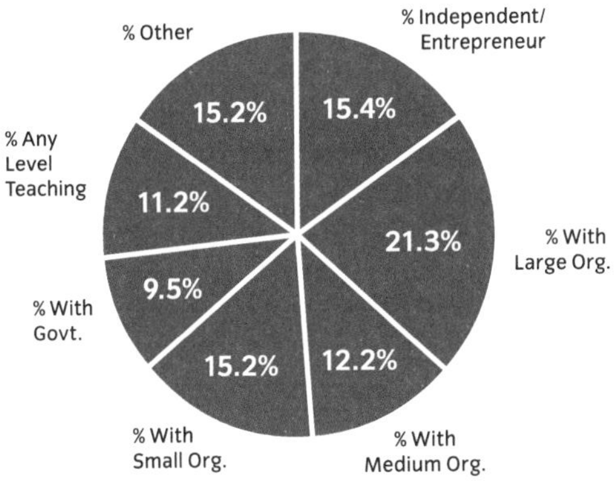
% Other
15.2%
% Independent/ Entrepreneur
15.4%
% With Large Org.
21.3%
% With Medium Org.
12.2%
% With Small Org.
15.2%
% With Govt.
9.5%
% Any Level Teaching
11.2%

Income Distribution of Graduates

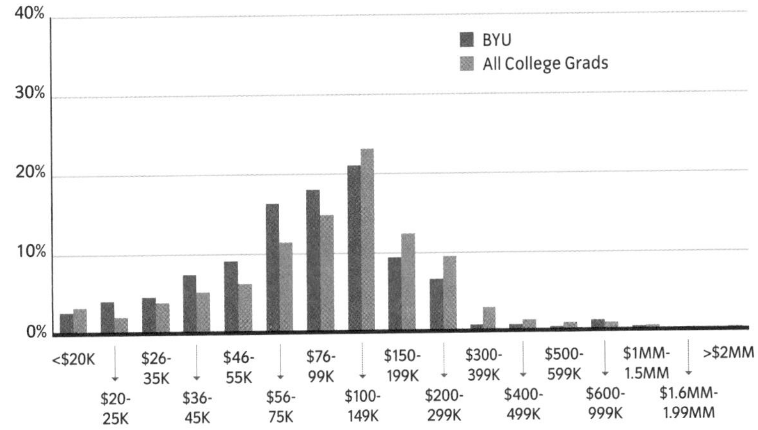
40%
30%
20%
10%
0%
BYU
All College Grads
<$20K
$20-25K
$26-35K
$36-45K
$46-55K
$56-75K
$76-99K
$100-149K
$150-199K
$200-299K
$300-399K
$400-499K
$500-599K
$600-999K
$1MM-1.5MM
$1.6MM-1.99MM
>$2MM

Current Selectivity & Demand Analysis for Brigham Young University

Attribute	% Accepted	% Accepted Who Enroll	Freshman Retention Rate	Graduation Rate	Demand Index	Reputation Index
Score	63.0%	80.0%	85.0%	78.0%	2.00	1.27
Rank	135	4	151	123	177	48

Where are the Graduates of Brigham Young University on the Political Spectrum?

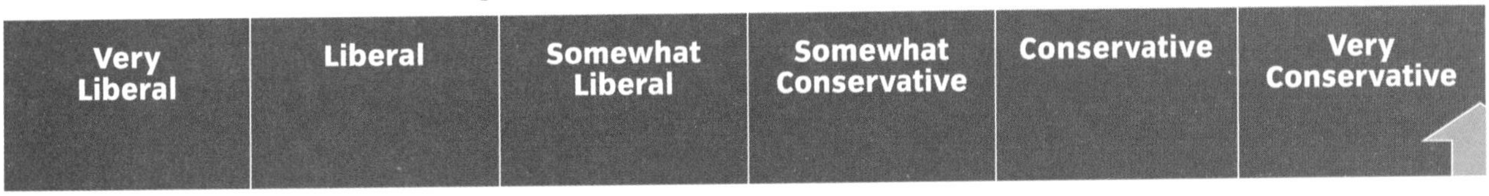
Very Liberal
Liberal
Somewhat Liberal
Somewhat Conservative
Conservative
Very Conservative

See pages 134–135 for detailed explanations and definitions.

Brown University

Location: Providence, RI
Campus Setting: City: Midsize
Total Expenses: $56,150
Estimated Average Discount: $33,407 (59%)
Estimated Net Price: $22,743

Type of Institution: National University
Number of Undergraduates: 6,318
SAT Score: Reading: 630–740, Math: 650–760
Student/Faculty Ratio: 9 to 1
Transfer Out Rate: Not Reported

Rank Among 104 National Universities	**14**
Overall Rank Among 177 *Alumni Factor* Schools	**31**

Overview

Ranked 14th among national universities and 5th among Ivy League Schools (behind Yale, Princeton Dartmouth and Cornell), Brown is truly a formidable player in global higher education today. The university proudly marches to its own beat – and its graduates follow suit. With a strong 6th ranking in the Ultimate Outcomes, Brown develops well-rounded and extraordinarily capable leaders and thinkers.

Brown grads are passionate about their undergrad experience. Ranked 13th in the College Experience (and 4th in the Ivy League), Brown grads strongly recommend the school today. Only Yale has a higher recommend rate than Brown within the Ivy League. However, with its strong liberal arts bent and resolute stance on having no required courses, grads give Brown less lofty marks on career preparation, job opportunities or Value for the Money. Those facts, however, do not prevent Brown grads from achieving Top 30 rankings in every key financial success metric and across each Ultimate Outcome. Nor does it deter grads from giving strong financial support (ranked 6th) to Brown. Brown grads are extremely successful and individualistic – Ivy leaguers with a uniquely positive twist.

Notable Alumni

John D. Rockefeller; Horace Mann; IBM's Thomas Watson; John F. Kennedy Jr.; CNN founder Ted Turner; Bank of America Chairman and CEO Brian Moynihan; former Penn State coach Joe Paterno; and scores more.

The Alumni Factor Rankings Summary

Attribute	University Rank	Overall Rank
College Experience	**13**	**43**
Intellectual Development	6	34
Social Development	9	34
Spiritual Development	9	42
Friendship Development	7	37
Preparation for Career Success	49	100
Immediate Job Opportunities	58	93
Overall Assessment	**28**	**60**
Would Personally Choose Again	34	66
Would Recommend to Student	19	35
Value for the Money	47	85
Financial Success	**24**	**42**
Income per Household	29	47
% Households with Income >$150K	25	45
Household Net Worth	23	43
% Households Net Worth >$1MM	23	45
Overall Happiness	**65**	**111**
Alumni Giving	**6**	**36**
Graduation Rate	**2**	**2**
Overall Rank	**14**	**31**

Other Key Alumni Outcomes

7.3% Are college professors
10.9% Teach at any level
71.8% Have post-graduate degrees
56.7% Live in dual-income homes
89.7% Are currently employed

See pages 134–135 for detailed explanations and definitions.

Alumni Activities During College

39.2% Community Service
24.7% Intramural Sports
24.2% Internships
22.2% Media Programs
25.3% Music Programs
38.7% Part-Time Jobs

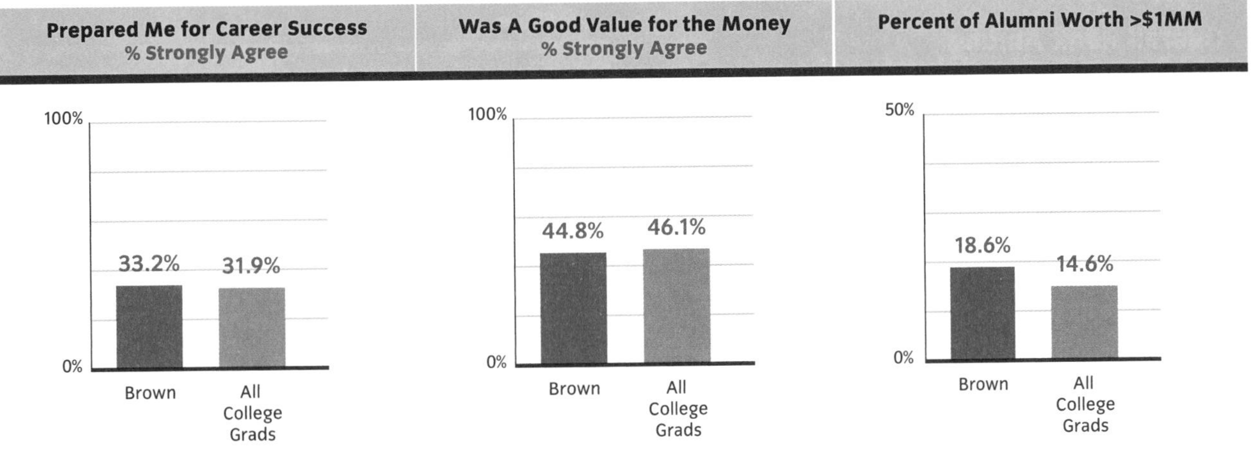

Alumni Employment

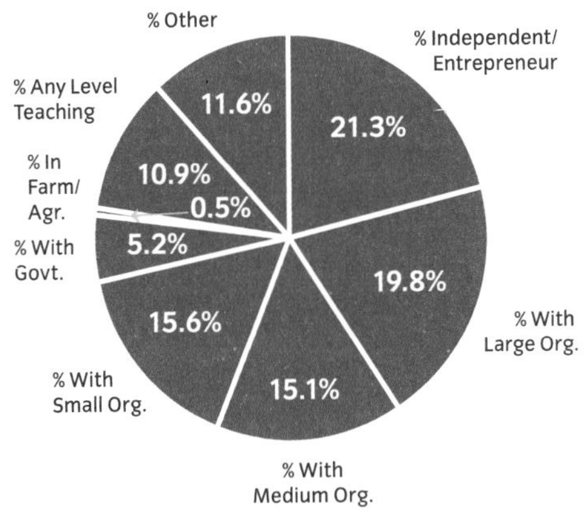

Income Distribution of Graduates

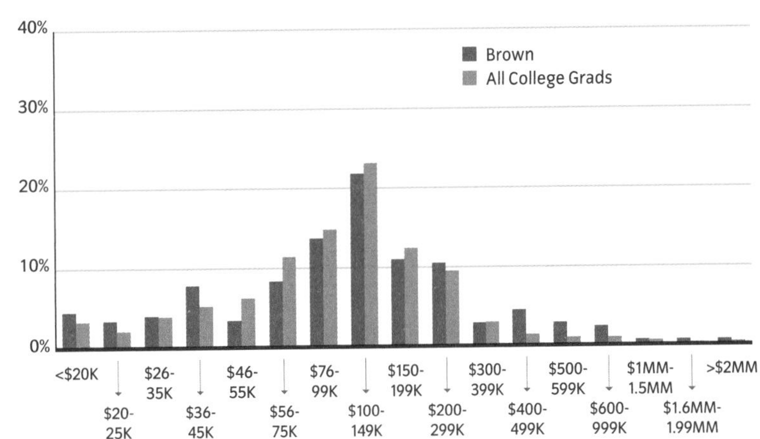

Current Selectivity & Demand Analysis for Brown University

Attribute	% Accepted	% Accepted Who Enroll	Freshman Retention Rate	Graduation Rate	Demand Index	Reputation Index
Score	9.0%	55.0%	97.0%	96.0%	20.53	6.11
Rank	6	14	13	2	5	9

Where are the Graduates of Brown University on the Political Spectrum?

Very Liberal	Liberal	Somewhat Liberal	Somewhat Conservative	Conservative	Very Conservative
↑					

See pages 134–135 for detailed explanations and definitions.

Bryn Mawr College

Location: Bryn Mawr, PA
Campus Setting: Suburb: Large
Total Expenses: $55,714
Estimated Average Discount: $29,923 (54%)
Estimated Net Price: $25,791

Type of Institution: Liberal Arts College
Number of Undergraduates: 1,289
SAT Score: Reading: 600–710, Math: 600–720
Student/Faculty Ratio: 8 to 1
Transfer Out Rate: Not Reported

Rank Among 53 Liberal Arts Colleges	**45**
Overall Rank Among 177 *Alumni Factor* Schools	**95**

Overview

The "smart sister" of the original Seven Sister colleges in the Northeast, Bryn Mawr has long been admired for intellectual excellence and rigor. Nearly 73% of graduates get a post-graduate degree, and grads are two times more likely to be a college professor than all college graduates.

Bryn Mawr ranks 9th among all liberal arts schools and 2nd among the all-women colleges in Intellectual Development. While also strong in Friendship Development (ranked 31st), Spiritual Development (20th), Preparation for Career Success (28th), and Job Opportunities (a very strong 11th), grads are less enthusiastic about Bryn Mawr's Social Development.

Ranked 23rd in Alumni Giving, Bryn Mawr produces strongly loyal, independent, accomplished women. After spending their undergraduate years on a stunningly beautiful campus in Philadelphia, near other top schools such as Haverford, Rosemont, Swarthmore, Penn and Villanova, Bryn Mawr women are serious scholars, well prepared for their future.

Notable Alumni

Actress Katharine Hepburn, Nobel Peace Prize winner Emily Greene Balch and Pulitzer Prize winner Margaret Ayer Barnes.

The Alumni Factor Rankings Summary

Attribute	Liberal Arts Rank	Overall Rank
College Experience	**26**	**44**
Intellectual Development	9	10
Social Development	49	138
Spiritual Development	20	45
Friendship Development	31	40
Preparation for Career Success	28	61
Immediate Job Opportunities	11	54
Overall Assessment	**37**	**106**
Would Personally Choose Again	43	137
Would Recommend to Student	41	123
Value for the Money	19	45
Financial Success	**45**	**138**
Income per Household	35	129
% Households with Income >$150K	41	132
Household Net Worth	51	171
% Households Net Worth >$1MM	38	99
Overall Happiness	**40**	**126**
Alumni Giving	**23**	**26**
Graduation Rate	**26**	**60**
Overall Rank	**45**	**95**

Other Key Alumni Outcomes

12.0% Are college professors
19.0% Teach at any level
72.5% Have post-graduate degrees
54.0% Live in dual-income homes
87.4% Are currently employed

See pages 134–135 for detailed explanations and definitions.

Alumni Activities During College

46.1% Community Service
10.8% Intramural Sports
29.4% Internships
20.6% Media Programs
22.6% Music Programs
40.2% Part-Time Jobs

Prepared Me for Career Success % Strongly Agree	Was A Good Value for the Money % Strongly Agree	Percent of Alumni Worth >$1MM
Bryn Mawr: 38.2%	Bryn Mawr: 52.0%	Bryn Mawr: 13.8%
All College Grads: 31.9%	All College Grads: 46.1%	All College Grads: 14.6%

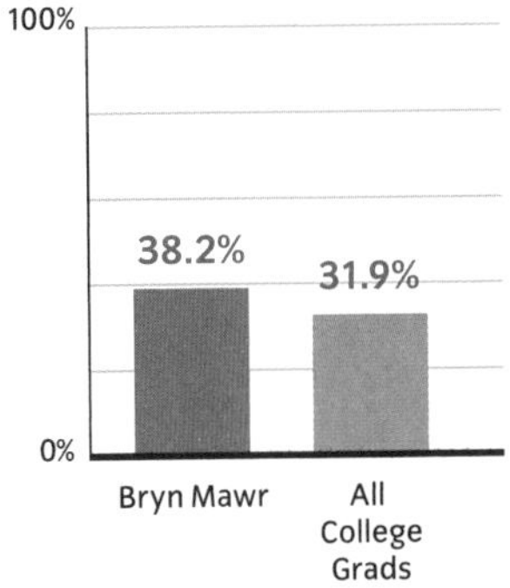

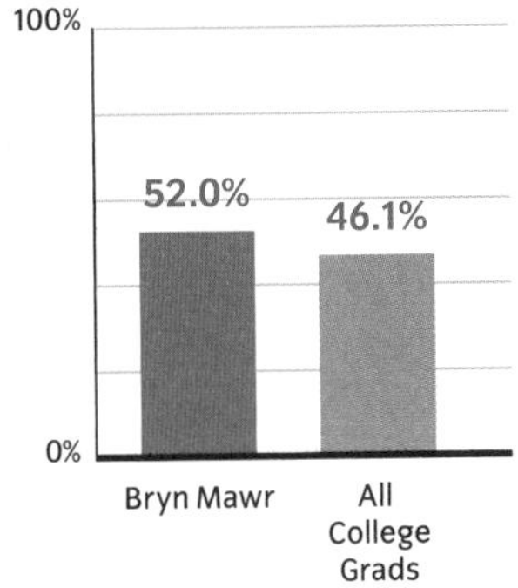

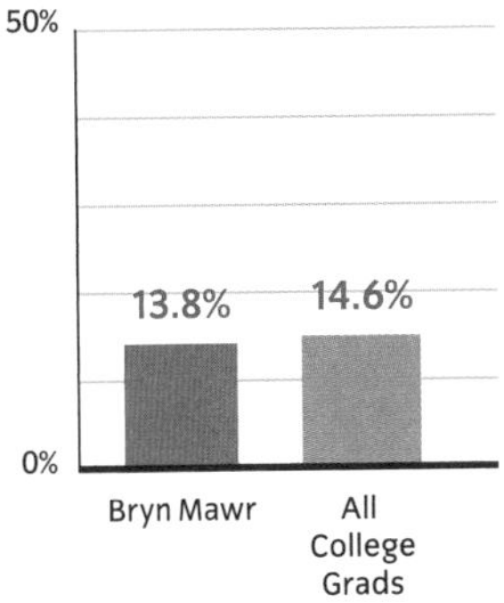

100%
0%
100%
0%
50%
0%

Alumni Employment

Category	%
% Independent/ Entrepreneur	15.0%
% With Large Org.	17.0%
% With Medium Org.	12.0%
% With Small Org.	12.0%
% With Govt.	5.0%
% Any Level Teaching	19.0%
% Other	20.0%

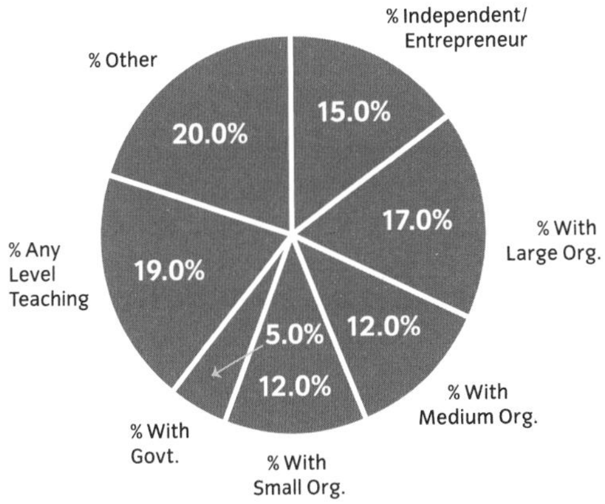

Income Distribution of Graduates

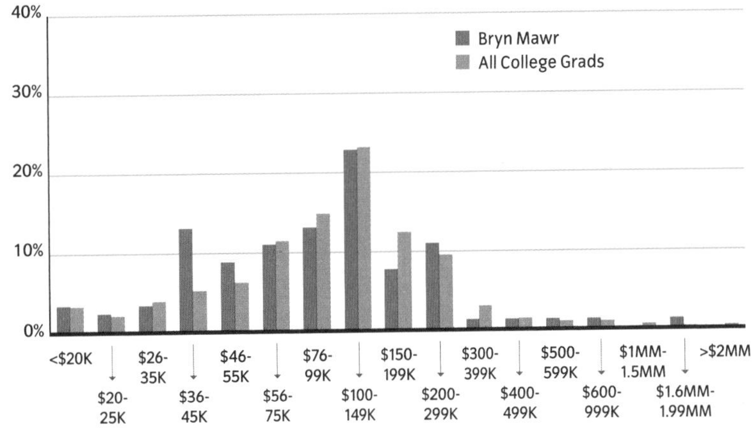

■ Bryn Mawr
■ All College Grads

40%
30%
20%
10%
0%

<$20K, $20-25K, $26-35K, $36-45K, $46-55K, $56-75K, $76-99K, $100-149K, $150-199K, $200-299K, $300-399K, $400-499K, $500-599K, $600-999K, $1MM-1.5MM, $1.6MM-1.99MM, >$2MM

Current Selectivity & Demand Analysis for Bryn Mawr College

Attribute	% Accepted	% Accepted Who Enroll	Freshman Retention Rate	Graduation Rate	Demand Index	Reputation Index
Score	46.0%	33.0%	93.0%	87.0%	6.47	0.72
Rank	96	83	73	60	120	82

Where are the Graduates of Bryn Mawr College on the Political Spectrum?

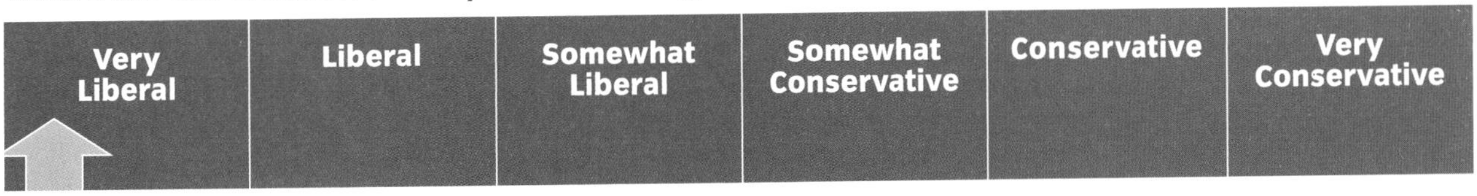

Very Liberal	Liberal	Somewhat Liberal	Somewhat Conservative	Conservative	Very Conservative
⇧					

Bucknell University

Location: Lewisburg, PA
Campus Setting: Town: Distant
Total Expenses: $57,140
Estimated Average Discount: $28,709 (50%)
Estimated Net Price: $28,431

Type of Institution: Liberal Arts College
Number of Undergraduates: 3,508
SAT Score: Reading: 590–680, Math: 630–720
Student/Faculty Ratio: 10 to 1
Transfer Out Rate: 2%

Rank Among 53 Liberal Arts Colleges	**16**
Overall Rank Among 177 *Alumni Factor* Schools	**23**

Overview

A liberal arts college with a university moniker, Bucknell aspires to offer a broad liberal arts education coupled with solid professional development. Based on graduate ratings and their real-world performance, it appears Bucknell is achieving its goal: it is ranked an impressive 16th overall among liberal arts colleges. Bucknell provides solid intellectual depth within a close community where Friendship (ranked 12th) and Social Development (11th) are among the highest of any college we measured. On the practical side, and a testament to their blend of liberal arts and university breadth, Bucknell ranks 6th in providing Immediate Job Opportunities to graduates – and is in the Top 30 in that measure among all 177 schools.

Despite a reputation for being a "safety school for Ivy League aspirers," Bucknell produces grads who achieve the enviable triad of financial success, deep friendships and overall happiness. Prospective students would be smart to radically reconsider how Bucknell fits into their plans, given the top-notch actual outcomes experienced by its grads. Bucknell is in the sterling company of only 21 schools to be ranked in the top third in at least 6 of the 7 major factors we measure. Only three Ivy League schools are ranked higher than Bucknell overall: Yale, Princeton and Dartmouth. Bucknell grads have long touted the unique magic of their alma mater in Lewisburg. We now understand why.

Notable Alumni

CBS CEO Les Moonves; Baron Funds founder Ronald Baron; and The Home Depot co-founder Ken Langone.

The Alumni Factor Rankings Summary

Attribute	Liberal Arts Rank	Overall Rank
College Experience	**17**	**29**
Intellectual Development	48	106
Social Development	11	16
Spiritual Development	40	72
Friendship Development	12	12
Preparation for Career Success	18	36
Immediate Job Opportunities	6	30
Overall Assessment	**34**	**84**
Would Personally Choose Again	11	22
Would Recommend to Student	36	88
Value for the Money	45	135
Financial Success	**15**	**36**
Income per Household	11	27
% Households with Income >$150K	6	11
Household Net Worth	22	60
% Households Net Worth >$1MM	27	64
Overall Happiness	**18**	**34**
Alumni Giving	**34**	**41**
Graduation Rate	**12**	**29**
Overall Rank	**16**	**23**

Other Key Alumni Outcomes

7.8% Are college professors
17.1% Teach at any level
55.8% Have post-graduate degrees
55.7% Live in dual-income homes
96.1% Are currently employed

See pages 134–135 for detailed explanations and definitions.

Alumni Activities During College

39.0% Community Service
33.7% Intramural Sports
18.0% Internships
18.1% Media Programs
21.9% Music Programs
18.5% Part-Time Jobs

Prepared Me for Career Success (% Strongly Agree)	Was A Good Value for the Money (% Strongly Agree)	Percent of Alumni Worth +$1MM
Bucknell 35.8%; All College Grads 31.9%	Bucknell 30.2%; All College Grads 46.1%	Bucknell 16.7%; All College Grads 14.6%

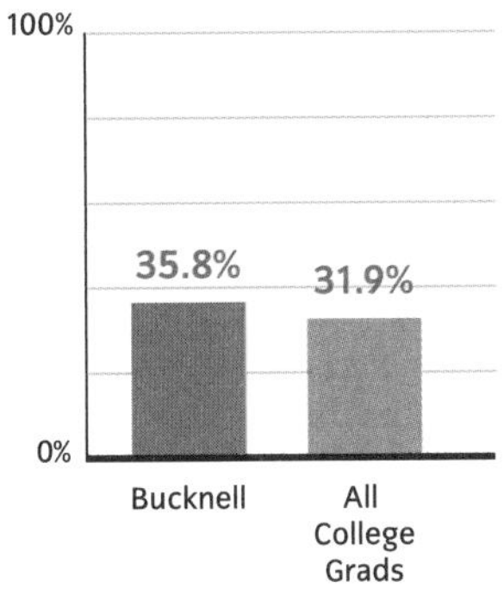

Alumni Employment

% Other 6.7%
% Independent/Entrepreneur 6.8%
% With Large Org. 25.4%
% With Medium Org. 17.6%
% With Small Org. 22.4%
% With Govt. 4.0%
% Any Level Teaching 17.1%

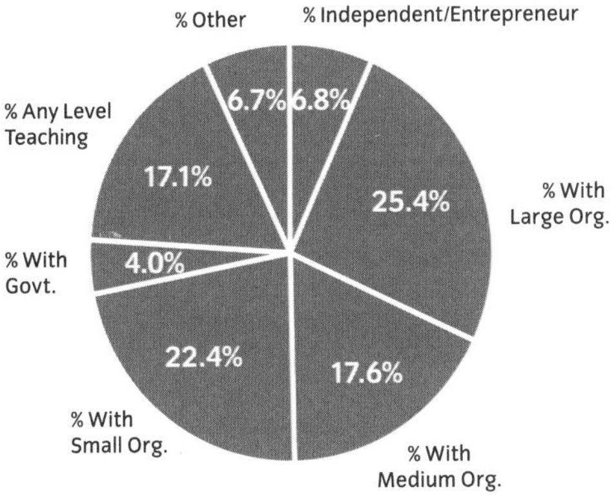

Income Distribution of Graduates

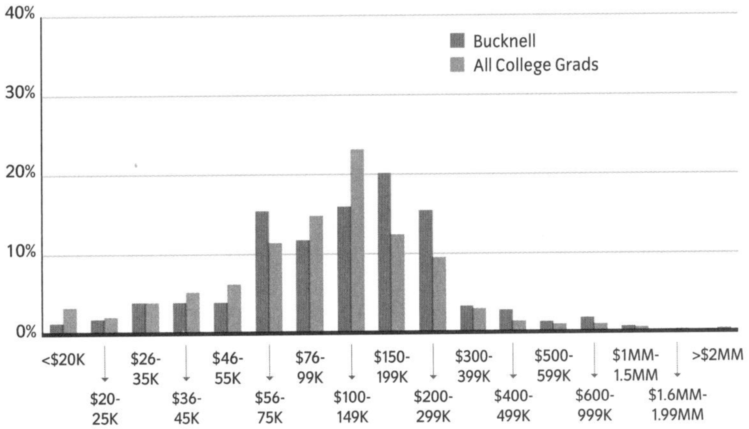

Bucknell / All College Grads

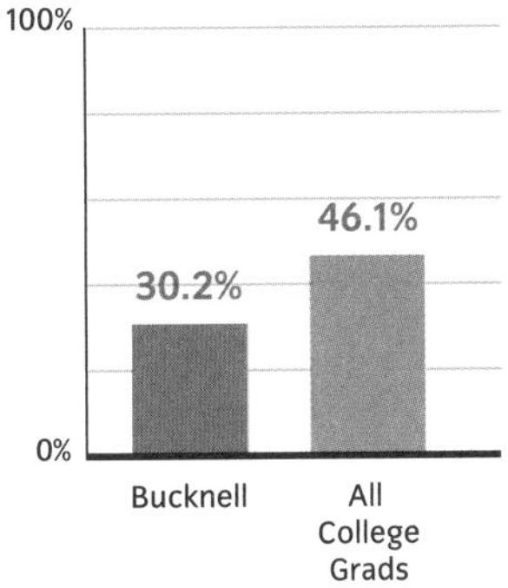

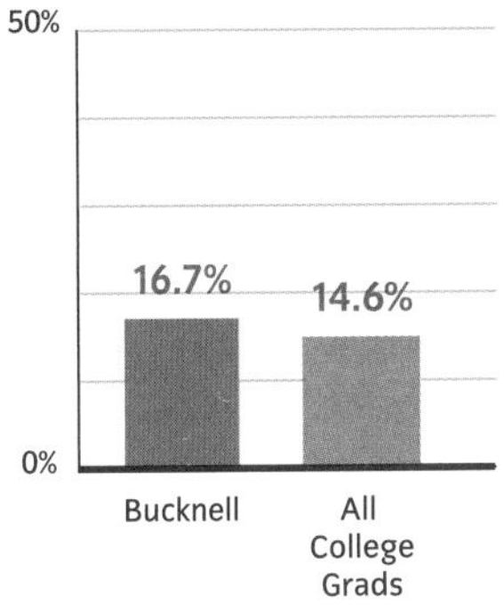

0% 10% 20% 30% 40%

<$20K, $20-25K, $26-35K, $36-45K, $46-55K, $56-75K, $76-99K, $100-149K, $150-199K, $200-299K, $300-399K, $400-499K, $500-599K, $600-999K, $1MM-1.5MM, $1.6MM-1.99MM, >$2MM

Current Selectivity & Demand Analysis for Bucknell University

Attribute	% Accepted	% Accepted Who Enroll	Freshman Retention Rate	Graduation Rate	Demand Index	Reputation Index
Score	28.0%	42.0%	94.0%	92.0%	8.67	1.50
Rank	46	33	58	29	91	38

Where are the Graduates of Bucknell University on the Political Spectrum?

Very Liberal	Liberal	Somewhat Liberal	Somewhat Conservative	Conservative	Very Conservative
			⇧		

California Institute of Technology

Location: Pasadena, CA
Campus Setting: City: Midsize
Total Expenses: $54,090
Estimated Average Discount: $28,708 (53%)
Estimated Net Price: $25,382

Type of Institution: National University
Number of Undergraduates: 967
SAT Score: Reading: 700–790, Math: 760–800
Student/Faculty Ratio: 3 to 1
Transfer Out Rate: Not Reported

Rank Among 104 National Universities	**20**
Overall Rank Among 177 *Alumni Factor* Schools	**41**

Overview

With the highest SAT scores of any college, Caltech grads are sizzlingly smart and superbly successful. While they appropriately give very high marks for Intellectual Development (ranked 4th), they do not rate their Social Development with such distinction (unless pulling off elaborately conceived technical pranks is considered "social development.") The Caltech undergraduate experience is unlike any other in the world – ranked 10th in the College Experience – and graduates recognize it. They also recognize that it is not for everyone – hence the 94th spot in Would Recommend.

Caltech graduates are undeniably brilliant and highly successful. With every Ultimate Outcome ranked in the Top 25 (10th overall in Ultimate Outcomes) and strong performance in all Financial Success measures (where it ranks 20th), Caltech grads are in high demand. The purity of Caltech's mission as "the world's best playground for math, science and engineering" fosters a close community and deep friendships (ranked an amazing 3rd). It is quite rare for technical schools to develop such deep friendships; Caltech and Harvey Mudd are the notable exceptions. As you would expect, Caltech compares quite well to its eleven peer technical schools in the Top 177, ranking 1st in Intellectual Development. Unlike many other schools, famous Caltech alumni tend to collect Nobel Prizes and have theorems and algorithms named after them. At the pinnacle of the technological elite, Caltech grads are at the forefront of redefining our future. Consider your future in capable hands.

Notable Alumni

Charlie Munger, Vice Chairman of Berkshire Hathaway; William Shockley, father of Silicon Valley; and C. Gordon Fullerton, astronaut.

The Alumni Factor Rankings Summary

Attribute	University Rank	Overall Rank
College Experience	**10**	**34**
Intellectual Development	4	25
Social Development	103	176
Spiritual Development	13	60
Friendship Development	3	24
Preparation for Career Success	3	11
Immediate Job Opportunities	3	6
Overall Assessment	**59**	**112**
Would Personally Choose Again	81	144
Would Recommend to Student	94	163
Value for the Money	10	17
Financial Success	**20**	**38**
Income per Household	20	37
% Households with Income >$150K	37	63
Household Net Worth	20	40
% Households Net Worth >$1MM	12	24
Overall Happiness	**71**	**123**
Alumni Giving	**10**	**49**
Graduation Rate	**24**	**39**
Overall Rank	**20**	**41**

Other Key Alumni Outcomes

12.0% Are college professors
12.0% Teach at any level
61.1% Have post-graduate degrees
41.7% Live in dual-income homes
93.5% Are currently employed

See pages 134–135 for detailed explanations and definitions.

Alumni Activities During College

20.8% Community Service
41.5% Intramural Sports
29.2% Internships
33.0% Media Programs
35.9% Music Programs
21.7% Part-Time Jobs

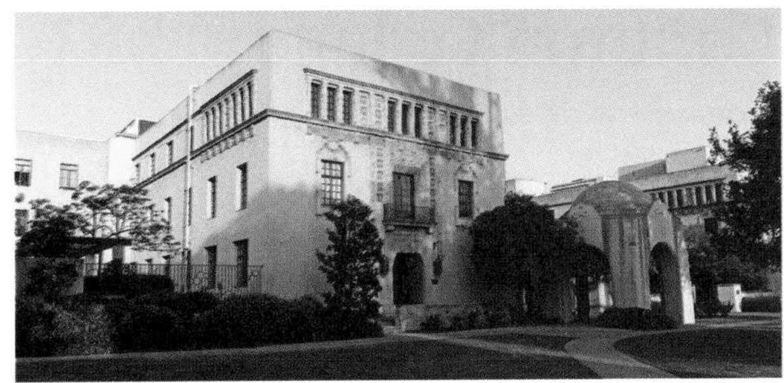

Prepared Me for Career Success % Strongly Agree	Was A Good Value for the Money % Strongly Agree	Percent of Alumni Worth >$1MM

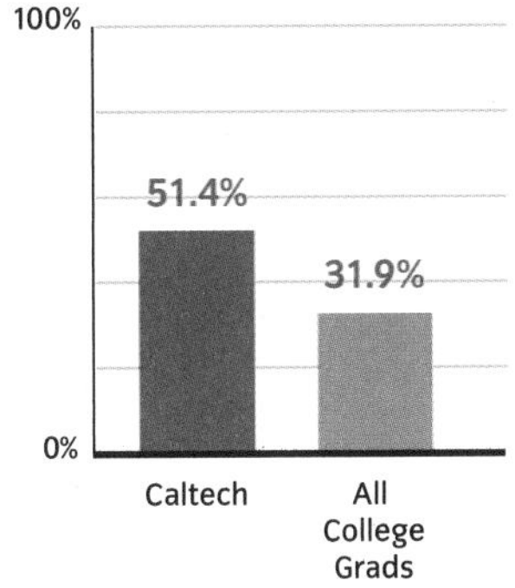
100%
51.4%
31.9%
0%
Caltech
All College Grads

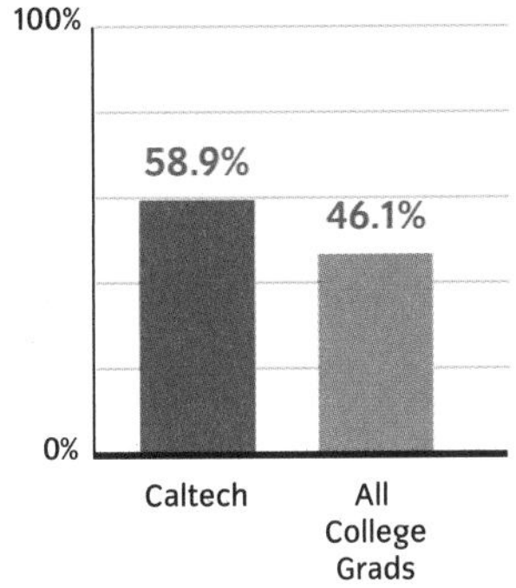
100%
58.9%
46.1%
0%
Caltech
All College Grads

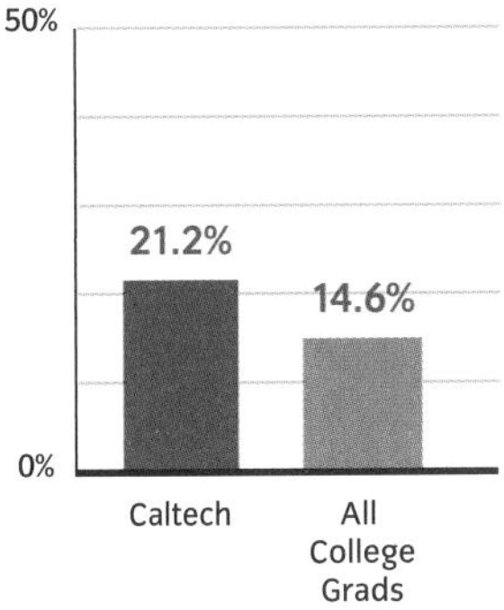
50%
21.2%
14.6%
0%
Caltech
All College Grads

Alumni Employment

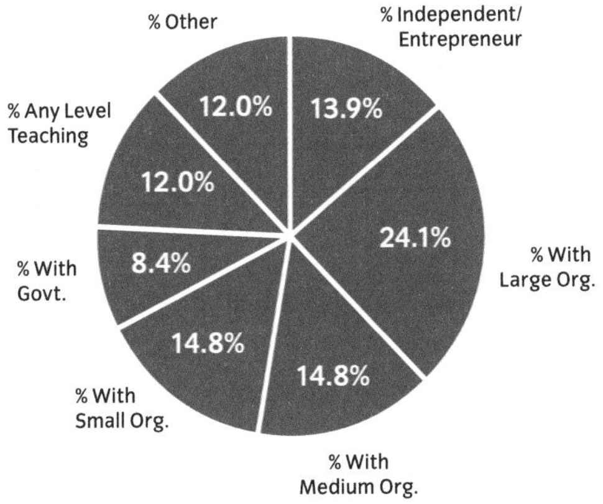
% Other
12.0%
% Independent/ Entrepreneur
13.9%
% With Large Org.
24.1%
% With Medium Org.
14.8%
% With Small Org.
14.8%
% With Govt.
8.4%
% Any Level Teaching
12.0%

Income Distribution of Graduates

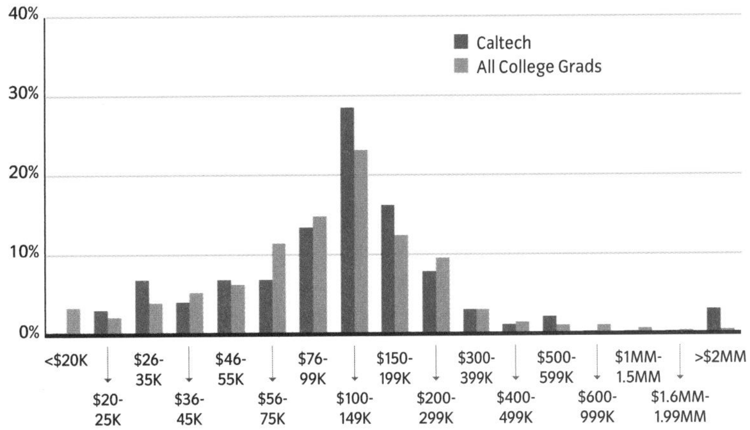
40%
30%
20%
10%
0%
Caltech
All College Grads
<$20K
$20-25K
$26-35K
$36-45K
$46-55K
$56-75K
$76-99K
$100-149K
$150-199K
$200-299K
$300-399K
$400-499K
$500-599K
$600-999K
$1MM-1.5MM
$1.6MM-1.99MM
>$2MM

Current Selectivity & Demand Analysis for California Institute of Technology

Attribute	% Accepted	% Accepted Who Enroll	Freshman Retention Rate	Graduation Rate	Demand Index	Reputation Index
Score	13.0%	37.0%	98.0%	90.0%	21.41	2.85
Rank	13	60	4	39	2	16

Where are the Graduates of California Institute of Technology on the Political Spectrum?

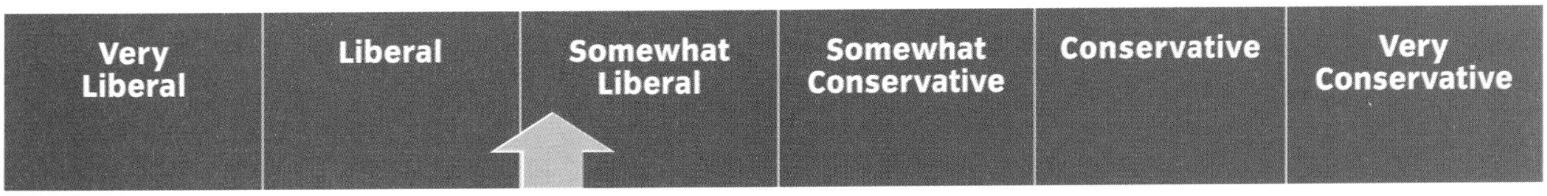
Very Liberal
Liberal
Somewhat Liberal
Somewhat Conservative
Conservative
Very Conservative

See pages 134–135 for detailed explanations and definitions.

Carleton College

Location: Northfield, MN
Campus Setting: Town: Distant
Total Expenses: $56,340
Estimated Average Discount: $27,522 (49%)
Estimated Net Price: $28,818

Type of Institution: Liberal Arts College
Number of Undergraduates: 2,020
SAT Score: Reading: 660–750, Math: 660–760
Student/Faculty Ratio: 9 to 1
Transfer Out Rate: Not Reported

Rank Among 53 Liberal Arts Colleges	**19**
Overall Rank Among 177 *Alumni Factor* Schools	**36**

Overview

The top liberal arts college in the country in Alumni Giving, Carleton produces grads who thoroughly embrace their school in its entirety. Intense and independent, Carleton grads are among the very few graduates of expensive liberal arts colleges who give their school high marks in Value for the Money (ranked 19th). That speaks volumes given Carleton's $50,000 plus annual price tag.

The strongest correlates to Alumni Giving across all colleges are Intellectual Development and the creation of deep friendships. Carleton is a perfect case in point. Carleton is ranked 10th in Intellectual Development; 19th in Friendship Development; and 16th in the Ultimate Outcome of Friendships & Intellectual Capability – all strong predictors of enduring alumni loyalty. Therefore, their 2nd rank in Alumni Giving among the Top 177 is not at all surprising.

There is something about the cold Minnesota air and progressive friendliness of the people that makes Carleton such a special place. Carleton has continually produced novelists, writers, academics and politicians of note. Grads are both happy with their lives (13th in Overall Happiness among liberal arts colleges) and are the 11th most liberal – an unusual combination in that happiness tends to skew a bit conservatively among college alumni. Carleton, once again, defies the odds.

Notable Alumni

Garrick Utley, former host of Meet the Press; Mary-Claire King, human geneticist, Kai Bird; Jonathan Capehart and T. J. Stiles, Pulitzer Prize winners; and Piotr Gajewski, artistic director for the National Philharmonic Orchestra.

The Alumni Factor Rankings Summary

Attribute	Liberal Arts Rank	Overall Rank
College Experience	**22**	**35**
Intellectual Development	10	11
Social Development	36	66
Spiritual Development	16	36
Friendship Development	19	21
Preparation for Career Success	12	21
Immediate Job Opportunities	44	156
Overall Assessment	**13**	**31**
Would Personally Choose Again	12	24
Would Recommend to Student	14	42
Value for the Money	19	45
Financial Success	**37**	**115**
Income per Household	44	141
% Households with Income >$150K	39	122
Household Net Worth	33	97
% Households Net Worth >$1MM	35	92
Overall Happiness	**13**	**22**
Alumni Giving	**1**	**2**
Graduation Rate	**5**	**16**
Overall Rank	**19**	**36**

Other Key Alumni Outcomes

7.7%	Are college professors
12.0%	Teach at any level
67.8%	Have post-graduate degrees
55.0%	Live in dual-income homes
88.1%	Are currently employed

See pages 134–135 for detailed explanations and definitions.

Alumni Activities During College

36.4% Community Service
52.1% Intramural Sports
14.9% Internships
41.3% Media Programs
37.2% Music Programs
19.8% Part-Time Jobs

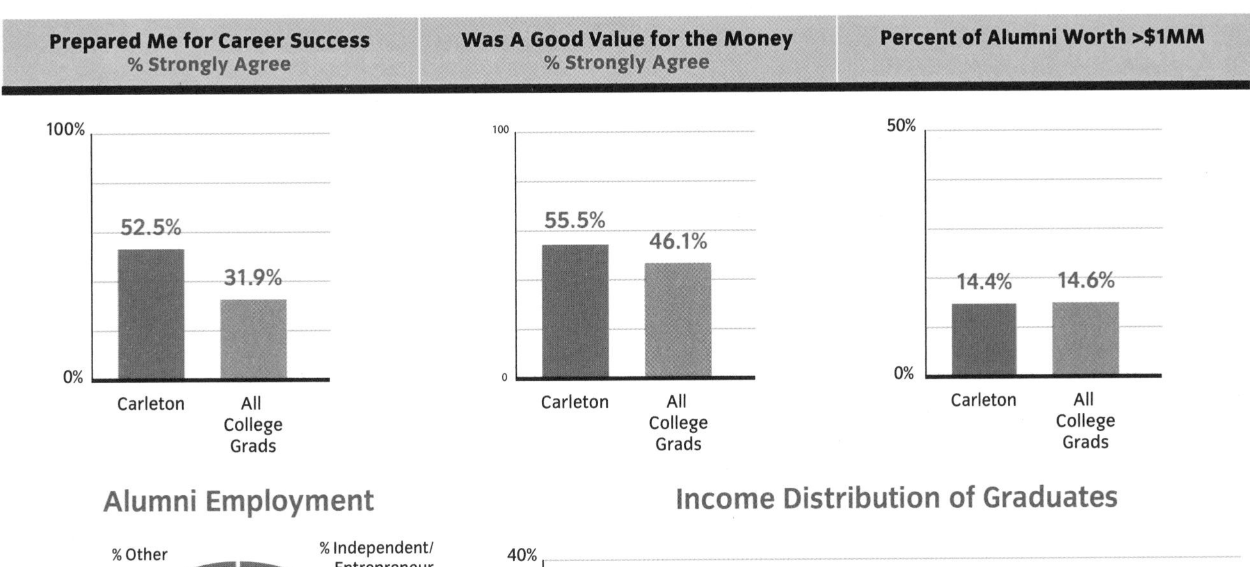

Alumni Employment

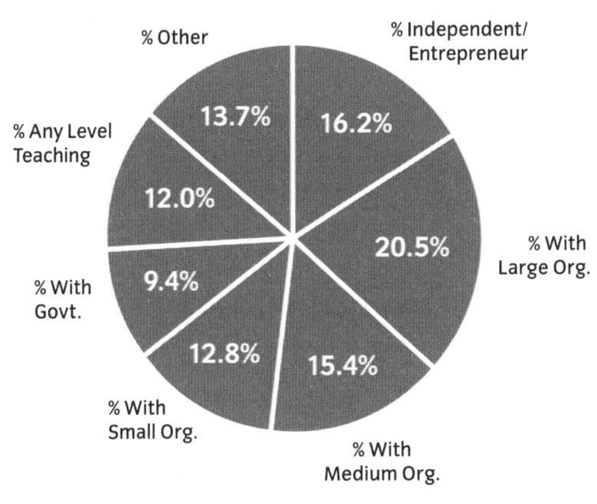

Income Distribution of Graduates

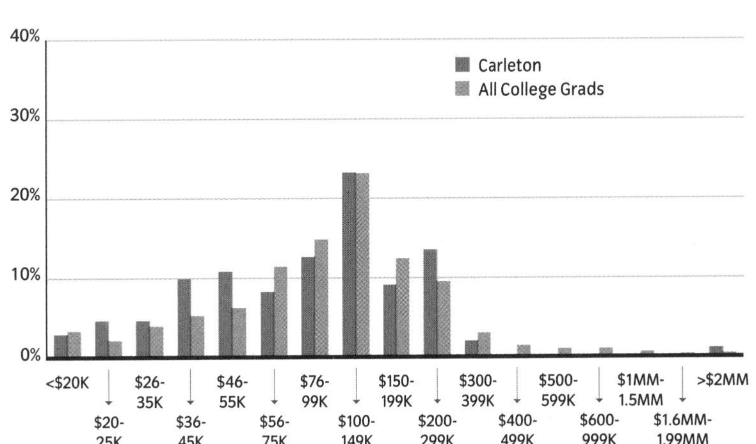

Current Selectivity & Demand Analysis for Carleton College

Attribute	% Accepted	% Accepted Who Enroll	Freshman Retention Rate	Graduation Rate	Demand Index	Reputation Index
Score	31.0%	34.0%	98.0%	93.0%	9.61	1.10
Rank	55	76	4	16	73	56

Where are the Graduates of Carleton College on the Political Spectrum?

Very Liberal	Liberal	Somewhat Liberal	Somewhat Conservative	Conservative	Very Conservative
↑					

See pages 134–135 for detailed explanations and definitions.

Carnegie Mellon University

Location: Pittsburgh, PA
Campus Setting: City: Large
Total Expenses: $57,520
Estimated Average Discount: $25,466 (44%)
Estimated Net Price: $32,054

Type of Institution: National University
Number of Undergraduates: 5,830
SAT Score: Reading: 630–730, Math: 680–780
Student/Faculty Ratio: 12 to 1
Transfer Out Rate: Not Reported

Rank Among 104 National Universities	**53**
Overall Rank Among 177 *Alumni Factor* Schools	**116**

Overview

Graduates of this stone-cold-serious science, engineering and research university are smart, hard-working pragmatists who are successful in a broad variety of fields – technical and non-technical. However, you might be surprised to know that this "technical" school has also produced some of America's favorite entertainment stars. Because Carnegie Mellon was multicultural well before it was fashionable, its graduates are among the most diverse of the Top 177 colleges – and because the school is refreshingly free of strong political ideology, CMU grads fall in the middle of the political spectrum, with just a slight tilt to the left.

CMU grads' strongest Ultimate Outcome is the combination of Financial Success & Intellectual Capability, where it ranks 32nd among national universities. Grads rank a strong 25th in Income per Household; 43rd in high-income grads and 38th in high net worth (millionaire) households. Financial Success is a clear outcome for undergraduates, and CMU alums excel in virtually all fields. They also perfectly illustrate the brilliant combination of art and science that defines the CMU experience.

Notable Alumni

Former Bank of America chairman David Coulter; Chairman & CEO of Zip Car Scott Griffith; former GM Chairman Charles Wilson; science luminary John Forbes Nash; astronaut Edgar Mitchell; and entertainment stars Stephen Schwartz, Steven Bochco, Ted Danson and Jack Klugman.

The Alumni Factor Rankings Summary

Attribute	University Rank	Overall Rank
College Experience	**55**	**123**
Intellectual Development	24	67
Social Development	98	171
Spiritual Development	93	165
Friendship Development	27	83
Preparation for Career Success	49	100
Immediate Job Opportunities	63	102
Overall Assessment	**81**	**146**
Would Personally Choose Again	64	117
Would Recommend to Student	83	152
Value for the Money	85	152
Financial Success	**40**	**71**
Income per Household	25	43
% Households with Income >$150K	43	75
Household Net Worth	62	107
% Households Net Worth >$1MM	38	69
Overall Happiness	**88**	**142**
Alumni Giving	**32**	**90**
Graduation Rate	**34**	**67**
Overall Rank	**53**	**116**

Other Key Alumni Outcomes

5.2% Are college professors
9.9% Teach at any level
51.0% Have post-graduate degrees
45.0% Live in dual-income homes
91.7% Are currently employed

See pages 134–135 for detailed explanations and definitions.

Alumni Activities During College

26.8% Community Service
30.0% Intramural Sports
34.2% Internships
22.6% Media Programs
21.5% Music Programs
29.5% Part-Time Jobs

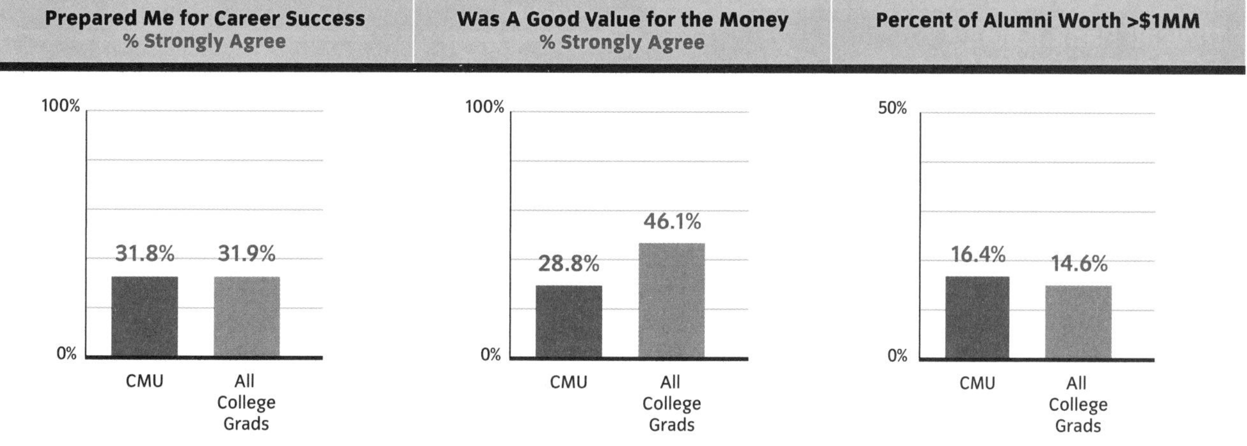

Alumni Employment

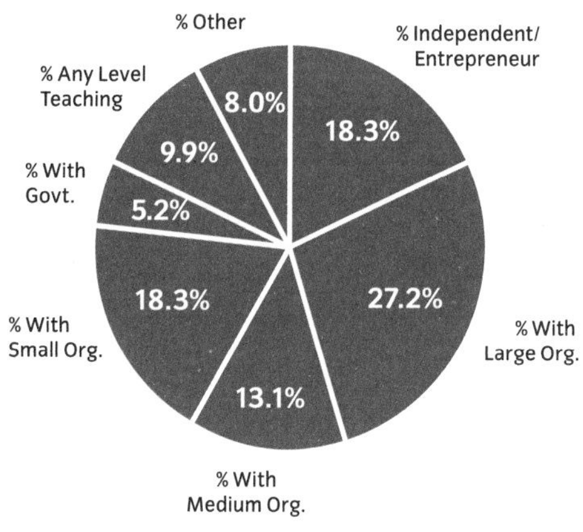

Income Distribution of Graduates

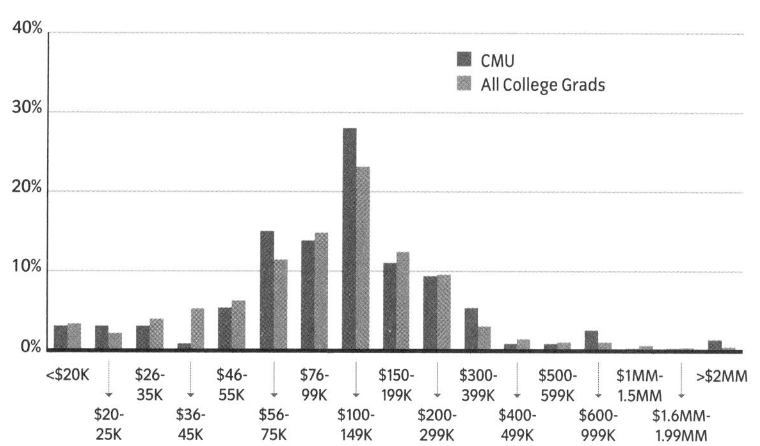

Current Selectivity & Demand Analysis for Carnegie Mellon University

Attribute	% Accepted	% Accepted Who Enroll	Freshman Retention Rate	Graduation Rate	Demand Index	Reputation Index
Score	30.0%	29.0%	96.0%	86.0%	11.51	0.97
Rank	51	107	27	67	49	62

Where are the Graduates of Carnegie Mellon University on the Political Spectrum?

Very Liberal	Liberal	Somewhat Liberal	Somewhat Conservative	Conservative	Very Conservative
		↑			

See pages 134–135 for detailed explanations and definitions.

Case Western Reserve University

Location: Cleveland, OH
Campus Setting: City: Large
Total Expenses: $54,133
Estimated Average Discount: $26,964 (50%)
Estimated Net Price: $27,169

Type of Institution: National University
Number of Undergraduates: 4,227
SAT Score: Reading: 590–700, Math: 650–740
Student/Faculty Ratio: 9 to 1
Transfer Out Rate: Not Reported

Rank Among 104 National Universities	**87**
Overall Rank Among 177 *Alumni Factor* Schools	**158**

Overview

Case graduates have the 39th highest reported SAT scores in the country, yet have just two attribute rankings – Intellectual Development (ranked 41st) and Overall Happiness (29th) – that are comparable to the SAT ranking. While Case certainly has the academic chops and respectability to earn a spot in the Top 177, its College Experience (71st) and its Overall Assessment by grads (103rd) is relatively low. This, of course, is among undergraduates, and we suspect it might be quite different for graduate students.

Like some other undergraduate technical schools, Case is working to find its niche within the contours of today's college landscape. Excruciatingly rigorous in its coursework, Case prepares its grads for Career Success (58th) and provides ample Immediate Job Opportunities (66th). Yet, among the twelve technical schools, Case is ranked near the bottom in Preparation for Career Success and Friendship Development, and is last in Would Recommend to a Prospective Student. On the positive side, Case ranks 4th among technical schools in Overall Happiness. Drawbacks aside, there is no doubt a CWRU diploma is valuable.

Notable Alumni

Henry Dow, founder of Dow Chemical; Craig Newmark, founder of Craigslist; and Barry Meyer, CEO of Warner Bros.

The Alumni Factor Rankings Summary

Attribute	University Rank	Overall Rank
College Experience	**71**	**141**
Intellectual Development	41	99
Social Development	96	168
Spiritual Development	66	138
Friendship Development	63	133
Preparation for Career Success	58	117
Immediate Job Opportunities	66	107
Overall Assessment	**103**	**175**
Would Personally Choose Again	97	165
Would Recommend to Student	104	177
Value for the Money	94	165
Financial Success	**89**	**150**
Income per Household	83	125
% Households with Income >$150K	81	135
Household Net Worth	96	163
% Households Net Worth >$1MM	95	158
Overall Happiness	**29**	**57**
Alumni Giving	**28**	**81**
Graduation Rate	**44**	**91**
Overall Rank	**87**	**158**

Other Key Alumni Outcomes

6.3% Are college professors
14.1% Teach at any level
70.6% Have post-graduate degrees
56.3% Live in dual-income homes
94.3% Are currently employed

See pages 134–135 for detailed explanations and definitions.

Alumni Activities During College

27.8% Community Service
29.4% Intramural Sports
20.6% Internships
19.9% Media Programs
31.6% Music Programs
32.5% Part-Time Jobs

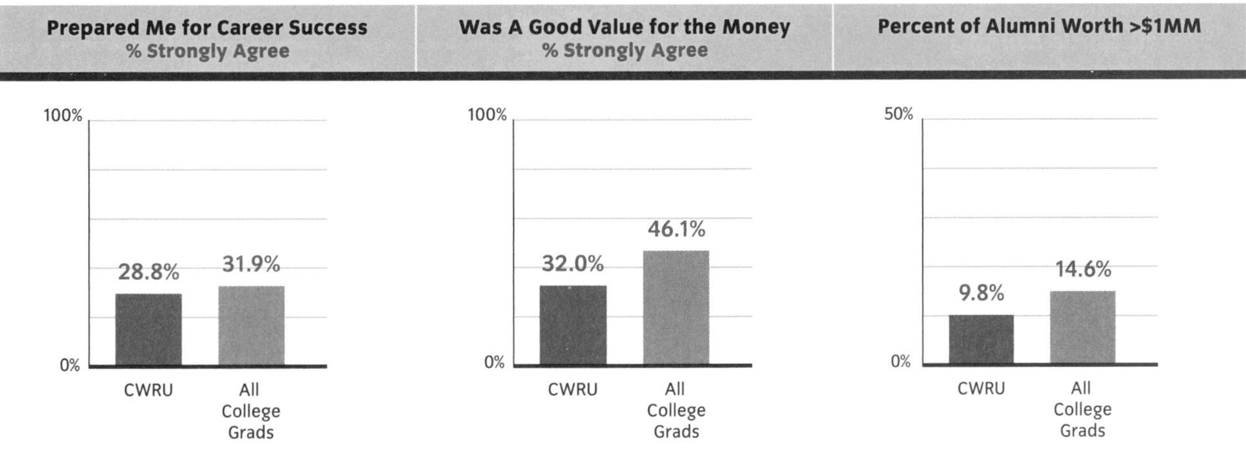

Alumni Employment

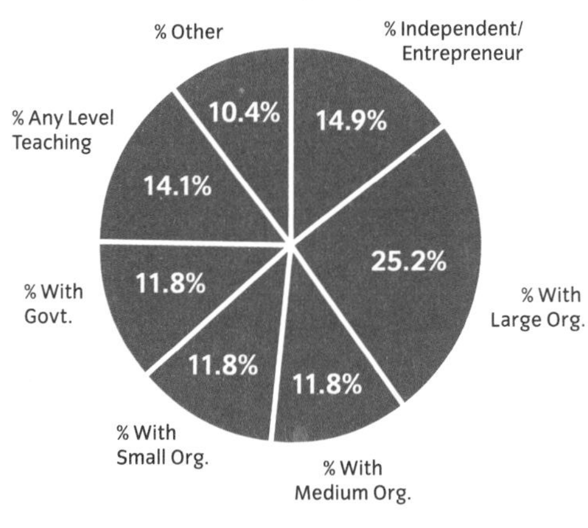

Income Distribution of Graduates

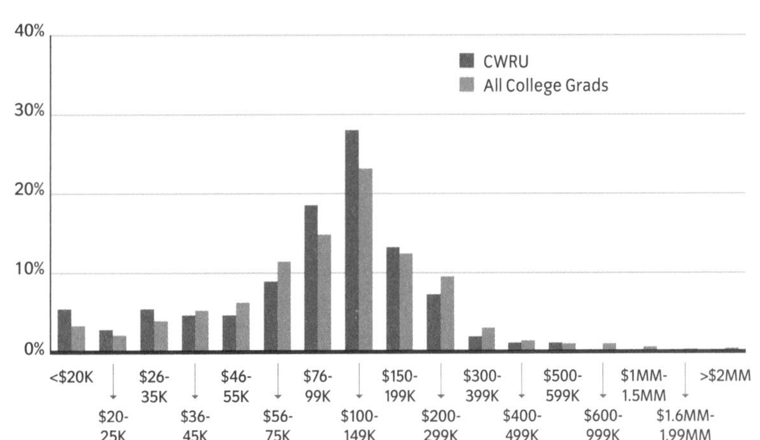

Current Selectivity & Demand Analysis for Case Western Reserve University

Attribute	% Accepted	% Accepted Who Enroll	Freshman Retention Rate	Graduation Rate	Demand Index	Reputation Index
Score	51.0%	13.0%	92.0%	82.0%	15.02	0.25
Rank	104	176	86	91	20	172

Where are the Graduates of Case Western Reserve University on the Political Spectrum?

Very Liberal	Liberal	Somewhat Liberal	Somewhat Conservative	Conservative	Very Conservative

See pages 134–135 for detailed explanations and definitions.

Centre College

Location: Danville, KY
Campus Setting: Town: Distant
Total Expenses: $45,100
Estimated Average Discount: $22,638 (50%)
Estimated Net Price: $22,462

Type of Institution: Liberal Arts College
Number of Undergraduates: 1,242
SAT Score: Reading: 560–690, Math: 560–670
Student/Faculty Ratio: 11 to 1
Transfer Out Rate: Not Reported

Rank Among 53 Liberal Arts Colleges	**11**
Overall Rank Among 177 *Alumni Factor* Schools	**18**

Overview

Centre College is likely one of the best colleges in the US of which you have never heard. One of only four schools in the country to rank in the Top 15 across all College Experience attributes and Overall Assessment attributes, Centre grads simply can't glow enough about their tiny academic gem in the geographic center of Kentucky (from which it derives its name). Centre grads are the happiest group of graduates in the country – not just among liberal arts colleges, but among all 177 colleges and universities we've measured. Centre also ranks an impressive 2nd in Alumni Giving among liberal arts colleges and 3rd among all colleges and universities. It has a strong showing at 6th on the Ultimate Outcome of Happiness & Friendship.

Centre mostly competes with other top Southern liberal arts colleges (Davidson, Furman, Richmond, Sewanee and Washington & Lee) and fares quite well in comparison across most of the key attributes. Centre ranks 1st in the Overall Assessment among the Southern liberal arts leaders. The heavy percent of Centre grads who become teachers suppresses its Financial Success rating, yet Centre still ranks 39th.

There truly is something special going on in the "Centre" of Kentucky – one of the finest liberal arts colleges in the country calls it home.

Notable Alumni

Former US chief justice Frederick Vinson, Adlai Stevenson and Bain Capital Managing Director Mark Nunnelly.

The Alumni Factor Rankings Summary

Attribute	Liberal Arts Rank	Overall Rank
College Experience	**5**	**5**
Intellectual Development	3	3
Social Development	2	2
Spiritual Development	14	34
Friendship Development	11	11
Preparation for Career Success	3	3
Immediate Job Opportunities	12	56
Overall Assessment	**3**	**7**
Would Personally Choose Again	13	26
Would Recommend to Student	4	9
Value for the Money	3	8
Financial Success	**39**	**119**
Income per Household	39	136
% Households with Income >$150K	34	95
Household Net Worth	38	134
% Households Net Worth >$1MM	39	101
Overall Happiness	**1**	**1**
Alumni Giving	**2**	**3**
Graduation Rate	**32**	**67**
Overall Rank	**11**	**18**

Other Key Alumni Outcomes

10.9% Are college professors
18.6% Teach at any level
58.0% Have post-graduate degrees
57.4% Live in dual-income homes
94.3% Are currently employed

See pages 134–135 for detailed explanations and definitions.

Alumni Activities During College

47.1% Community Service
56.1% Intramural Sports
24.2% Internships
22.3% Media Programs
23.6% Music Programs
22.9% Part-Time Jobs

Prepared Me for Career Success % Strongly Agree	Was A Good Value for the Money % Strongly Agree	Percent of Alumni Worth >$1MM
Centre: 57.7% All College Grads: 31.9%	Centre: 64.7% All College Grads: 46.1%	Centre: 13.7% All College Grads: 14.6%

Alumni Employment

Category	%
% Independent/ Entrepreneur	11.5%
% With Large Org.	18.6%
% With Medium Org.	12.8%
% With Small Org.	16.7%
% With Govt.	14.1%
% Any Level Teaching	18.6%
% Other	7.7%

Income Distribution of Graduates

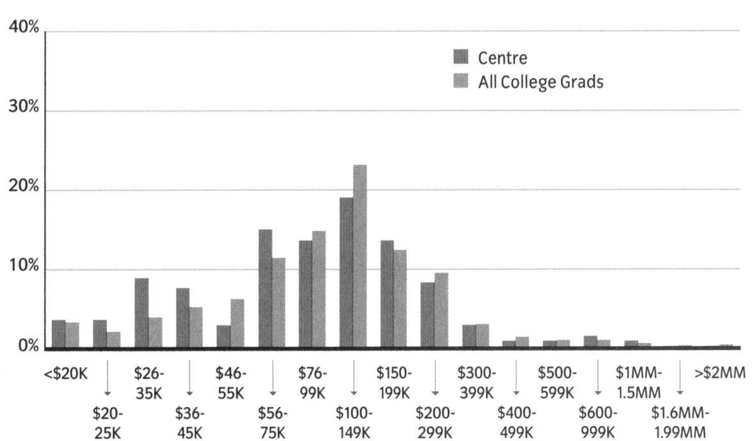

Current Selectivity & Demand Analysis for Centre College

Attribute	% Accepted	% Accepted Who Enroll	Freshman Retention Rate	Graduation Rate	Demand Index	Reputation Index
Score	71.0%	22.0%	92.0%	86.0%	6.45	0.31
Rank	155	149	86	67	121	166

Where are the Graduates of Centre College on the Political Spectrum?

Very Liberal	Liberal	Somewhat Liberal	Somewhat Conservative	Conservative	Very Conservative
				↑	

See pages 134–135 for detailed explanations and definitions.

Claremont McKenna College

Location: Claremont, CA
Campus Setting: Suburb: Large
Total Expenses: $57,865
Estimated Average Discount: $34,801 (60%)
Estimated Net Price: $23,064

Type of Institution: Liberal Arts College
Number of Undergraduates: 1,261
SAT Score: Reading: 630–720, Math: 670–760
Student/Faculty Ratio: 9 to 1
Transfer Out Rate: Not Reported

Overview

Often considered to be among the finest schools in the country (yet hardly a household name), Claremont McKenna College is one of only three schools in the country to achieve three #1 rankings (along with Princeton and West Point). It is ranked 1st in Financial Success and 5th in Ultimate Outcomes, driven by its 1st rankings in the Ultimate Outcomes of Happiness & Intellectual Development and Happiness & Friendships. CMC's uniquely strong programs in management, economics, government and public policy produce leaders throughout the world of business, politics, media, entertainment and a wide variety of other fields. Its 11th *Alumni Factor* ranking places it among the elite colleges in the US for graduate outcomes.

With Top 30 rankings in 19 of 26 attributes, and a centrist political environment, CMC delivers non-ideological excellence for its students, yielding smart, happy, successful and loyal graduates. CMC is a genuine surprise – an unabashed champion of commerce in the heart of California, and a global education leader whose graduates are among the most happy and successful of any college we measured.

Notable Alumni

Henry Kravis and George Roberts, two of three founders of blue chip investment firm KKR; Thomas Pritzker, Chairman of Hyatt Hotels; and Congressman David Dreier.

The Alumni Factor Rankings Summary

Attribute	Liberal Arts Rank	Overall Rank
College Experience	**31**	**55**
Intellectual Development	38	55
Social Development	26	44
Spiritual Development	52	132
Friendship Development	44	72
Preparation for Career Success	18	36
Immediate Job Opportunities	8	34
Overall Assessment	**32**	**81**
Would Personally Choose Again	31	87
Would Recommend to Student	43	126
Value for the Money	10	27
Financial Success	**1**	**2**
Income per Household	1	1
% Households with Income >$150K	1	2
Household Net Worth	2	4
% Households Net Worth >$1MM	5	10
Overall Happiness	**9**	**13**
Alumni Giving	**23**	**26**
Graduation Rate	**5**	**16**
Overall Rank	**6**	**11**

Other Key Alumni Outcomes

9.9% Are college professors
15.7% Teach at any level
66.3% Have post-graduate degrees
51.8% Live in dual-income homes
94.3% Are currently employed

See pages 134–135 for detailed explanations and definitions.

Alumni Activities During College

35.1% Community Service
41.2% Intramural Sports
28.9% Internships
37.0% Media Programs
8.7% Music Programs
29.9% Part-Time Jobs

Prepared Me for Career Success % Strongly Agree	Was A Good Value for the Money % Strongly Agree	Percent of Alumni Worth >$1MM
CMC 44.9%; All College Grads 31.9%	CMC 61.4%; All College Grads 46.1%	CMC 23.9%; All College Grads 14.6%

Alumni Employment

- % Independent/Entrepreneur: 24.1%
- % With Large Org.: 16.8%
- % With Medium Org.: 8.9%
- % With Small Org.: 13.1%
- % With Govt.: 8.9%
- % Any Level Teaching: 15.7%
- % Other: 12.5%

Income Distribution of Graduates

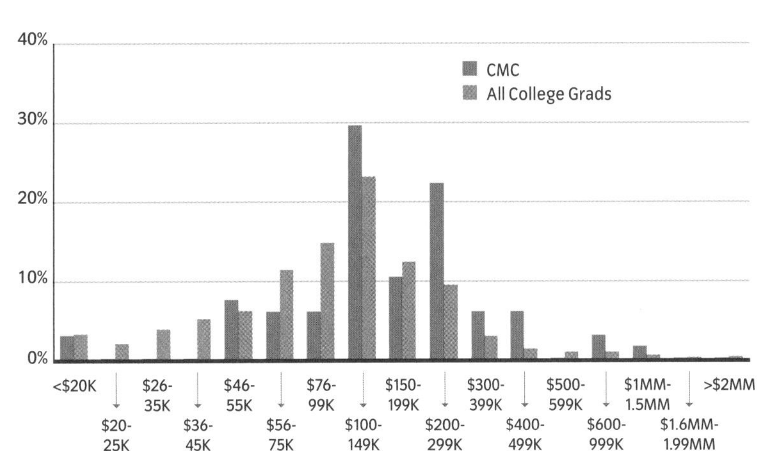

Current Selectivity & Demand Analysis for Claremont McKenna College

Attribute	% Accepted	% Accepted Who Enroll	Freshman Retention Rate	Graduation Rate	Demand Index	Reputation Index
Score	14.0%	49.0%	95.0%	93.0%	14.69	3.50
Rank	15	21	47	16	23	13

Where are the Graduates of Claremont McKenna College on the Political Spectrum?

Very Liberal	Liberal	Somewhat Liberal	Somewhat Conservative	Conservative	Very Conservative

Clark University

Location: Worcester, MA
Campus Setting: City: Midsize
Total Expenses: $46,200
Estimated Average Discount: $22,274 (48%)
Estimated Net Price: $23,926

Type of Institution: National University
Number of Undergraduates: 2,317
SAT Score: Reading: 540–660, Math: 530–640
Student/Faculty Ratio: 10 to 1
Transfer Out Rate: Not Reported

Rank Among 104 National Universities	**71**
Overall Rank Among 177 *Alumni Factor* Schools	**138**

Overview

It is difficult to get noticed as a small liberal arts research university in the middle of Massachusetts, surrounded by some of the best colleges in the country. But Clark has been able to carve out its own unique position among the New England colleges, and so have its graduates. It will surprise most readers that Clark ranks 6th in its percent of graduates with a Net Worth over $1 million. It also does quite well in its percent of Households with High Income (ranked 46th) and Intellectual Development (20th).

Clark is a small university with an orientation toward discovery and practical application. Its graduates pursue diverse career paths ranging from psychologist and politician to banker, entrepreneur and film producer. Interestingly, it does not score as well as expected in Preparation for Career Success (97th) and Immediate Job Opportunities (104th). It has mostly Top 50 rankings across the Ultimate Outcomes – despite the fact that its relatively low Overall Happiness rank depresses outcomes that include it.

Clark University prepares its graduates to "make a meaningful difference in a world hungry for change." Many of its graduates are quite successfully engaged in that very task.

Notable Alumni

Hollywood mogul and Philadelphia Eagles owner Jeffrey Lurie; actor John Heard; and private equity investor Marc Lasry.

The Alumni Factor Rankings Summary

Attribute	University Rank	Overall Rank
College Experience	**63**	**132**
Intellectual Development	20	66
Social Development	47	106
Spiritual Development	45	111
Friendship Development	39	102
Preparation for Career Success	97	169
Immediate Job Opportunities	104	175
Overall Assessment	**78**	**142**
Would Personally Choose Again	66	120
Would Recommend to Student	77	140
Value for the Money	83	148
Financial Success	**39**	**70**
Income per Household	86	129
% Households with Income >$150K	46	80
Household Net Worth	39	69
% Households Net Worth >$1MM	6	11
Overall Happiness	**95**	**161**
Alumni Giving	**39**	**99**
Graduation Rate	**65**	**127**
Overall Rank	**71**	**138**

Other Key Alumni Outcomes

4.1% Are college professors
10.7% Teach at any level
54.4% Have post-graduate degrees
51.2% Live in dual-income homes
86.9% Are currently employed

See pages 134–135 for detailed explanations and definitions.

Alumni Activities During College

37.9% Community Service
25.0% Intramural Sports
31.5% Internships
29.9% Media Programs
9.7% Music Programs
37.9% Part-Time Jobs

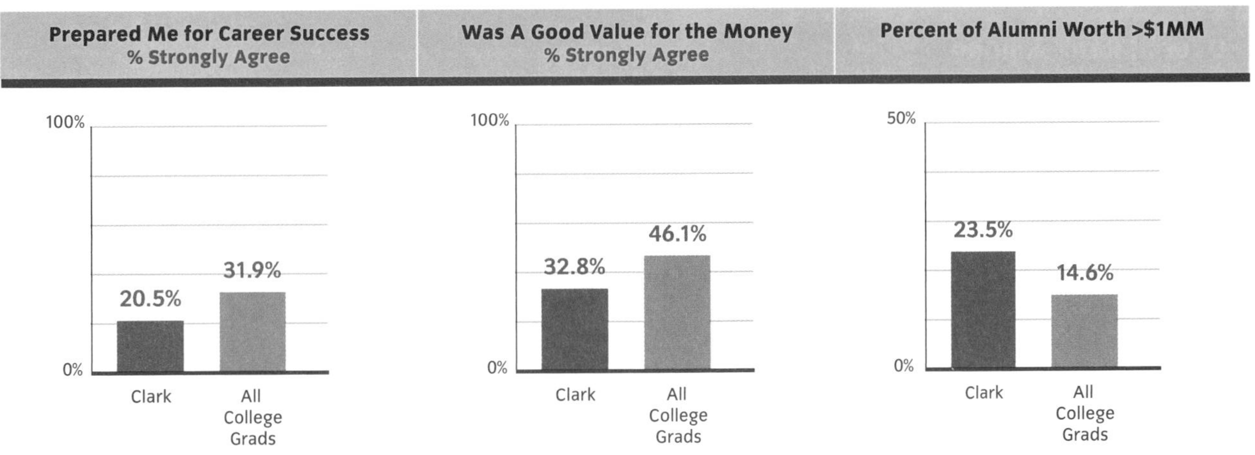

Alumni Employment

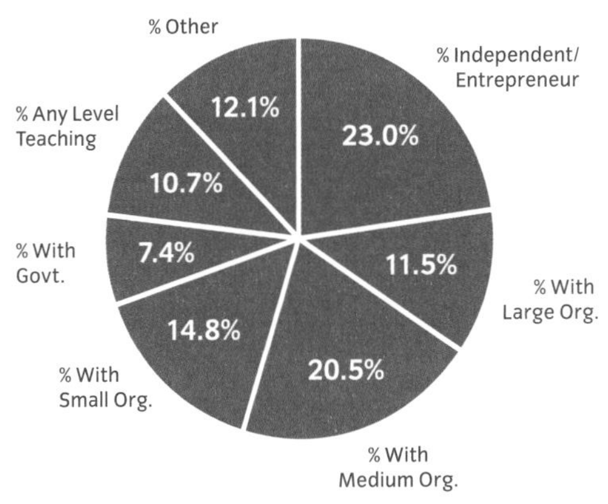

Income Distribution of Graduates

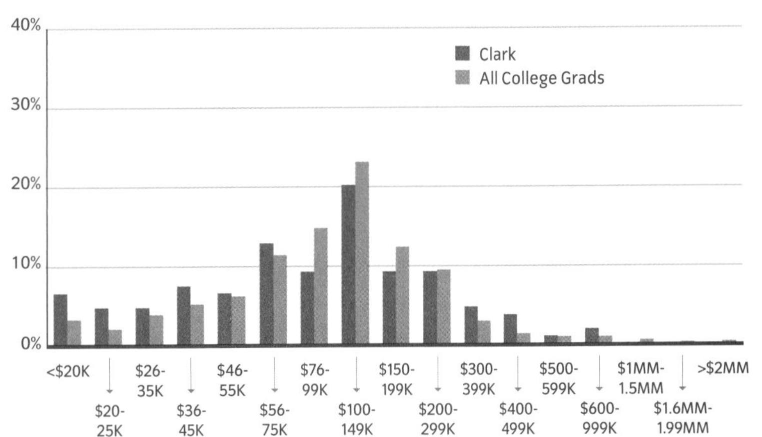

Current Selectivity & Demand Analysis for Clark University

Attribute	% Accepted	% Accepted Who Enroll	Freshman Retention Rate	Graduation Rate	Demand Index	Reputation Index
Score	68.0%	19.0%	90.0%	77.0%	7.56	0.28
Rank	145	167	113	127	107	170

Where are the Graduates of Clark University on the Political Spectrum?

Very Liberal	Liberal	Somewhat Liberal	Somewhat Conservative	Conservative	Very Conservative

See pages 134–135 for detailed explanations and definitions.

Clemson University

Location: Clemson, SC
Campus Setting: Town: Distant
Total Expenses: $26,626
Estimated Average Discount: $9,929 (37%)
Estimated Net Price: $16,697

Type of Institution: National University
Number of Undergraduates: 15,459
SAT Score: Reading: 550–650, Math: 590–680
Student/Faculty Ratio: 16 to 1
Transfer Out Rate: 8%

Rank Among 104 National Universities	**38**
Overall Rank Among 177 *Alumni Factor* Schools	**84**

Overview

Clemson is one of the finest public research universities in the country and a source of intense "Tiger Pride" that creates a lasting bond between the college, its students and alumni. Clemson is one of the rare universities that is able to have more than 10,000 undergraduates and still have high (Top 30) Alumni Giving rates. In fact, only 8 universities in the country are able to make that claim, and Clemson is 6th among them.

Clemson's strongest marks are in the College Experience (ranked 46th) and in the Overall Assessment by its graduates (24th). It ranks 8th among all national universities in alums' willingness to recommend it, and is 26th in Value for the Money and 46th in willingness to choose it again. Clemson graduates are quite happy (38th overall) and do well across the Ultimate Outcomes, ranking 49th on the pair of Financial Success & Happiness. Clemson graduates rank quite high in Financial Success (50th), driven by a 26th rank in the percentage of graduate households worth more than $1 million.

Clemson graduates are successful, happy and loyal alumni who have a lifelong bond to the Tigers. There is definitely life after "Death Valley" for Clemson graduates – perhaps less so for their competitors – regardless of the playing field.

Notable Alumni

Former senator Strom Thurmond; South Carolina Governor Nikki Haley; US Congressman Jeff Duncan; TV Host Nancy O'Dell; and NFL star Brian Dawkins and former NFL star William "Refrigerator" Perry.

The Alumni Factor Rankings Summary

Attribute	University Rank	Overall Rank
College Experience	**46**	**108**
Intellectual Development	76	148
Social Development	31	76
Spiritual Development	35	97
Friendship Development	57	123
Preparation for Career Success	42	92
Immediate Job Opportunities	40	64
Overall Assessment	**24**	**45**
Would Personally Choose Again	46	85
Would Recommend to Student	8	13
Value for the Money	26	50
Financial Success	**50**	**85**
Income per Household	78	120
% Households with Income >$150K	71	118
Household Net Worth	36	63
% Households Net Worth >$1MM	26	49
Overall Happiness	**38**	**66**
Alumni Giving	**26**	**79**
Graduation Rate	**71**	**134**
Overall Rank	**38**	**84**

Other Key Alumni Outcomes

1.3% Are college professors
8.6% Teach at any level
45.5% Have post-graduate degrees
53.3% Live in dual-income homes
91.5% Are currently employed

See pages 134–135 for detailed explanations and definitions.

Alumni Activities During College

26.0% Community Service
38.3% Intramural Sports
22.7% Internships
8.4% Media Programs
13.6% Music Programs
37.0% Part-Time Jobs

Prepared Me for Career Success % Strongly Agree	Was A Good Value for the Money % Strongly Agree	Percent of Alumni Worth >$1MM
Clemson 27.5%	Clemson 50.3%	Clemson 18.1%
All College Grads 31.9%	All College Grads 46.1%	All College Grads 14.6%

Alumni Employment

% Independent/ Entrepreneur 12.5%
% With Large Org. 27.6%
% With Medium Org. 18.4%
% With Small Org. 10.5%
% With Govt. 9.8%
% Any Level Teaching 8.6%
% Other 12.6%

Income Distribution of Graduates

Clemson
All College Grads

40%
30%
20%
10%
0%

<$20K, $20-25K, $26-35K, $36-45K, $46-55K, $56-75K, $76-99K, $100-149K, $150-199K, $200-299K, $300-399K, $400-499K, $500-599K, $600-999K, $1MM-1.5MM, $1.6MM-1.99MM, >$2MM

Current Selectivity & Demand Analysis for Clemson University

Attribute	% Accepted	% Accepted Who Enroll	Freshman Retention Rate	Graduation Rate	Demand Index	Reputation Index
Score	58.0%	31.0%	89.0%	76.0%	5.75	0.53
Rank	119	96	124	134	130	117

Where are the Graduates of Clemson University on the Political Spectrum?

Very Liberal	Liberal	Somewhat Liberal	Somewhat Conservative	Conservative	Very Conservative
					↑

Colby College

Location: Waterville, ME
Campus Setting: Rural: Fringe
Total Expenses: $55,400
Estimated Average Discount: $35,701 (64%)
Estimated Net Price: $19,699

Type of Institution: Liberal Arts College
Number of Undergraduates: 1,825
SAT Score: Reading: 620–710, Math: 630–710
Student/Faculty Ratio: 10 to 1
Transfer Out Rate: 7%

Rank Among 53 Liberal Arts Colleges	**32**
Overall Rank Among 177 *Alumni Factor* Schools	**63**

Overview

One of the three strong liberal arts colleges located in Maine, Colby produces alumni who are very happy (ranked 5th), highly developed intellectually (44th), financially successful (23rd) and are able to build strong friendships that last for decades (35th in Friendship Development). This mix of head and heart is what makes Colby so unique, and its graduates so successful. Colby grads rank 23rd in overall Financial Success, in a dead heat with Bates and slightly behind Bowdoin.

Colby grads lean strongly to the liberal side – less liberal than Bowdoin grads and more liberal than Bates. Since Colby earns Top 30 rankings across all the Ultimate Outcomes and Alumni Giving, its lower score in the Overall Assessment is puzzling. While the low Value for the Money is understandable given its price tag, this level of alumni love and loyalty typically leads to higher levels of recommendation and willingness to choose the college again. Maybe it's the Maine winters.

An excellent school with an increasingly strong national reputation, Colby grads transition well from their cold Camelot in Waterville.

Notable Alumni

Obama Chief of Staff Pete Rouse; Barclay's CEO Robert Diamond; former US senator from Florida Edward Gurney; novelist Annie Proulx; and *Gossip Girl* creator Cecily von Ziegesar.

The Alumni Factor Rankings Summary

Attribute	Liberal Arts Rank	Overall Rank
College Experience	**42**	**86**
Intellectual Development	44	73
Social Development	17	24
Spiritual Development	37	67
Friendship Development	35	46
Preparation for Career Success	47	126
Immediate Job Opportunities	48	162
Overall Assessment	**43**	**129**
Would Personally Choose Again	37	96
Would Recommend to Student	48	140
Value for the Money	47	142
Financial Success	**23**	**58**
Income per Household	24	75
% Households with Income >$150K	33	94
Household Net Worth	22	60
% Households Net Worth >$1MM	6	13
Overall Happiness	**5**	**8**
Alumni Giving	**29**	**32**
Graduation Rate	**16**	**39**
Overall Rank	**32**	**63**

Other Key Alumni Outcomes

7.5% Are college professors
13.1% Teach at any level
62.9% Have post-graduate degrees
56.7% Live in dual-income homes
98.1% Are currently employed

See pages 134–135 for detailed explanations and definitions.

Alumni Activities During College

23.6% Community Service
38.7% Intramural Sports
23.6% Internships
40.5% Media Programs
29.2% Music Programs
17.0% Part-Time Jobs

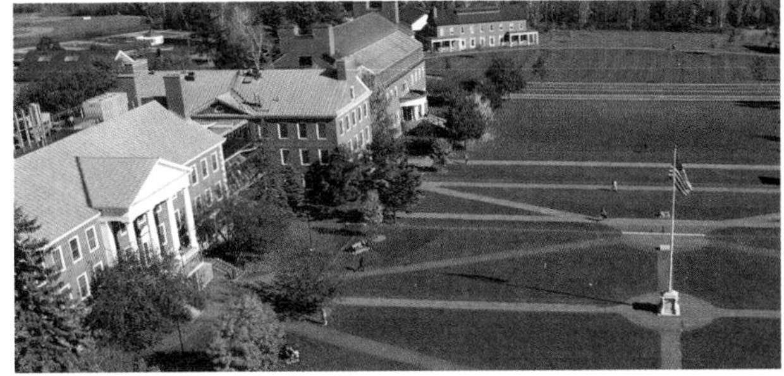

Prepared Me for Career Success % Strongly Agree	Was A Good Value for the Money % Strongly Agree	Percent of Alumni Worth >$1MM

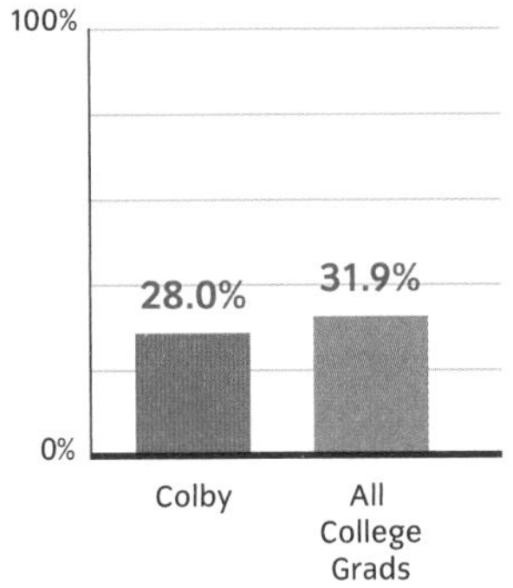

100%
0%
28.0%
31.9%
Colby
All College Grads

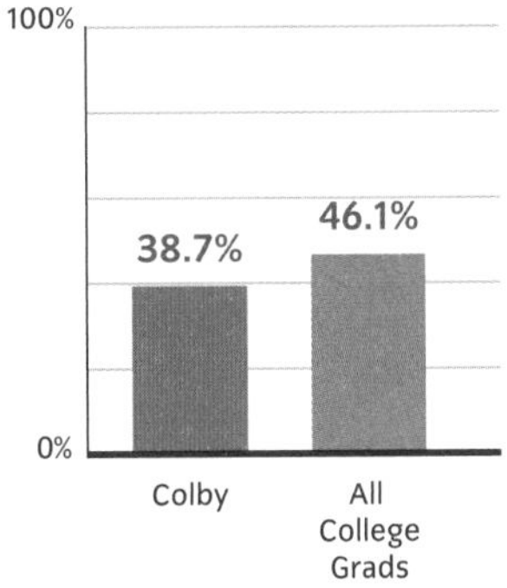

100%
0%
38.7%
46.1%
Colby
All College Grads

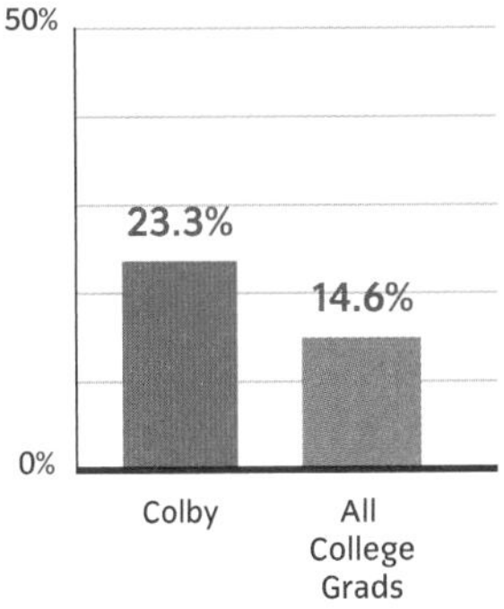

50%
0%
23.3%
14.6%
Colby
All College Grads

Alumni Employment

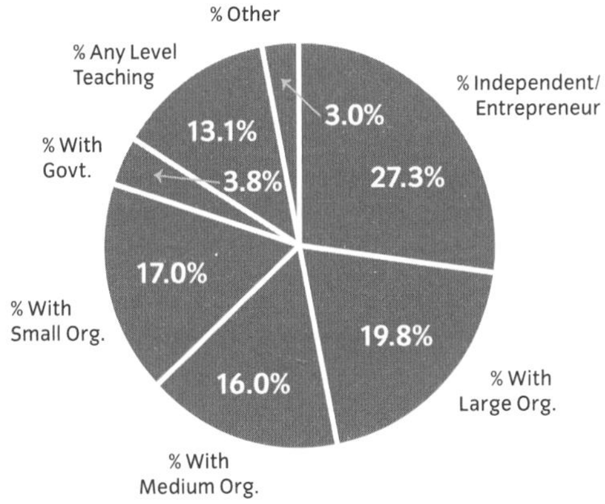

% Other
3.0%
% Independent/ Entrepreneur
27.3%
% With Large Org.
19.8%
% With Medium Org.
16.0%
% With Small Org.
17.0%
% With Govt.
3.8%
% Any Level Teaching
13.1%

Income Distribution of Graduates

40%
30%
20%
10%
0%
Colby
All College Grads
<$20K
$20-25K
$26-35K
$36-45K
$46-55K
$56-75K
$76-99K
$100-149K
$150-199K
$200-299K
$300-399K
$400-499K
$500-599K
$600-999K
$1MM-1.5MM
$1.6MM-1.99MM
>$2MM

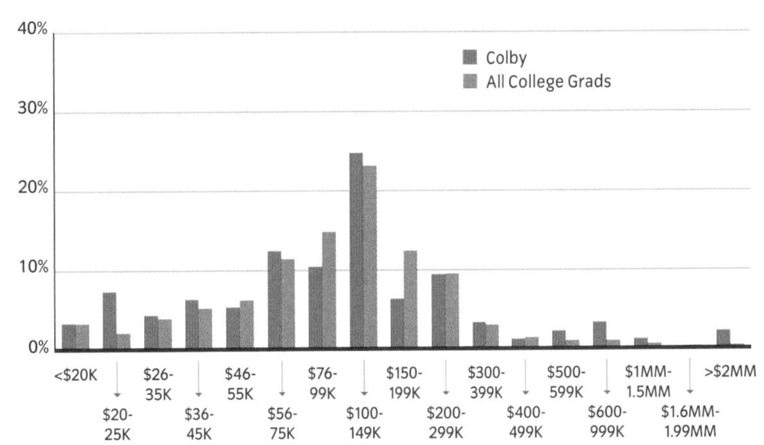

Current Selectivity & Demand Analysis for Colby College

Attribute	% Accepted	% Accepted Who Enroll	Freshman Retention Rate	Graduation Rate	Demand Index	Reputation Index
Score	29.0%	31.0%	95.0%	90.0%	11.10	1.07
Rank	48	96	47	39	58	58

Where are the Graduates of Colby College on the Political Spectrum?

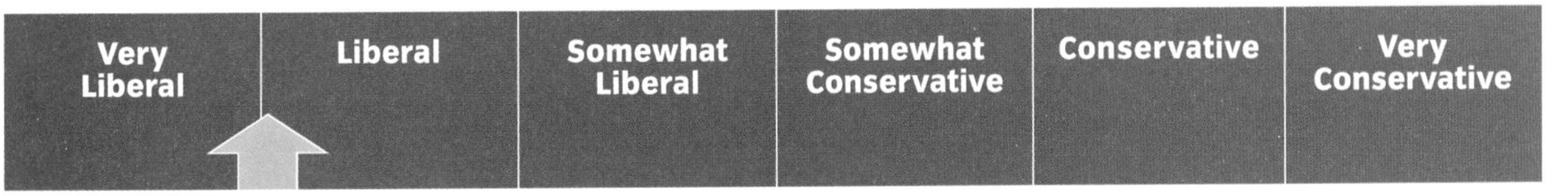

Very Liberal
Liberal
Somewhat Liberal
Somewhat Conservative
Conservative
Very Conservative

See pages 134–135 for detailed explanations and definitions.

Colgate University

Location: Hamilton, NY
Campus Setting: Town: Distant
Total Expenses: $55,570
Estimated Average Discount: $36,923 (66%)
Estimated Net Price: $18,647

Type of Institution: Liberal Arts College
Number of Undergraduates: 2,884
SAT Score: Reading: 620–720, Math: 640–720
Student/Faculty Ratio: 10 to 1
Transfer Out Rate: 12%

Rank Among 53 Liberal Arts Colleges	**38**
Overall Rank Among 177 *Alumni Factor* Schools	**72**

Overview

One of the most demanding colleges in the country, Colgate attracts excellent students and challenges them thoroughly. The result is a graduate who is successful, loyal and well prepared. Grads pursue a wide variety of careers and broadly excel in them. Colgate ranks 11th in Financial Success, and is in the Top 20 in every measure therein.

As to rigorous academics, there is no question that Colgate is demanding. It is ranked 4th among all schools in tough grading, behind only the Air Force Academy, the Naval Academy and Harvey Mudd College. Add to that a $55,000 price tag in an upstate NY climate and we could possibly be onto a few reasons graduates don't rate it as highly as expected in the Overall Assessment (ranked 44th).

There is no question, however, regarding the level of accomplishment Colgate grads enjoy after graduation. In addition to extraordinary Financial Success, Colgate is among the Top 25 schools in the overall Ultimate Outcome rankings. Add to that a strong proclivity to develop deep and lasting friendships (36th) and Colgate stacks up as one of the finest liberal arts schools in the country (38th overall). It is an excellent choice for the well-prepared student who expects to excel in life. The tough grading pays off for Colgate graduates – just as it does for graduates of all excellent schools.

Notable Alumni

Andy Rooney; Darius Bikoff, founder of vitaminwater; screenwriter Ted Griffin; commentator Monica Crowley; and Larry Bossidy, former CEO of Honeywell.

The Alumni Factor Rankings Summary

Attribute	Liberal Arts Rank	Overall Rank
College Experience	**43**	**90**
Intellectual Development	45	77
Social Development	38	76
Spiritual Development	34	62
Friendship Development	36	47
Preparation for Career Success	44	119
Immediate Job Opportunities	36	137
Overall Assessment	**44**	**137**
Would Personally Choose Again	41	127
Would Recommend to Student	47	139
Value for the Money	41	126
Financial Success	**11**	**28**
Income per Household	13	32
% Households with Income >$150K	12	28
Household Net Worth	15	30
% Households Net Worth >$1MM	17	41
Overall Happiness	**45**	**157**
Alumni Giving	**23**	**26**
Graduation Rate	**20**	**52**
Overall Rank	**38**	**72**

Other Key Alumni Outcomes

8.1%	Are college professors
15.3%	Teach at any level
64.8%	Have post-graduate degrees
49.2%	Live in dual-income homes
94.4%	Are currently employed

See pages 134–135 for detailed explanations and definitions.

Alumni Activities During College

37.6% Community Service
51.2% Intramural Sports
19.2% Internships
36.0% Media Programs
30.4% Music Programs
24.0% Part-Time Jobs

	Colgate	All College Grads
Prepared Me for Career Success (% Strongly Agree)	33.6%	31.9%
Was A Good Value for the Money (% Strongly Agree)	40.3%	46.1%
Percent of Alumni Worth >$1MM	19.7%	14.6%

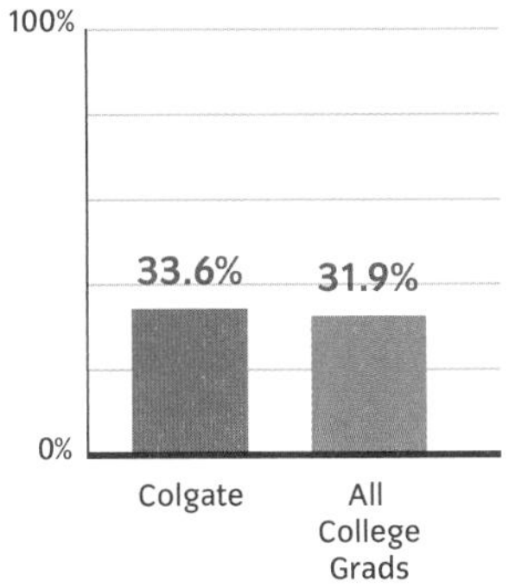

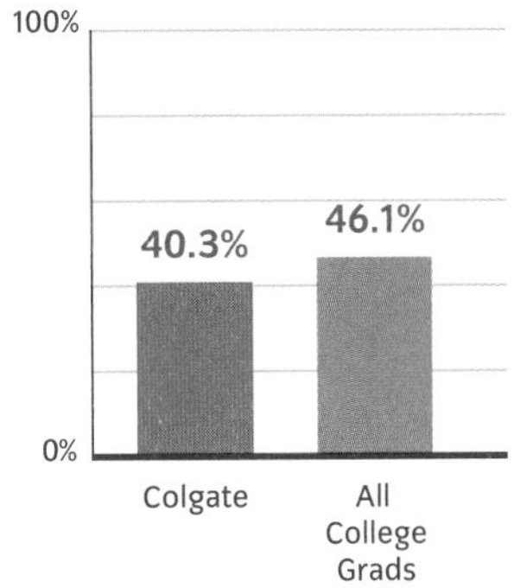

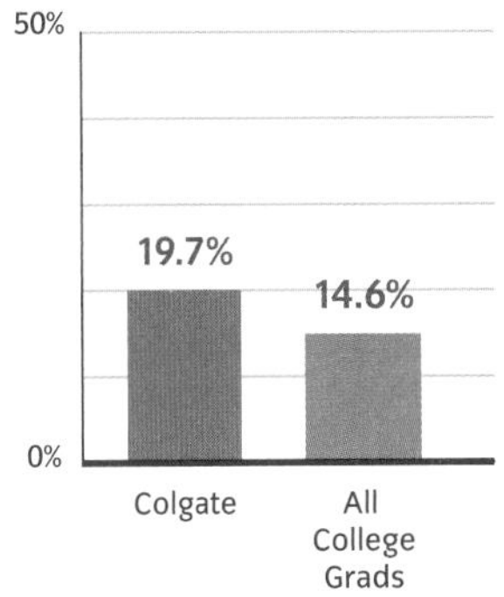

Alumni Employment

Category	%
% Independent/ Entrepreneur	15.4%
% With Large Org.	23.4%
% With Medium Org.	20.2%
% With Small Org.	9.7%
% With Govt.	7.2%
% Any Level Teaching	15.3%
% Other	8.8%

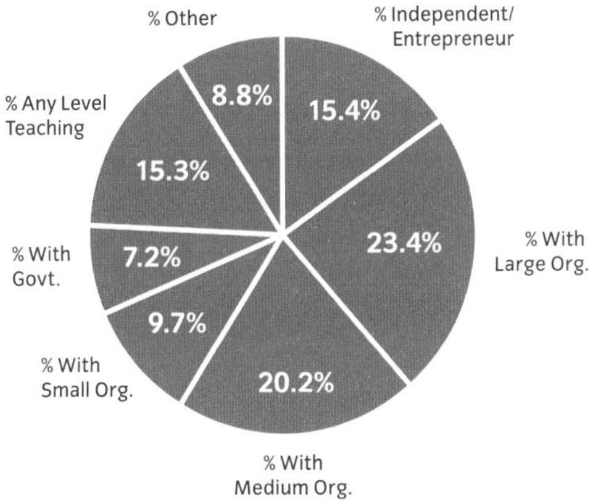

Income Distribution of Graduates

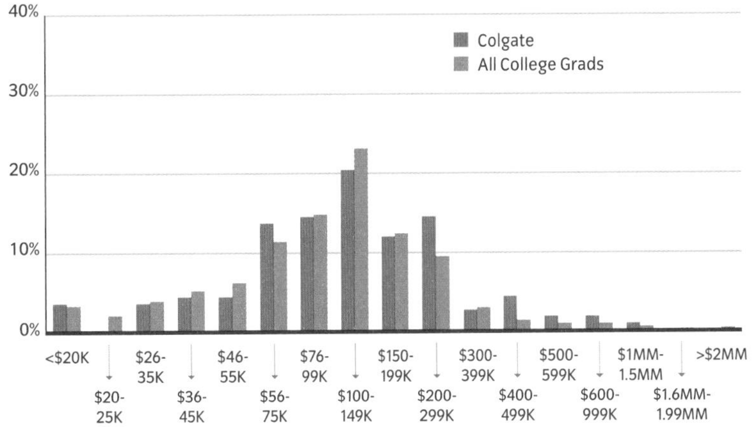

Current Selectivity & Demand Analysis for Colgate University

Attribute	% Accepted	% Accepted Who Enroll	Freshman Retention Rate	Graduation Rate	Demand Index	Reputation Index
Score	29.0%	33.0%	93.0%	88.0%	10.26	1.14
Rank	48	83	73	52	67	54

Where are the Graduates of Colgate University on the Political Spectrum?

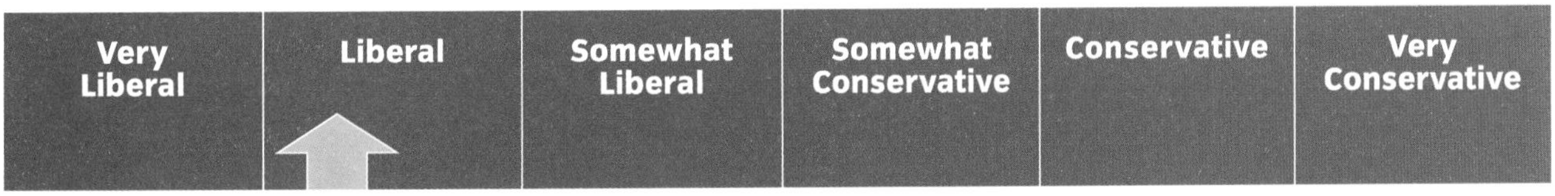

Very Liberal	Liberal	Somewhat Liberal	Somewhat Conservative	Conservative	Very Conservative
	↑				

See pages 134–135 for detailed explanations and definitions.

College of Charleston

Location: Charleston, SC
Campus Setting: City: Midsize
Total Expenses: $23,996
Estimated Average Discount: $7,977 (33%)
Estimated Net Price: $16,019

Type of Institution: Regional University
Number of Undergraduates: 10,121
SAT Score: Reading: 560–640, Math: 560–640
Student/Faculty Ratio: 16 to 1
Transfer Out Rate: 26%

Rank Among 20 Regional Universities	**17**
Overall Rank Among 177 *Alumni Factor* Schools	**142**

Overview

The College of Charleston has been around since 1770 – making it the 13th-oldest institution of higher learning in the country – but it has only recently taken its place on the national stage. Popular among its graduates (ranked 7th among all schools in Would Choose Again) and the recipient of strong scores in Social Development (ranked 69th among all 177 colleges and universities), C of C is a fun and friendly way to spend one's undergraduate years – and being in the heart of historic Charleston certainly doesn't hurt.

While not historically considered among the academic elite, C of C produces writers, artists, business leaders, political figures and educators who distinguish themselves throughout the South – and increasingly across the nation. With average scores in the Ultimate Outcomes (ranked 165th) and in Financial Success (153rd), C of C grads more than offset the college's lack of national reputation with a positive, engaged brand of modern conservatism that is progressive and practical.

A small number of schools in the country engender this type of love and level of alumni recommendation (11th). Most of those schools are among these 177, so C of C is being compared to the very best. As C of C continues to strengthen its academic programs and becomes even more selective in its admission standards (actions which are well underway), the city of Charleston will become a destination for much more than just its historic charm.

Notable Alumni

Allison Munn, actress (One Tree Hill); Matt Czuchry, actor (Gilmore Girls); baseball players Brett Gardner, Graham Godfrey and Michael Kohn.

The Alumni Factor Rankings Summary

Attribute	Overall Rank
College Experience	**127**
Intellectual Development	106
Social Development	69
Spiritual Development	98
Friendship Development	164
Preparation for Career Success	123
Immediate Job Opportunities	143
Overall Assessment	**27**
Would Personally Choose Again	7
Would Recommend to Student	11
Value for the Money	85
Financial Success	**153**
Income per Household	159
% Households with Income >$150K	109
Household Net Worth	140
% Households Net Worth >$1MM	175
Overall Happiness	**135**
Alumni Giving	**162**
Graduation Rate	**160**
Overall Rank	**142**

Other Key Alumni Outcomes

3.8% Are college professors
11.5% Teach at any level
38.5% Have post-graduate degrees
59.0% Live in dual-income homes
91.2% Are currently employed

See pages 134–135 for detailed explanations and definitions.

Alumni Activities During College

31.4% Community Service
26.5% Intramural Sports
22.5% Internships
7.8% Media Programs
5.9% Music Programs
57.8% Part-Time Jobs

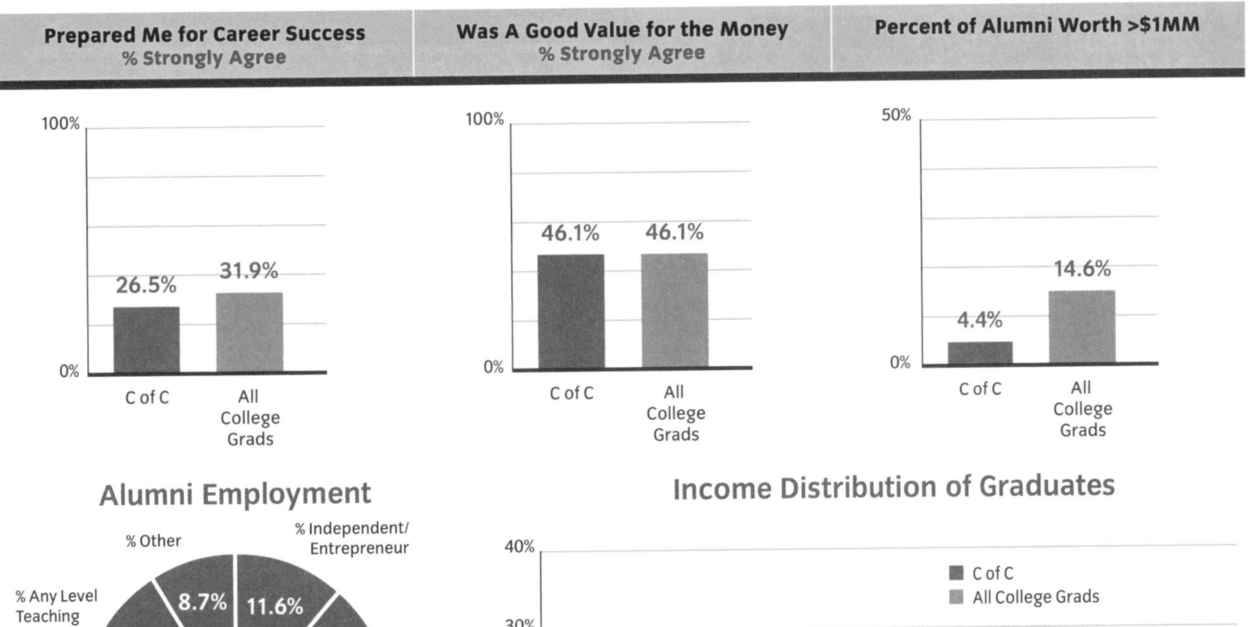

Alumni Employment

% Other 8.7%
% Independent/ Entrepreneur 11.6%
% With Large Org. 25.0%
% With Medium Org. 14.4%
% With Small Org. 18.3%
% With Govt. 10.5%
% Any Level Teaching 11.5%

Income Distribution of Graduates

C of C
All College Grads

40%
30%
20%
10%
0%

<$20K, $20-25K, $26-35K, $36-45K, $46-55K, $56-75K, $76-99K, $100-149K, $150-199K, $200-299K, $300-399K, $400-499K, $500-599K, $600-999K, $1MM-1.5MM, $1.6MM-1.99MM, >$2MM

Current Selectivity & Demand Analysis for College of Charleston

Attribute	% Accepted	% Accepted Who Enroll	Freshman Retention Rate	Graduation Rate	Demand Index	Reputation Index
Score	70.0%	25.0%	81.0%	66.0%	4.83	0.36
Rank	149	130	173	160	140	155

Where are the Graduates of College of Charleston on the Political Spectrum?

Very Liberal	Liberal	Somewhat Liberal	Somewhat Conservative	Conservative	Very Conservative
					↑

The College of New Jersey

Location: Ewing , NJ
Campus Setting: Suburb: Large
Total Expenses: $28,064
Estimated Average Discount: $8,488 (30%)
Estimated Net Price: $19,576

Type of Institution: Regional University
Number of Undergraduates: 6,460
SAT Score: Reading: 550–650, Math: 580–680
Student/Faculty Ratio: 13 to 1
Transfer Out Rate: 5%

Rank Among 20 Regional Universities	**13**
Overall Rank Among 177 *Alumni Factor* Schools	**112**

Overview

Historically New Jersey's premier school for teachers, The College of New Jersey is transforming itself into a regional university with a broader curriculum and greater academic breadth. However, the overall graduate population is still nearly twice as likely as the average college graduate to be a teacher (26% of TCNJ grads teach today, versus 14% of all grads).

Because of its historical focus on teaching, TCNJ gets high marks from grads in Career Preparation (ranked 51st) and in providing Job Opportunities (70th). It also gets high marks in graduate Willingness to Recommend (55th) and in Value for the Money (25th). The Overall Assessment rating by grads is quite strong.

TCNJ does surprisingly well in average household income and net worth, despite the heavy concentration of teachers and despite the fact that the large majority of its teachers teach at the primary and secondary level, with relatively few at the college level. Ranked among the Top 120 in all the Ultimate Outcomes and with 84% of its graduates earning above the US median income (versus 76% for all graduates), TCNJ graduates are successful not only as educators, but also as politicians, media personalities, business leaders and in the arts.

Notable Alumni

New Jersey's 49th Governor, James Florio, and the first African-American woman elected to the New Jersey legistature, Madaline A. Williams

The Alumni Factor Rankings Summary

Attribute	Overall Rank
College Experience	**110**
Intellectual Development	128
Social Development	124
Spiritual Development	130
Friendship Development	118
Preparation for Career Success	51
Immediate Job Opportunities	70
Overall Assessment	**56**
Would Personally Choose Again	94
Would Recommend to Student	55
Value for the Money	25
Financial Success	**118**
Income per Household	87
% Households with Income >$150K	123
Household Net Worth	91
% Households Net Worth >$1MM	164
Overall Happiness	**123**
Alumni Giving	**145**
Graduation Rate	**67**
Overall Rank	**112**

Other Key Alumni Outcomes

5.0%	Are college professors
26.5%	Teach at any level
46.7%	Have post-graduate degrees
60.4%	Live in dual-income homes
95.0%	Are currently employed

See pages 134–135 for detailed explanations and definitions.

Alumni Activities During College

29.5% Community Service
18.7% Intramural Sports
25.2% Internships
14.4% Media Programs
13.7% Music Programs
45.3% Part-Time Jobs

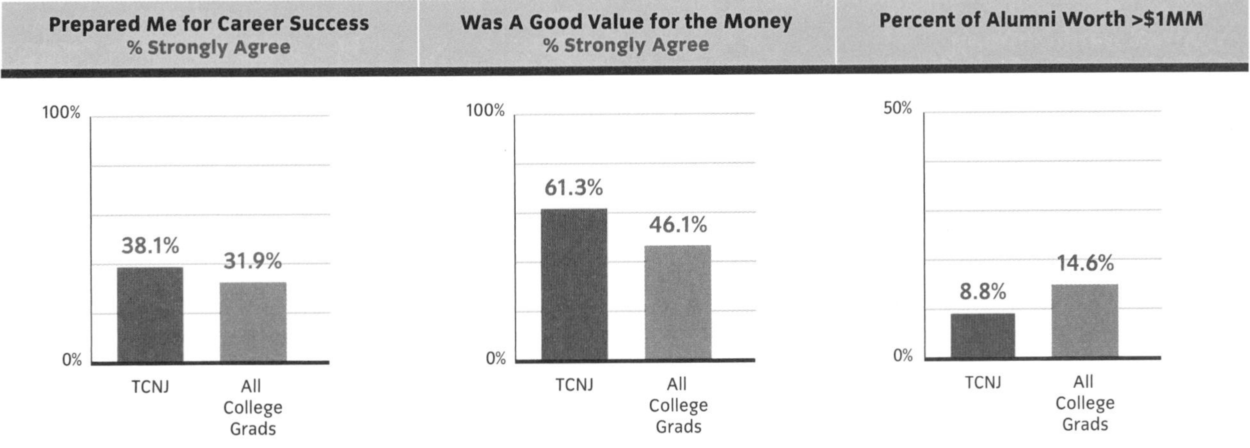

Alumni Employment

% Other 12.2%
% Independent/Entrepreneur 6.4%
% With Large Org. 20.7%
% With Medium Org. 18.6%
% With Small Org. 6.4%
% With Govt. 9.2%
% Any Level Teaching 26.5%

Income Distribution of Graduates

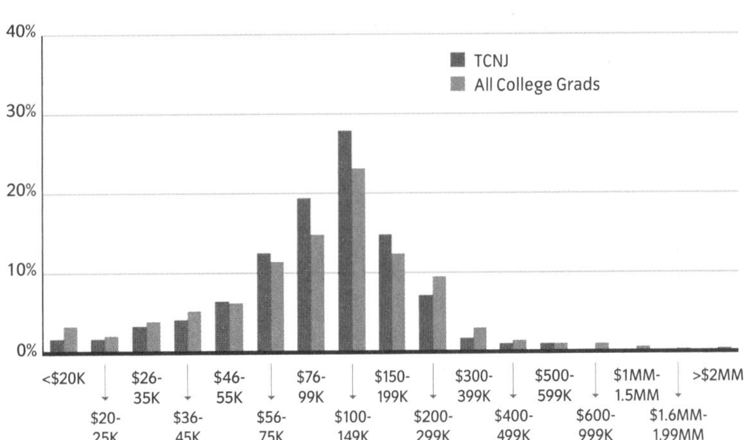

Current Selectivity & Demand Analysis for The College of New Jersey

Attribute	% Accepted	% Accepted Who Enroll	Freshman Retention Rate	Graduation Rate	Demand Index	Reputation Index
Score	46.0%	29.0%	93.0%	86.0%	7.40	0.63
Rank	96	107	73	67	110	96

Where are the Graduates of The College of New Jersey on the Political Spectrum?

Very Liberal	Liberal	Somewhat Liberal	Somewhat Conservative	Conservative	Very Conservative
			↑		

See pages 134–135 for detailed explanations and definitions.

College of the Holy Cross

Location: Worcester, MA
Campus Setting: City: Midsize
Total Expenses: $54,358
Estimated Average Discount: $31,580 (58%)
Estimated Net Price: $22,778

Type of Institution: Liberal Arts College
Number of Undergraduates: 2,899
SAT Score: Not Reported
Student/Faculty Ratio: 10 to 1
Transfer Out Rate: 4%

Rank Among 53 Liberal Arts Colleges	**2**
Overall Rank Among 177 *Alumni Factor* Schools	**5**

Overview

With a #2 ranking among liberal arts schools and the #5 spot overall, Holy Cross stands among the finest colleges in the country. HC excels at developing graduates who are highly successful (ranked 9th in Financial Success), comprehensively developed (ranked 8th in the College Experience), happy and loyal. Grads develop deep, lasting friendships with their classmates (12th) and have an extremely high regard for their college today (17th in the Overall Assessment). In fact, it is one of only 7 of 177 schools to receive rankings in the Top 30 in the 26 attributes we measure – along with Yale, Princeton, Notre Dame, Middlebury, Rice, and Washington & Lee.

This powerful combination of graduate success, happiness (16th) and broad development puts Holy Cross among the country's elite schools. HC is the top-rated among 12 Jesuit colleges and universities included in our ranking. In addition, HC is among the Top 10 schools in the country in the Graduation Rate of its varsity athletes, with a stellar overall rate of 97%.

Holy Cross produces grads that are happy, slightly conservative, tightly bound to one another and very successful. They repay their college with a Top 10 Alumni Giving rate that other colleges covet.

Notable Alumni

Supreme Court Justice Clarence Thomas; NBC Chairman Bob Wright; MSNBC's Chris Matthews; world-leading bio-engineer James Collins; Frontier Communications Chairman & CEO Maggie Wilderotter; JD Power founder Dave Power; and Celtic greats Bob Cousy and Tom Heinsohn.

The Alumni Factor Rankings Summary

Attribute	Liberal Arts Rank	Overall Rank
College Experience	**8**	**10**
Intellectual Development	18	21
Social Development	8	11
Spiritual Development	1	3
Friendship Development	12	12
Preparation for Career Success	13	22
Immediate Job Opportunities	22	93
Overall Assessment	**17**	**41**
Would Personally Choose Again	6	11
Would Recommend to Student	19	52
Value for the Money	26	69
Financial Success	**9**	**22**
Income per Household	12	30
% Households with Income >$150K	9	18
Household Net Worth	12	23
% Households Net Worth >$1MM	13	28
Overall Happiness	**16**	**29**
Alumni Giving	**7**	**8**
Graduation Rate	**5**	**16**
Overall Rank	**2**	**5**

Other Key Alumni Outcomes

4.6% Are college professors
13.4% Teach at any level
64.8% Have post-graduate degrees
54.2% Live in dual-income homes
93.4% Are currently employed

See pages 134–135 for detailed explanations and definitions.

Alumni Activities During College

45.5% Community Service
38.5% Intramural Sports
26.6% Internships
27.1% Media Programs
22.9% Music Programs
25.0% Part-Time Jobs

Prepared Me for Career Success % Strongly Agree	Was A Good Value for the Money % Strongly Agree	Percent of Alumni Worth >$1MM
Holy Cross 39.3%; All College Grads 31.9%	Holy Cross 49.8%; All College Grads 46.1%	Holy Cross 20.3%; All College Grads 14.6%

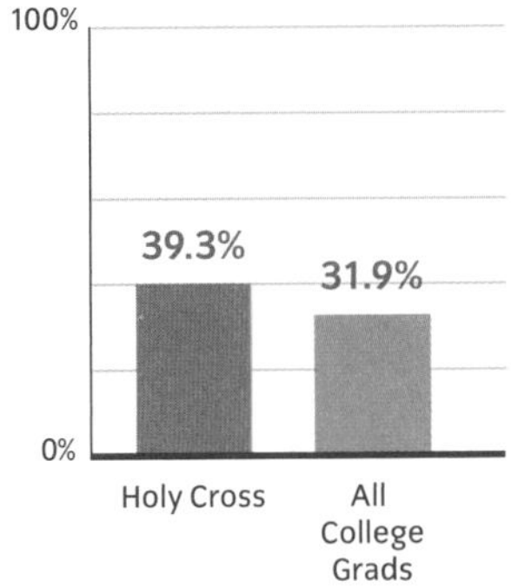

Alumni Employment

- % Independent/ Entrepreneur: 11.7%
- % With Large Org.: 22.9%
- % With Medium Org.: 17.9%
- % With Small Org.: 15.4%
- % With Govt.: 8.4%
- % Any Level Teaching: 13.4%
- % Other: 10.3%

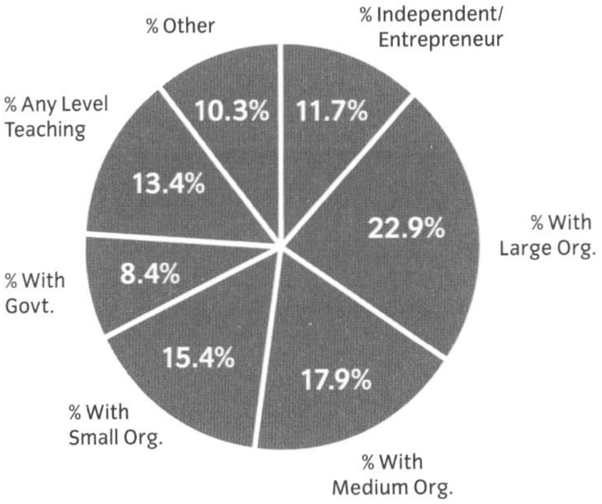

Income Distribution of Graduates

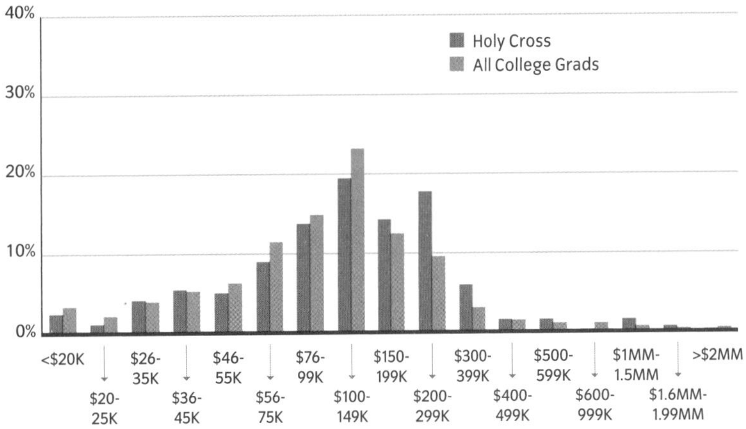

Holy Cross / All College Grads

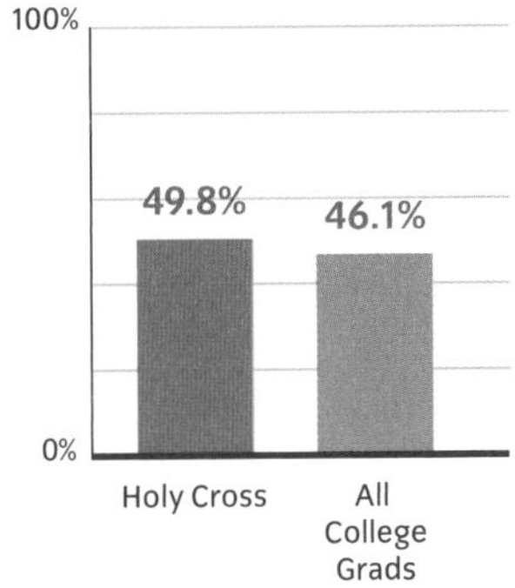

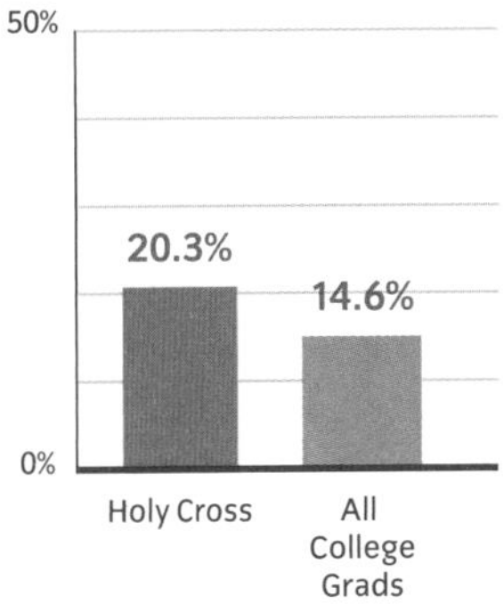

0% 10% 20% 30% 40%

<$20K, $20-25K, $26-35K, $36-45K, $46-55K, $56-75K, $76-99K, $100-149K, $150-199K, $200-299K, $300-399K, $400-499K, $500-599K, $600-999K, $1MM-1.5MM, $1.6MM-1.99MM, >$2MM

Current Selectivity & Demand Analysis for College of the Holy Cross

Attribute	% Accepted	% Accepted Who Enroll	Freshman Retention Rate	Graduation Rate	Demand Index	Reputation Index
Score	33.0%	31.0%	98.0%	93.0%	9.79	0.94
Rank	61	96	4	16	70	64

Where are the Graduates of College of the Holy Cross on the Political Spectrum?

Very Liberal	Liberal	Somewhat Liberal	Somewhat Conservative	Conservative	Very Conservative
			↑		

See pages 134–135 for detailed explanations and definitions.

The College of William & Mary

Location: Williamsburg, VA
Campus Setting: Suburb: Large
Total Expenses: $24,974
Estimated Average Discount: $12,314 (49%)
Estimated Net Price: $12,660

Type of Institution: National University
Number of Undergraduates: 5,898
SAT Score: Reading: 620–730, Math: 620–720
Student/Faculty Ratio: 11 to 1
Transfer Out Rate: 5%

Rank Among 104 National Universities	**16**
Overall Rank Among 177 *Alumni Factor* Schools	**33**

Overview

Founded in 1693 by royal charter as the second college in the country, William & Mary has an alumni pedigree that encompasses both historical greatness and modern excellence.

Ranked 17th among national universities and 35th among all 177 colleges, W&M produces graduates who are very happy (ranked 11th), quite successful (ranked 35th in Financial Success) and strong champions of their alma mater. W&M grads score their school 7th in Value for the Money and are among the Top 25 in their Willingness to Recommend it. Grads rate the Intellectual Development (7th), Friendship Development (14th) and Career Preparation (16th) in the Top 20 of all national universities. At less than $25,000 per year, William and Mary is one of the best values in the country as graduates enjoy very bright future prospects for a relatively low price.

The astounding aspect of W&M is that this historically rich college, founded by royal charter and located in the heart of American traditionalism, has produced some of the most progressive thinkers, artists, athletes, politicians and business leaders in America today – all at about 40% of the cost of America's most expensive colleges. Go Tribe!

Notable Alumni

Former US presidents Thomas Jefferson, James Monroe and John Tyler; comedian Jon Stewart; actress Glenn Close; and former secretary of defense Robert Gates.

The Alumni Factor Rankings Summary

Attribute	University Rank	Overall Rank
College Experience	**19**	**60**
Intellectual Development	7	35
Social Development	36	84
Spiritual Development	20	77
Friendship Development	14	55
Preparation for Career Success	16	39
Immediate Job Opportunities	60	98
Overall Assessment	**22**	**42**
Would Personally Choose Again	44	82
Would Recommend to Student	22	39
Value for the Money	7	11
Financial Success	**35**	**64**
Income per Household	40	66
% Households with Income >$150K	45	77
Household Net Worth	30	55
% Households Net Worth >$1MM	37	68
Overall Happiness	**11**	**25**
Alumni Giving	**20**	**70**
Graduation Rate	**24**	**39**
Overall Rank	**16**	**33**

Other Key Alumni Outcomes

9.8% Are college professors
19.3% Teach at any level
65.0% Have post-graduate degrees
52.7% Live in dual-income homes
91.7% Are currently employed

See pages 134–135 for detailed explanations and definitions.

Alumni Activities During College

32.0% Community Service
30.2% Intramural Sports
10.7% Internships
21.6% Media Programs
20.1% Music Programs
36.0% Part-Time Jobs

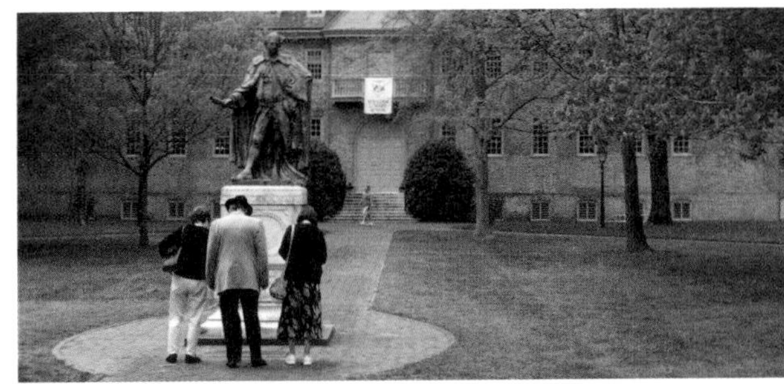

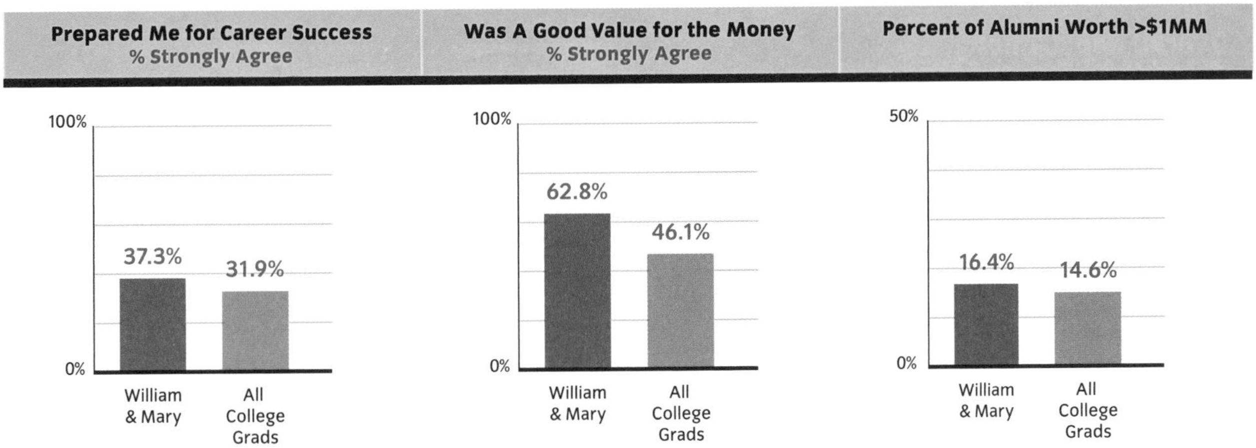

Prepared Me for Career Success
% Strongly Agree
100%
0%
37.3%
31.9%
William & Mary
All College Grads
Was A Good Value for the Money
% Strongly Agree
100%
0%
62.8%
46.1%
William & Mary
All College Grads
Percent of Alumni Worth >$1MM
50%
0%
16.4%
14.6%
William & Mary
All College Grads

Alumni Employment

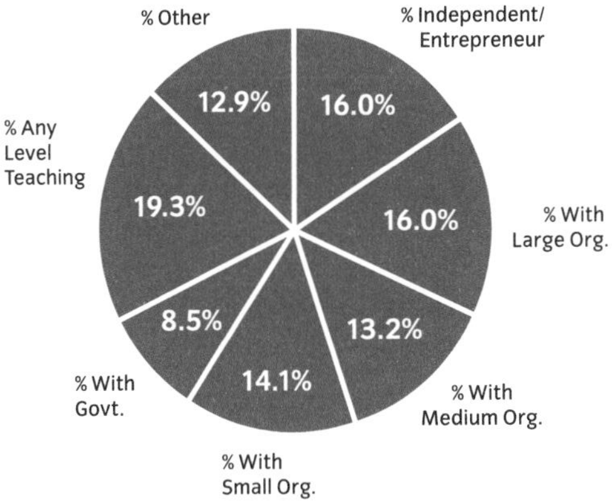

% Other
12.9%
% Independent/ Entrepreneur
16.0%
% With Large Org.
16.0%
% With Medium Org.
13.2%
% With Small Org.
14.1%
% With Govt.
8.5%
% Any Level Teaching
19.3%

Income Distribution of Graduates

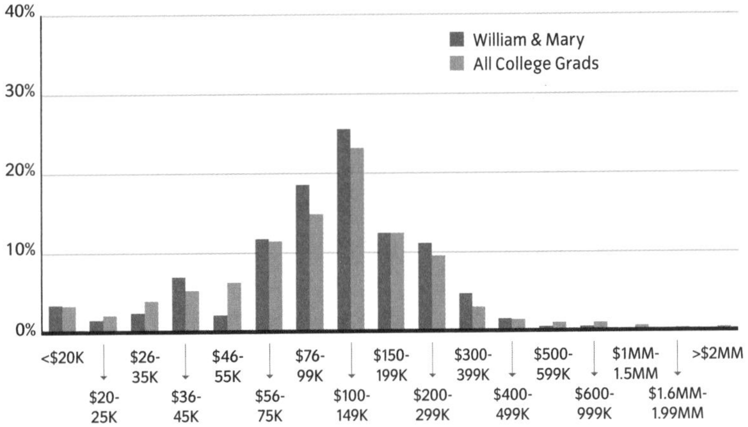

40%
30%
20%
10%
0%
William & Mary
All College Grads
<$20K
$20-25K
$26-35K
$36-45K
$46-55K
$56-75K
$76-99K
$100-149K
$150-199K
$200-299K
$300-399K
$400-499K
$500-599K
$600-999K
$1MM-1.5MM
$1.6MM-1.99MM
>$2MM

Current Selectivity & Demand Analysis for The College of William & Mary

Attribute	% Accepted	% Accepted Who Enroll	Freshman Retention Rate	Graduation Rate	Demand Index	Reputation Index
Score	35.0%	33.0%	95.0%	90.0%	8.64	0.94
Rank	67	83	47	39	92	64

Where are the Graduates of The College of William & Mary on the Political Spectrum?

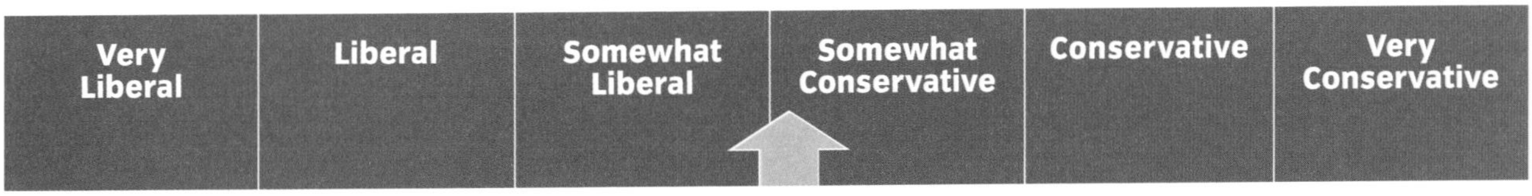

Very Liberal
Liberal
Somewhat Liberal
Somewhat Conservative
Conservative
Very Conservative

See pages 134–135 for detailed explanations and definitions.

Colorado College

Location: Colorado Springs, CO
Campus Setting: City: Large
Total Expenses: $52,150
Estimated Average Discount: $29,720 (57%)
Estimated Net Price: $22,430

Type of Institution: Liberal Arts College
Number of Undergraduates: 2,065
SAT Score: Reading: 610–710, Math: 610–700
Student/Faculty Ratio: 10 to 1
Transfer Out Rate: Not Reported

Rank Among 53 Liberal Arts Colleges	**20**
Overall Rank Among 177 *Alumni Factor* Schools	**39**

Overview

This private liberal arts college located in Colorado Springs at the foot of the Rockies, is called "A Unique Intellectual Adventure" for good reason. This is liberal arts with a western flair, and Colorado College grads are a reflection of that – happy, progressive, outdoor-loving, and successful on their own terms, defined in their own way.

With Top 40 rankings in each of the developmental attributes of the College Experience and Top 20 rankings in the Overall College Assessment attributes, grads have a deep appreciation for their school. The overall Financial Success (ranked 31st) among Colorado College grads is an interesting dichotomy – quite high in Household Net Worth (25th) but lower in Household Income (38th). This could possibly indicate a large number of grads who come from wealth and choose their careers based on passion more than economic reward.

The CC grad tends to gravitate more to the arts, to writing and to teaching. In fact, CC grads are 50% more likely to become college professors than all other grads. We are certain these professors will send their students on a "unique intellectual adventure" – just as they experienced in their undergraduate years.

Notable Alumni

Secretary of the Interior Ken Salazar and Lynne Cheney.

The Alumni Factor Rankings Summary

Attribute	Liberal Arts Rank	Overall Rank
College Experience	**23**	**38**
Intellectual Development	18	21
Social Development	6	9
Spiritual Development	29	55
Friendship Development	40	57
Preparation for Career Success	17	34
Immediate Job Opportunities	39	142
Overall Assessment	**11**	**28**
Would Personally Choose Again	16	31
Would Recommend to Student	9	26
Value for the Money	19	45
Financial Success	**31**	**93**
Income per Household	38	134
% Households with Income >$150K	40	130
Household Net Worth	27	69
% Households Net Worth >$1MM	25	57
Overall Happiness	**15**	**25**
Alumni Giving	**51**	**72**
Graduation Rate	**26**	**60**
Overall Rank	**20**	**39**

Other Key Alumni Outcomes

9.3% Are college professors
14.6% Teach at any level
62.1% Have post-graduate degrees
50.0% Live in dual-income homes
95.0% Are currently employed

See pages 134–135 for detailed explanations and definitions.

Alumni Activities During College

43.8% Community Service
47.3% Intramural Sports
10.3% Internships
17.8% Media Programs
17.8% Music Programs
35.6% Part-Time Jobs

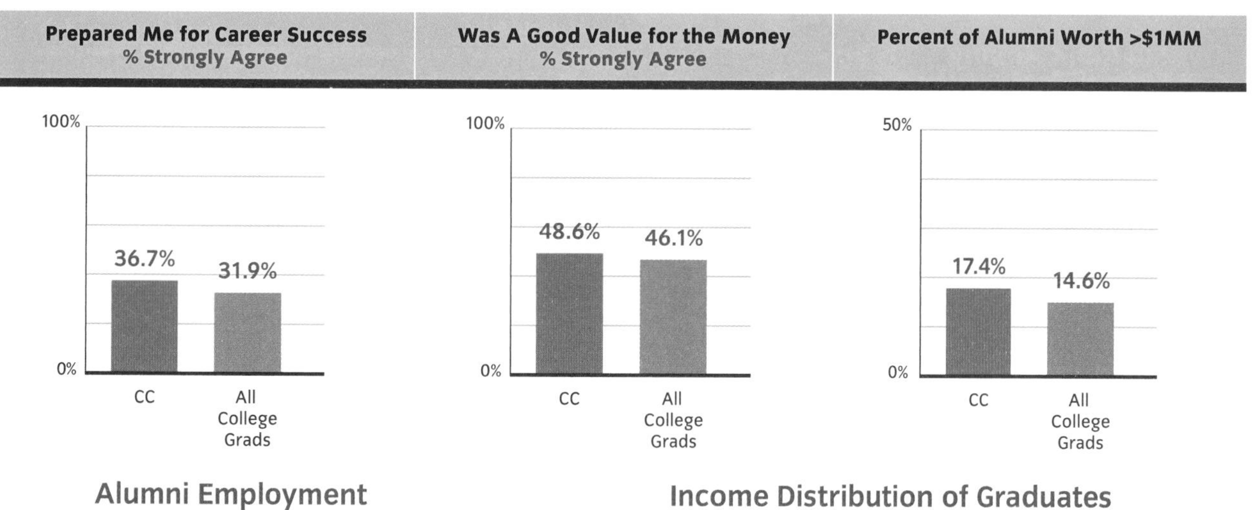

Alumni Employment

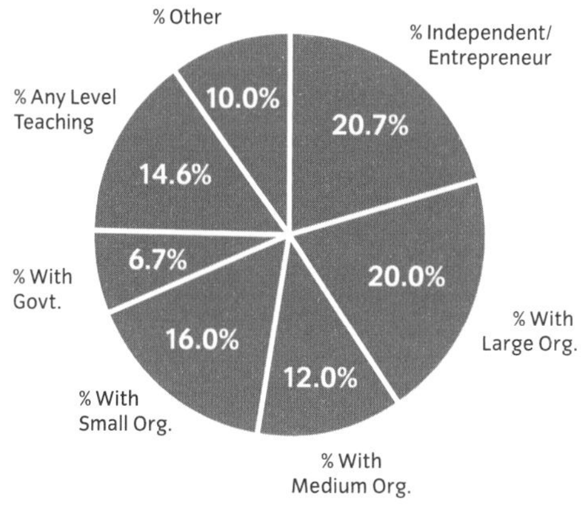

Income Distribution of Graduates

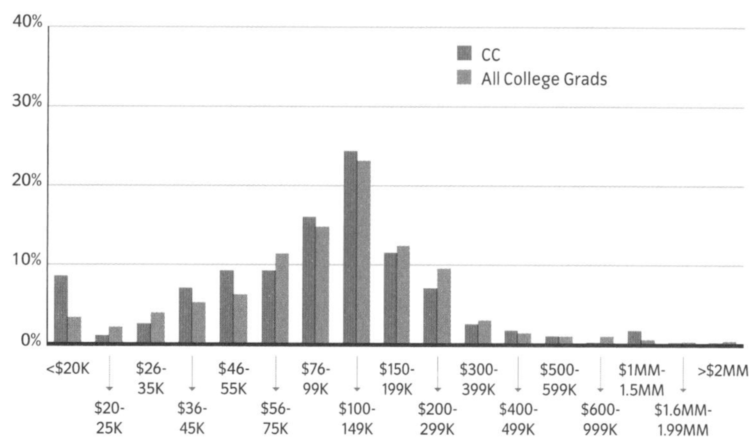

Current Selectivity & Demand Analysis for Colorado College

Attribute	% Accepted	% Accepted Who Enroll	Freshman Retention Rate	Graduation Rate	Demand Index	Reputation Index
Score	26.0%	39.0%	96.0%	87.0%	10.16	1.50
Rank	42	46	27	60	68	38

Where are the Graduates of Colorado College on the Political Spectrum?

Very Liberal	Liberal	Somewhat Liberal	Somewhat Conservative	Conservative	Very Conservative
↑					

See pages 134–135 for detailed explanations and definitions.

Colorado State University

Location: Fort Collins, CO
Campus Setting: City: Midsize
Total Expenses: $20,482
Estimated Average Discount: $8,017 (39%)
Estimated Net Price: $12,465

Type of Institution: National University
Number of Undergraduates: 22,831
SAT Score: Reading: 510–620, Math: 520–630
Student/Faculty Ratio: 18 to 1
Transfer Out Rate: 11%

Rank Among 104 National Universities	**97**
Overall Rank Among 177 *Alumni Factor* Schools	**170**

Overview

A large research university with a broad admissions policy and a wide choice of academic options, Colorado State University is chock-full of hard-working, practical, ambitious students – many of whom are first-generation college matriculates. CSU earns its place among the Top 177 for its quiet, unheralded excellence across a vast array of fields, with particular excellence in the sciences, technology, engineering and environmental sustainability. CSU's performance is actually much better than its brand reputation, and we expect that reputation will soon be growing.

CSU is often perceived as the conservative, dependable "work horse" to University of Colorado Boulder's "show horse." CSU outpunches its ranking weight (and equals Boulder) in three areas: Intellectual Development (ranked 81st versus Boulder's 85th), Preparation for Career Success (89th versus 96th) and Immediate Job Opportunities (85th versus 96th). CSU produces a happy graduate (69th) who would choose the school again (52nd) – and has a disproportionately large number of high net worth households (66th).

But, it is CSU's unsung grads are actually reflecting the most glory on this excellent university whose star is quickly rising. All hail to the Rams!

Notable Alumni

Former Colorado governor Roy Romer; and Berkshire Hathaway Director Walter Scott. Alumni also include professional athletes, astronauts and politicians.

The Alumni Factor Rankings Summary

Attribute	University Rank	Overall Rank
College Experience	**97**	**170**
Intellectual Development	81	153
Social Development	83	152
Spiritual Development	96	168
Friendship Development	82	152
Preparation for Career Success	89	160
Immediate Job Opportunities	85	140
Overall Assessment	**71**	**130**
Would Personally Choose Again	52	100
Would Recommend to Student	81	150
Value for the Money	70	128
Financial Success	**100**	**166**
Income per Household	104	177
% Households with Income >$150K	104	175
Household Net Worth	97	165
% Households Net Worth >$1MM	66	110
Overall Happiness	**69**	**119**
Alumni Giving	**91**	**162**
Graduation Rate	**93**	**164**
Overall Rank	**97**	**170**

Other Key Alumni Outcomes

2.6% Are college professors
11.4% Teach at any level
45.2% Have post-graduate degrees
48.2% Live in dual-income homes
89.7% Are currently employed

See pages 134–135 for detailed explanations and definitions.

Alumni Activities During College

30.2% Community Service
31.9% Intramural Sports
31.0% Internships
8.6% Media Programs
22.3% Music Programs
60.3% Part-Time Jobs

Prepared Me for Career Success % Strongly Agree	Was A Good Value for the Money % Strongly Agree	Percent of Alumni Worth >$1MM
CSU: 26.4% All College Grads: 31.9%	CSU: 39.3% All College Grads: 46.1%	CSU: 13.3% All College Grads: 14.6%

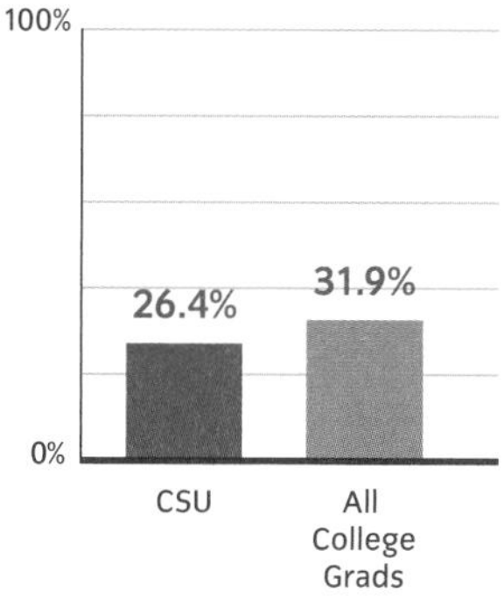

100%
0%
26.4%
31.9%
CSU
All College Grads

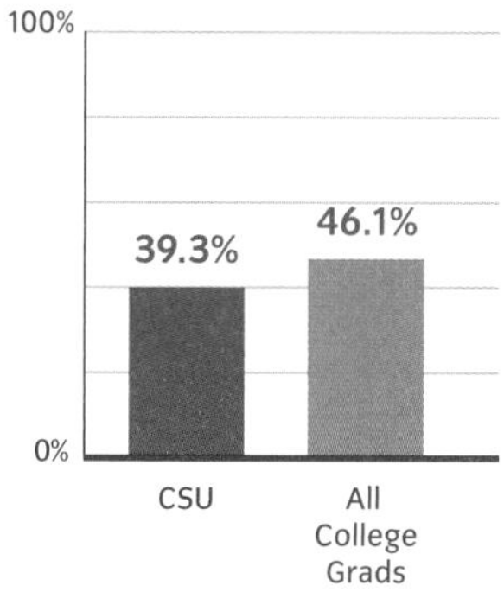

100%
0%
39.3%
46.1%
CSU
All College Grads

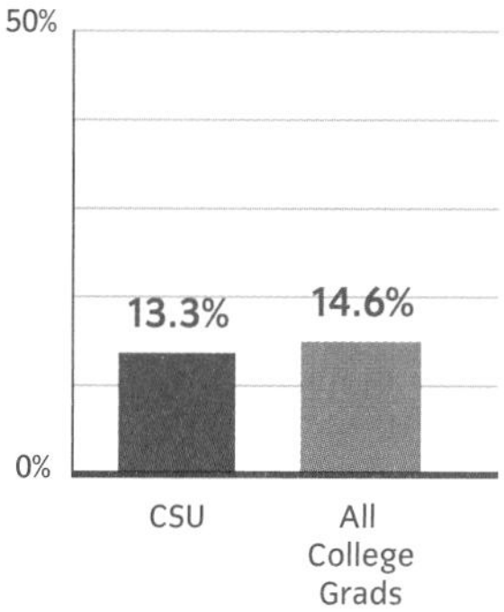

50%
0%
13.3%
14.6%
CSU
All College Grads

Alumni Employment

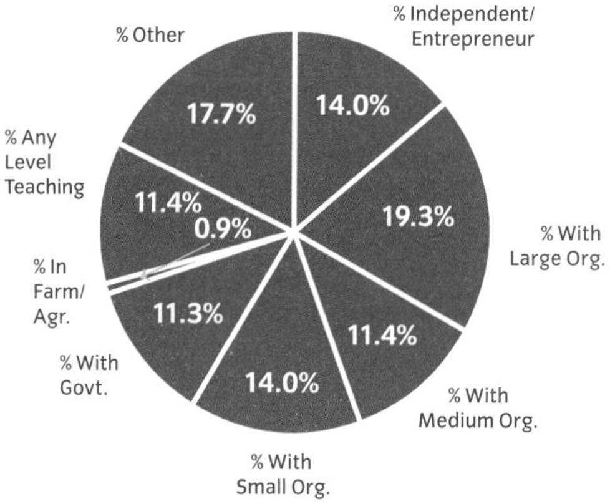

% Independent/ Entrepreneur 14.0%
% With Large Org. 19.3%
% With Medium Org. 11.4%
% With Small Org. 14.0%
% With Govt. 11.3%
% In Farm/ Agr. 0.9%
% Any Level Teaching 11.4%
% Other 17.7%

Income Distribution of Graduates

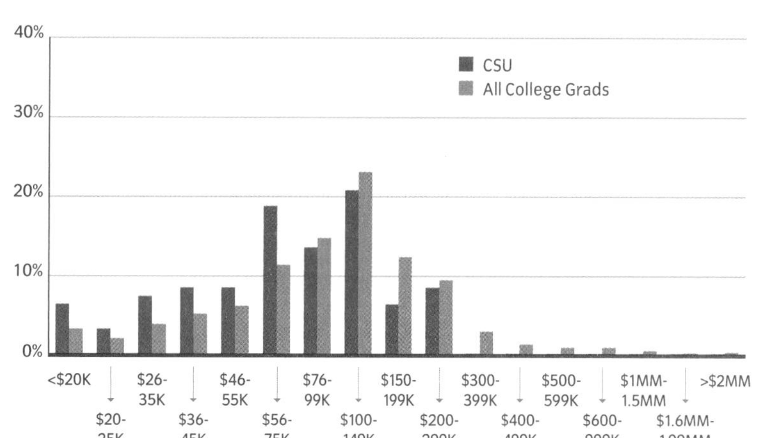

Current Selectivity & Demand Analysis for Colorado State University

Attribute	% Accepted	% Accepted Who Enroll	Freshman Retention Rate	Graduation Rate	Demand Index	Reputation Index
Score	76.0%	36.0%	83.0%	64.0%	3.68	0.47
Rank	162	68	161	164	159	130

Where are the Graduates of Colorado State University on the Political Spectrum?

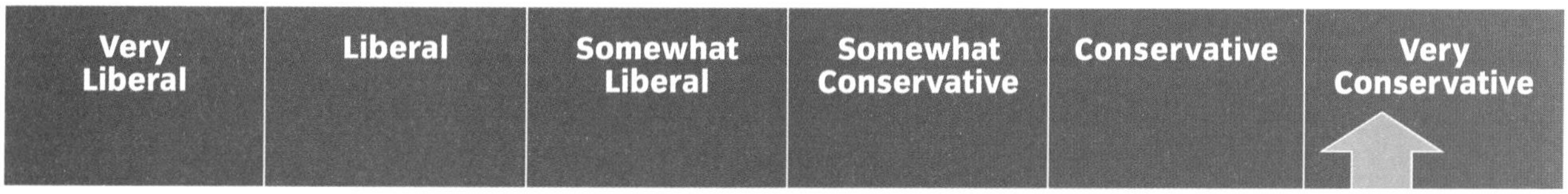

Very Liberal	Liberal	Somewhat Liberal	Somewhat Conservative	Conservative	Very Conservative
					↑

See pages 134–135 for detailed explanations and definitions.

Columbia University

Location: New York, NY
Campus Setting: City: Large
Total Expenses: $59,208
Estimated Average Discount: $40,135 (68%)
Estimated Net Price: $19,073

Type of Institution: National University
Number of Undergraduates: 7,950
SAT Score: Reading: 690–780, Math: 700–790
Student/Faculty Ratio: 6 to 1
Transfer Out Rate: Not Reported

Rank Among 104 National Universities	**42**
Overall Rank Among 177 *Alumni Factor* Schools	**91**

Overview

Considered to be among the world's finest universities, Columbia produces one of the most diverse graduate pools of any school in the Top 177 – diverse in race, creed, interests, occupations and even in how they view their college experience.

Ranked 42nd among national universities and 91st overall, most will be surprised that Columbia is not ranked higher, given its Ivy League reputation. Despite extremely high Intellectual Development scores (ranked 14th) and strong Financial Success (26th), Columbia grads are in the middle of the pack in judging their College Experience (44th) and in the Overall Assessment (51st). Also, Columbia grads claim to be less happy (102nd) than most other grads. This is likely correlated to its New York City location, since the bottom ranked schools in happiness include many NY schools. Add to that a mediocre score for Career Preparation (60th) and you end up with a rank (42nd) that most schools would covet, but which is lower than Columbia's reputation would suggest.

However, if you are exceptionally smart with a skin tough enough to withstand New York and the comparison to other Ivies, you just might thrive at Columbia – as indicated by its 9th ranking in the Ultimate Outcome Financial Success & Intellectual Capability.

Notable Alumni

Alexander Hamilton, John Jay, President Barack Obama, George Stephanopoulos, New England Patriots owner Robert Kraft, Oscar Hammerstein and many others who have made Columbia the global leader it is today.

The Alumni Factor Rankings Summary

Attribute	University Rank	Overall Rank
College Experience	**44**	**106**
Intellectual Development	14	52
Social Development	85	155
Spiritual Development	15	68
Friendship Development	36	98
Preparation for Career Success	60	119
Immediate Job Opportunities	66	107
Overall Assessment	**51**	**99**
Would Personally Choose Again	27	58
Would Recommend to Student	58	113
Value for the Money	63	116
Financial Success	**26**	**46**
Income per Household	17	34
% Households with Income >$150K	22	42
Household Net Worth	34	59
% Households Net Worth >$1MM	39	70
Overall Happiness	**102**	**175**
Alumni Giving	**45**	**108**
Graduation Rate	**12**	**16**
Overall Rank	**42**	**91**

Other Key Alumni Outcomes

9.0% Are college professors
13.5% Teach at any level
64.9% Have post-graduate degrees
49.2% Live in dual-income homes
88.1% Are currently employed

See pages 134–135 for detailed explanations and definitions.

Alumni Activities During College

28.4% Community Service
15.7% Intramural Sports
20.9% Internships
16.4% Media Programs
20.1% Music Programs
38.8% Part-Time Jobs

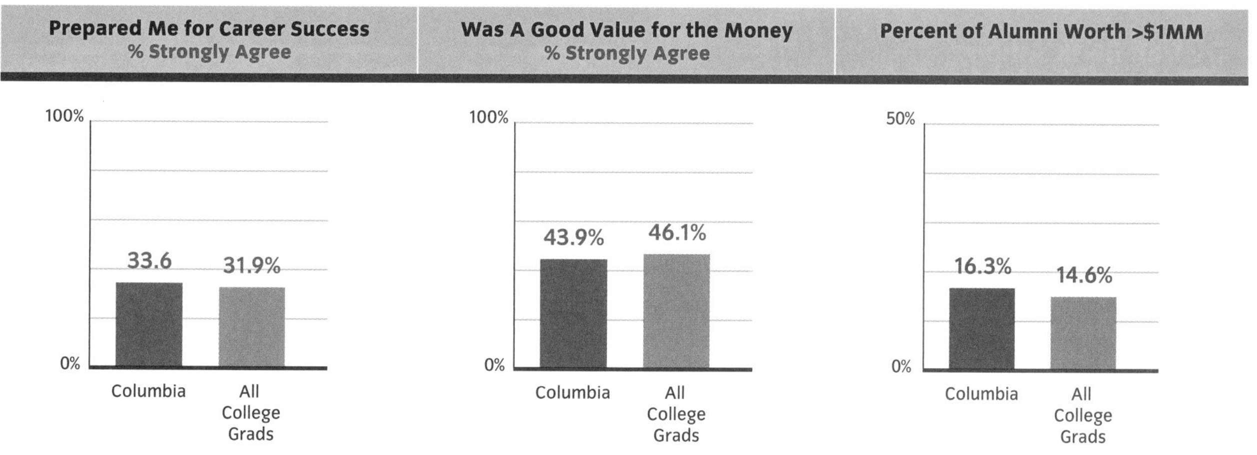

Alumni Employment

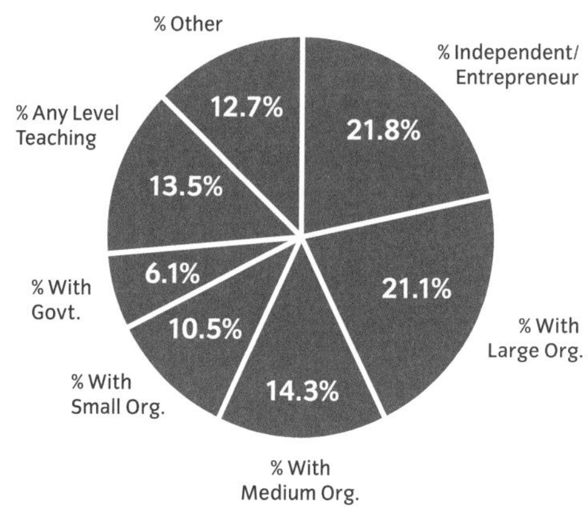

Income Distribution of Graduates

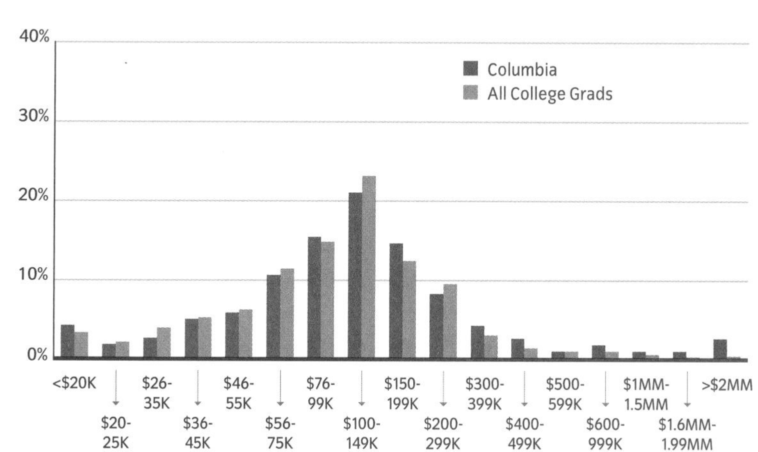

Current Selectivity & Demand Analysis for Columbia University

Attribute	% Accepted	% Accepted Who Enroll	Freshman Retention Rate	Graduation Rate	Demand Index	Reputation Index
Score	10.0%	56.0%	97.0%	93.0%	18.40	5.60
Rank	7	13	13	16	9	10

Where are the Graduates of Columbia University on the Political Spectrum?

Very Liberal	Liberal	Somewhat Liberal	Somewhat Conservative	Conservative	Very Conservative
		↑			

Connecticut College

Location: New London, CT
Campus Setting: City: Small
Total Expenses: $57,270
Estimated Average Discount: $33,461 (58%)
Estimated Net Price: $23,809

Type of Institution: Liberal Arts College
Number of Undergraduates: 1,880
SAT Score: Not Reported
Student/Faculty Ratio: 9 to 1
Transfer Out Rate: 10%

Rank Among 53 Liberal Arts Colleges	**42**
Overall Rank Among 177 *Alumni Factor* Schools	**89**

Overview

Located in southeastern Connecticut on the Thames River, Conn College is a small school with all of the expected charms of an exclusive New England liberal arts college. With a 42nd ranking among the liberal arts schools, Conn College grads are well balanced, happy (ranked 24th) and financially successful (27th). Their strongest performance is in the Ultimate Outcome of Happiness & Intellectual Capability, where they rank 26th among liberal arts colleges. Writers, artists, academicians and politicians are among the many accomplished Conn College grads.

Like many liberal arts colleges, Conn College gets lower scores in Career Preparation (51st) and Immediate Job Opportunities (also 51st). However, the strong Social Development and Friendship Development rankings lead to a loyal alumni group who give generously to the school (31st) and would promote it to prospective students today (32nd). Conn College has been producing excellent graduates for a century, and its national reputation will continue to grow based on its strong results.

Notable Alumni

Screenwriter Kevin Wade; Academy Award winning actress Estelle Parsons; fiction writer Gayl Jones; and NYC socialite Nan Kempner.

The Alumni Factor Rankings Summary

Attribute	Liberal Arts Rank	Overall Rank
College Experience	**47**	**104**
Intellectual Development	40	58
Social Development	37	69
Spiritual Development	45	96
Friendship Development	41	61
Preparation for Career Success	51	146
Immediate Job Opportunities	51	166
Overall Assessment	**41**	**119**
Would Personally Choose Again	42	130
Would Recommend to Student	32	85
Value for the Money	44	133
Financial Success	**27**	**75**
Income per Household	26	83
% Households with Income >$150K	24	65
Household Net Worth	32	88
% Households Net Worth >$1MM	28	67
Overall Happiness	**24**	**57**
Alumni Giving	**31**	**36**
Graduation Rate	**26**	**60**
Overall Rank	**42**	**89**

Other Key Alumni Outcomes

8.1% Are college professors
17.1% Teach at any level
58.9% Have post-graduate degrees
54.8% Live in dual-income homes
89.5% Are currently employed

See pages 134–135 for detailed explanations and definitions.

Alumni Activities During College

35.2% Community Service
25.6% Intramural Sports
24.0% Internships
24.0% Media Programs
26.4% Music Programs
15.2% Part-Time Jobs

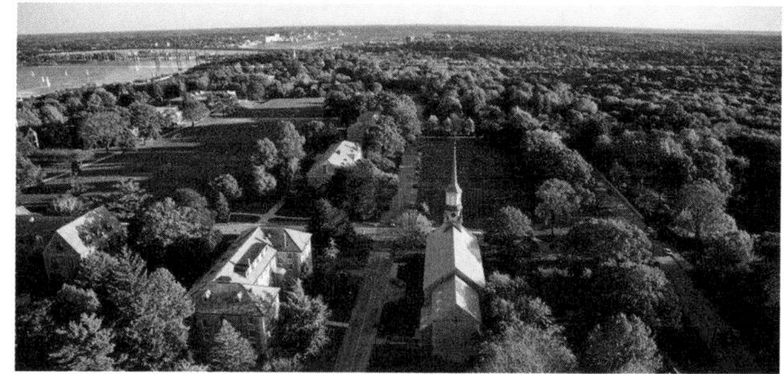

Prepared Me for Career Success
% Strongly Agree

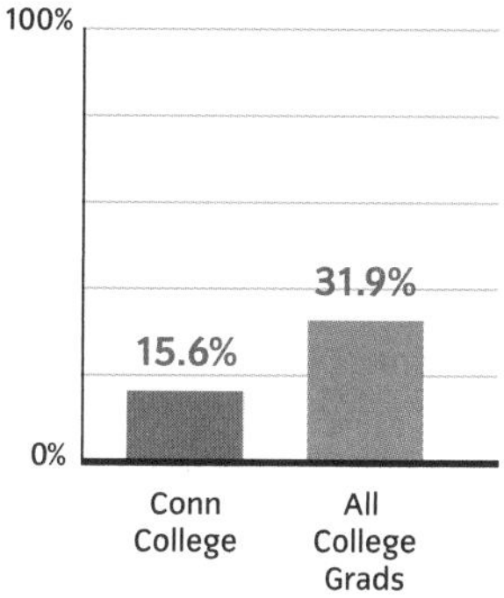
100%
0%
15.6%
31.9%
Conn College
All College Grads

Was A Good Value for the Money
% Strongly Agree

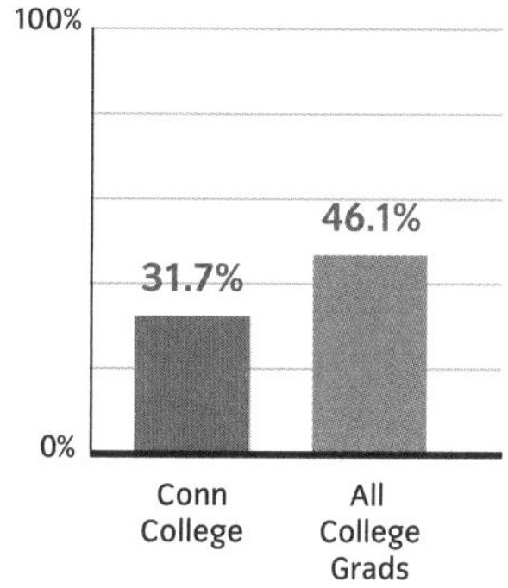
100%
0%
31.7%
46.1%
Conn College
All College Grads

Percent of Alumni Worth >$1MM

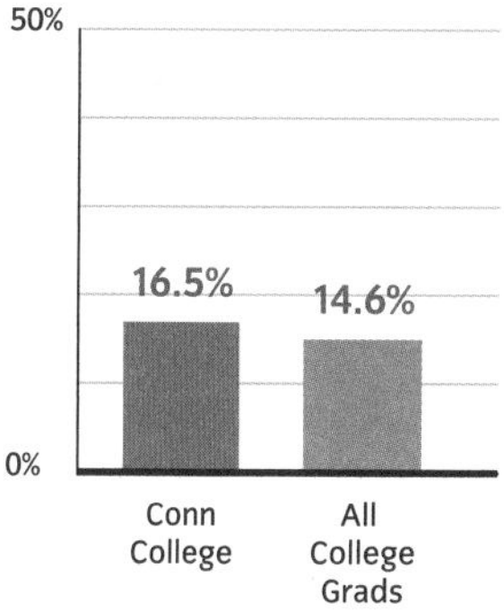
50%
0%
16.5%
14.6%
Conn College
All College Grads

Alumni Employment

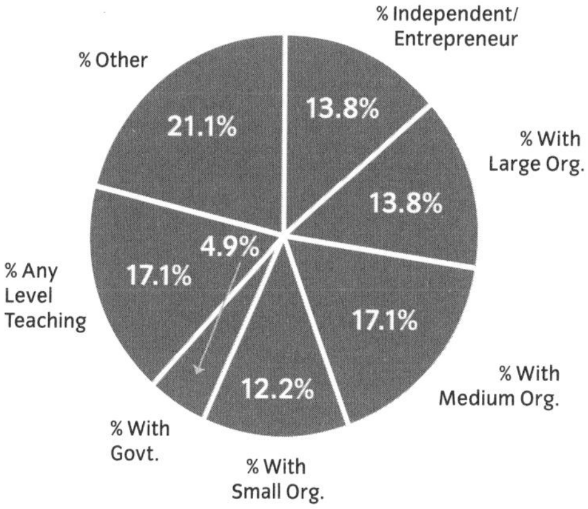
% Independent/ Entrepreneur
13.8%
% With Large Org.
13.8%
% With Medium Org.
17.1%
% With Small Org.
12.2%
% With Govt.
4.9%
% Any Level Teaching
17.1%
% Other
21.1%

Income Distribution of Graduates

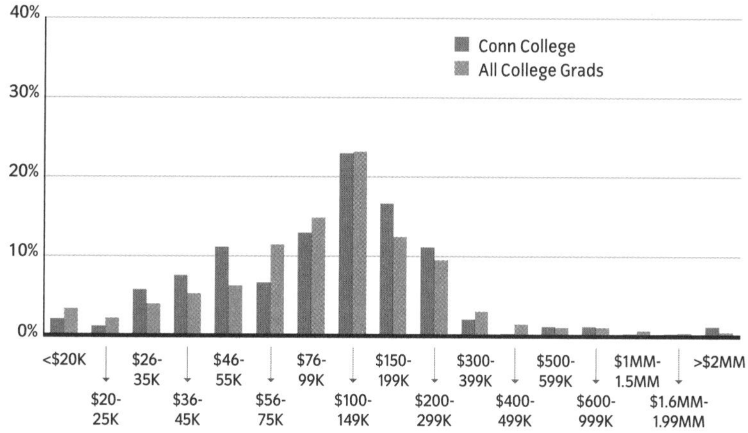
40%
30%
20%
10%
0%
Conn College
All College Grads
<$20K
$20-25K
$26-35K
$36-45K
$46-55K
$56-75K
$76-99K
$100-149K
$150-199K
$200-299K
$300-399K
$400-499K
$500-599K
$600-999K
$1MM-1.5MM
$1.6MM-1.99MM
>$2MM

Current Selectivity & Demand Analysis for Connecticut College

Attribute	% Accepted	% Accepted Who Enroll	Freshman Retention Rate	Graduation Rate	Demand Index	Reputation Index
Score	32.0%	29.0%	89.0%	87.0%	10.44	0.91
Rank	57	107	124	60	63	69

Where are the Graduates of Connecticut College on the Political Spectrum?

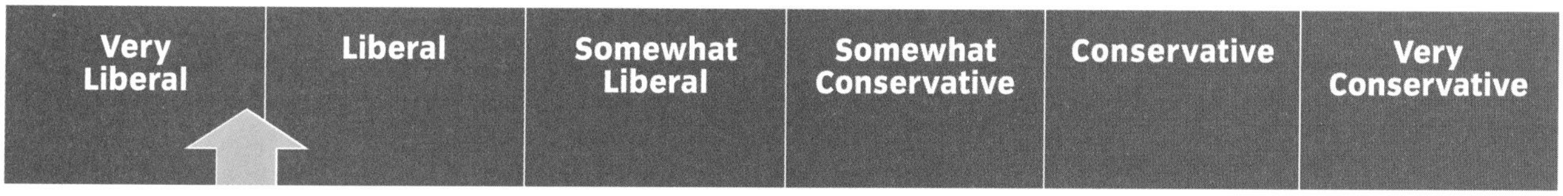
Very Liberal
Liberal
Somewhat Liberal
Somewhat Conservative
Conservative
Very Conservative

See pages 134–135 for detailed explanations and definitions.

Cornell University

Location: Ithaca, NY
Campus Setting: City: Small
Total Expenses: $57,125
Estimated Average Discount: $32,876 (58%)
Estimated Net Price: $24,249

Type of Institution: National University
Number of Undergraduates: 13,935
SAT Score: Reading: 630–730, Math: 670–770
Student/Faculty Ratio: 12 to 1
Transfer Out Rate: Not Reported

Rank Among 104 National Universities	**12**
Overall Rank Among 177 *Alumni Factor* Schools	**29**

Overview

The largest of the Ivy League schools and broadest in academic scope, Cornell has long been considered to be among the world's finest universities, and with good reason. Ranked 12th among all national universities and 29th overall, Cornell grads achieve extremely high Financial Success (ranked 12th), are fond of and loyal to their college (24th in Alumni Giving), and highly value their undergrad experience (ranked 18th in the College Experience). Cornell has as impressive an alumni list as any college in the country, and its graduates are leaders and innovators in virtually every field and discipline.

Cornell graduates rank 8th in average household income and 10th in high income households. Cornell ranks 5th in alumni giving among all colleges with more than 10,000 students, behind only USC, University of Pennsylvania, GA Tech, and UNC.

Cornell also performs well in the toughest comparison there is – the comparison to its Ivy League brethren. Cornell is 1st among the Ivies in the percentage of grads with income above the US median (88%); 4th in Value for the Money; and 3rd in Would Personally Choose Again.

Notable Alumni

Ruth Bader Ginsburg, Supreme Court Justice; Irene Rosenfeld, CEO of Kraft; Irwin Jacobs, co-founder of Qualcomm; and Sanford Weil, CEO of Citigroup.

The Alumni Factor Rankings Summary

Attribute	University Rank	Overall Rank
College Experience	**18**	**57**
Intellectual Development	17	61
Social Development	17	57
Spiritual Development	29	90
Friendship Development	10	45
Preparation for Career Success	34	79
Immediate Job Opportunities	31	47
Overall Assessment	**34**	**70**
Would Personally Choose Again	22	49
Would Recommend to Student	46	94
Value for the Money	39	69
Financial Success	**12**	**21**
Income per Household	8	15
% Households with Income >$150K	10	21
Household Net Worth	16	34
% Households Net Worth >$1MM	14	29
Overall Happiness	**48**	**90**
Alumni Giving	**24**	**75**
Graduation Rate	**12**	**16**
Overall Rank	**12**	**29**

Other Key Alumni Outcomes

9.2% Are college professors
12.9% Teach at any level
66.4% Have post-graduate degrees
53.1% Live in dual-income homes
94.5% Are currently employed

See pages 134–135 for detailed explanations and definitions.

Alumni Activities During College

31.0% Community Service
31.0% Intramural Sports
21.1% Internships
15.3% Media Programs
19.0% Music Programs
31.0% Part-Time Jobs

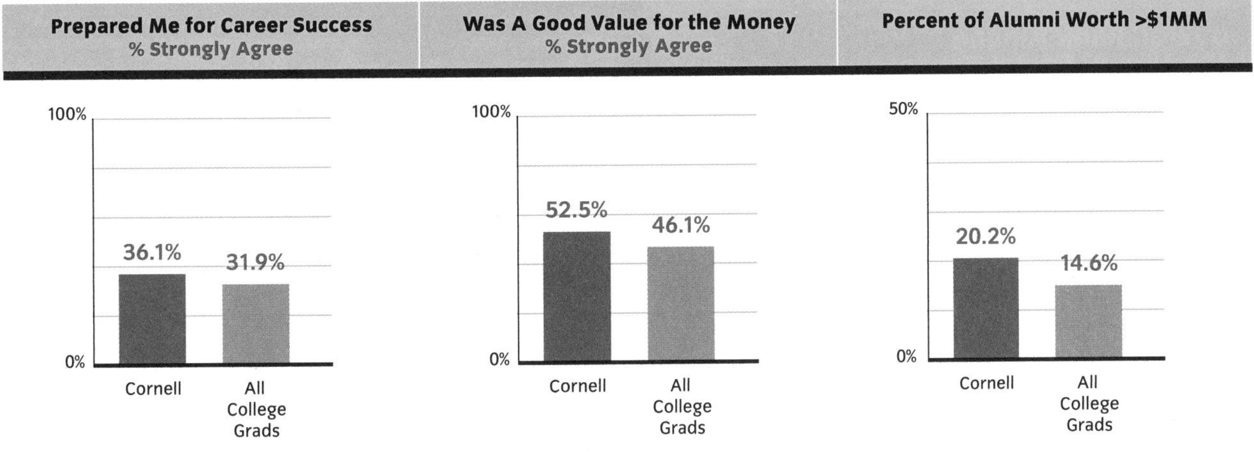

Alumni Employment

Income Distribution of Graduates

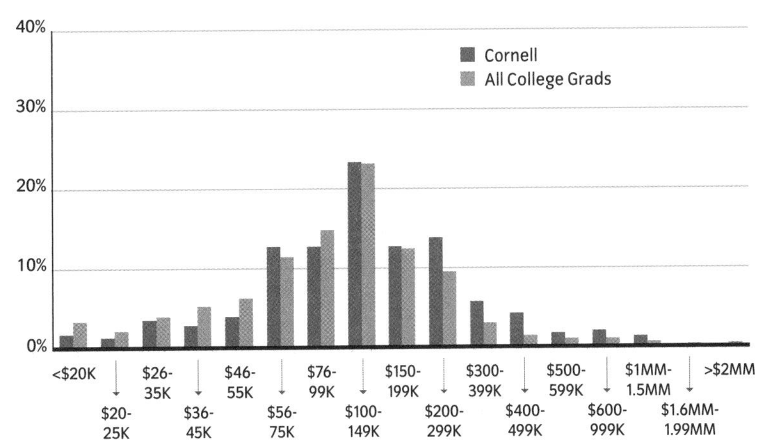

Current Selectivity & Demand Analysis for Cornell University

Attribute	% Accepted	% Accepted Who Enroll	Freshman Retention Rate	Graduation Rate	Demand Index	Reputation Index
Score	18.0%	51.0%	96.0%	93.0%	11.00	2.83
Rank	24	18	27	16	59	17

Where are the Graduates of Cornell University on the Political Spectrum?

Very Liberal	Liberal	Somewhat Liberal	Somewhat Conservative	Conservative	Very Conservative

See pages 134–135 for detailed explanations and definitions.

Creighton University

Location: Omaha, NE
Campus Setting: City: Large
Total Expenses: $45,132
Estimated Average Discount: $20,162 (45%)
Estimated Net Price: $24,970

Type of Institution: Regional University
Number of Undergraduates: 4,206
SAT Score: Reading: 520–640, Math: 550–660
Student/Faculty Ratio: 11 to 1
Transfer Out Rate: Not Reported

Rank Among 20 Regional Universities	**5**
Overall Rank Among 177 *Alumni Factor* Schools	**69**

Overview

One of 28 Jesuit colleges and universities in the US, Creighton is an excellent school with a practical, conservative Midwestern ethos. Creighton produces very successful graduates who are happy, spiritually developed, and loyal to their alma mater. Based on the overall ratings by grads and their performance in the real world, Creighton is ranked 69th among all colleges and 5th among the top regional universities.

Creighton graduates are well prepared for their careers (ranked 27th) and have very strong job opportunities upon graduation (18th). Its strongest Ultimate Outcome is the combination of Financial Success & Happiness – two areas where graduates excel. Creighton also does very well in comparison to the other 11 Jesuit colleges on our Top 177 list. It ranks 1st in Immediate Job Opportunities and 1st in the percentage of millionaire households. It also performs relatively well in Friendship and Social Development versus the other top Jesuit schools.

An impressive statistic for Creighton is its 18th ranking in grads with a net worth over $1 million. It is squarely within Creighton's midwestern, Jesuit ethic to have quiet wealth. This achievement says volumes about Creighton's character.

Notable Alumni

Legendary Coca-Cola President and board member Don Keough, and Chicago Cubs owner Joseph Ricketts.

The Alumni Factor Rankings Summary

Attribute	Overall Rank
College Experience	**58**
Intellectual Development	85
Social Development	124
Spiritual Development	7
Friendship Development	123
Preparation for Career Success	27
Immediate Job Opportunities	18
Overall Assessment	**102**
Would Personally Choose Again	105
Would Recommend to Student	82
Value for the Money	111
Financial Success	**55**
Income per Household	88
% Households with Income >$150K	72
Household Net Worth	63
% Households Net Worth >$1MM	18
Overall Happiness	**76**
Alumni Giving	**81**
Graduation Rate	**127**
Overall Rank	**69**

Other Key Alumni Outcomes

7.9% Are college professors
14.7% Teach at any level
55.6% Have post-graduate degrees
59.3% Live in dual-income homes
91.2% Are currently employed

See pages 134–135 for detailed explanations and definitions.

Alumni Activities During College

39.8% Community Service
33.0% Intramural Sports
20.5% Internships
13.6% Media Programs
21.6% Music Programs
55.7% Part-Time Jobs

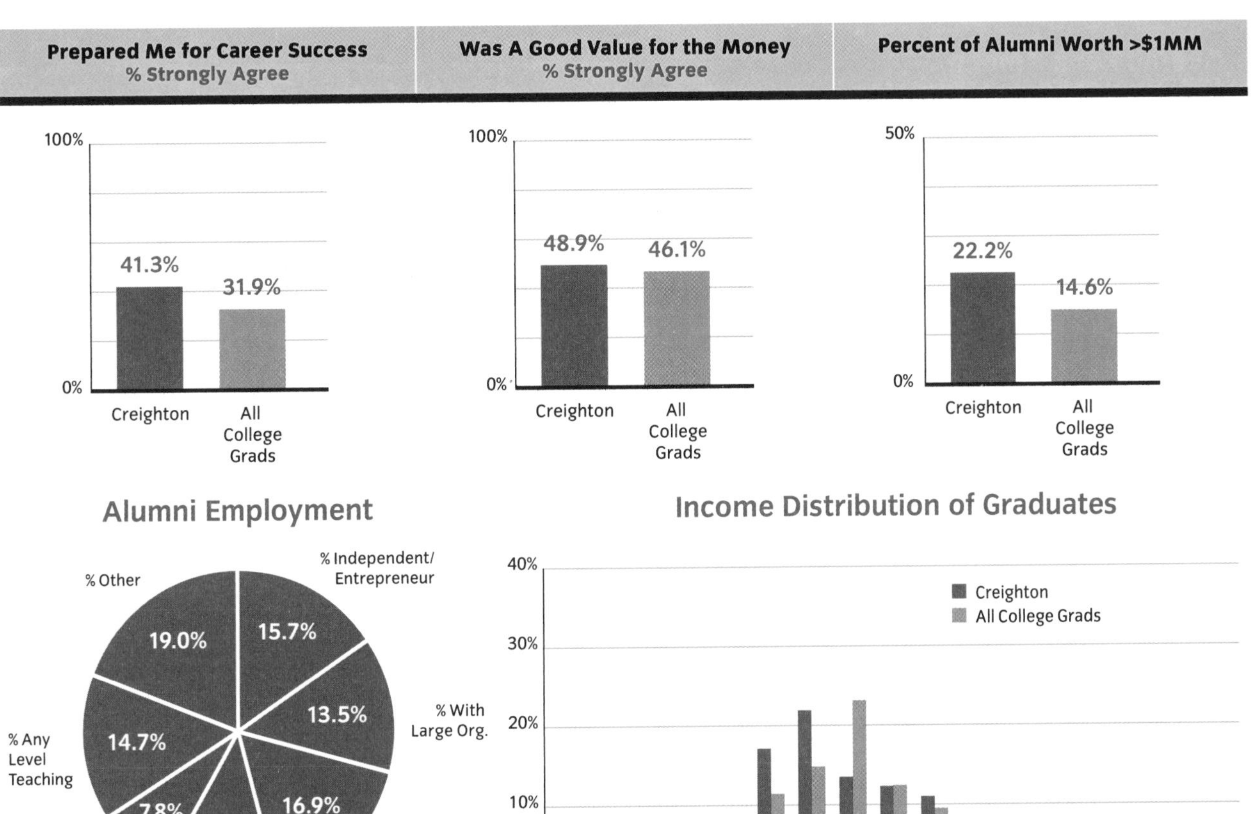

Current Selectivity & Demand Analysis for Creighton University

Attribute	% Accepted	% Accepted Who Enroll	Freshman Retention Rate	Graduation Rate	Demand Index	Reputation Index
Score	78.0%	25.0%	88.0%	77.0%	5.23	0.32
Rank	164	130	135	127	137	165

Where are the Graduates of Creighton University on the Political Spectrum?

Very Liberal	Liberal	Somewhat Liberal	Somewhat Conservative	Conservative	Very Conservative
				↑	

See pages 134–135 for detailed explanations and definitions.

Dartmouth College

Location: Hanover, NH
Campus Setting: Town: Remote
Total Expenses: $58,638
Estimated Average Discount: $37,824 (65%)
Estimated Net Price: $20,814

Type of Institution: National University
Number of Undergraduates: 4,248
SAT Score: Reading: 670–780, Math: 690–790
Student/Faculty Ratio: 8 to 1
Transfer Out Rate: Not Reported

Rank Among 104 National Universities	**7**
Overall Rank Among 177 *Alumni Factor* Schools	**14**

Overview

The smallest, most intimate, most spirited member of the prestigious Ivy League, Dartmouth famously excels at fully developing its undergraduates. It ranks 7th among national universities, 3rd (behind Yale and Princeton) in the Ivy League and 14th overall among all colleges and universities. Dartmouth and its graduates are a study in Renaissance excellence. From the boardrooms, to the courts and financial markets, to government and think tanks, Dartmouth grads can be found leading and shaping our world.

Dartmouth alumni results are even better than the school's current reputation – and that reputation is already among the nation's finest. The Dartmouth statistics are unassailable, with Top 25 rankings in many of our measures. In addition, Dartmouth is the 7th-toughest school in the country in terms of grading – and the toughest place in the Ivy league to get an "A." The tough grading may explain its relatively lower Overall Assessment ratings, which seem to contradict its 2nd ranking in Alumni Giving. Regardless, Dartmouth Alums are loyal and perform at an incredible level of excellence.

Something very special has been going on for generations in Hanover. The weather isn't perfect (unless Winter Carnival is your favorite time of year), and it is very difficult to get in, but you cannot find a more well-rounded, intensely tailored undergraduate experience anywhere.

Notable Alumni

Henry Paulson, Goldman Sachs; John Donahoe, eBay; Lou Gerstner, IBM; Jeff Imelt, GE; Salmon Chase; Timothy Geithner and Dr. Seuss.

The Alumni Factor Rankings Summary

Attribute	University Rank	Overall Rank
College Experience	**9**	**27**
Intellectual Development	12	50
Social Development	12	41
Spiritual Development	16	70
Friendship Development	8	43
Preparation for Career Success	14	34
Immediate Job Opportunities	21	30
Overall Assessment	**35**	**72**
Would Personally Choose Again	26	57
Would Recommend to Student	30	64
Value for the Money	54	99
Financial Success	**10**	**19**
Income per Household	13	23
% Households with Income >$150K	15	26
Household Net Worth	14	28
% Households Net Worth >$1MM	5	9
Overall Happiness	**25**	**48**
Alumni Giving	**2**	**13**
Graduation Rate	**7**	**7**
Overall Rank	**7**	**14**

Other Key Alumni Outcomes

10.0% Are college professors
11.2% Teach at any level
63.2% Have post-graduate degrees
46.0% Live in dual-income homes
90.3% Are currently employed

See pages 134–135 for detailed explanations and definitions.

Alumni Activities During College

41.8% Community Service
29.7% Intramural Sports
29.7% Internships
33.3% Media Programs
31.5% Music Programs
31.5% Part-Time Jobs

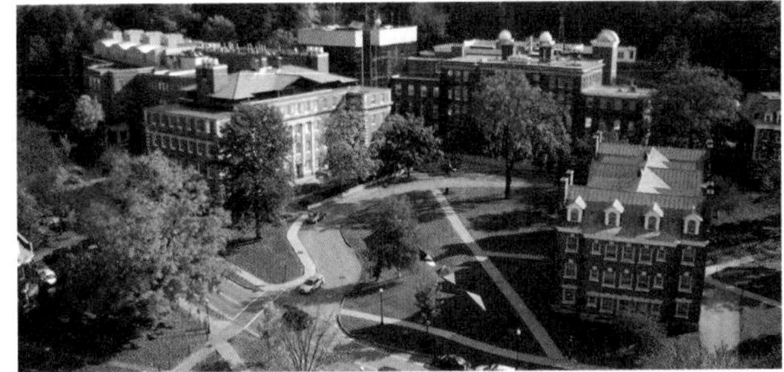

Prepared Me for Career Success % Strongly Agree	Was A Good Value for the Money % Strongly Agree	Percent of Alumni Worth >$1MM

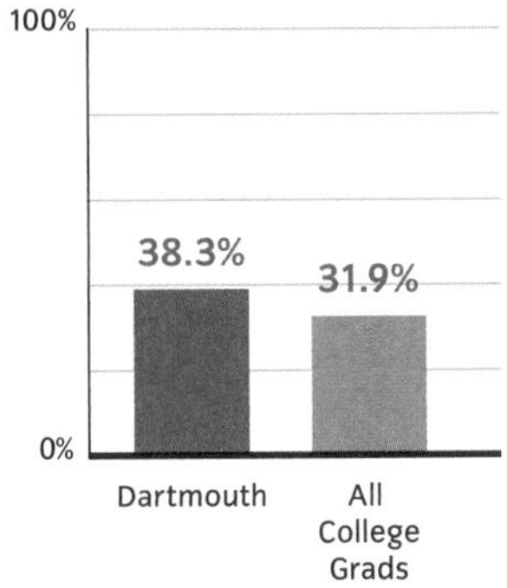

100%
0%
38.3%
31.9%
Dartmouth
All College Grads

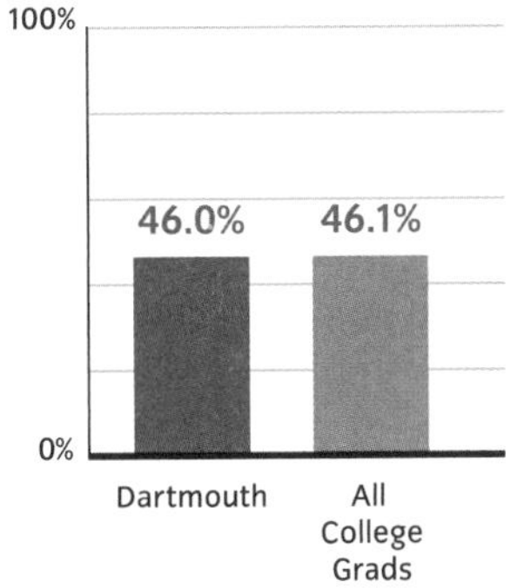

100%
0%
46.0%
46.1%
Dartmouth
All College Grads

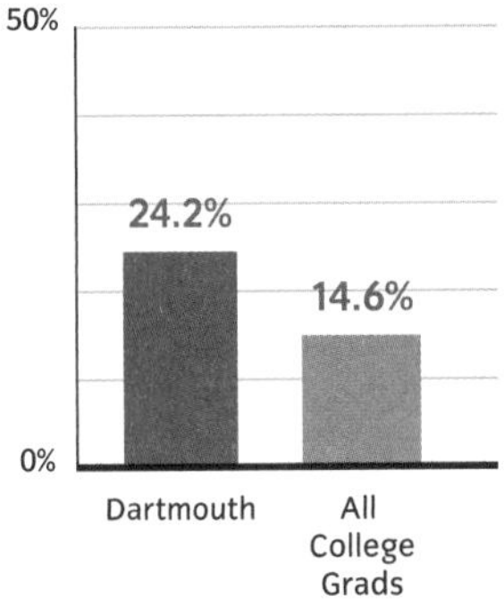

50%
0%
24.2%
14.6%
Dartmouth
All College Grads

Alumni Employment

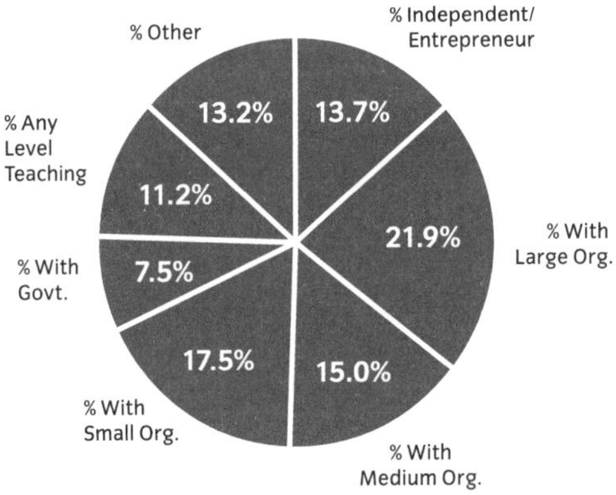

% Other
13.2%
% Independent/ Entrepreneur
13.7%
% With Large Org.
21.9%
% With Medium Org.
15.0%
% With Small Org.
17.5%
% With Govt.
7.5%
% Any Level Teaching
11.2%

Income Distribution of Graduates

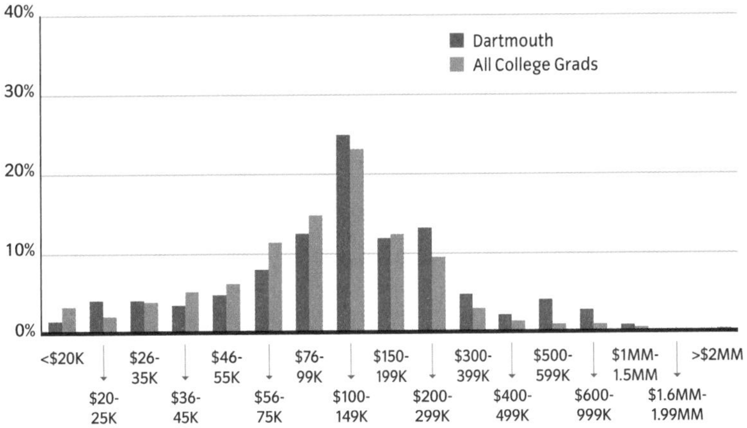

40%
30%
20%
10%
0%
Dartmouth
All College Grads
<$20K
$20-25K
$26-35K
$36-45K
$46-55K
$56-75K
$76-99K
$100-149K
$150-199K
$200-299K
$300-399K
$400-499K
$500-599K
$600-999K
$1MM-1.5MM
$1.6MM-1.99MM
>$2MM

Current Selectivity & Demand Analysis for Dartmouth College

Attribute	% Accepted	% Accepted Who Enroll	Freshman Retention Rate	Graduation Rate	Demand Index	Reputation Index
Score	12.0%	52.0%	97.0%	95.0%	16.89	4.33
Rank	11	16	13	7	13	12

Where are the Graduates of Dartmouth College on the Political Spectrum?

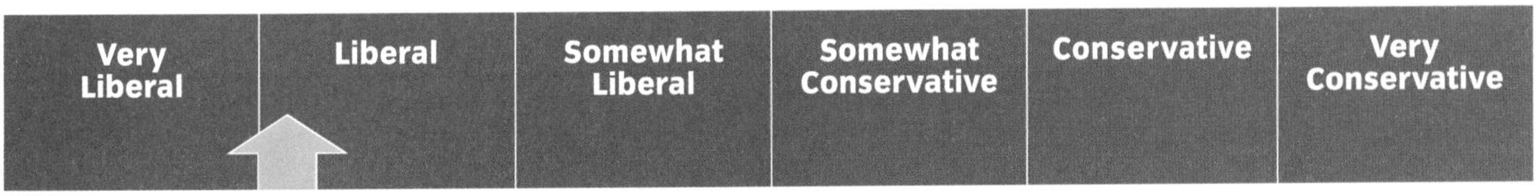

Very Liberal
Liberal
Somewhat Liberal
Somewhat Conservative
Conservative
Very Conservative

See pages 134–135 for detailed explanations and definitions.

Davidson College

Location: Davidson, NC
Campus Setting: Suburb: Large
Total Expenses: $52,498
Estimated Average Discount: $28,875 (55%)
Estimated Net Price: $23,623

Type of Institution: Liberal Arts College
Number of Undergraduates: 1,742
SAT Score: Reading: 630–730, Math: 640–718
Student/Faculty Ratio: 10 to 1
Transfer Out Rate: Not Reported

Rank Among 53 Liberal Arts Colleges	**13**
Overall Rank Among 177 *Alumni Factor* Schools	**20**

Overview

For 175 years, Davidson has been providing an intense liberal arts education to some of the finest minds. This has led to an impressive record of alumni achievement that ranks Davidson 13th in the country and among the finest liberal arts schools anywhere. Davidson grads are successful (ranked 25th in Financial Success), smart, spiritual, proud of their school, deeply connected to their undergraduate friends (ranked 17th in Friendship Development), and highly successful in business, politics, the arts, education and medicine. Davidson is also a prolific producer of Rhodes Scholars, with 23 in its history – only five liberal arts schools have more.

Davidson grads are quite proud of their small college, ranking 6th in Alumni Giving and 6th in their willingness to recommend their school. Davidson ranks in the Top 30 in all Ultimate Outcomes, with exceptional strength in Friendships & Intellectual Capability (ranked 4th) and in Happiness & Intellectual Capability (5th). Davidson also ranks 13th among all colleges in tough grading, as its academic programs are of legendary rigorousness.

Davidson grads are well known for being serious learners and strong leaders. This reputation clearly shows in Davidson alumni outcomes.

Notable Alumni

Dean Rusk; former Clinton counsel Vincent Foster; author Patricia Cornwell and Pulitzer Prize-winning poet Charles Wright.

The Alumni Factor Rankings Summary

Attribute	Liberal Arts Rank	Overall Rank
College Experience	**9**	**11**
Intellectual Development	13	14
Social Development	19	30
Spiritual Development	7	19
Friendship Development	17	19
Preparation for Career Success	8	12
Immediate Job Opportunities	10	47
Overall Assessment	**22**	**52**
Would Personally Choose Again	39	113
Would Recommend to Student	6	22
Value for the Money	13	37
Financial Success	**25**	**67**
Income per Household	27	92
% Households with Income >$150K	25	66
Household Net Worth	26	67
% Households Net Worth >$1MM	24	56
Overall Happiness	**23**	**57**
Alumni Giving	**6**	**7**
Graduation Rate	**14**	**32**
Overall Rank	**13**	**20**

Other Key Alumni Outcomes

8.8% Are college professors
12.5% Teach at any level
75.7% Have post-graduate degrees
49.3% Live in dual-income homes
88.4% Are currently employed

See pages 134–135 for detailed explanations and definitions.

Alumni Activities During College

43.1% Community Service
48.2% Intramural Sports
27.7% Internships
35.0% Media Programs
23.4% Music Programs
21.9% Part-Time Jobs

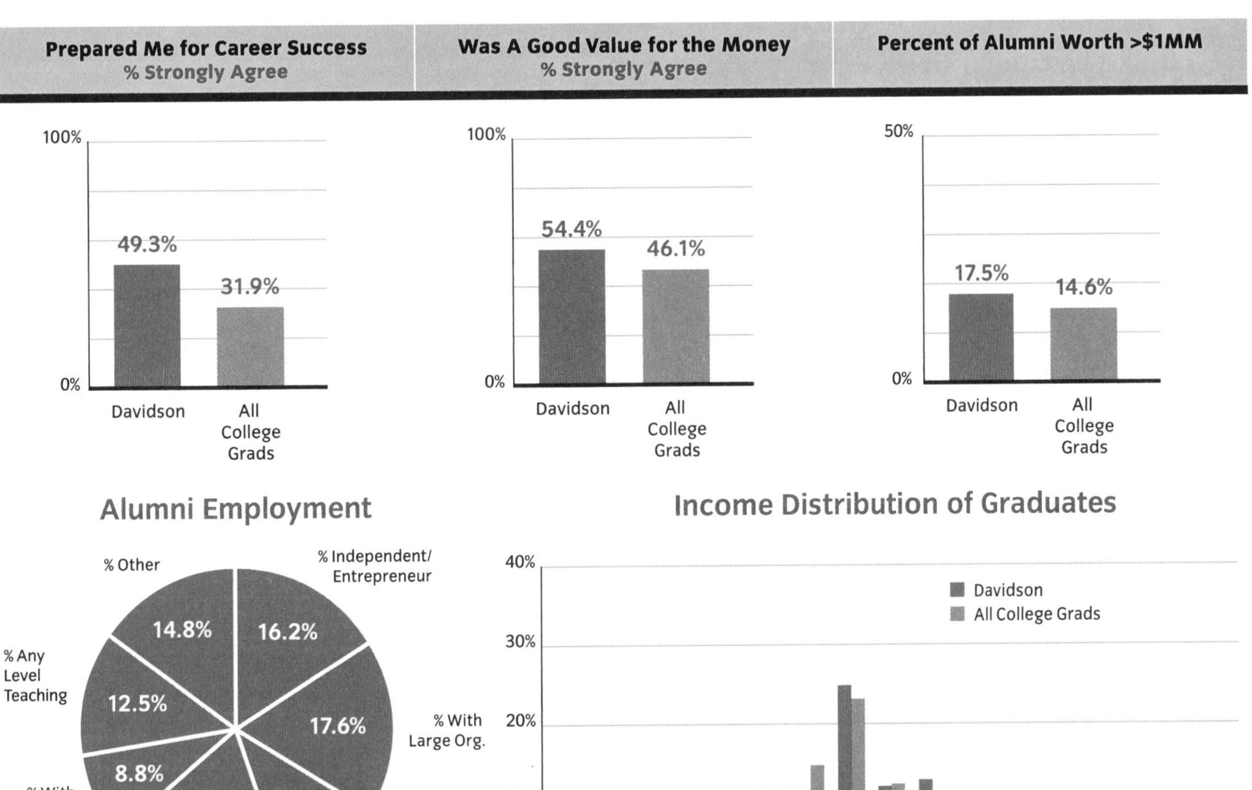

Current Selectivity & Demand Analysis for Davidson College

Attribute	% Accepted	% Accepted Who Enroll	Freshman Retention Rate	Graduation Rate	Demand Index	Reputation Index
Score	25.0%	40.0%	96.0%	91.0%	9.75	1.60
Rank	39	42	27	32	71	34

Where are the Graduates of Davidson College on the Political Spectrum?

Very Liberal	Liberal	Somewhat Liberal	Somewhat Conservative	Conservative	Very Conservative
		↑			

Denison University

Location: Grandville, OH
Campus Setting: Suburb: Small
Total Expenses: $52,020
Estimated Average Discount: $25,113 (48%)
Estimated Net Price: $26,907

Type of Institution: Liberal Arts College
Number of Undergraduates: 2,275
SAT Score: Reading: 600–690, Math: 590–670
Student/Faculty Ratio: 10 to 1
Transfer Out Rate: Not Reported

Rank Among 53 Liberal Arts Colleges	**49**
Overall Rank Among 177 *Alumni Factor* Schools	**107**

Overview

It is clear that Denison University, a small liberal arts school in Granville, Ohio, produces financially successful graduates. Denison ranks in the Top 20 for each of the four metrics of Financial Success we measure, and is 1st in Financial Success among the eight Ohio schools to make it onto our Top 177 list. Yet it is also clear that Denison's financial rankings outpace its scores across the rest of the attributes – particularly the College Experience (ranked 49th) and the Overall Assessment (49th). What can explain this "High Success/Lower Recommendation/Lower Experience" dynamic?

Interestingly, there are 16 schools like Denison with a Financial Success ranking in the top third and an Overall Assessment ranking in the bottom third. Most of these schools face a geographic challenge (like Denison) or some other cultural dynamic that drives this dichotomy. The Experience and Assessment rankings are the only elements preventing Denison from cracking the list of the Top 25 liberal arts schools or the Top 50 schools overall. Nevertheless, its results are strong enough to say that alumni outcomes well exceed the school's already strong reputation. This is a school we believe will continually climb in our rankings, given the progressive activity at Denison today.

Notable Alumni

Disney's Michael Eisner; Woody Hayes; Jennifer Garner; Steve Carell; and Senator Richard Lugar.

The Alumni Factor Rankings Summary

Attribute	Liberal Arts Rank	Overall Rank
College Experience	**49**	**116**
Intellectual Development	49	111
Social Development	44	96
Spiritual Development	49	117
Friendship Development	47	75
Preparation for Career Success	46	123
Immediate Job Opportunities	41	152
Overall Assessment	**49**	**154**
Would Personally Choose Again	53	175
Would Recommend to Student	44	130
Value for the Money	46	139
Financial Success	**16**	**37**
Income per Household	16	49
% Households with Income >$150K	19	39
Household Net Worth	14	29
% Households Net Worth >$1MM	19	44
Overall Happiness	**38**	**121**
Alumni Giving	**49**	**65**
Graduation Rate	**43**	**86**
Overall Rank	**49**	**107**

Other Key Alumni Outcomes

7.0% Are college professors
8.4% Teach at any level
48.9% Have post-graduate degrees
54.2% Live in dual-income homes
94.4% Are currently employed

See pages 134–135 for detailed explanations and definitions.

Alumni Activities During College

33.1% Community Service
32.4% Intramural Sports
26.8% Internships
21.8% Media Programs
16.2% Music Programs
15.5% Part-Time Jobs

Alumni Employment

Income Distribution of Graduates

Current Selectivity & Demand Analysis for Denison University

Attribute	% Accepted	% Accepted Who Enroll	Freshman Retention Rate	Graduation Rate	Demand Index	Reputation Index
Score	48.0%	26.0%	89.0%	83.0%	7.87	0.54
Rank	102	125	124	86	101	115

Where are the Graduates of Denison University on the Political Spectrum?

Very Liberal	Liberal	Somewhat Liberal	Somewhat Conservative	Conservative	Very Conservative
		↑			

See pages 134–135 for detailed explanations and definitions.

DePaul University

Location: Chicago, IL
Campus Setting: City: Large
Total Expenses: $45,618
Estimated Average Discount: $21,413 (47%)
Estimated Net Price: $24,205

Type of Institution: National University
Number of Undergraduates: 16,052
SAT Score: Reading: 530–640, Math: 520–620
Student/Faculty Ratio: 17 to 1
Transfer Out Rate: 13%

Rank Among 104 National Universities	**104**
Overall Rank Among 177 *Alumni Factor* Schools	**177**

Overview

The largest Catholic University in the nation with one of the country's most racially diverse campuses, DePaul is 36 inner-city acres of can-do attitude and optimism. When an inner-city school of this size – in this location and with its aggressively liberal admissions process – makes its way onto this Top 177 list, it is a noteworthy achievement. But don't tell that to DePaul grads and administrators – they likely never doubted the outcome. Ranked 104th among national universities, DePaul does not appear to stand out among this illustrious group of colleges – until you take a closer look.

DePaul truly differentiates itself by focusing on recruiting first-generation college students from moderate and disadvantaged backgrounds – and providing those students with a rigorous education. Few of the Top 177 can claim to do that on DePaul's scale or with DePaul's success.

An integral part of Chicago's history, DePaul has grown up with the city over the last 114 years and has experienced all of its ups and downs in parallel. As the past has proven, the future is bright for the Blue Demons.

Notable Alumni

Former mayors Richard M. and Richard J. Daley; CEOs of McDonald's, Kellogg, and the Chicago Board of Trade; athletes – 14 NBA stars and counting, and film and entertainment luminaries.

The Alumni Factor Rankings Summary

Attribute	University Rank	Overall Rank
College Experience	**90**	**163**
Intellectual Development	88	160
Social Development	81	150
Spiritual Development	28	89
Friendship Development	104	177
Preparation for Career Success	99	171
Immediate Job Opportunities	88	147
Overall Assessment	**95**	**165**
Would Personally Choose Again	79	140
Would Recommend to Student	88	157
Value for the Money	102	174
Financial Success	**99**	**165**
Income per Household	92	149
% Households with Income >$150K	97	161
Household Net Worth	91	156
% Households Net Worth >$1MM	97	160
Overall Happiness	**89**	**147**
Alumni Giving	**91**	**162**
Graduation Rate	**85**	**153**
Overall Rank	**104**	**177**

Other Key Alumni Outcomes

2.2% Are college professors
12.4% Teach at any level
40.3% Have post-graduate degrees
48.6% Live in dual-income homes
86.5% Are currently employed

See pages 134–135 for detailed explanations and definitions.

Alumni Activities During College

24.3% Community Service
10.7% Intramural Sports
17.9% Internships
6.4% Media Programs
9.3% Music Programs
41.4% Part-Time Jobs

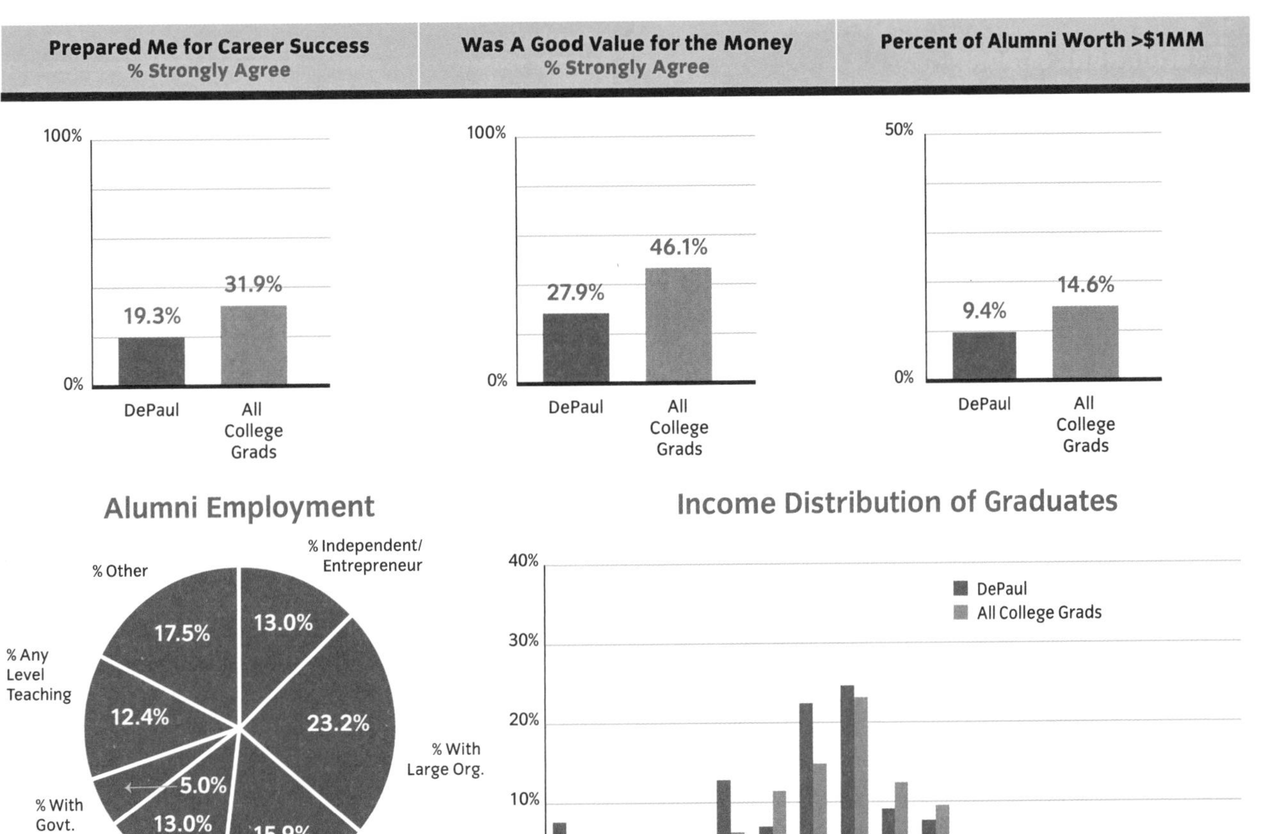

Current Selectivity & Demand Analysis for DePaul University

Attribute	% Accepted	% Accepted Who Enroll	Freshman Retention Rate	Graduation Rate	Demand Index	Reputation Index
Score	64.0%	23.0%	87.0%	68.0%	6.80	0.36
Rank	139	144	140	153	117	155

Where are the Graduates of DePaul University on the Political Spectrum?

Very Liberal	Liberal	Somewhat Liberal	Somewhat Conservative	Conservative	Very Conservative

See pages 134–135 for detailed explanations and definitions.

DePauw University

Location: Greencastle, IN
Campus Setting: Town: Distant
Total Expenses: $48,800
Estimated Average Discount: $24,767 (51%)
Estimated Net Price: $24,033

Type of Institution: Liberal Arts College
Number of Undergraduates: 2,390
SAT Score: Reading: 530–660, Math: 570–680
Student/Faculty Ratio: 10 to 1
Transfer Out Rate: Not Reported

Rank Among 53 Liberal Arts Colleges	**50**
Overall Rank Among 177 *Alumni Factor* Schools	**115**

Overview

A Top 50 Liberal Arts college with a tightly bound alumni group, DePauw has developed a reputation for delivering a powerful liberal arts education with a practical bent. Taking a cue from its central Indiana location, DePauw strives for a positive, sensible excellence in its education – and delivers it. DePauw grads are exceptionally hard-working and have the 4th best employment rate of any college or university we measure. With little fanfare or notoriety seeking, Depauw produces some of the best and brightest in business, government, science, journalism and entertainment.

Depauw grads are more Republican than the typical college graduate, yet place near the center of our graduate political spectrum in their political views. Strong Overall Happiness scores drive DePauw's success in Ultimate Outcomes (where it ranks 43rd overall), and DePauw's ability to provide ample Immediate Job Opportunities (27th) has long been a bright spot for the college. But it is the combination of work ethic and smarts that really differentiates DePauw from the typical college.

Notable Alumni

Research analyst extraordinaire Mary Meeker; Eli Lilly himself; Bill and Scott Rasmussen, founders of ESPN; billionaire Steven Rales; politician Dan Quayle and former N.O.W. president Patricia Ireland.

The Alumni Factor Rankings Summary

Attribute	Liberal Arts Rank	Overall Rank
College Experience	**44**	**91**
Intellectual Development	49	111
Social Development	22	36
Spiritual Development	41	76
Friendship Development	44	72
Preparation for Career Success	40	106
Immediate Job Opportunities	27	119
Overall Assessment	**47**	**144**
Would Personally Choose Again	46	147
Would Recommend to Student	45	137
Value for the Money	42	128
Financial Success	**40**	**126**
Income per Household	35	129
% Households with Income >$150K	36	106
Household Net Worth	44	145
% Households Net Worth >$1MM	42	116
Overall Happiness	**21**	**51**
Alumni Giving	**41**	**52**
Graduation Rate	**37**	**76**
Overall Rank	**50**	**115**

Other Key Alumni Outcomes

7.7% Are college professors
16.2% Teach at any level
50.4% Have post-graduate degrees
46.0% Live in dual-income homes
97.6% Are currently employed

See pages 134–135 for detailed explanations and definitions.

Alumni Activities During College

51.6% Community Service
42.2% Intramural Sports
34.4% Internships
34.4% Media Programs
36.7% Music Programs
27.3% Part-Time Jobs

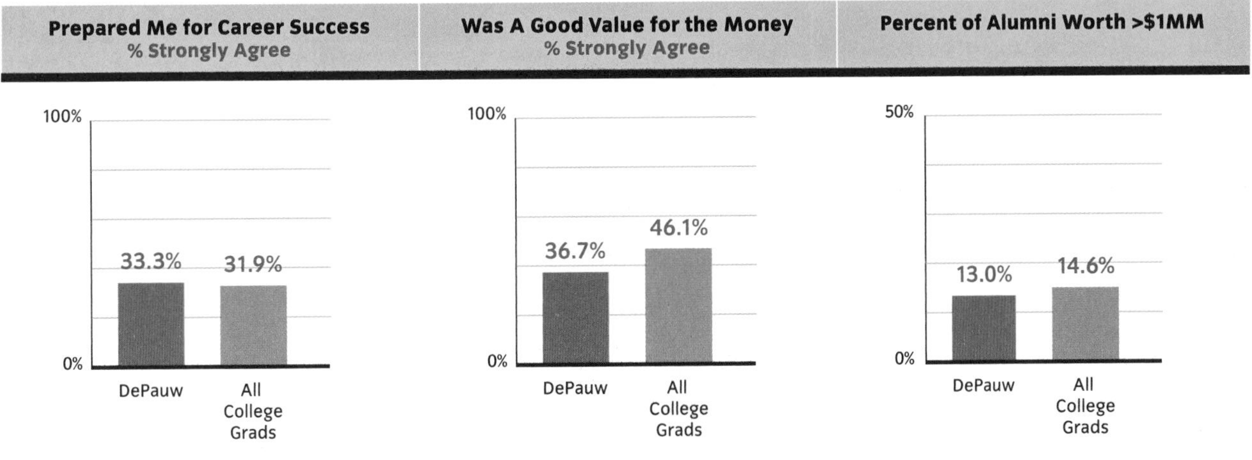

Alumni Employment

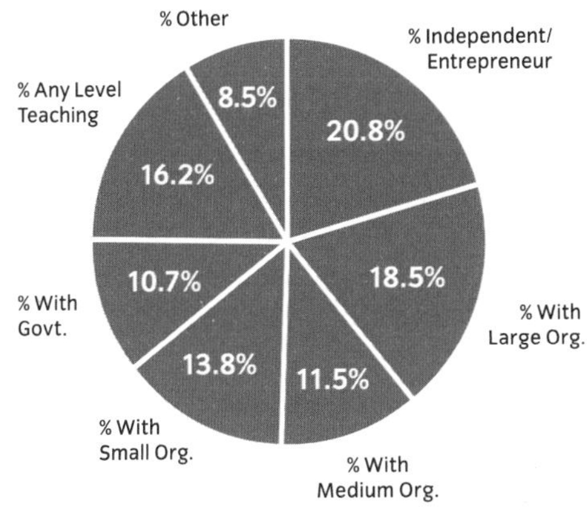

Income Distribution of Graduates

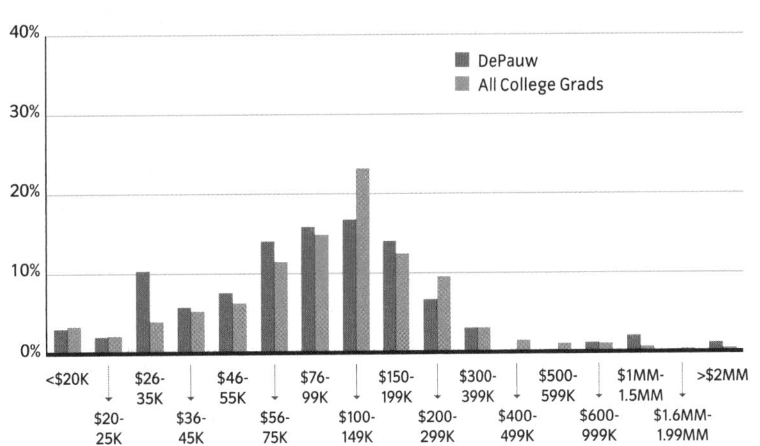

Current Selectivity & Demand Analysis for DePauw University

Attribute	% Accepted	% Accepted Who Enroll	Freshman Retention Rate	Graduation Rate	Demand Index	Reputation Index
Score	57.0%	20.0%	90.0%	85.0%	8.79	0.35
Rank	116	161	113	76	86	158

Where are the Graduates of DePauw University on the Political Spectrum?

Very Liberal	Liberal	Somewhat Liberal	Somewhat Conservative	Conservative	Very Conservative

See pages 134–135 for detailed explanations and definitions.

Dickinson College

Location: Carlisle, PA
Campus Setting: Town: Distant
Total Expenses: $56,360
Estimated Average Discount: $28,489 (51%)
Estimated Net Price: $27,871

Type of Institution: Liberal Arts College
Number of Undergraduates: 2,414
SAT Score: Reading: 600–690, Math: 590–680
Student/Faculty Ratio: 10 to 1
Transfer Out Rate: Not Reported

Rank Among 53 Liberal Arts Colleges	**52**
Overall Rank Among 177 *Alumni Factor* Schools	**150**

Overview

Founded by Benjamin Rush, signatory to the Declaration of Independence, as the 16th college in the US, Dickinson has long enjoyed a fine reputation as a liberal arts school with a global vision. It has produced a large number of journalists and public servants, as well as leaders in law, business and the arts. Nearly 8% of Dickinson grads become college professors (ranked 42nd).

Despite a lower Overall Assessment by graduates relative to the other top liberal arts colleges, Dickinson enjoys strong Alumni Giving (35th) and graduates perform quite well in Financial Success (33rd). Dickinson also ranks in the top half of all schools when it comes to the important Ultimate Outcomes of Financial Success & Intellectual Capability, Happiness & Intellectual Capability, and Friendships & Intellectual Capability. Notably, Dickinson recently celebrated its 125th anniversary of educating women – a rare co-educational achievement among the Top 177 colleges and universities.

Like some other liberal arts colleges, Dickinson does not get its highest marks in Immediate Job Opportunities (50th) or in Preparation for Career Success (52nd). But as its rankings on Financial Success and some Ultimate Outcomes illustrate, in the long run, it truly distinguishes itself in other unique ways to be among the best of the liberal arts colleges.

Notable Alumni

15th US president James Buchanan; 5th Supreme Court chief justice Roger Taney; talk-show host Rosie O'Donnell; and authors Jennifer Haigh and Jennifer Holm.

The Alumni Factor Rankings Summary

Attribute	Liberal Arts Rank	Overall Rank
College Experience	**52**	**143**
Intellectual Development	47	95
Social Development	52	154
Spiritual Development	47	101
Friendship Development	48	88
Preparation for Career Success	52	166
Immediate Job Opportunities	50	166
Overall Assessment	**53**	**176**
Would Personally Choose Again	52	174
Would Recommend to Student	53	169
Value for the Money	53	175
Financial Success	**33**	**96**
Income per Household	42	139
% Households with Income >$150K	29	86
Household Net Worth	30	81
% Households Net Worth >$1MM	34	85
Overall Happiness	**45**	**159**
Alumni Giving	**35**	**43**
Graduation Rate	**45**	**91**
Overall Rank	**52**	**150**

Other Key Alumni Outcomes

7.9% Are college professors
11.9% Teach at any level
56.3% Have post-graduate degrees
59.5% Live in dual-income homes
91.3% Are currently employed

See pages 134–135 for detailed explanations and definitions.

Alumni Activities During College

44.8% Community Service
36.0% Intramural Sports
31.2% Internships
27.2% Media Programs
23.2% Music Programs
25.6% Part-Time Jobs

Prepared Me for Career Success % Strongly Agree	Was A Good Value for the Money % Strongly Agree	Percent of Alumni Worth >$1MM
Dickinson: 16.9% All College Grads: 31.9%	Dickinson: 19.2% All College Grads: 46.1%	Dickinson: 14.8% All College Grads: 14.6%

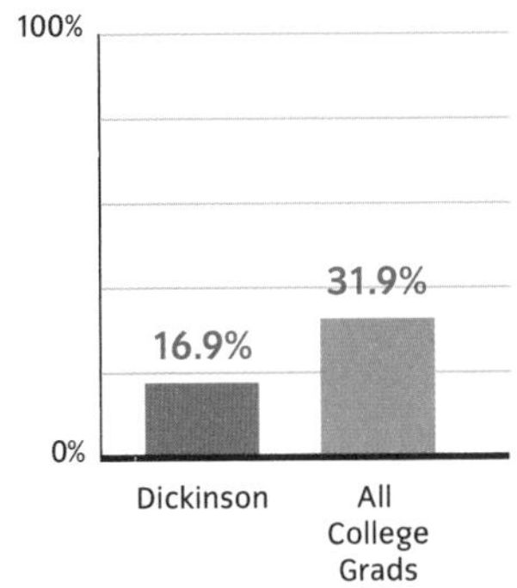

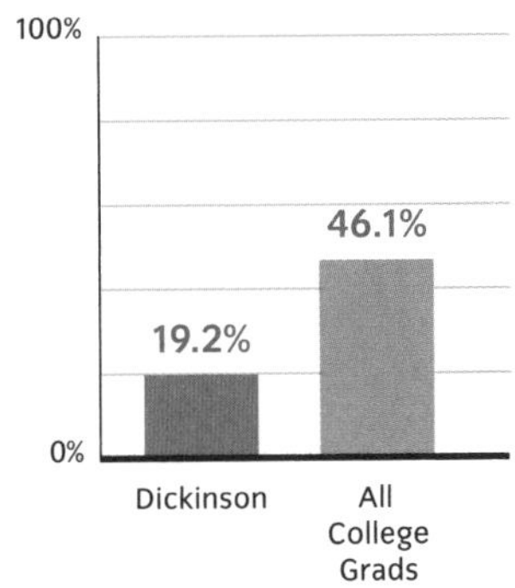

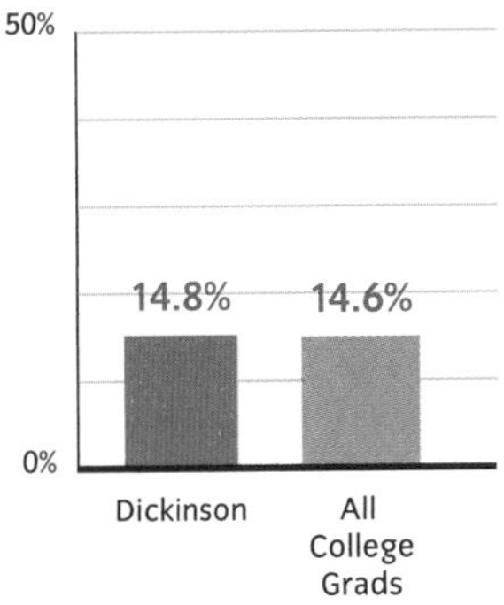

Alumni Employment

- % Independent/ Entrepreneur: 12.7%
- % With Large Org.: 20.6%
- % With Medium Org.: 13.5%
- % With Small Org.: 18.3%
- % With Govt.: 8.8%
- % Any Level Teaching: 11.9%
- % Other: 14.2%

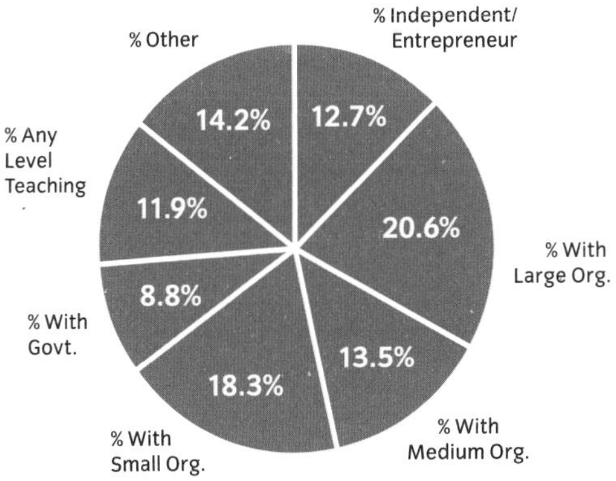

Income Distribution of Graduates

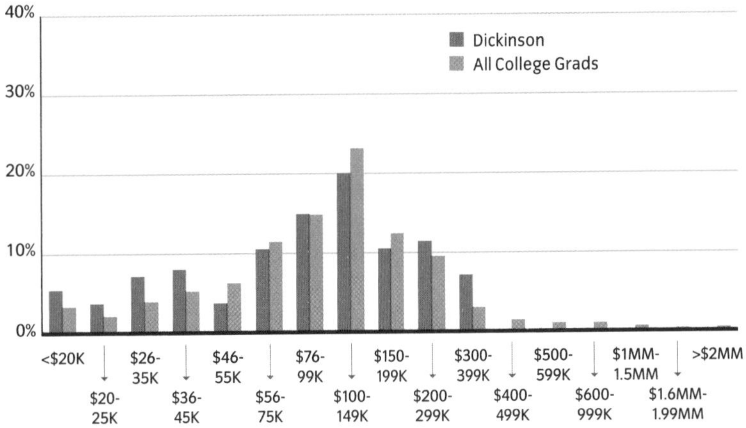

Dickinson / All College Grads

<$20K, $20-25K, $26-35K, $36-45K, $46-55K, $56-75K, $76-99K, $100-149K, $150-199K, $200-299K, $300-399K, $400-499K, $500-599K, $600-999K, $1MM-1.5MM, $1.6MM-1.99MM, >$2MM

Current Selectivity & Demand Analysis for Dickinson College

Attribute	% Accepted	% Accepted Who Enroll	Freshman Retention Rate	Graduation Rate	Demand Index	Reputation Index
Score	42.0%	26.0%	90.0%	82.0%	9.30	0.62
Rank	85	125	113	91	78	99

Where are the Graduates of Dickinson College on the Political Spectrum?

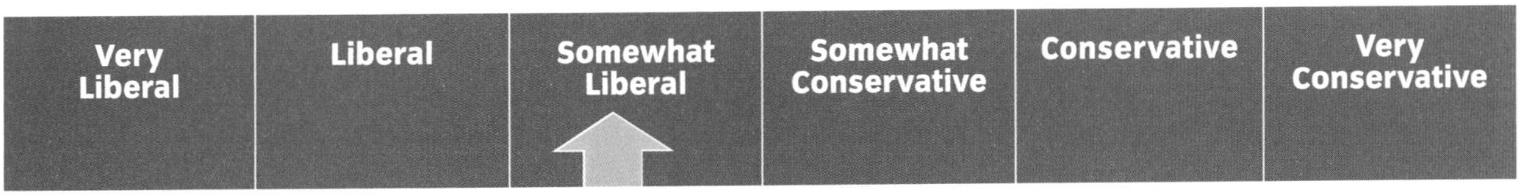

Very Liberal	Liberal	Somewhat Liberal	Somewhat Conservative	Conservative	Very Conservative
		↑			

Drexel University

Location: Philadelphia, PA
Campus Setting: City: Large
Total Expenses: $54,040
Estimated Average Discount: $19,380 (36%)
Estimated Net Price: $34,660

Type of Institution: National University
Number of Undergraduates: 13,980
SAT Score: Reading: 530–630, Math: 570–680
Student/Faculty Ratio: 10 to 1
Transfer Out Rate: 20%

Rank Among 104 National Universities	**69**
Overall Rank Among 177 *Alumni Factor* Schools	**134**

Overview

A rigorous science and engineering research university ranked 9th among national universities in providing Immediate Job Opportunities for its graduates, Drexel well prepares its alumni to succeed in their chosen fields. Grads of Drexel are financially successful (ranked 36th) as they apply a practical, demanding undergraduate education to their diverse careers. Drexel's co-op program is widely acclaimed.

Drexel grads skew to the right on the political spectrum, being 43% more likely to call themselves Republicans than the composite of all college graduates. Like many technical schools, Drexel grads are less likely to crow about their College Experience (69th) or stay as close to their undergraduate friends (92nd) as are graduates of the other Top 177 Colleges. Although exceptions do exist, technical schools generally do not have the close-knit campus life found at many of the liberal arts schools or even at some large universities.

Drexel certainly does, however, produce successful graduates. Ranked 32nd in high income households and 33rd in Household Net Worth, Drexel alumni compete very successfully.

Notable Alumni

Kenneth Dahlberg, CEO of SAIC; Raj Gupta, former CEO of Rohm & Haas; and many other leaders in medicine, politics and business.

The Alumni Factor Rankings Summary

Attribute	University Rank	Overall Rank
College Experience	**69**	**138**
Intellectual Development	99	171
Social Development	79	147
Spiritual Development	102	175
Friendship Development	92	162
Preparation for Career Success	29	70
Immediate Job Opportunities	9	13
Overall Assessment	**87**	**155**
Would Personally Choose Again	88	154
Would Recommend to Student	79	145
Value for the Money	79	142
Financial Success	**36**	**65**
Income per Household	53	85
% Households with Income >$150K	32	56
Household Net Worth	33	58
% Households Net Worth >$1MM	44	76
Overall Happiness	**93**	**148**
Alumni Giving	**39**	**99**
Graduation Rate	**85**	**153**
Overall Rank	**69**	**134**

Other Key Alumni Outcomes

1.9%	Are college professors
5.6%	Teach at any level
45.8%	Have post-graduate degrees
55.7%	Live in dual-income homes
88.0%	Are currently employed

See pages 134–135 for detailed explanations and definitions.

Alumni Activities During College

19.4% Community Service
23.1% Intramural Sports
42.6% Internships
12.0% Media Programs
9.2% Music Programs
37.0% Part-Time Jobs

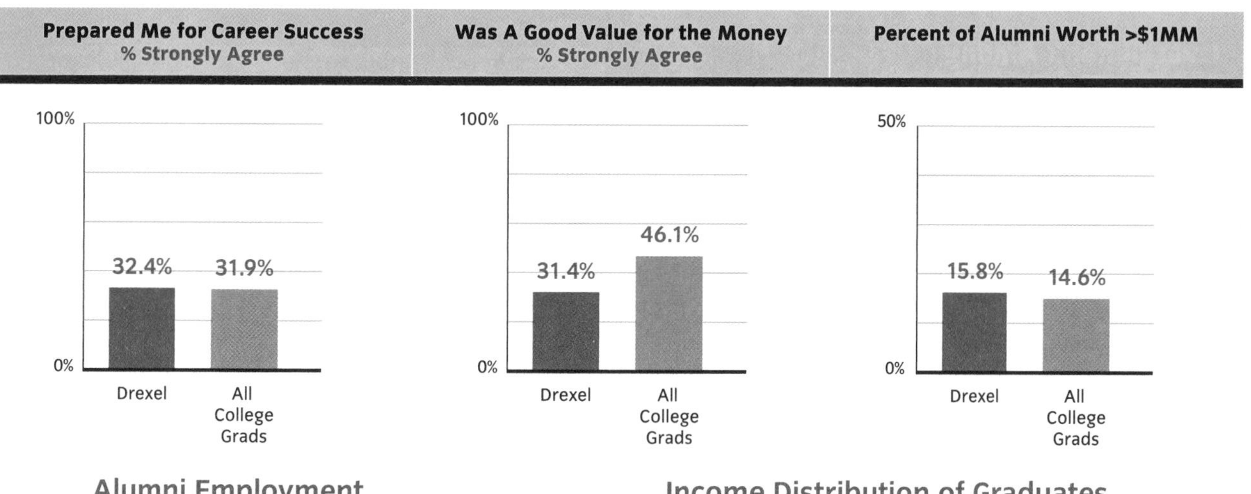

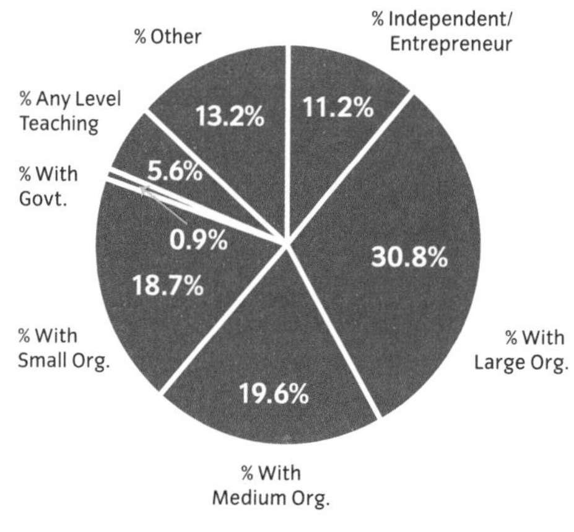

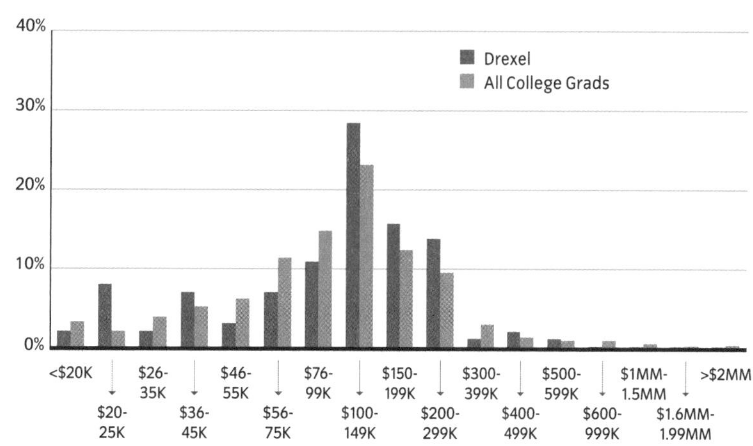

Current Selectivity & Demand Analysis for Drexel University

Attribute	% Accepted	% Accepted Who Enroll	Freshman Retention Rate	Graduation Rate	Demand Index	Reputation Index
Score	58.0%	11.0%	83.0%	68.0%	15.43	0.19
Rank	119	177	161	153	18	176

Where are the Graduates of Drexel University on the Political Spectrum?

Very Liberal	Liberal	Somewhat Liberal	Somewhat Conservative	Conservative	Very Conservative

See pages 134–135 for detailed explanations and definitions.

Duke University

Location: Durham, NC
Campus Setting: City: Midsize
Total Expenses: $57,325
Estimated Average Discount: $34,446 (60%)
Estimated Net Price: $22,879

Type of Institution: National University
Number of Undergraduates: 6,697
SAT Score: Reading: 660–750, Math: 690–780
Student/Faculty Ratio: 8 to 1
Transfer Out Rate: Not Reported

Rank Among 104 National Universities	**10**
Overall Rank Among 177 *Alumni Factor* Schools	**27**

Overview

Ranked 10th among national universities with strong performance across nearly all key attributes, Duke lives up to its stellar reputation for producing financially successful (ranked 8th) and loyal grads (4th in Alumni Giving) who are tightly bound to Duke and to one another (ranked 11th in Friendship Development). Despite its moderate value ranking (61st), it is definitely an excellent value based on actual alumni outcomes.

Duke's 3rd ranking in the Ultimate Outcomes is driven by its extraordinarily high performance in the trifecta that all colleges seek for their graduates: Financial Success, Intellectual Development and Friendship Development. Duke is also well known for having high-performing athletes who are also strong students. Duke is among the Top 10 schools in the country in the graduation rate of its varsity athletes, with a stellar rate of 97%.

It is hard to find a more accomplished alumni group than Duke's. Whether you love the Blue Devils or are on the wrong end of the score against their storied hoopsters, you can't deny the institutional excellence that defines Duke and its graduates.

Notable Alumni

Public servants Elizabeth Dole and Ron Paul; philanthropist Melinda Gates; Steve Pagliuca, Bain Capital; David Rubenstein, Carlyle Group; and William A. Hawkins, former CEO of Medtronic and current CEO of Immucor.

The Alumni Factor Rankings Summary

Attribute	University Rank	Overall Rank
College Experience	**22**	**69**
Intellectual Development	28	77
Social Development	22	63
Spiritual Development	23	81
Friendship Development	11	48
Preparation for Career Success	42	92
Immediate Job Opportunities	31	47
Overall Assessment	**41**	**85**
Would Personally Choose Again	32	64
Would Recommend to Student	40	78
Value for the Money	61	110
Financial Success	**8**	**16**
Income per Household	6	12
% Households with Income >$150K	11	22
Household Net Worth	11	23
% Households Net Worth >$1MM	10	20
Overall Happiness	**35**	**66**
Alumni Giving	**4**	**32**
Graduation Rate	**9**	**11**
Overall Rank	**10**	**27**

Other Key Alumni Outcomes

5.6% Are college professors
13.7% Teach at any level
67.6% Have post-graduate degrees
54.5% Live in dual-income homes
92.4% Are currently employed

See pages 134–135 for detailed explanations and definitions.

Alumni Activities During College

44.9% Community Service
32.6% Intramural Sports
24.6% Internships
19.1% Media Programs
20.4% Music Programs
30.1% Part-Time Jobs

Prepared Me for Career Success % Strongly Agree	Was A Good Value for the Money % Strongly Agree	Percent of Alumni Worth >$1MM
Duke: 29.5%	Duke: 39.7%	Duke: 22.0%
All College Grads: 31.9%	All College Grads: 46.1%	All College Grads: 14.6%

Alumni Employment

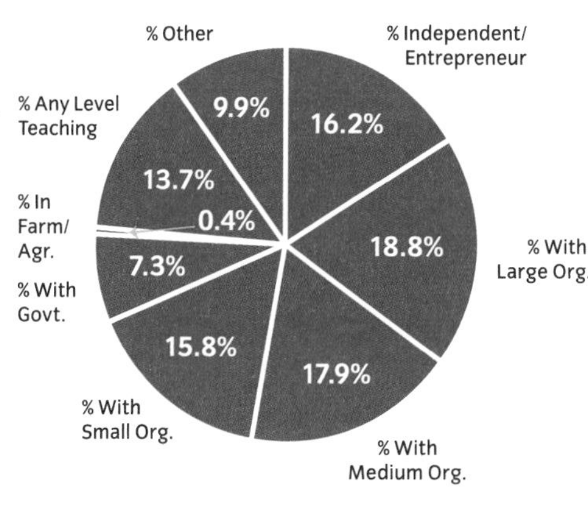

Income Distribution of Graduates

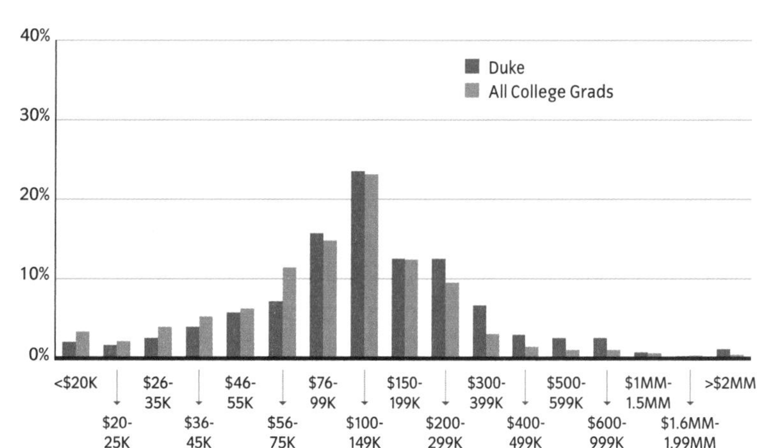

Current Selectivity & Demand Analysis for Duke University

Attribute	% Accepted	% Accepted Who Enroll	Freshman Retention Rate	Graduation Rate	Demand Index	Reputation Index
Score	16.0%	42.0%	97.0%	94.0%	14.79	2.63
Rank	18	33	13	11	22	19

Where are the Graduates of Duke University on the Political Spectrum?

Very Liberal	Liberal	Somewhat Liberal	Somewhat Conservative	Conservative	Very Conservative

See pages 134–135 for detailed explanations and definitions.

Elon University

Location: Elon, NC
Campus Setting: Rural: Fringe
Total Expenses: $40,471
Estimated Average Discount: $12,263 (30%)
Estimated Net Price: $28,208

Type of Institution: Regional University
Number of Undergraduates: 5,032
SAT Score: Reading: 560–660, Math: 560–660
Student/Faculty Ratio: 13 to 1
Transfer Out Rate: Not Reported

Rank Among 20 Regional Universities	**8**
Overall Rank Among 177 *Alumni Factor* Schools	**97**

Overview

Elon's prominence and reputation has been on the rise over the last decade. It is consistently producing happy graduates who are elated with their college experience (ranked 42nd among all colleges and universities). For Elon grads, the Intellectual Development (ranked 117th) is fine, but it is the Social and Friendship Development of their Elon years that truly differentiates the experience. Strong in Ultimate Outcomes, due to high Happiness (37th) and Friendship (24th) scores, Elon grads have yet to rise to the level of Financial Success (159th) that grads of other Top 177 colleges enjoy. Some of this is due to the high number of teachers that hail from Elon: Elon ranks 26th in its percent of grads who go on to the noble but relatively less remunerative vocation of teaching.

Surrounded by educational excellence – Wake Forest, Davidson, Duke and UNC Chapel Hill are all within a 2-hour drive – Elon will need to continue to diversify and elevate its academic offerings to climb further in these outcome-based rankings. Fortunately for Elon, they are firmly on that path. Alumni Giving continues to improve and is now ranked 93rd among all colleges and universities. Keep an eye on this fast riser.

Notable Alumni

Vice Admiral William Gortney and Emmy Award-winning writer Rich Blomquist.

The Alumni Factor Rankings Summary

Attribute	Overall Rank
College Experience	**42**
Intellectual Development	117
Social Development	27
Spiritual Development	28
Friendship Development	24
Preparation for Career Success	49
Immediate Job Opportunities	93
Overall Assessment	**71**
Would Personally Choose Again	108
Would Recommend to Student	34
Value for the Money	72
Financial Success	**159**
Income per Household	164
% Households with Income >$150K	150
Household Net Worth	151
% Households Net Worth >$1MM	137
Overall Happiness	**39**
Alumni Giving	**93**
Graduation Rate	**100**
Overall Rank	**97**

Other Key Alumni Outcomes

4.1% Are college professors
18.7% Teach at any level
32.5% Have post-graduate degrees
49.6% Live in dual-income homes
96.7% Are currently employed

See pages 134–135 for detailed explanations and definitions.

Alumni Activities During College

56.9% Community Service
31.7% Intramural Sports
40.7% Internships
21.9% Media Programs
17.1% Music Programs
49.6% Part-Time Jobs

Prepared Me for Career Success % Strongly Agree	Was A Good Value for the Money % Strongly Agree	Percent of Alumni Worth >$1MM
Elon: 33.1%	Elon: 45.5%	Elon: 11.2%
All College Grads: 31.9%	All College Grads: 46.1%	All College Grads: 14.6%

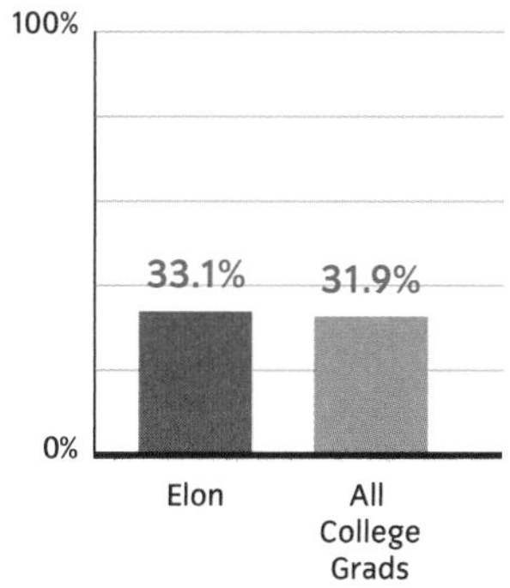

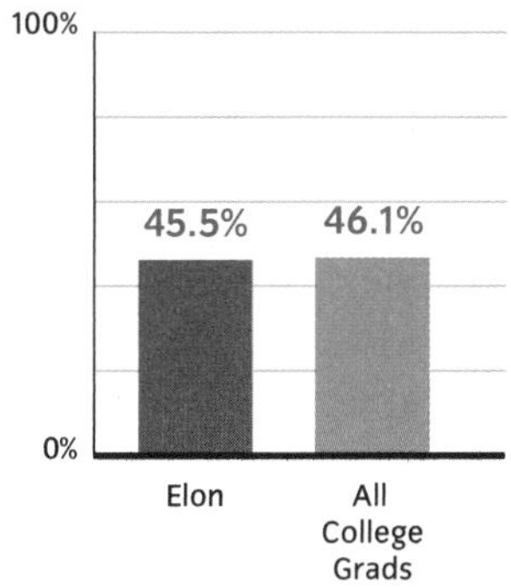

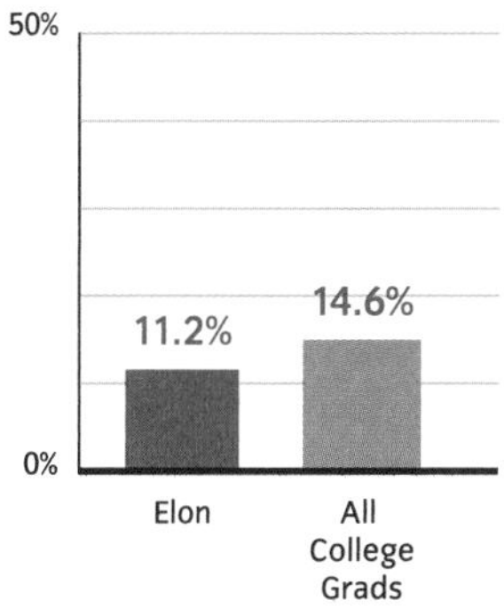

100% / 0% · 100% / 0% · 50% / 0%

Alumni Employment

Category	%
% Independent/ Entrepreneur	12.2%
% With Large Org.	17.1%
% With Medium Org.	17.9%
% With Small Org.	15.4%
% With Govt.	11.5%
% Any Level Teaching	18.7%
% Other	7.2%

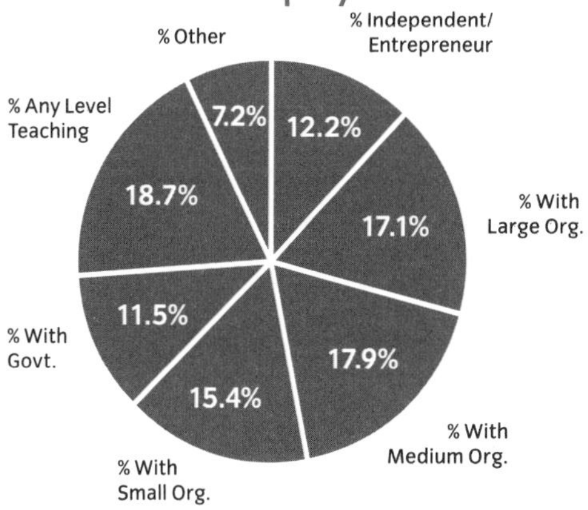

Income Distribution of Graduates

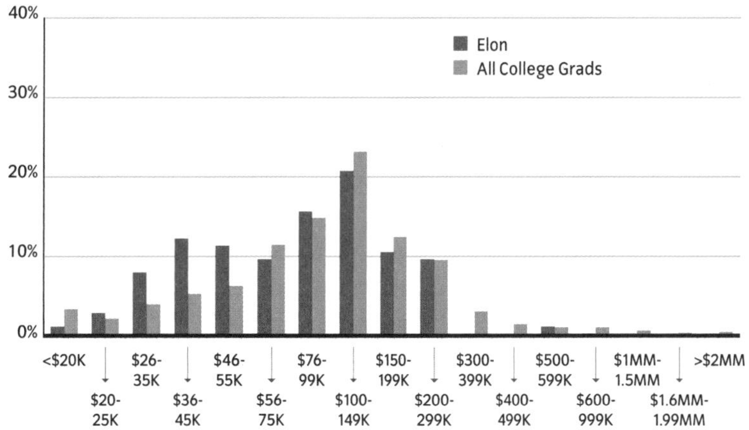

Elon
All College Grads

40%
30%
20%
10%
0%

<$20K, $20-25K, $26-35K, $36-45K, $46-55K, $56-75K, $76-99K, $100-149K, $150-199K, $200-299K, $300-399K, $400-499K, $500-599K, $600-999K, $1MM-1.5MM, $1.6MM-1.99MM, >$2MM

Current Selectivity & Demand Analysis for Elon University

Attribute	% Accepted	% Accepted Who Enroll	Freshman Retention Rate	Graduation Rate	Demand Index	Reputation Index
Score	58.0%	27.0%	90.0%	81.0%	6.41	0.47
Rank	119	119	113	100	122	130

Where are the Graduates of Elon University on the Political Spectrum?

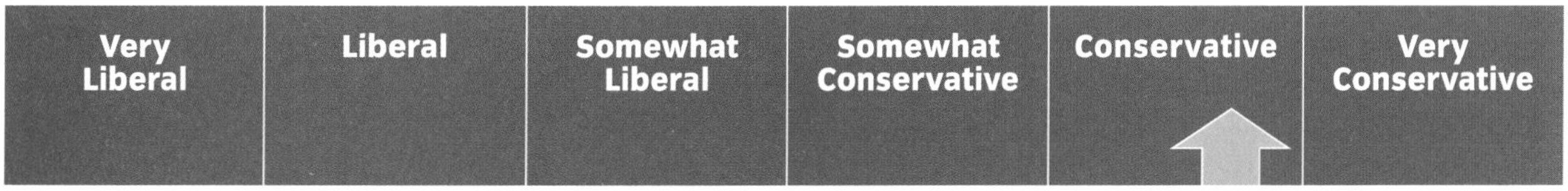

Very Liberal	Liberal	Somewhat Liberal	Somewhat Conservative	Conservative	Very Conservative
				↑	

See pages 134–135 for detailed explanations and definitions.

Emory University

Location: Atlanta, GA
Campus Setting: Suburb: Large
Total Expenses: $55,992
Estimated Average Discount: $30,898 (55%)
Estimated Net Price: $25,094

Type of Institution: National University
Number of Undergraduates: 7,231
SAT Score: *
Student/Faculty Ratio: 7 to 1
Transfer Out Rate: Not Reported

Rank Among 104 National Universities	**59**
Overall Rank Among 177 *Alumni Factor* Schools	**124**

Overview

Long known as one of the finest universities in the South, Emory shares the city of Atlanta with other educational standouts Georgia Tech, Morehouse and Spelman. Having produced an extraordinarily diverse and talented pool of graduates for decades, Emory stands as a mid-sized university with deep resources and a broad reach. Emory grads rank an impressive 28th in Financial Success and 18th in Alumni Giving – both strong indicators of the caliber and loyalty of Emory alumni. While they give the Emory College Experience lower ratings (ranked 70th), and are tough raters in the Overall Assessment (101st), Intellectual Development is a very strong 35th, which leads to strong performance in the Ultimate Outcomes (29th).

Ranked in the Top 25 in both high income and high net worth households, Emory grads are driven and financially successful. Like other universities without a powerful, unifying athletic program, Emory campus life is less collegiate in the traditional sense and, therefore, harder to define. Nonetheless, the Emory experience is life-changing for many.

*Editor's Note: In August, 2012, Emory University revealed that the SAT score ranges for incoming students had been misreported. They have reported a new composite score (Verbal, Math) range of 1270 to 1460. They did not report a corrected Writing score range.

Notable Alumni

Pulitzer Prize-winning historians Dumas Malone and C. Vann Woodward; entrepreneur Ely Callaway of Callaway Golf; designer Kenneth Cole; actor Jeff Goldblatt and former senators Sam Nunn and Newt Gingrich.

The Alumni Factor Rankings Summary

Attribute	University Rank	Overall Rank
College Experience	**70**	**139**
Intellectual Development	35	89
Social Development	65	128
Spiritual Development	27	86
Friendship Development	71	141
Preparation for Career Success	75	142
Immediate Job Opportunities	94	158
Overall Assessment	**101**	**173**
Would Personally Choose Again	103	173
Would Recommend to Student	97	168
Value for the Money	92	162
Financial Success	**28**	**51**
Income per Household	49	79
% Households with Income >$150K	24	44
Household Net Worth	37	67
% Households Net Worth >$1MM	22	43
Overall Happiness	**52**	**97**
Alumni Giving	**18**	**68**
Graduation Rate	**29**	**47**
Overall Rank	**59**	**124**

Other Key Alumni Outcomes

4.2% Are college professors
11.0% Teach at any level
64.1% Have post-graduate degrees
43.3% Live in dual-income homes
91.3% Are currently employed

See pages 134–135 for detailed explanations and definitions.

Alumni Activities During College

37.8% Community Service
30.1% Intramural Sports
25.9% Internships
17.1% Media Programs
23.8% Music Programs
33.2% Part-Time Jobs

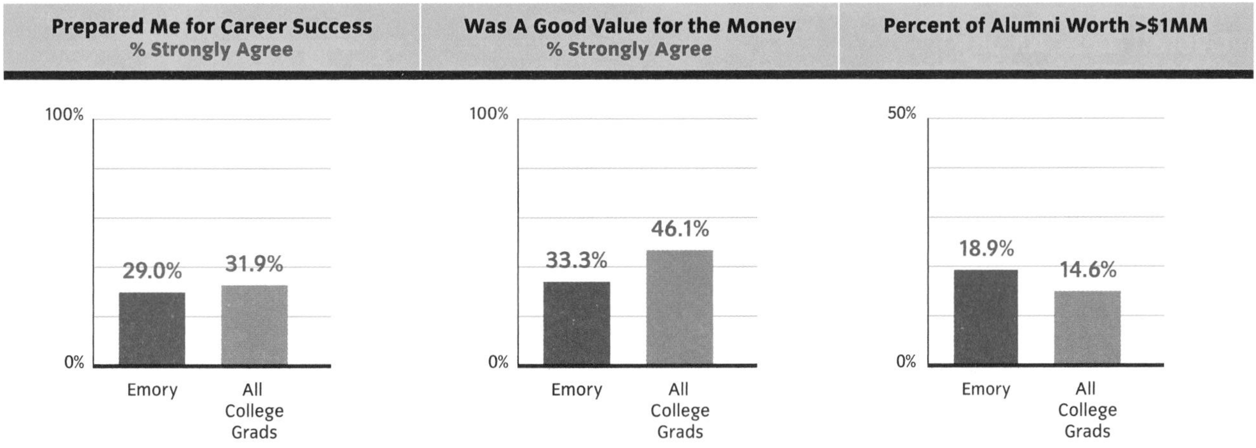

Alumni Employment

% Other 16.1%
% Independent/ Entrepreneur 16.2%
% With Large Org. 20.3%
% With Medium Org. 13.0%
% With Small Org. 17.2%
% With Govt. 6.2%
% Any Level Teaching 11.0%

Income Distribution of Graduates

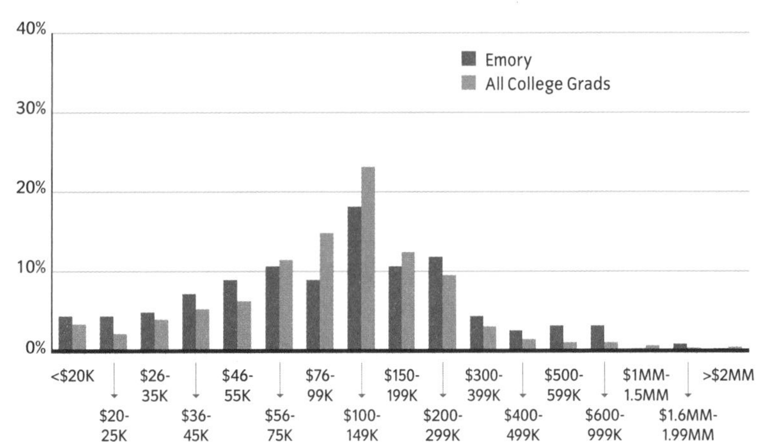

Current Selectivity & Demand Analysis for Emory University

Attribute	% Accepted	% Accepted Who Enroll	Freshman Retention Rate	Graduation Rate	Demand Index	Reputation Index
Score	29.0%	30.0%	94.0%	89.0%	8.74	1.03
Rank	48	103	58	47	88	59

Where are the Graduates of Emory University on the Political Spectrum?

Very Liberal	Liberal	Somewhat Liberal	Somewhat Conservative ↑	Conservative	Very Conservative

See pages 134–135 for detailed explanations and definitions.

Florida State University

Location: Tallahassee, FL
Campus Setting: City: Midsize
Total Expenses: $20,372
Estimated Average Discount: $7,908 (39%)
Estimated Net Price: $12,464

Type of Institution: National University
Number of Undergraduates: 31,418
SAT Score: Reading: 550–650, Math: 560–640
Student/Faculty Ratio: 26 to 1
Transfer Out Rate: 8%

Rank Among 104 National Universities **74**

Overall Rank Among 177 *Alumni Factor* Schools **141**

Overview

When a large state university such as Florida State has a high Overall Assessment (ranked 30th), yet a relatively lower rank in the College Experience (59th), it generally indicates an intangible bond between college and graduate that strengthens and grows over time, and is based less on academics and more on the social environment of the school. The bond between FSU and its grads is not about Intellectual Development (77th) or Preparation for Career Success (63rd). It is largely about an abiding love and passion for the Seminoles.

Florida State has historically fielded one of the top athletic programs in the country. More than 140 FSU footballers have played in the NFL, including two hall-of-famers (Fred Biletnikoff and Deion Sanders). FSU has won 12 national collegiate titles across all varsity sports and is second in winning percentage among all teams in college baseball. The success of the athletic program is what drives much of the connection to and the high regard for FSU among its grads. The fact that its highest aspect of the College Experience is Social Development (39th) underscores this fact.

FSU, however, is not only about sports. These grads are smart, hard-working (ranked 12th in employment rate) and lean to the conservative side. Whether it is for the chance to join the many notable luminaries and forever be a part of the Seminole Nation, or the great Value for the Money (23rd), the trip to Tallahassee proves, for many, to be the trip of a lifetime.

Notable Alumni

Former Florida governor Charlie Crist; NASA astronaut Norman Thagard; actor Burt Reynolds; and other business, military, academic and science leaders.

The Alumni Factor Rankings Summary

Attribute	University Rank	Overall Rank
College Experience	**59**	**128**
Intellectual Development	77	149
Social Development	39	91
Spiritual Development	53	120
Friendship Development	57	123
Preparation for Career Success	63	126
Immediate Job Opportunities	65	104
Overall Assessment	**30**	**63**
Would Personally Choose Again	41	77
Would Recommend to Student	36	72
Value for the Money	23	42
Financial Success	**98**	**164**
Income per Household	95	153
% Households with Income >$150K	90	147
Household Net Worth	93	158
% Households Net Worth >$1MM	94	157
Overall Happiness	**55**	**102**
Alumni Giving	**45**	**108**
Graduation Rate	**72**	**136**
Overall Rank	**74**	**141**

Other Key Alumni Outcomes

6.7% Are college professors
12.4% Teach at any level
49.1% Have post-graduate degrees
55.2% Live in dual-income homes
96.5% Are currently employed

See pages 134–135 for detailed explanations and definitions.

Alumni Activities During College

28.2% Community Service
27.8% Intramural Sports
26.4% Internships
10.6% Media Programs
15.5% Music Programs
55.6% Part-Time Jobs

THE
FLORIDA STATE
UNIVERSITY

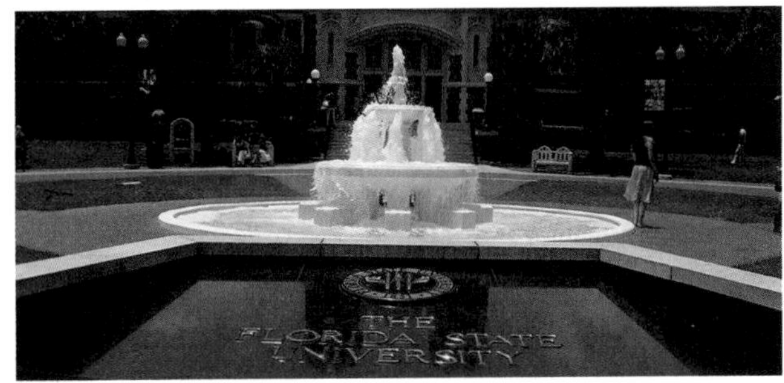

Prepared Me for Career Success % Strongly Agree	Was A Good Value for the Money % Strongly Agree	Percent of Alumni Worth >$1MM

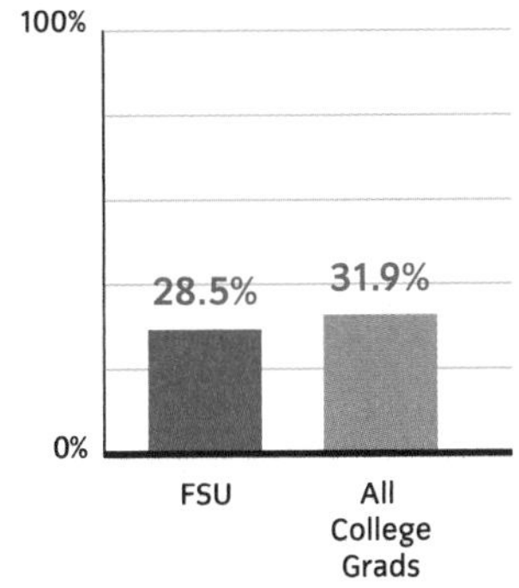
100%
0%
28.5%
31.9%
FSU
All College Grads

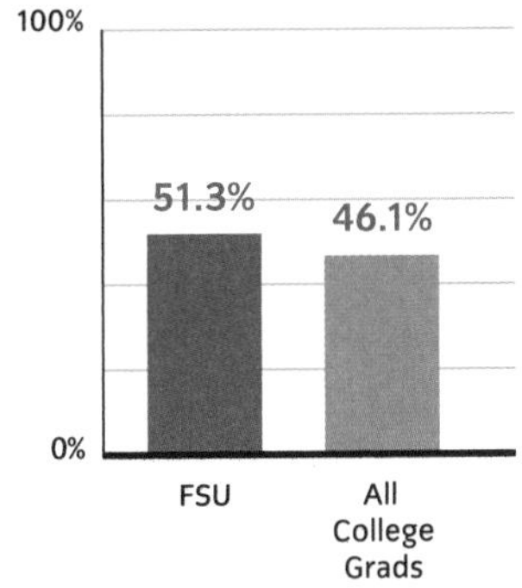
100%
0%
51.3%
46.1%
FSU
All College Grads

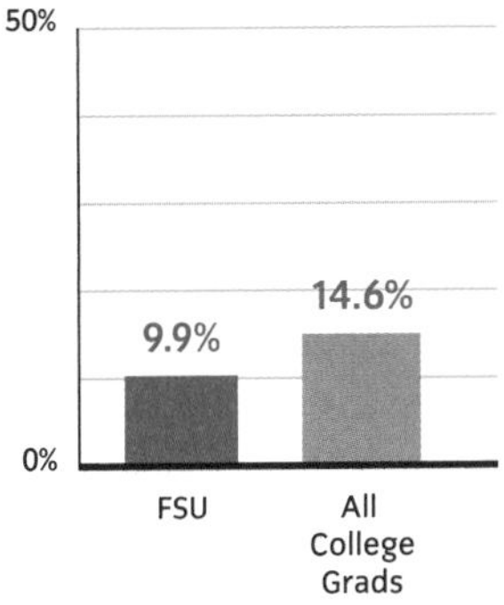
50%
0%
9.9%
14.6%
FSU
All College Grads

Alumni Employment

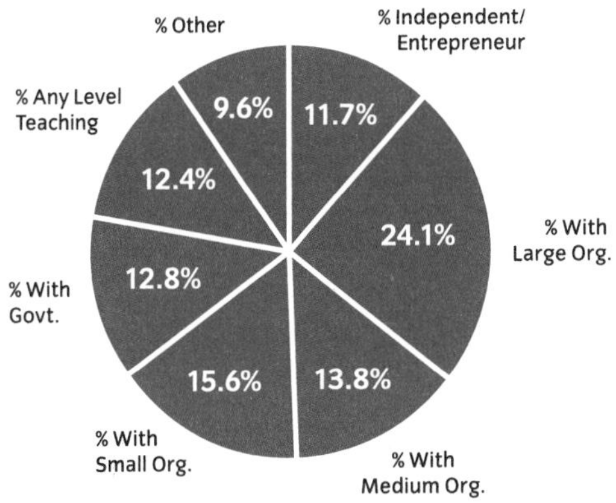
% Other
9.6%
% Independent/ Entrepreneur
11.7%
% With Large Org.
24.1%
% With Medium Org.
13.8%
% With Small Org.
15.6%
% With Govt.
12.8%
% Any Level Teaching
12.4%

Income Distribution of Graduates

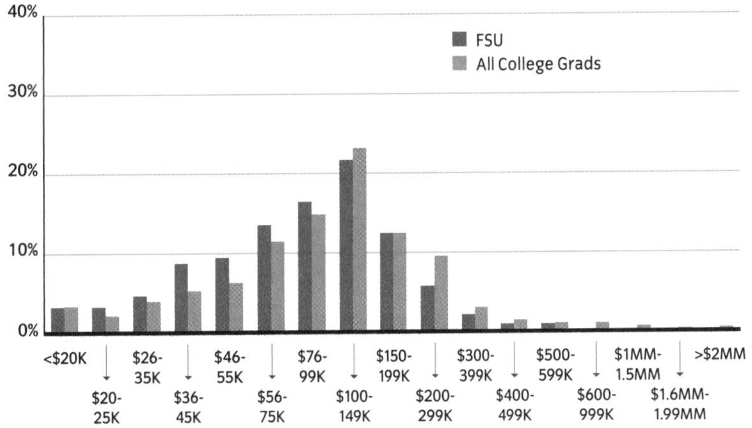
40%
30%
20%
10%
0%
FSU
All College Grads
<$20K
$20-25K
$26-35K
$36-45K
$46-55K
$56-75K
$76-99K
$100-149K
$150-199K
$200-299K
$300-399K
$400-499K
$500-599K
$600-999K
$1MM-1.5MM
$1.6MM-1.99MM
>$2MM

Current Selectivity & Demand Analysis for Florida State University

Attribute	% Accepted	% Accepted Who Enroll	Freshman Retention Rate	Graduation Rate	Demand Index	Reputation Index
Score	58.0%	37.0%	92.0%	74.0%	4.63	0.64
Rank	119	60	86	136	143	93

Where are the Graduates of Florida State University on the Political Spectrum?

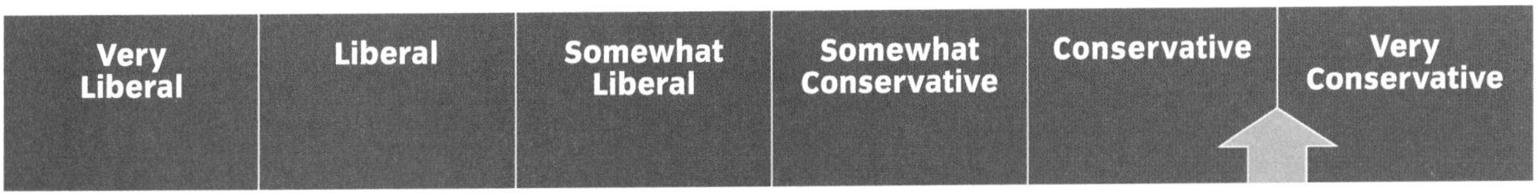
Very Liberal
Liberal
Somewhat Liberal
Somewhat Conservative
Conservative
Very Conservative

Franklin & Marshall College

Location: Lancaster, PA
Campus Setting: City: Small
Total Expenses: $56,580
Estimated Average Discount: $32,575 (58%)
Estimated Net Price: $24,005

Type of Institution: Liberal Arts College
Number of Undergraduates: 2,335
SAT Score: Not Reported
Student/Faculty Ratio: 10 to 1
Transfer Out Rate: Not Reported

Rank Among 53 Liberal Arts Colleges	**46**
Overall Rank Among 177 *Alumni Factor* Schools	**98**

Overview

The result of a merger between two small Pennsylvania colleges in 1853, each with a famous namesake (Benjamin Franklin and John Marshall), F&M is focused on the practical application of the liberal arts on a global basis. Ben Franklin would be very proud of the results. F&M takes very bright students (66th in SAT scores) and produces well-rounded, global thinkers and doers who succeed in a wide variety of fields.

Grads give F&M high marks in Intellectual (42nd) and Friendship Development (21st); are quite happy (ranked 31st); and do very well financially (ranked 28th in Financial Success) – particularly in household income (21st). Interestingly, F&M's income rankings are higher than their net worth rankings – generally a good sign, since income is typically driven solely by the graduates' effort, while net worth can be driven by both effort and inheritance. While grads give F&M lower marks in the Overall Assessment (51st), perhaps driven by the remote location, Alumni Giving ranks a strong 35th. The strong financial and professional success of its alumni across diverse fields ensures the impact of F&M extends well beyond its Pennsylvania Dutch setting.

Notable Alumni

Bowie Kuhn, former commissioner of Major League Baseball; and Mary Schapiro, Chair of US Securities & Exchange Commission.

The Alumni Factor Rankings Summary

Attribute	Liberal Arts Rank	Overall Rank
College Experience	**45**	**95**
Intellectual Development	42	60
Social Development	38	76
Spiritual Development	50	121
Friendship Development	21	24
Preparation for Career Success	44	119
Immediate Job Opportunities	38	140
Overall Assessment	**51**	**161**
Would Personally Choose Again	48	160
Would Recommend to Student	49	145
Value for the Money	49	150
Financial Success	**28**	**77**
Income per Household	21	62
% Households with Income >$150K	23	64
Household Net Worth	34	100
% Households Net Worth >$1MM	40	105
Overall Happiness	**31**	**82**
Alumni Giving	**35**	**43**
Graduation Rate	**26**	**60**
Overall Rank	**46**	**98**

Other Key Alumni Outcomes

7.4% Are college professors
15.7% Teach at any level
54.2% Have post-graduate degrees
57.0% Live in dual-income homes
91.6% Are currently employed

See pages 134–135 for detailed explanations and definitions.

Alumni Activities During College

41.1% Community Service
40.2% Intramural Sports
27.1% Internships
25.3% Media Programs
25.1% Music Programs
38.3% Part-Time Jobs

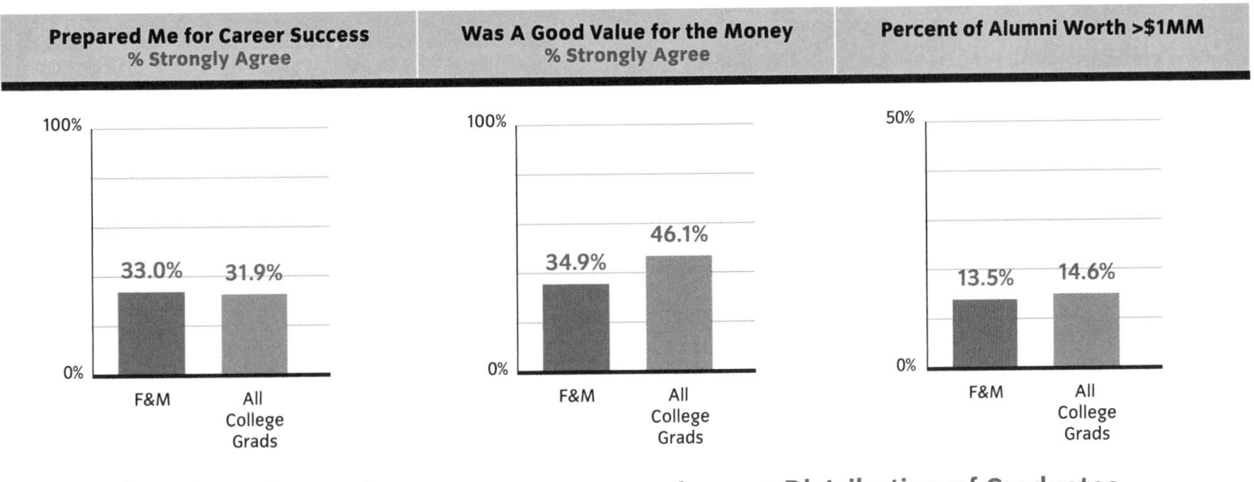

Alumni Employment

% Other: 13.0%
% Independent/ Entrepreneur: 19.5%
% With Large Org.: 19.4%
% With Medium Org.: 10.2%
% With Small Org.: 14.8%
% With Govt.: 7.4%
% Any Level Teaching: 15.7%

Income Distribution of Graduates

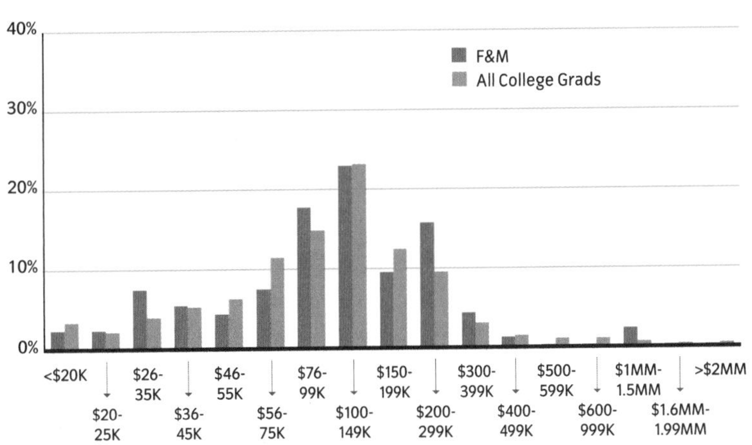

Current Selectivity & Demand Analysis for Franklin & Marshall College

Attribute	% Accepted	% Accepted Who Enroll	Freshman Retention Rate	Graduation Rate	Demand Index	Reputation Index
Score	45.0%	29.0%	94.0%	87.0%	8.26	0.64
Rank	91	107	58	60	95	93

Where are the Graduates of Franklin & Marshall College on the Political Spectrum?

Very Liberal	Liberal	Somewhat Liberal	Somewhat Conservative	Conservative	Very Conservative
		↑			

Furman University

Location: Greenville, SC
Campus Setting: Suburb: Large
Total Expenses: $53,096
Estimated Average Discount: $27,219 (51%)
Estimated Net Price: $25,877

Type of Institution: Liberal Arts College
Number of Undergraduates: 2,761
SAT Score: Reading: 580–690, Math: 570–690
Student/Faculty Ratio: 11 to 1
Transfer Out Rate: 11%

Rank Among 53 Liberal Arts Colleges	**33**
Overall Rank Among 177 *Alumni Factor* Schools	**64**

Overview

The oldest and most selective private college in South Carolina, Furman is a small, conservative, liberal arts school that produces well-rounded, loyal alumni who are extraordinarily happy (ranked 4th) and deeply appreciative of their College Experience (20th).

Furman's deep roots in the Baptist church have certainly influenced the culture of the Furman campus and its community. It follows that Furman grads are among the most conservative in the country and rank 10th in Spiritual Development. They are also bright, capable leaders who succeed in a broad array of careers. Furman athletes enjoy a 97% graduation success rate – among the Top 10 schools in the country.

Ranked 25th among liberal arts colleges in the Ultimate Outcomes and 35th in Alumni Giving, Furman grads are truly appreciative of their undergraduate years spent on one of the country's most beautiful campuses. The coursework is rigorous and "A's" are not easy to get (due to having the 20th-toughest grading in the country), but Furman's accomplished and happy grads are definitive proof that it is well worth the effort.

Notable Alumni

South Carolina Governor Mark Sanford; Frito-Lay founder Ken Lay; singer and songwriter Amy Grant; and former NFL coach Sam Wyche.

The Alumni Factor Rankings Summary

Attribute	Liberal Arts Rank	Overall Rank
College Experience	**20**	**32**
Intellectual Development	40	58
Social Development	26	44
Spiritual Development	10	30
Friendship Development	23	29
Preparation for Career Success	16	32
Immediate Job Opportunities	24	104
Overall Assessment	**31**	**77**
Would Personally Choose Again	19	41
Would Recommend to Student	34	88
Value for the Money	38	101
Financial Success	**42**	**131**
Income per Household	42	139
% Households with Income >$150K	49	159
Household Net Worth	24	63
% Households Net Worth >$1MM	49	145
Overall Happiness	**4**	**4**
Alumni Giving	**35**	**43**
Graduation Rate	**41**	**81**
Overall Rank	**33**	**64**

Other Key Alumni Outcomes

8.5% Are college professors
17.8% Teach at any level
57.6% Have post-graduate degrees
50.0% Live in dual-income homes
96.2% Are currently employed

Alumni Activities During College

45.4% Community Service
41.5% Intramural Sports
27.7% Internships
19.3% Media Programs
38.4% Music Programs
36.9% Part-Time Jobs

Prepared Me for Career Success % Strongly Agree	Was A Good Value for the Money % Strongly Agree	Percent of Alumni Worth >$1MM
Furman: 33.3%	Furman: 37.2%	Furman: 10.7%
All College Grads: 31.9%	All College Grads: 46.1%	All College Grads: 14.6%

Alumni Employment

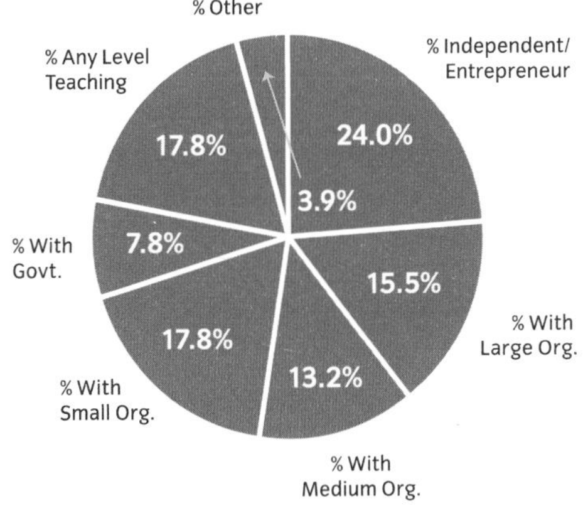

Income Distribution of Graduates

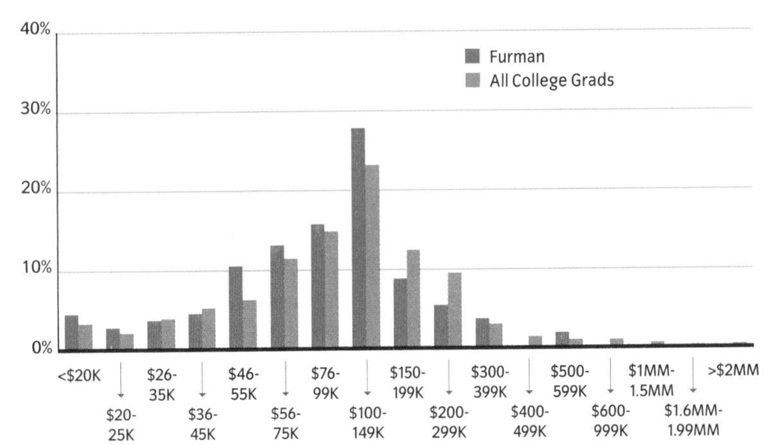

Current Selectivity & Demand Analysis for Furman University

Attribute	% Accepted	% Accepted Who Enroll	Freshman Retention Rate	Graduation Rate	Demand Index	Reputation Index
Score	70.0%	21.0%	89.0%	84.0%	5.87	0.30
Rank	149	156	124	81	128	168

Where are the Graduates of Furman University on the Political Spectrum?

Very Liberal	Liberal	Somewhat Liberal	Somewhat Conservative	Conservative	Very Conservative
					↑

See pages 134–135 for detailed explanations and definitions.

George Washington University

Location: Washington, D.C.
Campus Setting: City: Large
Total Expenses: $57,148
Estimated Average Discount: $29,355 (51%)
Estimated Net Price: $27,793

Type of Institution: National University
Number of Undergraduates: 10,358
SAT Score: Reading: 600–690, Math: 610–700
Student/Faculty Ratio: 13 to 1
Transfer Out Rate: Not Reported

Rank Among 104 National Universities	**101**
Overall Rank Among 177 *Alumni Factor* Schools	**174**

Overview

Located in the historic Foggy Bottom area of Washington, DC, George Washington University is the largest university and private land holder in the nation's capital. Despite average rankings across most measures that place GWU near the bottom overall (ranked 101st among 104 national universities), GWU grads are high achievers whose success is significant – it is simply that they are being compared to the absolute best. It has one of the most impressive undergraduate alumni lists of any college in the country. To be among the top national universities in the country is impressive – this just shows how tough the competition is.

Like other mid-to-large-sized colleges in metro areas (NYU, Boston U, Columbia), the College Experience (ranked 93rd) at GWU is as much about the city as the college itself. So, while its Overall Assessment ranking (104th) is somewhat low, GWU really shines by delivering the heady experience of intense intellectual debate among friends, steeped in the exciting political environment of our Nation's Capital. No wonder its strongest Ultimate Outcome – Friendships & Intellectual Capability – ranks an impressive 37th.

Notable Alumni

Billionaire developer Ted Lerner; Goldman Sachs analyst Abby Cohen; Virginia Senator Mark Warner; House Majority Leader Eric Cantor; J. Edgar Hoover; former Boston Celtic coach Red Auerbach; and Jackie Kennedy.

The Alumni Factor Rankings Summary

Attribute	University Rank	Overall Rank
College Experience	**93**	**166**
Intellectual Development	81	153
Social Development	56	117
Spiritual Development	92	164
Friendship Development	68	138
Preparation for Career Success	101	173
Immediate Job Opportunities	93	156
Overall Assessment	**104**	**177**
Would Personally Choose Again	102	172
Would Recommend to Student	99	171
Value for the Money	103	176
Financial Success	**97**	**163**
Income per Household	93	151
% Households with Income >$150K	94	155
Household Net Worth	99	167
% Households Net Worth >$1MM	80	133
Overall Happiness	**100**	**173**
Alumni Giving	**83**	**152**
Graduation Rate	**48**	**100**
Overall Rank	**101**	**174**

Other Key Alumni Outcomes

3.8% Are college professors
8.0% Teach at any level
50.0% Have post-graduate degrees
42.3% Live in dual-income homes
93.1% Are currently employed

See pages 134–135 for detailed explanations and definitions.

Alumni Activities During College

29.6% Community Service
19.6% Intramural Sports
44.2% Internships
17.6% Media Programs
12.1% Music Programs
53.3% Part-Time Jobs

Prepared Me for Career Success % Strongly Agree	Was A Good Value for the Money % Strongly Agree	Percent of Alumni Worth >$1MM
GW: 17.1%; All College Grads: 31.9%	GW: 21.3%; All College Grads: 46.1%	GW: 11.4%; All College Grads: 14.6%

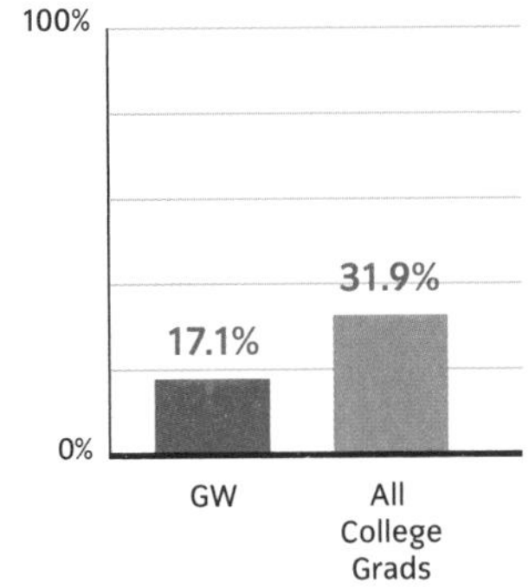

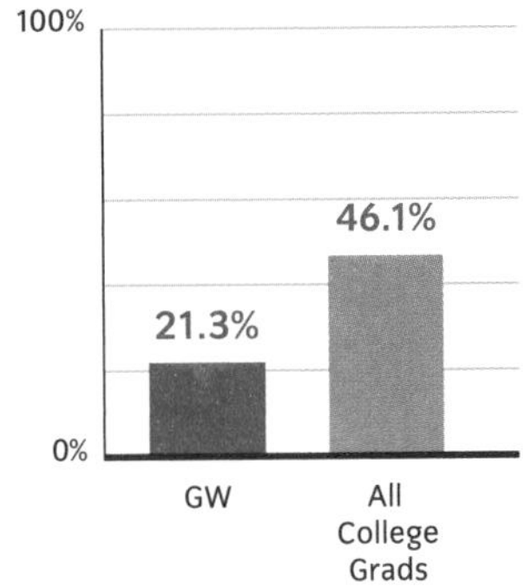

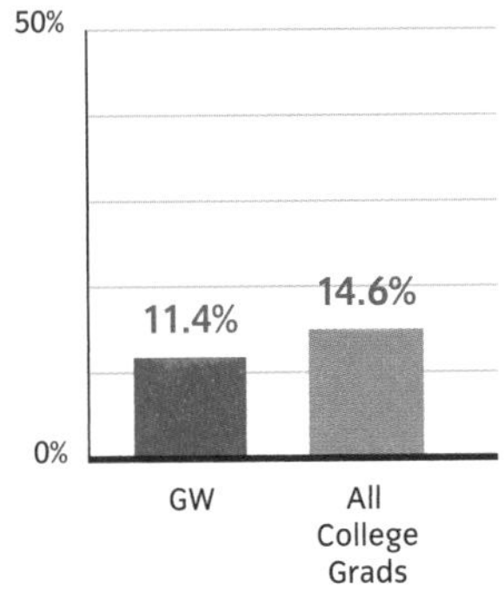

Alumni Employment

- % Independent/ Entrepreneur: 12.5%
- % With Large Org.: 15.9%
- % With Medium Org.: 18.0%
- % With Small Org.: 18.8%
- % With Govt.: 14.1%
- % Any Level Teaching: 8.0%
- % Other: 12.7%

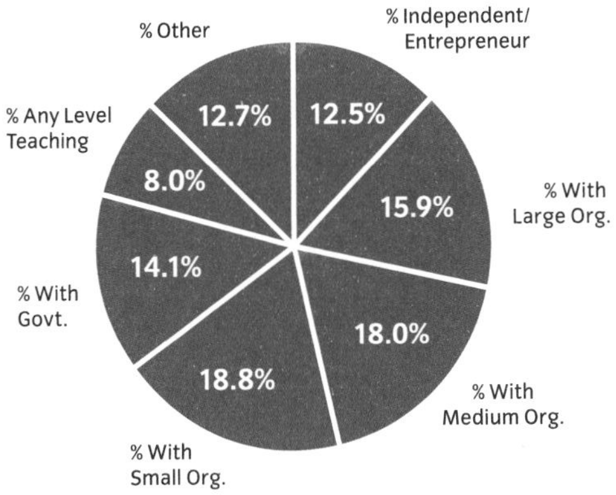

Income Distribution of Graduates

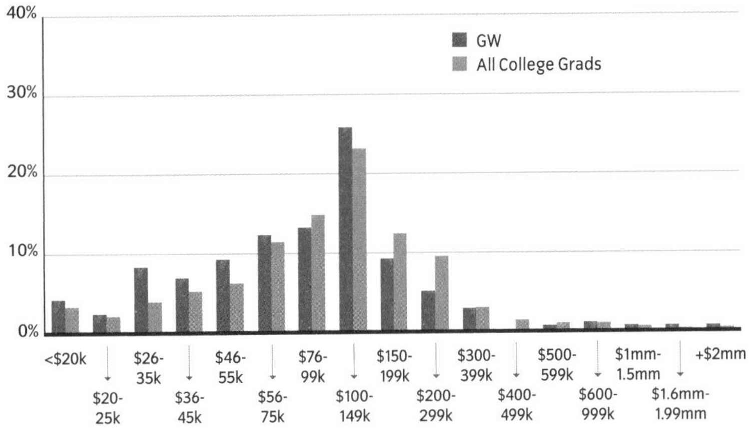

GW
All College Grads

40%
30%
20%
10%
0%

<$20k, $20-25k, $26-35k, $36-45k, $46-55k, $56-75k, $76-99k, $100-149k, $150-199k, $200-299k, $300-399k, $400-499k, $500-599k, $600-999k, $1mm-1.5mm, $1.6mm-1.99mm, +$2mm

Current Selectivity & Demand Analysis for George Washington University

Attribute	% Accepted	% Accepted Who Enroll	Freshman Retention Rate	Graduation Rate	Demand Index	Reputation Index
Score	32.0%	35.0%	94.0%	81.0%	9.56	1.09
Rank	57	70	58	100	75	57

Where are the Graduates of George Washington University on the Political Spectrum?

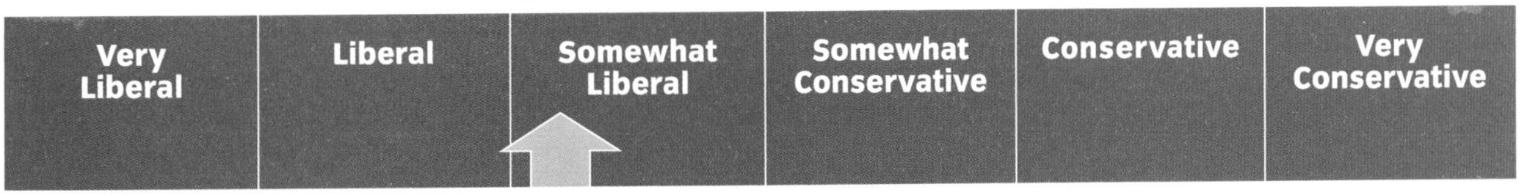

Very Liberal	Liberal	Somewhat Liberal	Somewhat Conservative	Conservative	Very Conservative
		↑			

See pages 134–135 for detailed explanations and definitions.

Georgetown University

Location: Washington, D.C.
Campus Setting: City: Large
Total Expenses: $58,125
Estimated Average Discount: $31,604 (54%)
Estimated Net Price: $26,521

Type of Institution: National University
Number of Undergraduates: 7,579
SAT Score: Reading: 640–750, Math: 650–750
Student/Faculty Ratio: 11 to 1
Transfer Out Rate: Not Reported

Rank Among 104 National Universities	**11**
Overall Rank Among 177 *Alumni Factor* Schools	**28**

Overview

Ranked 28th among all schools and in the Top 15 among national universities, Georgetown more than earns its well-deserved reputation as one of the finest schools in the country. Georgetown is a private, Jesuit university in the posh Georgetown section of Washington, DC. It is the oldest and one of the finest Catholic colleges in the country. Larger, more diverse and the most selective of the Jesuit colleges in the US, Georgetown has produced a group of stunning alumni that spans politics, the judicial branch, business, and entertainment. If it is Financial Success & Happiness you are looking for, Georgetown (ranked 3rd) delivers it as well as anyone.

Ranked 7th in the Ultimate Outcomes and 9th in Financial Success, there is no doubt that Georgetown alumni are powerfully leading and shaping their fields. Georgetown grads rank 3rd in high income households and 4th in average household income. Add to that their 10th ranking in Overall Happiness and their Top 15 College Experience, and you have the fundamentals for a world-class university that produces successful graduates of significance. The fact that alums' Overall Assessment, ranked 46th, lags its overall ranking is less significant when viewed in the context of an Alumni Giving rank that places Georgetown in the top quarter of all national universities. Go Hoyas!

Notable Alumni

Former president Bill Clinton; Supreme Court Justice Antonin Scalia; Ted Leonsis, owner of the Wizards, Capitals and Mystics; actor Bradley Cooper; and journalist Maria Shriver.

The Alumni Factor Rankings Summary

Attribute	University Rank	Overall Rank
College Experience	**15**	**46**
Intellectual Development	16	55
Social Development	41	96
Spiritual Development	4	22
Friendship Development	20	67
Preparation for Career Success	20	46
Immediate Job Opportunities	40	64
Overall Assessment	**46**	**92**
Would Personally Choose Again	40	76
Would Recommend to Student	53	107
Value for the Money	47	85
Financial Success	**9**	**17**
Income per Household	4	8
% Households with Income >$150K	3	7
Household Net Worth	13	27
% Households Net Worth >$1MM	20	38
Overall Happiness	**10**	**25**
Alumni Giving	**15**	**62**
Graduation Rate	**12**	**16**
Overall Rank	**11**	**28**

Other Key Alumni Outcomes

7.0% Are college professors
13.1% Teach at any level
58.9% Have post-graduate degrees
52.4% Live in dual-income homes
94.4% Are currently employed

See pages 134–135 for detailed explanations and definitions.

Alumni Activities During College

41.0% Community Service
23.4% Intramural Sports
35.2% Internships
22.5% Media Programs
16.1% Music Programs
49.6% Part-Time Jobs

Prepared Me for Career Success
% Strongly Agree

	%
Georgetown	35.5%
All College Grads	31.9%

Was A Good Value for the Money
% Strongly Agree

	%
Georgetown	46.5%
All College Grads	46.1%

Percent of Alumni Worth >$1MM

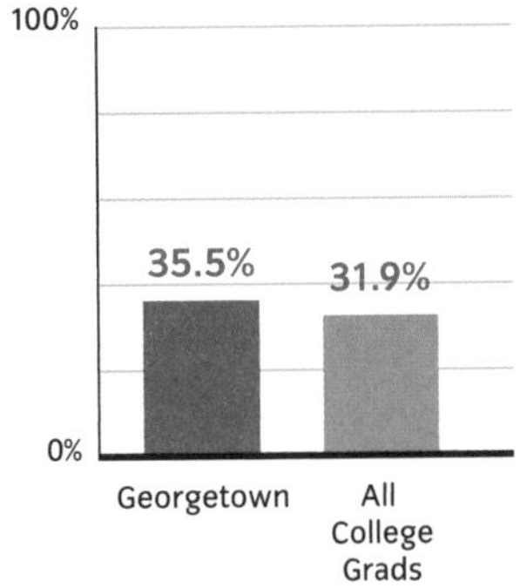

	%
Georgetown	19.7%
All College Grads	14.6%

Alumni Employment

% Independent/ Entrepreneur 19.3%
% With Large Org. 19.7%
% With Medium Org. 12.3%
% With Small Org. 13.5%
% With Govt. 12.3%
% In Farm/ Agr. 0.4%
% Any Level Teaching 13.1%
% Other 9.4%

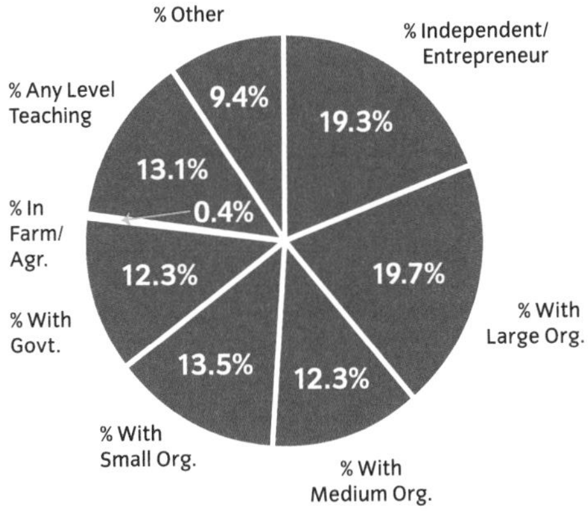

Income Distribution of Graduates

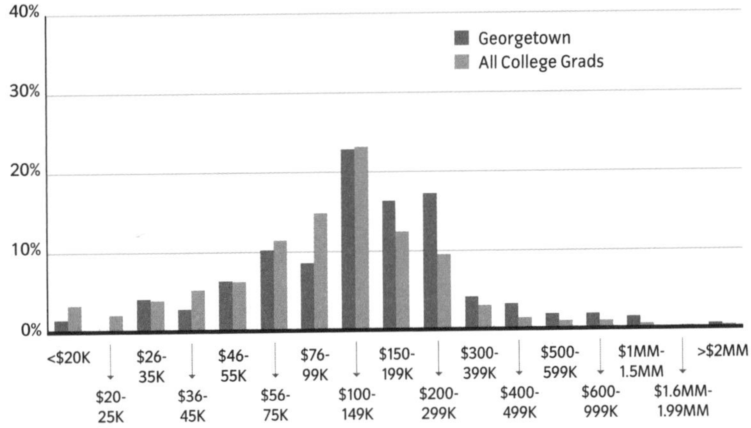

■ Georgetown
■ All College Grads

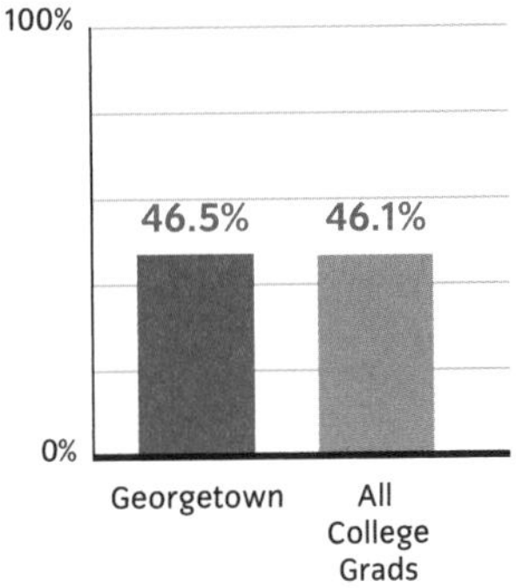

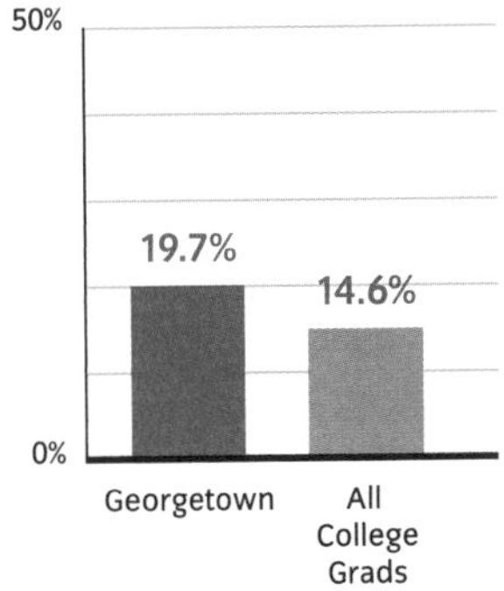

0% 10% 20% 30% 40%

<$20K, $20-25K, $26-35K, $36-45K, $46-55K, $56-75K, $76-99K, $100-149K, $150-199K, $200-299K, $300-399K, $400-499K, $500-599K, $600-999K, $1MM-1.5MM, $1.6MM-1.99MM, >$2MM

Current Selectivity & Demand Analysis for Georgetown University

Attribute	% Accepted	% Accepted Who Enroll	Freshman Retention Rate	Graduation Rate	Demand Index	Reputation Index
Score	20.0%	43.0%	96.0%	93.0%	11.31	2.15
Rank	29	31	27	16	55	26

Where are the Graduates of Georgetown University on the Political Spectrum?

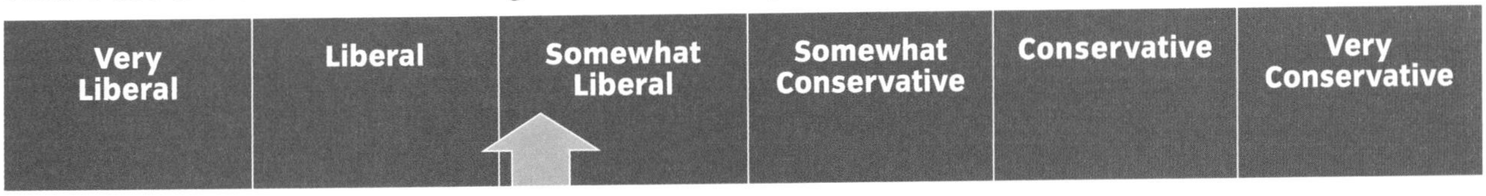

Very Liberal	Liberal	Somewhat Liberal	Somewhat Conservative	Conservative	Very Conservative
		↑			

See pages 134–135 for detailed explanations and definitions.

Georgia Institute of Technology

Location: Atlanta, GA
Campus Setting: City: Large
Total Expenses: $21,098
Estimated Average Discount: $12,653 (60%)
Estimated Net Price: $8,445

Type of Institution: National University
Number of Undergraduates: 13,750
SAT Score: Reading: 590–690, Math: 650–740
Student/Faculty Ratio: 19 to 1
Transfer Out Rate: Not Reported

Rank Among 104 National Universities	**9**
Overall Rank Among 177 *Alumni Factor* Schools	**25**

Overview

Georgia Tech is one of the finest technical schools in the country and the best value among them – 1st among technical schools and national universities, and 4th among all schools. Regardless of the method used to analyze graduate results, Georgia Tech comes out a winner. Since Tech grads will appreciate it, here is a strict, by-the-numbers look at Tech performance versus the 11 other technical schools on our list. Tech ranks:

- 1st in Preparation for Career Success
- 1st in Immediate Job Opportunities
- 1st in Value for the Money
- 1st in Overall Happiness
- 1st in Net Worth per Household
- 1st in Ultimate Outcome of Financial Success & Happiness
- 2nd in Willingness to Recommend
- 3rd in Financial Success (1st Harvey Mudd; 2nd MIT)
- 3rd in Income per Household
- 5th in College Experience

Not only does Georgia Tech place at the top of the technical schools, but it also ranks 9th overall among all national universities. GT is strong both in reputation and in performance – enough to be ranked in the Top 10 among all national universities and 25th overall. Ramble on!

Notable Alumni

Venture capitalist Brook Byers; Walmart CEO Mike Duke; 67th secretary of the Navy William Ball; comedian Jeff Foxworthy; and architects John Portman and Michael Arad.

The Alumni Factor Rankings Summary

Attribute	University Rank	Overall Rank
College Experience	**31**	**87**
Intellectual Development	17	61
Social Development	93	164
Spiritual Development	83	155
Friendship Development	49	112
Preparation for Career Success	1	7
Immediate Job Opportunities	1	4
Overall Assessment	**23**	**44**
Would Personally Choose Again	61	112
Would Recommend to Student	12	18
Value for the Money	1	4
Financial Success	**6**	**14**
Income per Household	6	12
% Households with Income >$150K	8	17
Household Net Worth	3	8
% Households Net Worth >$1MM	18	35
Overall Happiness	**4**	**15**
Alumni Giving	**18**	**68**
Graduation Rate	**50**	**106**
Overall Rank	**9**	**25**

Other Key Alumni Outcomes

3.9% Are college professors
4.3% Teach at any level
49.5% Have post-graduate degrees
54.0% Live in dual-income homes
91.7% Are currently employed

See pages 134–135 for detailed explanations and definitions.

Alumni Activities During College

25.4% Community Service
44.3% Intramural Sports
28.9% Internships
9.4% Media Programs
12.6% Music Programs
47.0% Part-Time Jobs

Prepared Me for Career Success % Strongly Agree	Was A Good Value for the Money % Strongly Agree	Percent of Alumni Worth >$1MM
Georgia Tech: 55.5% All College Grads: 31.9%	Georgia Tech: 73.9% All College Grads: 46.1%	Georgia Tech: 19.9% All College Grads: 14.6%

Alumni Employment

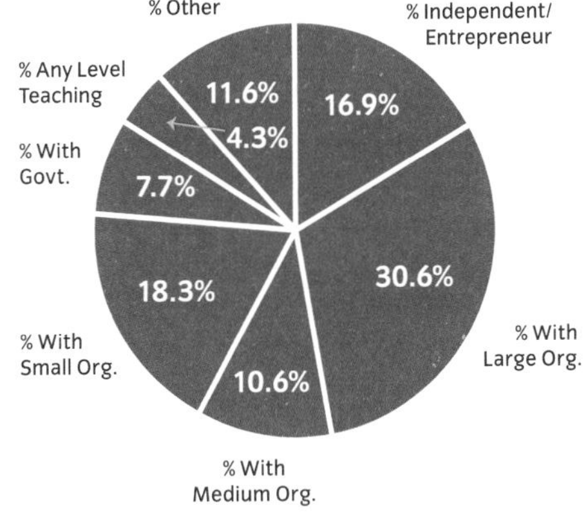

Income Distribution of Graduates

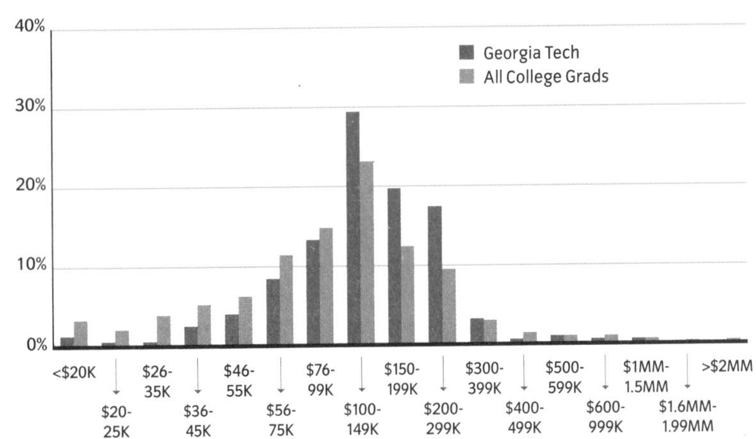

Current Selectivity & Demand Analysis for Georgia Institute of Technology

Attribute	% Accepted	% Accepted Who Enroll	Freshman Retention Rate	Graduation Rate	Demand Index	Reputation Index
Score	52.0%	39.0%	94.0%	80.0%	5.01	0.75
Rank	106	46	58	106	139	81

Where are the Graduates of Georgia Institute of Technology on the Political Spectrum?

Very Liberal	Liberal	Somewhat Liberal	Somewhat Conservative	Conservative	Very Conservative
					⇧

See pages 134–135 for detailed explanations and definitions.

Gettysburg College

Location: Gettysburg, PA
Campus Setting: Town: Distant
Total Expenses: $53,790
Estimated Average Discount: $26,199 (49%)
Estimated Net Price: $27,591

Type of Institution: Liberal Arts College
Number of Undergraduates: 2,485
SAT Score: Reading: 610–690, Math: 610–690
Student/Faculty Ratio: 10 to 1
Transfer Out Rate: 1%

Rank Among 53 Liberal Arts Colleges	**23**
Overall Rank Among 177 *Alumni Factor* Schools	**50**

Overview

With a Top 25 liberal arts college in town, Gettysburg has more to be proud of than just its historic battlefield. Gettysburg's 13th rank in Financial Success – along with its Top 30 rank in every Ultimate Outcome – means these hard-working grads are powerfully influencing every aspect of their world.

Gettysburg grads have a special relationship with one another and with the college. Immediate Job Opportunities (21st), Friendship Development (23rd) and Social Development (26th) are the hallmarks of the Gettysburg college experience, according to Gettysburg grads – clear indication that the Gettysburg community is close and caring. But it is the Financial Success of Gettysburg grads that is the school's strongest attribute. Ranked 7th in Household Net Worth and 13th in Financial Success overall, Gettysburg grads do unquestionably well. This Financial Success, coupled with strong Intellectual and Friendship Development, help give Gettysburg an 11th ranking in the Ultimate Outcomes overall and a Top 30 rank in each.

Notable Alumni

J. Michael Bishop, Nobel Laureate in Medicine; presidential candidate Ron Paul; Bruce Gordon, former head of the NAACP; and a large number of excellent teachers at all levels.

The Alumni Factor Rankings Summary

Attribute	Liberal Arts Rank	Overall Rank
College Experience	**37**	**70**
Intellectual Development	43	73
Social Development	26	44
Spiritual Development	38	69
Friendship Development	23	29
Preparation for Career Success	41	108
Immediate Job Opportunities	21	88
Overall Assessment	**45**	**140**
Would Personally Choose Again	36	95
Would Recommend to Student	50	145
Value for the Money	50	156
Financial Success	**13**	**30**
Income per Household	18	55
% Households with Income >$150K	21	51
Household Net Worth	7	11
% Households Net Worth >$1MM	11	22
Overall Happiness	**17**	**32**
Alumni Giving	**40**	**50**
Graduation Rate	**37**	**76**
Overall Rank	**23**	**50**

Other Key Alumni Outcomes

7.8% Are college professors
19.8% Teach at any level
58.5% Have post-graduate degrees
58.4% Live in dual-income homes
95.7% Are currently employed

See pages 134–135 for detailed explanations and definitions.

Alumni Activities During College

40.7% Community Service
37.3% Intramural Sports
27.1% Internships
29.7% Media Programs
43.2% Music Programs
23.7% Part-Time Jobs

Prepared Me for Career Success % Strongly Agree		Was A Good Value for the Money % Strongly Agree		Percent of Alumni Worth >$1MM	
Gettysburg	All College Grads	Gettysburg	All College Grads	Gettysburg	All College Grads
35.3%	31.9%	38.7%	46.1%	21.4%	14.6%

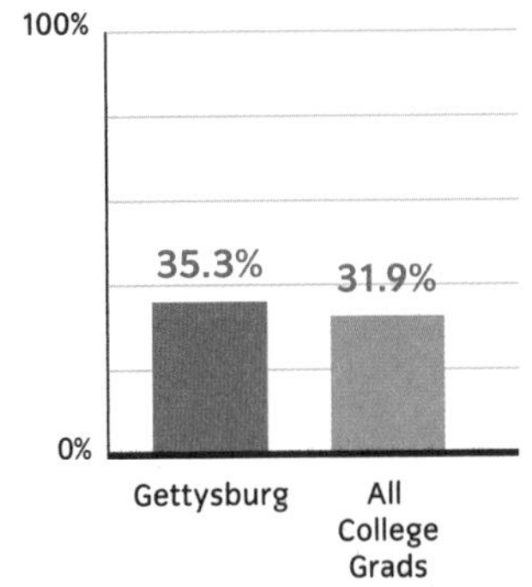

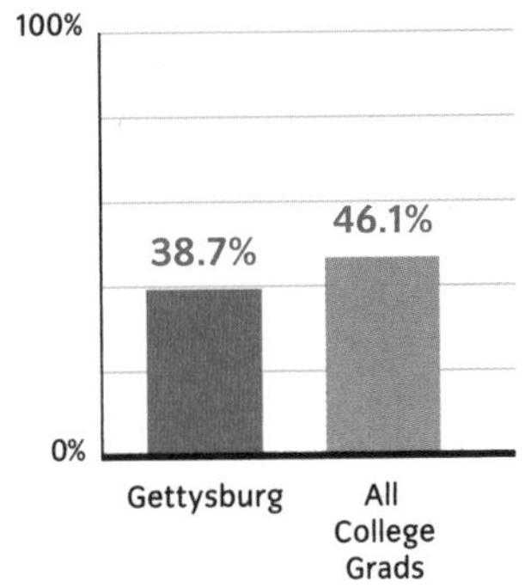

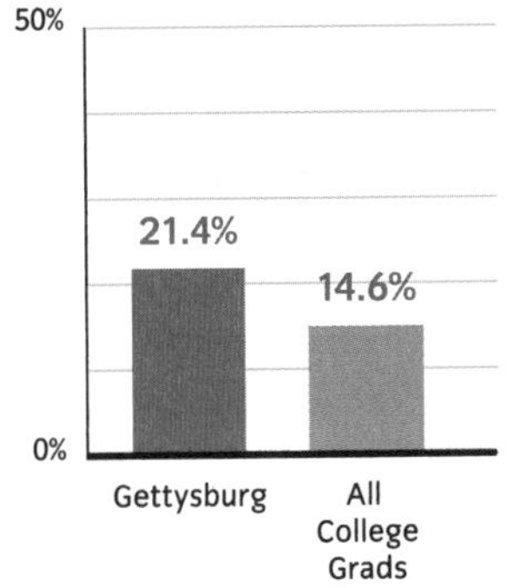

Alumni Employment

Category	%
% Independent/ Entrepreneur	12.9%
% With Large Org.	12.9%
% With Medium Org.	16.4%
% With Small Org.	13.8%
% With Govt.	10.3%
% Any Level Teaching	19.8%
% Other	13.9%

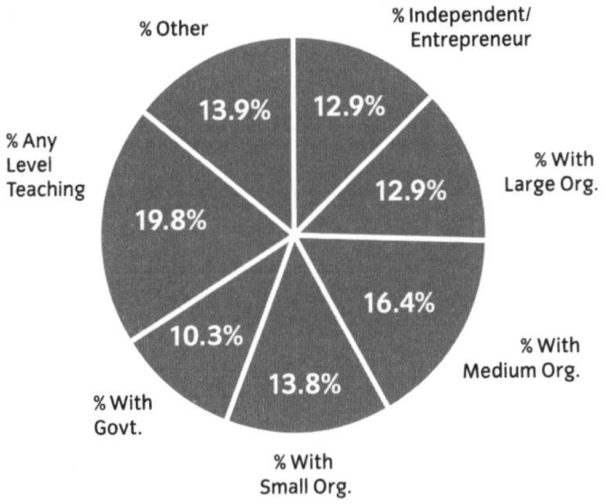

Income Distribution of Graduates

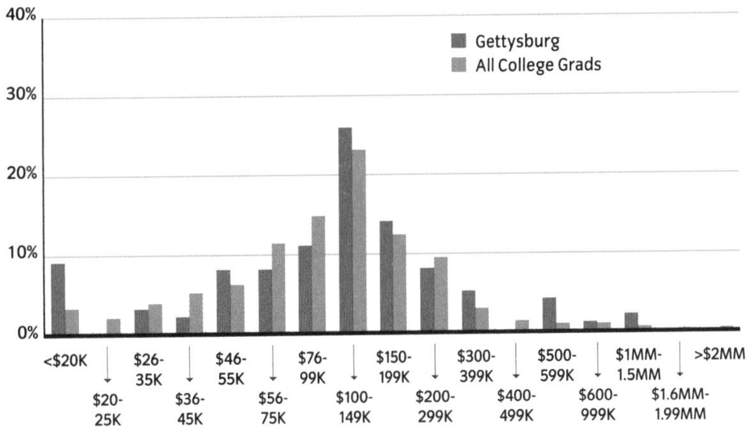

Gettysburg / All College Grads

0% 10% 20% 30% 40%

<$20K, $20-25K, $26-35K, $36-45K, $46-55K, $56-75K, $76-99K, $100-149K, $150-199K, $200-299K, $300-399K, $400-499K, $500-599K, $600-999K, $1MM-1.5MM, $1.6MM-1.99MM, >$2MM

Current Selectivity & Demand Analysis for Gettysburg College

Attribute	% Accepted	% Accepted Who Enroll	Freshman Retention Rate	Graduation Rate	Demand Index	Reputation Index
Score	40.0%	32.0%	89.0%	85.0%	7.73	0.80
Rank	77	92	124	76	105	74

Where are the Graduates of Gettysburg College on the Political Spectrum?

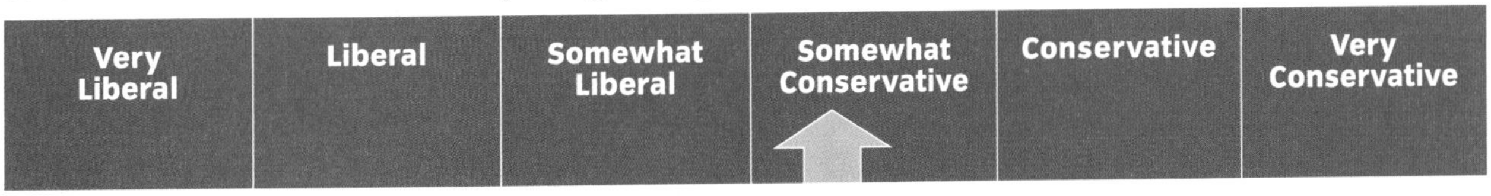

Very Liberal	Liberal	Somewhat Liberal	Somewhat Conservative	Conservative	Very Conservative
			↑		

See pages 134–135 for detailed explanations and definitions.

Gonzaga University

Location: Spokane, WA
Campus Setting: City: Midsize
Total Expenses: $44,849
Estimated Average Discount: $17,394 (39%)
Estimated Net Price: $27,455

Type of Institution: Regional University
Number of Undergraduates: 4,805
SAT Score: Reading: 550–700, Math: 560–690
Student/Faculty Ratio: 11 to 1
Transfer Out Rate: Not Reported

Rank Among 20 Regional Universities	**4**
Overall Rank Among 177 *Alumni Factor* Schools	**52**

Overview

A well-respected Jesuit university located just outside of downtown Spokane, Gonzaga University offers an education aimed at fully developing the mind, body and spirit. Ranked a very strong 52nd overall and 4th among all regional universities, Gonzaga produces an extraordinarily happy (ranked 6th among all schools) and well-rounded graduate who had a spectacular College Experience (ranked 12th) and who would strongly recommend it today to prospective students (31st).

Slightly conservative in perspective compared to all college graduates and highly spiritual (5th), the GU grad can be found in the fields of law, medicine, social services, teaching and many others. In fact, many Zags become elementary school teachers (ranked 21st among all schools), very much in keeping with the Jesuit goal of developing "men and women for others," and perhaps explaining GU alums' relatively lower Financial Success (147th).

Notable Alumni

Tom Foley, 57th Speaker of the House; the legendary Bing Crosby; and NBA great John Stockton.

The Alumni Factor Rankings Summary

Attribute	Overall Rank
College Experience	**12**
Intellectual Development	33
Social Development	6
Spiritual Development	5
Friendship Development	64
Preparation for Career Success	16
Immediate Job Opportunities	60
Overall Assessment	**24**
Would Personally Choose Again	20
Would Recommend to Student	31
Value for the Money	50
Financial Success	**147**
Income per Household	147
% Households with Income >$150K	146
Household Net Worth	128
% Households Net Worth >$1MM	148
Overall Happiness	**6**
Alumni Giving	**81**
Graduation Rate	**106**
Overall Rank	**52**

Other Key Alumni Outcomes

5.0% Are college professors
12.8% Teach at any level
48.3% Have post-graduate degrees
49.0% Live in dual-income homes
93.0% Are currently employed

See pages 134–135 for detailed explanations and definitions.

Alumni Activities During College

51.7% Community Service
37.1% Intramural Sports
24.5% Internships
21.7% Media Programs
14.0% Music Programs
56.6% Part-Time Jobs

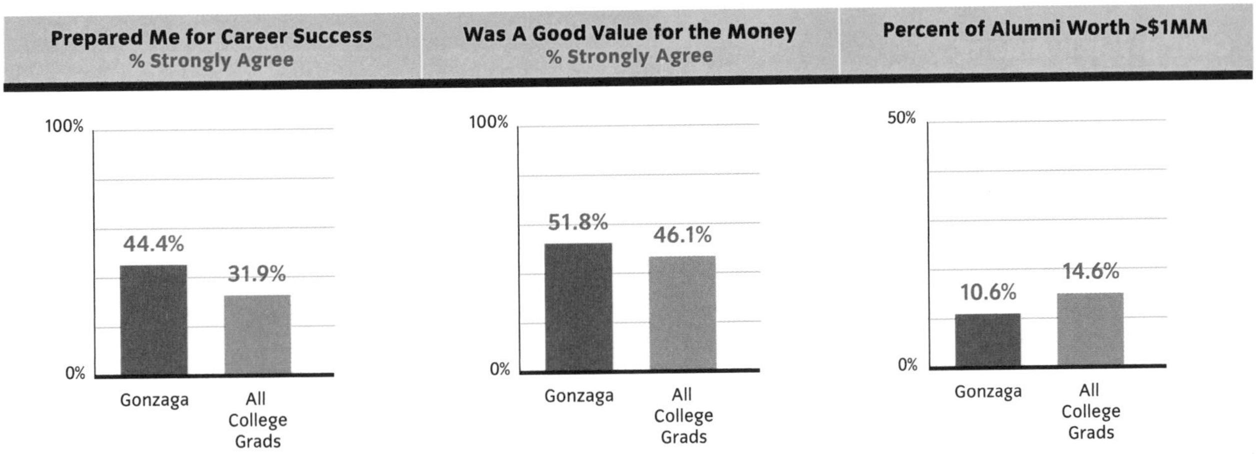

Prepared Me for Career Success (% Strongly Agree)	Was A Good Value for the Money (% Strongly Agree)	Percent of Alumni Worth >$1MM
Gonzaga: 44.4%	Gonzaga: 51.8%	Gonzaga: 10.6%
All College Grads: 31.9%	All College Grads: 46.1%	All College Grads: 14.6%

Alumni Employment

Category	%
% Other	12.0%
% Independent/Entrepreneur	11.4%
% With Large Org.	22.7%
% With Medium Org.	13.5%
% With Small Org.	14.9%
% With Govt.	12.7%
% Any Level Teaching	12.8%

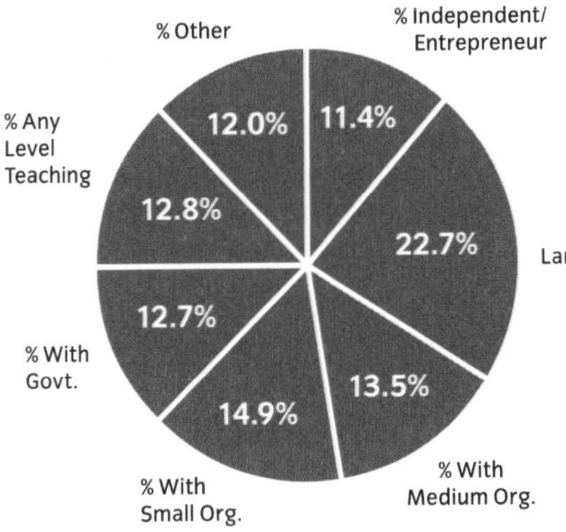

Income Distribution of Graduates

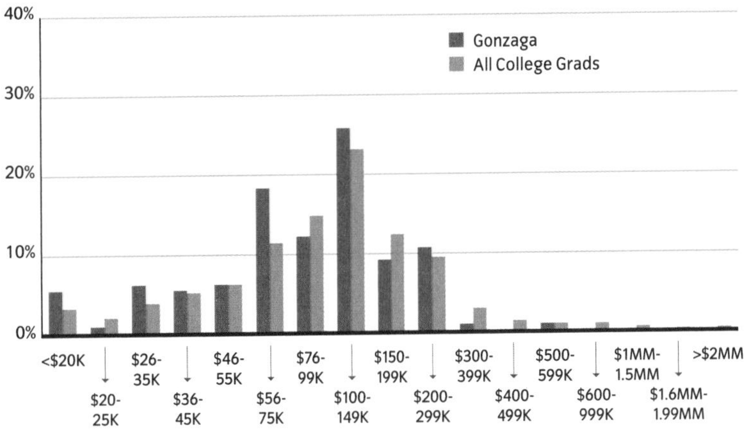

Current Selectivity & Demand Analysis for Gonzaga University

Attribute	% Accepted	% Accepted Who Enroll	Freshman Retention Rate	Graduation Rate	Demand Index	Reputation Index
Score	65.0%	26.0%	92.0%	80.0%	6.06	0.40
Rank	140	125	86	106	126	146

Where are the Graduates of Gonzaga University on the Political Spectrum?

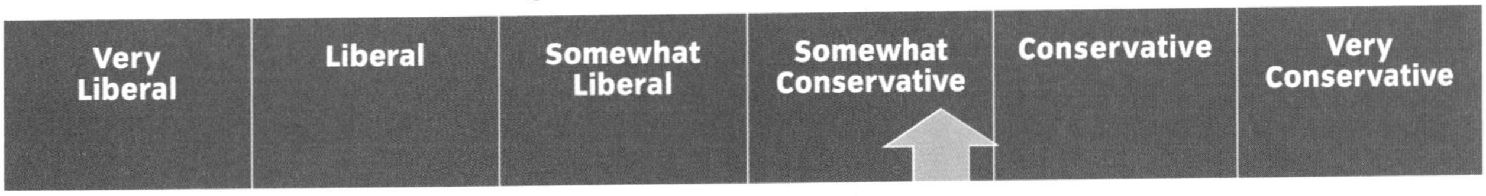

Very Liberal	Liberal	Somewhat Liberal	Somewhat Conservative	Conservative	Very Conservative
			⇧		

Grinnell College

Location: Grinnell, IA
Campus Setting: Town: Remote
Total Expenses: $51,844
Estimated Average Discount: $29,989 (58%)
Estimated Net Price: $21,855

Type of Institution: Liberal Arts College
Number of Undergraduates: 1,655
SAT Score: Reading: 600–720, Math: 610–710
Student/Faculty Ratio: 9 to 1
Transfer Out Rate: Not Reported

Rank Among 53 Liberal Arts Colleges	**25**
Overall Rank Among 177 *Alumni Factor* Schools	**54**

Overview

A demanding liberal arts college with a rich history of social consciousness and political activism, Grinnell is the nation's source for some of our best thinkers and teachers. Ranked 1st among all colleges in grads who become college professors and 2nd in teachers at any level, Grinnell produces serious, critical thinkers who combine the activism and smarts of a small, New England liberal arts college with the practical realism of its Midwest locale. This results in creative and innovative graduates who have their say across a wide swath of pursuits. It is among the 10 best schools in the country in Overall Assessment by its grads (4th among liberal arts colleges). Grinnell alumni are quite happy (ranked 18th) and are very loyal to their college (ranked 20th in Alumni Giving). Financial Success (52nd) is not a key outcome for Grinnell grads. With so many teaching, it is clear that many don't pursue wealth as a goal. Grinnell more than lives up to its reputation as a prime destination for smart, progressive, liberal thinkers who want to make an impact on their world.

In addition to its rich history of developing innovative educators, Grinnell has produced an amazingly talented pool of notable journalists, writers, politicians, science luminaries and business leaders. There is definitely vibrant, progressive life in the middle of Iowa – just find Grinnell.

Notable Alumni

Mary Sue Coleman, President of the University of Michigan and Robert Noyce, co-founder of Intel.

The Alumni Factor Rankings Summary

Attribute	Liberal Arts Rank	Overall Rank
College Experience	**14**	**24**
Intellectual Development	11	12
Social Development	14	19
Spiritual Development	9	27
Friendship Development	10	10
Preparation for Career Success	15	29
Immediate Job Opportunities	46	160
Overall Assessment	**4**	**10**
Would Personally Choose Again	8	17
Would Recommend to Student	5	14
Value for the Money	12	31
Financial Success	**52**	**174**
Income per Household	53	176
% Households with Income >$150K	53	176
Household Net Worth	52	175
% Households Net Worth >$1MM	47	140
Overall Happiness	**18**	**34**
Alumni Giving	**20**	**23**
Graduation Rate	**20**	**52**
Overall Rank	**25**	**54**

Other Key Alumni Outcomes

17.9% Are college professors
29.3% Teach at any level
65.4% Have post-graduate degrees
51.6% Live in dual-income homes
95.2% Are currently employed

See pages 134–135 for detailed explanations and definitions.

Alumni Activities During College

38.9% Community Service
32.5% Intramural Sports
26.2% Internships
52.4% Media Programs
40.5% Music Programs
25.4% Part-Time Jobs

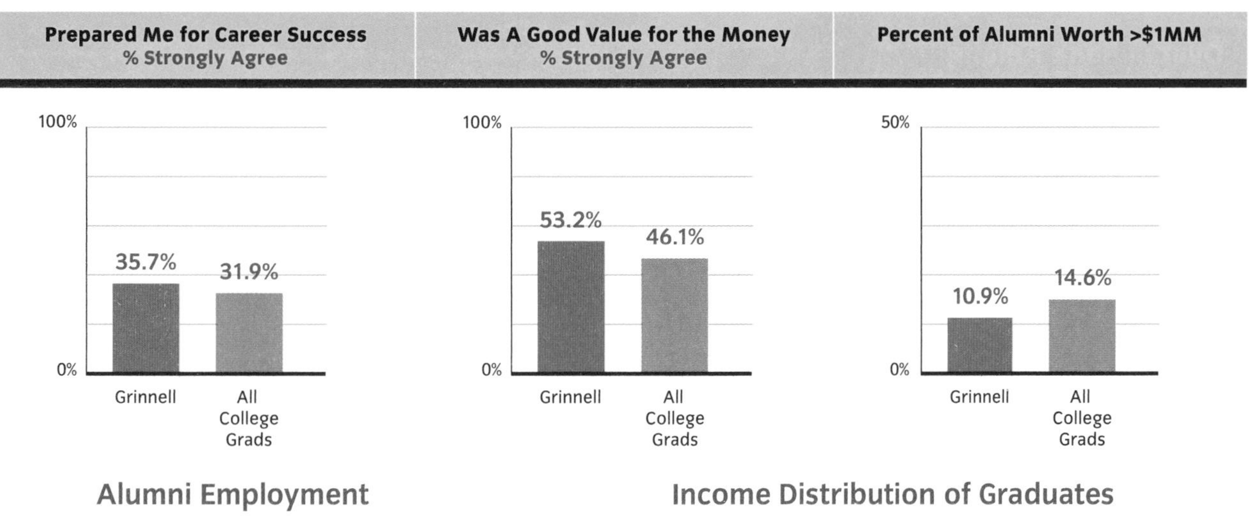

Alumni Employment

% Other: 13.0%
% Independent/ Entrepreneur: 14.6%
% With Large Org.: 9.8%
% With Medium Org.: 12.2%
% With Small Org.: 14.6%
% With Govt.: 6.5%
% Any Level Teaching: 29.3%

Income Distribution of Graduates

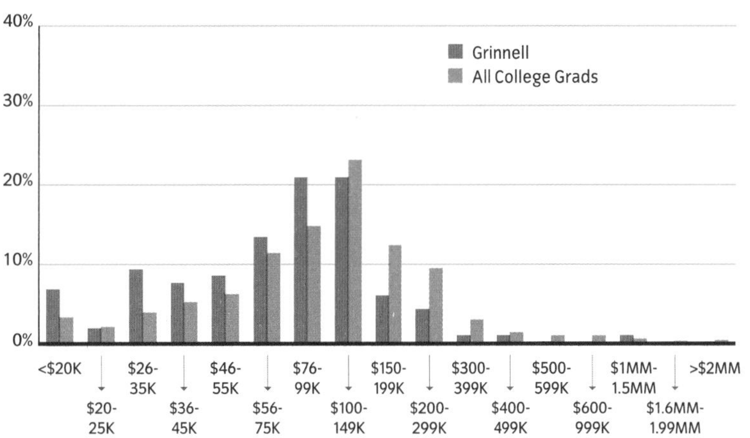

Current Selectivity & Demand Analysis for Grinnell College

Attribute	% Accepted	% Accepted Who Enroll	Freshman Retention Rate	Graduation Rate	Demand Index	Reputation Index
Score	45.0%	34.0%	93.0%	88.0%	6.63	0.76
Rank	91	76	73	52	119	78

Where are the Graduates of Grinnell College on the Political Spectrum?

Very Liberal	Liberal	Somewhat Liberal	Somewhat Conservative	Conservative	Very Conservative

See pages 134–135 for detailed explanations and definitions.

Hamilton College

Location: Clinton, NY
Campus Setting: Suburb: Midsize
Total Expenses: $55,270
Estimated Average Discount: $34,915 (63%)
Estimated Net Price: $20,355

Type of Institution: Liberal Arts College
Number of Undergraduates: 1,861
SAT Score: Reading: 650–740, Math: 660–730
Student/Faculty Ratio: 9 to 1
Transfer Out Rate: 8%

Rank Among 53 Liberal Arts Colleges	**43**
Overall Rank Among 177 *Alumni Factor* Schools	**93**

Overview

Blessed with an idyllic setting near the Adirondacks in upstate New York, stepping onto the Hamilton College campus feels like walking onto a movie set. It's no wonder grads rate Hamilton's Social Development 9th among all 177 schools and rate the overall College Experience 31st. With strong performance in Preparation for Career Success and Immediate Job Opportunities (14th and 16th, respectively, among liberal arts colleges) and in Intellectual (34th) and Friendship (26th) Development, Hamilton college produces accomplished writers, business leaders, academicians and public servants. Hamilton is ranked 43rd among the liberal arts colleges and 93rd overall.

While ranked 46th among liberal arts schools in graduates' Overall Assessment, Hamilton takes very bright students (70th in reported SAT scores) and produces highly skilled and left-leaning thinkers who succeed across a truly wide array of fields. Ranked 40th in the Ultimate Outcomes (11th in Friendships & Intellectual Capability), Hamilton succeeds in producing very well-balanced grads who are extremely loyal (10th in Alumni Giving).

Notable Alumni

Behavioral scientist B.F. Skinner, poet Ezra Pound, former Procter & Gamble CEO A.G. Lafley, and former Delaware governor Michael Castle.

The Alumni Factor Rankings Summary

Attribute	Liberal Arts Rank	Overall Rank
College Experience	**19**	**31**
Intellectual Development	34	45
Social Development	6	9
Spiritual Development	48	108
Friendship Development	26	34
Preparation for Career Success	14	27
Immediate Job Opportunities	16	67
Overall Assessment	**46**	**141**
Would Personally Choose Again	50	165
Would Recommend to Student	42	124
Value for the Money	40	116
Financial Success	**43**	**134**
Income per Household	40	137
% Households with Income >$150K	42	133
Household Net Worth	48	155
% Households Net Worth >$1MM	36	93
Overall Happiness	**52**	**169**
Alumni Giving	**10**	**11**
Graduation Rate	**20**	**52**
Overall Rank	**43**	**93**

Other Key Alumni Outcomes

4.8% Are college professors
13.7% Teach at any level
60.2% Have post-graduate degrees
45.0% Live in dual-income homes
88.5% Are currently employed

See pages 134–135 for detailed explanations and definitions.

Alumni Activities During College

38.4% Community Service
41.1% Intramural Sports
17.9% Internships
47.4% Media Programs
48.2% Music Programs
15.2% Part-Time Jobs

Theatre
Theatre

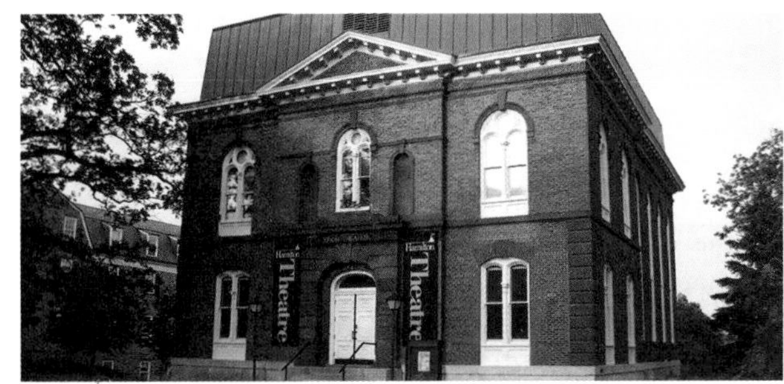

Prepared Me for Career Success
% Strongly Agree

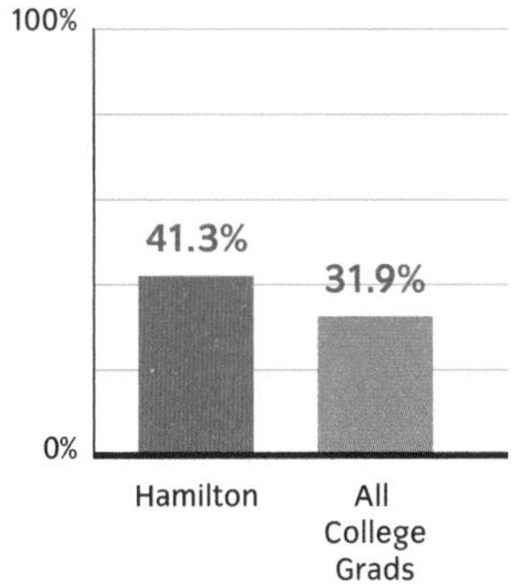

100%
0%
41.3%
31.9%
Hamilton
All College Grads

Was A Good Value for the Money
% Strongly Agree

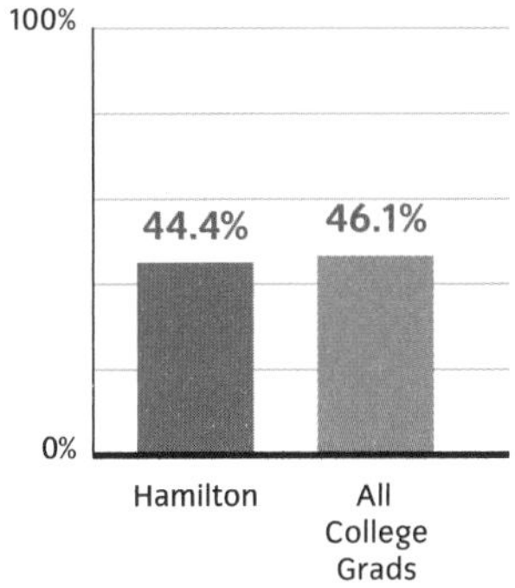

100%
0%
44.4%
46.1%
Hamilton
All College Grads

Percent of Alumni Worth >$1MM

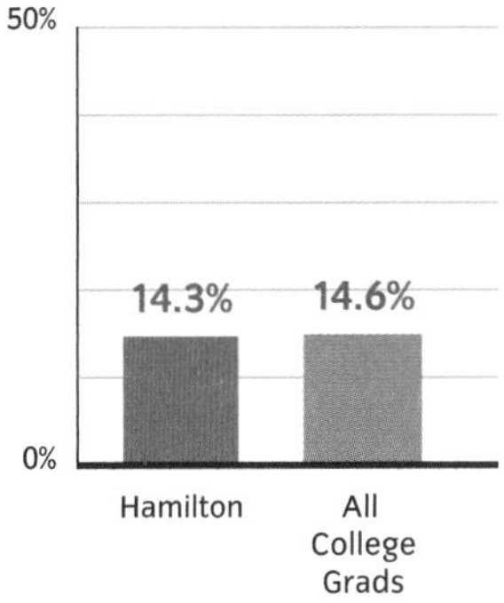

50%
0%
14.3%
14.6%
Hamilton
All College Grads

Alumni Employment

% Other
21.0%
% Independent/ Entrepreneur
21.0%
% With Large Org.
14.5%
% With Medium Org.
14.5%
% With Small Org.
12.1%
% With Govt.
3.2%
% Any Level Teaching
13.7%

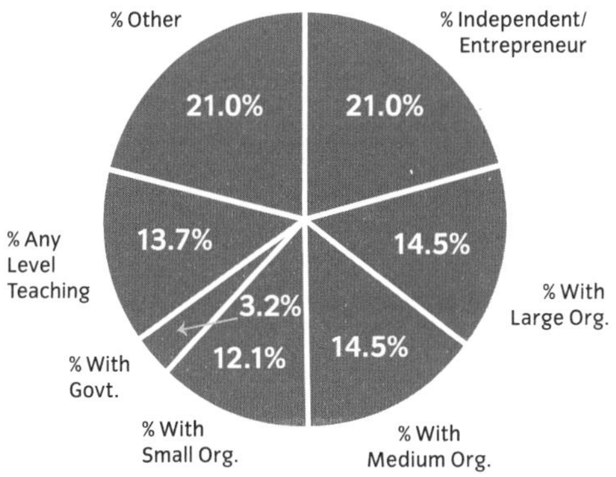

Income Distribution of Graduates

40%
30%
20%
10%
0%
Hamilton
All College Grads
<$20K
$20-25K
$26-35K
$36-45K
$46-55K
$56-75K
$76-99K
$100-149K
$150-199K
$200-299K
$300-399K
$400-499K
$500-599K
$600-999K
$1MM-1.5MM
$1.6MM-1.99MM
>$2MM

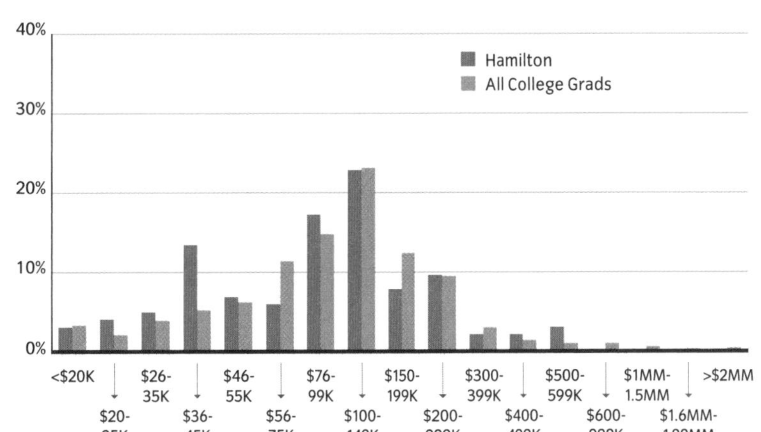

Current Selectivity & Demand Analysis for Hamilton College

Attribute	% Accepted	% Accepted Who Enroll	Freshman Retention Rate	Graduation Rate	Demand Index	Reputation Index
Score	27.0%	33.0%	95.0%	88.0%	10.95	1.22
Rank	44	83	47	52	60	50

Where are the Graduates of Hamilton College on the Political Spectrum?

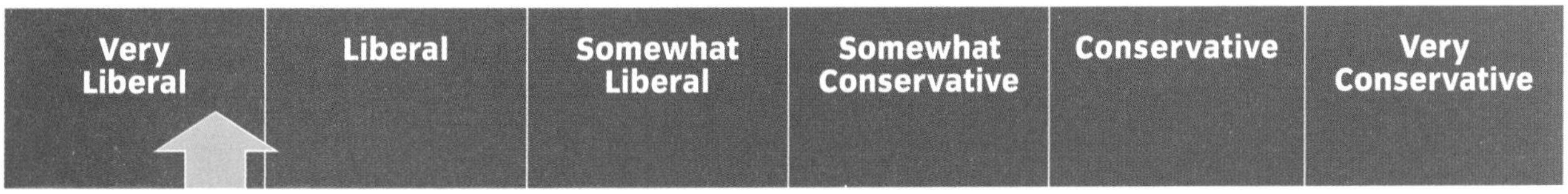

Very Liberal
Liberal
Somewhat Liberal
Somewhat Conservative
Conservative
Very Conservative

See pages 134–135 for detailed explanations and definitions.

Harvard University

Location: Cambridge, MA
Campus Setting: City: Midsize
Total Expenses: $56,000
Estimated Average Discount: $37,723 (67%)
Estimated Net Price: $18,277

Type of Institution: National University
Number of Undergraduates: 10,265
SAT Score: Reading: 690–790, Math: 700–800
Student/Faculty Ratio: 7 to 1
Transfer Out Rate: Not Reported

Rank Among 104 National Universities	**18**
Overall Rank Among 177 *Alumni Factor* Schools	**37**

Overview

The nation's oldest and most prestigious college, Harvard enjoys the finest reputation of any college or university on the planet. Its influence and power put it at the top of virtually every college ranking, and our analysis of graduate outcomes certainly confirms its place among the leaders. The biggest surprise for most readers will be that Harvard does not rise to the very top.

The facts speak for themselves – it actually does live up to its reputation. As expected, Harvard graduates fare exceptionally well upon graduation. They rank 3rd in high net worth grads; 5th in high income households; 1st in graduation rate and are in the Top 15 in five of the six Ultimate Outcomes, anchored by both strong intellectual and financial performance. What prevents Harvard from rising to the Top 10 is its rank in the Overall Assessment (48th), the College Experience (24th) and overall Happiness (77th). Proof of the Ivy League's staggering lead in graduate outcomes is the fact that Harvard ranks 6th among Ivies behind Yale, Princeton, Dartmouth, Cornell and Brown! Yet when it comes to having an impressive alumni list, there is no rival. The list is a veritable Who's Who roster for the globe. The world class performance on the Charles lives on.

Notable Alumni

Six US presidents were Crimson undergrads; 323 Rhodes Scholars; 50 Nobel Prize winners; numerous Supreme Court Justices, country leaders, science and political luminaries, business leaders and entertainment notables.

The Alumni Factor Rankings Summary

Attribute	University Rank	Overall Rank
College Experience	**24**	**74**
Intellectual Development	9	39
Social Development	52	111
Spiritual Development	25	84
Friendship Development	22	75
Preparation for Career Success	54	111
Immediate Job Opportunities	15	21
Overall Assessment	**48**	**95**
Would Personally Choose Again	67	121
Would Recommend to Student	43	88
Value for the Money	34	61
Financial Success	**5**	**12**
Income per Household	11	21
% Households with Income >$150K	5	13
Household Net Worth	7	17
% Households Net Worth >$1MM	3	7
Overall Happiness	**77**	**131**
Alumni Giving	**29**	**81**
Graduation Rate	**1**	**1**
Overall Rank	**18**	**37**

Other Key Alumni Outcomes

9.8% Are college professors
15.2% Teach at any level
64.8% Have post-graduate degrees
47.5% Live in dual-income homes
91.5% Are currently employed

See pages 134–135 for detailed explanations and definitions.

Alumni Activities During College

42.6% Community Service
36.5% Intramural Sports
17.7% Internships
29.3% Media Programs
33.5% Music Programs
37.5% Part-Time Jobs

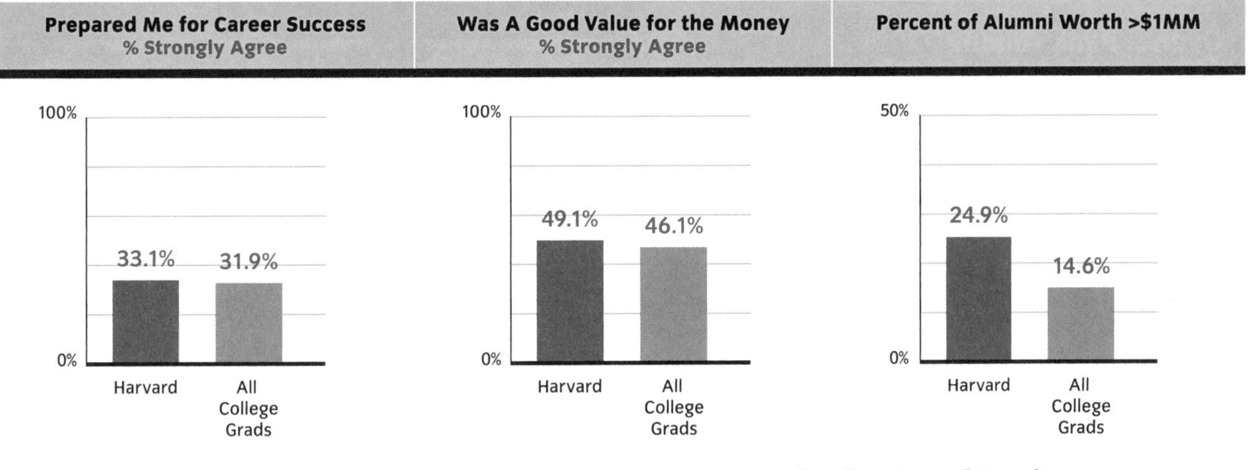

Alumni Employment

% Other 11.3%
% Independent/Entrepreneur 19.2%
% With Large Org. 19.2%
% With Medium Org. 13.0%
% With Small Org. 17.4%
% With Govt. 4.7%
% Any Level Teaching 15.2%

Income Distribution of Graduates

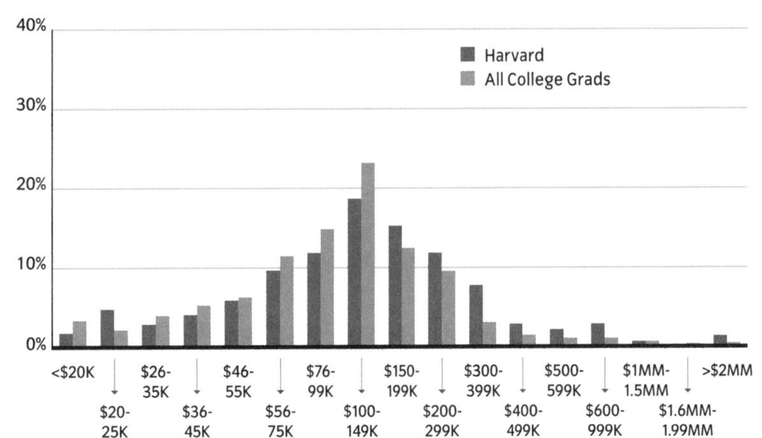

Current Selectivity & Demand Analysis for Harvard University

Attribute	% Accepted	% Accepted Who Enroll	Freshman Retention Rate	Graduation Rate	Demand Index	Reputation Index
Score	6.0%	76.0%	98.0%	97.0%	21.09	12.67
Rank	1	5	4	1	3	1

Where are the Graduates of Harvard University on the Political Spectrum?

Very Liberal	Liberal	Somewhat Liberal	Somewhat Conservative	Conservative	Very Conservative
⇧					

See pages 134–135 for detailed explanations and definitions.

Harvey Mudd College

Location: Claremont, CA
Campus Setting: Suburb: Large
Total Expenses: $57,968
Estimated Average Discount: $27,797 (48%)
Estimated Net Price: $30,171

Type of Institution: Liberal Arts College
Number of Undergraduates: 773
SAT Score: Reading: 690–770, Math: 740–800
Student/Faculty Ratio: 8 to 1
Transfer Out Rate: Not Reported

Rank Among 53 Liberal Arts Colleges	**10**
Overall Rank Among 177 *Alumni Factor* Schools	**17**

Overview

There is broad agreement that Harvey Mudd is among the finest undergraduate engineering programs in the country – and many consider it the best. Our data concur. When it comes to graduate outcomes, there is no better undergraduate engineering school. Ranked 10th among all liberal arts colleges and 17th overall, HMC is truly unique. It provides liberal arts training in the humanities to uber-smart (6th highest SAT scores) math and science whiz-kids. The result is a "Mudder" who has been rigorously trained (3rd toughest college in grading) and deeply understands the impact of their work on society. With a ranking of 5th in Financial Success and 8th in Ultimate Outcomes, HMC grads do extremely well. They rank 3rd in Immediate Job Opportunities, have the best employment rate of any group of college grads, and are 1st in Would Personally Choose their College Again. But here is what makes a HMC education so unique – nearly 63% of grads say they developed deep friendships, versus 37% for all college graduates. Most engineering schools are at or below that 37% average – Caltech (53%) and MIT (47%) also stand out, but fall well short of Harvey Mudd.

HMC has mastered the blend of providing art and science to its talented undergrads – and it is reflected in HMC alumni excellence.

Notable Alumni

Astronauts George "Pinky" Nelson and Stan Love; and diplomat Richard H. Jones, Deputy Executive Director of the International Energy Agency.

The Alumni Factor Rankings Summary

Attribute	Liberal Arts Rank	Overall Rank
College Experience	**21**	**33**
Intellectual Development	37	52
Social Development	53	168
Spiritual Development	21	46
Friendship Development	9	9
Preparation for Career Success	11	18
Immediate Job Opportunities	3	7
Overall Assessment	**7**	**18**
Would Personally Choose Again	1	1
Would Recommend to Student	17	45
Value for the Money	14	38
Financial Success	**5**	**6**
Income per Household	4	6
% Households with Income >$150K	3	4
Household Net Worth	5	9
% Households Net Worth >$1MM	8	16
Overall Happiness	**50**	**167**
Alumni Giving	**35**	**43**
Graduation Rate	**26**	**60**
Overall Rank	**10**	**17**

Other Key Alumni Outcomes

10.6% Are college professors
14.4% Teach at any level
59.2% Have post-graduate degrees
53.9% Live in dual-income homes
90.2% Are currently employed

See pages 134–135 for detailed explanations and definitions.

Alumni Activities During College

16.7% Community Service
40.2% Intramural Sports
22.5% Internships
19.6% Media Programs
24.5% Music Programs
17.6% Part-Time Jobs

Prepared Me for Career Success % Strongly Agree	Was A Good Value for the Money % Strongly Agree	Percent of Alumni Worth >$1MM

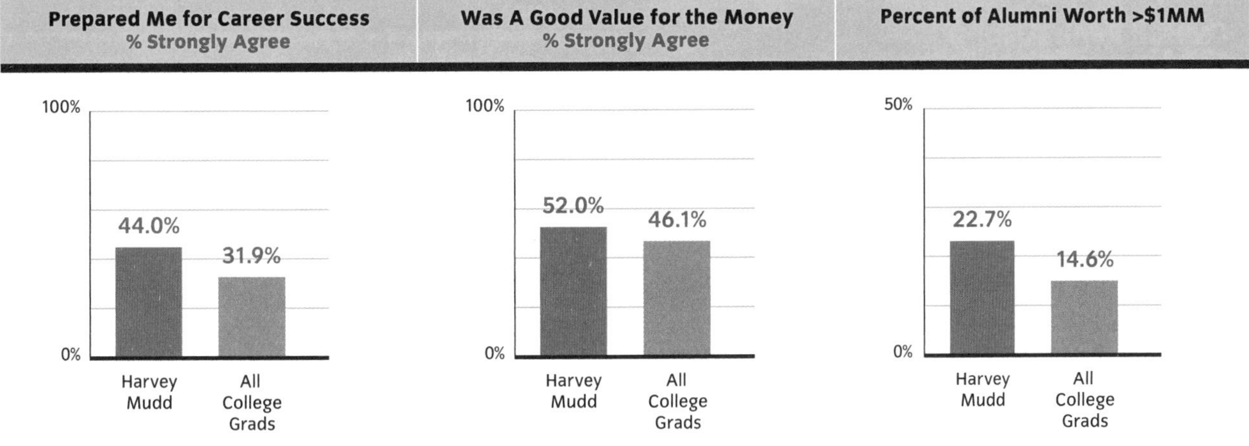

Alumni Employment

% Other 11.5%
% Independent/ Entrepreneur 18.3%
% With Large Org. 20.2%
% With Medium Org. 10.6%
% With Small Org. 18.3%
% With Govt. 6.7%
% Any Level Teaching 14.4%

Income Distribution of Graduates

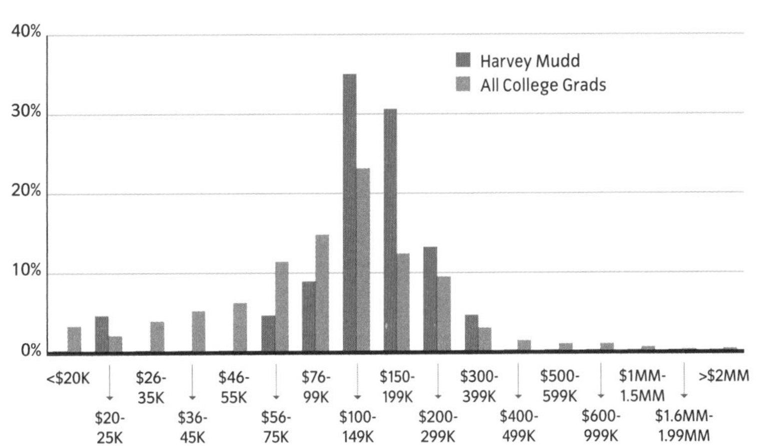

Current Selectivity & Demand Analysis for Harvey Mudd College

Attribute	% Accepted	% Accepted Who Enroll	Freshman Retention Rate	Graduation Rate	Demand Index	Reputation Index
Score	21.0%	29.0%	99.0%	87.0%	16.12	1.38
Rank	30	107	1	60	14	42

Where are the Graduates of Harvey Mudd College on the Political Spectrum?

Very Liberal	Liberal	Somewhat Liberal	Somewhat Conservative	Conservative	Very Conservative

See pages 134–135 for detailed explanations and definitions.

Haverford College

Location: Haverford, PA
Campus Setting: Suburb: Large
Total Expenses: $57,712
Estimated Average Discount: $36,263 (63%)
Estimated Net Price: $21,449

Type of Institution: Liberal Arts College
Number of Undergraduates: 1,177
SAT Score: Reading: 650–750, Math: 650–750
Student/Faculty Ratio: 8 to 1
Transfer Out Rate: 2%

Rank Among 53 Liberal Arts Colleges	**41**
Overall Rank Among 177 *Alumni Factor* Schools	**87**

Overview

A small, highly-respected liberal arts college just outside Philadelphia, Haverford has always been as concerned with the development of its students' character as with their intellect – a holdover from its Quaker heritage that is reflected in its 8th ranking for Spiritual Development. Haverford grads tout the strong Intellectual (15th) and Friendship Development (39th) they experienced in their undergrad years. This is significant since these are also some of the smartest grads anywhere (18th in reported SAT scores). They are also fiercely loyal to Haverford (ranked 18th in Alumni Giving). In fact, it is the combined intensity of the intellectual development and close friendships that truly differentiates Haverford and its graduates, earning it a 7th ranking on the Ultimate Outcome of Happiness & Intellectual Capability.

Haverford alumni can be found wherever people are serving others, including the fields of medicine, law, academics and the Peace Corps. Haverfordians are also journalists, writers and business leaders. Super-smart and well-prepared to serve the world while solving its problems, Haverford grads have broad interests and expansive capabilities that are put to very good use.

Notable Alumni

Norman Pearlstine, previous editor-in-chief of Time, Inc.; Pulitzer Prize-winning humorist Dave Barry; and Cantor-Fitzgerald CEO Howard Lutnick.

The Alumni Factor Rankings Summary

Attribute	Liberal Arts Rank	Overall Rank
College Experience	**33**	**61**
Intellectual Development	15	17
Social Development	40	88
Spiritual Development	8	21
Friendship Development	39	55
Preparation for Career Success	34	83
Immediate Job Opportunities	34	134
Overall Assessment	**23**	**53**
Would Personally Choose Again	15	29
Would Recommend to Student	26	72
Value for the Money	25	68
Financial Success	**46**	**139**
Income per Household	35	129
% Households with Income >$150K	35	104
Household Net Worth	42	141
% Households Net Worth >$1MM	50	161
Overall Happiness	**45**	**157**
Alumni Giving	**18**	**21**
Graduation Rate	**12**	**29**
Overall Rank	**41**	**87**

Other Key Alumni Outcomes

8.9% Are college professors
20.9% Teach at any level
64.4% Have post-graduate degrees
57.6% Live in dual-income homes
93.1% Are currently employed

See pages 134–135 for detailed explanations and definitions.

Alumni Activities During College

40.2% Community Service
38.2% Intramural Sports
17.6% Internships
37.3% Media Programs
32.3% Music Programs
24.5% Part-Time Jobs

Prepared Me for Career Success % Strongly Agree	Was A Good Value for the Money % Strongly Agree	Percent of Alumni Worth >$1MM
Haverford 25.0%; All College Grads 31.9%	Haverford 42.1%; All College Grads 46.1%	Haverford 9.2%; All College Grads 14.6%

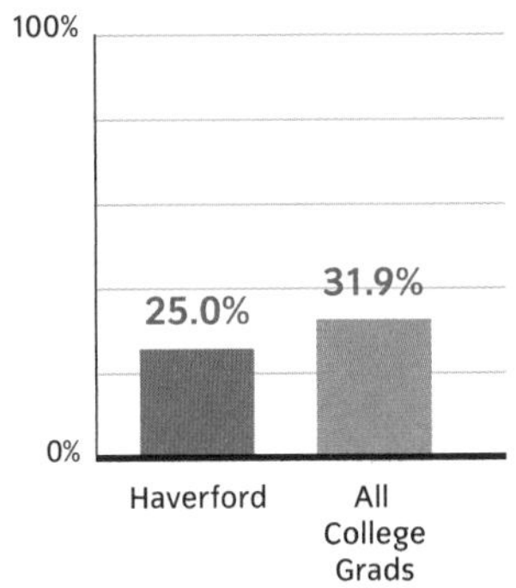

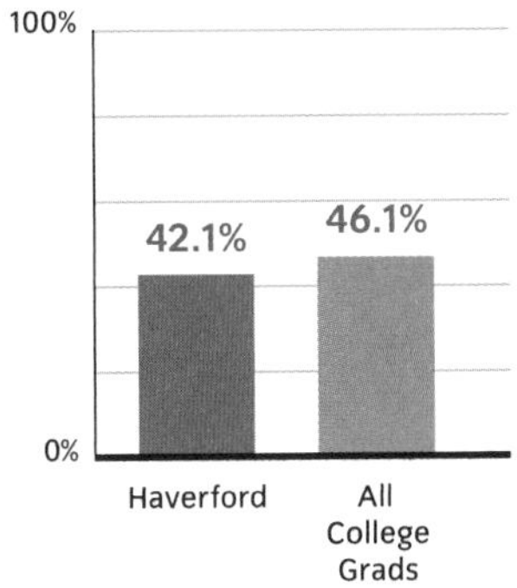

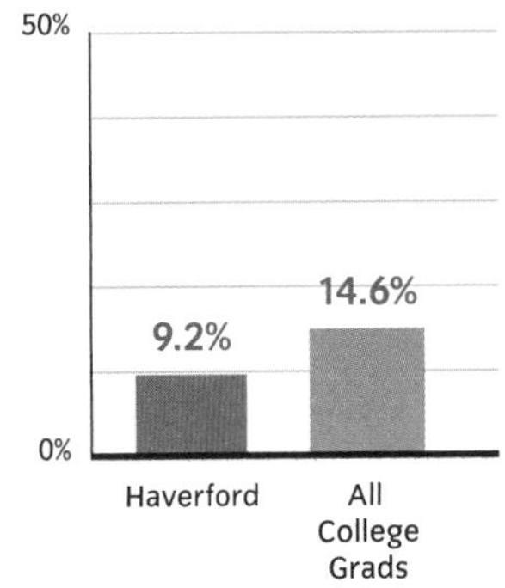

Alumni Employment

Category	%
% Independent/ Entrepreneur	9.9%
% With Large Org.	17.8%
% With Medium Org.	18.8%
% With Small Org.	16.8%
% With Govt.	7.0%
% Any Level Teaching	20.9%
% Other	8.8%

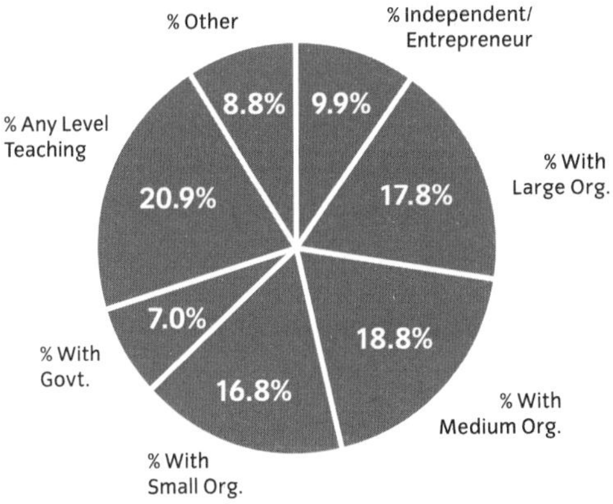

Income Distribution of Graduates

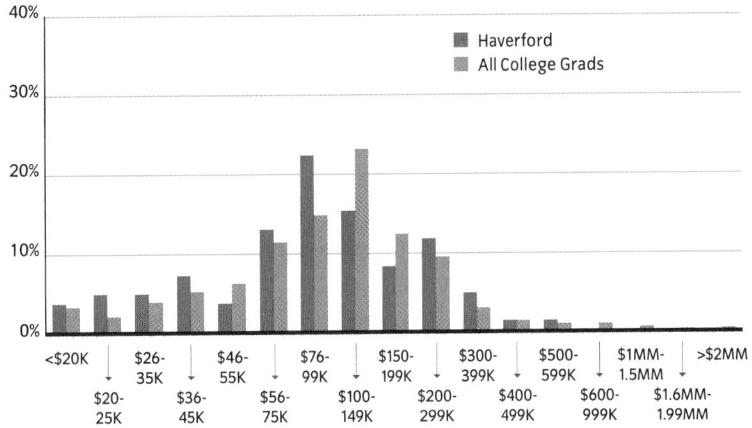

Current Selectivity & Demand Analysis for Haverford College

Attribute	% Accepted	% Accepted Who Enroll	Freshman Retention Rate	Graduation Rate	Demand Index	Reputation Index
Score	25.0%	39.0%	96.0%	92.0%	10.39	1.56
Rank	39	46	27	29	65	36

Where are the Graduates of Haverford College on the Political Spectrum?

Very Liberal	Liberal	Somewhat Liberal	Somewhat Conservative	Conservative	Very Conservative
↑					

See pages 134–135 for detailed explanations and definitions.

Howard University

Location: Washington, D.C.
Campus Setting: City: Large
Total Expenses: $39,237
Estimated Average Discount: $22,466 (57%)
Estimated Net Price: $16,771

Type of Institution: National University
Number of Undergraduates: 6,932
SAT Score: Reading: 480–580, Math: 470–570
Student/Faculty Ratio: 10 to 1
Transfer Out Rate: 3%

Rank Among 104 National Universities	**39**
Overall Rank Among 177 *Alumni Factor* Schools	**85**

Overview

Simply scan the list of consequential alumni from this historic school to see the role Howard University has played in our nation's upbringing. From Brown v. Board of Education, to "Black Power," to Lyndon Johnson's 1965 speech to Howard graduates on affirmative action, Howard has been instrumental in the education of historically aware, distinguished African Americans since it was chartered in 1867. It is a deeply transformational experience for its graduates, who rank it 3rd among all national universities in the College Experience.

Considered to be among the Top 3 historically Black colleges in the country, along with Morehouse and Spelman, Howard produces a fiercely loyal, accomplished graduate whose actual success exceeds the already strong reputation of the school. The mean income of the Howard grad is higher than that of the composite of all college grads (and significantly higher than the average of all Black graduates).

By producing so many scholars and influential leaders on the frontlines of American progress, Howard continues to be a powerful force for positive change.

Notable Alumni

Benjamin Hooks, Andrew Young, Phylicia Rashad, Debbie Allen, Toni Morrison, Mike Espy, David Dinkins, Shirley Franklin, Elijah Cummings, Roberta Flack, and Colbert King.

The Alumni Factor Rankings Summary

Attribute	University Rank	Overall Rank
College Experience	**3**	**13**
Intellectual Development	33	85
Social Development	4	13
Spiritual Development	6	24
Friendship Development	2	21
Preparation for Career Success	8	24
Immediate Job Opportunities	17	23
Overall Assessment	**16**	**29**
Would Personally Choose Again	17	41
Would Recommend to Student	12	18
Value for the Money	24	45
Financial Success	**87**	**145**
Income per Household	66	101
% Households with Income >$150K	84	140
Household Net Worth	85	144
% Households Net Worth >$1MM	104	173
Overall Happiness	**91**	**148**
Alumni Giving	**91**	**162**
Graduation Rate	**81**	**148**
Overall Rank	**39**	**85**

Other Key Alumni Outcomes

4.4% Are college professors
10.0% Teach at any level
48.2% Have post-graduate degrees
45.1% Live in dual-income homes
90.7% Are currently employed

See pages 134–135 for detailed explanations and definitions.

Alumni Activities During College

35.3% Community Service
10.7% Intramural Sports
30.4% Internships
28.6% Media Programs
21.4% Music Programs
51.8% Part-Time Jobs

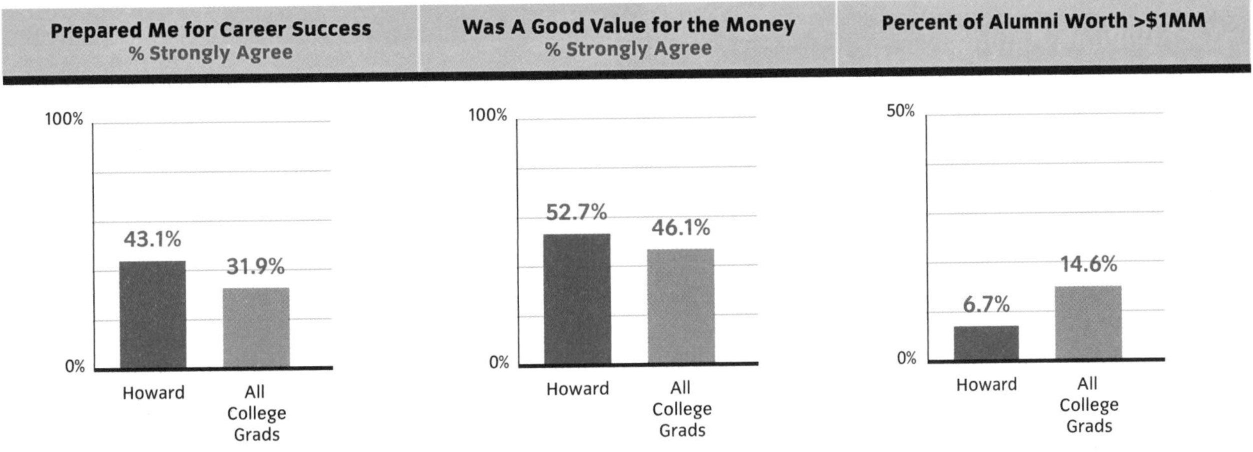

Alumni Employment

% Other 15.2%
% Independent/ Entrepreneur 18.1%
% With Large Org. 21.7%
% With Medium Org. 10.2%
% With Small Org. 9.7%
% With Govt. 14.7%
% In Farm/ Agr. 0.4%
% Any Level Teaching 10.0%

Income Distribution of Graduates

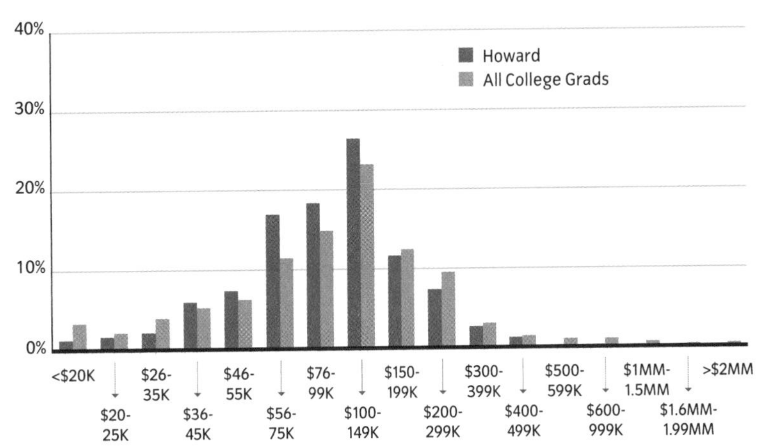

Current Selectivity & Demand Analysis for Howard University

Attribute	% Accepted	% Accepted Who Enroll	Freshman Retention Rate	Graduation Rate	Demand Index	Reputation Index
Score	54.0%	31.0%	83.0%	69.0%	5.69	0.57
Rank	110	96	161	148	131	109

Where are the Graduates of Howard University on the Political Spectrum?

Very Liberal	Liberal	Somewhat Liberal	Somewhat Conservative	Conservative	Very Conservative
	⬆				

Indiana University Bloomington

Location: Bloomington, IN
Campus Setting: City: Small
Total Expenses: $22,049
Estimated Average Discount: $11,725 (53%)
Estimated Net Price: $10,324

Type of Institution: National University
Number of Undergraduates: 32,367
SAT Score: Reading: 510–630, Math: 540–650
Student/Faculty Ratio: 19 to 1
Transfer Out Rate: 18%

Rank Among 104 National Universities	**64**
Overall Rank Among 177 *Alumni Factor* Schools	**129**

Overview

One of America's most beautiful large college campuses, sitting on the thick bed of off-white Indiana limestone used to construct many of the historic buildings on campus, Indiana University Bloomington is a collegiate treasure – and not simply because of its architecture. Its graduates (mostly Indianans) adore it, giving it high scores in all areas of the Overall Assessment (ranked 32nd). Its highest ranking is in graduates who Would Personally Choose it Again (24th).

With a 64th ranking among national universities and ranked 129th overall, IU is a Midwestern-friendly campus in a college town that is progressive, open minded and dynamic. Graduates fare moderately well in Financial Success (73rd) and succeed in a broad variety of fields – as expected from graduates of a large teaching and research university. It ranks 25th in the country in the percentage of grads who teach and does a very good job overall (57th) in placing graduates in jobs. IU's highest ranked Ultimate Outcome is Friendships & Intellectual Capability, where it ranks 76th among national universities.

Notable Alumni

Actor Kevin Kline; journalist Jane Pauley; Dallas Maverick's owner Mark Cuban; composer Hoagy Carmichael; Smithsonian Chairwoman Patty Stonesifer; and Senator Evan Bayh.

The Alumni Factor Rankings Summary

Attribute	University Rank	Overall Rank
College Experience	**61**	**130**
Intellectual Development	67	137
Social Development	31	76
Spiritual Development	64	135
Friendship Development	74	144
Preparation for Career Success	69	135
Immediate Job Opportunities	57	92
Overall Assessment	**32**	**68**
Would Personally Choose Again	24	51
Would Recommend to Student	30	64
Value for the Money	52	94
Financial Success	**73**	**120**
Income per Household	75	115
% Households with Income >$150K	49	83
Household Net Worth	83	135
% Households Net Worth >$1MM	81	134
Overall Happiness	**79**	**135**
Alumni Giving	**52**	**115**
Graduation Rate	**75**	**141**
Overall Rank	**64**	**129**

Other Key Alumni Outcomes

5.9% Are college professors
19.7% Teach at any level
52.6% Have post-graduate degrees
58.2% Live in dual-income homes
92.7% Are currently employed

See pages 134–135 for detailed explanations and definitions.

Alumni Activities During College

22.4% Community Service
32.1% Intramural Sports
18.5% Internships
13.4% Media Programs
15.4% Music Programs
49.1% Part-Time Jobs

Prepared Me for Career Success % Strongly Agree	Was A Good Value for the Money % Strongly Agree	Percent of Alumni Worth >$1MM
IU Bloomington 24.2%; All College Grads 31.9%	IU Bloomington 41.1%; All College Grads 46.1%	IU Bloomington 11.3%; All College Grads 14.6%

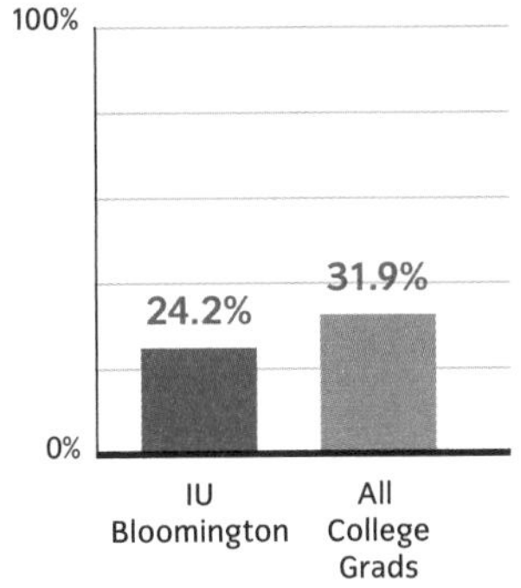

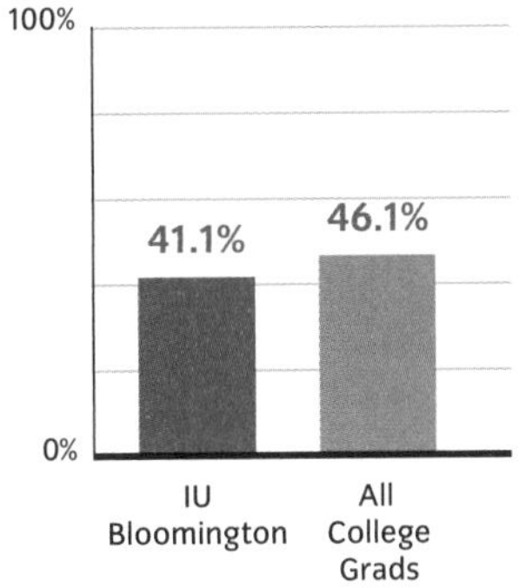

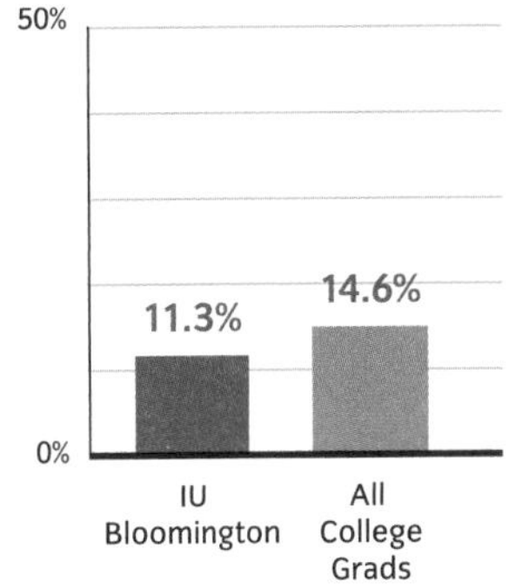

Alumni Employment

- % Other: 11.6%
- % Independent/ Entrepreneur: 16.1%
- % With Large Org.: 20.1%
- % With Medium Org.: 11.7%
- % With Small Org.: 13.6%
- % With Govt.: 7.2%
- % Any Level Teaching: 19.7%

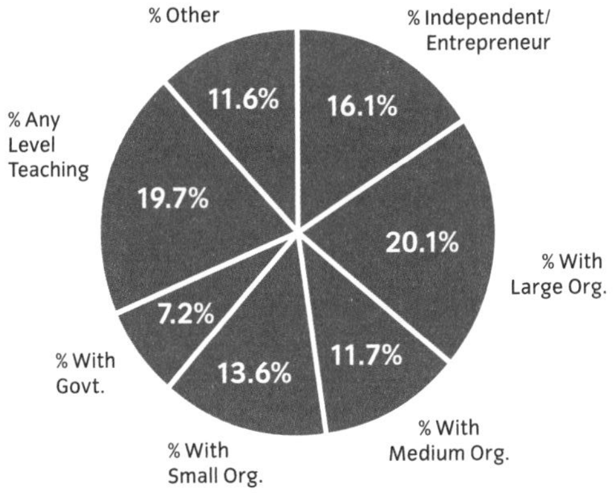

Income Distribution of Graduates

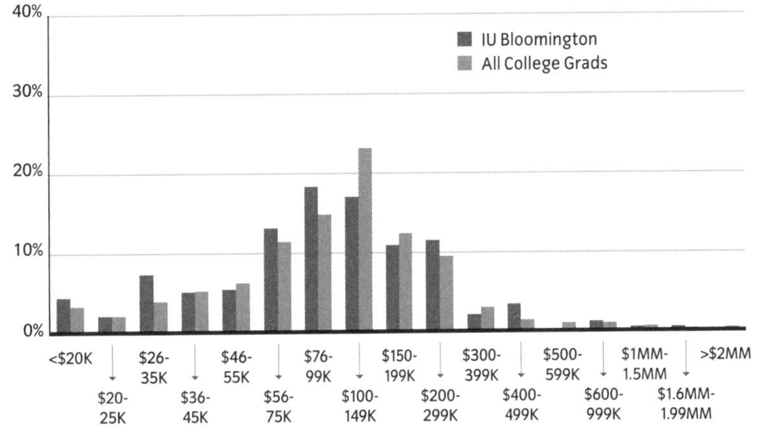

Current Selectivity & Demand Analysis for Indiana University Bloomington

Attribute	% Accepted	% Accepted Who Enroll	Freshman Retention Rate	Graduation Rate	Demand Index	Reputation Index
Score	72.0%	29.0%	90.0%	71.0%	4.74	0.40
Rank	156	107	113	141	141	146

Where are the Graduates of Indiana University Bloomington on the Political Spectrum?

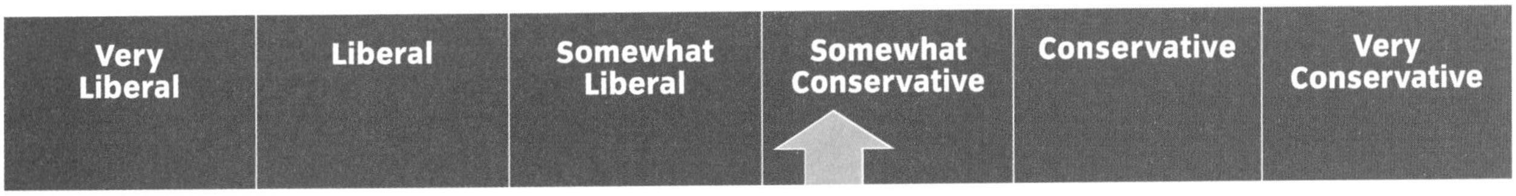

Very Liberal	Liberal	Somewhat Liberal	Somewhat Conservative	Conservative	Very Conservative
			↑		

Iowa State University

Location: Ames, IA
Campus Setting: City: Small
Total Expenses: $18,521
Estimated Average Discount: $4,967 (27%)
Estimated Net Price: $13,554

Type of Institution: National University
Number of Undergraduates: 23,104
SAT Score: Reading: 460–640, Math: 530–670
Student/Faculty Ratio: 17 to 1
Transfer Out Rate: 16%

Rank Among 104 National Universities **84**

Overall Rank Among 177 *Alumni Factor* Schools **153**

Overview

Like many large state schools, Iowa State University offers a practical, economical, hands-on education to its largely rural Iowa student base. Consequently, its strengths are in agriculture and engineering (particularly mechanical, agricultural and aerospace engineering), where it has some of the top programs in the country. Add to those strengths a warm, friendly atmosphere and a school spirit that is abuzz year round and you can see why ISU produces a very happy graduate (ranked 49th in Overall Happiness) who is hard working, conservative and reliable. ISU grads are astronauts, scientists, engineers, business leaders and Pulitzer Prize-winning writers.

ISU's highest ranking is in providing students Immediate Job Opportunities (ranked 54th); its highest ranked Ultimate Outcome is Financial Success & Happiness (81st). It also scores quite well in the percentage of grads who would recommend the university (49th). These strengths, along with respectable rankings across the remaining attributes, earn ISU an 84th overall ranking among national universities and a top spot among the finest research universities in the country.

Notable Alumni

US Senator Tom Harkin; Pulitzer Prize winner Ted Kooser; and current Director of the National Science Foundation, Subra Suresh.

The Alumni Factor Rankings Summary

Attribute	University Rank	Overall Rank
College Experience	**77**	**149**
Intellectual Development	93	165
Social Development	54	114
Spiritual Development	60	129
Friendship Development	89	159
Preparation for Career Success	71	137
Immediate Job Opportunities	54	86
Overall Assessment	**61**	**114**
Would Personally Choose Again	60	111
Would Recommend to Student	49	98
Value for the Money	65	119
Financial Success	**86**	**141**
Income per Household	78	120
% Households with Income >$150K	78	128
Household Net Worth	88	149
% Households Net Worth >$1MM	86	146
Overall Happiness	**49**	**94**
Alumni Giving	**67**	**131**
Graduation Rate	**77**	**143**
Overall Rank	**84**	**153**

Other Key Alumni Outcomes

3.1% Are college professors
10.5% Teach at any level
37.4% Have post-graduate degrees
59.7% Live in dual-income homes
92.2% Are currently employed

See pages 134–135 for detailed explanations and definitions.

Alumni Activities During College

20.5% Community Service
44.6% Intramural Sports
26.0% Internships
17.5% Media Programs
12.5% Music Programs
55.4% Part-Time Jobs

Prepared Me for Career Success (% Strongly Agree)	Was A Good Value for the Money (% Strongly Agree)	Percent of Alumni Worth >$1MM
ISU: 25.0%	ISU: 38.7%	ISU: 10.7%
All College Grads: 31.9%	All College Grads: 46.1%	All College Grads: 14.6%

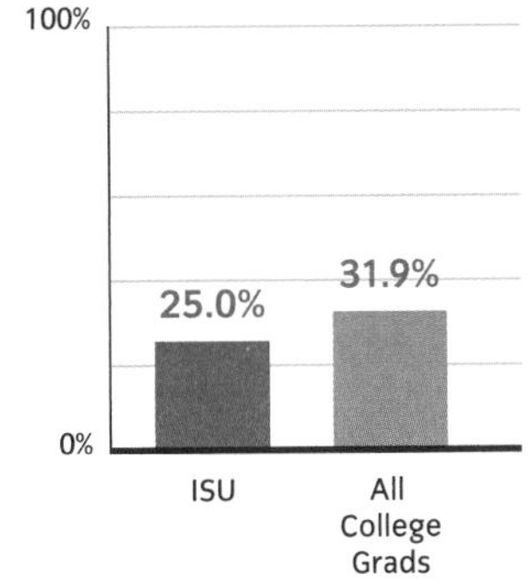

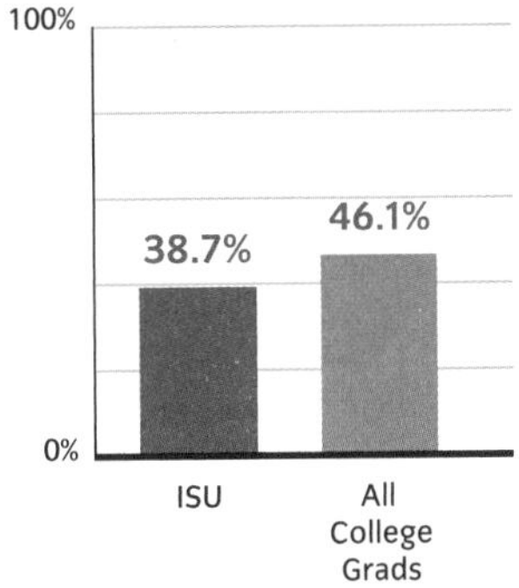

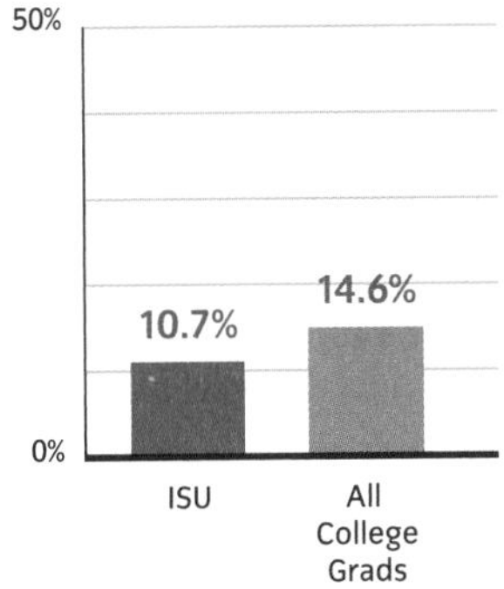

Alumni Employment

- % Independent/ Entrepreneur: 10.9%
- % With Large Org.: 25.3%
- % With Medium Org.: 11.7%
- % With Small Org.: 12.5%
- % With Govt.: 12.8%
- % In Farm/ Agr.: 0.4%
- % Any Level Teaching: 10.5%
- % Other: 15.9%

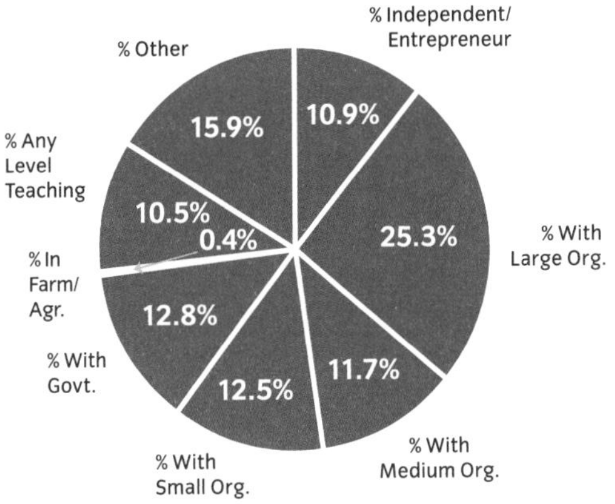

Income Distribution of Graduates

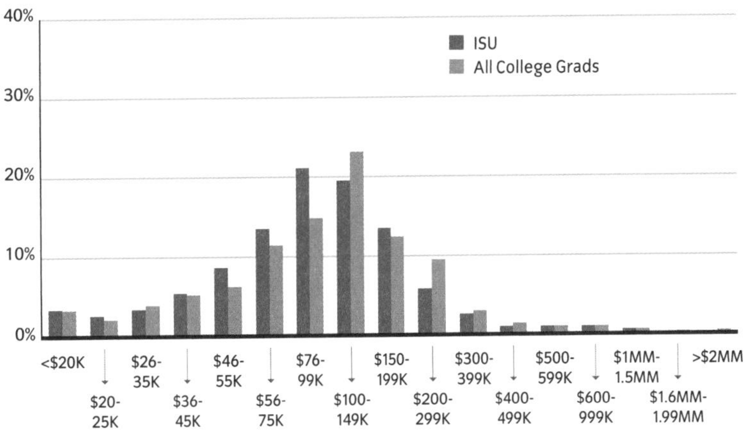

ISU
All College Grads

0% 10% 20% 30% 40%

<$20K, $20-25K, $26-35K, $36-45K, $46-55K, $56-75K, $76-99K, $100-149K, $150-199K, $200-299K, $300-399K, $400-499K, $500-599K, $600-999K, $1MM-1.5MM, $1.6MM-1.99MM, >$2MM

Current Selectivity & Demand Analysis for Iowa State University

Attribute	% Accepted	% Accepted Who Enroll	Freshman Retention Rate	Graduation Rate	Demand Index	Reputation Index
Score	81.0%	38.0%	86.0%	70.0%	2.98	0.47
Rank	168	55	146	143	170	130

Where are the Graduates of Iowa State University on the Political Spectrum?

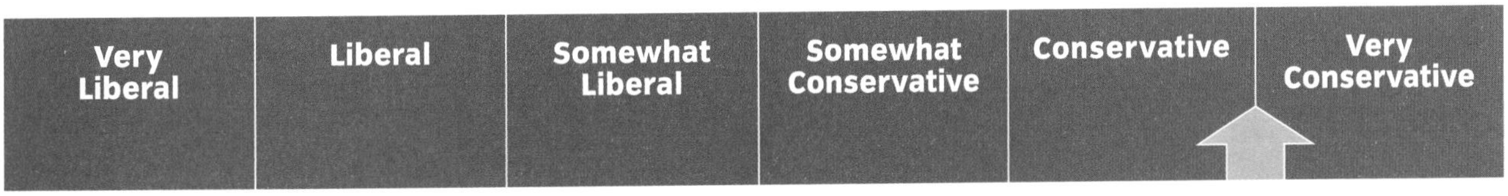

Very Liberal	Liberal	Somewhat Liberal	Somewhat Conservative	Conservative	Very Conservative
				↑	

James Madison University

Location: Harrisonburg, VA
Campus Setting: City: Small
Total Expenses: $21,214
Estimated Average Discount: $8,339 (39%)
Estimated Net Price: $12,875

Type of Institution: Regional University
Number of Undergraduates: 17,657
SAT Score: Reading: 540–640, Math: 550–650
Student/Faculty Ratio: 16 to 1
Transfer Out Rate: 7%

Rank Among 20 Regional Universities	**9**
Overall Rank Among 177 *Alumni Factor* Schools	**101**

Overview

James Madison University has had a tradition of preparing excellent teachers since its founding in 1908. That tradition and passion continues today, as JMU is the #1 ranked school among the 177 we analyzed in the percent of graduates who teach at any level. This fundamental strength propels JMU to its 27th rank in its ability to help grads land jobs; its 54th ranking in Preparation for Career Success; its 31st rank in the percent of grads who are college professors and its 22nd rank for employment rate. However, JMU graduates much more than teachers – it produces writers, musicians, entertainers, business leaders and government officials.

JMU grads have a deep passion for their alma mater, as indicated by their College Experience rating (52nd among all schools). JMU's highest experience attribute ranking is Social Development (ranked 30th), and its highest Ultimate Outcome ranking is Happiness & Friendships (67th). Also considered a strong value for the money (61st), JMU graduates tend to be very happy (57th) in life. Overall, 65% of grads strongly agree they would recommend it to a prospective student (45th). In all, JMU is one of the Top 10 regional universities in the US – and just keeps getting stronger.

Notable Alumni

Jim Acosta, reporter for CNN's American Morning; Dave Matthews Band founding member Leroi Moore; and long-time Dave Matthews Band guest musician, Butch Taylor.

The Alumni Factor Rankings Summary

Attribute	Overall Rank
College Experience	**52**
Intellectual Development	133
Social Development	30
Spiritual Development	64
Friendship Development	61
Preparation for Career Success	54
Immediate Job Opportunities	26
Overall Assessment	**82**
Would Personally Choose Again	135
Would Recommend to Student	45
Value for the Money	61
Financial Success	**142**
Income per Household	126
% Households with Income >$150K	166
Household Net Worth	102
% Households Net Worth >$1MM	149
Overall Happiness	**57**
Alumni Giving	**162**
Graduation Rate	**91**
Overall Rank	**101**

Other Key Alumni Outcomes

8.6% Are college professors
28.6% Teach at any level
47.9% Have post-graduate degrees
52.9% Live in dual-income homes
95.7% Are currently employed

See pages 134–135 for detailed explanations and definitions.

Alumni Activities During College

36.0% Community Service
28.1% Intramural Sports
20.9% Internships
13.7% Media Programs
23.0% Music Programs
38.8% Part-Time Jobs

Prepared Me for Career Success % Strongly Agree	Was A Good Value for the Money % Strongly Agree	Percent of Alumni Worth >$1MM
JMU 37.9% / All College Grads 31.9%	JMU 48.6% / All College Grads 46.1%	JMU 10.6% / All College Grads 14.6%

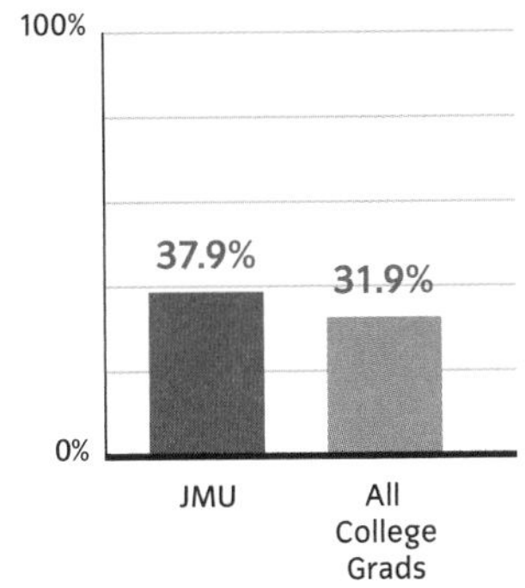

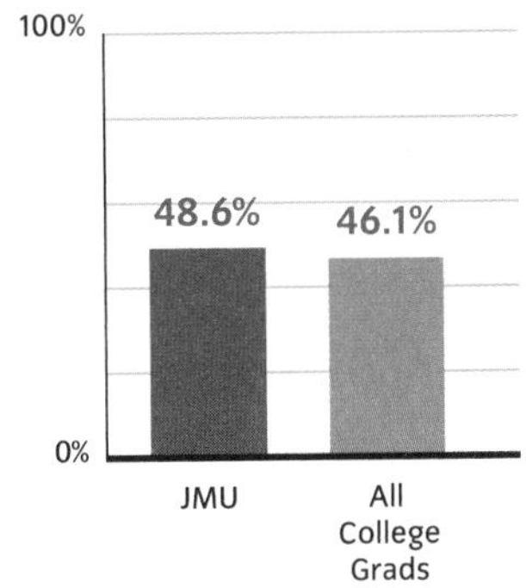

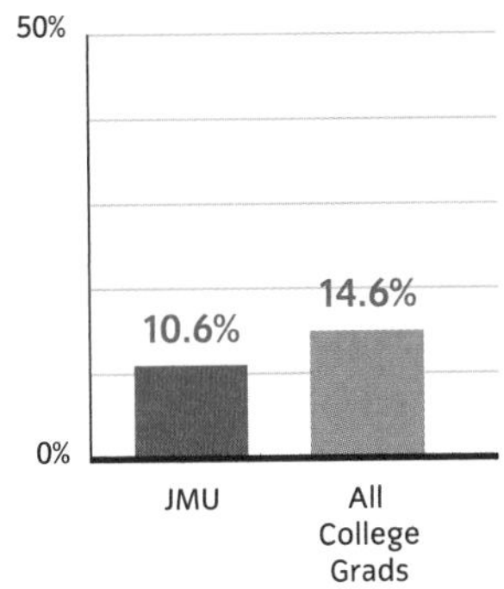

Alumni Employment

- % Other: 10.5%
- % Independent/ Entrepreneur: 10.0%
- % With Large Org.: 20.7%
- % With Medium Org.: 8.6%
- % With Small Org.: 13.6%
- % With Govt.: 8.0%
- % Any Level Teaching: 28.6%

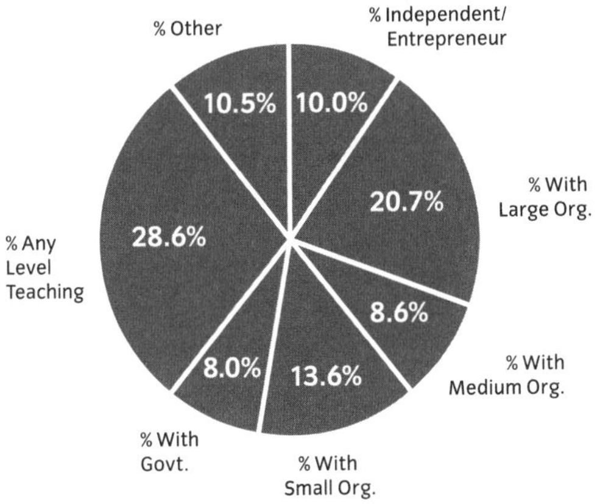

Income Distribution of Graduates

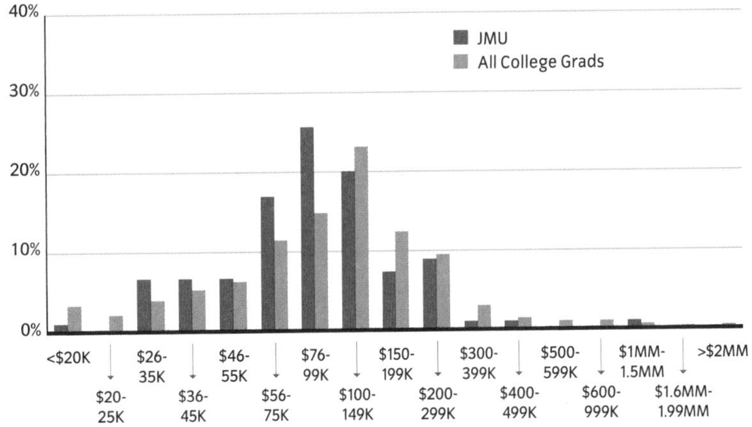

■ JMU
■ All College Grads

<$20K, $20-25K, $26-35K, $36-45K, $46-55K, $56-75K, $76-99K, $100-149K, $150-199K, $200-299K, $300-399K, $400-499K, $500-599K, $600-999K, $1MM-1.5MM, $1.6MM-1.99MM, >$2MM

Current Selectivity & Demand Analysis for James Madison University

Attribute	% Accepted	% Accepted Who Enroll	Freshman Retention Rate	Graduation Rate	Demand Index	Reputation Index
Score	60.0%	30.0%	91.0%	82.0%	5.52	0.50
Rank	129	103	102	91	136	121

Where are the Graduates of James Madison University on the Political Spectrum?

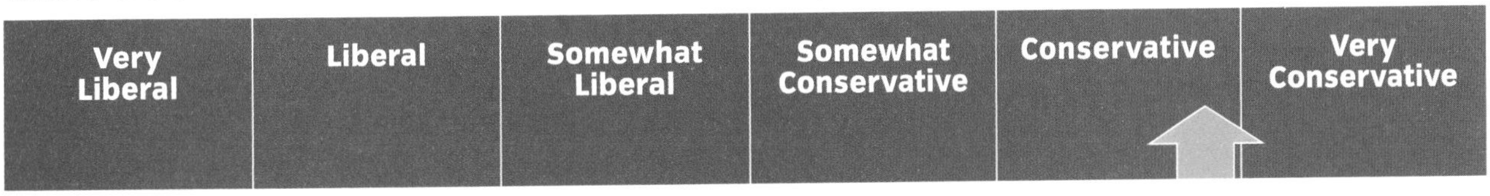

Very Liberal	Liberal	Somewhat Liberal	Somewhat Conservative	Conservative	Very Conservative

Johns Hopkins University

Location: Baltimore, MD
Campus Setting: City: Large
Total Expenses: $57,442
Estimated Average Discount: $31,647 (55%)
Estimated Net Price: $25,795

Type of Institution: National University
Number of Undergraduates: 5,820
SAT Score: Reading: 630–730, Math: 670–770
Student/Faculty Ratio: 9 to 1
Transfer Out Rate: 5%

Rank Among 104 National Universities	**45**
Overall Rank Among 177 *Alumni Factor* Schools	**100**

Overview

Generally acknowledged to be among the preeminent academic institutions in the country, Johns Hopkins graduates are extremely successful (Top 15 in Financial Success) and faithful in opening their pocketbooks (32nd in Alumni Giving). Yet their rating of the College Experience itself (ranked 68th) and all aspects of their Overall Assessment (99th) indicate that graduates have a less glowing view of their experience. As hinted at by the school's 65th and 99th rankings in Friendship and Social Development, respectively, much of this is likely due to its difficult location and the lack of the close campus community students experience at many other schools – the perennially strong lacrosse team notwithstanding.

This apparent shortcoming, however, does not prevent strong Intellectual Development (21st); Top 10 household income results; the 13th best employment rate and an impressive showing in the Ultimate Outcomes (22nd). If Financial Success & Intellectual Capability are your goal, JHU is one of the top destinations in the country (ranked 13th in this Ultimate Outcome). JHU is also ranked 9th in the country in grads with a post-graduate degree.

Notable Alumni

NYC Mayor Michael Bloomberg, former vice president Spiro Agnew, IBM CEO Sam Palmisano, Pulitzer Prize winners Murray Kempton and Richard Ben Cramer, and a long list of other academic, business and political leaders.

The Alumni Factor Rankings Summary

Attribute	University Rank	Overall Rank
College Experience	**68**	**137**
Intellectual Development	21	67
Social Development	99	172
Spiritual Development	95	167
Friendship Development	65	135
Preparation for Career Success	48	100
Immediate Job Opportunities	59	97
Overall Assessment	**99**	**170**
Would Personally Choose Again	98	167
Would Recommend to Student	101	173
Value for the Money	79	142
Financial Success	**14**	**24**
Income per Household	9	18
% Households with Income >$150K	9	19
Household Net Worth	15	32
% Households Net Worth >$1MM	17	34
Overall Happiness	**61**	**109**
Alumni Giving	**32**	**90**
Graduation Rate	**24**	**39**
Overall Rank	**45**	**100**

Other Key Alumni Outcomes

7.4% Are college professors
12.4% Teach at any level
71.2% Have post-graduate degrees
60.0% Live in dual-income homes
96.3% Are currently employed

See pages 134–135 for detailed explanations and definitions.

Alumni Activities During College

25.8% Community Service
23.9% Intramural Sports
19.5% Internships
13.2% Media Programs
22.6% Music Programs
42.8% Part-Time Jobs

Prepared Me for Career Success % Strongly Agree	Was A Good Value for the Money % Strongly Agree	Percent of Alumni Worth >$1MM
Johns Hopkins 33.1%; All College Grads 31.9%	Johns Hopkins 38.0%; All College Grads 46.1%	Johns Hopkins 19.9%; All College Grads 14.6%

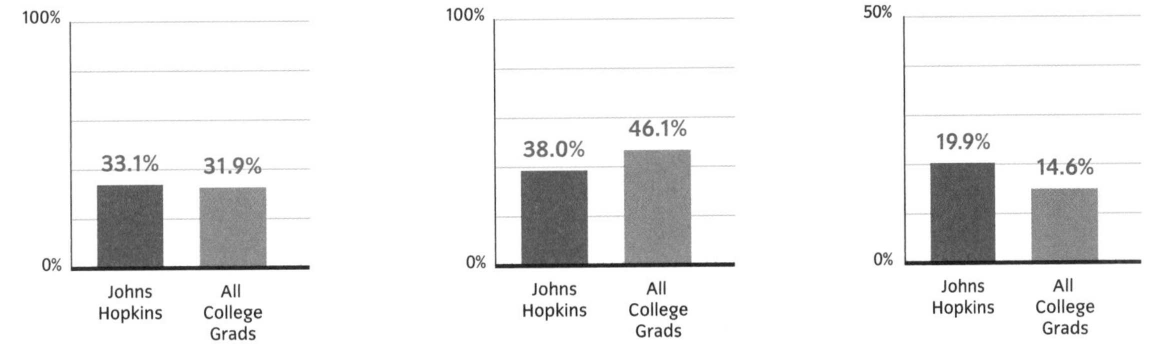

Alumni Employment

- % Independent/ Entrepreneur: 17.3%
- % With Large Org.: 17.9%
- % With Medium Org.: 13.0%
- % With Small Org.: 17.3%
- % With Govt.: 15.4%
- % Any Level Teaching: 12.4%
- % Other: 6.7%

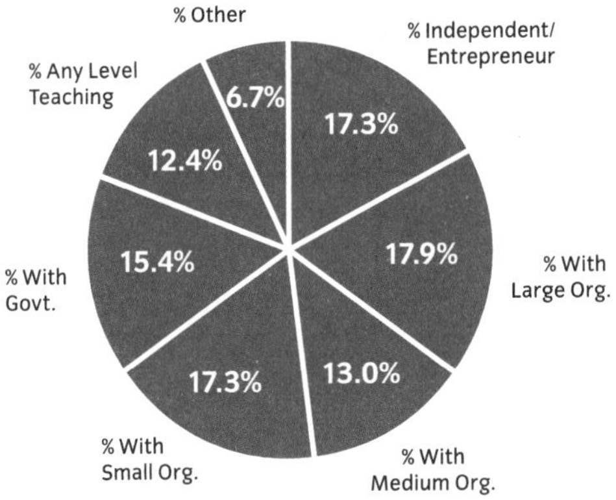

Income Distribution of Graduates

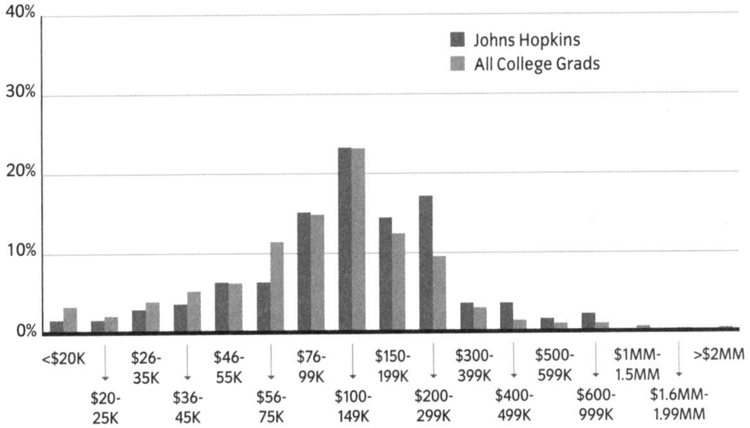

■ Johns Hopkins ■ All College Grads

0% 10% 20% 30% 40%

<$20K, $20-25K, $26-35K, $36-45K, $46-55K, $56-75K, $76-99K, $100-149K, $150-199K, $200-299K, $300-399K, $400-499K, $500-599K, $600-999K, $1MM-1.5MM, $1.6MM-1.99MM, >$2MM

Current Selectivity & Demand Analysis for Johns Hopkins University

Attribute	% Accepted	% Accepted Who Enroll	Freshman Retention Rate	Graduation Rate	Demand Index	Reputation Index
Score	19.0%	35.0%	96.0%	90.0%	14.89	1.84
Rank	26	70	27	39	21	29

Where are the Graduates of Johns Hopkins University on the Political Spectrum?

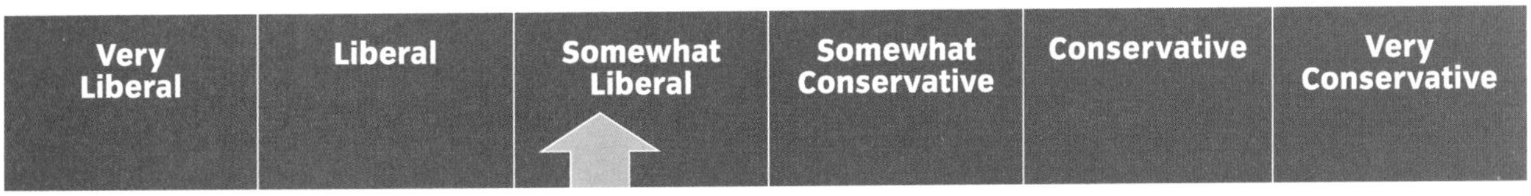

Very Liberal	Liberal	Somewhat Liberal	Somewhat Conservative	Conservative	Very Conservative
		⇧			

Kansas State University

Location: Manhattan, KS
Campus Setting: Town: Remote
Total Expenses: $19,629
Estimated Average Discount: $5,277 (27%)
Estimated Net Price: $14,352

Type of Institution: National University
Number of Undergraduates: 19,205
SAT Score: Not Reported
Student/Faculty Ratio: 21 to 1
Transfer Out Rate: Not Reported

Rank Among 104 National Universities	**42**
Overall Rank Among 177 *Alumni Factor* Schools	**92**

Overview

Among the very first of the 106 land-grant colleges in the US, Kansas State has been at the forefront of public education since its founding in 1863. One of the friendliest and most egalitarian campuses in the country (women have been admitted since its inception – the 2nd public institution in the US to admit women), KSU is an upbeat, highly spirited, conservative community that produces a very happy (ranked 7th overall), industrious and loyal graduate who would do it all again (ranked 10th in Would Personally Choose Again). KSU graduates well outperform the school's reputation. The Overall Assessment scores from graduates are top notch (ranked 25th among national universities) and the College Experience attributes also rank quite high (ranked 36th) for a large university with over 15,000 undergraduates.

Given its origins as an agriculture and science institution, it is not surprising that its strongest programs – and the source of many of its most influential graduates – are in agriculture, the biosciences, physics, and engineering. Smart and capable, KSU grads get it done in whatever field they choose to enter.

Notable Alumni

George "Bud" Peterson, President of Georgia Tech; Warren Staley, former president and CEO of Cargill; Reagan's Press Secretary Marlin Fitzwater; and former Chair of the Joint Chiefs of Staff, Richard Myers.

The Alumni Factor Rankings Summary

Attribute	University Rank	Overall Rank
College Experience	**36**	**94**
Intellectual Development	74	146
Social Development	31	76
Spiritual Development	41	106
Friendship Development	35	96
Preparation for Career Success	29	70
Immediate Job Opportunities	24	38
Overall Assessment	**25**	**46**
Would Personally Choose Again	10	28
Would Recommend to Student	27	58
Value for the Money	34	61
Financial Success	**75**	**122**
Income per Household	87	133
% Households with Income >$150K	96	160
Household Net Worth	46	84
% Households Net Worth >$1MM	63	107
Overall Happiness	**7**	**17**
Alumni Giving	**29**	**81**
Graduation Rate	**96**	**167**
Overall Rank	**42**	**92**

Other Key Alumni Outcomes

3.7% Are college professors
11.2% Teach at any level
40.5% Have post-graduate degrees
62.0% Live in dual-income homes
96.3% Are currently employed

See pages 134–135 for detailed explanations and definitions.

Alumni Activities During College

27.3% Community Service
40.0% Intramural Sports
20.0% Internships
16.7% Media Programs
22.3% Music Programs
53.7% Part-Time Jobs

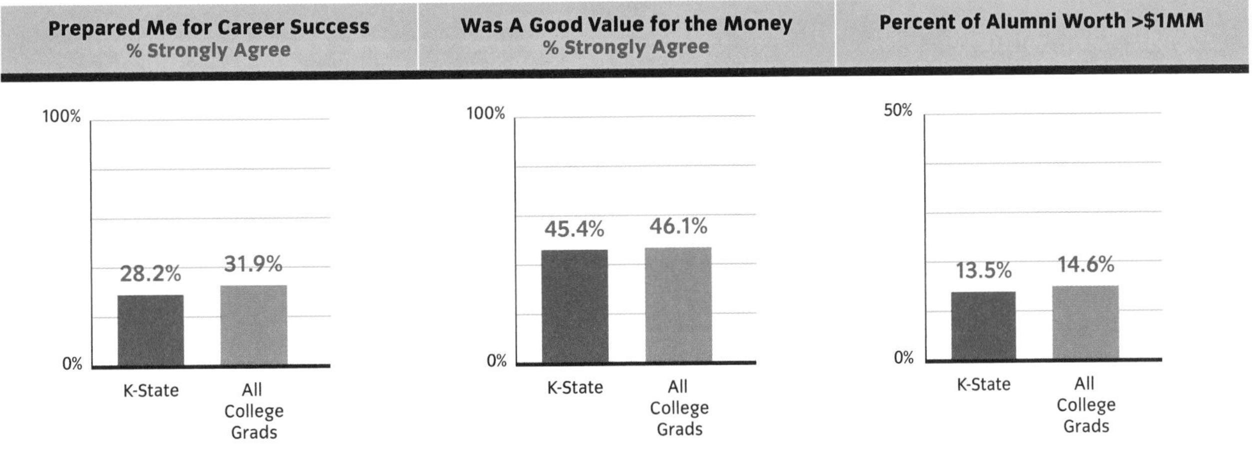

Alumni Employment

% Other 10.7%
% Independent/ Entrepreneur 16.6%
% With Large Org. 19.3%
% With Medium Org. 12.5%
% With Small Org. 16.6%
% With Govt. 12.8%
% In Farm/ Agr. 0.3%
% Any Level Teaching 11.2%

Income Distribution of Graduates

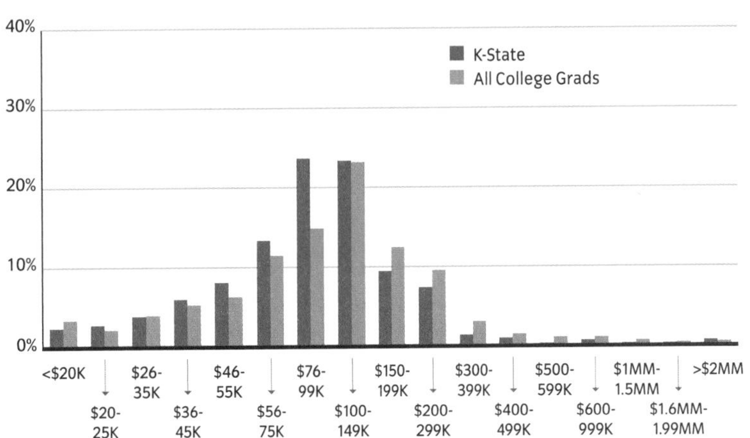

Current Selectivity & Demand Analysis for Kansas State University

Attribute	% Accepted	% Accepted Who Enroll	Freshman Retention Rate	Graduation Rate	Demand Index	Reputation Index
Score	99.0%	44.0%	81.0%	60.0%	2.28	0.44
Rank	177	26	173	167	176	138

Where are the Graduates of Kansas State University on the Political Spectrum?

Very Liberal	Liberal	Somewhat Liberal	Somewhat Conservative	Conservative	Very Conservative
					↑

See pages 134–135 for detailed explanations and definitions.

Kenyon College

Location: Grambier, OH
Campus Setting: Rural: Fringe
Total Expenses: $55,680
Estimated Average Discount: $24,901 (45%)
Estimated Net Price: $30,779

Type of Institution: Liberal Arts College
Number of Undergraduates: 1,632
SAT Score: Reading: 640–740, Math: 610–690
Student/Faculty Ratio: 10 to 1
Transfer Out Rate: Not Reported

Rank Among 53 Liberal Arts Colleges	**31**
Overall Rank Among 177 *Alumni Factor* Schools	**62**

Overview

Kenyon is the quintessential small, exclusive liberal arts college tucked away in a charming town in central Ohio. Kenyon's location, coupled with an extraordinarily bright student body (in the Top 50 in SAT scores), forces an unusually strong bond between the students themselves and between students and the faculty (ranked 7th in Friendship Development). It results in one of the most intense intellectual experiences in the country (ranked 4th in Intellectual Development) and a rank of 5th in the Ultimate Outcome of Friendships & Intellectual Capability. Like other liberal arts colleges with a large percentage of graduates who majored in English, the classics, drama/theatre and the social sciences, Kenyon grads are not as enthusiastic about the school's ability to get them Immediate Job Opportunities (ranked 52nd). However, Kenyon grads have the 5th highest employment rate of any school in the country – so these graduates are very successful in landing and thriving in a variety of fields (ranked 29th in Financial Success). In all, Kenyon's reputation is strong, but its results are even stronger. The intellectual center of Ohio's collegiate system, Kenyon is everything a liberal arts college should be.

Notable Alumni

Former US president Rutherford B. Hayes, actors Paul Newman and Allison Janney, cartoonist Jim Borgman, Calvin & Hobbes creator Bill Watterson, and Pulitzer Prize-winning poet James Wright.

The Alumni Factor Rankings Summary

Attribute	Liberal Arts Rank	Overall Rank
College Experience	**32**	**59**
Intellectual Development	4	4
Social Development	31	53
Spiritual Development	22	47
Friendship Development	7	7
Preparation for Career Success	37	100
Immediate Job Opportunities	52	176
Overall Assessment	**25**	**59**
Would Personally Choose Again	22	55
Would Recommend to Student	17	45
Value for the Money	31	82
Financial Success	**29**	**84**
Income per Household	30	107
% Households with Income >$150K	28	79
Household Net Worth	30	81
% Households Net Worth >$1MM	32	79
Overall Happiness	**49**	**161**
Alumni Giving	**27**	**30**
Graduation Rate	**32**	**67**
Overall Rank	**31**	**62**

Other Key Alumni Outcomes

6.8%	Are college professors
12.7%	Teach at any level
58.0%	Have post-graduate degrees
50.8%	Live in dual-income homes
97.4%	Are currently employed

See pages 134–135 for detailed explanations and definitions.

Alumni Activities During College

37.8% Community Service
24.4% Intramural Sports
11.8% Internships
36.9% Media Programs
36.9% Music Programs
21.8% Part-Time Jobs

	Prepared Me for Career Success (% Strongly Agree)	Was A Good Value for the Money (% Strongly Agree)	Percent of Alumni Worth >$1MM
Kenyon	36.8%	44.1%	15.6%
All College Grads	31.9%	46.1%	14.6%

Alumni Employment

Category	%
% Independent/ Entrepreneur	22.1%
% Other	5.0%
% With Large Org.	17.8%
% With Medium Org.	15.3%
% With Small Org.	18.6%
% With Govt.	8.5%
% Any Level Teaching	12.7%

Income Distribution of Graduates

Current Selectivity & Demand Analysis for Kenyon College

Attribute	% Accepted	% Accepted Who Enroll	Freshman Retention Rate	Graduation Rate	Demand Index	Reputation Index
Score	33.0%	33.0%	92.0%	86.0%	9.13	1.00
Rank	61	83	86	67	83	60

Where are the Graduates of Kenyon College on the Political Spectrum?

Very Liberal	Liberal	Somewhat Liberal	Somewhat Conservative	Conservative	Very Conservative
⇧					

See pages 134–135 for detailed explanations and definitions.

Lafayette College

Location: Easton, PA
Campus Setting: Suburb: Large
Total Expenses: $55,720
Estimated Average Discount: $29,757 (53%)
Estimated Net Price: $25,963

Type of Institution: Liberal Arts College
Number of Undergraduates: 2,414
SAT Score: Reading: 590–680, Math: 620–700
Student/Faculty Ratio: 10 to 1
Transfer Out Rate: 9%

Rank Among 53 Liberal Arts Colleges	**40**
Overall Rank Among 177 *Alumni Factor* Schools	**77**

Overview

A fierce battle known simply as "The Rivalry" has occupied eastern Pennsylvania since the 1880s. This rivalry between Lafayette College and Lehigh University – two schools separated by 17 miles and a century of competition – began as a football contest and has since spread to every aspect of life between the two schools. While competition has made both schools very strong, Lafayette takes a close second in our analysis of alumni results, ranking 77th versus Lehigh's 75th ranking. However, graduates of both of these fine schools perform well above their strong reputations.

The financial success of Lafayette grads is truly astounding. They are the number one college in the country in average graduate Household Net Worth and rank 8th overall in Financial Success. This leads to Top 15 rankings in each Ultimate Outcome in which Financial Success is included. They are slightly behind Lehigh in the College Experience (121st) and in the Overall Assessment (166th). Lafayette leads by a substantial margin, however, in Alumni Giving (43rd).

Notable Alumni

Former US Department of the Treasury secretary William Simon; founder of Dow Jones Charles Bergstresser; CEO of Rockefeller Group Jonathan Green; and Nobel Prize winners Haldan Hartline and Philip Hench.

The Alumni Factor Rankings Summary

Attribute	Liberal Arts Rank	Overall Rank
College Experience	**51**	**121**
Intellectual Development	52	126
Social Development	45	101
Spiritual Development	53	136
Friendship Development	50	94
Preparation for Career Success	42	115
Immediate Job Opportunities	26	117
Overall Assessment	**52**	**166**
Would Personally Choose Again	49	164
Would Recommend to Student	51	149
Value for the Money	52	159
Financial Success	**8**	**18**
Income per Household	10	23
% Households with Income >$150K	14	30
Household Net Worth	1	1
% Households Net Worth >$1MM	12	26
Overall Happiness	**24**	**57**
Alumni Giving	**35**	**43**
Graduation Rate	**18**	**47**
Overall Rank	**40**	**77**

Other Key Alumni Outcomes

3.8% Are college professors
7.5% Teach at any level
55.0% Have post-graduate degrees
54.9% Live in dual-income homes
95.3% Are currently employed

See pages 134–135 for detailed explanations and definitions.

Alumni Activities During College

37.4% Community Service
35.5% Intramural Sports
25.2% Internships
23.3% Media Programs
23.3% Music Programs
22.4% Part-Time Jobs

Prepared Me for Career Success % Strongly Agree	Was A Good Value for the Money % Strongly Agree	Percent of Alumni Worth >$1MM

	Prepared Me for Career Success	Was A Good Value for the Money	Percent of Alumni Worth >$1MM
Lafayette	30.6%	27.8%	21.1%
All College Grads	31.9%	46.1%	14.6%

Alumni Employment

Category	Percent
% Independent/ Entrepreneur	21.7%
% With Large Org.	23.6%
% With Medium Org.	23.6%
% With Small Org.	9.4%
% With Govt.	3.7%
% Any Level Teaching	7.5%
% Other	10.5%

Income Distribution of Graduates

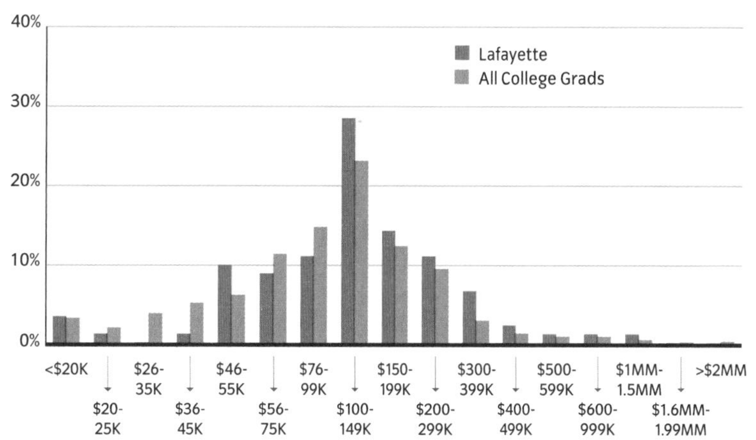

Current Selectivity & Demand Analysis for Lafayette College

Attribute	% Accepted	% Accepted Who Enroll	Freshman Retention Rate	Graduation Rate	Demand Index	Reputation Index
Score	40.0%	28.0%	94.0%	89.0%	8.96	0.70
Rank	77	117	58	47	84	85

Where are the Graduates of Lafayette College on the Political Spectrum?

Very Liberal	Liberal	Somewhat Liberal	Somewhat Conservative	Conservative	Very Conservative

See pages 134–135 for detailed explanations and definitions.

Lehigh University

Location: Bethlehem, PA
Campus Setting: City: Small
Total Expenses: $54,020
Estimated Average Discount: $29,510 (55%)
Estimated Net Price: $24,510

Type of Institution: National University
Number of Undergraduates: 4,781
SAT Score: Reading: 580–680, Math: 640–720
Student/Faculty Ratio: 10 to 1
Transfer Out Rate: Not Reported

Rank Among 104 National Universities	**31**
Overall Rank Among 177 *Alumni Factor* Schools	**75**

Overview

A very strong engineering, math and finance university with extraordinarily successful graduates (ranked 7th in Financial Success), Lehigh University is a small but powerful force in education at the national level. Ranked slightly ahead of its arch-competitor Lafayette (ranked 75th overall versus Lafayette's 77th ranking), Lehigh is neck and neck with Lafayette in the College Experience (ranked 120th), but surpasses Lafayette in Preparation for Career Success, and in the percentage of graduates who go on to become millionaires (where Lehigh is ranked 1st among all national universities and 3rd overall). Lehigh graduates also have higher SAT scores (ranked 81st versus Lafayette's 92nd ranking). But Lehigh is not an easy path for students – it ranks 16th among all colleges in tough grading, where it is an estimated 13% tougher in giving out "A"s than other colleges with equally capable students. Students seem to be tough graders, too, giving Lehigh a 93rd ranking in Overall Assessment that is belied by its Top 20 showing in Alumni Giving among national universities.

But like all colleges with tough grading policies, it proves to be a benefit in ultimately producing successful grads. Competition sharpens all players – and Lehigh is as competitive as they come.

Notable Alumni

Business and racing legend Roger Penske; former Chrysler chairman Lee Iacocca; Chairman and CEO of Turner Broadcasting Philip Kent; former Space Shuttle astronaut John-David Bartoe and scores of other notable leaders.

The Alumni Factor Rankings Summary

Attribute	University Rank	Overall Rank
College Experience	**53**	**120**
Intellectual Development	64	133
Social Development	72	138
Spiritual Development	86	158
Friendship Development	42	105
Preparation for Career Success	34	79
Immediate Job Opportunities	26	41
Overall Assessment	**93**	**163**
Would Personally Choose Again	94	161
Would Recommend to Student	85	154
Value for the Money	85	152
Financial Success	**7**	**15**
Income per Household	14	25
% Households with Income >$150K	18	36
Household Net Worth	6	15
% Households Net Worth >$1MM	1	3
Overall Happiness	**30**	**57**
Alumni Giving	**20**	**70**
Graduation Rate	**32**	**52**
Overall Rank	**31**	**75**

Other Key Alumni Outcomes

5.9% Are college professors
8.9% Teach at any level
55.1% Have post-graduate degrees
50.7% Live in dual-income homes
91.3% Are currently employed

See pages 134–135 for detailed explanations and definitions.

Alumni Activities During College

30.7% Community Service
42.4% Intramural Sports
21.0% Internships
17.6% Media Programs
21.0% Music Programs
26.3% Part-Time Jobs

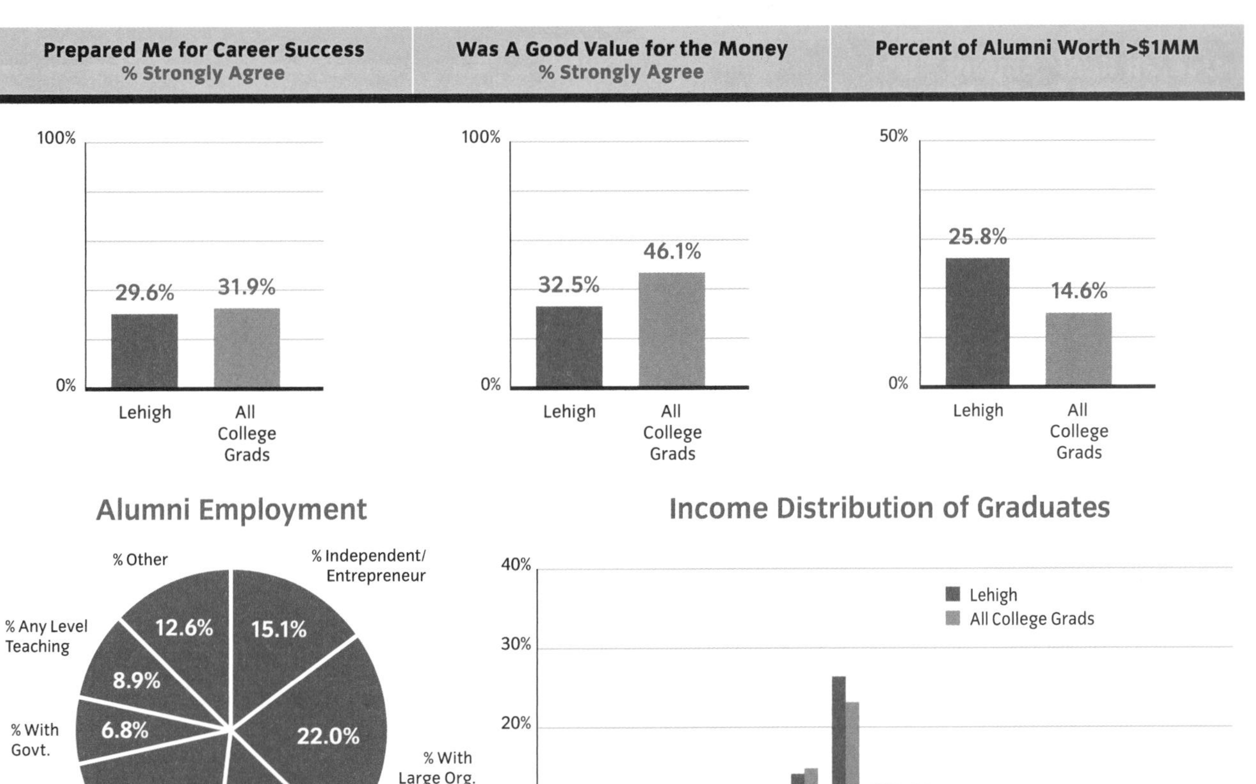

Current Selectivity & Demand Analysis for Lehigh University

Attribute	% Accepted	% Accepted Who Enroll	Freshman Retention Rate	Graduation Rate	Demand Index	Reputation Index
Score	33.0%	31.0%	93.0%	88.0%	9.59	0.94
Rank	61	96	73	52	74	64

Where are the Graduates of Lehigh University on the Political Spectrum?

Very Liberal	Liberal	Somewhat Liberal	Somewhat Conservative	Conservative	Very Conservative

Loyola Marymount University

Location: Los Angeles, CA
Campus Setting: Citiy: Large
Total Expenses: $55,299
Estimated Average Discount: $21,314 (39%)
Estimated Net Price: $33,985

Type of Institution: Regional University
Number of Undergraduates: 5,950
SAT Score: Reading: 540–630, Math: 560–650
Student/Faculty Ratio: 11 to 1
Transfer Out Rate: Not Reported

Rank Among 20 Regional Universities	**11**
Overall Rank Among 177 *Alumni Factor* Schools	**108**

Overview

Sitting on a bluff above Marina Del Rey overlooking the Pacific Ocean, Loyola Marymount University has one of the most stunningly beautiful campuses to be found anywhere. Add to that a well-rounded, Jesuit academic and social experience (ranked 81st in the College Experience and 97th in the Overall Assessment) and excellent Financial Success for graduates (ranked 82nd), and you can understand Loyola Marymount's rapid ascension in esteem and popularity over the last decade.

LMU's strongest Ultimate Outcome is Financial Success & Friendships (89th), and it ranks 55th in graduates who would recommend the school to prospective students. Film and entertainment industry internships are plentiful at LMU, driven by its excellent School of Film and Television, as well as by the underlying strength of its core academic requirements. Long famous for its Law School, LMU is quickly developing a reputation for its undergraduate programs as well.

Notable Alumni

Minnesota Timberwolves head Coach Rick Adelman and many Hollywood notables, including James Bond film producer Barbara Broccoli; actor Bob Denver of Gilligan's Island fame; actors Colin Hanks, Mindy Cohn and Mila Kunis; as well as many other Emmy and Academy Award winning producers, writers and directors.

The Alumni Factor Rankings Summary

Attribute	Overall Rank
College Experience	**81**
Intellectual Development	102
Social Development	75
Spiritual Development	15
Friendship Development	112
Preparation for Career Success	79
Immediate Job Opportunities	88
Overall Assessment	**97**
Would Personally Choose Again	104
Would Recommend to Student	55
Value for the Money	124
Financial Success	**82**
Income per Household	83
% Households with Income >$150K	71
Household Net Worth	75
% Households Net Worth >$1MM	114
Overall Happiness	**155**
Alumni Giving	**99**
Graduation Rate	**106**
Overall Rank	**108**

Other Key Alumni Outcomes

4.9%	Are college professors
14.1%	Teach at any level
49.5%	Have post-graduate degrees
51.7%	Live in dual-income homes
90.0%	Are currently employed

See pages 134–135 for detailed explanations and definitions.

Alumni Activities During College

32.2% Community Service
28.8% Intramural Sports
27.3% Internships
24.0% Media Programs
9.3% Music Programs
49.8% Part-Time Jobs

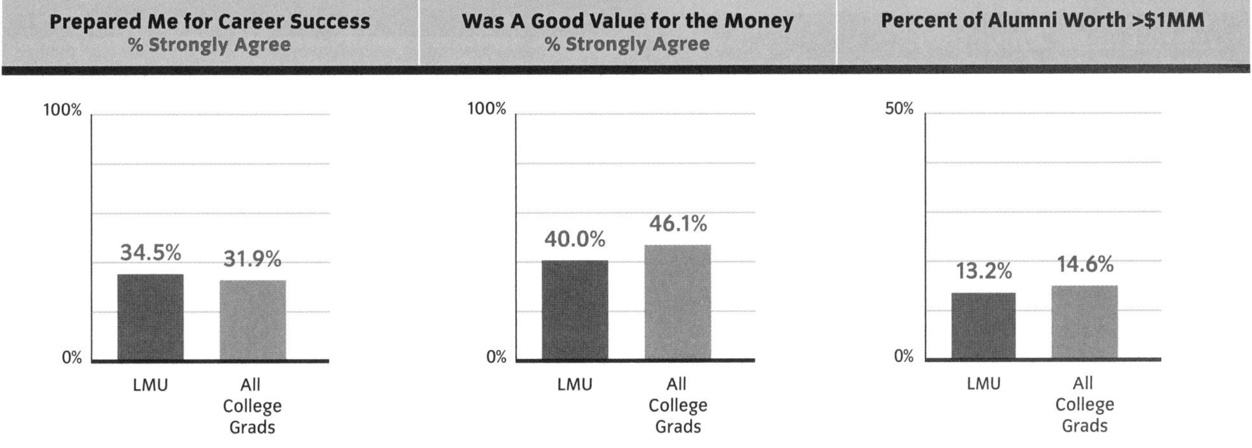

Alumni Employment

% Other 11.1%
% Independent/ Entrepreneur 19.0%
% With Large Org. 19.9%
% With Medium Org. 15.5%
% With Small Org. 13.6%
% With Govt. 6.8%
% Any Level Teaching 14.1%

Income Distribution of Graduates

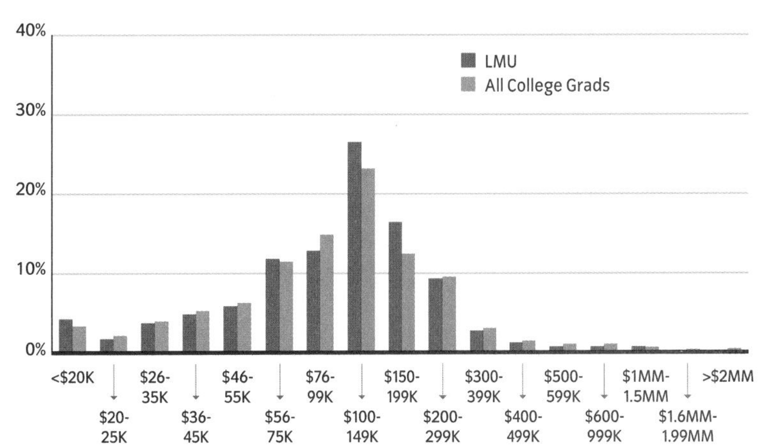

Current Selectivity & Demand Analysis for Loyola Marymount University

Attribute	% Accepted	% Accepted Who Enroll	Freshman Retention Rate	Graduation Rate	Demand Index	Reputation Index
Score	53.0%	21.0%	89.0%	80.0%	8.78	0.40
Rank	107	156	124	106	87	146

Where are the Graduates of Loyola Marymount University on the Political Spectrum?

Very Liberal	Liberal	Somewhat Liberal	Somewhat Conservative	Conservative	Very Conservative
			↑		

Loyola University Chicago

Location: Chicago, IL
Campus Setting: City: Large
Total Expenses: $47,664
Estimated Average Discount: $18,688 (39%)
Estimated Net Price: $28,976

Type of Institution: Regional University
Number of Undergraduates: 9,747
SAT Score: Reading: 540–660, Math: 540–650
Student/Faculty Ratio: 14 to 1
Transfer Out Rate: Not Reported

Rank Among 20 Regional Universities	**20**
Overall Rank Among 177 *Alumni Factor* Schools	**168**

Overview

The second largest of the 28 US Jesuit colleges, Loyola University is an academic stalwart in Chicago, and its prominence is growing nationally. Ranked 20th among the regional universities, with above average rankings in both the College Experience (ranked 140th among all colleges) and in the Overall Assessment (ranked 133rd – driven by a 114th ranking in Value for the Money) Loyola grads are bright and successful, and have a tight affinity to this Chicago-based icon.

Loyola's highest ranking is Spiritual Development (ranked 20th), but it also does quite well in high income households (88th). Roughly two-thirds of Loyola's grads are female. Its nursing school produces some of the finest nurses in medicine, and it ranks 10th in the percent of grads who become college professors.

Notable Alumni

Retired McDonald's chairman Michael Quinlan; legendary actor and comedian Bob Newhart; former US congressman Dan Rostenkowski; Pulitzer prize-winning reporter and author Philip Caputo; Fr. Daniel Coughlin, former chaplain of the US House of Representatives; and Ian Brennan, co-creator of *Glee*.

The Alumni Factor Rankings Summary

Attribute	Overall Rank
College Experience	**140**
Intellectual Development	111
Social Development	156
Spiritual Development	20
Friendship Development	174
Preparation for Career Success	142
Immediate Job Opportunities	143
Overall Assessment	**133**
Would Personally Choose Again	137
Would Recommend to Student	130
Value for the Money	114
Financial Success	**154**
Income per Household	153
% Households with Income >$150K	88
Household Net Worth	164
% Households Net Worth >$1MM	177
Overall Happiness	**164**
Alumni Giving	**141**
Graduation Rate	**158**
Overall Rank	**168**

Other Key Alumni Outcomes

11.8% Are college professors
11.8% Teach at any level
63.5% Have post-graduate degrees
57.7% Live in dual-income homes
93.9% Are currently employed

See pages 134–135 for detailed explanations and definitions.

Alumni Activities During College

30.8% Community Service
21.2% Intramural Sports
25.0% Internships
25.0% Media Programs
8.8% Music Programs
48.1% Part-Time Jobs

Prepared Me for Career Success % Strongly Agree	Was A Good Value for the Money % Strongly Agree	Percent of Alumni Worth >$1MM
Loyola Chicago 17.6%; All College Grads 31.9%	Loyola Chicago 37.3%; All College Grads 46.1%	Loyola Chicago 0.0%; All College Grads 14.6%

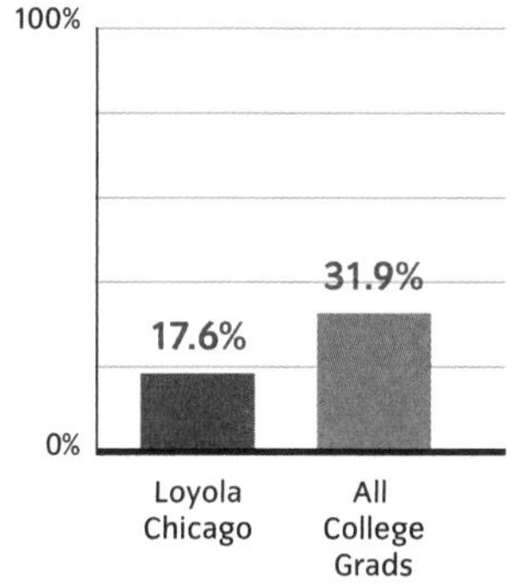

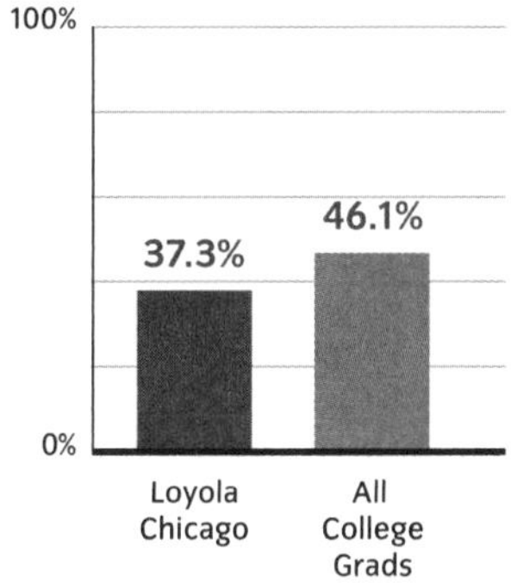

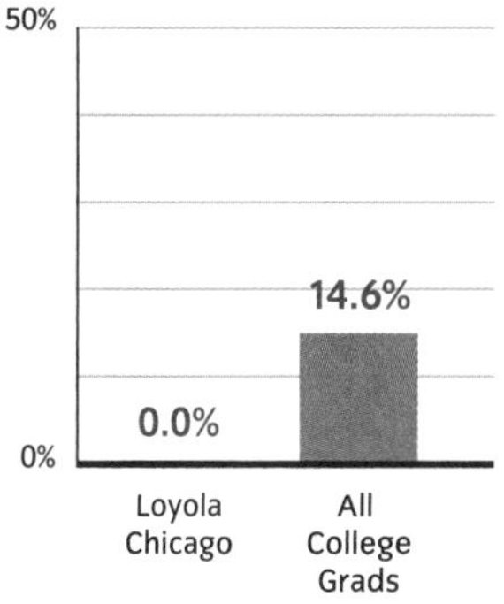

Alumni Employment

Category	%
% Independent/Entrepreneur	7.8%
% With Large Org.	27.5%
% With Medium Org.	15.7%
% With Small Org.	21.6%
% With Govt.	4.0%
% Any Level Teaching	11.8%
% Other	11.6%

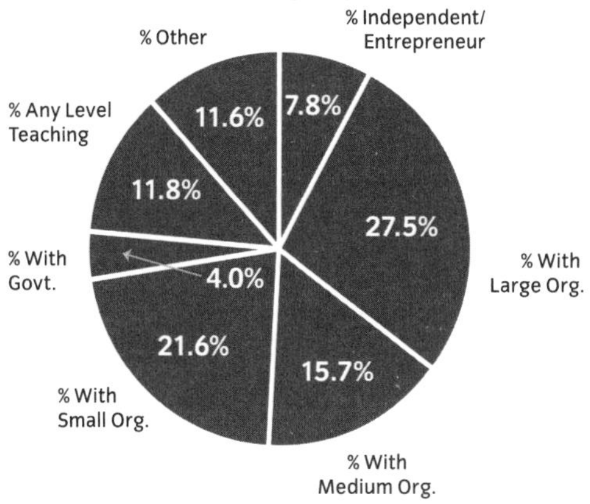

Income Distribution of Graduates

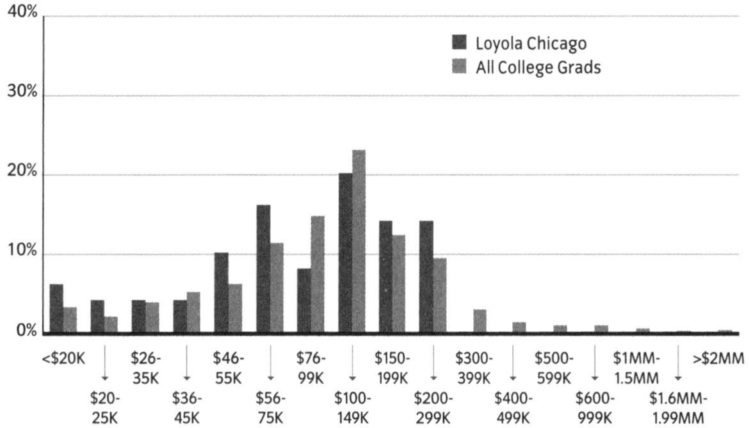

Current Selectivity & Demand Analysis for Loyola University Chicago

Attribute	% Accepted	% Accepted Who Enroll	Freshman Retention Rate	Graduation Rate	Demand Index	Reputation Index
Score	55.0%	20.0%	85.0%	67.0%	9.24	0.36
Rank	113	161	151	158	79	155

Where are the Graduates of Loyola University Chicago on the Political Spectrum?

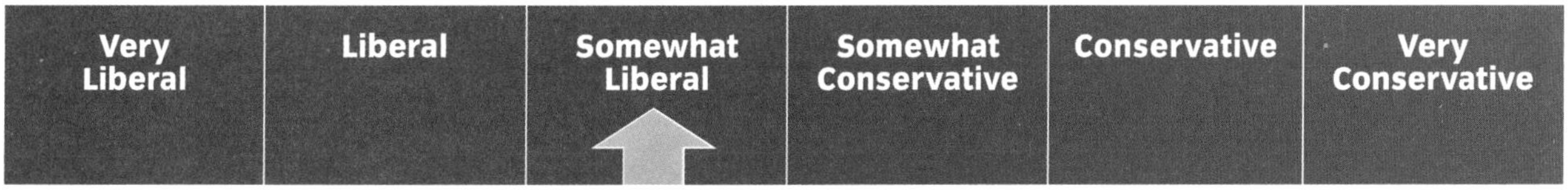

Very Liberal	Liberal	Somewhat Liberal	Somewhat Conservative	Conservative	Very Conservative
		↑			

See pages 134–135 for detailed explanations and definitions.

Loyola University Maryland

Location: Baltimore, MD
Campus Setting: City: Large
Total Expenses: $54,700
Estimated Average Discount: $26,582 (49%)
Estimated Net Price: $28,118

Type of Institution: Regional University
Number of Undergraduates: 3,807
SAT Score: Reading: 540–640, Math: 550–650
Student/Faculty Ratio: 13 to 1
Transfer Out Rate: Not Reported

Rank Among 20 Regional Universities	**16**
Overall Rank Among 177 *Alumni Factor* Schools	**137**

Overview

One of four Loyola colleges across the country (all four are in our 177 Top Colleges), Loyola University Maryland is a Jesuit school on the outskirts of Baltimore that competes with the other Northeastern Catholic colleges. Graduates have a high regard for their experience (ranked 96th in the College Experience) and do quite well financially (62nd in Financial Success). Its highest ranking, outside of its 29th ranking in Spiritual Development, is its 45th ranking in Household Net Worth. Its strongest Ultimate Outcome is Financial Success & Friendships (ranked 55th).

Loyola operates somewhat under the radar on the national education scene, but that is changing as its programs strengthen and its reputation builds. Its toughest challenge is the lackluster Overall Assessment ratings by its graduates (172nd). Even while it is becoming more selective (graduates' SAT scores rank 164th among the 177 colleges), Loyola grads already have a strong history of success in politics, business, writing, law and academics.

Notable Alumni

Legendary sportscaster Jim McKay; authors Tom Clancy and Mark Bowden; and Maryland's 51st governor, Herbert O'Conor.

The Alumni Factor Rankings Summary

Attribute	Overall Rank
College Experience	**96**
Intellectual Development	93
Social Development	114
Spiritual Development	29
Friendship Development	75
Preparation for Career Success	152
Immediate Job Opportunities	88
Overall Assessment	**172**
Would Personally Choose Again	177
Would Recommend to Student	174
Value for the Money	146
Financial Success	**62**
Income per Household	58
% Households with Income >$150K	50
Household Net Worth	45
% Households Net Worth >$1MM	111
Overall Happiness	**172**
Alumni Giving	**152**
Graduation Rate	**91**
Overall Rank	**137**

Other Key Alumni Outcomes

1.4% Are college professors
11.5% Teach at any level
56.5% Have post-graduate degrees
59.4% Live in dual-income homes
94.2% Are currently employed

See pages 134–135 for detailed explanations and definitions.

Alumni Activities During College

47.1% Community Service
40.0% Intramural Sports
40.0% Internships
27.1% Media Programs
18.5% Music Programs
40.0% Part-Time Jobs

Prepared Me for Career Success % Strongly Agree	Was A Good Value for the Money % Strongly Agree	Percent of Alumni Worth >$1MM
Loyola Maryland: 28.6% All College Grads: 31.9%	Loyola Maryland: 37.1% All College Grads: 46.1%	Loyola Maryland: 13.2% All College Grads: 14.6%

Alumni Employment

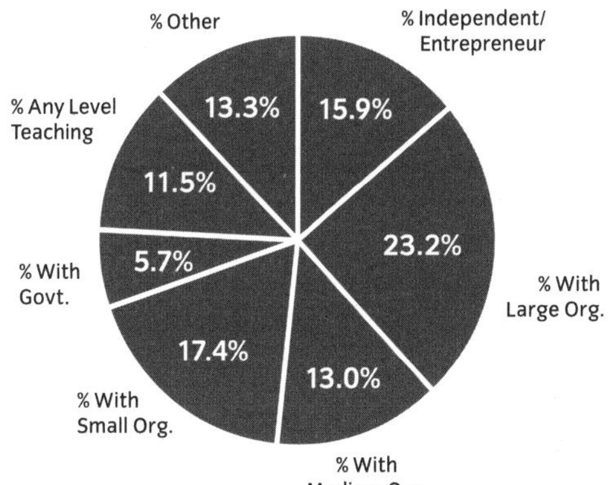

Income Distribution of Graduates

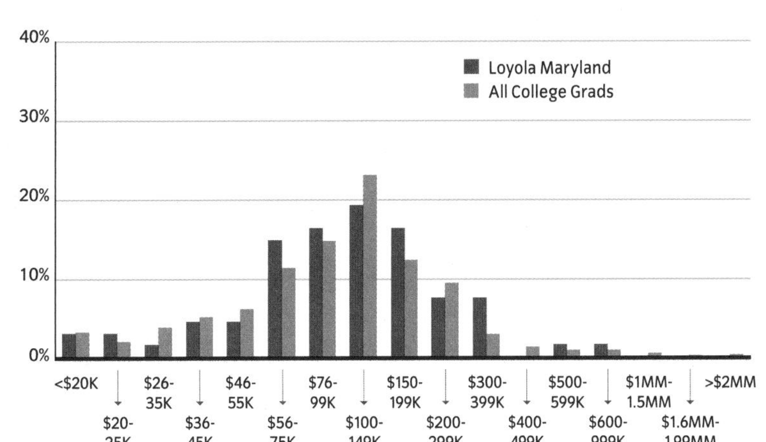

Current Selectivity & Demand Analysis for Loyola University Maryland

Attribute	% Accepted	% Accepted Who Enroll	Freshman Retention Rate	Graduation Rate	Demand Index	Reputation Index
Score	63.0%	14.0%	87.0%	82.0%	11.27	0.22
Rank	135	174	140	91	57	175

Where are the Graduates of Loyola University Maryland on the Political Spectrum?

Very Liberal	Liberal	Somewhat Liberal	Somewhat Conservative	Conservative	Very Conservative
				↑	

See pages 134–135 for detailed explanations and definitions.

Loyola University New Orleans

Location: New Orleans, LA
Campus Setting: City: Large
Total Expenses: $46,802
Estimated Average Discount: $23,994 (51%)
Estimated Net Price: $22,808

Type of Institution: Regional University
Number of Undergraduates: 2,922
SAT Score: Reading: 590–630, Math: 560–610
Student/Faculty Ratio: 9 to 1
Transfer Out Rate: Not Reported

Rank Among 20 Regional Universities	**10**
Overall Rank Among 177 *Alumni Factor* Schools	**105**

Overview

The highest ranked of the four Loyola colleges in the US, Loyola New Orleans gets very high marks from its graduates for the College Experience (ranked 40th) and in the Overall Assessment (39th). Located next door to Tulane University, Loyola's campus is just close enough to the finest of New Orleans' food, fun and music, driving its 36th ranking in Social Development. Despite the New Orleans atmosphere, Loyola produces a hard- working (33rd in employment), happy (96th in Happiness), Spiritual (6th) and well-rounded graduate who sees the education as a great value (ranked 1st among the 12 Jesuit colleges in Value for the Money) and would gladly recommend it to students today (ranked 30th among all colleges).

Now fully recovered from Hurricane Katrina, enrollment is again strong, and the campus is more beautiful than ever. Loyola's history of producing some of Louisiana's best and brightest continues. Graduates enjoy success in many fields, including politics, entertainment, academics, journalism, business, religion and government. This just may be one of the best combinations of academic, spiritual and social experiences to be found anywhere in the country.

Notable Alumni

Among the well-known graduates are Donald Wetzel, inventor of the ATM Machine, and former NASA administrator Sean O'Keefe.

The Alumni Factor Rankings Summary

Attribute	Overall Rank
College Experience	**40**
Intellectual Development	87
Social Development	36
Spiritual Development	6
Friendship Development	90
Preparation for Career Success	51
Immediate Job Opportunities	60
Overall Assessment	**39**
Would Personally Choose Again	75
Would Recommend to Student	30
Value for the Money	25
Financial Success	**144**
Income per Household	159
% Households with Income >$150K	101
Household Net Worth	142
% Households Net Worth >$1MM	150
Overall Happiness	**97**
Alumni Giving	**145**
Graduation Rate	**174**
Overall Rank	**105**

Other Key Alumni Outcomes

4.8% Are college professors
12.5% Teach at any level
43.0% Have post-graduate degrees
48.6% Live in dual-income homes
95.2% Are currently employed

See pages 134–135 for detailed explanations and definitions.

Alumni Activities During College

37.7% Community Service
18.9% Intramural Sports
31.1% Internships
24.6% Media Programs
19.9% Music Programs
51.9% Part-Time Jobs

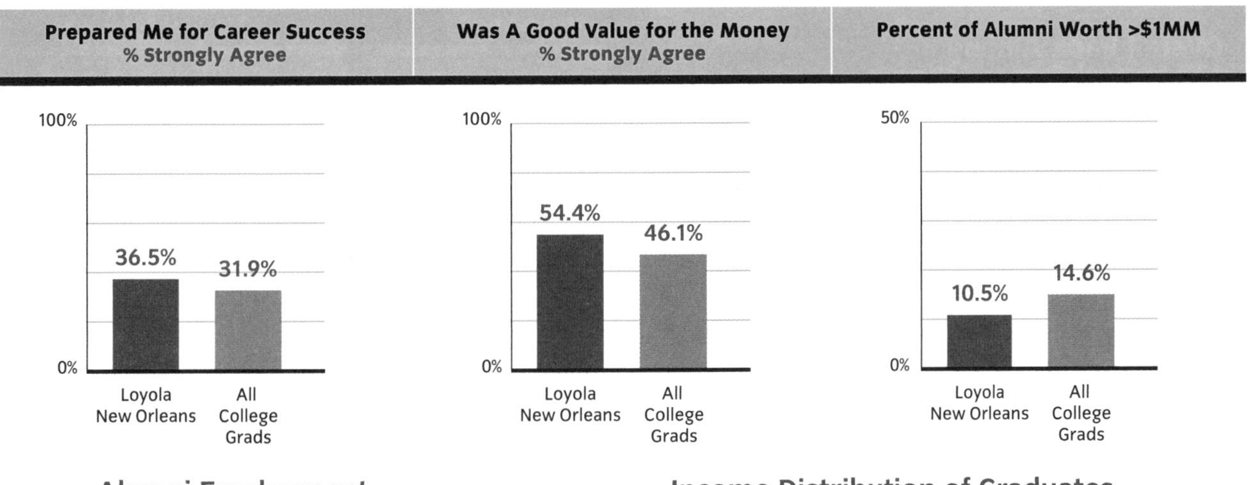

Alumni Employment

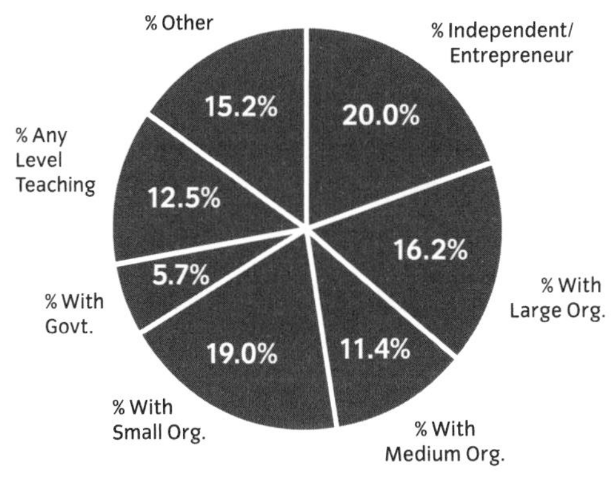

Income Distribution of Graduates

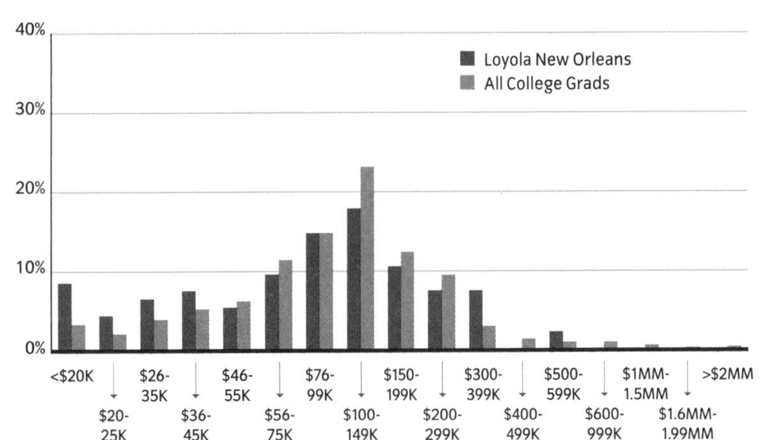

Current Selectivity & Demand Analysis for Loyola University New Orleans

Attribute	% Accepted	% Accepted Who Enroll	Freshman Retention Rate	Graduation Rate	Demand Index	Reputation Index
Score	65.0%	25.0%	82.0%	57.0%	7.43	0.38
Rank	140	130	167	174	109	151

Where are the Graduates of Loyola University New Orleans on the Political Spectrum?

Very Liberal	Liberal	Somewhat Liberal	Somewhat Conservative	Conservative	Very Conservative
				↑	

See pages 134–135 for detailed explanations and definitions.

Macalester College

Location: St. Paul, MN
Campus Setting: City: Large
Total Expenses: $53,315
Estimated Average Discount: $30,939 (58%)
Estimated Net Price: $22,376

Type of Institution: Liberal Arts College
Number of Undergraduates: 2,033
SAT Score: Reading: 650–740, Math: 630–710
Student/Faculty Ratio: 11 to 1
Transfer Out Rate: 8%

Rank Among 53 Liberal Arts Colleges	**48**
Overall Rank Among 177 *Alumni Factor* Schools	**103**

Overview

Macalester College has seen a surge in its reputation and its applicants over the last decade, driven by its globally focused, social justice-minded liberal arts mission. Ranked 103rd overall and 48th among liberal arts schools, Macalester delivers a powerful Intellectual Development experience (ranked 35th) for its extremely bright students (ranked 31st in SAT scores). Macalester grads give the school excellent marks in the Overall Assessment (27th), with a 14th ranking in Would Recommend to a Prospective Student. Its strongest Ultimate Outcome is Happiness & Intellectual Capability (36th), as its intimate community, intense academic environment and progressive social stance make for a uniquely liberal and loyal Mac culture. It is the 3rd most liberal of all 177 colleges, behind only Reed and Oberlin colleges. It also ranks 23rd among all liberal arts colleges in Alumni Giving – a clear indication of the love and affection Mac grads have for their alma mater.

Notable Alumni

William Morris Endeavor CEO (and uber-agent) Ari Emanuel; film director, producer and writer Peter Berg; Nobel Peace Prize winner Kofi Annan; and former US vice president Walter Mondale.

The Alumni Factor Rankings Summary

Attribute	Liberal Arts Rank	Overall Rank
College Experience	**46**	**102**
Intellectual Development	35	48
Social Development	42	93
Spiritual Development	32	59
Friendship Development	51	98
Preparation for Career Success	49	131
Immediate Job Opportunities	41	152
Overall Assessment	**27**	**65**
Would Personally Choose Again	29	80
Would Recommend to Student	14	42
Value for the Money	29	76
Financial Success	**38**	**117**
Income per Household	40	137
% Households with Income >$150K	26	70
Household Net Worth	47	154
% Households Net Worth >$1MM	37	96
Overall Happiness	**45**	**159**
Alumni Giving	**23**	**26**
Graduation Rate	**20**	**52**
Overall Rank	**48**	**103**

Other Key Alumni Outcomes

8.1% Are college professors
12.1% Teach at any level
63.9% Have post-graduate degrees
58.8% Live in dual-income homes
91.2% Are currently employed

See pages 134–135 for detailed explanations and definitions.

Alumni Activities During College

41.5% Community Service
34.0% Intramural Sports
38.1% Internships
32.6% Media Programs
27.2% Music Programs
39.5% Part-Time Jobs

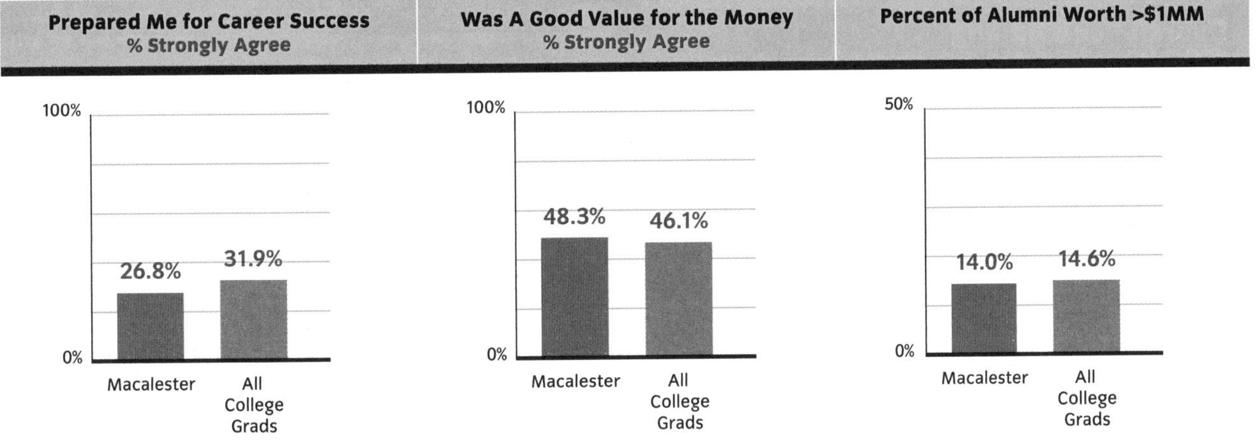

Alumni Employment

% Other 15.3%
% Independent/Entrepreneur 20.2%
% With Large Org. 15.4%
% With Medium Org. 13.4%
% With Small Org. 12.8%
% With Govt. 10.8%
% Any Level Teaching 12.1%

Income Distribution of Graduates

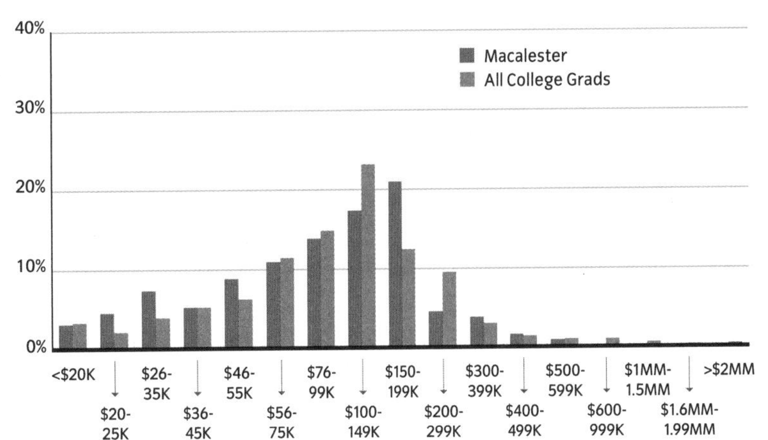

Current Selectivity & Demand Analysis for Macalester College

Attribute	% Accepted	% Accepted Who Enroll	Freshman Retention Rate	Graduation Rate	Demand Index	Reputation Index
Score	35.0%	22.0%	96.0%	88.0%	12.78	0.63
Rank	67	149	27	52	38	96

Where are the Graduates of Macalester College on the Political Spectrum?

Very Liberal	Liberal	Somewhat Liberal	Somewhat Conservative	Conservative	Very Conservative

Marquette University

Location: Milwaukee, WI
Campus Setting: City: Large
Total Expenses: $44,922
Estimated Average Discount: $16,176 (36%)
Estimated Net Price: $28,746

Type of Institution: Regional University
Number of Undergraduates: 8,113
SAT Score: Reading: 520–630, Math: 530–650
Student/Faculty Ratio: 14 to 1
Transfer Out Rate: 0%

Rank Among 20 Regional Universities	**6**
Overall Rank Among 177 *Alumni Factor* Schools	**82**

Overview

A Jesuit University located in the heart of Milwaukee, Marquette is Wisconsin's largest private university and among its finest. Of the dozen Jesuit colleges in our Top 177, Marquette ranks 3rd in graduates with income above the US Median, 5th in Preparation for Career Success and is 5th in Intellectual Development. The College Experience at Marquette is ranked a very strong 48th among all colleges, its highest rankings being Preparation for Career Success (46th) and, not suprisingly, Spiritual Development (12th).

Marquette grads do quite well financially (ranked 87th overall in Financial Success), and the school's strongest Ultimate Outcome is Financial Success & Happiness, where it is ranked 60th. Marquette grads are also very happy (ranked 48th among all colleges) and hard working, with the 54th highest employment rate. Grads lean to the conservative side politically, like those of many of the Jesuit colleges (among Jesuit colleges, only Georgetown and Loyola-Chicago are left of center on *The Alumni Factor* Political Spectrum).

Notable Alumni

Tony Award-winning actor Anthony Crivello; former Saturday Night Live comedian Chris Farley; actress Amy Madigan, and former Sears chairman Edward Brennan.

The Alumni Factor Rankings Summary

Attribute	Overall Rank
College Experience	**48**
Intellectual Development	81
Social Development	96
Spiritual Development	12
Friendship Development	79
Preparation for Career Success	46
Immediate Job Opportunities	47
Overall Assessment	**117**
Would Personally Choose Again	116
Would Recommend to Student	101
Value for the Money	121
Financial Success	**87**
Income per Household	72
% Households with Income >$150K	98
Household Net Worth	69
% Households Net Worth >$1MM	123
Overall Happiness	**48**
Alumni Giving	**75**
Graduation Rate	**100**
Overall Rank	**82**

Other Key Alumni Outcomes

4.4%	Are college professors
10.8%	Teach at any level
47.0%	Have post-graduate degrees
53.0%	Live in dual-income homes
94.1%	Are currently employed

See pages 134–135 for detailed explanations and definitions.

Alumni Activities During College

43.8% Community Service
34.0% Intramural Sports
28.1% Internships
24.1% Media Programs
20.2% Music Programs
52.2% Part-Time Jobs

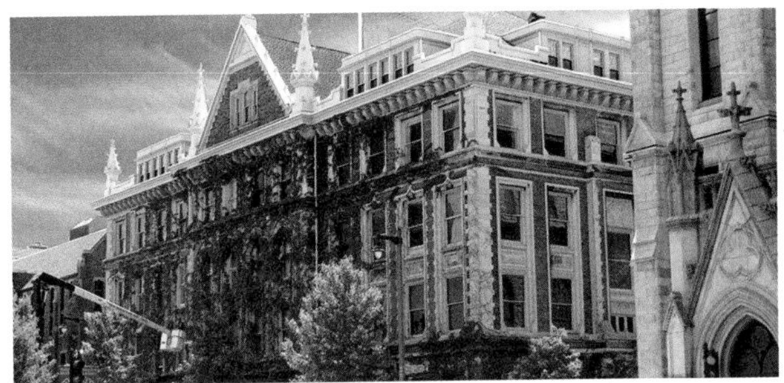

Prepared Me for Career Success % Strongly Agree	Was A Good Value for the Money % Strongly Agree	Percent of Alumni Worth >$1MM

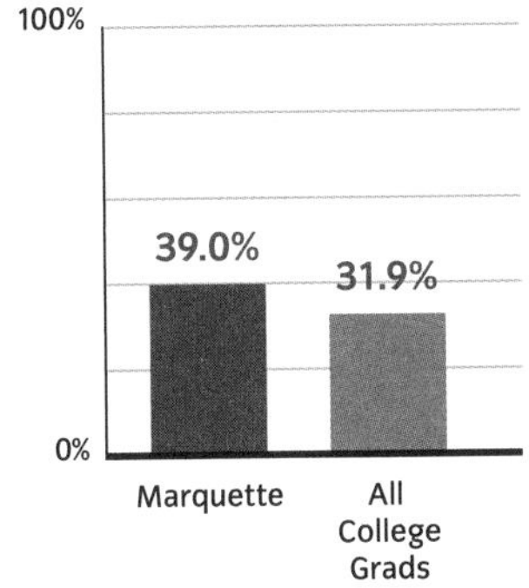
100%
39.0%
31.9%
0%
Marquette
All College Grads

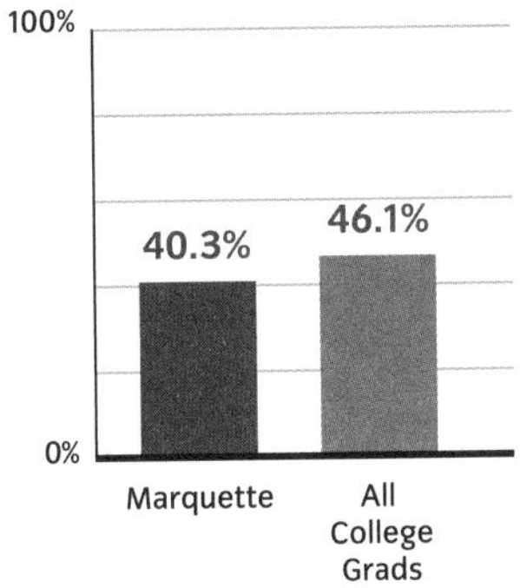
100%
40.3%
46.1%
0%
Marquette
All College Grads

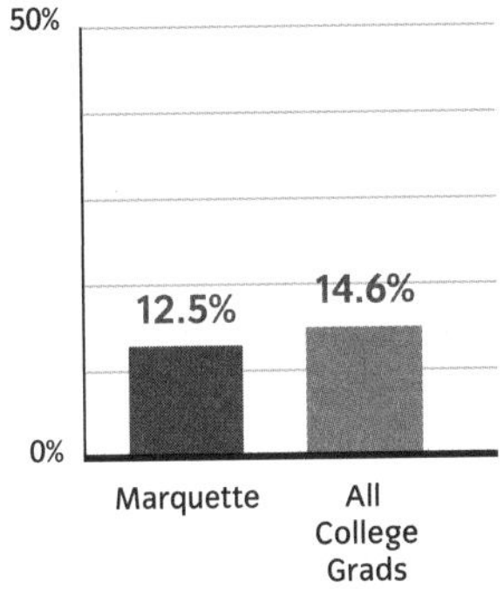
50%
12.5%
14.6%
0%
Marquette
All College Grads

Alumni Employment

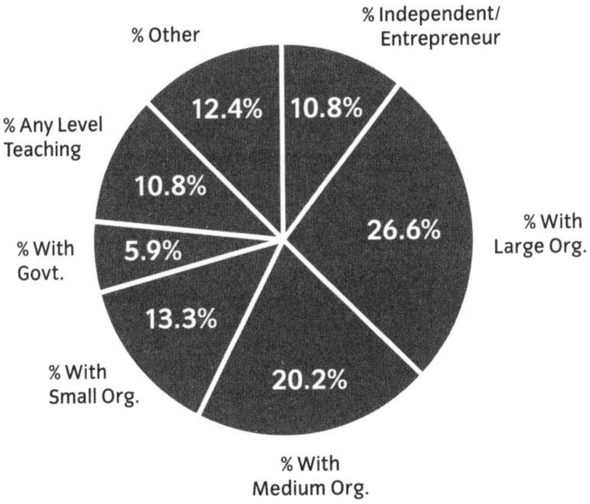
% Other
12.4%
% Independent/ Entrepreneur
10.8%
% Any Level Teaching
10.8%
% With Large Org.
26.6%
% With Govt.
5.9%
% With Small Org.
13.3%
% With Medium Org.
20.2%

Income Distribution of Graduates

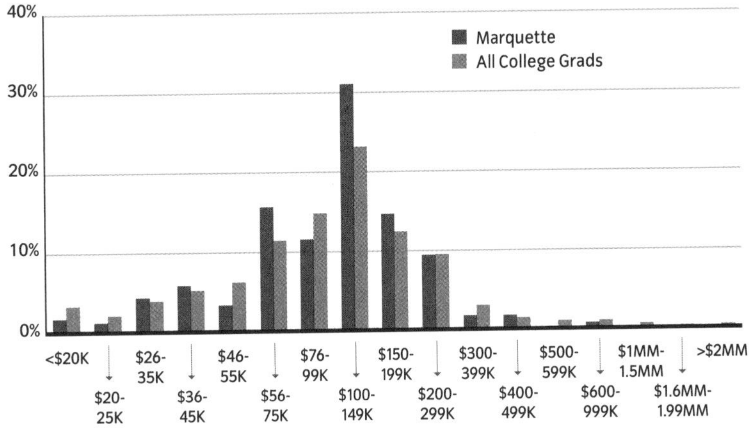
40%
30%
20%
10%
0%
Marquette
All College Grads
<$20K
$20-25K
$26-35K
$36-45K
$46-55K
$56-75K
$76-99K
$100-149K
$150-199K
$200-299K
$300-399K
$400-499K
$500-599K
$600-999K
$1MM-1.5MM
$1.6MM-1.99MM
>$2MM

Current Selectivity & Demand Analysis for Marquette University

Attribute	% Accepted	% Accepted Who Enroll	Freshman Retention Rate	Graduation Rate	Demand Index	Reputation Index
Score	57.0%	16.0%	88.0%	81.0%	10.81	0.28
Rank	116	172	135	100	61	170

Where are the Graduates of Marquette University on the Political Spectrum?

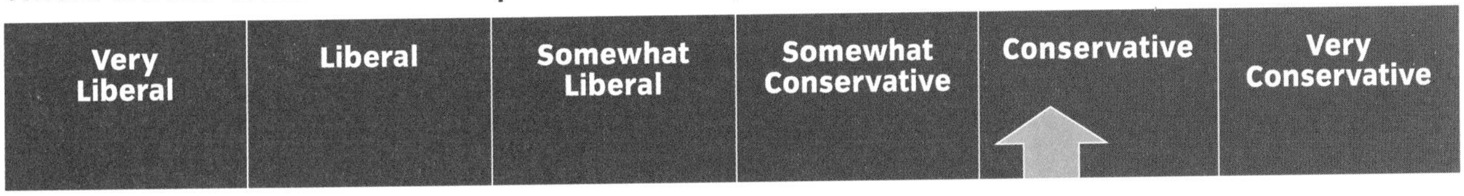
Very Liberal
Liberal
Somewhat Liberal
Somewhat Conservative
Conservative
Very Conservative

See pages 134–135 for detailed explanations and definitions.

Massachusetts Institute of Technology

Location: Cambridge, MA
Campus Setting: City: Midsize
Total Expenses: $55,270
Estimated Average Discount: $34,610 (63%)
Estimated Net Price: $20,660

Type of Institution: National University
Number of Undergraduates: 4,299
SAT Score: Reading: 670–770, Math: 740–800
Student/Faculty Ratio: 8 to 1
Transfer Out Rate: Not Reported

Rank Among 104 National Universities	**15**
Overall Rank Among 177 *Alumni Factor* Schools	**32**

Overview

Known the world over for its excellence in engineering, math and science, MIT is THE source for some of the world's most creatively brilliant leaders in technology, science, business, education and the arts. Ranked in the Top 10 in every Financial Success attribute (and 2nd in Financial Success overall) and in the Top 25 in each of the six Ultimate Outcomes (11th overall in the Ultimate Outcomes), MIT more than lives up to its sterling reputation, with a 13th ranking overall among national universities and a 32nd ranking among all schools.

MIT starts with great raw material – its alums report the 3rd highest SAT scores of any school. In addition, there is no question that the MIT academic requirements are rigorous, as zero intellectual lethargy is tolerated. An impressive 8th ranking in Intellectual Development underscores this fact. Perhaps more surprising for a technical school is that other aspects of the College Experience also rate so well, painting a picture that is more than just an academic grind. This has allowed MIT to produce one of the most impressive alumni lists of any school anywhere.

Notable Alumni

Architect I.M. Pei; astronaut Buzz Aldrin; former White House chief of staff John Sununu; Israeli Prime Minister Benjamin Netanyahu; Federal Reserve Bank Chairman Ben Bernanke; 3Com founder Robert Metcalf; Digital Equipment founder Ken Olsen; Bose founder Amar Bose; and Campbell's Soup founder John Dorrance.

The Alumni Factor Rankings Summary

Attribute	University Rank	Overall Rank
College Experience	**23**	**72**
Intellectual Development	8	37
Social Development	102	175
Spiritual Development	55	124
Friendship Development	15	57
Preparation for Career Success	13	32
Immediate Job Opportunities	2	5
Overall Assessment	**50**	**98**
Would Personally Choose Again	53	101
Would Recommend to Student	62	117
Value for the Money	38	66
Financial Success	**2**	**7**
Income per Household	2	4
% Households with Income >$150K	4	8
Household Net Worth	5	14
% Households Net Worth >$1MM	7	12
Overall Happiness	**78**	**131**
Alumni Giving	**9**	**43**
Graduation Rate	**12**	**16**
Overall Rank	**15**	**32**

Other Key Alumni Outcomes

5.1% Are college professors
5.8% Teach at any level
64.5% Have post-graduate degrees
53.7% Live in dual-income homes
93.5% Are currently employed

See pages 134–135 for detailed explanations and definitions.

Alumni Activities During College

34.1% Community Service
54.3% Intramural Sports
34.8% Internships
18.1% Media Programs
23.2% Music Programs
33.3% Part-Time Jobs

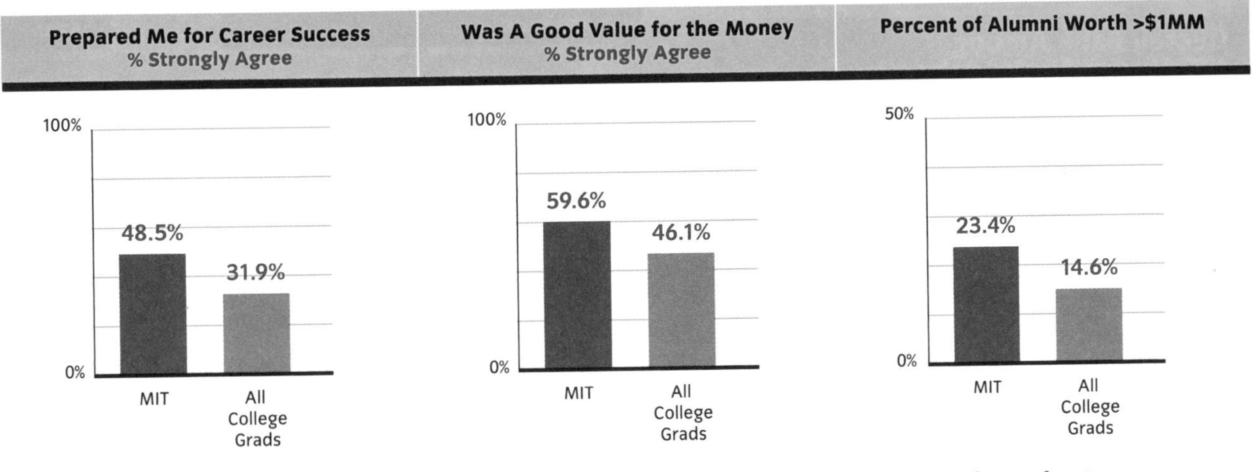

Alumni Employment

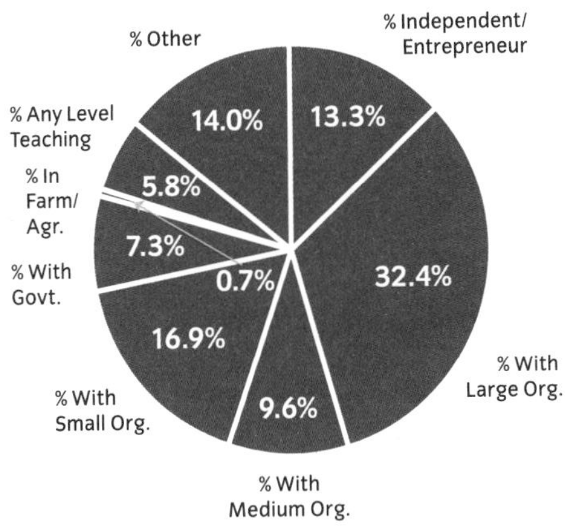

Income Distribution of Graduates

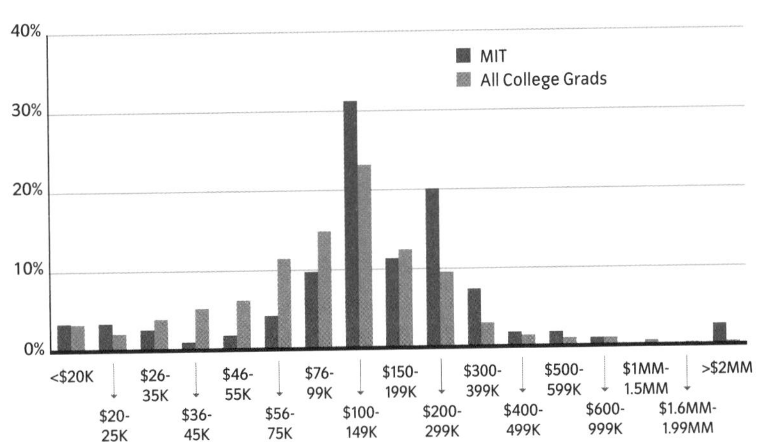

Current Selectivity & Demand Analysis for Massachusetts Institute of Technology

Attribute	% Accepted	% Accepted Who Enroll	Freshman Retention Rate	Graduation Rate	Demand Index	Reputation Index
Score	10.0%	65.0%	97.0%	93.0%	15.90	6.50
Rank	7	9	13	16	16	8

Where are the Graduates of Massachusetts Institute of Technology on the Political Spectrum?

Very Liberal	Liberal	Somewhat Liberal	Somewhat Conservative	Conservative	Very Conservative
	↑				

Miami University

Location: Oxford, OH
Campus Setting: City: Distant
Total Expenses: $30,536
Estimated Average Discount: $8,326 (27%)
Estimated Net Price: $22,210

Type of Institution: National University
Number of Undergraduates: 14,872
SAT Score: Reading: 530–620, Math: 560–660
Student/Faculty Ratio: 17 to 1
Transfer Out Rate: Not Reported

Rank Among 104 National Universities	**47**
Overall Rank Among 177 *Alumni Factor* Schools	**104**

Overview

The 10th-oldest public university in the country, Miami University lays legitimate claim to being the original Miami University, as U Miami in Florida was founded 116 years later in Coral Gables. For more than 200 years, Miami has been producing successful, happy and loyal graduates from one of the country's most classically beautiful college campuses. Its highest rankings are Happiness (ranked 21st) and Social Development (17th) – two of the universal characteristics of Miami graduates. Ranked 47th overall among national universities, real world outcomes for Miami grads are even stronger than the school's reputation. Miamians are a hard-working bunch, ranking 26th in employment rate. When compared to its Mid-American Conference rivals, Miami is in a league of its own, as none of the other schools – many of them excellent – make it into our 177 Top Colleges.

Notable Alumni

Former US president Benjamin Harrison; former Procter & Gamble chairman and CEO John Smale; US senator Maria Cantwell; entrepeneur extraordinaire Fred Mayerson and satirist P. J. O'Rourke.

However, Miami may be most famous for its alumni who became legendary football coaches: Bo Schembechler, Ara Parseghian, Paul Brown, Weeb Ewbank, John Harbaugh, Johnny Pont, Carmen Cozza and John McVay.

The Alumni Factor Rankings Summary

Attribute	University Rank	Overall Rank
College Experience	**38**	**98**
Intellectual Development	67	137
Social Development	17	57
Spiritual Development	57	126
Friendship Development	27	83
Preparation for Career Success	40	89
Immediate Job Opportunities	42	67
Overall Assessment	**40**	**80**
Would Personally Choose Again	49	92
Would Recommend to Student	33	67
Value for the Money	42	76
Financial Success	**76**	**123**
Income per Household	70	107
% Households with Income >$150K	70	117
Household Net Worth	69	117
% Households Net Worth >$1MM	87	147
Overall Happiness	**21**	**42**
Alumni Giving	**52**	**115**
Graduation Rate	**50**	**106**
Overall Rank	**47**	**104**

Other Key Alumni Outcomes

5.2% Are college professors
16.4% Teach at any level
52.1% Have post-graduate degrees
57.0% Live in dual-income homes
95.4% Are currently employed

See pages 134–135 for detailed explanations and definitions.

Alumni Activities During College

29.7% Community Service
37.9% Intramural Sports
15.9% Internships
14.1% Media Programs
18.5% Music Programs
36.4% Part-Time Jobs

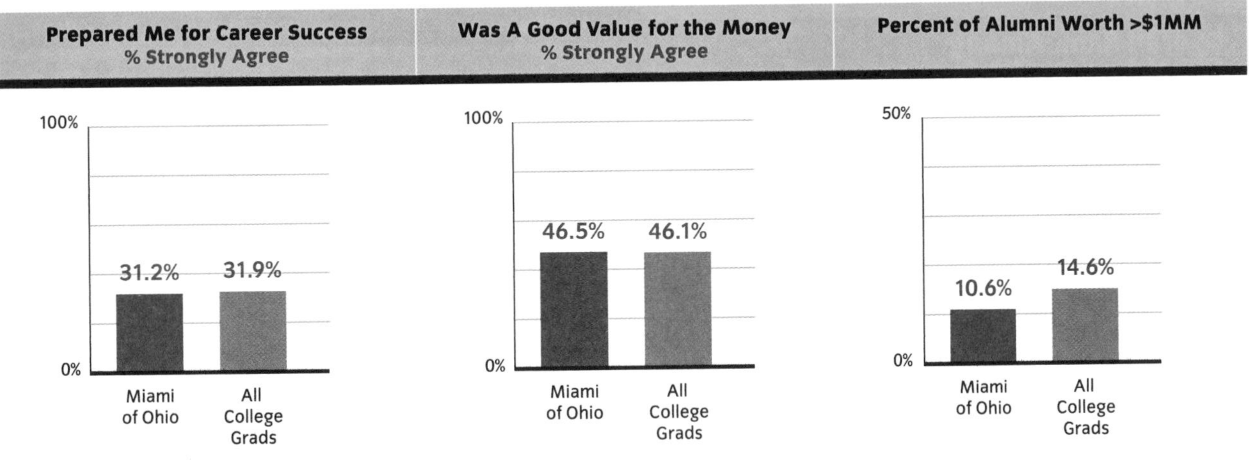

Alumni Employment

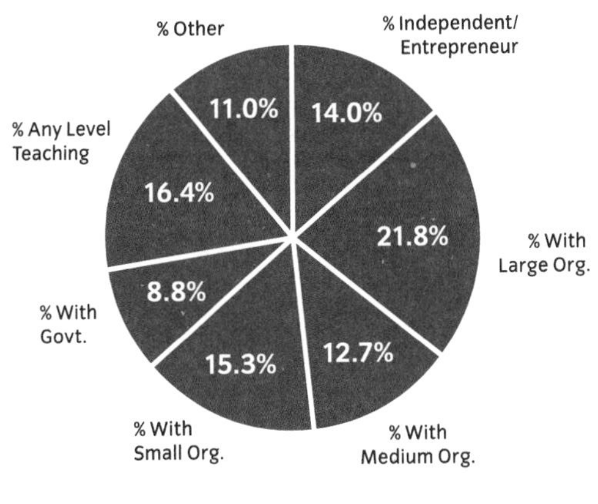

Income Distribution of Graduates

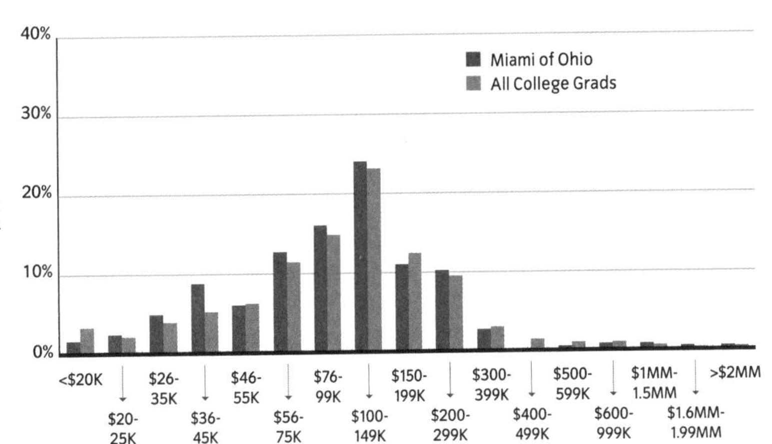

Current Selectivity & Demand Analysis for Miami University

Attribute	% Accepted	% Accepted Who Enroll	Freshman Retention Rate	Graduation Rate	Demand Index	Reputation Index
Score	74.0%	26.0%	89.0%	80.0%	5.16	0.35
Rank	158	125	124	106	138	158

Where are the Graduates of Miami University on the Political Spectrum?

Very Liberal	Liberal	Somewhat Liberal	Somewhat Conservative	Conservative	Very Conservative
			⇧		

See pages 134–135 for detailed explanations and definitions.

Michigan State University

Location: East Lansing, MI
Campus Setting: Rural: Fringe
Total Expenses: $23,202
Estimated Average Discount: $10,836 (47%)
Estimated Net Price: $12,366

Type of Institution: National University
Number of Undergraduates: 35,921
SAT Score: Reading: 440–600, Math: 540–670
Student/Faculty Ratio: 16 to 1
Transfer Out Rate: 17%

Rank Among 104 National Universities	**49**
Overall Rank Among 177 *Alumni Factor* Schools	**110**

Overview

The original prototype for President Lincoln's land-grant colleges under the Morrill Act, Michigan State University began as an agricultural college in 1855. Like many of the other land-grant schools, MSU is larger and more technically focused than its cross-state competitor, the University of Michigan. Yet MSU performs quite well against its Big Ten competitors on all fronts – academics, athletics and alumni performance post-graduation. It ranks 49th among national universities and ranks 7th among the Big Ten's twelve schools, ahead of Iowa, Indiana, Ohio State, Nebraska and Minnesota. Grads tend to be somewhat politically conservative and are very happy with their lives (ranked 39th).

MSU's highest ranking comes in the Overall Assessment, where it ranks 29th; it ranks 20th in grads who Would Personally Choose it Again. MSU also does very well in providing Immediate Job Opportunities for grads (43rd) and Preparation for Career Success (36th). Above average in Financial Success (74th) and ranked 63rd in Average Household Income, MSU's strongest Ultimate Outcome is Financial Success & Happiness, where it is ranked 60th among national universities.

Interestingly, Michigan State produces a large number of teachers (33rd overall). But that is not the only field in which alums shine.

Notable Alumni

Billionaire businessman and philanthropist Eli Broad; Michigan Governor John Engler and former governor James Blanchard; prolific filmmaker Walter Hill; and Quicken Loans founder Dan Gilbert.

The Alumni Factor Rankings Summary

Attribute	University Rank	Overall Rank
College Experience	**51**	**115**
Intellectual Development	47	106
Social Development	27	69
Spiritual Development	79	151
Friendship Development	72	142
Preparation for Career Success	36	83
Immediate Job Opportunities	43	70
Overall Assessment	**29**	**61**
Would Personally Choose Again	20	45
Would Recommend to Student	30	64
Value for the Money	43	79
Financial Success	**74**	**121**
Income per Household	63	98
% Households with Income >$150K	73	121
Household Net Worth	65	111
% Households Net Worth >$1MM	82	138
Overall Happiness	**39**	**76**
Alumni Giving	**59**	**122**
Graduation Rate	**65**	**127**
Overall Rank	**49**	**110**

Other Key Alumni Outcomes

4.6% Are college professors
18.2% Teach at any level
54.8% Have post-graduate degrees
57.3% Live in dual-income homes
93.8% Are currently employed

See pages 134–135 for detailed explanations and definitions.

Alumni Activities During College

24.1% Community Service
32.2% Intramural Sports
23.7% Internships
7.3% Media Programs
11.5% Music Programs
51.7% Part-Time Jobs

	Prepared Me for Career Success % Strongly Agree	Was A Good Value for the Money % Strongly Agree	Percent of Alumni Worth >$1MM
MSU	29.5%	42.5%	11.2%
All College Grads	31.9%	46.1%	14.6%

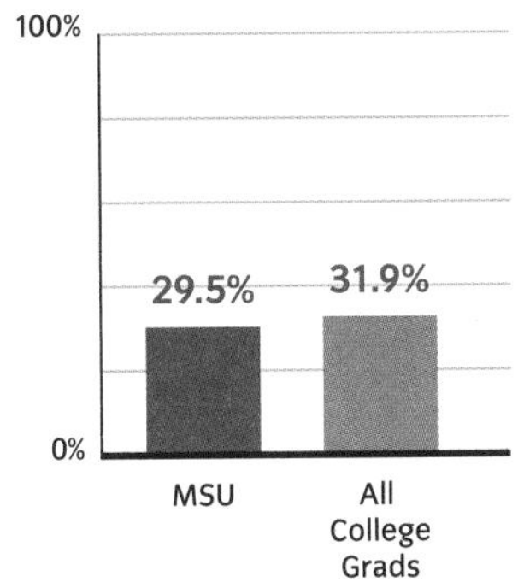

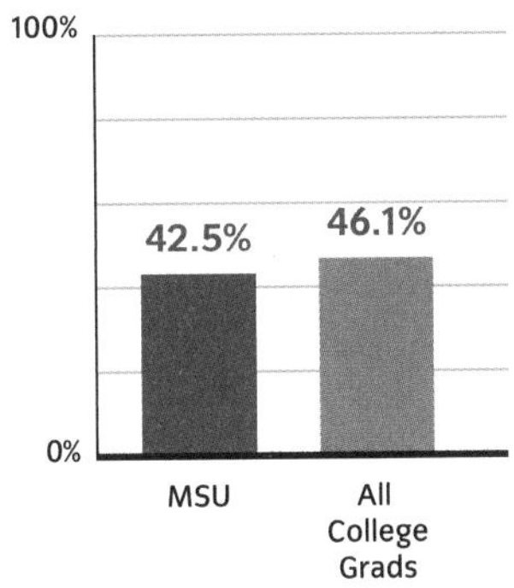

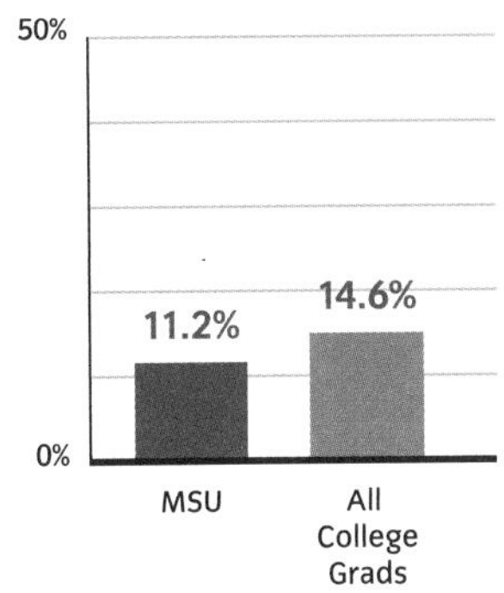

Alumni Employment

Category	%
% Independent/ Entrepreneur	12.5%
% With Large Org.	24.7%
% With Medium Org.	11.3%
% With Small Org.	9.4%
% With Govt.	11.3%
% Any Level Teaching	18.2%
% Other	12.6%

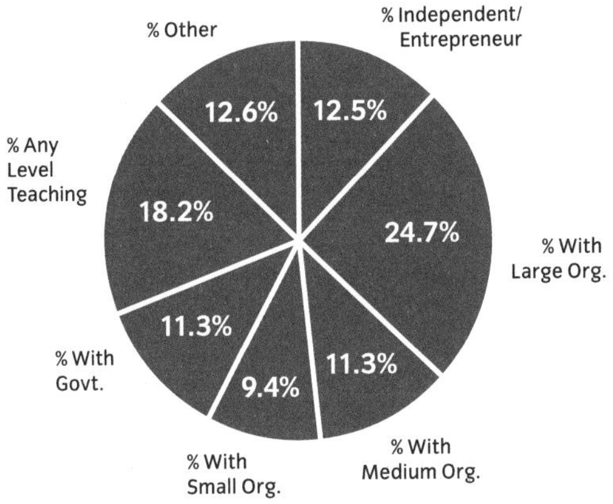

Income Distribution of Graduates

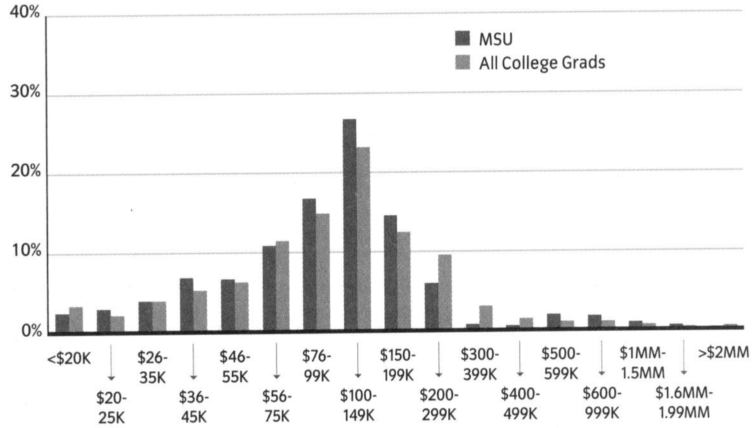

Current Selectivity & Demand Analysis for Michigan State University

Attribute	% Accepted	% Accepted Who Enroll	Freshman Retention Rate	Graduation Rate	Demand Index	Reputation Index
Score	73.0%	39.0%	91.0%	77.0%	3.56	0.53
Rank	157	46	102	127	163	117

Where are the Graduates of Michigan State University on the Political Spectrum?

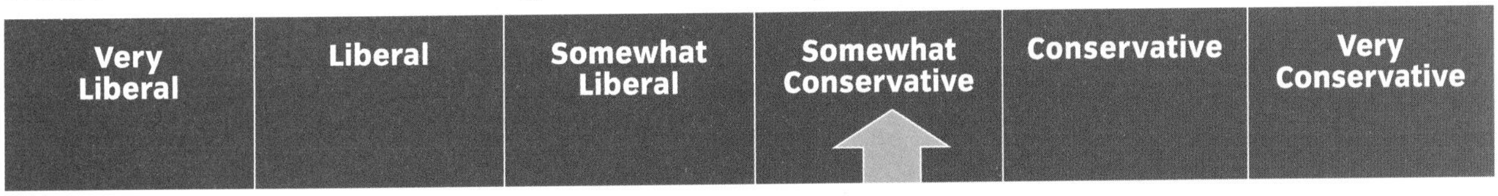

See pages 134–135 for detailed explanations and definitions.

Middlebury College

Location: Middlebury, VT
Campus Setting: Rural: Fringe
Total Expenses: $57,050
Estimated Average Discount: $33,687 (59%)
Estimated Net Price: $23,363

Type of Institution: Liberal Arts College
Number of Undergraduates: 2,532
SAT Score: Reading: 640–740, Math: 650–740
Student/Faculty Ratio: 9 to 1
Transfer Out Rate: Not Reported

Rank Among 53 Liberal Arts Colleges	**3**
Overall Rank Among 177 *Alumni Factor* Schools	**7**

Overview

Founded in 1800, Middlebury College is consistently ranked as one of the premier liberal arts colleges in the country – and for very good reason. Our results not only confirm that reputation, but also place Middlebury among the top ten of ALL colleges and universities in America based on extraordinary outcomes for their graduates. This superb school is 3rd among the liberal arts schools in the Northeast; 3rd among all liberal arts schools in the country; and 7th overall in our rankings. Middlebury has a higher percentage of millionaire graduates than any other college we've measured. But it is not only financial success that the Middlebury grad accrues. These fortunate (and extremely bright) grads are happy (ranked 12th), thoroughly developed intellectually, socially and spiritually, and develop lasting friendships that create a loyal bond to their school. This loyalty generates the 5th highest Alumni Giving percentage among all colleges in the US. It also puts Middlebury in the 2nd spot for Ultimate Outcomes. With a Top 30 ranking in an astonishing 25 of 26 attributes, Middlebury is the consummate college for America's brightest.

Alums are liberal and with a Top 30 rank in employment, are hard working in a number of fields.

Notable Alumni

Investment banker Felix Rohatyn; Midocean Partners founder and former CEO Ted Virtue; former US commerce secretary Ron Brown; former US Supreme Court justice Samuel Nelson; and farm equipment company founder John Deere.

The Alumni Factor Rankings Summary

Attribute	Liberal Arts Rank	Overall Rank
College Experience	**24**	**39**
Intellectual Development	22	25
Social Development	16	22
Spiritual Development	23	48
Friendship Development	28	36
Preparation for Career Success	27	58
Immediate Job Opportunities	32	132
Overall Assessment	**16**	**37**
Would Personally Choose Again	7	13
Would Recommend to Student	22	58
Value for the Money	22	53
Financial Success	**4**	**5**
Income per Household	7	14
% Households with Income >$150K	7	12
Household Net Worth	3	5
% Households Net Worth >$1MM	1	1
Overall Happiness	**12**	**17**
Alumni Giving	**4**	**5**
Graduation Rate	**14**	**32**
Overall Rank	**3**	**7**

Other Key Alumni Outcomes

4.9% Are college professors
13.3% Teach at any level
60.8% Have post-graduate degrees
53.1% Live in dual-income homes
93.9% Are currently employed

See pages 134–135 for detailed explanations and definitions.

Alumni Activities During College

36.2% Community Service
45.0% Intramural Sports
24.2% Internships
36.2% Media Programs
24.2% Music Programs
34.2% Part-Time Jobs

Prepared Me for Career Success % Strongly Agree	Was A Good Value for the Money % Strongly Agree	Percent of Alumni Worth >$1MM
Middlebury: 36.1% All College Grads: 31.9%	Middlebury: 45.4% All College Grads: 46.1%	Middlebury: 29.4% All College Grads: 14.6%

Alumni Employment

Income Distribution of Graduates

Current Selectivity & Demand Analysis for Middlebury College

Attribute	% Accepted	% Accepted Who Enroll	Freshman Retention Rate	Graduation Rate	Demand Index	Reputation Index
Score	17.0%	42.0%	96.0%	91.0%	13.26	2.47
Rank	22	33	27	32	31	22

Where are the Graduates of Middlebury College on the Political Spectrum?

Very Liberal	Liberal	Somewhat Liberal	Somewhat Conservative	Conservative	Very Conservative

Morehouse College

Location: Atlanta, GA
Campus Setting: City: Large
Total Expenses: $43,601
Estimated Average Discount: $20,277 (47%)
Estimated Net Price: $23,324

Type of Institution: Liberal Arts College
Number of Undergraduates: 2,586
SAT Score: Reading: 460–590, Math: 470–580
Student/Faculty Ratio: 14 to 1
Transfer Out Rate: Not Reported

Rank Among 53 Liberal Arts Colleges	**24**
Overall Rank Among 177 *Alumni Factor* Schools	**53**

Overview

For inspiration, read Morehouse president Dr. Robert Michael Franklin's opening address to new students in 2008 in which he describes the "Morehouse Man" as a "Renaissance Man with a Social Conscience," whose purpose is to bring excellence, leadership and service to the world – a stirring call. The Morehouse experience is truly a transformative educational experience for its graduates. It is why the Morehouse College Experience ranks 2nd among all colleges (behind only West Point) as well as 2nd in the Overall Assessment. Morehouse ranks 1st in the country in Friendship Development and 3rd in the Ultimate Outcome of Happiness & Friendships.

Proof of the life-altering potential Morehouse provides is this fact: in comparing all Morehouse grads to all African American graduates of the Ivy League, Morehouse grads outperform their Ivy League brethren in each of the ten Experience and Overall Assessment attributes; are significantly happier; and have incomes that are above the average of all college grads and nearly equal to that of Black Ivy Leaguers. While the numbers are impressive, Morehouse excellence is perhaps best displayed via their impressive alumni list. Excellence, bold leadership and service are personified in the "Morehouse Man."

Notable Alumni

Dr. Martin Luther King, Jr.; Spike Lee; Samuel L. Jackson; Edwin Moses; Herman Cain; and Fellow and past president of the American Association for the Advancement of Science Walter Massey, who also serves on the Boards of Motorola, Bank of America, McDonald's, and BP p.l.c.

The Alumni Factor Rankings Summary

Attribute	Liberal Arts Rank	Overall Rank
College Experience	**2**	**2**
Intellectual Development	24	29
Social Development	5	5
Spiritual Development	4	10
Friendship Development	1	1
Preparation for Career Success	4	5
Immediate Job Opportunities	5	23
Overall Assessment	**2**	**3**
Would Personally Choose Again	4	9
Would Recommend to Student	3	8
Value for the Money	4	12
Financial Success	**48**	**148**
Income per Household	28	103
% Households with Income >$150K	43	134
Household Net Worth	50	170
% Households Net Worth >$1MM	51	167
Overall Happiness	**40**	**126**
Alumni Giving	**53**	**99**
Graduation Rate	**53**	**174**
Overall Rank	**24**	**53**

Other Key Alumni Outcomes

4.2% Are college professors
14.7% Teach at any level
45.1% Have post-graduate degrees
51.8% Live in dual-income homes
90.8% Are currently employed

See pages 134–135 for detailed explanations and definitions.

Alumni Activities During College

49.6% Community Service
24.8% Intramural Sports
30.5% Internships
24.8% Media Programs
29.1% Music Programs
60.3% Part-Time Jobs

Prepared Me for Career Success % Strongly Agree	Was A Good Value for the Money % Strongly Agree	Percent of Alumni Worth >$1MM

100%
56.0%
31.9%
0%
Morehouse
All College Grads

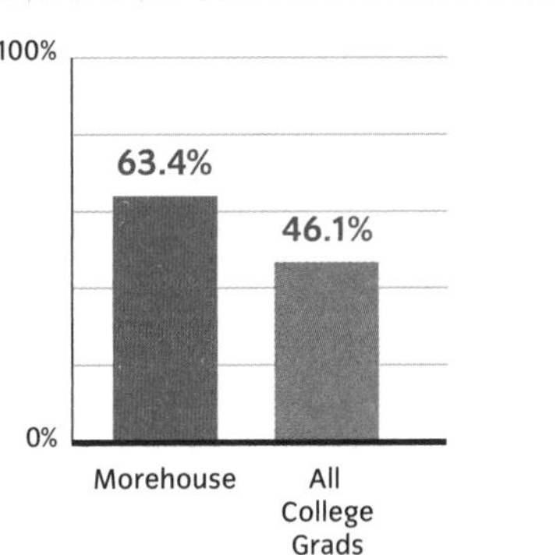

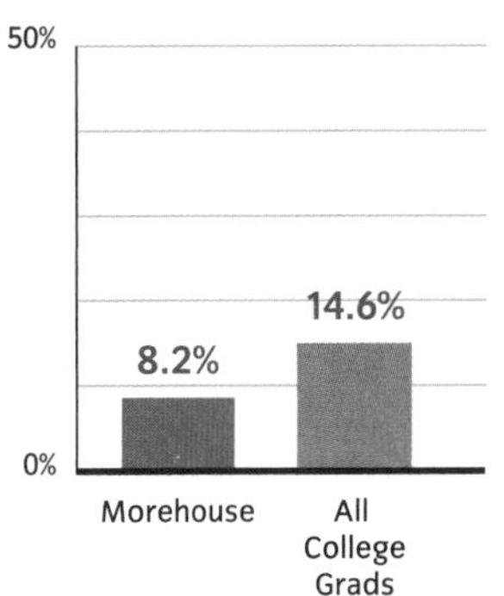

Alumni Employment

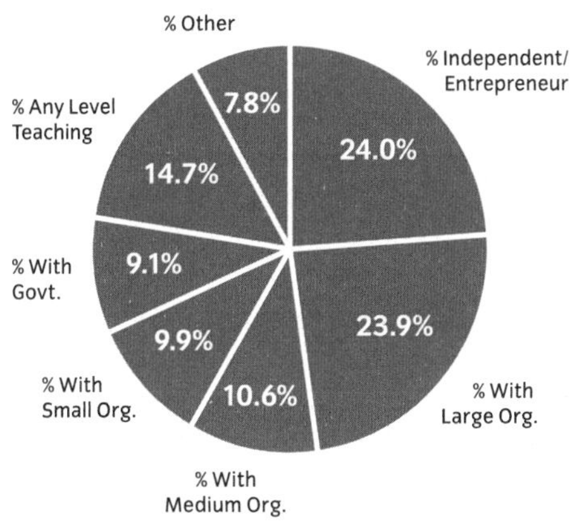

Income Distribution of Graduates

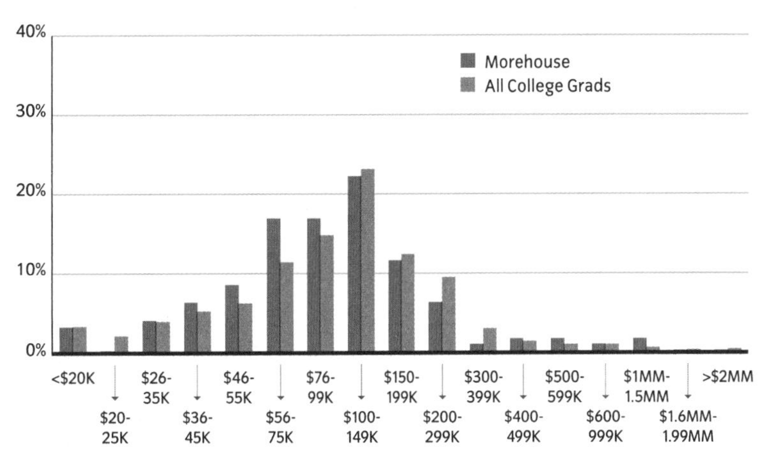

Current Selectivity & Demand Analysis for Morehouse College

Attribute	% Accepted	% Accepted Who Enroll	Freshman Retention Rate	Graduation Rate	Demand Index	Reputation Index
Score	62.0%	37.0%	83.0%	57.0%	4.39	0.60
Rank	134	60	161	174	147	103

Where are the Graduates of Morehouse College on the Political Spectrum?

Very Liberal	Liberal	Somewhat Liberal	Somewhat Conservative	Conservative	Very Conservative

Mount Holyoke College

Location: South Hadley, MA
Campus Setting: Suburb: Large
Total Expenses: $55,496
Estimated Average Discount: $31,586 (57%)
Estimated Net Price: $23,910

Type of Institution: Liberal Arts College
Number of Undergraduates: 2,332
SAT Score: Not Reported
Student/Faculty Ratio: 9 to 1
Transfer Out Rate: 15%

Rank Among 53 Liberal Arts Colleges	**17**
Overall Rank Among 177 *Alumni Factor* Schools	**26**

Overview

One of the original Seven Sisters of female higher education, Mt. Holyoke is one of the top schools in the country and ranks 17th among all liberal arts colleges. Mt. Holyoke has been appropriately heralded as a source of bright, globally focused, politically active, progressive women who succeed in a wide variety of fields. This strong women's school gets excellent ratings from its graduates for the College Experience (ranked 10th), receives a strong 20th ranking in the Overall Assessment and a 26th ranking in Financial Success. Mt. Holyoke is among the top third in each of the Ultimate Outcomes – one of only two Women's Colleges to achieve that distinction (Wellesley is the other).

Versus the other top women's colleges, Mt. Holyoke has the happiest grads (ranked 13th among liberal arts schools), is second in Household Net Worth (16th among liberal arts schools), and is second in Millionaire Households (18th within liberal arts schools). Strong, powerful, courageous women are the hallmark of Mt. Holyoke.

Notable Alumni

Legendary poet Emily Dickinson; Wonder Woman co-creator Elizabeth Holloway Marston; Director of the film *The Princess Diaries,* Debra Martin Chase; Academy Award-winning film producer Julia Phillips; former CEO of the Global Fund for Women Kavita Ramdas; former US congresswoman Shirley Chisolm; Peace Corps head Elaine Chao; Apple/Mac graphics designer Susan Kare; and Nancy Kissinger.

The Alumni Factor Rankings Summary

Attribute	Liberal Arts Rank	Overall Rank
College Experience	**10**	**14**
Intellectual Development	11	12
Social Development	22	36
Spiritual Development	15	35
Friendship Development	29	37
Preparation for Career Success	9	13
Immediate Job Opportunities	12	56
Overall Assessment	**20**	**49**
Would Personally Choose Again	25	67
Would Recommend to Student	25	67
Value for the Money	8	23
Financial Success	**26**	**69**
Income per Household	33	116
% Households with Income >$150K	32	93
Household Net Worth	16	36
% Households Net Worth >$1MM	18	42
Overall Happiness	**13**	**22**
Alumni Giving	**31**	**36**
Graduation Rate	**45**	**91**
Overall Rank	**17**	**26**

Other Key Alumni Outcomes

8.5% Are college professors
16.5% Teach at any level
61.7% Have post-graduate degrees
49.7% Live in dual-income homes
93.8% Are currently employed

See pages 134–135 for detailed explanations and definitions.

Alumni Activities During College

38.6% Community Service
21.0% Intramural Sports
39.2% Internships
36.9% Media Programs
27.9% Music Programs
30.7% Part-Time Jobs

Prepared Me for Career Success % Strongly Agree	Was A Good Value for the Money % Strongly Agree	Percent of Alumni Worth >$1MM
Mount Holyoke: 44.6%	Mount Holyoke: 59.9%	Mount Holyoke: 19.2%
All College Grads: 31.9%	All College Grads: 46.1%	All College Grads: 14.6%

Alumni Employment

% Other: 14.5%
% Independent/ Entrepreneur: 19.2%
% With Large Org.: 13.6%
% With Medium Org.: 17.5%
% With Small Org.: 16.4%
% With Govt.: 2.3%
% Any Level Teaching: 16.5%

Income Distribution of Graduates

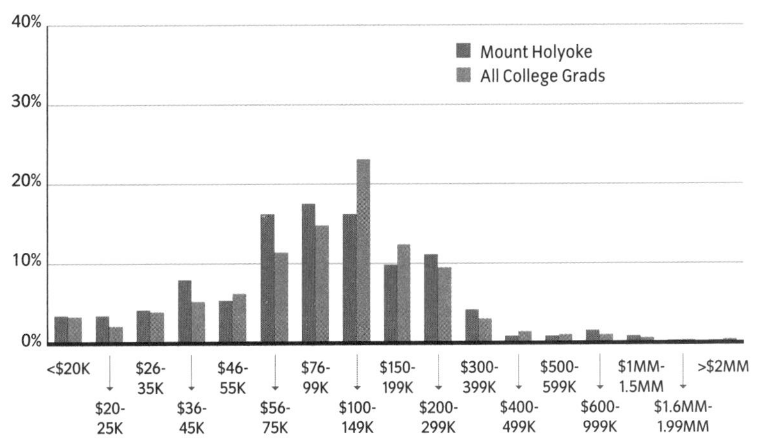

Current Selectivity & Demand Analysis for Mount Holyoke College

Attribute	% Accepted	% Accepted Who Enroll	Freshman Retention Rate	Graduation Rate	Demand Index	Reputation Index
Score	51.0%	34.0%	91.0%	82.0%	5.77	0.67
Rank	104	76	102	91	129	91

Where are the Graduates of Mount Holyoke College on the Political Spectrum?

Very Liberal	Liberal	Somewhat Liberal	Somewhat Conservative	Conservative	Very Conservative
⇧					

New York University

Location: New York, NY
Campus Setting: City: Large
Total Expenses: $58,858
Estimated Average Discount: $22,024 (37%)
Estimated Net Price: $36,834

Type of Institution: National University
Number of Undergraduates: 22,097
SAT Score: Reading: 630–720, Math: 630–740
Student/Faculty Ratio: 11 to 1
Transfer Out Rate: Not Reported

Rank Among 104 National Universities	**93**
Overall Rank Among 177 *Alumni Factor* Schools	**165**

Overview

The New York University brand name looms large, due to its stellar academic reputation, its center-of-the-action Manhattan location, and its alumni roll that reads like a Who's Who list of Hollywood, business, entertainment, government and medicine. NYU ranks 48th in Financial Success and 33rd in the Ultimate Outcome of Financial Success & Intellectual Capability.

Like other metropolitan campuses, it is difficult to separate NYU from its surroundings, which makes the undergraduate experience like none other in the world – but not for everyone. You shouldn't expect a close, collegial undergraduate experience or an expansive quad with a lush lawn. But you can expect to be around some of the brightest, most fiercely driven strivers who will make their mark in the world. New York, New York!

Notable Alumni

Former senator Jacob Javits; CNBC Market Week host Maria Bartiromo; billionaire industrialist Marvin Davis; sportscaster Howard Cosell; former American Express chairman Harvey Golub; former Federal Reserve chairman Alan Greenspan; CEO of the Hartz Group Leonard Stern; billionaire Laurence Tisch; supermodel Christy Turlington; actors and entertainers Alec Baldwin, Billy Crystal, Bridget Fonda, Philip Seymour Hoffman and Lou Gossett; Dreamworks founder Jeffrey Katz; filmmaker Martin Scorsese; Broadway hit-maker Alan Menken; and songwriter Carole Bayer Sager.

The Alumni Factor Rankings Summary

Attribute	University Rank	Overall Rank
College Experience	**101**	**174**
Intellectual Development	77	149
Social Development	87	158
Spiritual Development	78	150
Friendship Development	102	175
Preparation for Career Success	103	175
Immediate Job Opportunities	100	171
Overall Assessment	**100**	**171**
Would Personally Choose Again	93	159
Would Recommend to Student	92	161
Value for the Money	104	177
Financial Success	**48**	**81**
Income per Household	65	100
% Households with Income >$150K	42	74
Household Net Worth	55	95
% Households Net Worth >$1MM	42	74
Overall Happiness	**104**	**177**
Alumni Giving	**91**	**162**
Graduation Rate	**34**	**67**
Overall Rank	**93**	**165**

Other Key Alumni Outcomes

3.9% Are college professors
10.0% Teach at any level
50.4% Have post-graduate degrees
43.3% Live in dual-income homes
88.0% Are currently employed

Alumni Activities During College

23.5% Community Service
7.8% Intramural Sports
32.6% Internships
11.2% Media Programs
8.3% Music Programs
50.0% Part-Time Jobs

	Prepared Me for Career Success % Strongly Agree	Was A Good Value for the Money % Strongly Agree	Percent of Alumni Worth >$1MM
NYU	19.4%	22.7%	16.0%
All College Grads	31.9%	46.1%	14.6%

Alumni Employment

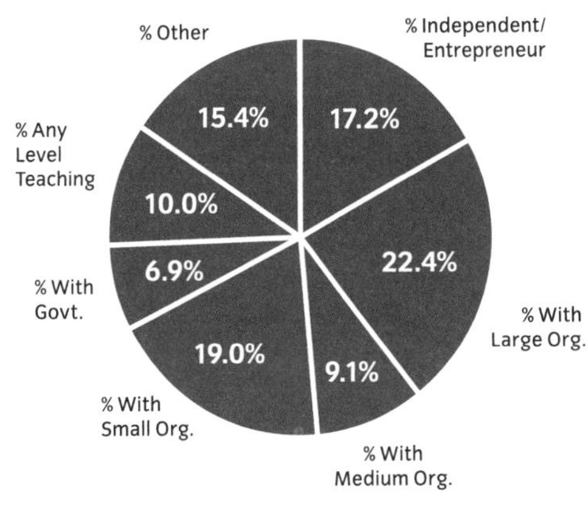

Income Distribution of Graduates

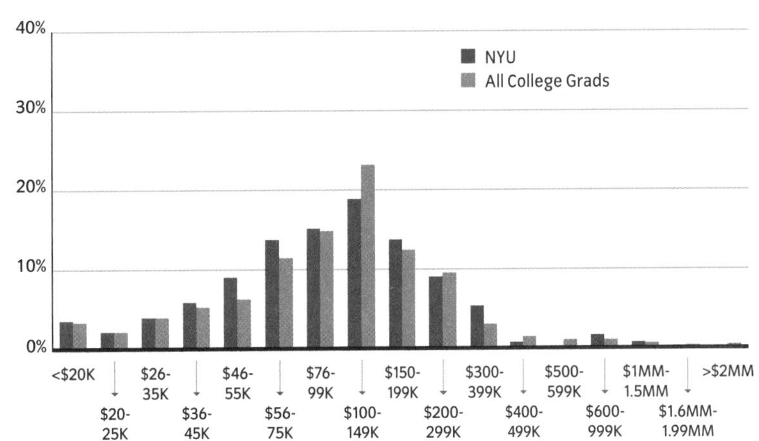

Current Selectivity & Demand Analysis for New York University

Attribute	% Accepted	% Accepted Who Enroll	Freshman Retention Rate	Graduation Rate	Demand Index	Reputation Index
Score	32.0%	37.0%	92.0%	86.0%	8.40	1.16
Rank	57	60	86	67	94	53

Where are the Graduates of New York University on the Political Spectrum?

Very Liberal	Liberal	Somewhat Liberal	Somewhat Conservative	Conservative	Very Conservative

North Carolina State University

Location: Raleigh, NC
Campus Setting: City: Large
Total Expenses: $19,388
Estimated Average Discount: $9,541 (49%)
Estimated Net Price: $9,847

Type of Institution: National University
Number of Undergraduates: 25,247
SAT Score: Reading: 530–620, Math: 560–660
Student/Faculty Ratio: 18 to 1
Transfer Out Rate: 10%

Rank Among 104 National Universities	**44**
Overall Rank Among 177 *Alumni Factor* Schools	**96**

Overview

When you are a university located in Raleigh, North Carolina, within an hour of Duke, Wake Forest and UNC Chapel Hill (ranked 10th, 21st and 12th respectively among all national universities), you had better be very good, or prepare to suffer the inevitable comparisons. Fortunately for NC State, it can stand proudly beside these other schools as an excellent science, engineering, agricultural and technical university. The practical, hard-working NC State grad is a conservative, loyal and enthusiastic member of the Wolfpack. Compared to other state universities, NC State ranks second in Value for the Money. It also ranks third in Overall Happiness, Immediate Job Opportunities, Would Choose Again and Would Recommend to a Prospective Student. It rates in the Top 30 on 7 metrics when compared to all national universities, signalling the school's ability to compete on a wider playing field.

Notable Alumni

NFL Pro-Bowl quarterback Philip Rivers; former Pittsburgh Steelers head coach Bill Cowher; musician John Tesh; former chairman of the US Joint Chiefs of Staff Hugh Shelton; former White House press secretary for President Obama Robert Gibbs; 4-term former governor of North Carolina James Hunt; CEO of Citrix Systems Mark Templeton; and many other leaders in science, business and the military.

The Alumni Factor Rankings Summary

Attribute	University Rank	Overall Rank
College Experience	**35**	**93**
Intellectual Development	62	131
Social Development	22	63
Spiritual Development	43	109
Friendship Development	51	114
Preparation for Career Success	29	70
Immediate Job Opportunities	28	44
Overall Assessment	**20**	**38**
Would Personally Choose Again	14	37
Would Recommend to Student	16	26
Value for the Money	36	64
Financial Success	**77**	**124**
Income per Household	74	114
% Households with Income >$150K	85	141
Household Net Worth	59	103
% Households Net Worth >$1MM	79	130
Overall Happiness	**27**	**54**
Alumni Giving	**59**	**122**
Graduation Rate	**74**	**138**
Overall Rank	**44**	**96**

Other Key Alumni Outcomes

3.7% Are college professors
8.9% Teach at any level
46.60% Have post-graduate degrees
57.9% Live in dual-income homes
92.2% Are currently employed

See pages 134–135 for detailed explanations and definitions.

Alumni Activities During College

22.0% Community Service
38.2% Intramural Sports
22.5% Internships
10.0% Media Programs
21.4% Music Programs
49.2% Part-Time Jobs

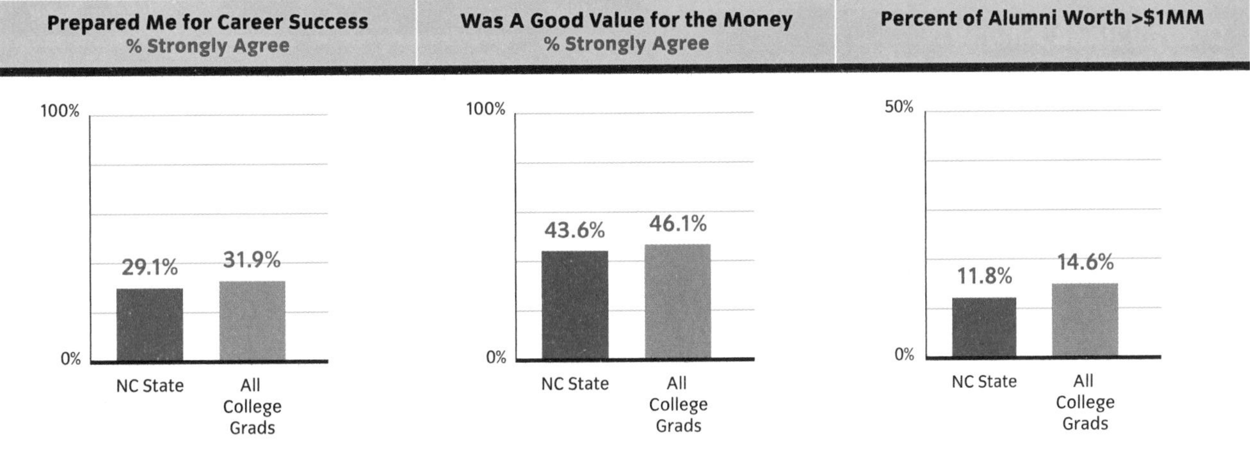

Alumni Employment

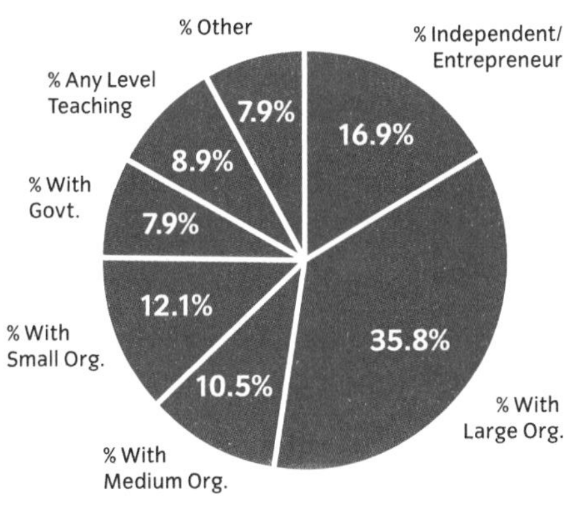

Income Distribution of Graduates

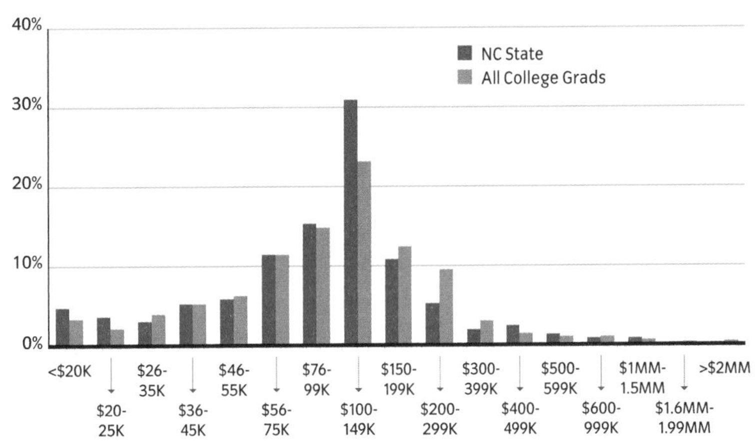

Current Selectivity & Demand Analysis for North Carolina State University

Attribute	% Accepted	% Accepted Who Enroll	Freshman Retention Rate	Graduation Rate	Demand Index	Reputation Index
Score	54.0%	44.0%	88.0%	73.0%	4.21	0.81
Rank	110	26	135	138	152	73

Where are the Graduates of North Carolina State University on the Political Spectrum?

Very Liberal	Liberal	Somewhat Liberal	Somewhat Conservative	Conservative	Very Conservative
					↑

See pages 134–135 for detailed explanations and definitions.

Northeastern University

Location: Boston, MA
Campus Setting: City: Large
Total Expenses: $53,812
Estimated Average Discount: $21,319 (40%)
Estimated Net Price: $32,493

Type of Institution: National University
Number of Undergraduates: 19,435
SAT Score: Reading: 610–700, Math: 640–730
Student/Faculty Ratio: 13 to 1
Transfer Out Rate: Not Reported

Rank Among 104 National Universities **79**

Overall Rank Among 177 *Alumni Factor* Schools **147**

Overview

An institutional renaissance over the last 25 years has elevated Northeastern University into the upper echelons of US higher education. While maintaining its experience-based foundation, rooted in its history of educating via close connections with local commerce, government and other institutions, Northeastern has upgraded and modernized every aspect of its offering – unlike many colleges with a similar history. In addition, it has continually improved its student body.

This transformation has allowed Northeastern to maintain its excellence in providing practical experiences that prepare its grads for success (ranked 6th in Immediate Job Opportunities, 28th in Preparation for Career Success, and 42nd in employment), while also dramatically upgrading their career outcomes (ranked 38th in Income per Household and 46th in Overall Financial Success). Northeastern's strongest Ultimate Outcome is Financial Success & Happiness, where it is ranked 67th.

Notable Alumni

Co-founder of Twitter Biz Stone; founder of Napster Shawn Fanning; co-founder of EMC Richard Egan; former *Saturday Night Live* star Jane Curtin; political activist Lyndon LaRouche; and Boston Globe sportswriter Will McDonough.

The Alumni Factor Rankings Summary

Attribute	University Rank	Overall Rank
College Experience	**64**	**133**
Intellectual Development	103	176
Social Development	74	142
Spiritual Development	104	177
Friendship Development	89	159
Preparation for Career Success	28	68
Immediate Job Opportunities	6	10
Overall Assessment	**94**	**164**
Would Personally Choose Again	84	148
Would Recommend to Student	88	157
Value for the Money	90	159
Financial Success	**46**	**79**
Income per Household	38	64
% Households with Income >$150K	41	73
Household Net Worth	57	97
% Households Net Worth >$1MM	59	102
Overall Happiness	**97**	**164**
Alumni Giving	**67**	**131**
Graduation Rate	**65**	**127**
Overall Rank	**79**	**147**

Other Key Alumni Outcomes

2.0% Are college professors
6.5% Teach at any level
45.2% Have post-graduate degrees
49.8% Live in dual-income homes
94.4% Are currently employed

See pages 134–135 for detailed explanations and definitions.

Alumni Activities During College

15.7% Community Service
20.2% Intramural Sports
31.8% Internships
12.6% Media Programs
8.0% Music Programs
48.0% Part-Time Jobs

Prepared Me for Career Success (% Strongly Agree)	Was A Good Value for the Money (% Strongly Agree)	Percent of Alumni Worth >$1MM
Northeastern: 34.2%; All College Grads: 31.9%	Northeastern: 32.6%; All College Grads: 46.1%	Northeastern: 13.7%; All College Grads: 14.6%

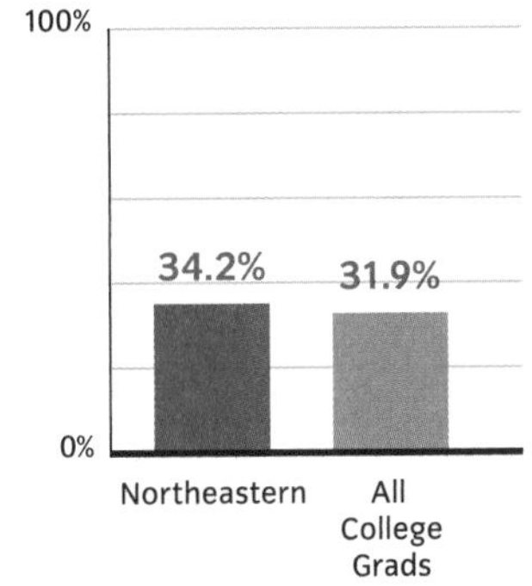

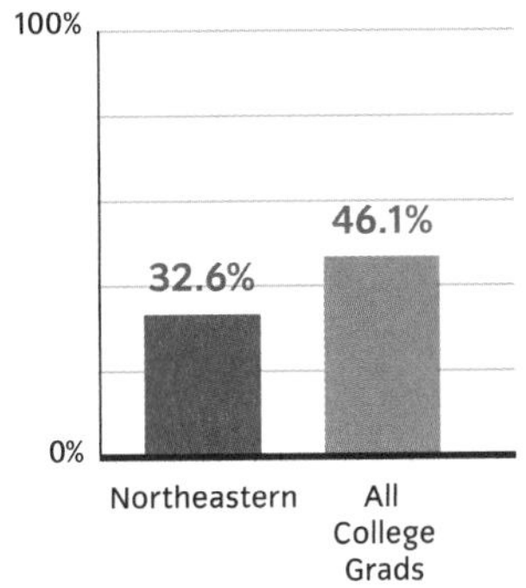

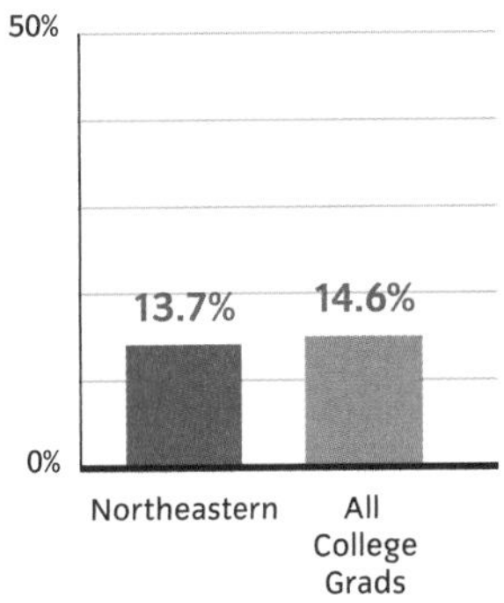

Alumni Employment

- % Independent/Entrepreneur: 9.1%
- % With Large Org.: 31.0%
- % With Medium Org.: 21.8%
- % With Small Org.: 15.2%
- % With Govt.: 6.5%
- % Any Level Teaching: 6.5%
- % Other: 9.9%

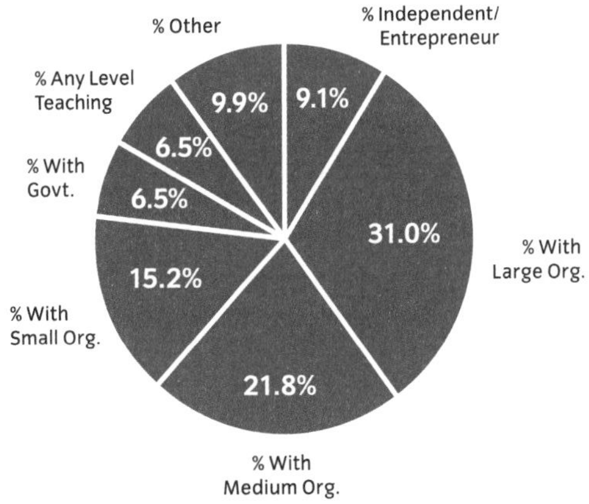

Income Distribution of Graduates

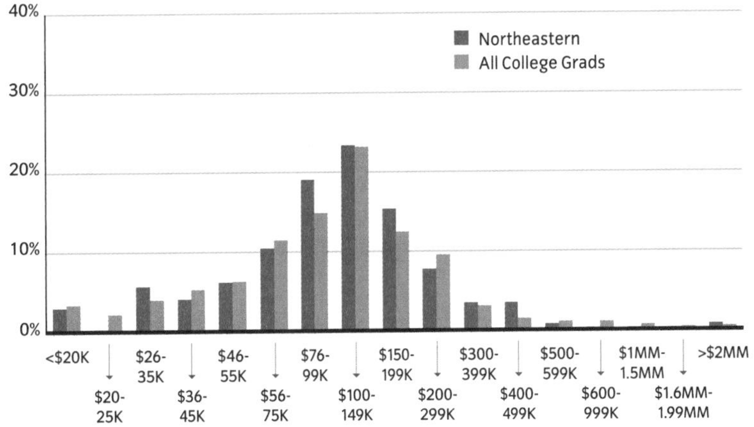

Current Selectivity & Demand Analysis for Northeastern University

Attribute	% Accepted	% Accepted Who Enroll	Freshman Retention Rate	Graduation Rate	Demand Index	Reputation Index
Score	35.0%	21.0%	93.0%	77.0%	14.03	0.60
Rank	67	156	73	127	25	103

Where are the Graduates of Northeastern University on the Political Spectrum?

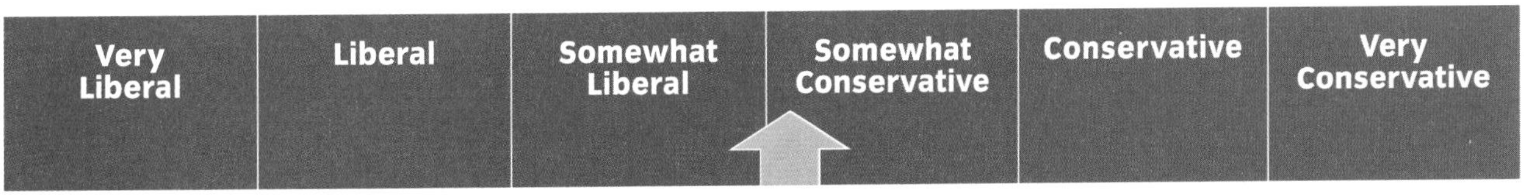

Very Liberal	Liberal	Somewhat Liberal	Somewhat Conservative	Conservative	Very Conservative
			↑		

Northwestern University

Location: Evanston, IL
Campus Setting: City: Small
Total Expenses: $58,829
Estimated Average Discount: $31,716 (54%)
Estimated Net Price: $27,113

Type of Institution: National University
Number of Undergraduates: 9,535
SAT Score: Reading: 680–750, Math: 700–780
Student/Faculty Ratio: 7 to 1
Transfer Out Rate: Not Reported

Rank Among 104 National Universities	**37**
Overall Rank Among 177 *Alumni Factor* Schools	**83**

Overview

Founded in 1850, when "Northwestern" referred to the Northwest Territory of an expanding America, Northwestern earns its reputation as one of the finest schools in the country. Located in the upscale Chicago suburb of Evanston on the shores of Lake Michigan, there is not a finer setting for a college campus anywhere. This setting, and its worldwide reputation, draws the best and brightest to Northwestern (32nd highest in SAT scores) and produces talented graduates in all fields. Also, its varsity athlete graduation rate is among the Top 5 of all Division I programs in the country.

NWU is a shining star within the twelve Big Ten Conference schools: It ranks 1st in Intellectual Development, Net Worth, and Financial Success. Among national universities, it ranks 22nd in Financial Success, 18th in Income per Household, 28th in Millionaires, and in the Ultimate Outcome of Financial Success & Intellectual Capabilility it ranks 19th overall.

And while the Big Ten comparisons are relevant, it is worth remembering NWU can hold its own on the national stage, ranking in the Top 30 among all schools for its Graduation Rate and its leading Ultimate Outcome.

Notable Alumni

Saul Bellow; Charlton Heston; Supreme Court Justice John Paul Stevens; Chicago Bulls and White Sox owner Jerry Reinsdorf; actor David Schwimmer; comedian Stephen Colbert; George McGovern; and founders of Booz-Allen, James Allen and Edwin Booz.

The Alumni Factor Rankings Summary

Attribute	University Rank	Overall Rank
College Experience	**50**	**114**
Intellectual Development	26	73
Social Development	47	106
Spiritual Development	56	125
Friendship Development	53	119
Preparation for Career Success	56	113
Immediate Job Opportunities	56	88
Overall Assessment	**67**	**124**
Would Personally Choose Again	63	115
Would Recommend to Student	62	117
Value for the Money	70	128
Financial Success	**22**	**40**
Income per Household	18	35
% Households with Income >$150K	23	43
Household Net Worth	21	41
% Households Net Worth >$1MM	28	52
Overall Happiness	**85**	**142**
Alumni Giving	**36**	**93**
Graduation Rate	**9**	**11**
Overall Rank	**37**	**83**

Other Key Alumni Outcomes

9.3% Are college professors
14.2% Teach at any level
62.1% Have post-graduate degrees
54.2% Live in dual-income homes
92.2% Are currently employed

See pages 134–135 for detailed explanations and definitions.

Alumni Activities During College

30.2% Community Service
23.7% Intramural Sports
26.7% Internships
26.7% Media Programs
25.4% Music Programs
42.2% Part-Time Jobs

Prepared Me for Career Success % Strongly Agree	Was A Good Value for the Money % Strongly Agree	Percent of Alumni Worth >$1MM
Northwestern 28.7%; All College Grads 31.9%	Northwestern 37.3%; All College Grads 46.1%	Northwestern 17.7%; All College Grads 14.6%

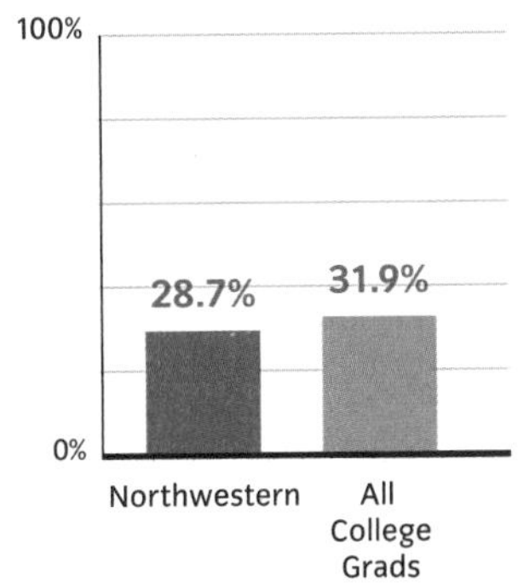

Alumni Employment

Category	%
% Independent/ Entrepreneur	15.1%
% With Large Org.	22.6%
% With Medium Org.	16.4%
% With Small Org.	13.7%
% With Govt.	4.0%
% Any Level Teaching	14.2%
% Other	14.0%

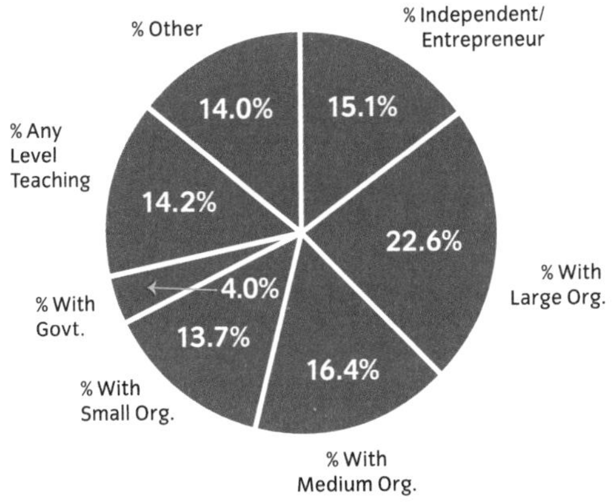

Income Distribution of Graduates

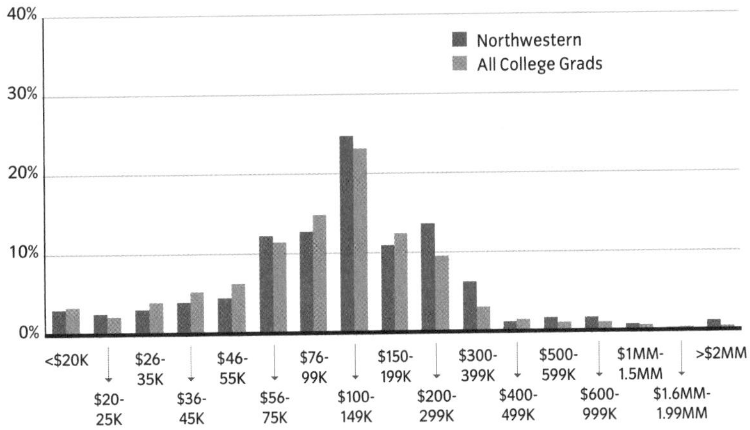

Northwestern / All College Grads

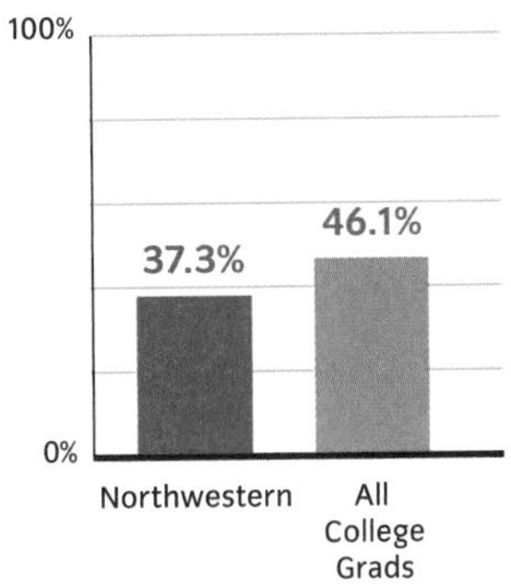

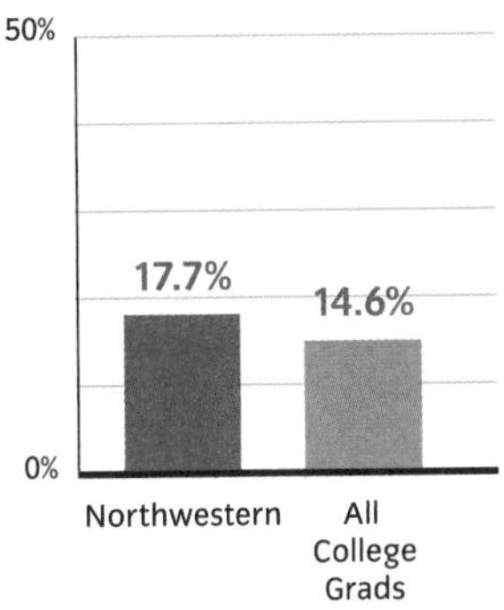

<$20K, $20-25K, $26-35K, $36-45K, $46-55K, $56-75K, $76-99K, $100-149K, $150-199K, $200-299K, $300-399K, $400-499K, $500-599K, $600-999K, $1MM-1.5MM, $1.6MM-1.99MM, >$2MM

Current Selectivity & Demand Analysis for Northwestern University

Attribute	% Accepted	% Accepted Who Enroll	Freshman Retention Rate	Graduation Rate	Demand Index	Reputation Index
Score	23.0%	33.0%	96.0%	94.0%	13.07	1.43
Rank	34	83	27	11	34	41

Where are the Graduates of Northwestern University on the Political Spectrum?

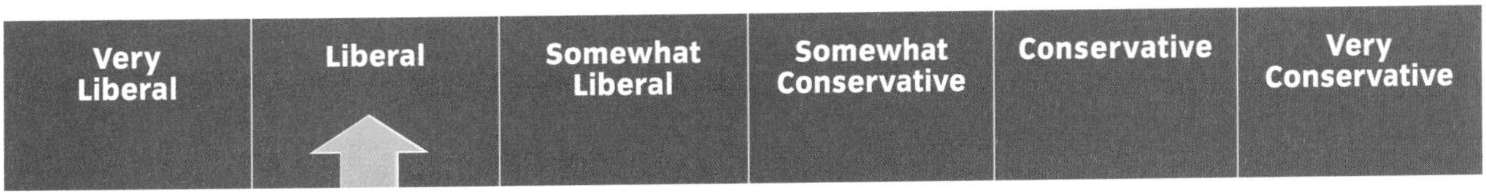

Very Liberal	Liberal	Somewhat Liberal	Somewhat Conservative	Conservative	Very Conservative
	↑				

See pages 134–135 for detailed explanations and definitions.

Oberlin College

Location: Oberlin, OH
Campus Setting: Suburb: Midsize
Total Expenses: $57,268
Estimated Average Discount: $22,471 (39%)
Estimated Net Price: $34,797

Type of Institution: Liberal Arts College
Number of Undergraduates: 2,974
SAT Score: Reading: 650–740, Math: 630–720
Student/Faculty Ratio: 9 to 1
Transfer Out Rate: Not Reported

Rank Among 53 Liberal Arts Colleges	**39**
Overall Rank Among 177 *Alumni Factor* Schools	**73**

Overview

A small, highly acclaimed liberal arts college in the middle of Ohio, Oberlin has long been at the forefront of social and political progressivism. It was the first college in the country to admit Black students (1835) and the first to become co-educational, admitting women in 1837. Its graduates today are the 2nd most liberal among the 177 schools we measure.

With a ranking of 18th in Intellectual Development, 21st in Overall Assessment and 44th in Alumni Giving, there is no doubt that Oberlin grads have abounding love for and loyalty to their school. This is a place that expands and stretches the mind in ways that most other colleges cannot. It also inspires its graduates to transfer that experience by teaching others – and Oberlin grads do this prolifically. They are tenth among all colleges in earning post-grad degrees; third in percent of grads who become college professors and tenth in the percent who teach at any level.

It is, therefore, not surprising that many notable Oberlin grads can be found in academia, education, journalism, law, government and politics.

Notable Alumni

Academy Award-winning screenwriter Mark Boal (*The Hurt Locker*); creator/producer of *Cheers, Wings* and *Will & Grace* James Burrows; and Spelman College's first female African American president, Johnnetta B. Cole.

The Alumni Factor Rankings Summary

Attribute	Liberal Arts Rank	Overall Rank
College Experience	**25**	**41**
Intellectual Development	18	21
Social Development	19	30
Spiritual Development	18	39
Friendship Development	20	23
Preparation for Career Success	36	89
Immediate Job Opportunities	34	134
Overall Assessment	**21**	**51**
Would Personally Choose Again	20	52
Would Recommend to Student	29	81
Value for the Money	14	38
Financial Success	**44**	**136**
Income per Household	49	167
% Households with Income >$150K	46	152
Household Net Worth	43	142
% Households Net Worth >$1MM	26	63
Overall Happiness	**38**	**119**
Alumni Giving	**44**	**55**
Graduation Rate	**20**	**52**
Overall Rank	**39**	**73**

Other Key Alumni Outcomes

16.3% Are college professors
22.9% Teach at any level
71.1% Have post-graduate degrees
52.5% Live in dual-income homes
92.9% Are currently employed

See pages 134–135 for detailed explanations and definitions.

Alumni Activities During College

42.3% Community Service
24.0% Intramural Sports
21.4% Internships
32.1% Media Programs
48.5% Music Programs
28.6% Part-Time Jobs

Prepared Me for Career Success % Strongly Agree	Was A Good Value for the Money % Strongly Agree	Percent of Alumni Worth >$1MM
Oberlin 36.0% All College Grads 31.9%	Oberlin 53.3% All College Grads 46.1%	Oberlin 16.9% All College Grads 14.6%

Alumni Employment

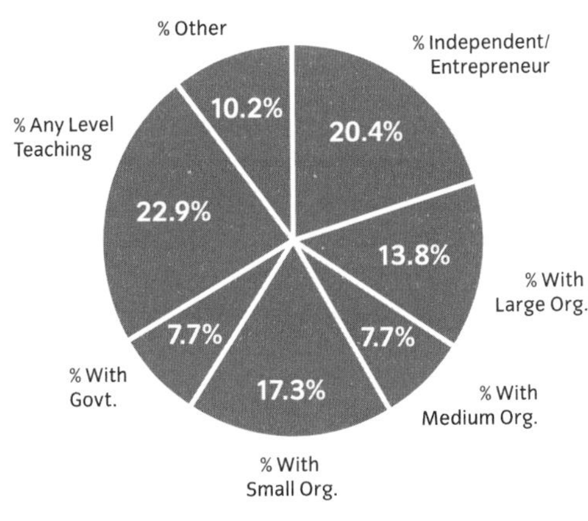

Income Distribution of Graduates

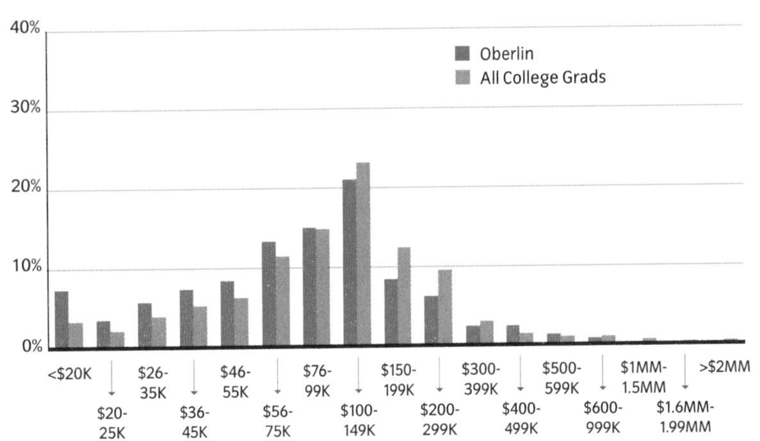

Current Selectivity & Demand Analysis for Oberlin College

Attribute	% Accepted	% Accepted Who Enroll	Freshman Retention Rate	Graduation Rate	Demand Index	Reputation Index
Score	30.0%	35.0%	94.0%	88.0%	9.85	1.17
Rank	51	70	58	52	69	51

Where are the Graduates of Oberlin College on the Political Spectrum?

Very Liberal	Liberal	Somewhat Liberal	Somewhat Conservative	Conservative	Very Conservative

See pages 134–135 for detailed explanations and definitions.

Occidental College

Location: Los Angeles, CA
Campus Setting: City: Large
Total Expenses: $58,343
Estimated Average Discount: $30,497 (52%)
Estimated Net Price: $27,846

Type of Institution: Liberal Arts College
Number of Undergraduates: 2,089
SAT Score: Reading: 600–700, Math: 610–690
Student/Faculty Ratio: 9 to 1
Transfer Out Rate: Not Reported

Rank Among 53 Liberal Arts Colleges	**44**
Overall Rank Among 177 *Alumni Factor* Schools	**94**

Overview

One of the West Coast's oldest and finest liberal arts colleges, Occidental College has a long history of academic excellence and social activism. With a 44th ranking among the liberal arts colleges, "Oxy" grads are well rounded and extraordinarily happy (17th among all colleges and 11th among liberal arts schools). Oxy ranks a strong 33rd in Alumni Giving – a clear sign of the esteem in which alumni hold their school.

The Financial Success of Oxy grads is above the average for all colleges – ranked 41st. This is somewhat suppressed by the large percentage of grads who go on to teach (ranked 13th in the country in graduates who teach at any level). It does particularly well in the Ultimate Outcomes of Happiness & Intellectual Capability (ranked 18th) and Happiness & Friendships (33rd).

Notable Alumni

Former Pro-Football quarterback, US congressman and HUD secretary Jack Kemp; former NFL head coach Jim Mora; actor Luke Wilson; and former US congressman from California, Al Bell, Jr. Of course, President Barack Obama also attended Oxy for two years before transferring to Columbia.

The Alumni Factor Rankings Summary

Attribute	Liberal Arts Rank	Overall Rank
College Experience	**39**	**75**
Intellectual Development	32	42
Social Development	31	53
Spiritual Development	35	65
Friendship Development	44	72
Preparation for Career Success	33	79
Immediate Job Opportunities	33	133
Overall Assessment	**40**	**116**
Would Personally Choose Again	45	143
Would Recommend to Student	37	94
Value for the Money	37	99
Financial Success	**41**	**127**
Income per Household	45	145
% Households with Income >$150K	45	139
Household Net Worth	40	135
% Households Net Worth >$1MM	30	77
Overall Happiness	**11**	**17**
Alumni Giving	**33**	**40**
Graduation Rate	**37**	**76**
Overall Rank	**44**	**94**

Other Key Alumni Outcomes

6.8% Are college professors
21.1% Teach at any level
54.1% Have post-graduate degrees
55.8% Live in dual-income homes
93.2% Are currently employed

See pages 134–135 for detailed explanations and definitions.

Alumni Activities During College

35.1% Community Service
23.0% Intramural Sports
23.0% Internships
25.0% Media Programs
23.1% Music Programs
43.2% Part-Time Jobs

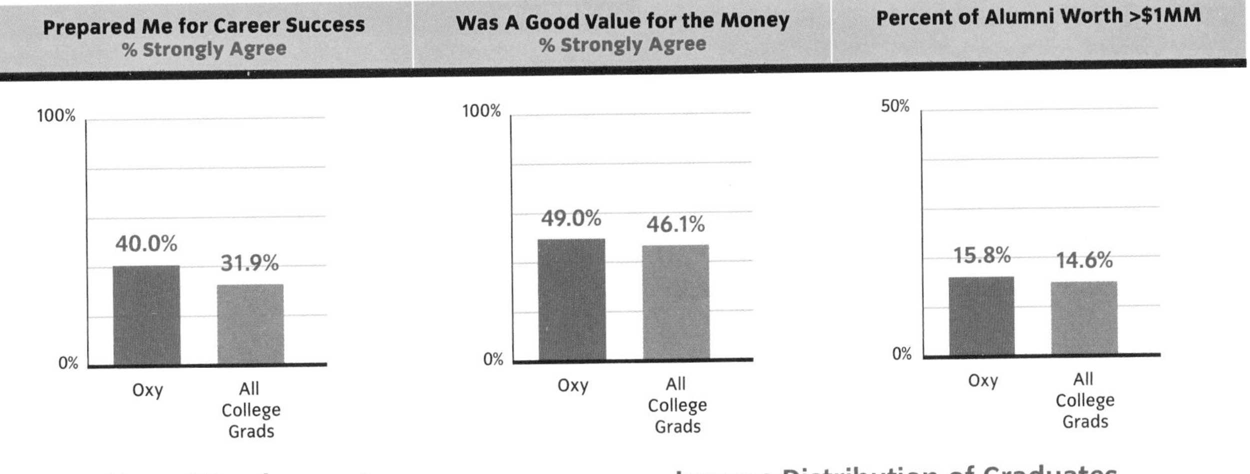

Alumni Employment

% Other 10.1%
% Independent/ Entrepreneur 23.1%
% With Large Org. 15.0%
% With Medium Org. 7.5%
% With Small Org. 17.7%
% With Govt. 5.5%
% Any Level Teaching 21.1%

Income Distribution of Graduates

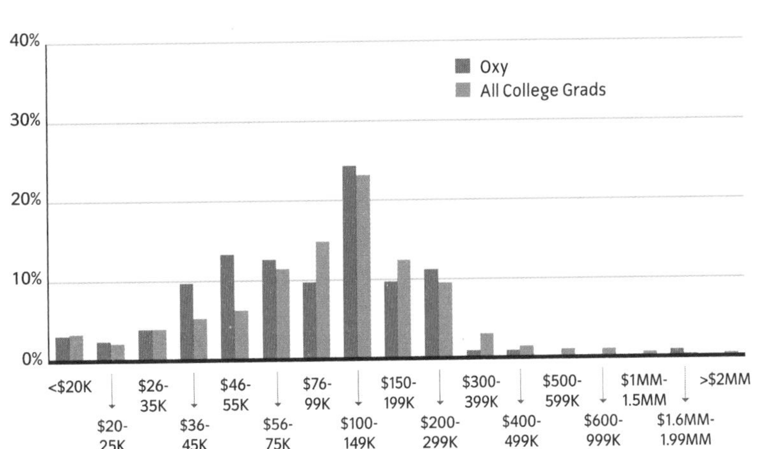

Current Selectivity & Demand Analysis for Occidental College

Attribute	% Accepted	% Accepted Who Enroll	Freshman Retention Rate	Graduation Rate	Demand Index	Reputation Index
Score	39.0%	23.0%	94.0%	85.0%	11.40	0.59
Rank	75	144	58	76	52	106

Where are the Graduates of Occidental College on the Political Spectrum?

Very Liberal	Liberal	Somewhat Liberal	Somewhat Conservative	Conservative	Very Conservative
	↑				

See pages 134–135 for detailed explanations and definitions.

Ohio Northern University

Location: Ada, OH
Campus Setting: Town: Distant
Total Expenses: $47,944
Estimated Average Discount: $23,273 (49%)
Estimated Net Price: $24,671

Type of Institution: Regional University
Number of Undergraduates: 2,610
SAT Score: Reading: 520–620, Math: 550–660
Student/Faculty Ratio: 11 to 1
Transfer Out Rate: 26%

Rank Among 20 Regional Universities	**18**
Overall Rank Among 177 *Alumni Factor* Schools	**154**

Overview

A regional university with a growing reputation, Ohio Northern University is primarily focused on training undergraduates in the areas of pharmacy, business, engineering and law. It enrolls an above average caliber student who has a specific career track in mind and gives them practical training in lucrative and growing fields. ONU's focus is narrower than many other colleges on our list of 177, and that fact drives many of the rankings to the lower end of our spectrum. However, graduates rank the College Experience a strong 73rd – and perhaps not surprisingly, given the school's focus – a powerful 30th in Immediate Job Opportunities (its highest ranking). Its strongest Ultimate Outcome is Happiness & Friendships, where it ranks 99th. Alumni loyalty is strong, with a ranking of 81st in Alumni Giving.

Although its reach is broadening, ONU sources most of its students from the surrounding Northwest Ohio area. This geographic sphere leans toward the conservative side politically and socially, which is reflected in the political views of ONU's alums.

Notable Alumni

US Senator from Ohio Mike DeWine; former mayor of Cleveland and cabinet member under both the Kennedy and Johnson administrations, Anthony Celebrezze; and Bruce Mays, Director of Football Operations for the Dallas Cowboys.

The Alumni Factor Rankings Summary

Attribute	Overall Rank
College Experience	**73**
Intellectual Development	137
Social Development	84
Spiritual Development	43
Friendship Development	67
Preparation for Career Success	70
Immediate Job Opportunities	30
Overall Assessment	**150**
Would Personally Choose Again	129
Would Recommend to Student	140
Value for the Money	162
Financial Success	**177**
Income per Household	171
% Households with Income >$150K	177
Household Net Worth	174
% Households Net Worth >$1MM	170
Overall Happiness	**153**
Alumni Giving	**81**
Graduation Rate	**160**
Overall Rank	**154**

Other Key Alumni Outcomes

7.4% Are college professors
13.8% Teach at any level
55.8% Have post-graduate degrees
54.3% Live in dual-income homes
92.6% Are currently employed

See pages 134–135 for detailed explanations and definitions.

Alumni Activities During College

34.0% Community Service
33.0% Intramural Sports
23.4% Internships
34.0% Media Programs
46.9% Music Programs
33.0% Part-Time Jobs

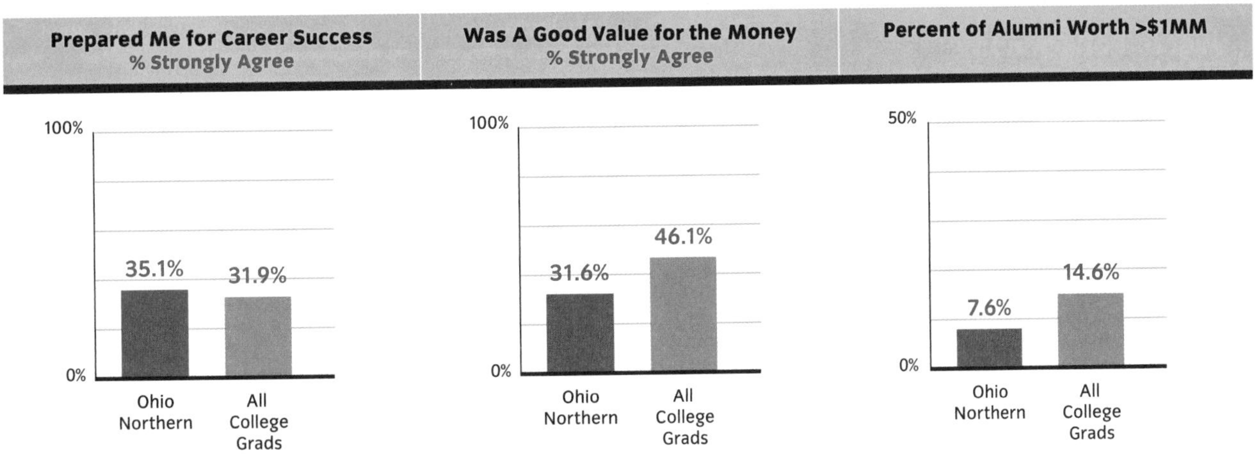

	Ohio Northern	All College Grads
Prepared Me for Career Success (% Strongly Agree)	35.1%	31.9%
Was A Good Value for the Money (% Strongly Agree)	31.6%	46.1%
Percent of Alumni Worth >$1MM	7.6%	14.6%

Alumni Employment

Category	%
% Independent/ Entrepreneur	10.7%
% With Large Org.	25.5%
% With Medium Org.	17.0%
% With Small Org.	8.5%
% With Govt.	7.4%
% Any Level Teaching	13.8%
% Other	17.1%

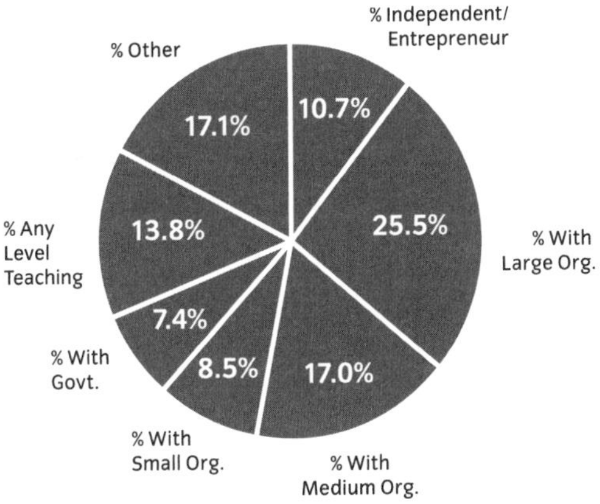

Income Distribution of Graduates

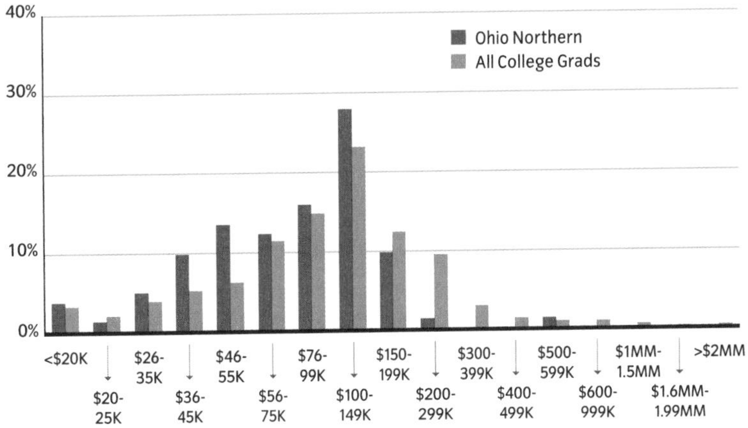

Ohio Northern
All College Grads

40%, 30%, 20%, 10%, 0%

<$20K, $20-25K, $26-35K, $36-45K, $46-55K, $56-75K, $76-99K, $100-149K, $150-199K, $200-299K, $300-399K, $400-499K, $500-599K, $600-999K, $1MM-1.5MM, $1.6MM-1.99MM, >$2MM

Current Selectivity & Demand Analysis for Ohio Northern University

Attribute	% Accepted	% Accepted Who Enroll	Freshman Retention Rate	Graduation Rate	Demand Index	Reputation Index
Score	82.0%	27.0%	84.0%	66.0%	4.57	0.33
Rank	170	119	158	160	144	162

Where are the Graduates of Ohio Northern University on the Political Spectrum?

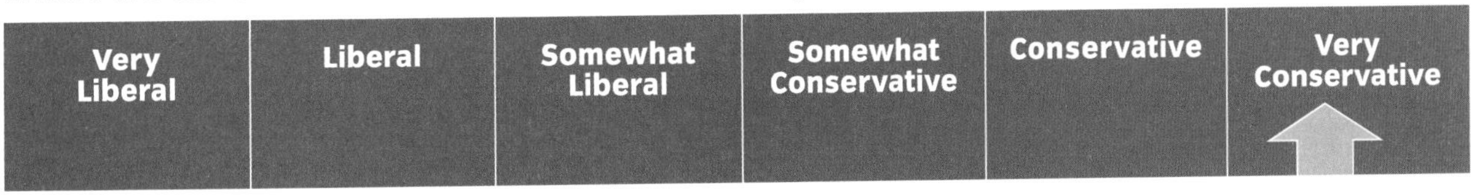

Very Liberal	Liberal	Somewhat Liberal	Somewhat Conservative	Conservative	Very Conservative
					↑

Ohio State University

Location: Columbus, OH
Campus Setting: City: Large
Total Expenses: $26,871
Estimated Average Discount: $7,789 (29%)
Estimated Net Price: $19,082

Type of Institution: National University
Number of Undergraduates: 42,082
SAT Score: Reading: 540–660, Math: 600–700
Student/Faculty Ratio: 19 to 1
Transfer Out Rate: Not Reported

Rank Among 104 National Universities	**60**
Overall Rank Among 177 *Alumni Factor* Schools	**125**

Overview

The 2nd largest university among our 177 top colleges (only Arizona State has more undergraduates), Ohio State has made significant strides over the last decade in enhancing its academic credentials and its overall student offering. The real-world outcomes for its undergraduates are quite strong, and OSU alumni hold the school in very high regard (and not just for the athletic program). OSU has a strong 39th ranking in the Overall Assessment. It ranks 67th in Financial Success (59th in Income per Household), which is quite high for a school of this size with as diverse an alumni base, and even more impressive in light of the high percentage of its grads who are in the teaching profession.

The real test, of course, is how well OSU performs versus its Big Ten competitors. While it ranks 8th among the 12 Big Ten schools overall, it is in the top five in Preparation for Career Success (4th), and Would Recommend to a Student (5th). Be careful not to assume the coursework is easy at OSU. It actually ranks 3rd in the Big Ten (behind only Northwestern and Michigan) in rigorous grading.

Notable Alumni

CEOs, senators, governors, and academicians; as well as innumerable athletes such as legends Jesse Owens, Jerry Lucas, Bobby Knight, John Havlicek, Archie Griffin, Urban Meyer and Jack Nicklaus.

The Alumni Factor Rankings Summary

Attribute	University Rank	Overall Rank
College Experience	**62**	**131**
Intellectual Development	70	137
Social Development	47	106
Spiritual Development	65	137
Friendship Development	81	151
Preparation for Career Success	52	108
Immediate Job Opportunities	50	81
Overall Assessment	**39**	**79**
Would Personally Choose Again	38	72
Would Recommend to Student	33	67
Value for the Money	52	94
Financial Success	**67**	**109**
Income per Household	59	94
% Households with Income >$150K	59	102
Household Net Worth	64	109
% Households Net Worth >$1MM	73	124
Overall Happiness	**81**	**135**
Alumni Giving	**45**	**108**
Graduation Rate	**62**	**123**
Overall Rank	**60**	**125**

Other Key Alumni Outcomes

6.1% Are college professors
18.0% Teach at any level
51.0% Have post-graduate degrees
56.6% Live in dual-income homes
91.3% Are currently employed

See pages 134–135 for detailed explanations and definitions.

Alumni Activities During College

23.5% Community Service
28.0% Intramural Sports
20.1% Internships
11.2% Media Programs
18.3% Music Programs
51.5% Part-Time Jobs

Prepared Me for Career Success % Strongly Agree	Was A Good Value for the Money % Strongly Agree	Percent of Alumni Worth >$1MM
Ohio State: 31.2%; All College Grads: 31.9%	Ohio State: 43.3%; All College Grads: 46.1%	Ohio State: 12.3%; All College Grads: 14.6%

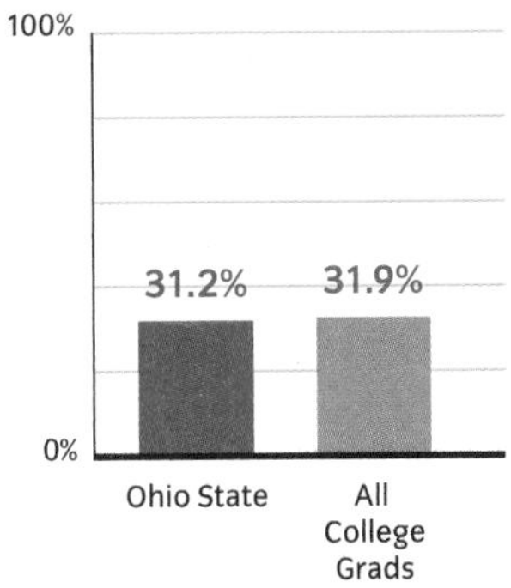

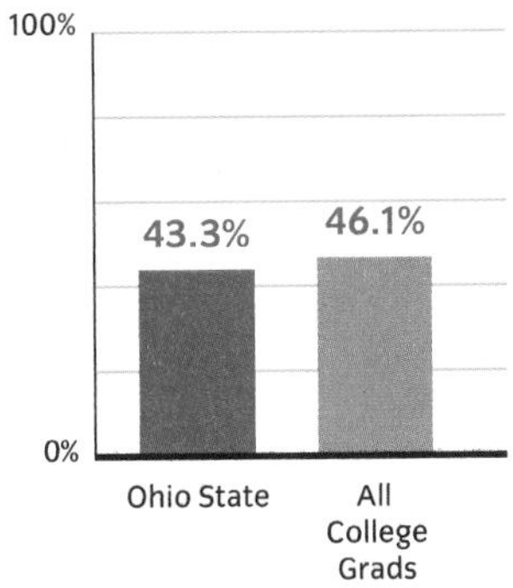

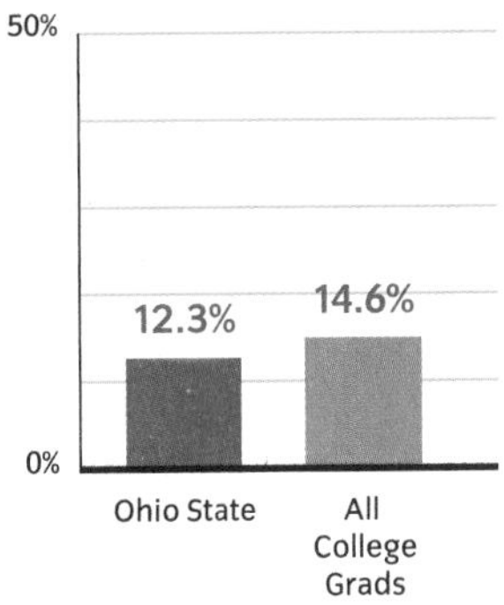

Alumni Employment

Category	%
% Independent/ Entrepreneur	14.3%
% With Large Org.	21.1%
% With Medium Org.	10.5%
% With Small Org.	12.2%
% With Govt.	6.7%
% In Farm/ Agr.	0.3%
% Any Level Teaching	18.0%
% Other	16.9%

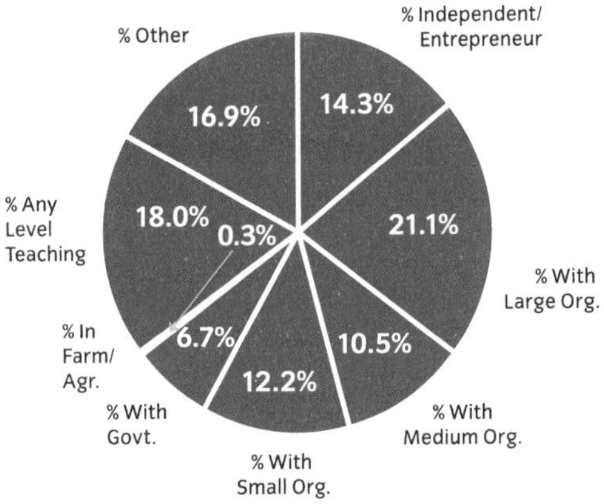

Income Distribution of Graduates

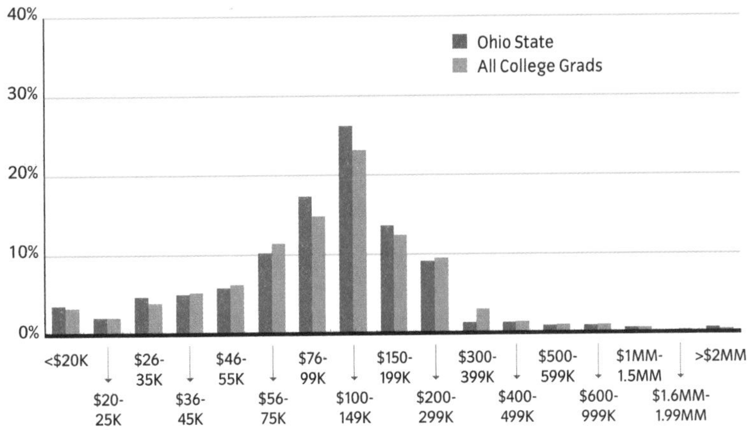

Current Selectivity & Demand Analysis for Ohio State University

Attribute	% Accepted	% Accepted Who Enroll	Freshman Retention Rate	Graduation Rate	Demand Index	Reputation Index
Score	63.0%	43.0%	93.0%	78.0%	3.68	0.68
Rank	135	31	73	123	160	88

Where are the Graduates of Ohio State University on the Political Spectrum?

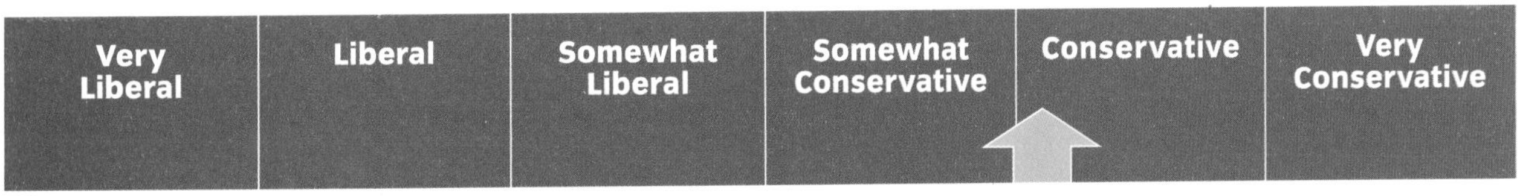

Very Liberal	Liberal	Somewhat Liberal	Somewhat Conservative	Conservative	Very Conservative
				↑	

See pages 134–135 for detailed explanations and definitions.

Oregon State University

Location: Corvallis, OR
Campus Setting: City: Small
Total Expenses: $21,475
Estimated Average Discount: $5,955 (28%)
Estimated Net Price: $15,520

Type of Institution: National University
Number of Undergraduates: 19,557
SAT Score: Reading: 470–600, Math: 490–620
Student/Faculty Ratio: 26 to 1
Transfer Out Rate: 10%

Rank Among 104 National Universities	**62**
Overall Rank Among 177 *Alumni Factor* Schools	**127**

Overview

Appearance and perception can be distorted. A university with a strong history in agriculture and research that has historically played second fiddle to the University of Oregon in esteem and reputation, OSU can now take pride in the fact that its alumni outperform those of their rival on virtually all key attributes. This excellent university has blossomed well beyond its agricultural beginning. Its strongest performance is in the Overall Assessment (ranked 38th), and it ranks an amazing 9th among all national universities in Would Personally Choose the School Again. Add to that a friendly, down-to-earth atmosphere and a decidedly slower pace than that of its main competitor in Eugene, and you have a college and culture that alumni love.

OSU outperforms Oregon in the College Experience (ranked 75th vs. 96th), the Overall Assessment (38th vs. 65th), Financial Success (55th vs. 101st), Overall Happiness (41st vs. 101st) and in the Ultimate Outcomes (71st vs. 94th): a clean sweep in all key categories. Overall, OSU's ranking is 62nd versus Oregon's 98th. Quite impressive!

Notable Alumni

Two-time Nobel Prize winner Linus Pauling; computer mouse inventor Douglas Engelbart; co-founder of E*Trade Bernie Newcomb; and many other lumniaries in science, academics and business.

The Alumni Factor Rankings Summary

Attribute	University Rank	Overall Rank
College Experience	**75**	**146**
Intellectual Development	89	160
Social Development	61	122
Spiritual Development	63	134
Friendship Development	74	144
Preparation for Career Success	62	123
Immediate Job Opportunities	62	101
Overall Assessment	**38**	**78**
Would Personally Choose Again	9	18
Would Recommend to Student	46	94
Value for the Money	63	116
Financial Success	**55**	**92**
Income per Household	81	123
% Households with Income >$150K	68	115
Household Net Worth	46	84
% Households Net Worth >$1MM	33	61
Overall Happiness	**41**	**76**
Alumni Giving	**67**	**131**
Graduation Rate	**96**	**167**
Overall Rank	**62**	**127**

Other Key Alumni Outcomes

4.9% Are college professors
11.8% Teach at any level
41.5% Have post-graduate degrees
50.8% Live in dual-income homes
92.9% Are currently employed

See pages 134–135 for detailed explanations and definitions.

Alumni Activities During College

26.5% Community Service
38.4% Intramural Sports
26.5% Internships
9.7% Media Programs
17.8% Music Programs
44.3% Part-Time Jobs

Prepared Me for Career Success % Strongly Agree	Was A Good Value for the Money % Strongly Agree	Percent of Alumni Worth >$1MM
Oregon State 28.1%; All College Grads 31.9%	Oregon State 38.4%; All College Grads 46.1%	Oregon State 17.0%; All College Grads 14.6%

Alumni Employment

- % Independent/Entrepreneur: 19.1%
- % With Large Org.: 16.9%
- % With Medium Org.: 10.4%
- % With Small Org.: 12.6%
- % With Govt.: 15.3%
- % In Farm/Agr.: 0.5%
- % Any Level Teaching: 11.8%
- % Other: 13.4%

Income Distribution of Graduates

Oregon State / All College Grads

0% 10% 20% 30% 40%

<$20K, $20-25K, $26-35K, $36-45K, $46-55K, $56-75K, $76-99K, $100-149K, $150-199K, $200-299K, $300-399K, $400-499K, $500-599K, $600-999K, $1MM-1.5MM, $1.6MM-1.99MM, >$2MM

Current Selectivity & Demand Analysis for Oregon State University

Attribute	% Accepted	% Accepted Who Enroll	Freshman Retention Rate	Graduation Rate	Demand Index	Reputation Index
Score	81.0%	40.0%	83.0%	60.0%	3.26	0.49
Rank	168	42	161	167	166	125

Where are the Graduates of Oregon State University on the Political Spectrum?

Very Liberal	Liberal	Somewhat Liberal	Somewhat Conservative	Conservative	Very Conservative
				↑	

See pages 134–135 for detailed explanations and definitions.

Pennsylvania State University

Location: University Park, PA
Campus Setting: City: Small
Total Expenses: $31,002
Estimated Average Discount: $9,660 (31%)
Estimated Net Price: $21,342

Type of Institution: National University
Number of Undergraduates: 38,594
SAT Score: Reading: 530–630, Math: 560–670
Student/Faculty Ratio: 17 to 1
Transfer Out Rate: Not Reported

Rank Among 104 National Universities	**46**
Overall Rank Among 177 *Alumni Factor* Schools	**102**

Overview

A tightly-knit community with incredibly strong ties to the Nittany Lions, Penn State has a storied tradition of excellence in academics and athletics. Its graduates are happy (ranked 28th), financially successful (58th) and are transparent in their love for and loyalty to Penn State (Overall Assessment ranked 42nd). Its strongest Ultimate Outcome is Financial Success & Happiness – where it ranks 47th. Many will be surprised to see that, despite its middle Pennsylvania location, it ranks 36th (its highest experiential attribute ranking) in Immediate Job Opportunities.

Now that it is in the Big Ten, Penn State has a new set of competitors for comparison – and the competition is tough. Overall, it ranks 6th among the Big Ten's 12 schools. It ranks 2nd in Overall Happiness, 7th in Willingness to Recommend and 3rd in Developing Deep Friendships.

Time will tell if the tragic events which recently came to light will come to weigh on alumni assessment. Regardless, the academic, social and job placement record of the school speaks for itself.

Notable Alumni

Fisher-Price founder Herman Fisher; Nike CEO Mark Parker; Chairman & CEO of US Steel John Surma; CEO of Archer Daniels Midland Patricia Woertz; pro-footballer and composer Mike Reid; former secretary of defense William Perry; and former Pro Bowl running back Franco Harris.

The Alumni Factor Rankings Summary

Attribute	University Rank	Overall Rank
College Experience	**52**	**118**
Intellectual Development	77	149
Social Development	41	96
Spiritual Development	49	115
Friendship Development	42	105
Preparation for Career Success	60	119
Immediate Job Opportunities	36	54
Overall Assessment	**42**	**86**
Would Personally Choose Again	46	85
Would Recommend to Student	36	72
Value for the Money	50	91
Financial Success	**58**	**98**
Income per Household	55	88
% Households with Income >$150K	53	89
Household Net Worth	57	97
% Households Net Worth >$1MM	70	120
Overall Happiness	**28**	**54**
Alumni Giving	**52**	**115**
Graduation Rate	**37**	**76**
Overall Rank	**46**	**102**

Other Key Alumni Outcomes

5.8% Are college professors
12.7% Teach at any level
51.1% Have post-graduate degrees
60.9% Live in dual-income homes
93.6% Are currently employed

See pages 134–135 for detailed explanations and definitions.

Alumni Activities During College

24.7% Community Service
31.1% Intramural Sports
25.6% Internships
16.4% Media Programs
16.5% Music Programs
45.3% Part-Time Jobs

Prepared Me for Career Success % Strongly Agree	Was A Good Value for the Money % Strongly Agree	Percent of Alumni Worth >$1MM
Penn State: 25.8%; All College Grads: 31.9%	Penn State: 43.0%; All College Grads: 46.1%	Penn State: 12.7%; All College Grads: 14.6%

Alumni Employment

- % Independent/ Entrepreneur: 12.5%
- % With Large Org.: 26.5%
- % With Medium Org.: 13.0%
- % With Small Org.: 14.1%
- % With Govt.: 9.4%
- % In Farm/ Agr.: 0.3%
- % Any Level Teaching: 12.7%
- % Other: 11.5%

Income Distribution of Graduates

Penn State / All College Grads

<$20K, $20-25K, $26-35K, $36-45K, $46-55K, $56-75K, $76-99K, $100-149K, $150-199K, $200-299K, $300-399K, $400-499K, $500-599K, $600-999K, $1MM-1.5MM, $1.6MM-1.99MM, >$2MM

Current Selectivity & Demand Analysis for Pennsylvania State University

Attribute	% Accepted	% Accepted Who Enroll	Freshman Retention Rate	Graduation Rate	Demand Index	Reputation Index
Score	55.0%	32.0%	92.0%	85.0%	5.63	0.58
Rank	113	92	86	76	133	107

Where are the Graduates of Pennsylvania State University on the Political Spectrum?

Very Liberal	Liberal	Somewhat Liberal	Somewhat Conservative	Conservative	Very Conservative
				↑	

Pepperdine University

Location: Malibu, CA
Campus Setting: Suburb: Large
Total Expenses: $55,296
Estimated Average Discount: $32,864 (59%)
Estimated Net Price: $22,432

Type of Institution: National University
Number of Undergraduates: 3,447
SAT Score: Reading: 540–650, Math: 560–680
Student/Faculty Ratio: 13 to 1
Transfer Out Rate: Not Reported

Rank Among 104 National Universities	**53**
Overall Rank Among 177 *Alumni Factor* Schools	**117**

Overview

Most are surprised to hear that Pepperdine, renowned for stunning views of the Pacific from its Malibu perch, is a Christian, conservative school – yet it is – decidedly so. It ranks 7th in Spiritual Development and ranks 12th among the 177 Top Colleges in graduates who regularly vote Republican. Pepperdine's Christian roots are deep, propelling a laudable number of alumni into lives of service and social contribution. Pepperdine's combination of Christian values and academic excellence translates to a 117th overall *Alumni Factor* ranking and a rank of 53rd among national universities. Graduates give fairly high marks for both the College Experience (ranked 45th) and the Overall Assessment (57th).

Pepperdine's strongest Ultimate Outcome is the combination of Happiness & Friendships, for which it is ranked 41st. Graduates are quite happy overall (32nd) and develop lifelong friendships (47th). Financial Success is also evident among graduates (47th), driven by high Income per Household (41st) and a very impressive ranking of 24th in the percent of households that are worth over $1 million. College life in Malibu seems somewhat surreal, but the Pepperdine experience is a quality one.

Notable Alumni

Actors Chace Crawford and Kim Fields, and eHarmony founder and CEO Neil Clark Warren.

The Alumni Factor Rankings Summary

Attribute	University Rank	Overall Rank
College Experience	**45**	**107**
Intellectual Development	49	111
Social Development	31	76
Spiritual Development	7	25
Friendship Development	47	110
Preparation for Career Success	63	126
Immediate Job Opportunities	90	150
Overall Assessment	**57**	**110**
Would Personally Choose Again	13	33
Would Recommend to Student	69	126
Value for the Money	85	152
Financial Success	**47**	**80**
Income per Household	41	67
% Households with Income >$150K	61	105
Household Net Worth	75	123
% Households Net Worth >$1MM	24	46
Overall Happiness	**32**	**65**
Alumni Giving	**75**	**141**
Graduation Rate	**50**	**106**
Overall Rank	**53**	**117**

Other Key Alumni Outcomes

5.6% Are college professors
14.6% Teach at any level
49.3% Have post-graduate degrees
52.8% Live in dual-income homes
93.1% Are currently employed

See pages 134–135 for detailed explanations and definitions.

Alumni Activities During College

36.4% Community Service
17.5% Intramural Sports
23.1% Internships
17.5% Media Programs
18.9% Music Programs
39.2% Part-Time Jobs

Prepared Me for Career Success % Strongly Agree	Was A Good Value for the Money % Strongly Agree	Percent of Alumni Worth >$1MM
Pepperdine: 23.1%; All College Grads: 31.9%	Pepperdine: 28.7%; All College Grads: 46.1%	Pepperdine: 18.3%; All College Grads: 14.6%

Alumni Employment

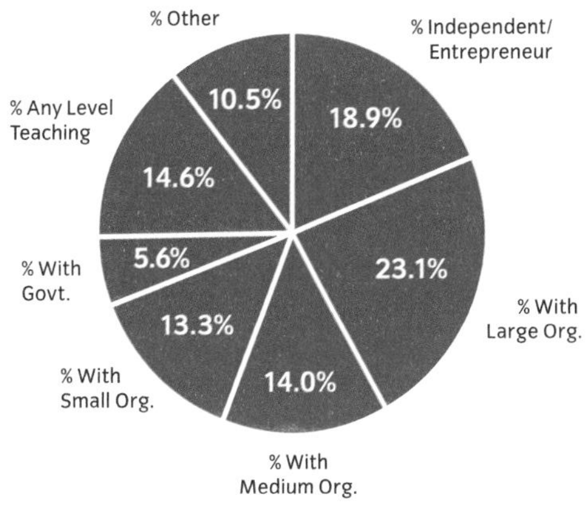

Income Distribution of Graduates

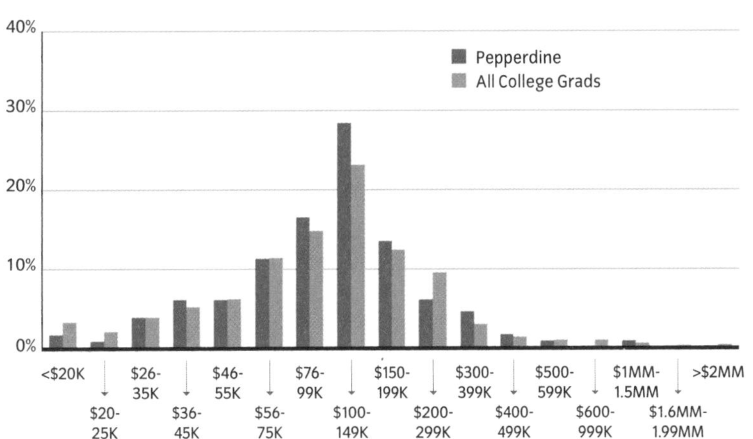

Current Selectivity & Demand Analysis for Pepperdine University

Attribute	% Accepted	% Accepted Who Enroll	Freshman Retention Rate	Graduation Rate	Demand Index	Reputation Index
Score	32.0%	23.0%	89.0%	80.0%	13.88	0.72
Rank	57	144	124	106	27	82

Where are the Graduates of Pepperdine University on the Political Spectrum?

Very Liberal	Liberal	Somewhat Liberal	Somewhat Conservative	Conservative	Very Conservative

See pages 134–135 for detailed explanations and definitions.

Pitzer College

Location: Claremont, CA
Campus Setting: Suburb: Large
Total Expenses: $56,988
Estimated Average Discount: $35,351 (62%)
Estimated Net Price: $21,637

Type of Institution: Liberal Arts College
Number of Undergraduates: 1,080
SAT Score: Reading: 610–685, Math: 600–679
Student/Faculty Ratio: 12 to 1
Transfer Out Rate: Not Reported

Rank Among 53 Liberal Arts Colleges	**35**
Overall Rank Among 177 *Alumni Factor* Schools	**67**

The Alumni Factor Rankings Summary

Attribute	Liberal Arts Rank	Overall Rank
College Experience	**36**	**66**
Intellectual Development	30	39
Social Development	26	44
Spiritual Development	19	41
Friendship Development	43	70
Preparation for Career Success	32	77
Immediate Job Opportunities	37	139
Overall Assessment	**24**	**54**
Would Personally Choose Again	21	53
Would Recommend to Student	10	31
Value for the Money	33	85
Financial Success	**36**	**110**
Income per Household	30	107
% Households with Income >$150K	44	136
Household Net Worth	39	135
% Households Net Worth >$1MM	21	51
Overall Happiness	**6**	**9**
Alumni Giving	**48**	**62**
Graduation Rate	**49**	**118**
Overall Rank	**35**	**67**

Overview

Pitzer has the happiest graduates among the five schools in the world-class Claremont College constellation (including Claremont McKenna, Harvey Mudd, Pitzer, Pomona and Scripps). Pitzer is a small, liberal arts college benefitting from the vast resources of the Claremont University Consortium. Often considered the most liberal among the five schools (it is not – Pitzer graduates actually rank 3rd behind Scripps and Pomona), Pitzer ranks a very strong 67th among all colleges, 35th among liberal arts colleges and 5th among the five Claremont Colleges – more an indication of the strength of the Claremont Consortium than any weakness at Pitzer. Consider the fact that three of the five consortium colleges (Claremont, Pomona and Harvey Mudd) are all ranked among the Top 10 liberal arts colleges.

Pitzer produces grads that are very satisfied with their education – ranked 36th among liberal arts colleges in the College Experience and 24th in the Overall Assessment. From a Financial Success standpoint (ranked 36th), Pitzer grads do quite well, but suffer from comparison to the other Consortium members who are extraordinary in this regard. For instance, Pitzer ranks a strong 21st in the percent of grads who become millionaires, but ranks 4th among the Claremont colleges.

Notable Alumni

Actress Anne Archer; former NBC News anchor David Bloom; and former US attorney Debra Wong Yang.

Other Key Alumni Outcomes

10.0% Are college professors
19.2% Teach at any level
58.4% Have post-graduate degrees
47.2% Live in dual-income homes
90.2% Are currently employed

See pages 134–135 for detailed explanations and definitions.

Alumni Activities During College

44.9% Community Service
20.5% Intramural Sports
29.9% Internships
24.4% Media Programs
8.7% Music Programs
37.0% Part-Time Jobs

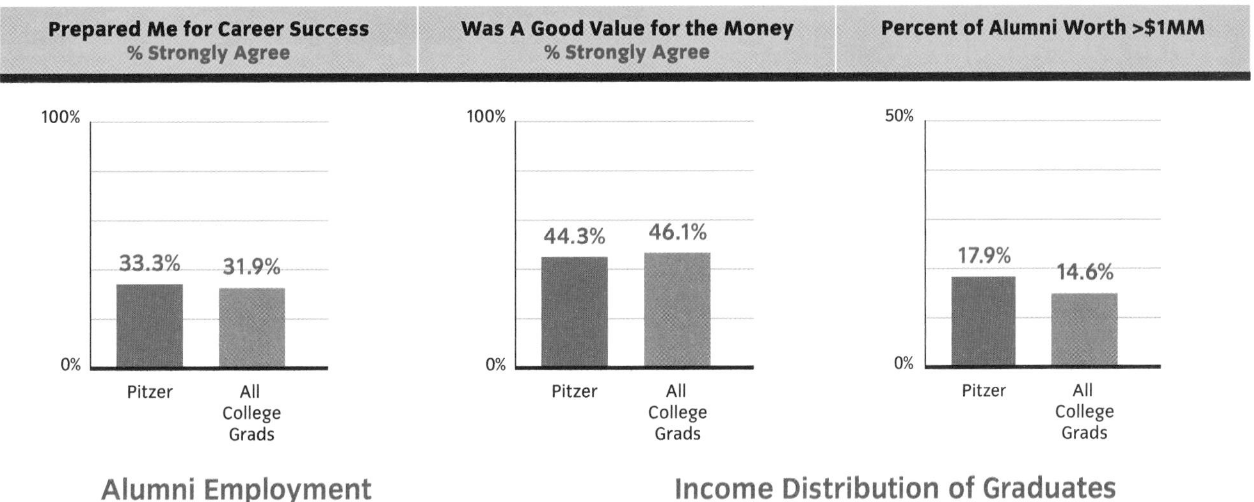

Alumni Employment

% Other 10.8%
% Independent/ Entrepreneur 24.6%
% With Large Org. 10.0%
% With Medium Org. 13.1%
% With Small Org. 13.1%
% With Govt. 9.2%
% Any Level Teaching 19.2%

Income Distribution of Graduates

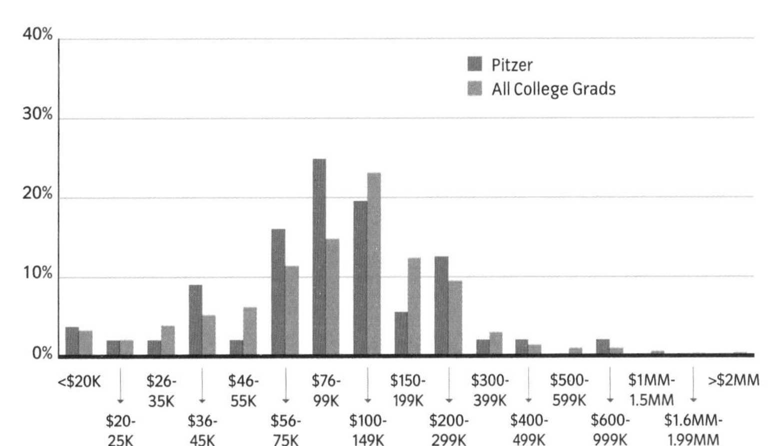

Current Selectivity & Demand Analysis for Pitzer College

Attribute	% Accepted	% Accepted Who Enroll	Freshman Retention Rate	Graduation Rate	Demand Index	Reputation Index
Score	24.0%	30.0%	93.0%	79.0%	13.46	1.25
Rank	37	103	73	118	30	49

Where are the Graduates of Pitzer College on the Political Spectrum?

Very Liberal	Liberal	Somewhat Liberal	Somewhat Conservative	Conservative	Very Conservative
	↑				

Pomona College

Location: Claremont, CA
Campus Setting: Suburb: Large
Total Expenses: $55,319
Estimated Average Discount: $37,064 (67%)
Estimated Net Price: $18,255

Type of Institution: Liberal Arts College
Number of Undergraduates: 1,560
SAT Score: Reading: 680–780, Math: 690–770
Student/Faculty Ratio: 7 to 1
Transfer Out Rate: Not Reported

Rank Among 53 Liberal Arts Colleges	**9**
Overall Rank Among 177 *Alumni Factor* Schools	**16**

Overview

One of the Top 10 liberal arts colleges in the country, with evident strengths across each of the core attributes we measure, Pomona's sterling reputation is well deserved. The Pomona College Experience (ranked 18th) is heralded by its graduates, with Intellectual, Social and Friendship Development all ranked within the Top 25 among liberal arts colleges. Pomona ranks a very impressive 9th in the Overall Assessment by graduates and is 17th in Overall Financial Success (ranked 9th in percent of grads who are millionaires). This leads to an overall ranking of 10th in the Ultimate Outcomes and a top 25 ranking in each of the individual Ultimate Outcomes. There are only 18 schools in the country that can boast of that accomplishment. Pomona is truly a liberal arts powerhouse of the West – and among the finest liberal arts schools in the country.

Pomona is small and highly selective (among the 15 most selective colleges in the country); therefore, its graduates are highly capable intellectually (ranked 14th in SAT scores), fiercely loyal (ranked 16th in Alumni Giving) and succeed in a wide variety of fields.

Notable Alumni

Civil rights and former NAACP leader Myrlie Evers-Williams; Academy Award winning screenwriters Jim Taylor and Robert Towne; entertainment industry legends Roy Disney and Ted Field; singer/actor Kris Kristofferson; and Pulitzer Prize-winning journalist Bill Keller.

The Alumni Factor Rankings Summary

Attribute	Liberal Arts Rank	Overall Rank
College Experience	**18**	**30**
Intellectual Development	16	18
Social Development	11	16
Spiritual Development	31	58
Friendship Development	15	17
Preparation for Career Success	24	54
Immediate Job Opportunities	30	124
Overall Assessment	**9**	**21**
Would Personally Choose Again	14	27
Would Recommend to Student	11	31
Value for the Money	16	41
Financial Success	**17**	**43**
Income per Household	17	52
% Households with Income >$150K	22	62
Household Net Worth	19	49
% Households Net Worth >$1MM	9	17
Overall Happiness	**31**	**82**
Alumni Giving	**16**	**18**
Graduation Rate	**3**	**11**
Overall Rank	**9**	**16**

Other Key Alumni Outcomes

7.4% Are college professors
12.2% Teach at any level
56.0% Have post-graduate degrees
54.4% Live in dual-income homes
94.2% Are currently employed

See pages 134–135 for detailed explanations and definitions.

Alumni Activities During College

34.9% Community Service
31.8% Intramural Sports
26.0% Internships
41.1% Media Programs
33.3% Music Programs
31.8% Part-Time Jobs

Prepared Me for Career Success % Strongly Agree	Was A Good Value for the Money % Strongly Agree	Percent of Alumni Worth >$1MM
Pomona: 37.6% All College Grads: 31.9%	Pomona: 50.0% All College Grads: 46.1%	Pomona: 22.4% All College Grads: 14.6%

Alumni Employment

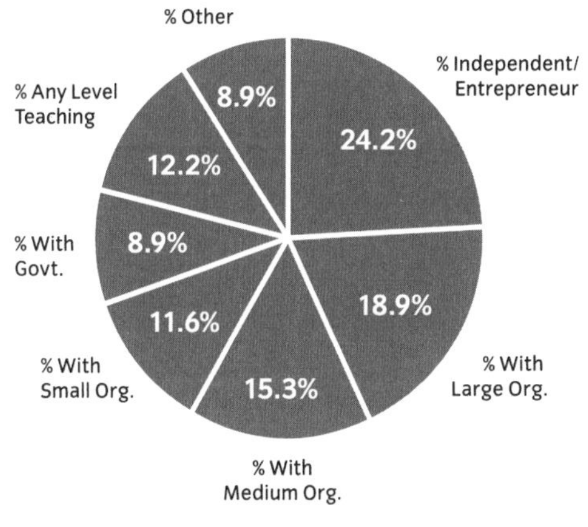

Income Distribution of Graduates

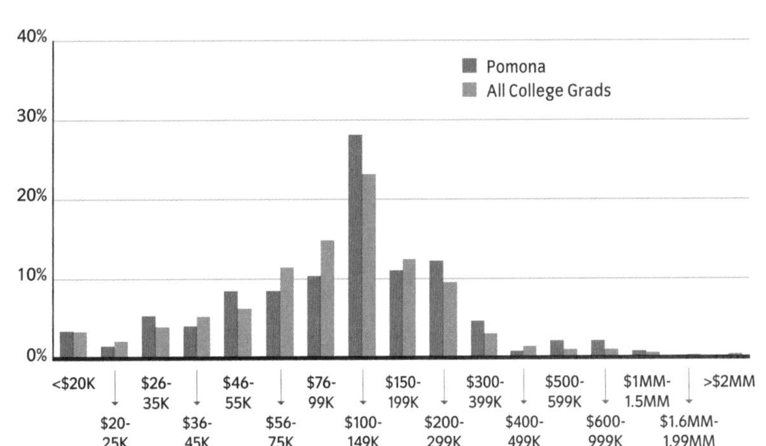

Current Selectivity & Demand Analysis for Pomona College

Attribute	% Accepted	% Accepted Who Enroll	Freshman Retention Rate	Graduation Rate	Demand Index	Reputation Index
Score	14.0%	39.0%	97.0%	94.0%	18.29	2.79
Rank	15	46	13	11	11	18

Where are the Graduates of Pomona College on the Political Spectrum?

Very Liberal ⇧	Liberal	Somewhat Liberal	Somewhat Conservative	Conservative	Very Conservative

Princeton University

Location: Princeton, NJ
Campus Setting: Suburb: Large
Total Expenses: $53,934
Estimated Average Discount: $35,121 (65%)
Estimated Net Price: $18,813

Type of Institution: National University
Number of Undergraduates: 5,142
SAT Score: Reading: 700–790, Math: 710–800
Student/Faculty Ratio: 6 to 1
Transfer Out Rate: Not Reported

Rank Among 104 National Universities	**2**
Overall Rank Among 177 *Alumni Factor* Schools	**3**

Overview

Whether the measure is prestige, reputation, endowed wealth, selectivity, academic superiority or any other indicator of college excellence, Princeton is counted among the super elite. That brilliance continues, not surprisingly, with analyses of actual alumni results. Ranked 2nd overall among all national universities and 1st in the Financial Success of its graduates, Princeton delivers on its reputation as one of the world's finest universities. Princeton is one of only three schools (along with Yale and Washington & Lee) to be ranked in the Top 5 in all six Ultimate Outcomes. Princeton produces graduates with the winning trifecta of Financial Success, Intellectual Development and Friendship Development. A staggering 50% of Princeton grads have household income above $150,000 – versus just 27% of all college graduates and only 8% of all US Households. Princeton ranks 2nd in reported SAT scores and 3rd in earning post-graduate degrees. All hail, Tigers!

Notable Alumni

Two former US presidents (Madison and Wilson); three current Supreme Court Justices (Alito, Kagan, Sotomayor); and First Lady Michelle Obama are all illustrious Princeton grads, but that is just a start. Other alumni include James Baker, Aaron Burr, Bill Bradley, John Foster Dulles, Meg Whitman, Pierre DuPont, Donald Rumsfeld, Brooke Shields, George Schultz, Adlai Stevenson, Kate Betts, Paul Volcker, Jeff Bezos, writer Jodi Picoult, Malcolm and Steve Forbes, Bill Ford, Jr., Molly Ephraim, and scores more.

The Alumni Factor Rankings Summary

Attribute	University Rank	Overall Rank
College Experience	**4**	**16**
Intellectual Development	4	25
Social Development	11	36
Spiritual Development	14	63
Friendship Development	5	29
Preparation for Career Success	11	29
Immediate Job Opportunities	13	18
Overall Assessment	**13**	**22**
Would Personally Choose Again	17	41
Would Recommend to Student	19	35
Value for the Money	10	17
Financial Success	**1**	**1**
Income per Household	1	3
% Households with Income >$150K	1	1
Household Net Worth	1	2
% Households Net Worth >$1MM	2	6
Overall Happiness	**26**	**51**
Alumni Giving	**1**	**1**
Graduation Rate	**2**	**2**
Overall Rank	**2**	**3**

Other Key Alumni Outcomes

14.0% Are college professors
17.5% Teach at any level
74.5% Have post-graduate degrees
42.7% Live in dual-income homes
90.9% Are currently employed

See pages 134–135 for detailed explanations and definitions.

Alumni Activities During College

25.0% Community Service
25.0% Intramural Sports
11.4% Internships
22.1% Media Programs
29.3% Music Programs
30.0% Part-Time Jobs

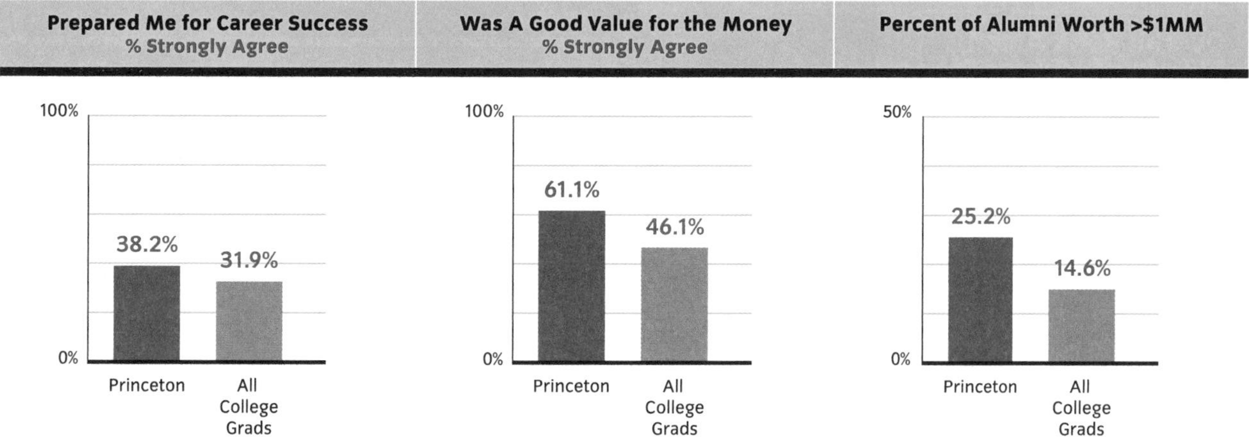

Alumni Employment

% Other 13.9%
% Independent/ Entrepreneur 21.0%
% With Large Org. 19.6%
% With Medium Org. 8.4%
% With Small Org. 14.7%
% With Govt. 4.9%
% Any Level Teaching 17.5%

Income Distribution of Graduates

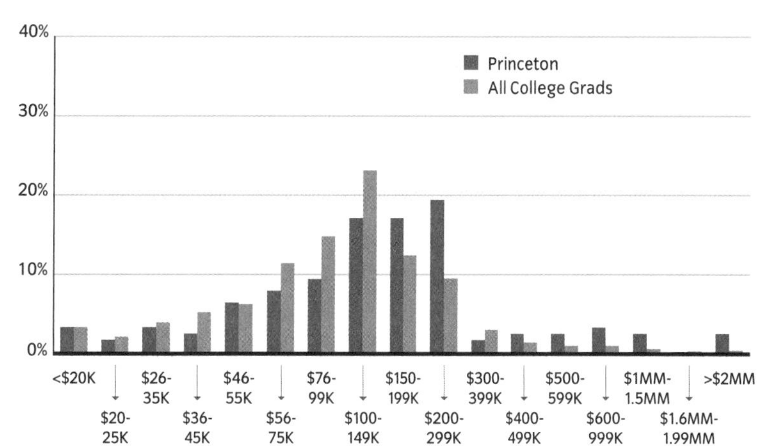

Current Selectivity & Demand Analysis for Princeton University

Attribute	% Accepted	% Accepted Who Enroll	Freshman Retention Rate	Graduation Rate	Demand Index	Reputation Index
Score	8.0%	57.0%	99.0%	96.0%	20.95	7.13
Rank	4	12	1	2	4	7

Where are the Graduates of Princeton University on the Political Spectrum?

Very Liberal	Liberal	Somewhat Liberal	Somewhat Conservative	Conservative	Very Conservative
	↑				

See pages 134–135 for detailed explanations and definitions.

Purdue University

Location: West Lafayette, IN
Campus Setting: Suburb: Midsize
Total Expenses: $22,748
Estimated Average Discount: $10,214 (45%)
Estimated Net Price: $12,534

Type of Institution: National University
Number of Undergraduates: 32,173
SAT Score: Reading: 490–610, Math: 550–690
Student/Faculty Ratio: 14 to 1
Transfer Out Rate: 21%

Rank Among 104 National Universities	**33**
Overall Rank Among 177 *Alumni Factor* Schools	**78**

Overview

A strong science, engineering and technology school with a friendly, spirited student body, Purdue ranks 33rd among national universities and 78th overall. Like many other large, technically-focused schools, the graduate base of Purdue skews conservative relative to other college grads. The real story at Purdue, however, is its academic rigor and excellence. Of the 68 schools in our database with more than 10,000 graduates, Purdue is one of only 17 to crack the Top 50 in Intellectual Development (ranked 39th). With more than 30,000 undergraduates, Purdue is one of America's largest universities, while simultaneously being one of the best – an admirable accomplishment.

Purdue's excellent ranking in College Experience (34th) is driven by strengths in Preparation for Career Success (18th) and Immediate Job Opportunities (12th). Purdue grads also do well in Financial Success (52nd) and receive very high scores in Overall Happiness (14th). Purdue's strongest Ultimate Outcome is Financial Success & Happiness, where it ranks 37th.

Notable Alumni

The first person to walk on the moon, Neil Armstrong, and the last, Eugene Cernan; as well as Nobel Prize-winning physicists Edward Purcell, Ben Mottelson and Julian Schwinger; Bechtel founder Stephen Bechtel; legendary coach John Wooden; and NFL quarterback Drew Brees.

The Alumni Factor Rankings Summary

Attribute	University Rank	Overall Rank
College Experience	**34**	**92**
Intellectual Development	39	97
Social Development	40	93
Spiritual Development	72	144
Friendship Development	68	138
Preparation for Career Success	18	43
Immediate Job Opportunities	12	16
Overall Assessment	**33**	**69**
Would Personally Choose Again	55	103
Would Recommend to Student	23	45
Value for the Money	30	57
Financial Success	**52**	**88**
Income per Household	47	75
% Households with Income >$150K	58	100
Household Net Worth	54	94
% Households Net Worth >$1MM	60	103
Overall Happiness	**14**	**32**
Alumni Giving	**45**	**108**
Graduation Rate	**81**	**148**
Overall Rank	**33**	**78**

Other Key Alumni Outcomes

4.8% Are college professors
9.8% Teach at any level
43.2% Have post-graduate degrees
55.8% Live in dual-income homes
93.3% Are currently employed

See pages 134–135 for detailed explanations and definitions.

Alumni Activities During College

23.7% Community Service
32.1% Intramural Sports
20.3% Internships
13.1% Media Programs
12.8% Music Programs
40.8% Part-Time Jobs

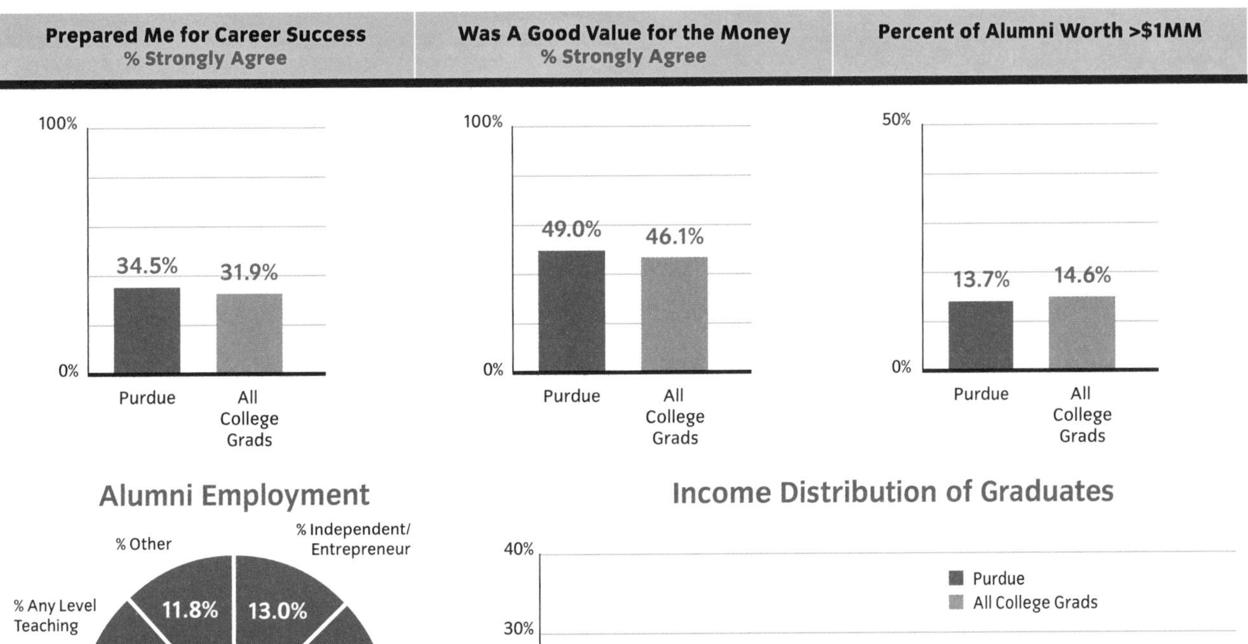

Alumni Employment

% Other: 11.8%
% Independent/Entrepreneur: 13.0%
% With Large Org.: 30.5%
% With Medium Org.: 13.2%
% With Small Org.: 14.1%
% With Govt.: 7.6%
% Any Level Teaching: 9.8%

Income Distribution of Graduates

40%
30%
20%
10%
0%
Purdue
All College Grads
<$20K | $20-25K | $26-35K | $36-45K | $46-55K | $56-75K | $76-99K | $100-149K | $150-199K | $200-299K | $300-399K | $400-499K | $500-599K | $600-999K | $1MM-1.5MM | $1.6MM-1.99MM | >$2MM

Current Selectivity & Demand Analysis for Purdue University

Attribute	% Accepted	% Accepted Who Enroll	Freshman Retention Rate	Graduation Rate	Demand Index	Reputation Index
Score	68.0%	34.0%	88.0%	69%	4.36	0.50
Rank	145	76	135	148	149	121

Where are the Graduates of Purdue University on the Political Spectrum?

Very Liberal	Liberal	Somewhat Liberal	Somewhat Conservative	Conservative	Very Conservative
					↑

See pages 134–135 for detailed explanations and definitions.

Reed College

Location: Portland, OR
Campus Setting: City: Large
Total Expenses: $55,700
Estimated Average Discount: $35,933 (65%)
Estimated Net Price: $19,767

Type of Institution: Liberal Arts College
Number of Undergraduates: 1,447
SAT Score: Reading: 670–750, Math: 630–720
Student/Faculty Ratio: 10 to 1
Transfer Out Rate: Not Reported

Rank Among 53 Liberal Arts Colleges	**47**
Overall Rank Among 177 *Alumni Factor* Schools	**99**

Overview

When you gather 1500 brilliant students in a fiercely permissive environment on a Portland, Oregon campus, the result is an unpredictable mix of intellectual curiosity, cultural experimentation and academic intensity. Reed and its graduates would not want it any other way. Reed graduates are unapologetically the most liberal of all the grads we have measured and among the absolute brightest. They are the 2nd most likely to become college professors, the 2nd highest in Intellectual Development, and 2nd in Would Choose their College Again. Graduates love the atmosphere and the friends they developed at Reed, but it is certainly not for everyone. Because Reed is the 12th toughest school in terms of grading, only the resolutely self-directed need apply. It should not be a surprise that Reed does not appear at the top of the financial success ladder – that is rarely a goal for many grads. Intense mental and personal development are the more likely goals for Reed grads. Their highest Ultimate Outcome is Happiness & Friendship (ranked 39th), followed closely by Friendships & Intellectual Capability (44th).

Notable Alumni

Deliciously quirky, Reed grads would likely scoff at being famous, so their list of notable alums is somewhat small. It is chock full of brilliant academicians, artists, writers and, appropriately, Wikipedia founder Larry Sanger. Steve Jobs also spent 24 months dropping in and out of Reed classes in the mid-1970s.

The Alumni Factor Rankings Summary

Attribute	Liberal Arts Rank	Overall Rank
College Experience	**41**	**84**
Intellectual Development	2	2
Social Development	51	148
Spiritual Development	24	49
Friendship Development	27	35
Preparation for Career Success	39	105
Immediate Job Opportunities	45	159
Overall Assessment	**10**	**26**
Would Personally Choose Again	2	2
Would Recommend to Student	28	78
Value for the Money	8	23
Financial Success	**47**	**146**
Income per Household	50	168
% Households with Income >$150K	50	163
Household Net Worth	37	116
% Households Net Worth >$1MM	43	117
Overall Happiness	**36**	**106**
Alumni Giving	**41**	**52**
Graduation Rate	**49**	**118**
Overall Rank	**47**	**99**

Other Key Alumni Outcomes

16.3% Are college professors
23.1% Teach at any level
63.7% Have post-graduate degrees
45.6% Live in dual-income homes
94.0% Are currently employed

See pages 134–135 for detailed explanations and definitions.

Alumni Activities During College

28.0% Community Service
25.0% Intramural Sports
20.0% Internships
39.0% Media Programs
14.0% Music Programs
38.0% Part-Time Jobs

Prepared Me for Career Success % Strongly Agree	Was A Good Value for the Money % Strongly Agree	Percent of Alumni Worth >$1MM
Reed 30.1%; All College Grads 31.9%	Reed 57.7%; All College Grads 46.1%	Reed 12.9%; All College Grads 14.6%

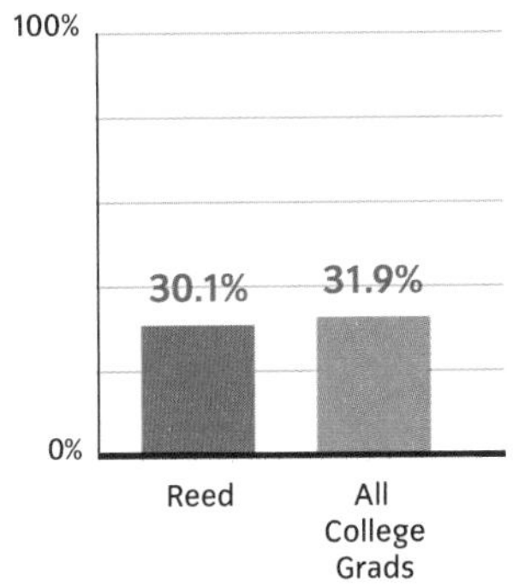

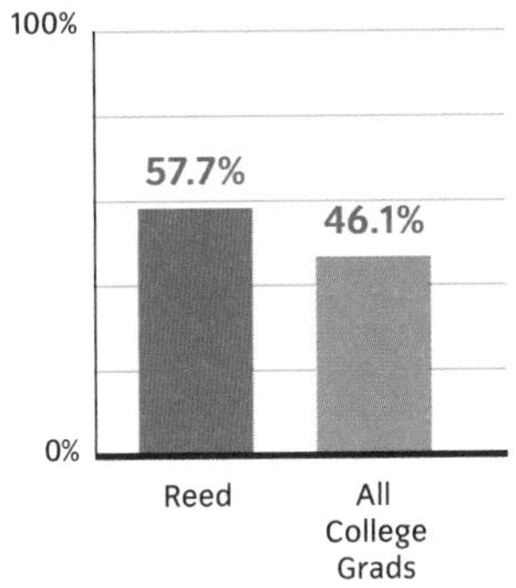

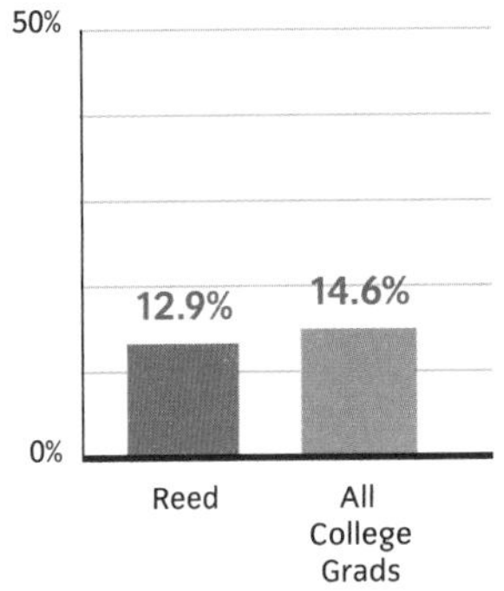

Alumni Employment

% Other 10.6%
% Independent/ Entrepreneur 22.1%
% With Large Org. 13.5%
% With Medium Org. 11.5%
% With Small Org. 15.4%
% With Govt. 3.8%
% Any Level Teaching 23.1%

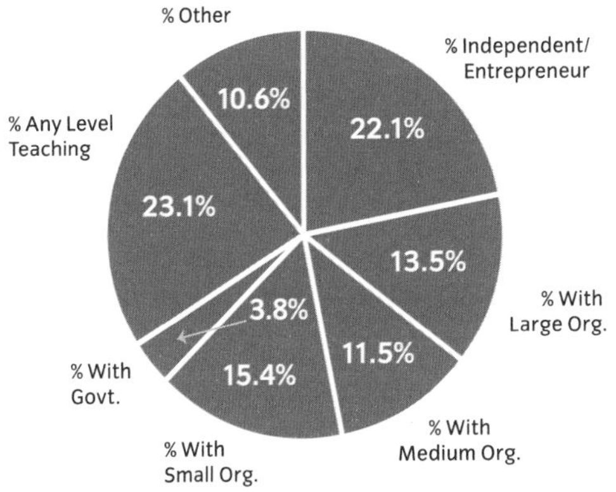

Income Distribution of Graduates

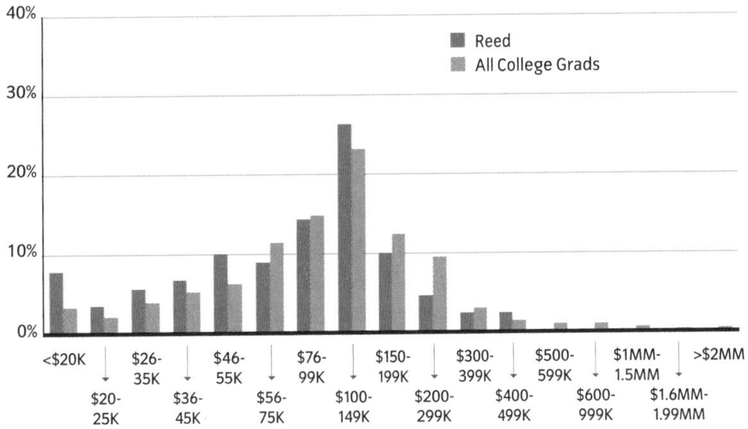

40%
30%
20%
10%
0%

Reed
All College Grads

<$20K
$20-25K
$26-35K
$36-45K
$46-55K
$56-75K
$76-99K
$100-149K
$150-199K
$200-299K
$300-399K
$400-499K
$500-599K
$600-999K
$1MM-1.5MM
$1.6MM-1.99MM
>$2MM

Current Selectivity & Demand Analysis for Reed College

Attribute	% Accepted	% Accepted Who Enroll	Freshman Retention Rate	Graduation Rate	Demand Index	Reputation Index
Score	40.0%	31.0%	90.0%	79.0%	8.20	0.78
Rank	77	96	113	118	96	77

Where are the Graduates of Reed College on the Political Spectrum?

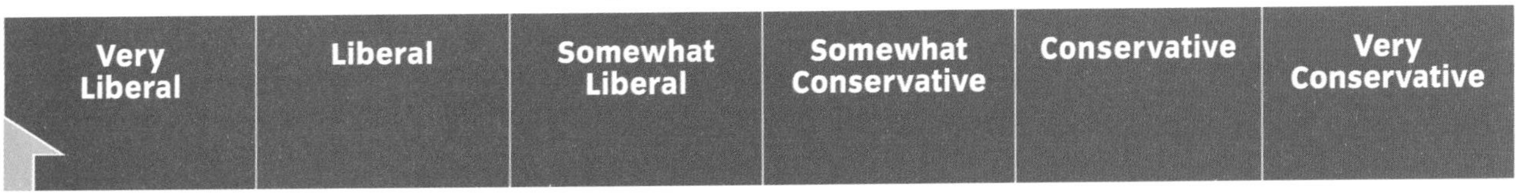

Very Liberal	Liberal	Somewhat Liberal	Somewhat Conservative	Conservative	Very Conservative

See pages 134–135 for detailed explanations and definitions.

Rensselaer Polytechnic Institute

Location: Troy, NY
Campus Setting: City: Small
Total Expenses: $57,179
Estimated Average Discount: $23,922 (42%)
Estimated Net Price: $33,257

Type of Institution: National University
Number of Undergraduates: 5,431
SAT Score: Reading: 610–710, Math: 670–760
Student/Faculty Ratio: 16 to 1
Transfer Out Rate: 3%

Rank Among 104 National Universities	**56**
Overall Rank Among 177 *Alumni Factor* Schools	**120**

Overview

Rensselaer Polytechnic Institute's purpose, since its beginning in 1824, has been "the application of science to the common purposes of life." It rightly prides itself on the transfer of its ideas to the marketplace through its graduates and professors. Intellectually rigorous and highly selective (grads have the 29th highest SAT scores), RPI is a veritable petri dish of inventive ideas. Consider that each of the following inventions originated at RPI: the ferris wheel, the cathode ray tube for TVs, the fire sprinkler, the plastic telephone wire, the microprocessor, sunscreen, the digital camera, baking soda, email and many other of life's utilities.

It is not surprising that RPI grads are in high demand (ranked 4th in Immediate Job Opportunities) and do quite well financially (43rd overall and 25th among national universities in income). They are also quite happy – ranked 34th in Overall Happiness. RPI ranks in the Top 40 in all of the Ultimate Outcomes, getting its highest ranking in Happiness & Friendships (27th).

Notable Alumni

Garmin founder Gary Burrell; co-founder of Texas Instruments J. Erik Jonsson; founder of Union Carbide George Knapp; founder of Gerber Scientific Joseph Gerber; film director Bobby Farrelly; Robert Widmer, designer of the B-58 bomber; and former US Air Force general Arthur McCullough.

The Alumni Factor Rankings Summary

Attribute	University Rank	Overall Rank
College Experience	**57**	**125**
Intellectual Development	95	167
Social Development	104	177
Spiritual Development	103	176
Friendship Development	22	75
Preparation for Career Success	42	92
Immediate Job Opportunities	4	8
Overall Assessment	**97**	**168**
Would Personally Choose Again	86	150
Would Recommend to Student	100	172
Value for the Money	89	156
Financial Success	**43**	**74**
Income per Household	25	43
% Households with Income >$150K	48	82
Household Net Worth	50	88
% Households Net Worth >$1MM	49	86
Overall Happiness	**34**	**66**
Alumni Giving	**45**	**108**
Graduation Rate	**44**	**91**
Overall Rank	**56**	**120**

Other Key Alumni Outcomes

4.1% Are college professors
5.7% Teach at any level
56.1% Have post-graduate degrees
51.7% Live in dual-income homes
91.8% Are currently employed

See pages 134–135 for detailed explanations and definitions.

Alumni Activities During College

25.6% Community Service
46.3% Intramural Sports
24.8% Internships
14.8% Media Programs
13.2% Music Programs
21.5% Part-Time Jobs

Prepared Me for Career Success (% Strongly Agree)	Was A Good Value for the Money (% Strongly Agree)	Percent of Alumni Worth >$1MM
Rensselaer: 30.9%	Rensselaer: 24.6%	Rensselaer: 14.8%
All College Grads: 31.9%	All College Grads: 46.1%	All College Grads: 14.6%

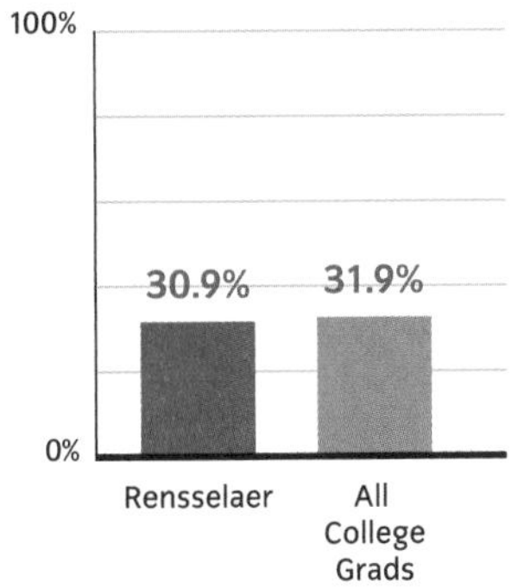

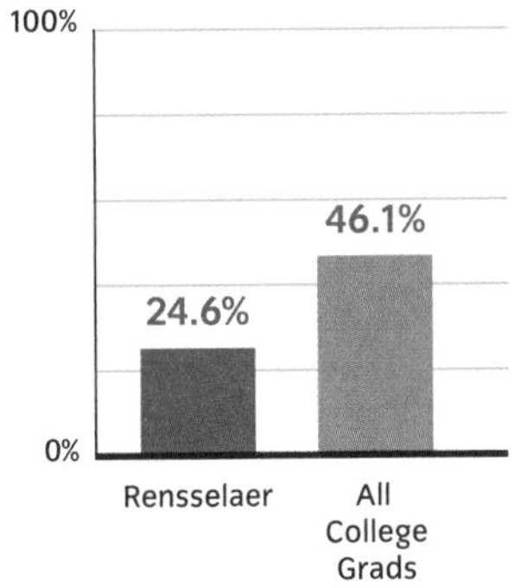

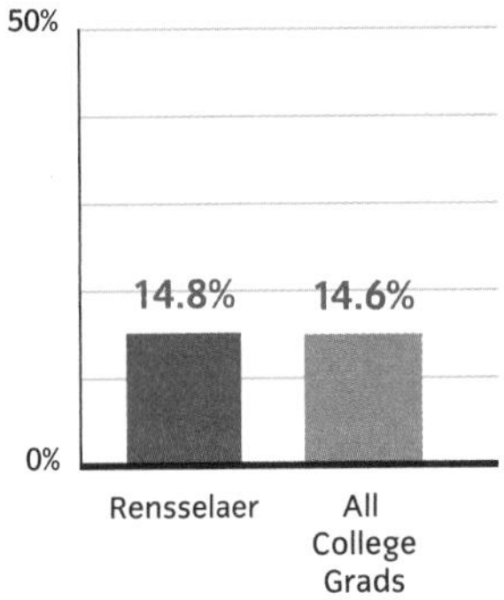

Alumni Employment

- % Independent/Entrepreneur: 10.6%
- % With Large Org.: 30.3%
- % With Medium Org.: 18.9%
- % With Small Org.: 10.7%
- % With Govt.: 9.8%
- % Any Level Teaching: 5.7%
- % Other: 14.0%

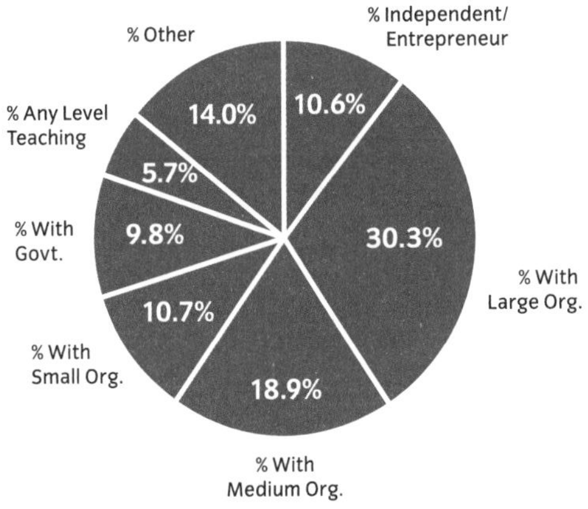

Income Distribution of Graduates

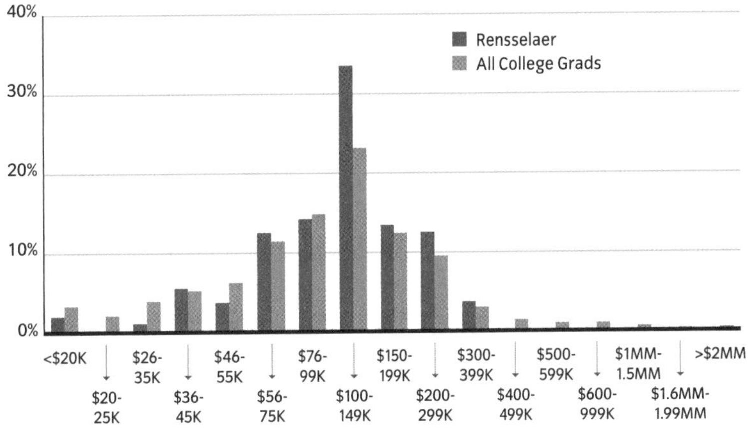

Current Selectivity & Demand Analysis for Rensselaer Polytechnic Institute

Attribute	% Accepted	% Accepted Who Enroll	Freshman Retention Rate	Graduation Rate	Demand Index	Reputation Index
Score	40.0%	21.0%	91.0%	82.0%	12.30	0.53
Rank	77	156	102	91	41	117

Where are the Graduates of Rensselaer Polytechnic Institute on the Political Spectrum?

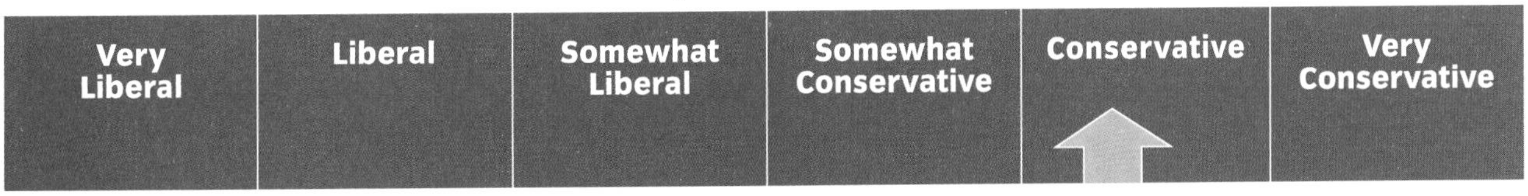

Very Liberal	Liberal	Somewhat Liberal	Somewhat Conservative	Conservative	Very Conservative
				↑	

See pages 134–135 for detailed explanations and definitions.

Rice University

Location: Houston, TX
Campus Setting: City: Large
Total Expenses: $50,171
Estimated Average Discount: $30,496 (61%)
Estimated Net Price: $19,675

Type of Institution: National University
Number of Undergraduates: 3,529
SAT Score: Reading: 650–750, Math: 680–780
Student/Faculty Ratio: 8 to 1
Transfer Out Rate: Not Reported

Rank Among 104 National Universities **3**

Overall Rank Among 177 *Alumni Factor* Schools **4**

Overview

Without doubt, Rice is one of the finest universities in the country and among the leaders worldwide. While it is certainly highly regarded, its performance is even better than its reputation. Rice's intense focus on undergraduate education results in alumni success that is nearly unmatched in the world of higher education. Among the national universities, only two schools perform better than Rice (Yale and Princeton), and Rice is one of only 4 schools to receive a Top 20 ranking in 25 of 26 attributes.

Rice has strengths across every major set of attributes we measure. It is among the very best in College Experience (ranked 5th), Overall Assessment (5th), Financial Success (13th), Happiness (8th) and Graduation Rate (18th). While Rice ranks 12th overall in the Ultimate Outcomes, its strongest Ultimate Outcome is Financial Success & Happiness (8th). Rice grads are extremely loyal to their school (11th in Alumni Giving) and have a broad appreciation for the Preparation for Career Success (2nd) and Immediate Job Opportunities (14th) that Rice afforded them.

Notable Alumni

US Attorney General Alberto Gonzalez; founder of Koch Industries Fred Koch; former president of Coca-Cola and Carter's secretary of energy Charles Duncan; NASA astronaut Peggy Whitson; US Congressman John Kline; brilliant Silicon Valley entrepreneur John Doerr; Nobel Prize-winning chemists Richard Smalley and Bob Curl; Representative Pete Olson and Houston Mayor Annise Parker.

The Alumni Factor Rankings Summary

Attribute	University Rank	Overall Rank
College Experience	**5**	**19**
Intellectual Development	2	14
Social Development	15	49
Spiritual Development	36	99
Friendship Development	11	48
Preparation for Career Success	2	10
Immediate Job Opportunities	14	20
Overall Assessment	**5**	**8**
Would Personally Choose Again	11	30
Would Recommend to Student	6	10
Value for the Money	2	5
Financial Success	**13**	**23**
Income per Household	16	29
% Households with Income >$150K	12	23
Household Net Worth	7	17
% Households Net Worth >$1MM	15	31
Overall Happiness	**8**	**22**
Alumni Giving	**11**	**50**
Graduation Rate	**18**	**29**
Overall Rank	**3**	**4**

Other Key Alumni Outcomes

10.9% Are college professors
13.6% Teach at any level
70.5% Have post-graduate degrees
55.2% Live in dual-income homes
93.3% Are currently employed

See pages 134–135 for detailed explanations and definitions.

Alumni Activities During College

30.2% Community Service
51.0% Intramural Sports
17.4% Internships
30.3% Media Programs
31.5% Music Programs
28.2% Part-Time Jobs

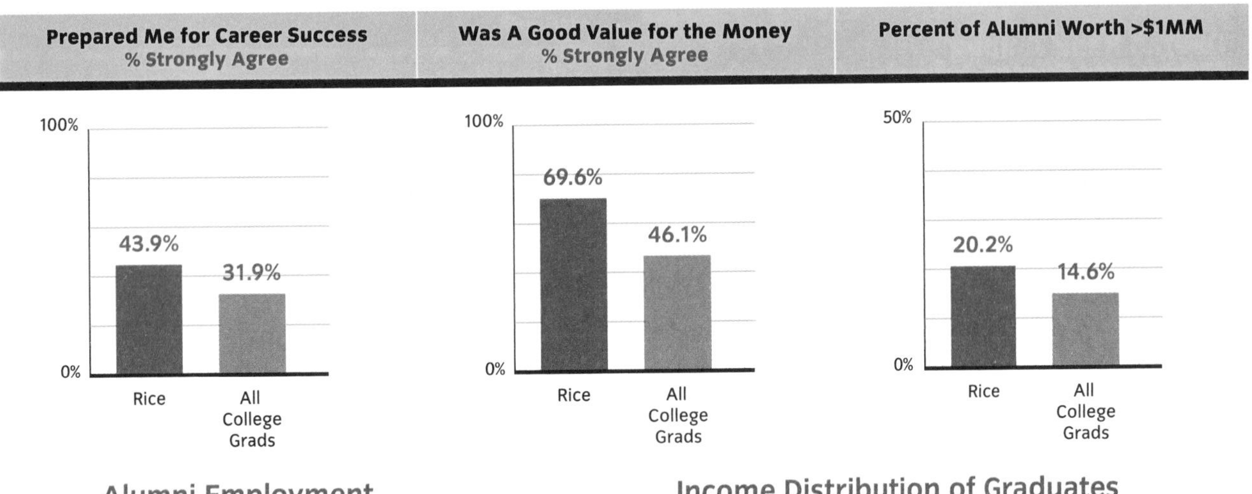

Alumni Employment

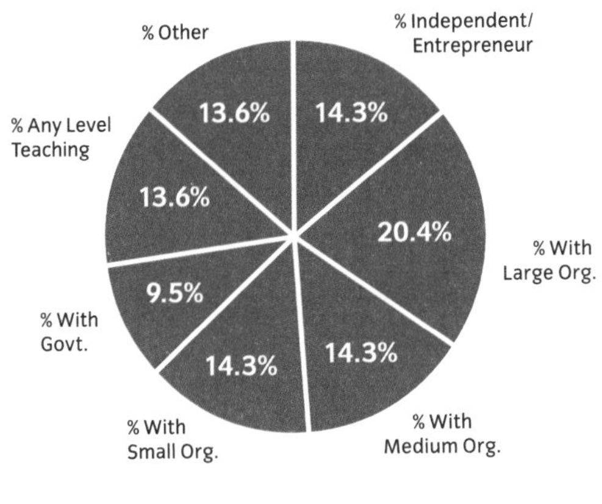

Income Distribution of Graduates

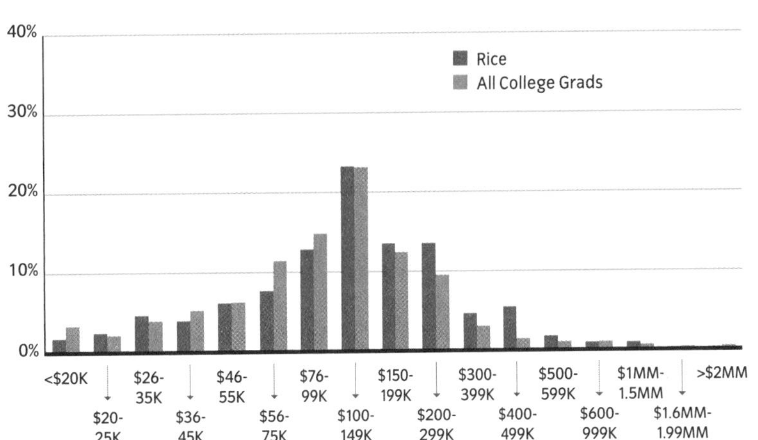

Current Selectivity & Demand Analysis for Rice University

Attribute	% Accepted	% Accepted Who Enroll	Freshman Retention Rate	Graduation Rate	Demand Index	Reputation Index
Score	19.0%	38.0%	95.0%	92.0%	13.84	2.00
Rank	26	55	47	29	28	28

Where are the Graduates of Rice University on the Political Spectrum?

Very Liberal	Liberal	Somewhat Liberal	Somewhat Conservative	Conservative	Very Conservative

See pages 134–135 for detailed explanations and definitions.

Rollins College

Location: Winter Park, FL
Campus Setting: Suburb: Large
Total Expenses: $55,100
Estimated Average Discount: $27,706 (50%)
Estimated Net Price: $27,394

Type of Institution: Regional University
Number of Undergraduates: 2,505
SAT Score: Reading: 550–640, Math: 545-640
Student/Faculty Ratio: 10 to 1
Transfer Out Rate: Not Reported

Rank Among 20 Regional Universities	**15**
Overall Rank Among 177 *Alumni Factor* Schools	**136**

Overview

Rollins is Florida's oldest college, with one of the newest, most beautiful campuses. Trying hard to shed its reputation as a sports and party school for affluent kids, Rollins has made recent strides in improving its academic gravitas. Graduates are conservative, well-prepared for career success (ranked 70th) and would choose Rollins all over again (22nd). It is somewhat surprising that Rollins does not perform better in Friendship Development (168th), given its small size and its social reputation.

Rollins ranks 130th overall in Financial Success, with graduates performing better in Net Worth (103rd) than in Income per Household (165th), which often indicates a privileged population. One other reason incomes are not higher is the prevalence of graduates who teach (52nd). Rollins' strongest Ultimate Outcome is Happiness & Intellectual Capability, where it ranks 88th among all colleges and universities.

Notable Alumni

Golf course architect Pete Dye; television actor Buddy Ebsen; co-founder of the National Organization for Women (NOW) Muriel Fox; former tennis pro Gigi Fernandez; Nobel Prize-winning Chemist Donald Cram; and former BellSouth CEO F. Duane Ackerman.

The Alumni Factor Rankings Summary

Attribute	Overall Rank
College Experience	**117**
Intellectual Development	91
Social Development	111
Spiritual Development	88
Friendship Development	168
Preparation for Career Success	70
Immediate Job Opportunities	112
Overall Assessment	**66**
Would Personally Choose Again	22
Would Recommend to Student	67
Value for the Money	114
Financial Success	**130**
Income per Household	165
% Households with Income >$150K	151
Household Net Worth	103
% Households Net Worth >$1MM	89
Overall Happiness	**131**
Alumni Giving	**152**
Graduation Rate	**148**
Overall Rank	**136**

Other Key Alumni Outcomes

2.9% Are college professors
15.7% Teach at any level
37.3% Have post-graduate degrees
54.6% Live in dual-income homes
96.0% Are currently employed

See pages 134–135 for detailed explanations and definitions.

Alumni Activities During College

41.4% Community Service
12.1% Intramural Sports
22.2% Internships
29.3% Media Programs
17.1% Music Programs
49.5% Part-Time Jobs

Prepared Me for Career Success % Strongly Agree	Was A Good Value for the Money % Strongly Agree	Percent of Alumni Worth >$1MM
Rollins: 30.7% All College Grads: 31.9%	Rollins: 41.2% All College Grads: 46.1%	Rollins: 14.6% All College Grads: 14.6%

Alumni Employment

% Independent/ Entrepreneur 18.6%
% With Large Org. 16.7%
% With Medium Org. 9.8%
% With Small Org. 17.6%
% With Govt. 7.8%
% Any Level Teaching 15.7%
% Other 13.8%

Income Distribution of Graduates

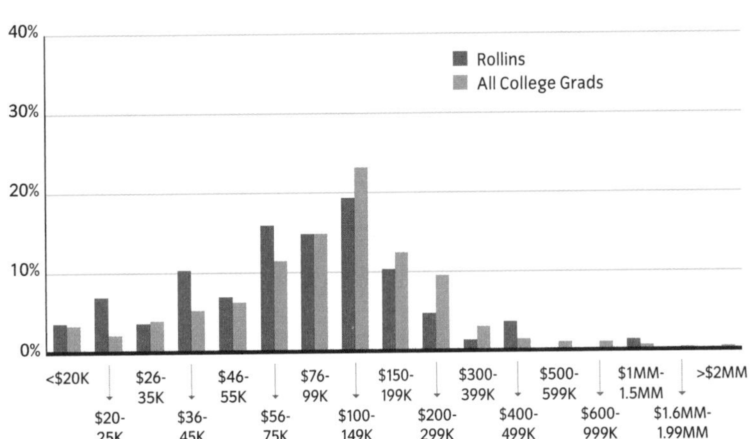

Current Selectivity & Demand Analysis for Rollins College

Attribute	% Accepted	% Accepted Who Enroll	Freshman Retention Rate	Graduation Rate	Demand Index	Reputation Index
Score	54.0%	23.0%	82.0%	69.0%	7.96	0.43
Rank	110	144	167	148	100	142

Where are the Graduates of Rollins College on the Political Spectrum?

Very Liberal	Liberal	Somewhat Liberal	Somewhat Conservative	Conservative	Very Conservative
					↑

See pages 134–135 for detailed explanations and definitions.

Rutgers University

Location: New Brunswick, NJ
Campus Setting: City: Small
Total Expenses: $28,253
Estimated Average Discount: $12,348 (44%)
Estimated Net Price: $15,905

Type of Institution: National University
Number of Undergraduates: 30,351
SAT Score: Reading: 520–630, Math: 560–680
Student/Faculty Ratio: 15 to 1
Transfer Out Rate: 9%

Rank Among 104 National Universities	**68**
Overall Rank Among 177 *Alumni Factor* Schools	**133**

Overview

The eighth oldest college in the US and New Jersey's largest, Rutgers has a rich history of educational breadth and excellence that dates back to our country's colonial beginning. Rutgers offers a wide variety of intellectual, social and cultural options that allow graduates to excel in many fields, including teaching, science, business, the arts, politics, government, athletics and journalism.

Rutgers grads do very well financially – ranked 34th in overall Financial Success and 27th in Income per Household. Rutgers' strongest Ultimate Outcome is Financial Success & Happiness (ranked 30th). It is notable that Rutgers has one of the highest-ranking Happiness scores among colleges in the greater New York area (behind only Princeton).

Notable Alumni

Nobel Laureates Milton Friedman and Selman Waksman; famous architect Henry Janeway Hardenburgh; Poet Laureate Robert Pinsky; former FBI director Louis Freeh; seven New Jersey governors; founder of The Home Depot Bernie Marcus; and film and television stars such as James Gandolfini, Calista Flockhart and Kristen Davis.

The Alumni Factor Rankings Summary

Attribute	University Rank	Overall Rank
College Experience	**85**	**158**
Intellectual Development	71	143
Social Development	72	138
Spiritual Development	85	157
Friendship Development	92	162
Preparation for Career Success	73	139
Immediate Job Opportunities	70	113
Overall Assessment	**60**	**113**
Would Personally Choose Again	85	149
Would Recommend to Student	64	119
Value for the Money	30	57
Financial Success	**34**	**63**
Income per Household	27	45
% Households with Income >$150K	36	61
Household Net Worth	26	48
% Households Net Worth >$1MM	65	109
Overall Happiness	**63**	**111**
Alumni Giving	**83**	**152**
Graduation Rate	**65**	**127**
Overall Rank	**68**	**133**

Other Key Alumni Outcomes

6.8% Are college professors
16.0% Teach at any level
55.6% Have post-graduate degrees
58.6% Live in dual-income homes
92.9% Are currently employed

See pages 134–135 for detailed explanations and definitions.

Alumni Activities During College

25.7% Community Service
19.7% Intramural Sports
24.3% Internships
19.9% Media Programs
12.7% Music Programs
46.8% Part-Time Jobs

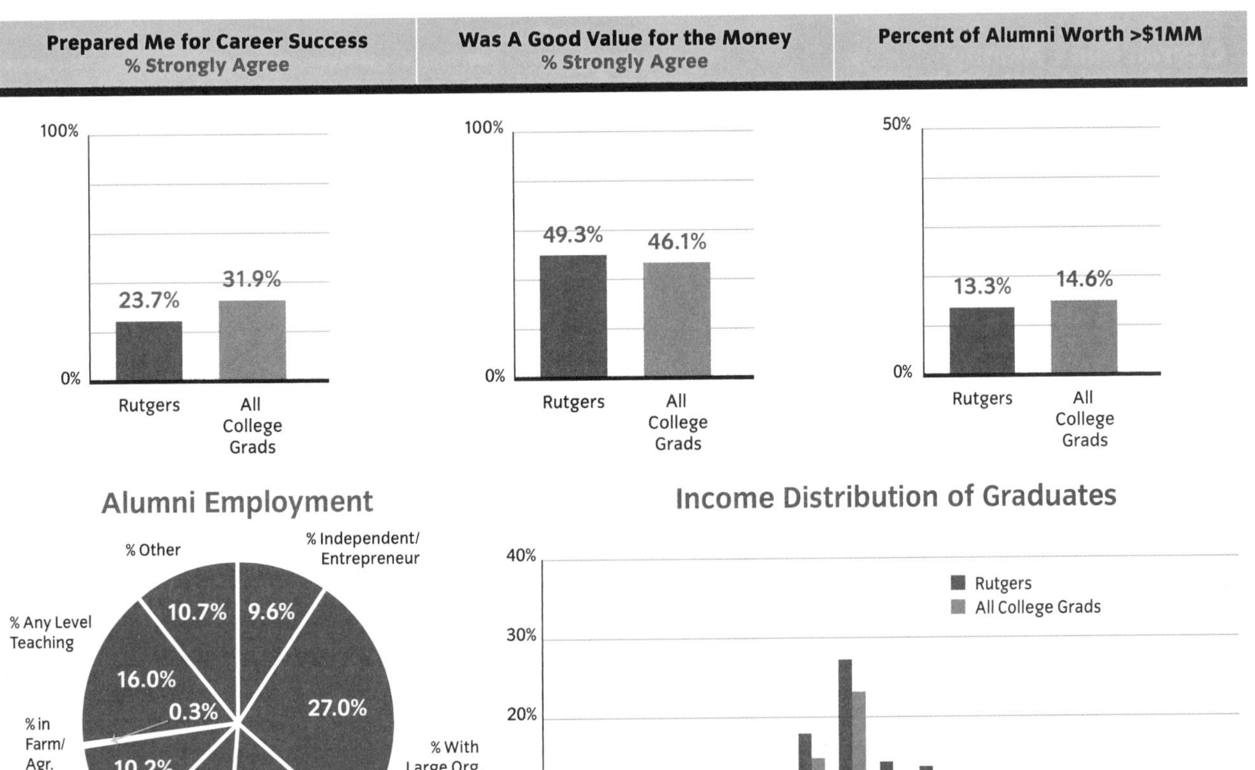

Current Selectivity & Demand Analysis for Rutgers University

Attribute	% Accepted	% Accepted Who Enroll	Freshman Retention Rate	Graduation Rate	Demand Index	Reputation Index
Score	61.0%	35.0%	91.0%	77.0%	4.71	0.57
Rank	130	70	102	127	142	109

Where are the Graduates of Rutgers University on the Political Spectrum?

Very Liberal	Liberal	Somewhat Liberal	Somewhat Conservative	Conservative	Very Conservative
		↑			

See pages 134–135 for detailed explanations and definitions.

San Diego State University

Location: San Diego, CA
Campus Setting: City: Large
Total Expenses: $23,756
Estimated Average Discount: $15,229 (64%)
Estimated Net Price: $8,527

Type of Institution: National University
Number of Undergraduates: 23,960
SAT Score: Reading: 480–580, Math: 500–610
Student/Faculty Ratio: 25 to 1
Transfer Out Rate: 7%

Rank Among 104 National Universities	**89**
Overall Rank Among 177 *Alumni Factor* Schools	**160**

Overview

Some will wonder how San Diego State made its way onto our list of 177 Top schools. A part of the extensive Cal State system, and now the fifth largest university in the state of California, SDSU is a growing force in California education and will play an even greater role in the future. Most importantly, its numerous alumni perform very well. It is the financial success of SDSU graduates that stands out, ranking 63rd in overall Financial Success and 39th in Household Net Worth. Its highest Ultimate Outcome is Financial Success & Happiness (62nd), driven by its strong performance in overall Financial Success and Overall Happiness (75th). SDSU has a growing reputation as a technology leader and has long been considered a fine research institution.

Notable Alumni

Film producer Kathleen Kennedy (ET and Jurassic Park); entertainer Art Linkletter; Marion Ross of Happy Days; founder of Jack-in-the Box chain Robert Peterson; founder of Price Club Sol Price; CEO of Costco Jim Sinegal; founder of Rubio's Fresh Mexican Grill Ralph Rubio; distinguished professor and environmentalist Dr. J. Michael Scott; legendary NFL coach Joe Gibbs; and athletes Marshall Faulk, Tony Gwynn, Brian Sipe and Fred Dryer.

The Alumni Factor Rankings Summary

Attribute	University Rank	Overall Rank
College Experience	**91**	**164**
Intellectual Development	92	164
Social Development	68	133
Spiritual Development	90	162
Friendship Development	98	170
Preparation for Career Success	71	137
Immediate Job Opportunities	78	127
Overall Assessment	**74**	**135**
Would Personally Choose Again	82	145
Would Recommend to Student	91	160
Value for the Money	46	82
Financial Success	**63**	**104**
Income per Household	71	110
% Households with Income >$150K	67	113
Household Net Worth	39	69
% Households Net Worth >$1MM	68	115
Overall Happiness	**75**	**126**
Alumni Giving	**104**	**177**
Graduation Rate	**91**	**160**
Overall Rank	**89**	**160**

Other Key Alumni Outcomes

2.3% Are college professors
13.7% Teach at any level
48.5% Have post-graduate degrees
44.7% Live in dual-income homes
89.5% Are currently employed

See pages 134–135 for detailed explanations and definitions.

Alumni Activities During College

22.0% Community Service
18.2% Intramural Sports
21.2% Internships
7.5% Media Programs
13.6% Music Programs
59.1% Part-Time Jobs

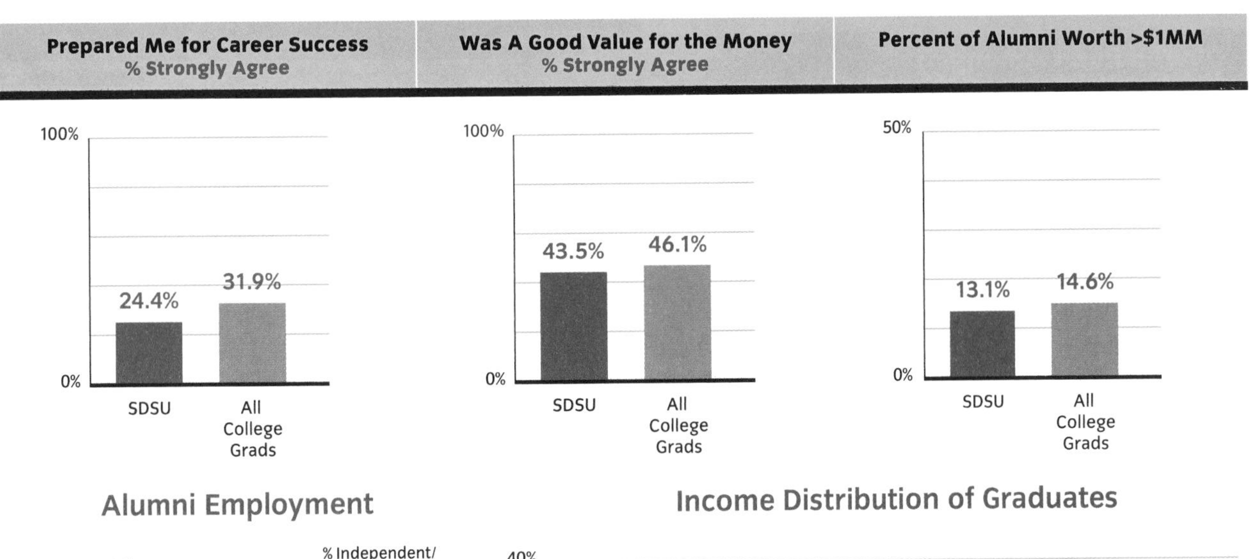

Alumni Employment

% Other 17.3%
% Independent/ Entrepreneur 14.4%
% With Large Org. 18.9%
% With Medium Org. 16.7%
% With Small Org. 9.1%
% With Govt. 9.9%
% Any Level Teaching 13.7%

Income Distribution of Graduates

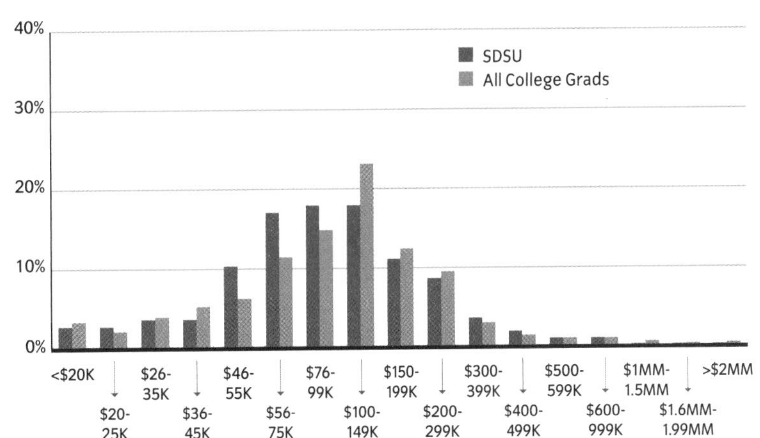

Current Selectivity & Demand Analysis for San Diego State University

Attribute	% Accepted	% Accepted Who Enroll	Freshman Retention Rate	Graduation Rate	Demand Index	Reputation Index
Score	30.0%	25.0%	86.0%	66.0%	11.30	0.83
Rank	51	130	146	160	56	71

Where are the Graduates of San Diego State University on the Political Spectrum?

Very Liberal	Liberal	Somewhat Liberal	Somewhat Conservative	Conservative	Very Conservative
			↑		

See pages 134–135 for detailed explanations and definitions.

Santa Clara University

Location: Santa Clara, CA
Campus Setting: City: Midsize
Total Expenses: $55,797
Estimated Average Discount: $21,907 (39%)
Estimated Net Price: $33,890

Type of Institution: Regional University
Number of Undergraduates: 5,107
SAT Score: Reading: 560–660, Math: 590–690
Student/Faculty Ratio: 13 to 1
Transfer Out Rate: Not Reported

Rank Among 20 Regional Universities	**1**
Overall Rank Among 177 *Alumni Factor* Schools	**43**

Overview

One of the nation's 28 Jesuit schools, Santa Clara is California's oldest college and a West Coast Jesuit powerhouse. It is small in numbers, with an intimate community feel, but large in impact. Its graduates, on the whole, lean conservative in their political and social views. Santa Clara is quite diverse, drawing broadly from both public and private high schools. It ranks 43rd among all colleges; 1st among the 20 regional schools; and 3rd among the 12 Jesuit schools (behind only Holy Cross and Georgetown) on our list of 177 Top colleges and universities.

This is an excellent school that is emerging on the national scene and will rapidly grow in popularity and notoriety. Santa Clara grads do very well in the market and are accomplished in many fields.

Santa Clara ranks a stunning 35th among all colleges in Financial Success – a statistic that would surprise many – and ranks 3rd in Financial Success among the Jesuit schools. This doesn't surprise Santa Clara graduates at all – they've experienced the quality of the student body firsthand. Santa Clara's increasing diversity is now making this opportunity available to a broader pool of candidates.

Notable Alumni

Creator of Java Script Brendan Eich; producer and director of *Seinfeld*, Andy Ackerman; founder of Farmer's Insurance Thomas Leavey ; former White House spokesperson Dee Dee Myers; Secretary of Defense Leon Panetta; and Secretary of Homeland Security Janet Napolitano.

The Alumni Factor Rankings Summary

Attribute	Overall Rank
College Experience	**68**
Intellectual Development	89
Social Development	91
Spiritual Development	16
Friendship Development	130
Preparation for Career Success	51
Immediate Job Opportunities	41
Overall Assessment	**50**
Would Personally Choose Again	25
Would Recommend to Student	35
Value for the Money	104
Financial Success	**35**
Income per Household	31
% Households with Income >$150K	59
Household Net Worth	30
% Households Net Worth >$1MM	36
Overall Happiness	**88**
Alumni Giving	**93**
Graduation Rate	**60**
Overall Rank	**43**

Other Key Alumni Outcomes

5.2% Are college professors
10.4% Teach at any level
59.6% Have post-graduate degrees
53.1% Live in dual-income homes
92.9% Are currently employed

See pages 134–135 for detailed explanations and definitions.

Alumni Activities During College

47.5% Community Service
30.3% Intramural Sports
27.3% Internships
28.3% Media Programs
12.1% Music Programs
55.6% Part-Time Jobs

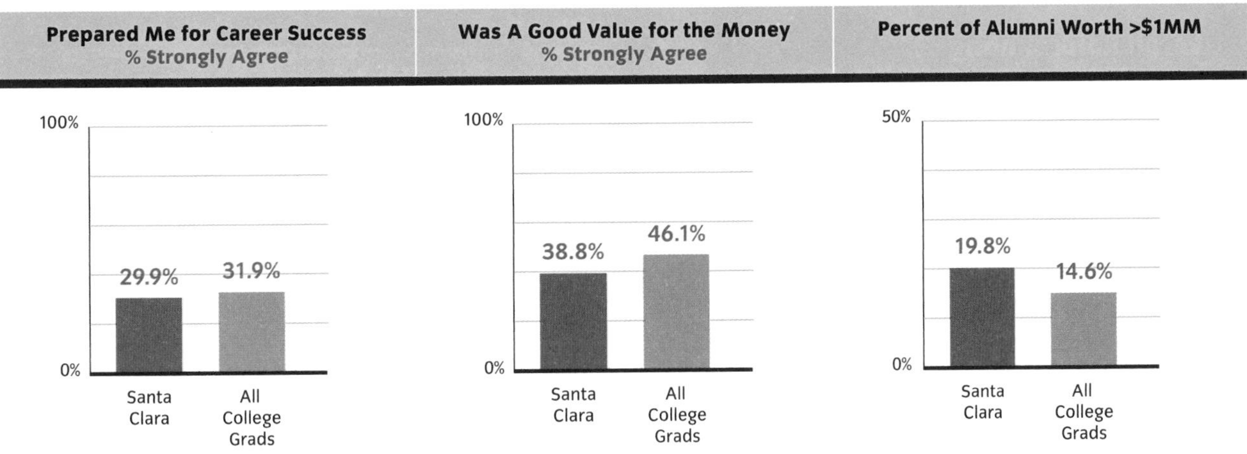

Alumni Employment

% Other 13.3%
% Independent/ Entrepreneur 19.6%
% With Large Org. 12.4%
% With Medium Org. 16.5%
% With Small Org. 23.7%
% With Govt. 4.1%
% Any Level Teaching 10.4%

Income Distribution of Graduates

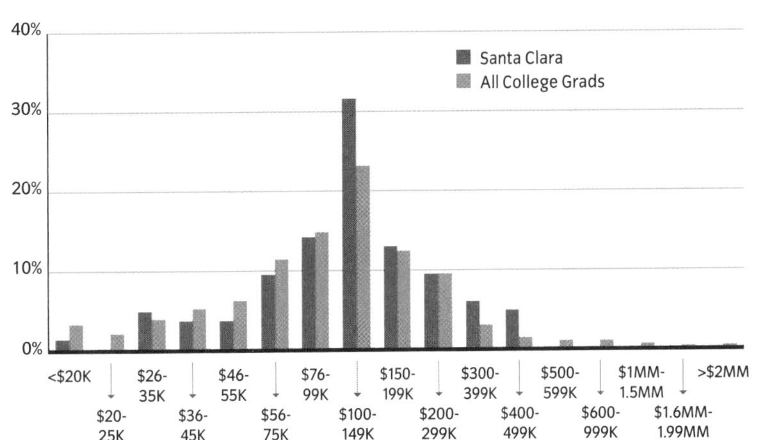

Current Selectivity & Demand Analysis for Santa Clara University

Attribute	% Accepted	% Accepted Who Enroll	Freshman Retention Rate	Graduation Rate	Demand Index	Reputation Index
Score	58.0%	19.0%	93.0%	87.0%	9.19	0.33
Rank	119	167	73	60	82	162

Where are the Graduates of Santa Clara University on the Political Spectrum?

Very Liberal	Liberal	Somewhat Liberal	Somewhat Conservative	Conservative	Very Conservative

See pages 134–135 for detailed explanations and definitions.

Scripps College

Location: Claremont, CA
Campus Setting: Suburb: Large
Total Expenses: $56,700
Estimated Average Discount: $34,259 (60%)
Estimated Net Price: $22,441

Type of Institution: Liberal Arts College
Number of Undergraduates: 956
SAT Score: Reading: 640–740, Math: 640–710
Student/Faculty Ratio: 10 to 1
Transfer Out Rate: 9%

Rank Among 53 Liberal Arts Colleges	**26**
Overall Rank Among 177 *Alumni Factor* Schools	**55**

Overview

Scripps is the all-female college among the five schools in the Claremont Consortium. Scripps women may have the best of all worlds – an all-female student body for focus and support, intertwined with four other strong co-ed colleges for interaction and intellectual expansion. This allows for excellent Intellectual Development (ranked 6th among liberal arts schools). Impressively, Scripps ranks 1st among women's colleges on Intellectual Development, which is typically very high in all-female schools. Also among women's colleges, Scripps is ranked 1st in Household Income (20th among the liberal arts colleges) and 2nd in Overall Happiness (behind Mt. Holyoke). In all, Scripps ranks 26th among the liberal arts colleges, and 3rd among the all-female colleges behind Wellesley and Mt. Holyoke.

Scripps' strongest Ultimate Outcome is Happiness & Intellectual Capability (9th). This is a very good thing for America's classrooms since many Scripps grads become teachers (3rd among all colleges). Scripps is also strong in the Ultimate Outcome of Financial Success & Intellectual Capability (22nd) – an indication that many grads perform well in the private sector.

Notable Alumni

Zen Buddhism leader Anne Hopkins Aitken and the awe-inspiring former Arizona congresswoman Gabrielle Giffords.

The Alumni Factor Rankings Summary

Attribute	Liberal Arts Rank	Overall Rank
College Experience	**38**	**71**
Intellectual Development	4	4
Social Development	11	16
Spiritual Development	36	66
Friendship Development	42	67
Preparation for Career Success	38	100
Immediate Job Opportunities	49	163
Overall Assessment	**26**	**62**
Would Personally Choose Again	26	69
Would Recommend to Student	19	52
Value for the Money	26	69
Financial Success	**32**	**94**
Income per Household	20	60
% Households with Income >$150K	38	119
Household Net Worth	34	100
% Households Net Worth >$1MM	41	112
Overall Happiness	**20**	**42**
Alumni Giving	**13**	**15**
Graduation Rate	**45**	**91**
Overall Rank	**26**	**55**

Other Key Alumni Outcomes

11.6% Are college professors
26.8% Teach at any level
58.8% Have post-graduate degrees
53.6% Live in dual-income homes
96.4% Are currently employed

See pages 134–135 for detailed explanations and definitions.

Alumni Activities During College

35.1% Community Service
9.9% Intramural Sports
27.9% Internships
26.1% Media Programs
27.0% Music Programs
35.1% Part-Time Jobs

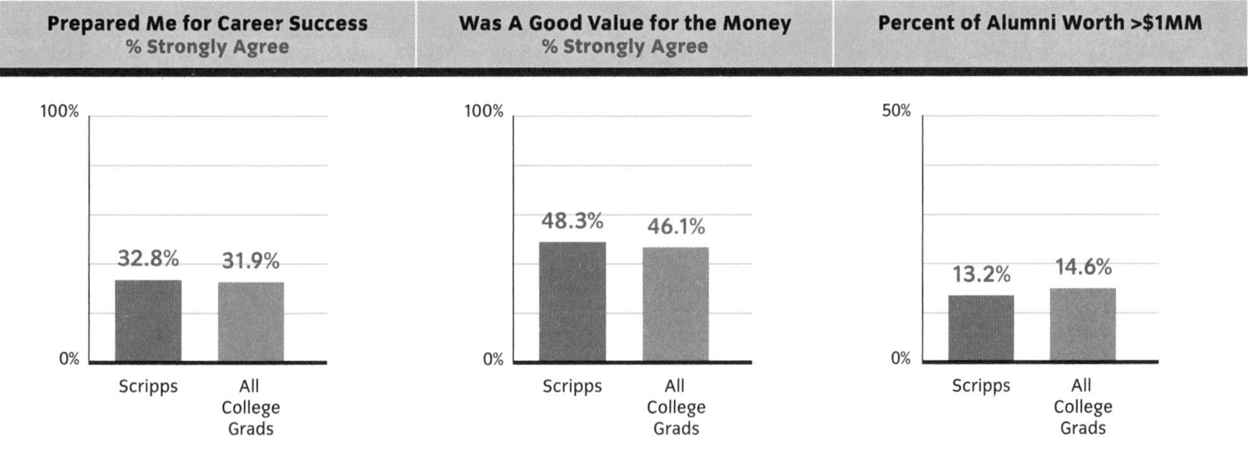

Alumni Employment

% Other 11.5%
% Independent/ Entrepreneur 16.1%
% With Large Org. 12.5%
% With Medium Org. 8.9%
% With Small Org. 10.7%
% With Govt. 12.6%
% In Farm/ Agr. 0.9%
% Any Level Teaching 26.8%

Income Distribution of Graduates

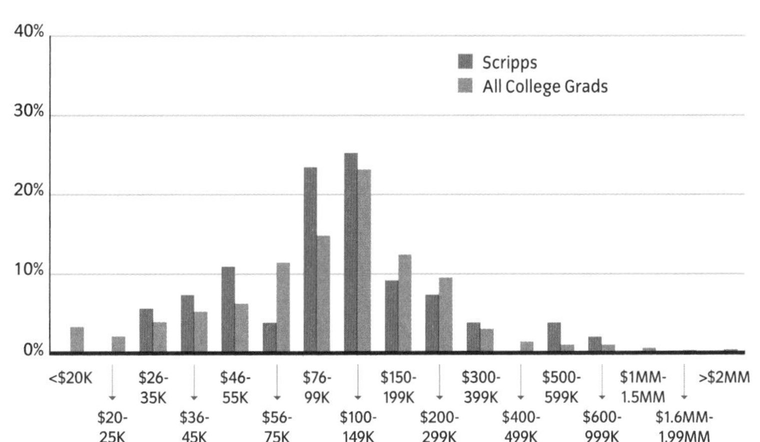

Current Selectivity & Demand Analysis for Scripps College

Attribute	% Accepted	% Accepted Who Enroll	Freshman Retention Rate	Graduation Rate	Demand Index	Reputation Index
Score	36.0%	33.0%	96.0%	82.0%	8.42	0.92
Rank	71	83	27	91	93	68

Where are the Graduates of Scripps College on the Political Spectrum?

Very Liberal	Liberal	Somewhat Liberal	Somewhat Conservative	Conservative	Very Conservative
↑					

See pages 134–135 for detailed explanations and definitions.

Sewanee: The University of the South

Location: Sewanee, TN
Campus Setting: Rural: Distant
Total Expenses: $43,418
Estimated Average Discount: $19,567 (45%)
Estimated Net Price: $23,851

Type of Institution: Liberal Arts College
Number of Undergraduates: 1,455
SAT Score: Reading: 580–680, Math: 560–650
Student/Faculty Ratio: 11 to 1
Transfer Out Rate: Not Reported

Rank Among 53 Liberal Arts Colleges	**18**
Overall Rank Among 177 *Alumni Factor* Schools	**35**

Overview

A casual stroll around the beautiful Sewanee campus is a serene awakening. Undergraduate study there is a transformative life experience. Located on 13,000 acres of the Cumberland Plateau in middle Tennessee, the Sewanee "Domain" is awash in natural beauty. It is also home to one of the finest College Experiences available anywhere (ranked 4th among all colleges). Ranked in the Top 5 for each developmental attribute among liberal arts colleges, and, notably, ranked 1st in both Intellectual and Social Development among all schools, Sewanee earns its place among the finest liberal arts colleges in the country (18th) and among the most profound intellectual experiences to be found. It produces extraordinarily happy (10th), loyal (21st in Alumni Giving) and proud graduates (2nd in Would Recommend to Student). Sewanee is academically rigorous and grading is tough but well worth the work in terms of graduate outcomes. Sewanee ranks 17th in grads who become professors and 20th in grads who become teachers. With more than 20% of graduates in the teaching profession, Financial Success (49th) is understandably ranked lower than other attributes. However, there are scores of accomplished alumni in business, politics, journalism, the arts and education – strongly bent towards service for others. It has also produced more Rhodes Scholars than all but four other liberal arts colleges. Watch this space – Sewanee's historic excellence is ever improving, and its stature will continue to rise.

Notable Alumni

Grayson Hall, President and CEO of Regions Bank; former editor of *Newsweek* and Pulitzer Prize-winning author Jon Meacham; National Geographic photographer Stephen Alvarez; Actor Anson Mount; and Professor Samuel F. Pickering, the inspiration for Mr. Keating in the film *Dead Poets Society*.

The Alumni Factor Rankings Summary

Attribute	Liberal Arts Rank	Overall Rank
College Experience	**4**	**4**
Intellectual Development	1	1
Social Development	1	1
Spiritual Development	3	8
Friendship Development	2	2
Preparation for Career Success	6	8
Immediate Job Opportunities	19	77
Overall Assessment	**5**	**11**
Would Personally Choose Again	18	36
Would Recommend to Student	2	2
Value for the Money	10	27
Financial Success	**49**	**155**
Income per Household	46	148
% Households with Income >$150K	47	157
Household Net Worth	40	135
% Households Net Worth >$1MM	48	141
Overall Happiness	**10**	**15**
Alumni Giving	**21**	**24**
Graduation Rate	**48**	**100**
Overall Rank	**18**	**35**

Other Key Alumni Outcomes

9.8% Are college professors
20.6% Teach at any level
67.6% Have post-graduate degrees
54.8% Live in dual-income homes
94.1% Are currently employed

See pages 134–135 for detailed explanations and definitions.

Alumni Activities During College

53.8% Community Service
47.1% Intramural Sports
15.4% Internships
41.4% Media Programs
28.7% Music Programs
24.0% Part-Time Jobs

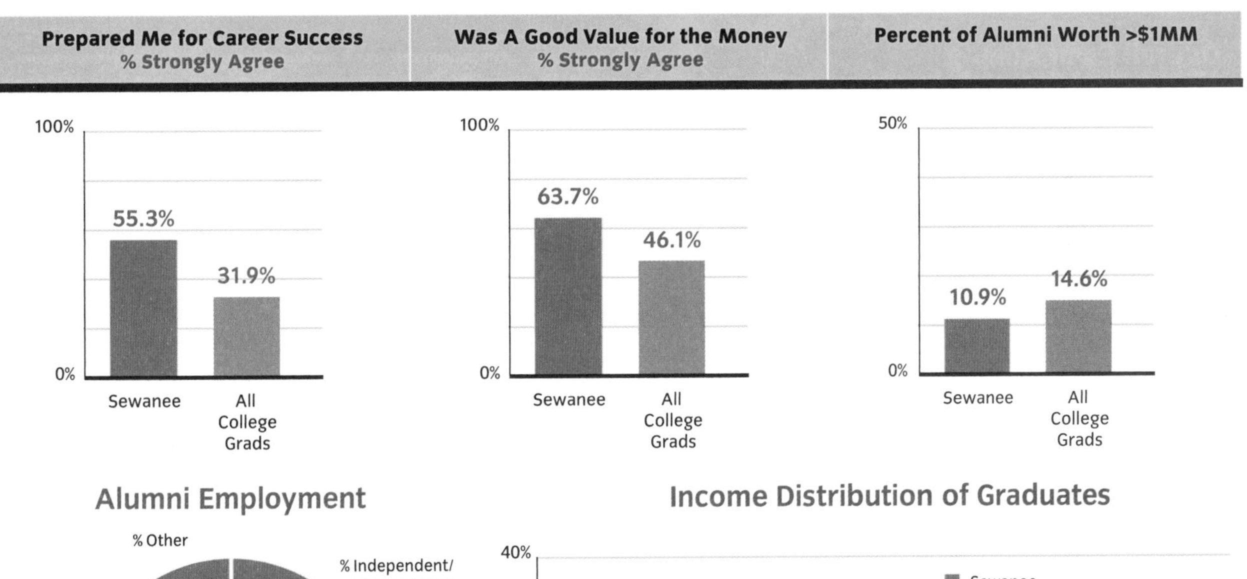

Alumni Employment

% Other 8.9%
% Independent/ Entrepreneur 21.5%
% With Large Org. 17.6%
% With Medium Org. 9.8%
% With Small Org. 11.8%
% With Govt. 9.8%
% Any Level Teaching 20.6%

Income Distribution of Graduates

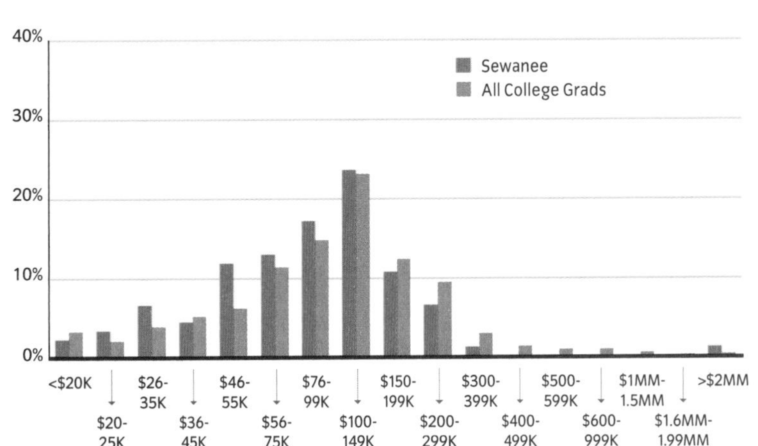

Current Selectivity & Demand Analysis for Sewanee: The University of the South

Attribute	% Accepted	% Accepted Who Enroll	Freshman Retention Rate	Graduation Rate	Demand Index	Reputation Index
Score	61.0%	24.0%	85.0%	81.0%	6.74	0.39
Rank	130	138	151	100	118	150

Where are the Graduates of Sewanee: The University of the South on the Political Spectrum?

Very Liberal	Liberal	Somewhat Liberal	Somewhat Conservative	Conservative	Very Conservative
		↑			

Skidmore College

Location: Saratoga Springs, NY
Campus Setting: Suburb: Small
Total Expenses: $56,500
Estimated Average Discount: $34,671 (61%)
Estimated Net Price: $21,829

Type of Institution: Liberal Arts College
Number of Undergraduates: 2,734
SAT Score: Reading: 570–680, Math: 580–670
Student/Faculty Ratio: 9 to 1
Transfer Out Rate: Not Reported

Rank Among 53 Liberal Arts Colleges	**51**
Overall Rank Among 177 *Alumni Factor* Schools	**119**

Overview

Artistically disposed and merrily non-conformist, Skidmore grads are on a deeply personal journey. This journey may take them into the arts, journalism, business, academics or other passions that stir their souls. Wherever the destination, be assured they will arrive in über-style via their own individual path. This kind of freedom is often a privilege of the well-heeled (notice the rank of 11th in Net Worth paired with an Income per Household rank of 32nd), or the result of unbridled creativity. Both have their place at Skidmore.

Grads give fairly high scores to their College Experience (ranked 53rd) – with a consistent view across all experiential attributes we measured. Skidmore's 51st rank in Would Personally Choose Again reflects the experience-hungry Skidmore grad likely wanting to try something new.

Notable Alumni

Former CBS executive Barbara Bloom; Anglo American CEO Cynthia Carroll; iVillage founder Nancy Evans; Vineyard Vines founder Shep Murray; MIT professor/oceanographer Sallie Chisholm; and brilliant indie musician Julia Nunes.

The Alumni Factor Rankings Summary

Attribute	Liberal Arts Rank	Overall Rank
College Experience	**53**	**148**
Intellectual Development	49	111
Social Development	48	136
Spiritual Development	51	123
Friendship Development	52	123
Preparation for Career Success	50	140
Immediate Job Opportunities	41	152
Overall Assessment	**48**	**149**
Would Personally Choose Again	51	170
Would Recommend to Student	40	111
Value for the Money	48	149
Financial Success	**22**	**56**
Income per Household	32	110
% Households with Income >$150K	31	92
Household Net Worth	11	20
% Households Net Worth >$1MM	10	21
Overall Happiness	**33**	**90**
Alumni Giving	**41**	**52**
Graduation Rate	**41**	**81**
Overall Rank	**51**	**119**

Other Key Alumni Outcomes

6.1%	Are college professors
17.3%	Teach at any level
45.0%	Have post-graduate degrees
56.0%	Live in dual-income homes
91.9%	Are currently employed

See pages 134–135 for detailed explanations and definitions.

Alumni Activities During College

30.9% Community Service
10.3% Intramural Sports
21.6% Internships
23.7% Media Programs
20.7% Music Programs
30.9% Part-Time Jobs

	Skidmore	All College Grads
Prepared Me for Career Success (% Strongly Agree)	28.0%	31.9%
Was A Good Value for the Money (% Strongly Agree)	32.0%	46.1%
Percent of Alumni Worth >$1MM	21.8%	14.6%

Alumni Employment

Category	%
% Independent/ Entrepreneur	20.4%
% With Large Org.	8.2%
% With Medium Org.	13.3%
% With Small Org.	19.4%
% With Govt.	8.2%
% Any Level Teaching	17.3%
% Other	13.2%

Income Distribution of Graduates

Current Selectivity & Demand Analysis for Skidmore College

Attribute	% Accepted	% Accepted Who Enroll	Freshman Retention Rate	Graduation Rate	Demand Index	Reputation Index
Score	42.0%	27.0%	94.0%	84.0%	8.72	0.64
Rank	85	119	58	81	89	93

Where are the Graduates of Skidmore College on the Political Spectrum?

Very Liberal	Liberal	Somewhat Liberal	Somewhat Conservative	Conservative	Very Conservative

See pages 134–135 for detailed explanations and definitions.

Smith College

Location: Northampton, MA
Campus Setting: Suburb: Large
Total Expenses: $55,993
Estimated Average Discount: $33,407 (60%)
Estimated Net Price: $22,586

Type of Institution: Liberal Arts College
Number of Undergraduates: 2,588
SAT Score: Not Reported
Student/Faculty Ratio: 9 to 1
Transfer Out Rate: Not Reported

Rank Among 53 Liberal Arts Colleges	**27**
Overall Rank Among 177 *Alumni Factor* Schools	**56**

Overview

One of the original Seven Sisters of women's secondary education, Smith develops women who make a difference. From Gloria Steinem to Julia Child to Nancy Reagan, Smithies are consequential women who have gone a long way in, as they say, changing the "old boys' network" to an "ageless women's network." This exemplifies the mission of Smith and drives many Smith alumni to excel and achieve. Ranking 27th among liberal arts schools, Smith produces smart, loyal, focused women who succeed in a wide variety of fields.

Among all the all-women colleges in our study, Smith ranks 4th overall (behind Wellesley, Mt. Holyoke and Scripps), is one of the most liberal (Bryn Mawr is slightly more liberal and Scripps slightly less), and is the largest with nearly 2,600 undergrads. Smith's highest experiential ranking is in Intellectual Development (ranked 24th), and its strongest Ultimate Outcome is Friendships & Intellectual Capability (21st).

Notable Alumni

In addition to the women mentioned above, some of the other notable Smith alumni include Barbara Bush, Molly Ivins, Laura Tyson, and Betty Friedan; US Cultural attache, Helen Le Fave; Pakistan National Assembly member, Sherry Rehman; environmental journalist Simran Seth; as well as best-selling and award-winning authors Madeleine L'Engle, Sarah Maclean, Virginia Wolf, Jane Yolen, Margaret Mitchell and Sylvia Plath.

The Alumni Factor Rankings Summary

Attribute	Liberal Arts Rank	Overall Rank
College Experience	**16**	**28**
Intellectual Development	24	29
Social Development	22	36
Spiritual Development	33	61
Friendship Development	29	37
Preparation for Career Success	22	43
Immediate Job Opportunities	15	64
Overall Assessment	**29**	**73**
Would Personally Choose Again	32	88
Would Recommend to Student	30	82
Value for the Money	22	53
Financial Success	**35**	**107**
Income per Household	34	119
% Households with Income >$150K	27	78
Household Net Worth	45	147
% Households Net Worth >$1MM	33	80
Overall Happiness	**37**	**115**
Alumni Giving	**27**	**30**
Graduation Rate	**43**	**86**
Overall Rank	**27**	**56**

Other Key Alumni Outcomes

7.9% Are college professors
13.0% Teach at any level
58.0% Have post-graduate degrees
46.5% Live in dual-income homes
91.7% Are currently employed

See pages 134–135 for detailed explanations and definitions.

Alumni Activities During College

33.8% Community Service
16.2% Intramural Sports
37.5% Internships
21.3% Media Programs
33.8% Music Programs
33.8% Part-Time Jobs

Prepared Me for Career Success % Strongly Agree	Was A Good Value for the Money % Strongly Agree	Percent of Alumni Worth >$1MM
Smith 40.8%; All College Grads 31.9%	Smith 56.7%; All College Grads 46.1%	Smith 15.4%; All College Grads 14.6%

Alumni Employment

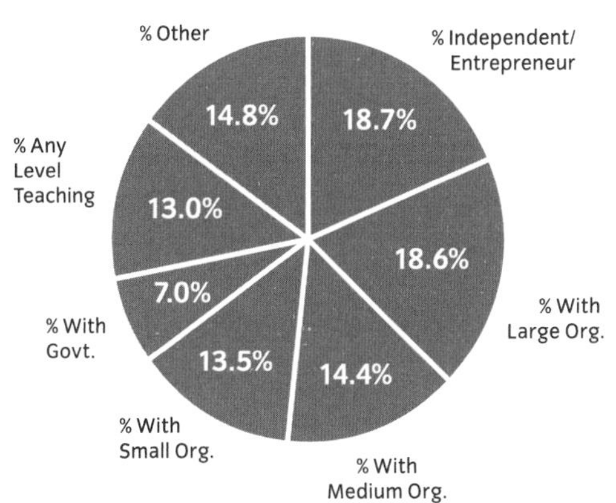

Income Distribution of Graduates

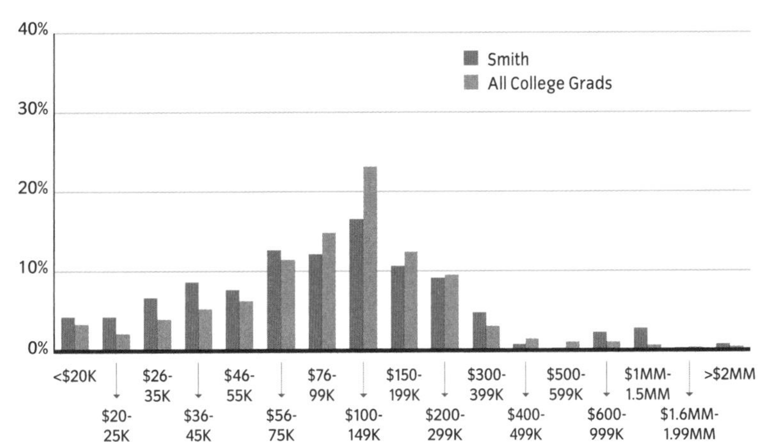

Current Selectivity & Demand Analysis for Smith College

Attribute	% Accepted	% Accepted Who Enroll	Freshman Retention Rate	Graduation Rate	Demand Index	Reputation Index
Score	45.0%	37.0%	91.0%	830.%	5.95	0.82
Rank	91	60	102	86	127	72

Where are the Graduates of Smith College on the Political Spectrum?

Very Liberal	Liberal	Somewhat Liberal	Somewhat Conservative	Conservative	Very Conservative
↑					

See pages 134–135 for detailed explanations and definitions.

Southern Methodist University

Location: Dallas, TX
Campus Setting: Suburb: Large
Total Expenses: $55,955
Estimated Average Discount: $26,815 (48%)
Estimated Net Price: $29,140

Type of Institution: National University
Number of Undergraduates: 6,192
SAT Score: Reading: 580–680, Math: 600–690
Student/Faculty Ratio: 12 to 1
Transfer Out Rate: Not Reported

Rank Among 104 National Universities	**75**
Overall Rank Among 177 *Alumni Factor* Schools	**143**

Overview

Southern Methodist University has been busy shedding its reputation as a well-endowed haven for wealthy, White, conservative fraternity and sorority socialites. That was yesterday's image and is, therefore, somewhat reflected in SMU's alumni. Today's reality, however, is quite different, as SMU has made fundamental changes over the last 25 years to strengthen its academic offering and diversify its student body. Located in the heart of Dallas, SMU offers a wide array of academic options across its seven degree-granting schools – and its alumni reflect that diversity in their broad success. This is a school with a very good reputation, whose alumni actually outperform that reputation in the marketplace – particularly in Financial Success.

SMU grads experience significant Financial Success – ranked 30th in the percent of grads who are millionaires (SMU's highest ranking) and 38th in overall Financial Success. However, the College Experience and Overall Assessment attributes are more moderate, and overall graduate happiness ranks 53rd.

Notable Alumni

KC Chiefs owner Lamar Hunt; Colts owner Jim Irsay; former First Lady Laura Bush; billionaire banker Gerald Ford; former Enron CEO Jeff Skilling; and former George W. Bush chief counsel Harriet Miers.

The Alumni Factor Rankings Summary

Attribute	University Rank	Overall Rank
College Experience	**82**	**154**
Intellectual Development	81	153
Social Development	56	117
Spiritual Development	47	113
Friendship Development	83	153
Preparation for Career Success	78	146
Immediate Job Opportunities	78	127
Overall Assessment	**91**	**160**
Would Personally Choose Again	78	137
Would Recommend to Student	85	154
Value for the Money	90	159
Financial Success	**38**	**68**
Income per Household	45	72
% Households with Income >$150K	47	81
Household Net Worth	39	69
% Households Net Worth >$1MM	30	58
Overall Happiness	**53**	**97**
Alumni Giving	**41**	**99**
Graduation Rate	**72**	**136**
Overall Rank	**75**	**143**

Other Key Alumni Outcomes

3.0% Are college professors
6.5% Teach at any level
45.1% Have post-graduate degrees
50.0% Live in dual-income homes
89.4% Are currently employed

See pages 134–135 for detailed explanations and definitions.

Alumni Activities During College

41.5% Community Service
29.3% Intramural Sports
27.3% Internships
11.3% Media Programs
11.3% Music Programs
41.5% Part-Time Jobs

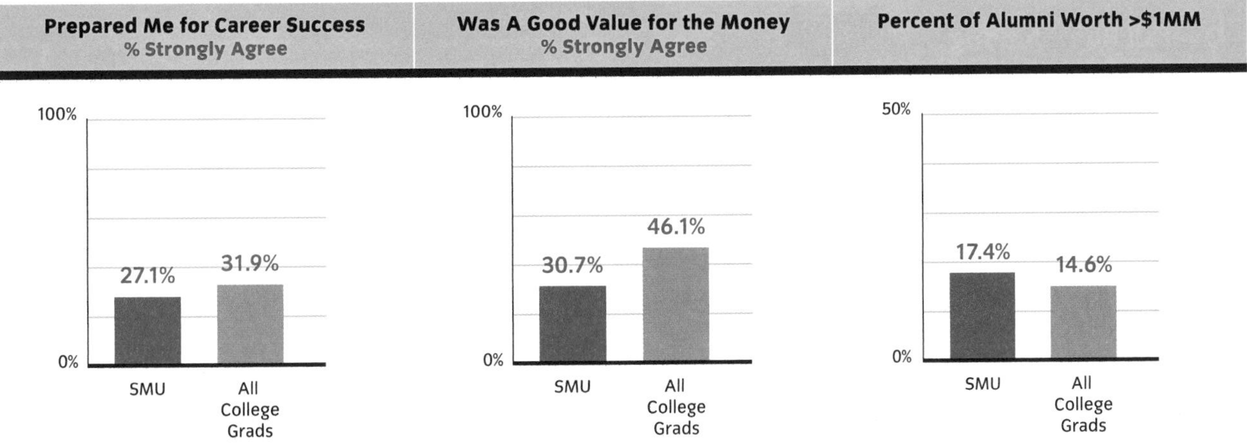

Alumni Employment

% Other 14.2%
% Independent/ Entrepreneur 24.1%
% Any Level Teaching 6.5%
% With Govt. 5.5%
% With Small Org. 16.7%
% With Medium Org. 11.3%
% With Large Org. 21.7%

Income Distribution of Graduates

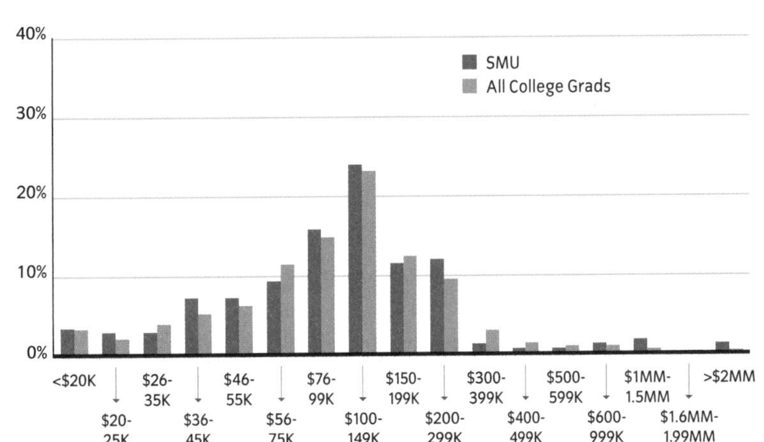

Current Selectivity & Demand Analysis for Southern Methodist University

Attribute	% Accepted	% Accepted Who Enroll	Freshman Retention Rate	Graduation Rate	Demand Index	Reputation Index
Score	55.0%	24.0%	89.0%	74.0%	7.48	0.44
Rank	113	138	124	136	108	138

Where are the Graduates of Southern Methodist University on the Political Spectrum?

Very Liberal	Liberal	Somewhat Liberal	Somewhat Conservative	Conservative	Very Conservative

See pages 134–135 for detailed explanations and definitions.

Spelman College

Location: Atlanta, GA
Campus Setting: City: Large
Total Expenses: $40,540
Estimated Average Discount: $12,892 (32%)
Estimated Net Price: $27,648

Type of Institution: Liberal Arts College
Number of Undergraduates: 2,177
SAT Score: Reading: 480–560, Math: 460–550
Student/Faculty Ratio: 10 to 1
Transfer Out Rate: Not Reported

Rank Among 53 Liberal Arts Colleges	**28**
Overall Rank Among 177 *Alumni Factor* Schools	**57**

Overview

When you are a graduate of the nation's oldest and most prestigious historically Black college for women, extraordinary accomplishments are expected of you. Spelman seeks to empower Black women by fully developing their intellectual, ethical and leadership potential. By all indications, it is doing so quite well. Ranked an impressive 3rd in the College Experience and 1st among liberal arts colleges in the Overall Assessment (including 1st in Would Recommend to Student), the Spelman experience is obviously life-altering. Spelman exists to fully develop not only the wealthy or the brilliant, but also all those who are seriously committed to learning and to ethically serving others and their communities.

Spelman measures a graduate's success not in financial terms, but by their ability to lead positive social change. When compared to Black Ivy League female grads, Spelman grads are happier; two times as likely to be a teacher; rank Spelman higher on EVERY Experience and Overall Assessment attribute we measure and get post-grad degrees at about the same rate. They are less likely to be high income or high net worth, but only slightly so.

Notable Alumni

Pulitzer Prize winner Alice Walker; Marian Wright Edelman; Harvard Dean Evelynn Hammonds; Audrey Manley; Marcelite Harris and actress Keshia Knight Pulliam.

The Alumni Factor Rankings Summary

Attribute	Liberal Arts Rank	Overall Rank
College Experience	**3**	**3**
Intellectual Development	32	42
Social Development	3	3
Spiritual Development	2	4
Friendship Development	4	4
Preparation for Career Success	4	5
Immediate Job Opportunities	4	16
Overall Assessment	**1**	**2**
Would Personally Choose Again	5	10
Would Recommend to Student	1	1
Value for the Money	4	12
Financial Success	**53**	**176**
Income per Household	51	172
% Households with Income >$150K	48	158
Household Net Worth	53	177
% Households Net Worth >$1MM	53	176
Overall Happiness	**44**	**155**
Alumni Giving	**29**	**32**
Graduation Rate	**52**	**138**
Overall Rank	**28**	**57**

Other Key Alumni Outcomes

8.6%	Are college professors
24.2%	Teach at any level
64.0%	Have post-graduate degrees
40.2%	Live in dual-income homes
95.0%	Are currently employed

See pages 134–135 for detailed explanations and definitions.

Alumni Activities During College

53.5% Community Service
8.6% Intramural Sports
34.6% Internships
11.3% Media Programs
27.0% Music Programs
53.5% Part-Time Jobs

Prepared Me for Career Success % Strongly Agree	Was A Good Value for the Money % Strongly Agree	Percent of Alumni Worth >$1MM
Spelman 57.6%; All College Grads 31.9%	Spelman 63.2%; All College Grads 46.1%	Spelman 2.3%; All College Grads 14.6%

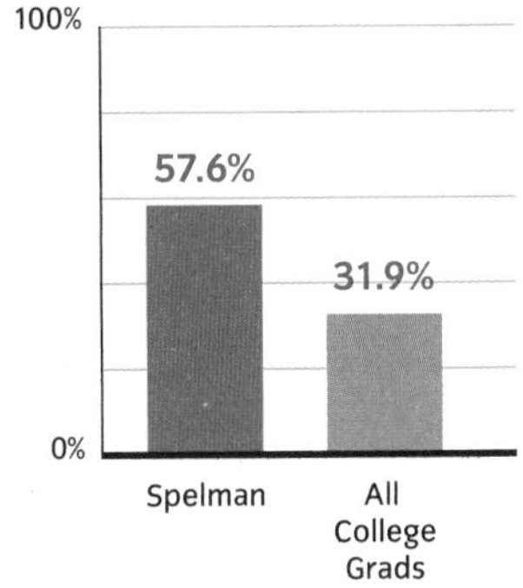

Alumni Employment

- % Independent/Entrepreneur: 8.6%
- % With Large Org.: 25.4%
- % With Medium Org.: 9.7%
- % With Small Org.: 11.4%
- % With Govt.: 14.1%
- % Any Level Teaching: 24.2%
- % Other: 6.6%

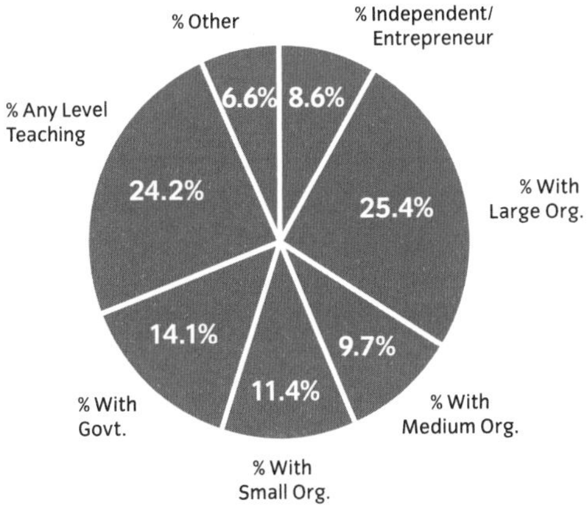

Income Distribution of Graduates

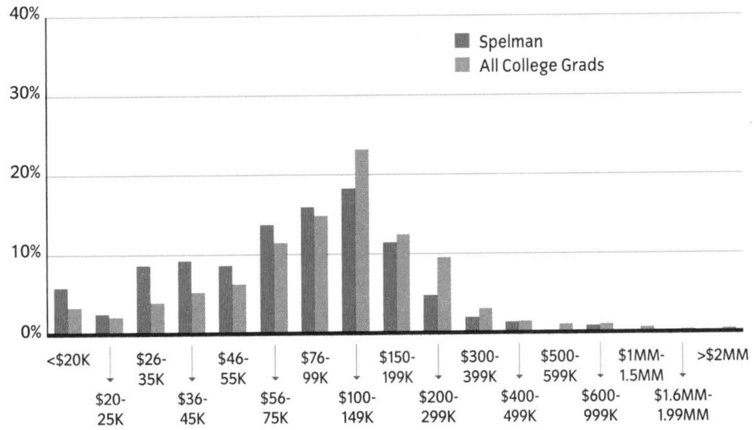

Spelman / All College Grads

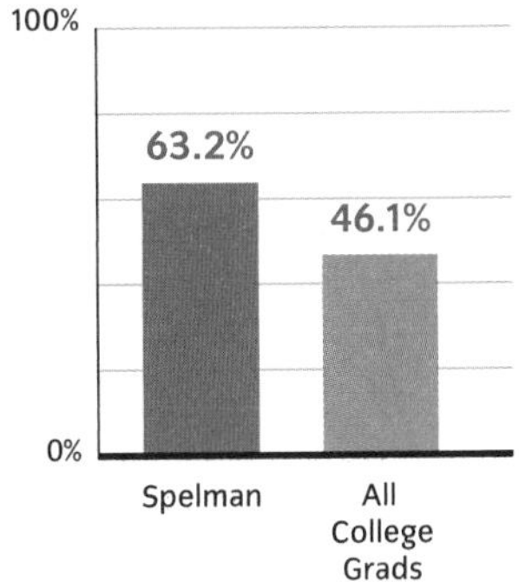

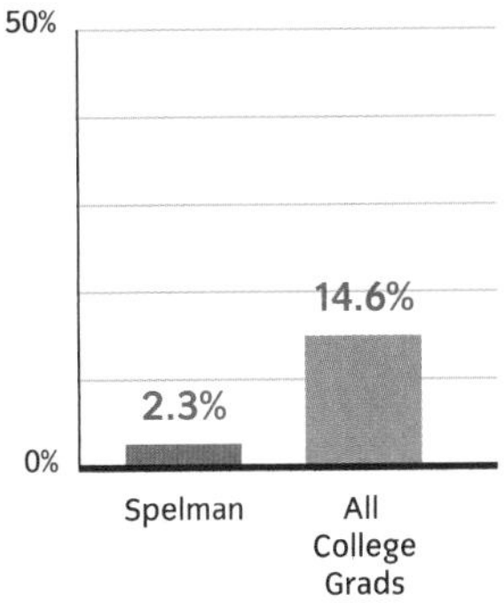

0% 10% 20% 30% 40%

<$20K, $20-25K, $26-35K, $36-45K, $46-55K, $56-75K, $76-99K, $100-149K, $150-199K, $200-299K, $300-399K, $400-499K, $500-599K, $600-999K, $1MM-1.5MM, $1.6MM-1.99MM, >$2MM

Current Selectivity & Demand Analysis for Spelman College

Attribute	% Accepted	% Accepted Who Enroll	Freshman Retention Rate	Graduation Rate	Demand Index	Reputation Index
Score	39.0%	27.0%	88.0%	73.0%	9.66	0.69
Rank	75	119	135	138	72	86

Where are the Graduates of Spelman College on the Political Spectrum?

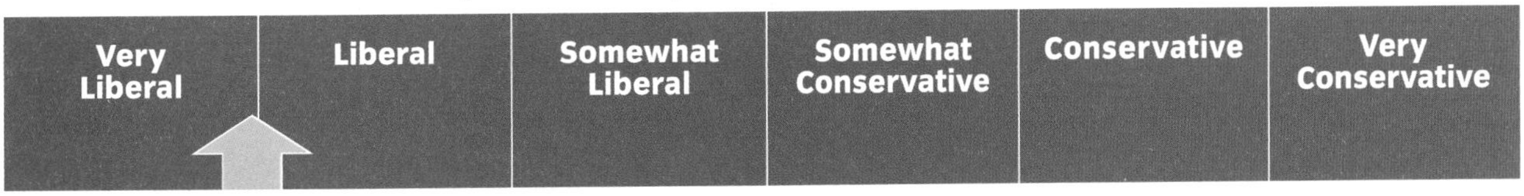

Very Liberal	Liberal	Somewhat Liberal	Somewhat Conservative	Conservative	Very Conservative

See pages 134–135 for detailed explanations and definitions.

St. Olaf College

Location: Northfield, MN
Campus Setting: Town: Distant
Total Expenses: $48,850
Estimated Average Discount: $22,574 (46%)
Estimated Net Price: $26,276

Type of Institution: Liberal Arts College
Number of Undergraduates: 3,156
SAT Score: Reading: 590–720, Math: 600–710
Student/Faculty Ratio: 12 to 1
Transfer Out Rate: Not Reported

Rank Among 53 Liberal Arts Colleges	**37**
Overall Rank Among 177 *Alumni Factor* Schools	**70**

Overview

There are three small, highly acclaimed liberal arts colleges in the Minneapolis area that compete for students, reputation and athletic glory: Carleton College (ranked 19th), Macalester College (48th) and St. Olaf College (37th). While Carleton and Macalester have been recognized on the national liberal arts scene for some time, St. Olaf is now making its way into prominence. St. Olaf grads are among the happiest in the country (7th) and thoroughly enjoyed their College Experience (11th) – ahead of Carleton and Macalester on both counts.

Even though St. Olaf grads lag Carleton and Macalester in Financial Success (51st), they were strong in Immediate Job Opportunties (18th) and in the Ultimate Outcome of Happiness & Friendships (ranked 9th versus Carleton's 10th and Macalester's 52nd). While leaning to the liberal side, St. Olaf grads are significantly less so than Macalester or Carleton grads. The school is globally known for its excellence in all things musical, and the campus is overflowing in song throughout the year.

Notable Alumni

There are a large number of accomplished alumni in all musical fields and across many other wide ranging pursuits, including Pulitzer Prize-winning financial author Gretchen Morgenson and former Minnesota governor Al Quie.

The Alumni Factor Rankings Summary

Attribute	Liberal Arts Rank	Overall Rank
College Experience	**11**	**15**
Intellectual Development	26	31
Social Development	19	30
Spiritual Development	5	11
Friendship Development	8	8
Preparation for Career Success	20	39
Immediate Job Opportunities	18	70
Overall Assessment	**30**	**76**
Would Personally Choose Again	23	56
Would Recommend to Student	32	85
Value for the Money	33	85
Financial Success	**51**	**171**
Income per Household	48	161
% Households with Income >$150K	52	173
Household Net Worth	46	150
% Households Net Worth >$1MM	52	169
Overall Happiness	**7**	**10**
Alumni Giving	**46**	**57**
Graduation Rate	**37**	**76**
Overall Rank	**37**	**70**

Other Key Alumni Outcomes

6.7% Are college professors
20.7% Teach at any level
59.3% Have post-graduate degrees
63.0% Live in dual-income homes
94.4% Are currently employed

See pages 134–135 for detailed explanations and definitions.

Alumni Activities During College

38.4% Community Service
32.9% Intramural Sports
19.5% Internships
23.8% Media Programs
60.9% Music Programs
27.4% Part-Time Jobs

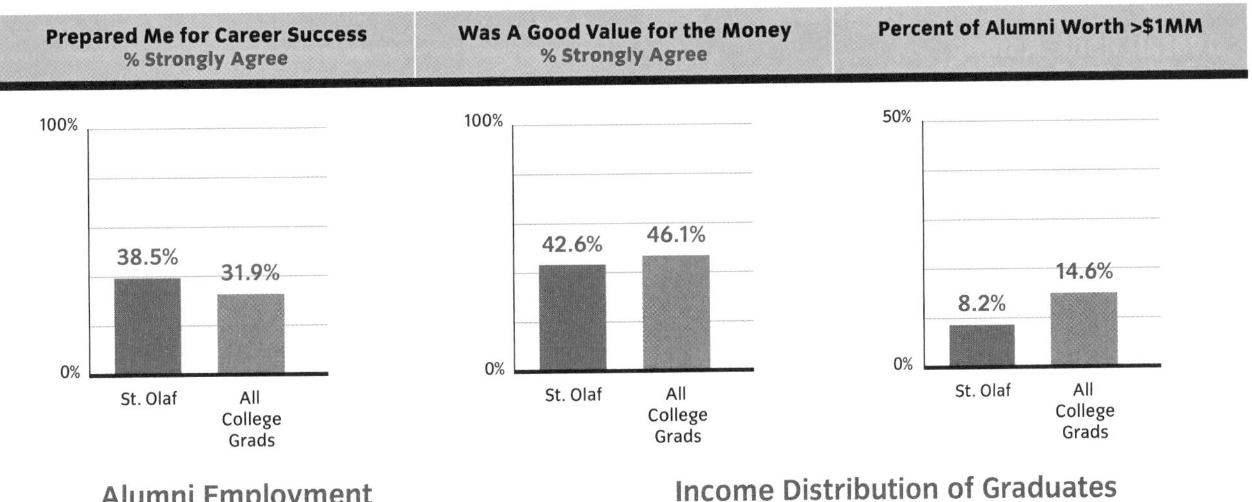

Alumni Employment

% Other 11.0%
% Independent/ Entrepreneur 19.5%
% With Large Org. 11.6%
% With Medium Org. 10.4%
% With Small Org. 18.9%
% With Govt. 7.3%
% In Farm/ Agr. 0.6%
% Any Level Teaching 20.7%

Income Distribution of Graduates

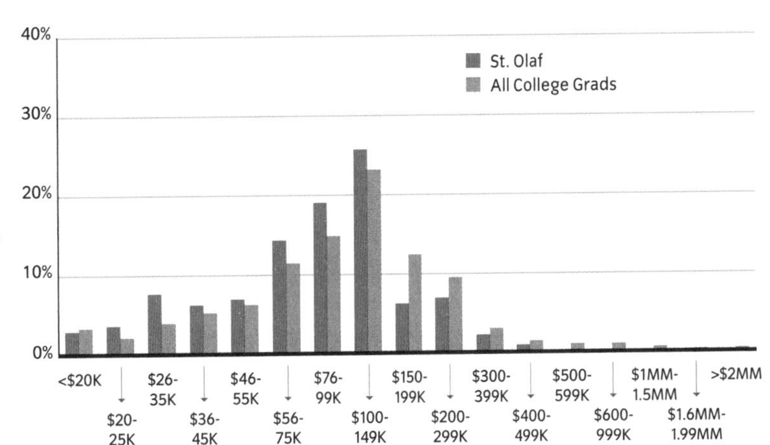

Current Selectivity & Demand Analysis for St. Olaf College

Attribute	% Accepted	% Accepted Who Enroll	Freshman Retention Rate	Graduation Rate	Demand Index	Reputation Index
Score	53.0%	33.0%	93.0%	85.0%	5.66	0.62
Rank	107	83	73	76	132	99

Where are the Graduates of St. Olaf College on the Political Spectrum?

Very Liberal	Liberal	Somewhat Liberal	Somewhat Conservative	Conservative	Very Conservative
	⇧				

See pages 134–135 for detailed explanations and definitions.

Stanford University

Location: Stanford, CA
Campus Setting: Suburb: Large
Total Expenses: $57,755
Estimated Average Discount: $36,334 (63%)
Estimated Net Price: $21,421

Type of Institution: National University
Number of Undergraduates: 6,940
SAT Score: Reading: 670–770, Math: 690–780
Student/Faculty Ratio: 10 to 1
Transfer Out Rate: Not Reported

Rank Among 104 National Universities	**5**
Overall Rank Among 177 *Alumni Factor* Schools	**10**

Overview

Broadly considered to be one of the world's finest universities, Stanford produces alumni results that actually exceed the school's sterling reputation. Stanford has all of the brains and power of the East Coast Ivy League schools, but sports West Coast cool that distinguishes it from the often intensely uptight Ivy League scene. In our outcomes-based assessment, Stanford outperforms all but Yale and Princeton within the Ivy League. With stellar Financial Success (ranked 4th among national universities) and amazing performance in the Ultimate Outcomes (ranked 5th), it is clear that Stanford grads perform exceptionally well in all walks of life. They can boast (although they likely wouldn't) of the 9th highest SAT scores; an athletic program that stands proudly in concert with their academic credentials; and a reputation for aggressive humility.

Notable Alumni

Luminaries such as Herbert Hoover; Derek Bok, 25th Harvard president; Rick Levin, 22nd and current President of Yale; Nobel Prize winner Eric Cornell; Sigourney Weaver; astronaut Sally Ride and, impressively, the following business leaders: Craig Barrett, Richard Fairbank, Brian Farrell, Carly Fiorina, Steve Fossett, Reid Hoffman, Victor Li, Robert Mondavi, David Packard, Peter Thiel and Jerry Yang.

The Alumni Factor Rankings Summary

Attribute	University Rank	Overall Rank
College Experience	**16**	**47**
Intellectual Development	19	64
Social Development	25	66
Spiritual Development	21	78
Friendship Development	15	57
Preparation for Career Success	25	63
Immediate Job Opportunities	19	26
Overall Assessment	**15**	**25**
Would Personally Choose Again	12	31
Would Recommend to Student	9	14
Value for the Money	30	57
Financial Success	**4**	**10**
Income per Household	10	20
% Households with Income >$150K	6	14
Household Net Worth	2	7
% Households Net Worth >$1MM	4	8
Overall Happiness	**44**	**82**
Alumni Giving	**6**	**36**
Graduation Rate	**7**	**7**
Overall Rank	**5**	**10**

Other Key Alumni Outcomes

6.2% Are college professors
9.9% Teach at any level
66.5% Have post-graduate degrees
48.5% Live in dual-income homes
92.6% Are currently employed

See pages 134–135 for detailed explanations and definitions.

Alumni Activities During College

34.0% Community Service
25.8% Intramural Sports
22.5% Internships
17.6% Media Programs
18.9% Music Programs
33.6% Part-Time Jobs

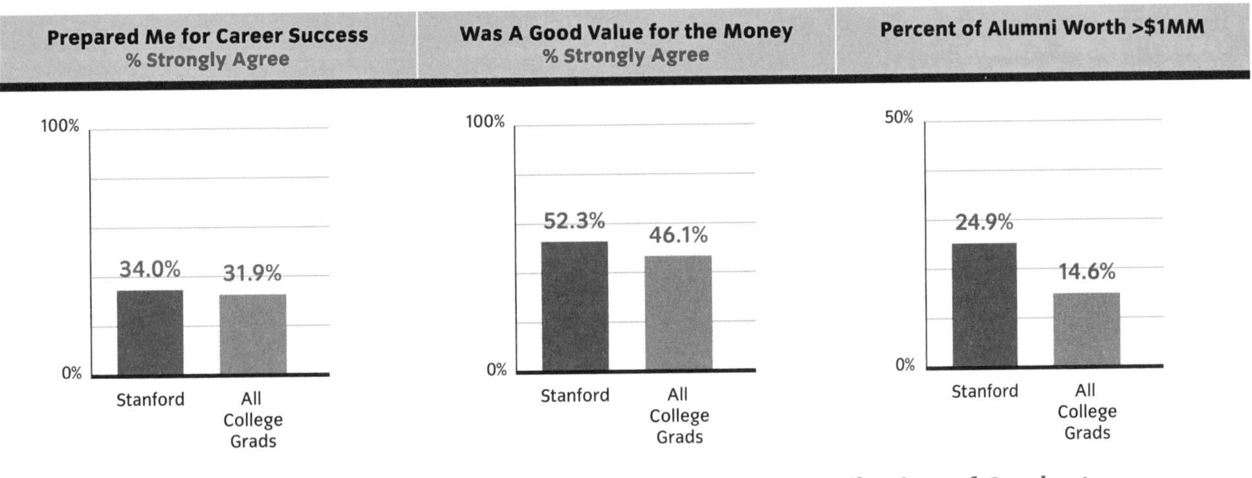

Alumni Employment

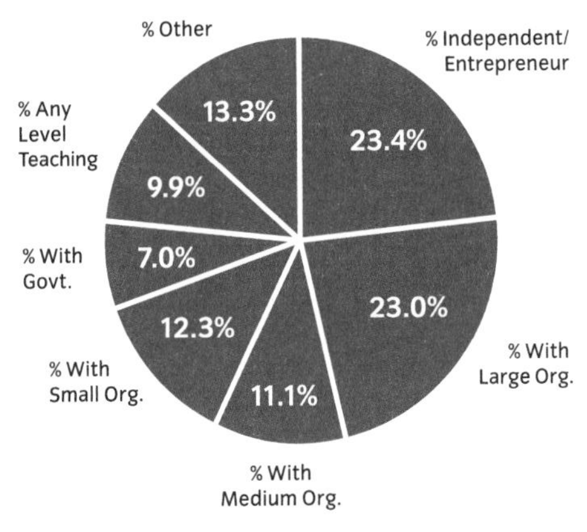

Income Distribution of Graduates

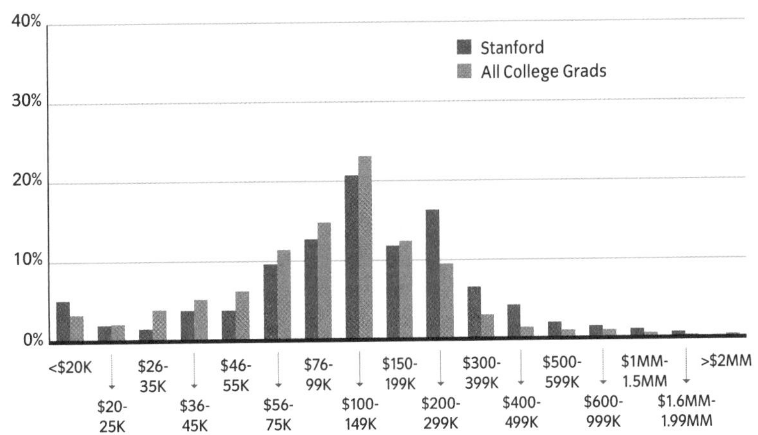

Current Selectivity & Demand Analysis for Stanford University

Attribute	% Accepted	% Accepted Who Enroll	Freshman Retention Rate	Graduation Rate	Demand Index	Reputation Index
Score	7.0%	70.0%	98.0%	95.0%	20.16	10.00
Rank	2	6	4	7	6	3

Where are the Graduates of Stanford University on the Political Spectrum?

Very Liberal	Liberal	Somewhat Liberal	Somewhat Conservative	Conservative	Very Conservative

See pages 134–135 for detailed explanations and definitions.

Swarthmore College

Location: Swarthmore, PA
Campus Setting: Suburb: Large
Total Expenses: $55,895
Estimated Average Discount: $35,468 (63%)
Estimated Net Price: $20,427

Type of Institution: Liberal Arts College
Number of Undergraduates: 1,524
SAT Score: Reading: 680–770, Math: 670–760
Student/Faculty Ratio: 8 to 1
Transfer Out Rate: Not Reported

Rank Among 53 Liberal Arts Colleges	**14**
Overall Rank Among 177 *Alumni Factor* Schools	**21**

Overview

Since 1864, on a serenely beautiful campus just southwest of Philadelphia, a relatively small number of undergraduates have gone through the uniquely transformational Swarthmore experience. Armed with blistering intellects (8th in SAT scores) and supported by superbly caring professors (ranked 4th in Intellectual Development), these graduates achieve results that no other liberal arts college, and only two other colleges in the country (Harvard and Yale), are able to achieve. Swarthmore graduates are simultaneously among the Top 25 in Financial Success (ranked 9th overall and 6th among liberal arts colleges) and the 30 most liberal colleges in the country in social and political views (ranked 6th most liberal). Not one of the other 23 liberal arts colleges or the other six national universities on the 30 most liberal list can make that claim. With Ultimate Outcomes ranked 4th (Top 20 in all Ultimate Outcomes), Swarthmore is a Top 15 liberal arts school and a Top 25 overall school for *The Alumni Factor*. The "Little Ivy" moniker is well-deserved.

Notable Alumni

T. Rowe Price founder Thomas Rowe Price; billionaire KKR founder Jerome Kohlberg; the former and 7th president of Stanford Richard Wall Lyman; and astronomy pioneer Nancy Roman.

The Alumni Factor Rankings Summary

Attribute	Liberal Arts Rank	Overall Rank
College Experience	**28**	**51**
Intellectual Development	4	4
Social Development	49	138
Spiritual Development	13	33
Friendship Development	14	14
Preparation for Career Success	24	54
Immediate Job Opportunities	30	124
Overall Assessment	**28**	**67**
Would Personally Choose Again	30	83
Would Recommend to Student	30	82
Value for the Money	18	44
Financial Success	**6**	**9**
Income per Household	5	9
% Households with Income >$150K	2	3
Household Net Worth	10	19
% Households Net Worth >$1MM	7	14
Overall Happiness	**29**	**76**
Alumni Giving	**13**	**15**
Graduation Rate	**5**	**16**
Overall Rank	**14**	**21**

Other Key Alumni Outcomes

12.4% Are college professors
18.6% Teach at any level
73.8% Have post-graduate degrees
55.1% Live in dual-income homes
94.3% Are currently employed

See pages 134–135 for detailed explanations and definitions.

Alumni Activities During College

33.1% Community Service
26.9% Intramural Sports
15.0% Internships
43.2% Media Programs
43.2% Music Programs
20.6% Part-Time Jobs

Prepared Me for Career Success % Strongly Agree	Was A Good Value for the Money % Strongly Agree	Percent of Alumni Worth >$1MM
Swarthmore 34.4%	Swarthmore 51.0%	Swarthmore 23.2%
All College Grads 31.9%	All College Grads 46.1%	All College Grads 14.6%

Alumni Employment

% Other 15.6%
% Independent/ Entrepreneur 20.5%
% With Large Org. 14.9%
% With Medium Org. 10.6%
% With Small Org. 12.4%
% With Govt. 6.8%
% In Farm/ Agr. 0.6%
% Any Level Teaching 18.6%

Income Distribution of Graduates

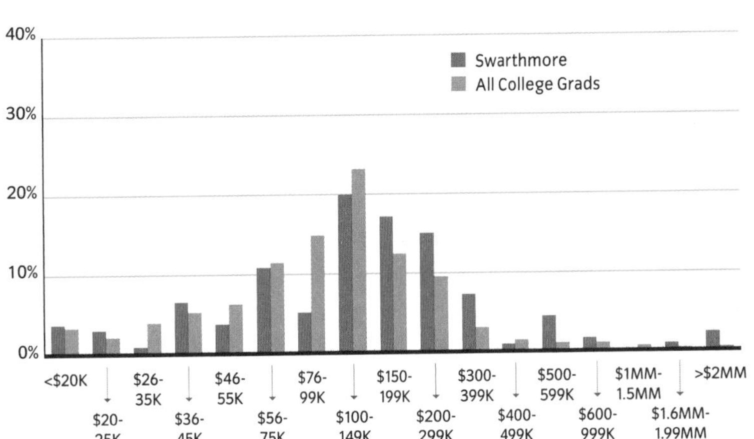

Current Selectivity & Demand Analysis for Swarthmore College

Attribute	% Accepted	% Accepted Who Enroll	Freshman Retention Rate	Graduation Rate	Demand Index	Reputation Index
Score	15.0%	39.0%	94.0%	93.0%	16.96	2.60
Rank	17	46	58	16	12	20

Where are the Graduates of Swarthmore College on the Political Spectrum?

Very Liberal	Liberal	Somewhat Liberal	Somewhat Conservative	Conservative	Very Conservative

See pages 134–135 for detailed explanations and definitions.

Syracuse University

Location: Syracuse, NY
Campus Setting: City: Midsize
Total Expenses: $53,790
Estimated Average Discount: $25,796 (48%)
Estimated Net Price: $27,994

Type of Institution: National University
Number of Undergraduates: 14,201
SAT Score: Reading: 510–620, Math: 540–650
Student/Faculty Ratio: 16 to 1
Transfer Out Rate: Not Reported

Rank Among 104 National Universities	**76**
Overall Rank Among 177 *Alumni Factor* Schools	**144**

Overview

A large private university in upstate NY, within a short drive of the Finger Lakes and the Adirondacks, Syracuse's goal is to put "scholarship into action" – and it certainly does with SU graduates. However, Syracuse's consistent excellence is often overlooked since a number of smaller, elite liberal arts schools are all within a short drive (Colgate, Amherst, Williams, Hamilton, Cornell, Skidmore and Vassar). Ranked 43rd in the country in millionaire households (75th among all colleges and universities) and 48th in Immediate Job Opportunities, Syracuse is well known for the strength of its communications, architecture and social sciences departments. Of course, it also has nationally acclaimed athletics, including one of the finest lacrosse programs in the country.

SU's strongest Ultimate Outcome is Friendships & Intellectual Capability (ranked 26th), and it ranks 25th in the Social Development of its graduates. Everyone at SU loves the Orangemen and that drives alumni loyalty (83rd in Alumni Giving).

Notable Alumni

Many of SU's notable alumni define broadcasting excellence, such as Ted Koppel, Bob Costas, Sean McDonough, Dick Clark, Vanessa Williams, Washington Post editor Harry Rosenfeld and television executive Fred Silverman. In addition, Syracuse can boast of legendary athletes Larry Csonka, Jim Brown, Ernie Davis, Derrick Coleman, Floyd Little, Donovan McNabb and Art Monk; musician Lou Reed; and screenwriter Aaron Sorkin.

The Alumni Factor Rankings Summary

Attribute	University Rank	Overall Rank
College Experience	**43**	**105**
Intellectual Development	60	128
Social Development	25	66
Spiritual Development	62	133
Friendship Development	40	103
Preparation for Career Success	42	92
Immediate Job Opportunities	48	77
Overall Assessment	**84**	**151**
Would Personally Choose Again	87	151
Would Recommend to Student	72	130
Value for the Money	85	152
Financial Success	**70**	**113**
Income per Household	81	123
% Households with Income >$150K	69	116
Household Net Worth	81	132
% Households Net Worth >$1MM	43	75
Overall Happiness	**103**	**175**
Alumni Giving	**83**	**152**
Graduation Rate	**44**	**91**
Overall Rank	**76**	**144**

Other Key Alumni Outcomes

1.4% Are college professors
7.1% Teach at any level
55.2% Have post-graduate degrees
45.8% Live in dual-income homes
89.7% Are currently employed

See pages 134–135 for detailed explanations and definitions.

Alumni Activities During College

28.3% Community Service
22.8% Intramural Sports
35.2% Internships
38.8% Media Programs
11.8% Music Programs
40.0% Part-Time Jobs

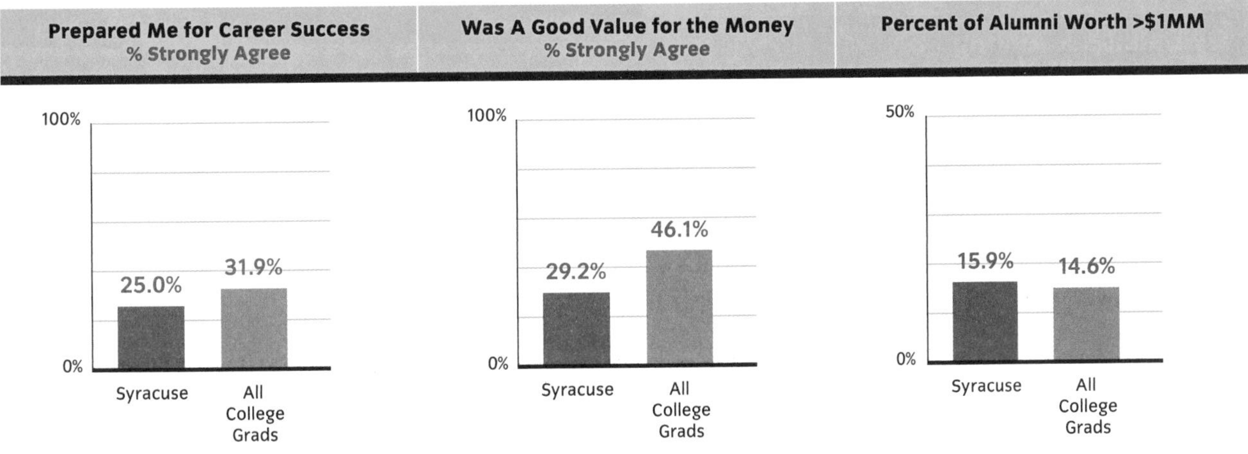

Alumni Employment

Category	Percent
% Independent/ Entrepreneur	17.1%
% With Large Org.	23.6%
% With Medium Org.	15.7%
% With Small Org.	17.1%
% With Govt.	4.9%
% Any Level Teaching	7.1%
% Other	14.5%

Income Distribution of Graduates

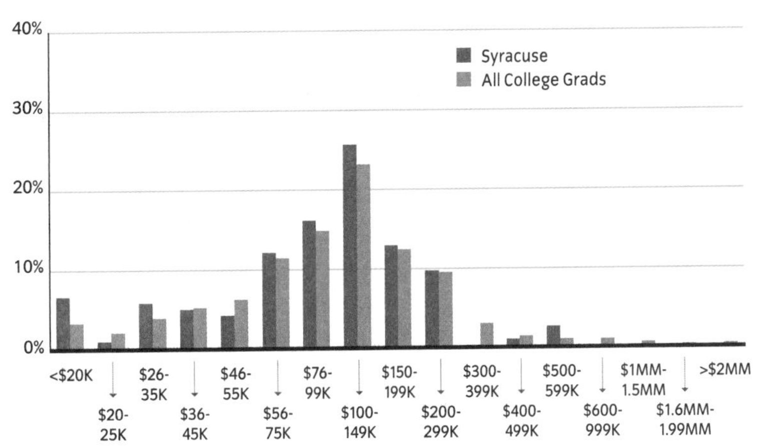

Current Selectivity & Demand Analysis for Syracuse University

Attribute	% Accepted	% Accepted Who Enroll	Freshman Retention Rate	Graduation Rate	Demand Index	Reputation Index
Score	49.0%	27.0%	91.0%	82.0%	7.59	0.55
Rank	103	119	102	91	106	112

Where are the Graduates of Syracuse University on the Political Spectrum?

Very Liberal	Liberal	Somewhat Liberal	Somewhat Conservative	Conservative	Very Conservative
	↑				

See pages 134–135 for detailed explanations and definitions.

Texas A&M University

Location: College Station, TX
Campus Setting: City: Small
Total Expenses: $20,723
Estimated Average Discount: $9,173 (44%)
Estimated Net Price: $11,550

Type of Institution: National University
Number of Undergraduates: 39,148
SAT Score: Reading: 530–650, Math: 570–670
Student/Faculty Ratio: 20 to 1
Transfer Out Rate: 14%

Rank Among 104 National Universities	**28**
Overall Rank Among 177 *Alumni Factor* Schools	**65**

Overview

Established in 1876 as the state's first public university, Texas A&M is a true research university, exhibiting excellence in engineering, the physical and biological sciences and biomedical research. While not as famous as its Austin competitor, Texas A&M more than holds its own in a faceoff with UT. They are distinctly different schools with unique cultures. Relative to all colleges, both schools produce conservative alumni, with Texas A&M further to the right than UT. This reflects the general trend of engineering and science grads leaning more conservatively than liberal arts grads.

From a College Experience standpoint, TAMU wins hands-down, with a 23rd ranking (8th among national universities) versus UT's 101st ranking. In fact, TAMU ranks higher than UT in every element of the College Experience. Both are excellent in the Overall Assessment, with the slight edge going to UT (13th versus TAMU's 15th). From a Financial Success stand-point, UT ranks higher in Income, and TAMU ranks higher in net worth, but they are quite similar overall. TAMU has a slight edge in the Ultimate Outcomes (ranked 63rd), but they are identical in Graduation Rates.

Notable Alumni

Texas Governor Rick Perry; singer Lyle Lovett; Emmy Award winners Patricia Gras and Melinda Murphy; Actor Rip Torn; and radio personality Neal Boortz.

The Alumni Factor Rankings Summary

Attribute	University Rank	Overall Rank
College Experience	**8**	**23**
Intellectual Development	37	93
Social Development	7	27
Spiritual Development	12	57
Friendship Development	13	53
Preparation for Career Success	5	16
Immediate Job Opportunities	5	9
Overall Assessment	**10**	**15**
Would Personally Choose Again	28	59
Would Recommend to Student	1	3
Value for the Money	9	16
Financial Success	**79**	**128**
Income per Household	59	94
% Households with Income >$150K	87	143
Household Net Worth	63	108
% Households Net Worth >$1MM	91	154
Overall Happiness	**74**	**125**
Alumni Giving	**62**	**125**
Graduation Rate	**50**	**106**
Overall Rank	**28**	**65**

Other Key Alumni Outcomes

3.8% Are college professors
10.8% Teach at any level
44.4% Have post-graduate degrees
50.6% Live in dual-income homes
90.3% Are currently employed

See pages 134–135 for detailed explanations and definitions.

Alumni Activities During College

37.1% Community Service
41.9% Intramural Sports
17.2% Internships
8.2% Media Programs
7.5% Music Programs
47.3% Part-Time Jobs

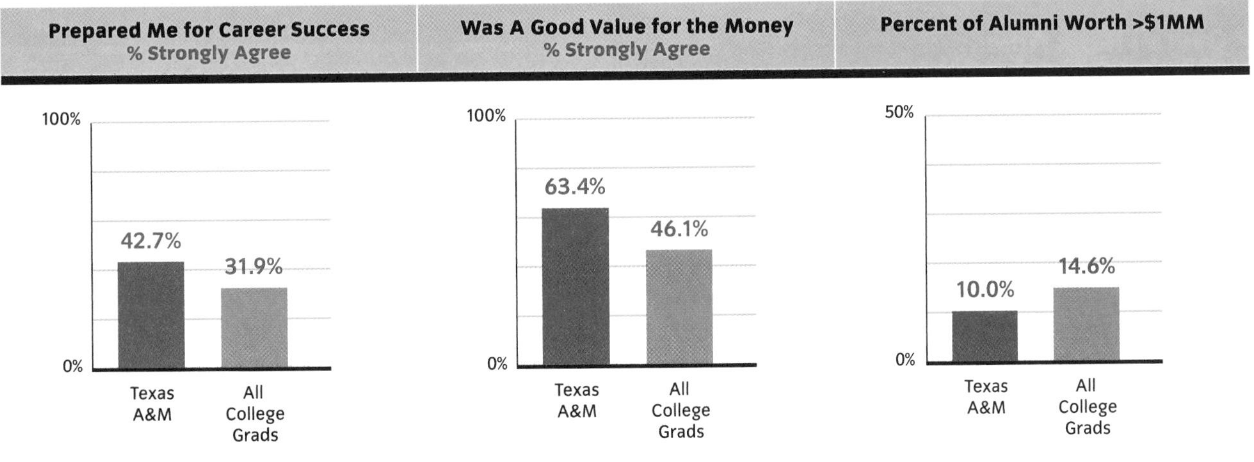

Alumni Employment

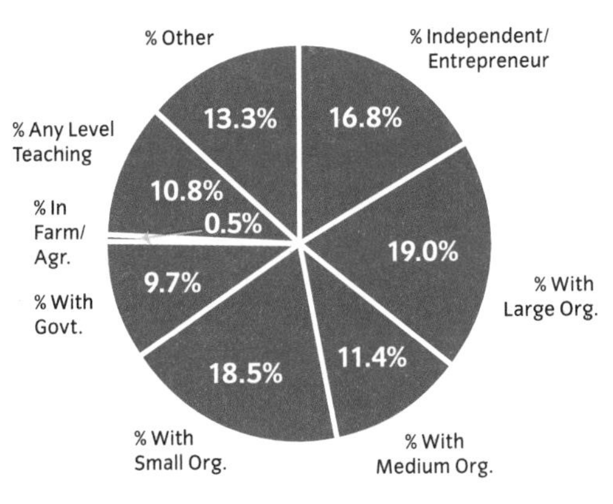

Income Distribution of Graduates

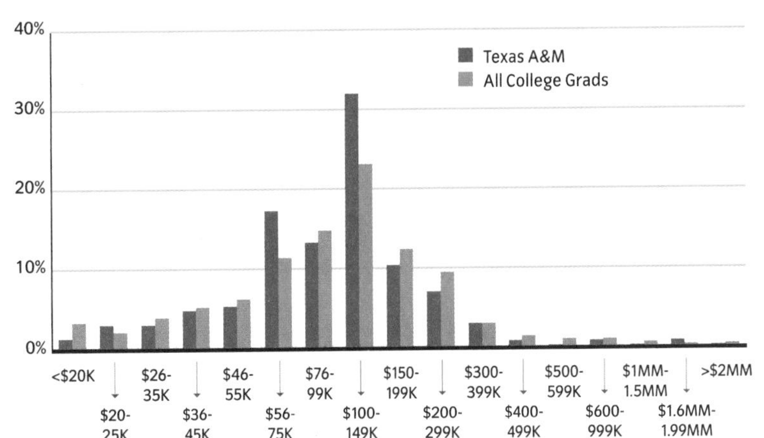

Current Selectivity & Demand Analysis for Texas A&M University

Attribute	% Accepted	% Accepted Who Enroll	Freshman Retention Rate	Graduation Rate	Demand Index	Reputation Index
Score	63.0%	50.0%	91.0%	80.0%	3.15	0.79
Rank	135	19	102	106	169	76

Where are the Graduates of Texas A&M University on the Political Spectrum?

Very Liberal	Liberal	Somewhat Liberal	Somewhat Conservative	Conservative	Very Conservative
					⇧

See pages 134–135 for detailed explanations and definitions.

Trinity College

Location: Hartford, CT
Campus Setting: City: Midsize
Total Expenses: $57,575
Estimated Average Discount: $39,158 (68%)
Estimated Net Price: $18,417

Type of Institution: Liberal Arts College
Number of Undergraduates: 2,292
SAT Score: Reading: 580–680, Math: 600–690
Student/Faculty Ratio: 10 to 1
Transfer Out Rate: 7%

Rank Among 53 Liberal Arts Colleges	**36**
Overall Rank Among 177 *Alumni Factor* Schools	**68**

Overview

Sometimes it pays to be number two. Trinity College is the second oldest college in Connecticut (behind Yale); ranked second among Connecticut liberal arts colleges (behind Wesleyan); and has a reputation of being second choice, or backup school, to Yale for many talented and striving individuals. All of that competitive rivalry appears to drive Trinity grads to astonishing Financial Success (ranked 4th among all schools and 3rd among liberal arts colleges) and a level of professional accomplishment that any other school would covet. A little Yale envy can go a long way.

Trinity grads show gratitude to their alma mater with an Alumni Giving percentage that is in the Top 10 in the nation. That gratitude, however, is not driven by particularly high marks in Overall Assessment (50th) or College Experience (50th). This creates an inexplicable dissonance when analyzing this school. For alumni to rank Intellectual Development 53rd and then go on to such post-graduate financial accomplishment likely means that Trinity grads are simply tough customers with high expectations.

Notable Alumni

Pulitzer Prize winners George Will and Charles McLean Andrews; Governors Jane Swift (MA) and Thomas Meskill (CT); and many others at the top of their fields.

The Alumni Factor Rankings Summary

Attribute	Liberal Arts Rank	Overall Rank
College Experience	**50**	**119**
Intellectual Development	53	133
Social Development	40	88
Spiritual Development	42	79
Friendship Development	53	123
Preparation for Career Success	47	126
Immediate Job Opportunities	22	93
Overall Assessment	**50**	**157**
Would Personally Choose Again	47	153
Would Recommend to Student	52	165
Value for the Money	42	128
Financial Success	**3**	**4**
Income per Household	3	5
% Households with Income >$150K	8	15
Household Net Worth	4	6
% Households Net Worth >$1MM	3	4
Overall Happiness	**30**	**81**
Alumni Giving	**8**	**9**
Graduation Rate	**32**	**67**
Overall Rank	**36**	**68**

Other Key Alumni Outcomes

2.5% Are college professors
7.5% Teach at any level
52.9% Have post-graduate degrees
49.6% Live in dual-income homes
87.4% Are currently employed

See pages 134–135 for detailed explanations and definitions.

Alumni Activities During College

38.8% Community Service
30.6% Intramural Sports
33.1% Internships
19.0% Media Programs
18.2% Music Programs
31.4% Part-Time Jobs

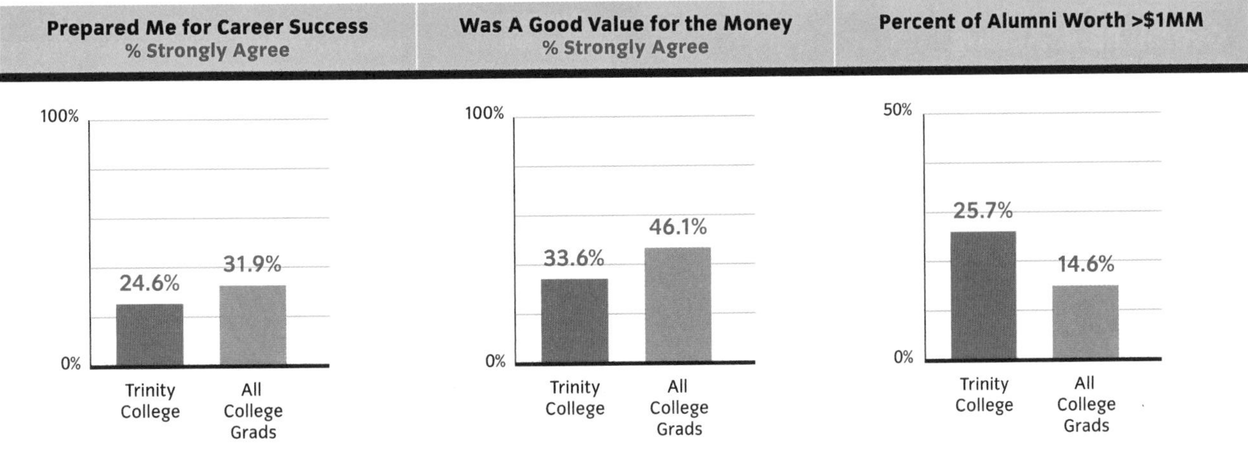

Alumni Employment

% Other 16.3%
% Independent/ Entrepreneur 19.0%
% With Large Org. 20.7%
% With Medium Org. 14.9%
% With Small Org. 17.4%
% With Govt. 4.2%
% Any Level Teaching 7.5%

Income Distribution of Graduates

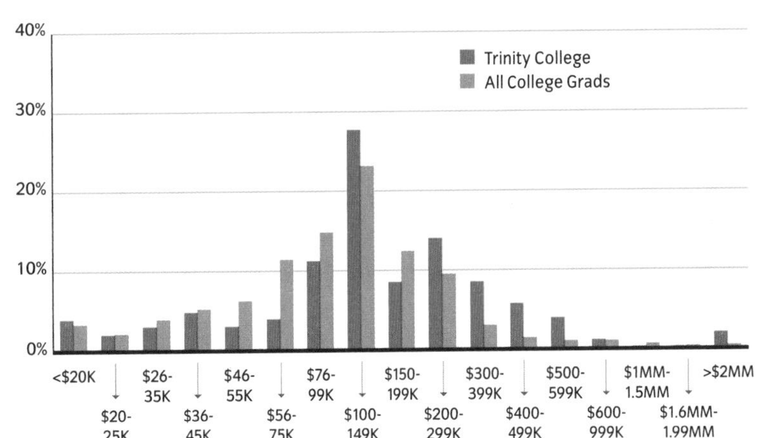

Current Selectivity & Demand Analysis for Trinity College

Attribute	% Accepted	% Accepted Who Enroll	Freshman Retention Rate	Graduation Rate	Demand Index	Reputation Index
Score	30.0%	28.0%	92.0%	86.0%	11.81	0.93
Rank	51	117	86	67	47	67

Where are the Graduates of Trinity College on the Political Spectrum?

Very Liberal	Liberal	Somewhat Liberal	Somewhat Conservative	Conservative	Very Conservative
	⇧				

See pages 134–135 for detailed explanations and definitions.

Trinity University

Location: San Antonio, TX
Campus Setting: City: Large
Total Expenses: $44,422
Estimated Average Discount: $19,580 (44%)
Estimated Net Price: $24,842

Type of Institution: Regional University
Number of Undergraduates: 2,296
SAT Score: Reading: 570–680, Math: 590–680
Student/Faculty Ratio: 9 to 1
Transfer Out Rate: Not Reported

Rank Among 20 Regional Universities	**12**
Overall Rank Among 177 *Alumni Factor* Schools	**109**

Overview

With a positive view of their College Experience and the opportunities it provided them, Trinity University graduates are happy and content in their lives. Trinity alumni Would Personally Choose It Again (ranked 38th) and Would Recommend It to Student (45th), driving the overall rank of 107th and 12th among the 20 regional universities in our study. While the lower Financial Success ranking (175th) is expected from a selective, Texas-based regional college competing with the finest colleges in the country, Trinity grads are hard working (24th in employment rate) and prepared for a wide variety of careers – from engineering and operations to journalism and teaching. Trinity also has a very strong tennis program that has sent many players on the pro tour.

Trinity's strongest Ultimate Outcome is in Happiness & Friendships (58th) – a clear indication of the inclusive, friendly environment on campus and the type of student drawn to this well-endowed Texas institution. Trinity grads give high marks for their Intellectual Development (64th), and many of them pursue post-graduate degrees (65th).

Notable Alumni

Actress and designer Jaclyn Smith; co-owner of the Sacramento Kings Gavin Maloof; and Crystal Bridges Museum of American Art founder Alice Walton.

The Alumni Factor Rankings Summary

Attribute	Overall Rank
College Experience	**50**
Intellectual Development	64
Social Development	49
Spiritual Development	40
Friendship Development	64
Preparation for Career Success	63
Immediate Job Opportunities	84
Overall Assessment	**58**
Would Personally Choose Again	38
Would Recommend to Student	45
Value for the Money	94
Financial Success	**175**
Income per Household	166
% Households with Income >$150K	170
Household Net Worth	160
% Households Net Worth >$1MM	174
Overall Happiness	**54**
Alumni Giving	**99**
Graduation Rate	**123**
Overall Rank	**109**

Other Key Alumni Outcomes

7.5%	Are college professors
16.6%	Teach at any level
58.6%	Have post-graduate degrees
43.1%	Live in dual-income homes
95.4%	Are currently employed

See pages 134–135 for detailed explanations and definitions.

Alumni Activities During College

42.1% Community Service
45.9% Intramural Sports
23.3% Internships
25.5% Media Programs
21.8% Music Programs
35.3% Part-Time Jobs

Prepared Me for Career Success % Strongly Agree	Was A Good Value for the Money % Strongly Agree	Percent of Alumni Worth >$1MM
Trinity University: 29.5%	Trinity University: 40.2%	Trinity University: 6.4%
All College Grads: 31.9%	All College Grads: 46.1%	All College Grads: 14.6%

Alumni Employment

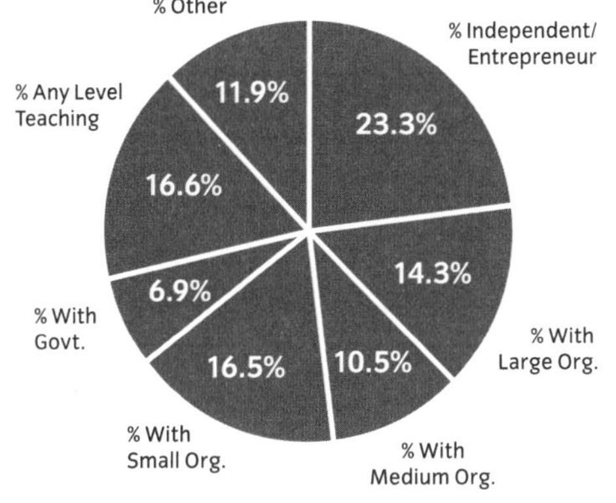

Income Distribution of Graduates

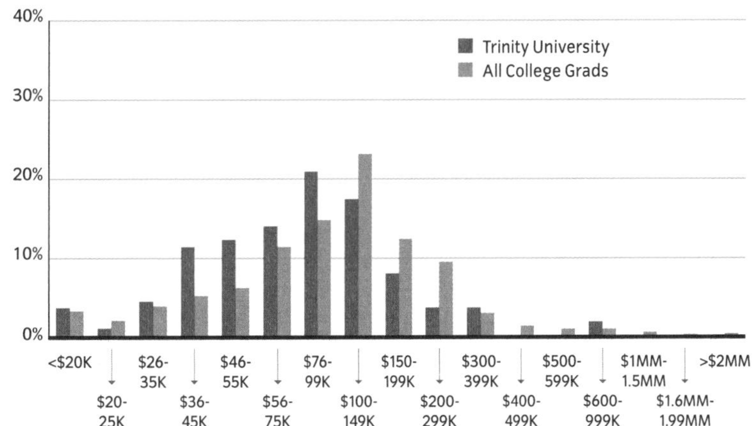

Current Selectivity & Demand Analysis for Trinity University

Attribute	% Accepted	% Accepted Who Enroll	Freshman Retention Rate	Graduation Rate	Demand Index	Reputation Index
Score	61.0%	23.0%	90.0%	78.0%	7.09	0.38
Rank	130	144	113	123	113	151

Where are the Graduates of Trinity University on the Political Spectrum?

Very Liberal	Liberal	Somewhat Liberal	Somewhat Conservative	Conservative	Very Conservative

See pages 134–135 for detailed explanations and definitions.

Tufts University

Location: Medford, MA
Campus Setting: Suburb: Large
Total Expenses: $56,600
Estimated Average Discount: $30,326 (54%)
Estimated Net Price: $26,274

Type of Institution: National University
Number of Undergraduates: 5,224
SAT Score: Reading: 680–740, Math: 680–760
Student/Faculty Ratio: 9 to 1
Transfer Out Rate: 5%

Rank Among 104 National Universities	**50**
Overall Rank Among 177 *Alumni Factor* Schools	**111**

Overview

A highly acclaimed and selective university in a metro area (Boston) awash in similarly qualified universities, Tufts has managed to carve its own uniquely excellent niche in higher education. Like other strong schools inaccurately viewed as "safety schools" to the Ivies (an occupational hazard if you are a highly selective college in the Northeast corridor), Tufts produces a super-smart (34th in SAT scores), loyal (26th in Alumni Giving) and highly successful graduate (29th in Financial Success). Tufts alumni enjoy the winning trifecta of Intellectual Development, Financial Success and Friendship Development, as evidenced by their formidable 17th ranking in the Ultimate Outcomes.

So why do alums judge the College Experience (56th) and Overall Assessment (80th) relatively lower? These rankings, we believe, are more indicative of unusually high standards by alumni than a lackluster experience. What suppresses the ratings are career-related factors on the one hand, and a lower Value for the Money rating on the other. It seems that in the long run, Tufts alums make up for any lack of career preparation, given their Financial Success. And perhaps the relatively steep tuition comes into play in assessing value. In the ultimate loyalty test – Alumni Giving – Tufts grad are voting positively with their pocketbooks (ranked 26th). Proof that the school holds its own amid the multitude of excellent schools in the greater Boston – and national – arenas.

Notable Alumni

Pierre Omidyar, Jamie Dimon, Meredith Vieira, Jessica Biel, Michelle Kwan, Jonathan Tisch, Laura Lang (Time, Inc. CEO), Ellen Kullman (DuPont CEO) and New Mexico Governor Bill Richardson.

The Alumni Factor Rankings Summary

Attribute	University Rank	Overall Rank
College Experience	**56**	**124**
Intellectual Development	36	91
Social Development	56	117
Spiritual Development	51	118
Friendship Development	18	61
Preparation for Career Success	94	165
Immediate Job Opportunities	86	145
Overall Assessment	**80**	**145**
Would Personally Choose Again	70	125
Would Recommend to Student	66	121
Value for the Money	96	167
Financial Success	**29**	**52**
Income per Household	21	38
% Households with Income >$150K	33	57
Household Net Worth	42	75
% Households Net Worth >$1MM	35	65
Overall Happiness	**70**	**121**
Alumni Giving	**26**	**79**
Graduation Rate	**19**	**32**
Overall Rank	**50**	**111**

Other Key Alumni Outcomes

5.7% Are college professors
10.8% Teach at any level
58.2% Have post-graduate degrees
48.0% Live in dual-income homes
91.5% Are currently employed

See pages 134–135 for detailed explanations and definitions.

Alumni Activities During College

33.9% Community Service
20.1% Intramural Sports
27.6% Internships
26.9% Media Programs
31.8% Music Programs
38.5% Part-Time Jobs

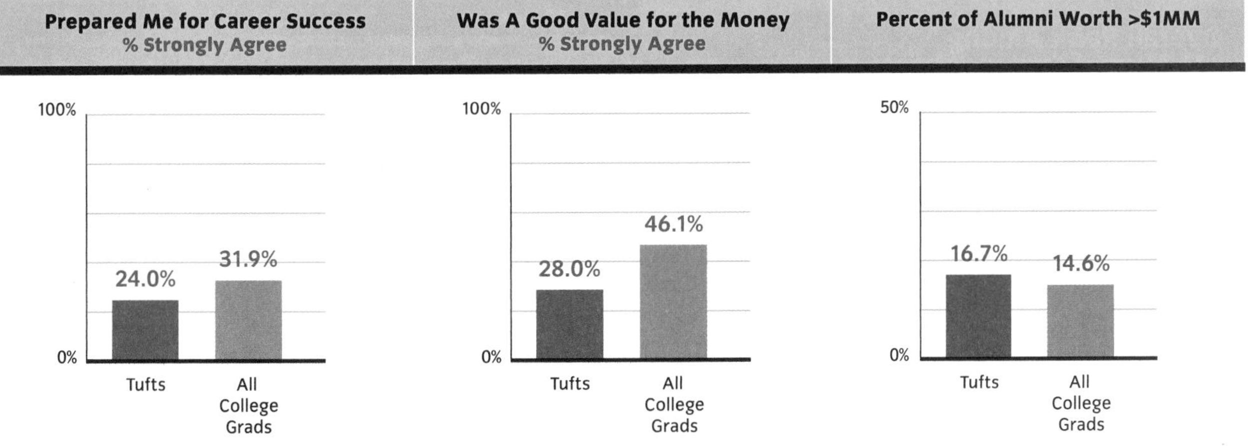

Alumni Employment

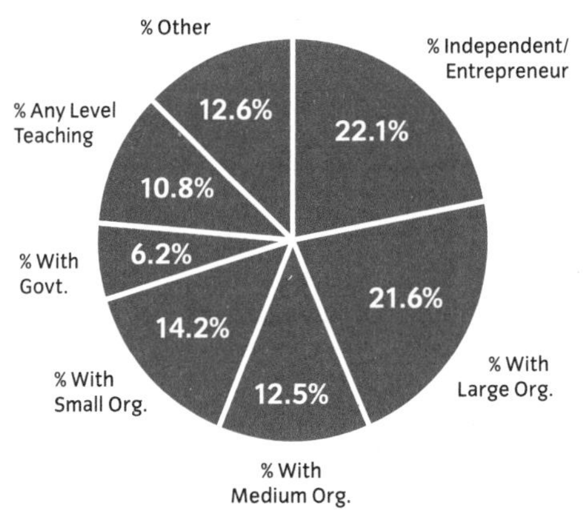

Income Distribution of Graduates

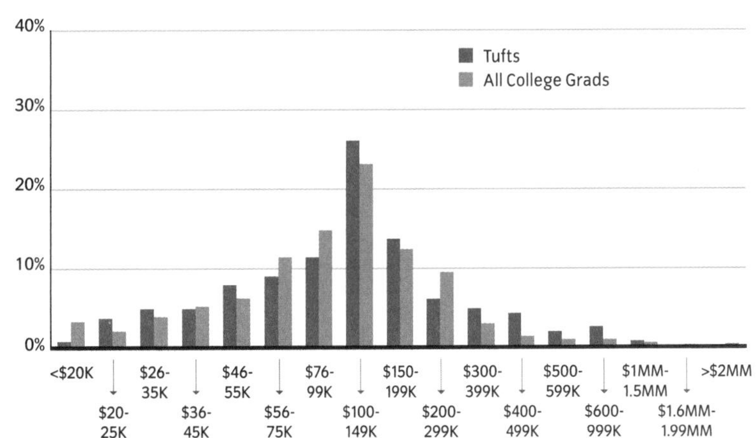

Current Selectivity & Demand Analysis for Tufts University

Attribute	% Accepted	% Accepted Who Enroll	Freshman Retention Rate	Graduation Rate	Demand Index	Reputation Index
Score	22.0%	35.0%	97.0%	91.0%	13.03	1.59
Rank	33	70	13	32	35	35

Where are the Graduates of Tufts University on the Political Spectrum?

Very Liberal	Liberal	Somewhat Liberal	Somewhat Conservative	Conservative	Very Conservative
	↑				

Tulane University

Location: New Orleans, LA
Campus Setting: City: Large
Total Expenses: $56,484
Estimated Average Discount: $27,629 (49%)
Estimated Net Price: $28,855

Type of Institution: National University
Number of Undergraduates: 7,754
SAT Score: Reading: 620–710, Math: 620–700
Student/Faculty Ratio: 11 to 1
Transfer Out Rate: 24%

Rank Among 104 National Universities	**77**
Overall Rank Among 177 *Alumni Factor* Schools	**145**

Overview

There is definitely academic excellence in the city known for Mardi Gras and Bourbon Street, but you have to go a bit southwest of the party to find it. In the New Orleans Garden District about 5 miles west of the French Quarter sits Tulane, side by side with Loyola University on a park-like campus. New Orleans and serious scholarship do not often co-exist, but they do live comfortably side by side at Tulane.

Ranked 88th in SAT scores, Tulane grads are sharp and capable. They are also quite happy (ranked 43rd) and do very well financially (53rd). It is hard to decipher why grads rank the College Experience 72nd and the Overall Assessment 76th when Loyola, right next door, ranks 40th and 39th respectively. We believe it has more to do with the high expectations and ambitions of the Tulane alumni than the experience itself, and also shows Loyola's strength. Tulane's strongest Ultimate Outcome is Financial Success & Intellectual Capability (38th) – a good pair to be armed with for success in life.

Notable Alumni

Paul Michael Glaser, Jerry Springer, Lauren Hutton, Ira Sorkin, Yahoo co-founder David Filo, and many Pulitzer Prize-winning authors and journalists.

The Alumni Factor Rankings Summary

Attribute	University Rank	Overall Rank
College Experience	**72**	**142**
Intellectual Development	47	106
Social Development	56	117
Spiritual Development	58	127
Friendship Development	27	83
Preparation for Career Success	89	160
Immediate Job Opportunities	97	166
Overall Assessment	**76**	**138**
Would Personally Choose Again	51	98
Would Recommend to Student	69	126
Value for the Money	93	164
Financial Success	**53**	**89**
Income per Household	66	101
% Households with Income >$150K	38	67
Household Net Worth	67	114
% Households Net Worth >$1MM	54	94
Overall Happiness	**43**	**82**
Alumni Giving	**78**	**145**
Graduation Rate	**77**	**143**
Overall Rank	**77**	**145**

Other Key Alumni Outcomes

5.6% Are college professors
10.7% Teach at any level
51.0% Have post-graduate degrees
46.2% Live in dual-income homes
90.3% Are currently employed

Alumni Activities During College

32.3% Community Service
24.3% Intramural Sports
24.7% Internships
18.2% Media Programs
16.1% Music Programs
36.2% Part-Time Jobs

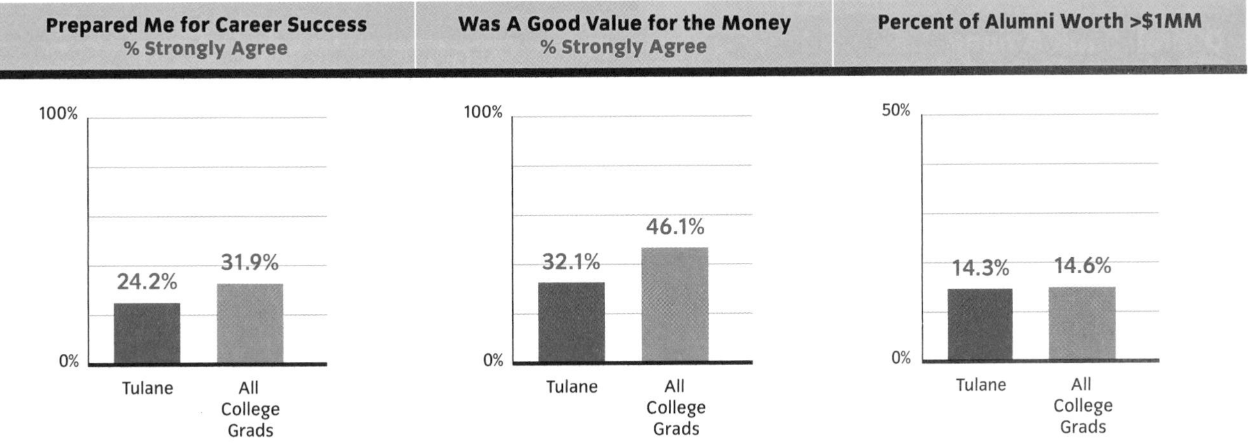

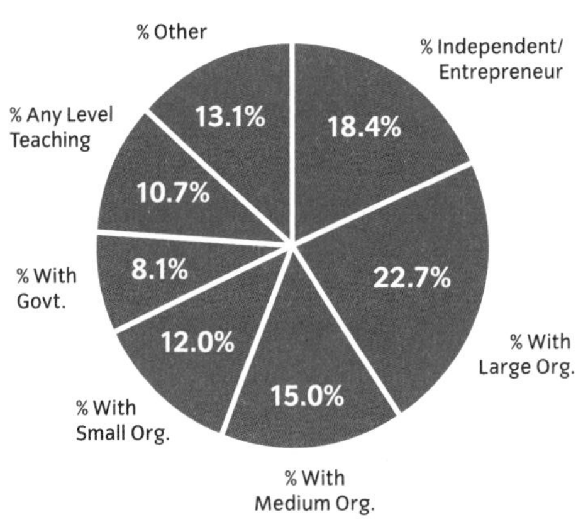

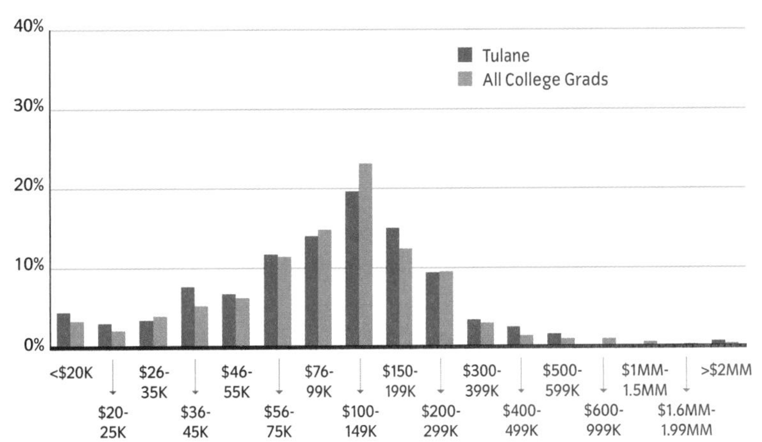

Current Selectivity & Demand Analysis for Tulane University

Attribute	% Accepted	% Accepted Who Enroll	Freshman Retention Rate	Graduation Rate	Demand Index	Reputation Index
Score	25.0%	17.0%	90.0%	70.0%	23.00	0.68
Rank	39	170	113	143	1	88

Where are the Graduates of Tulane University on the Political Spectrum?

Very Liberal	Liberal	Somewhat Liberal	Somewhat Conservative	Conservative	Very Conservative

See pages 134–135 for detailed explanations and definitions.

United States Air Force Academy

Location: Colorado Springs, CO
Campus Setting: Suburb: Large
Total Expenses: $0
Estimated Average Discount: N/A
Estimated Net Price: $0

Type of Institution: Regional University
Number of Undergraduates: 4,619
SAT Score: Reading: 590–680, Math: 630–710
Student/Faculty Ratio: 8 to 1
Transfer Out Rate: Not Reported

Rank Among 20 Regional Universities	**2**
Overall Rank Among 177 *Alumni Factor* Schools	**45**

Overview

The US Air Force Academy is not a lighthearted undergraduate experience. However, if you are disciplined and tough enough to make it through, you are likely to have a lifetime of happiness, friendship and success waiting for you. To be clear, this is the toughest grading undergraduate college in the nation, with only 7% of graduates reporting a GPA above a 3.5 – and these are some of the brightest students around (49th in SAT scores). There is a huge reward for all the hard work, as Air Force grads rank 2nd (behind only the US Naval Academy) in Immediate Job Opportunities; 9th in Employment rate; 4th in Preparation for Career Success; 7th in Overall Happiness; 13th in the Ultimate Outcomes and 53rd in Financial Success.

Like all of the military academies, Air Force is a patriotic, conservative institution, and its graduates reflect that fact. Social Development is not something graduates rate highly at the Academy (it was male-only until 1976), and graduates are careful to not recommend it to just anyone, since it is not intended for everyone.

Notable Alumni

The Air Force Academy has produced a star-studded list of military leaders, astronauts, engineers, government leaders and successful business leaders throughout its long and proud history.

The Alumni Factor Rankings Summary

Attribute	Overall Rank
College Experience	**25**
Intellectual Development	45
Social Development	167
Spiritual Development	26
Friendship Development	15
Preparation for Career Success	4
Immediate Job Opportunities	2
Overall Assessment	**88**
Would Personally Choose Again	118
Would Recommend to Student	136
Value for the Money	3
Financial Success	**53**
Income per Household	26
% Households with Income >$150K	46
Household Net Worth	33
% Households Net Worth >$1MM	135
Overall Happiness	**7**
Alumni Giving	**131**
Graduation Rate	**100**
Overall Rank	**45**

Other Key Alumni Outcomes

2.4% Are college professors
4.4% Teach at any level
65.5% Have post-graduate degrees
51.0% Live in dual-income homes
96.6% Are currently employed

See pages 134–135 for detailed explanations and definitions.

Alumni Activities During College

18.4% Community Service
82.0% Intramural Sports
5.8% Internships
9.7% Media Programs
29.1% Music Programs
0.0% Part-Time Jobs

Prepared Me for Career Success % Strongly Agree	Was A Good Value for the Money % Strongly Agree	Percent of Alumni Worth >$1MM
USAFA: 61.7% All College Grads: 31.9%	USAFA: 86.9% All College Grads: 46.1%	USAFA: 11.3% All College Grads: 14.6%

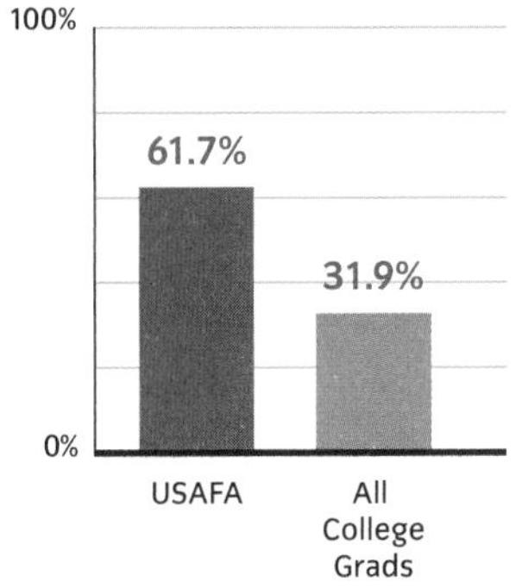

100%
0%
100%
0%
50%
0%

Alumni Employment

% With Govt. 34.2%
% With Large Org. 26.8%
% With Medium Org. 10.7%
% With Small Org. 10.7%
% Independent/ Entrepreneur 8.3%
% Other 4.9%
% Any Level Teaching 4.4%

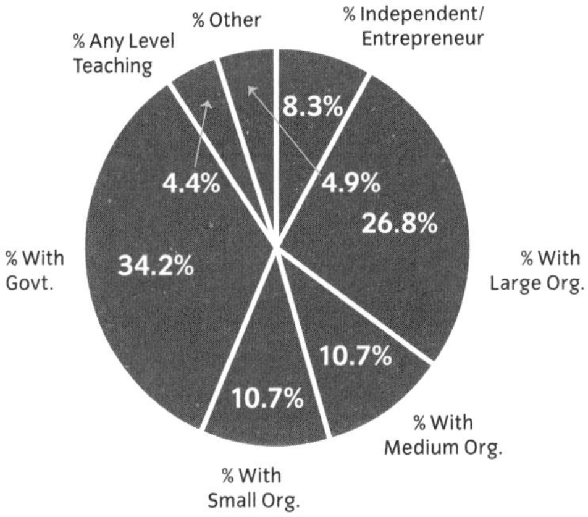

Income Distribution of Graduates

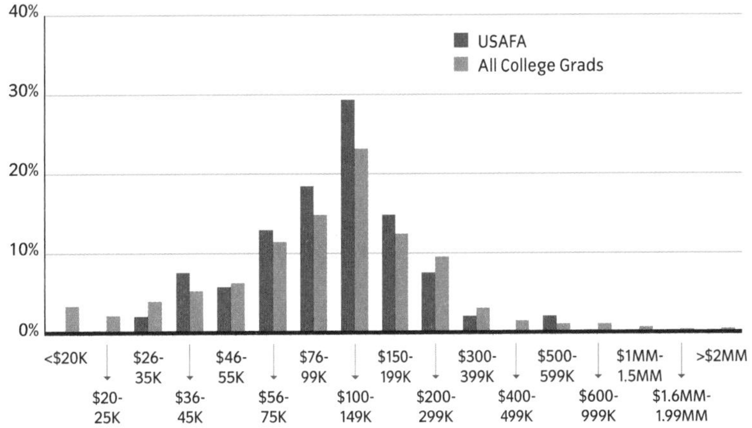

■ USAFA
■ All College Grads

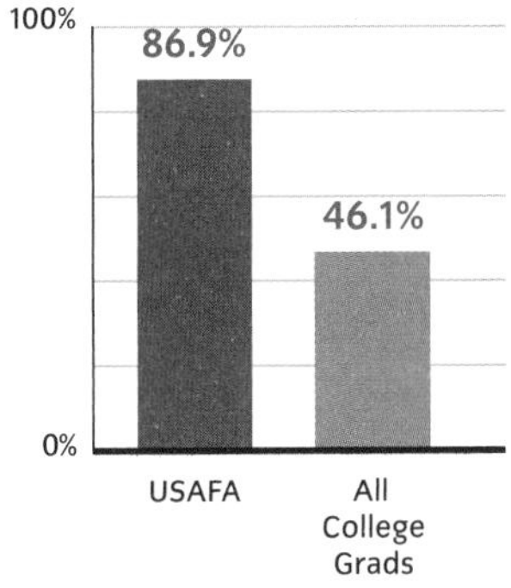

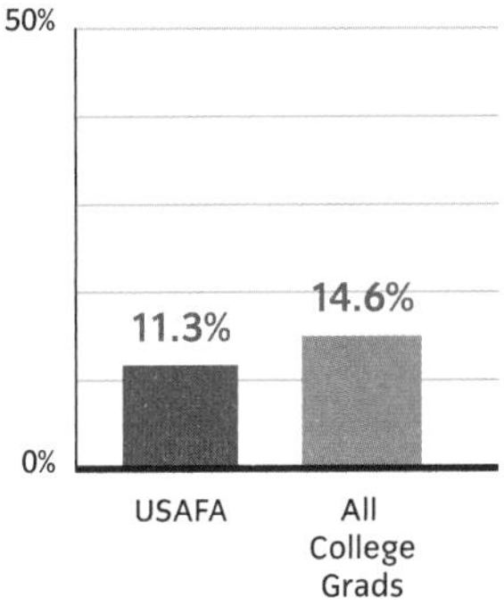

40%
30%
20%
10%
0%

<$20K | $20-25K | $26-35K | $36-45K | $46-55K | $56-75K | $76-99K | $100-149K | $150-199K | $200-299K | $300-399K | $400-499K | $500-599K | $600-999K | $1MM-1.5MM | $1.6MM-1.99MM | >$2MM

Current Selectivity & Demand Analysis for United States Air Force Academy

Attribute	% Accepted	% Accepted Who Enroll	Freshman Retention Rate	Graduation Rate	Demand Index	Reputation Index
Score	11.0%	82.0%	90.0%	81.0%	11.89	7.45
Rank	9	3	113	100	46	6

Where are the Graduates of United States Air Force Academy on the Political Spectrum?

Very Liberal	Liberal	Somewhat Liberal	Somewhat Conservative	Conservative	Very Conservative

See pages 134–135 for detailed explanations and definitions.

United States Military Academy

Location: West Point, NY
Campus Setting: Suburb: Large
Total Expenses: $0
Estimated Average Discount: N/A
Estimated Net Price: $0

Type of Institution: Liberal Arts College
Number of Undergraduates: 4,686
SAT Score: Reading: 560–680, Math: 590–690
Student/Faculty Ratio: 8 to 1
Transfer Out Rate: Not Reported

Overview

Fifty miles north of Manhattan, perched atop a gorgeous bluff with a stunning view of the Hudson River, sits a national treasure worthy of its reputation. The US Military Academy (West Point) may have the most beautiful campus in the country, and is home to one of the finest, most well-rounded educational experiences anywhere. West Point is transformational in every way (ranked 1st in the College Experience). It is among the Top 15 colleges in every attribute of the College Experience and produces happy (2nd in Overall Happiness) and successful graduates (ranked 19th in Financial Success and 8th in Income per Household) who lead and excel in virtually every field. These are truly some of America's finest hero-citizens.

There are two major challenges with West Point – getting in and getting out. Less than 15% of applicants are admitted, and once admitted, the experience is one of the most rigorous and demanding anywhere. This is the 6th most difficult academic environment in the country, according to our data, and the physical and emotional requirements are legendary.

Notable Alumni

Two former US presidents, Eisenhower and Grant; former generals Robert E. Lee, Douglas MacArthur, and William Westmoreland, among many others; CIA Director David Petraeus; astronaut Buzz Aldrin; and Heisman Trophy winner Pete Dawkins. West Point graduates also occupy America's executive suites and boardrooms: Bob McDonald, P&G CEO; Joe DePinto, 7-11 CEO; and Kleiner Perkins co-founder Frank Caufield.

The Alumni Factor Rankings Summary

Attribute	Liberal Arts Rank	Overall Rank
College Experience	**1**	**1**
Intellectual Development	13	14
Social Development	9	13
Spiritual Development	6	13
Friendship Development	3	3
Preparation for Career Success	1	1
Immediate Job Opportunities	2	2
Overall Assessment	**15**	**36**
Would Personally Choose Again	24	61
Would Recommend to Student	24	58
Value for the Money	1	1
Financial Success	**19**	**47**
Income per Household	8	16
% Households with Income >$150K	10	20
Household Net Worth	18	43
% Households Net Worth >$1MM	44	131
Overall Happiness	**2**	**2**
Alumni Giving	**46**	**57**
Graduation Rate	**32**	**67**
Overall Rank	**5**	**9**

Other Key Alumni Outcomes

2.2% Are college professors
3.1% Teach at any level
57.6% Have post-graduate degrees
43.9% Live in dual-income homes
96.5% Are currently employed

See pages 134–135 for detailed explanations and definitions.

Alumni Activities During College

19.5% Community Service
80.1% Intramural Sports
13.0% Internships
7.7% Media Programs
20.3% Music Programs
1.7% Part-Time Jobs

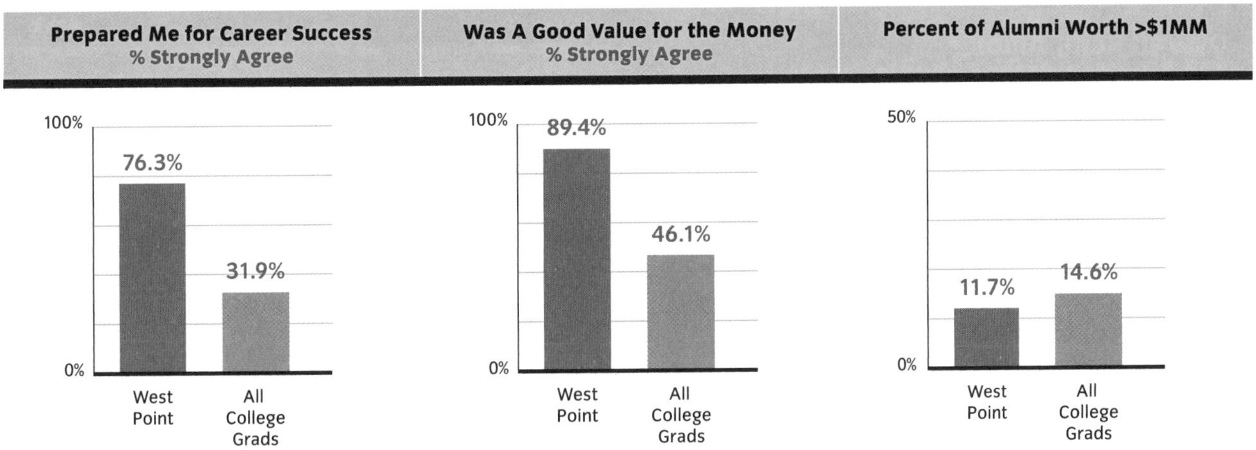

Prepared Me for Career Success — % Strongly Agree

West Point: 76.3%
All College Grads: 31.9%

Was A Good Value for the Money — % Strongly Agree

West Point: 89.4%
All College Grads: 46.1%

Percent of Alumni Worth >$1MM

West Point: 11.7%
All College Grads: 14.6%

Alumni Employment

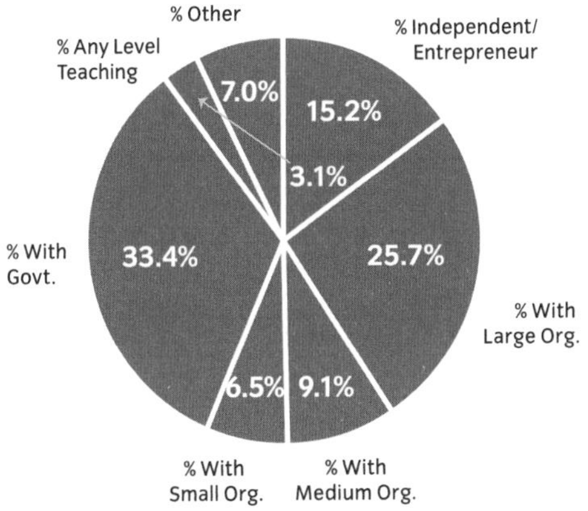

Income Distribution of Graduates

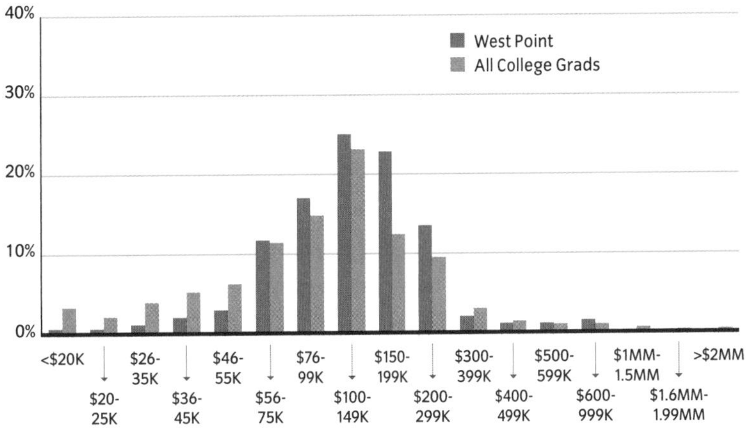

Current Selectivity & Demand Analysis for United States Military Academy

Attribute	% Accepted	% Accepted Who Enroll	Freshman Retention Rate	Graduation Rate	Demand Index	Reputation Index
Score	11.0%	84.0%	95.0%	86.0%	11.34	7.64
Rank	9	2	47	67	54	5

Where are the Graduates of United States Military Academy on the Political Spectrum?

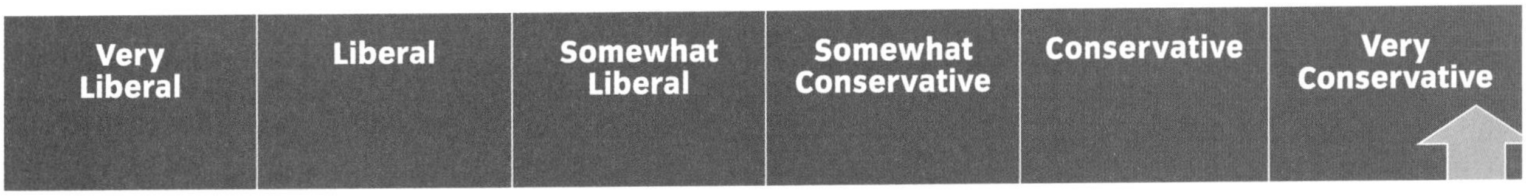

Very Liberal	Liberal	Somewhat Liberal	Somewhat Conservative	Conservative	Very Conservative
					↑

United States Naval Academy

Location: Annapolis, MD
Campus Setting: Suburb: Large
Total Expenses: $0
Estimated Average Discount: N/A
Estimated Net Price: $0

Type of Institution: Liberal Arts College
Number of Undergraduates: 4,603
SAT Score: Reading: 560–680, Math: 600–700
Student/Faculty Ratio: 9 to 1
Transfer Out Rate: Not Reported

Rank Among 53 Liberal Arts Colleges	**4**
Overall Rank Among 177 *Alumni Factor* Schools	**8**

Overview

Ranked 4th among all liberal arts colleges and 8th overall, the US Naval Academy is one of the finest educational institutions in the country. Like West Point, Annapolis is a life-changing experience that transforms a young man or woman (ranked 7th in College Experience) into an honorable leader who serves our country. As you would expect, it well earns its reputation for academic rigor, structured regimen and discipline in thought and action. Those attributes prepare Naval Academy graduates for a lifetime of happiness (ranked 2nd), friendship (5th), and extraordinary success (3rd in the Ultimate Outcomes and 10th in Financial Success) across a wide variety of fields – both military and non-military.

With Top 10 rankings in every Ultimate Outcome, Navy grads are among the most sought after alumni anywhere. A quick glance at some of the astonishingly talented alumni from Annapolis shows the power of this institution. Anchors aweigh!

Notable Alumni

Former president Jimmy Carter; former admirals James Holloway, Stansfield Turner and Dennis Blair; former astronaut Alan Shepard and current astronaut Kay Hire; athletes Roger Staubach, David Robinson and Napoleon McCallum; business leaders Ross Perot, John McMullen and Richard Armitage; officer and author James Webb; and government leaders John McCain, Charlie Wilson and John Poindexter.

The Alumni Factor Rankings Summary

Attribute	Liberal Arts Rank	Overall Rank
College Experience	**7**	**9**
Intellectual Development	26	31
Social Development	42	93
Spiritual Development	11	31
Friendship Development	5	5
Preparation for Career Success	2	2
Immediate Job Opportunities	1	1
Overall Assessment	**14**	**32**
Would Personally Choose Again	27	74
Would Recommend to Student	12	39
Value for the Money	2	2
Financial Success	**10**	**25**
Income per Household	8	16
% Households with Income >$150K	16	33
Household Net Worth	9	16
% Households Net Worth >$1MM	20	47
Overall Happiness	**2**	**2**
Alumni Giving	**52**	**75**
Graduation Rate	**18**	**47**
Overall Rank	**4**	**8**

Other Key Alumni Outcomes

1.7% Are college professors
2.9% Teach at any level
57.4% Have post-graduate degrees
44.1% Live in dual-income homes
95.3% Are currently employed

See pages 134–135 for detailed explanations and definitions.

Alumni Activities During College

15.2% Community Service
78.9% Intramural Sports
6.4% Internships
12.9% Media Programs
28.7% Music Programs
2.3% Part-Time Jobs

Prepared Me for Career Success % Strongly Agree	Was A Good Value for the Money % Strongly Agree	Percent of Alumni Worth >$1MM
USNA: 69.0%	USNA: 91.2%	USNA: 18.2%
All College Grads: 31.9%	All College Grads: 46.1%	All College Grads: 14.6%

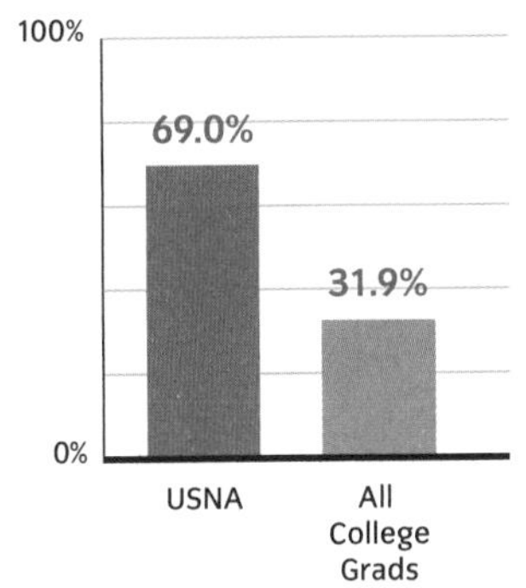

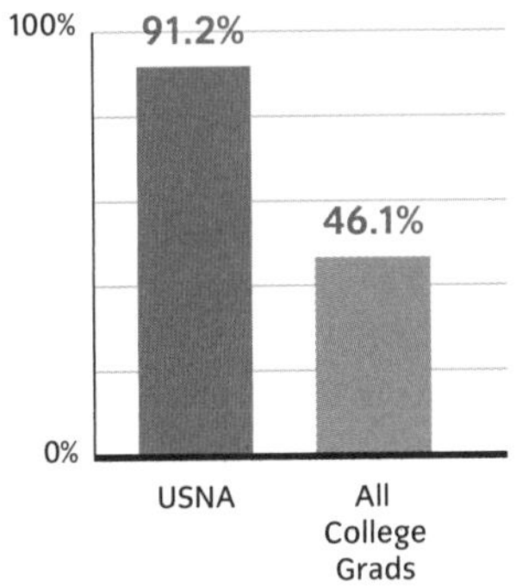

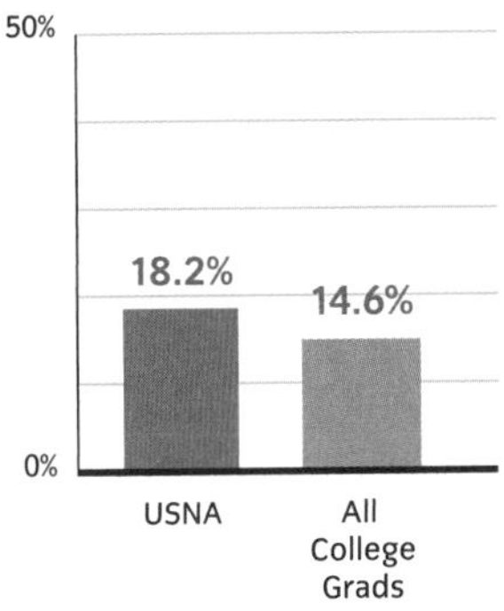

Alumni Employment

Category	%
% Independent/ Entrepreneur	12.8%
% With Large Org.	23.8%
% With Medium Org.	10.5%
% With Small Org.	10.5%
% With Govt.	32.5%
% Any Level Teaching	2.9%
% Other	7.0%

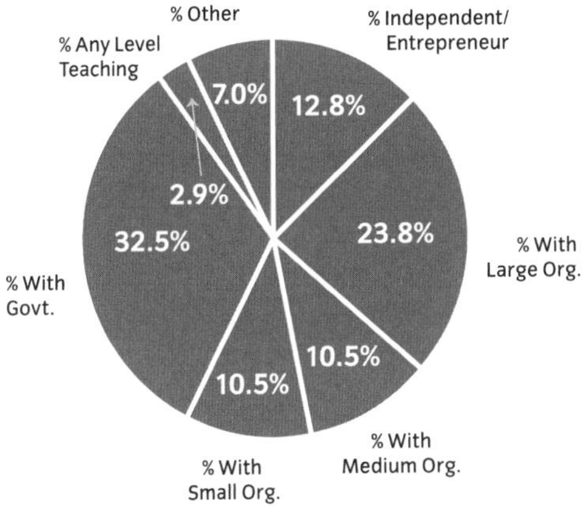

Income Distribution of Graduates

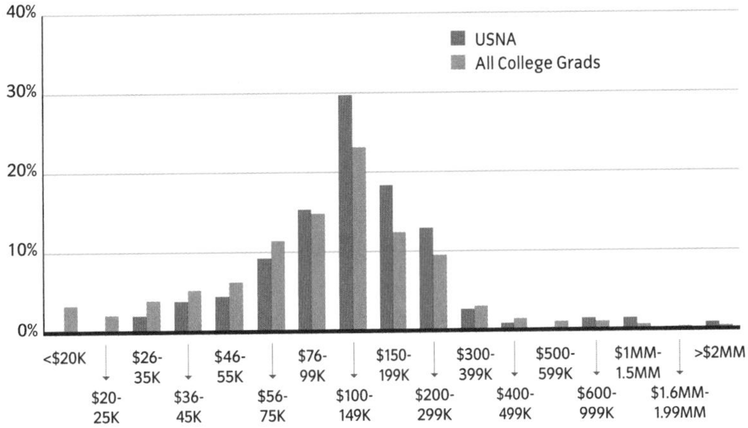

Current Selectivity & Demand Analysis for United States Naval Academy

Attribute	% Accepted	% Accepted Who Enroll	Freshman Retention Rate	Graduation Rate	Demand Index	Reputation Index
Score	7.0%	86.0%	97.0%	89.0%	16.03	12.29
Rank	2	1	13	47	15	2

Where are the Graduates of United States Naval Academy on the Political Spectrum?

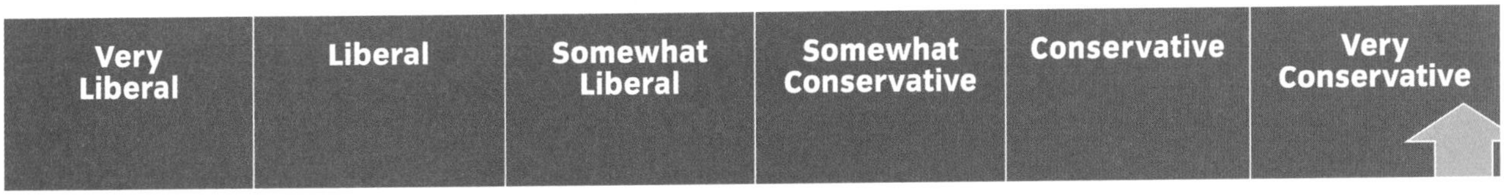

Very Liberal	Liberal	Somewhat Liberal	Somewhat Conservative	Conservative	Very Conservative
					↑

See pages 134–135 for detailed explanations and definitions.

University of Alabama

Location: Tuscaloosa, AL
Campus Setting: City: Small
Total Expenses: $23,939
Estimated Average Discount: $7,684 (32%)
Estimated Net Price: $16,255

Type of Institution: National University
Number of Undergraduates: 24,882
SAT Score: Reading: 500–620, Math: 500–640
Student/Faculty Ratio: 19 to 1
Transfer Out Rate: 18%

Rank Among 104 National Universities	**27**
Overall Rank Among 177 *Alumni Factor* Schools	**61**

Overview

Beautifully spread across 1,800 acres in the heart of Tuscaloosa sits a university that has historically been best known for its football program. That will change as the world recognizes the accomplishments of University of Alabama graduates and their outcomes – strong enough to rank the school 27th among national universities and 3rd in the famous SEC Conference, behind only Auburn (22nd) and Vanderbilt (17th). UA alumni are very happy (18th), successful (49th in Financial Success) and appreciative of their time spent in Tuscaloosa – a true college town. The highest ranked attribute for UA is in Social Development (6th) – not surprising given the friendly Southern charm of the campus and the community's loyal support of the Crimson Tide. Alabama's strongest Ultimate Outcome is Happiness & Friendships, where it ranks a strong 7th.

With rankings in the Top 55 across all measures of Financial Success (a very strong result given the Southern location of many graduates and the relatively low cost of living and wages), Alabama produces a higher percentage of millionaire households than all SEC schools except Vanderbilt.

Notable Alumni

There are far too many notable alumni athletes to list, but here are a few non-athletic notables: author Gay Talese; actors Sela Ward and Jim Nabors; Senator Richard Shelby; and the brilliant Pulitzer Prize-winning socio-biologist E. O. Wilson.

The Alumni Factor Rankings Summary

Attribute	University Rank	Overall Rank
College Experience	**14**	**45**
Intellectual Development	55	122
Social Development	6	22
Spiritual Development	17	73
Friendship Development	4	28
Preparation for Career Success	22	58
Immediate Job Opportunities	27	43
Overall Assessment	**31**	**64**
Would Personally Choose Again	43	81
Would Recommend to Student	23	45
Value for the Money	36	64
Financial Success	**49**	**83**
Income per Household	51	81
% Households with Income >$150K	54	91
Household Net Worth	52	91
% Households Net Worth >$1MM	46	82
Overall Happiness	**18**	**39**
Alumni Giving	**52**	**115**
Graduation Rate	**90**	**158**
Overall Rank	**27**	**61**

Other Key Alumni Outcomes

7.0% Are college professors
15.6% Teach at any level
48.1% Have post-graduate degrees
50.3% Live in dual-income homes
92.5% Are currently employed

See pages 134–135 for detailed explanations and definitions.

Alumni Activities During College

24.9% Community Service
34.1% Intramural Sports
24.3% Internships
15.1% Media Programs
21.6% Music Programs
50.3% Part-Time Jobs

	Prepared Me for Career Success % Strongly Agree	Was A Good Value for the Money % Strongly Agree	Percent of Alumni Worth >$1MM
Alabama	30.3%	46.7%	15.1%
All College Grads	31.9%	46.1%	14.6%

Alumni Employment

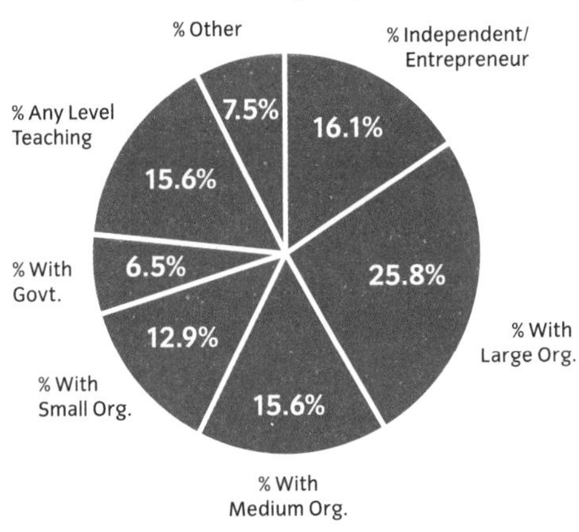

Income Distribution of Graduates

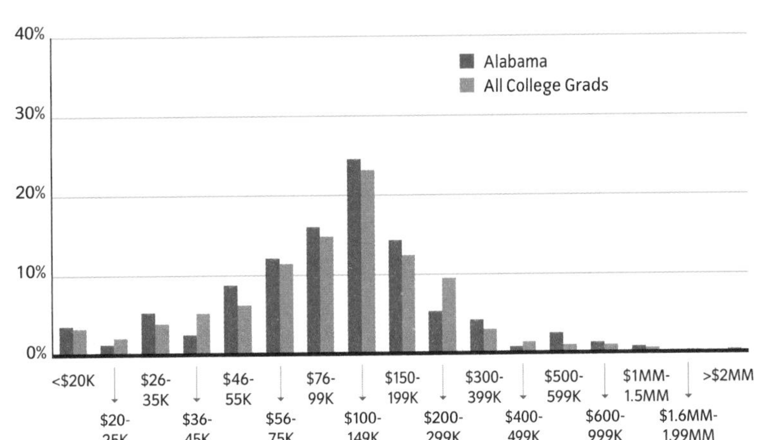

Current Selectivity & Demand Analysis for University of Alabama

Attribute	% Accepted	% Accepted Who Enroll	Freshman Retention Rate	Graduation Rate	Demand Index	Reputation Index
Score	44.0%	60.0%	85.0%	67.0%	3.86	1.36
Rank	89	11	151	158	152	43

Where are the Graduates of University of Alabama on the Political Spectrum?

Very Liberal	Liberal	Somewhat Liberal	Somewhat Conservative	Conservative	Very Conservative
					↑

See pages 134–135 for detailed explanations and definitions.

University of Arizona

Location: Tucson, AZ
Campus Setting: City: Large
Total Expenses: $22,366
Estimated Average Discount: $10,181 (46%)
Estimated Net Price: $12,185

Type of Institution: National University
Number of Undergraduates: 30,592
SAT Score: Reading: 480–610, Math: 490–620
Student/Faculty Ratio: 21 to 1
Transfer Out Rate: Not Reported

Rank Among 104 National Universities	**86**
Overall Rank Among 177 *Alumni Factor* Schools	**157**

Overview

A popular destination for many Arizona and California students, University of Arizona captivates with its beautiful campus, stunning natural environment and relaxed atmosphere. Ranked 86th among national universities and 157th overall, Arizona grads see it as a very good value (40th) and would recommend it to prospective students (43rd). Despite the year-round sunny climate and its reputation for serious partying, Arizona does produce a very high number of intellectually serious and capable graduates who are high achievers and quite accomplished in a broad range of fields. They are also quite happy (ranked 50th). Arizona's strongest Ultimate Outcome is Financial Success & Happiness (77th). Versus its in-state competitor ASU, Arizona performs quite well, out-performing ASU in 25 of the 26 attributes measured. The one attribute where ASU is slightly better is Percentage of Households Net Worth >$1MM, where ASU ranks 74th versus Arizona's 77th ranking.

Notable Alumni

Barry Goldwater; legendary producer Jerry Bruckheimer; Sesame Street founder Joan Cooney; Geraldo Rivera; actor Greg Kinnear; New York Jets owner Woody Johnson; and Phoenix Suns owner Robert Sarver.

The Alumni Factor Rankings Summary

Attribute	University Rank	Overall Rank
College Experience	**86**	**159**
Intellectual Development	86	157
Social Development	74	142
Spiritual Development	76	148
Friendship Development	94	165
Preparation for Career Success	83	153
Immediate Job Opportunities	60	98
Overall Assessment	**44**	**89**
Would Personally Choose Again	53	101
Would Recommend to Student	43	88
Value for the Money	40	72
Financial Success	**84**	**137**
Income per Household	78	120
% Households with Income >$150K	86	142
Household Net Worth	84	139
% Households Net Worth >$1MM	77	128
Overall Happiness	**50**	**96**
Alumni Giving	**98**	**171**
Graduation Rate	**96**	**167**
Overall Rank	**86**	**157**

Other Key Alumni Outcomes

6.0% Are college professors
14.6% Teach at any level
51.5% Have post-graduate degrees
52.2% Live in dual-income homes
91.1% Are currently employed

See pages 134–135 for detailed explanations and definitions.

Alumni Activities During College

25.1% Community Service
23.7% Intramural Sports
21.1% Internships
10.4% Media Programs
14.3% Music Programs
50.2% Part-Time Jobs

Prepared Me for Career Success % Strongly Agree	Was A Good Value for the Money % Strongly Agree	Percent of Alumni Worth >$1MM
Arizona: 22.3% All College Grads: 31.9%	Arizona: 45.5% All College Grads: 46.1%	Arizona: 12.0% All College Grads: 14.6%

Alumni Employment

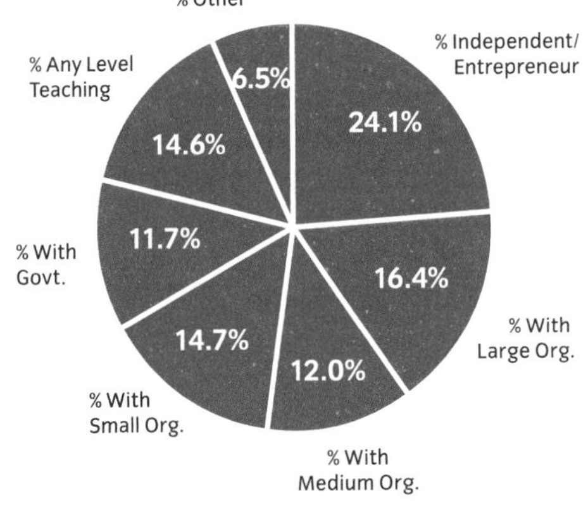

Income Distribution of Graduates

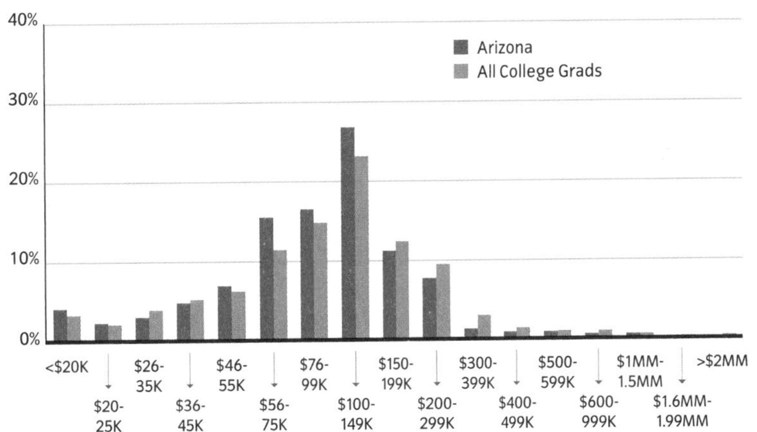

Current Selectivity & Demand Analysis for University of Arizona

Attribute	% Accepted	% Accepted Who Enroll	Freshman Retention Rate	Graduation Rate	Demand Index	Reputation Index
Score	75.0%	35.0%	77.0%	60.0%	3.65	0.47
Rank	160	70	176	167	161	130

Where are the Graduates of University of Arizona on the Political Spectrum?

Very Liberal	Liberal	Somewhat Liberal	Somewhat Conservative	Conservative	Very Conservative
				↑	

See pages 134–135 for detailed explanations and definitions.

University of California, Berkeley

Location: Berkeley, CA
Campus Setting: City: Midsize
Total Expenses: $32,632
Estimated Average Discount: $17,043 (52%)
Estimated Net Price: $15,589

Type of Institution: National University
Number of Undergraduates: 25,540
SAT Score: Reading: 600–730, Math: 630–760
Student/Faculty Ratio: 16 to 1
Transfer Out Rate: Not Reported

Rank Among 104 National Universities	**26**
Overall Rank Among 177 *Alumni Factor* Schools	**59**

Overview

One of the world's best-known and most prestigious universities, UC Berkeley is among the most selective colleges in the country. Providing the highest caliber of intellectual challenge and development to its nearly 25,000 undergrads, Berkeley is one of the rare large institutions capable of excellence on a mass scale. There are only 33 schools among our Top 177 colleges that have more than 20,000 undergraduates. Among those 33 schools, Berkeley is ranked 1st in Intellectual Development; 1st in Graduation Rate; 2nd in Value for the Money; 7th in Income per Household; and 3rd in Percentage of Households Net Worth >$1MM, and SAT scores.

Of course, the rapid ascent of technology in our lives has made Berkeley even more relevant as an institution. If there is a "birthplace" of high-tech founders, Berkeley and Stanford are certainly the dominant cradles in the nursery. But Berkeley's excellence extends well beyond technology into the humanities, physical and biological sciences and the liberal arts.

Notable Alumni

Gordon Moore of Intel; Steve Wozniak of Apple; former chief justice Earl Warren; Governor Jerry Brown; Robert McNamara; Gregory Peck; Eric Schmidt of Google; and Jennifer Granholm.

The Alumni Factor Rankings Summary

Attribute	University Rank	Overall Rank
College Experience	**37**	**97**
Intellectual Development	12	50
Social Development	47	106
Spiritual Development	19	75
Friendship Development	65	135
Preparation for Career Success	51	106
Immediate Job Opportunities	54	86
Overall Assessment	**11**	**17**
Would Personally Choose Again	16	40
Would Recommend to Student	19	35
Value for the Money	6	10
Financial Success	**32**	**60**
Income per Household	43	69
% Households with Income >$150K	29	53
Household Net Worth	46	84
% Households Net Worth >$1MM	27	50
Overall Happiness	**60**	**109**
Alumni Giving	**83**	**152**
Graduation Rate	**19**	**32**
Overall Rank	**26**	**59**

Other Key Alumni Outcomes

8.2% Are college professors
15.2% Teach at any level
59.5% Have post-graduate degrees
52.4% Live in dual-income homes
91.4% Are currently employed

See pages 134–135 for detailed explanations and definitions.

Alumni Activities During College

36.1% Community Service
21.6% Intramural Sports
26.8% Internships
7.9% Media Programs
11.2% Music Programs
53.4% Part-Time Jobs

	Prepared Me for Career Success (% Strongly Agree)	Was A Good Value for the Money (% Strongly Agree)	Percent of Alumni Worth >$1MM
UC Berkeley	37.0%	67.3%	18.0%
All College Grads	31.9%	46.1%	14.6%

Alumni Employment

Category	%
% Independent/ Entrepreneur	25.2%
% With Large Org.	22.4%
% With Medium Org.	8.4%
% With Small Org.	14.7%
% With Govt.	7.2%
% Any Level Teaching	15.2%
% Other	6.9%

Income Distribution of Graduates

Current Selectivity & Demand Analysis for University of California, Berkeley

Attribute	% Accepted	% Accepted Who Enroll	Freshman Retention Rate	Graduation Rate	Demand Index	Reputation Index
Score	21.0%	38.0%	97.0%	91.0%	11.34	1.81
Rank	30	55	13	32	53	31

Where are the Graduates of University of California, Berkeley on the Political Spectrum?

Very Liberal	Liberal	Somewhat Liberal	Somewhat Conservative	Conservative	Very Conservative
⇧					

See pages 134–135 for detailed explanations and definitions.

University of California, Davis

Location: Davis, CA
Campus Setting: Suburb: Small
Total Expenses: $31,199
Estimated Average Discount: $17,127 (55%)
Estimated Net Price: $14,072

Type of Institution: National University
Number of Undergraduates: 24,670
SAT Score: Reading: 520–650, Math: 570–680
Student/Faculty Ratio: 16 to 1
Transfer Out Rate: Not Reported

Rank Among 104 National Universities	**66**
Overall Rank Among 177 *Alumni Factor* Schools	**131**

Overview

Ranked 66th among national universities and 4th within the University of California system, UC Davis is a world-class school in a system created for California's top students. Like all the UC schools, UC Davis is considered a very good value by its graduates (ranked 28th) and produces successful alumni across a wide variety of fields. While not as selective as Berkeley, UCLA, UC Irvine or UC San Diego, UC Davis excels in many key areas versus the other UC schools. From its beginning, UC Davis has been focused on the agricultural and life sciences, as well as engineering. Within the UC System, UC Davis ranks 2nd in Preparation for Career Success; 2nd in Friendship Development; 3rd in Would Recommend to Student; 3rd in Value for the Money; and 4th in College Experience. Its highest ranking is in Household Net Worth, where it ranks 46th among all national universities.

Notable Alumni

Renowned cancer researcher H. Michael Shepard; screenwriter Christopher Markus; TV Chef Martin Yan; Olympic gold medalist Catherin Carr; chairman & CEO of Chevron John Watson; CEO of Agilent Technolgies William Sullivan; California Chief Justice Tani Cantil- Sakauye; and celebrated wine expert Heidi Barrett.

The Alumni Factor Rankings Summary

Attribute	University Rank	Overall Rank
College Experience	**74**	**145**
Intellectual Development	51	117
Social Development	65	128
Spiritual Development	73	145
Friendship Development	63	133
Preparation for Career Success	66	132
Immediate Job Opportunities	71	114
Overall Assessment	**43**	**87**
Would Personally Choose Again	56	106
Would Recommend to Student	43	88
Value for the Money	28	53
Financial Success	**61**	**102**
Income per Household	71	110
% Households with Income >$150K	75	125
Household Net Worth	46	84
% Households Net Worth >$1MM	50	87
Overall Happiness	**80**	**135**
Alumni Giving	**91**	**162**
Graduation Rate	**44**	**91**
Overall Rank	**66**	**131**

Other Key Alumni Outcomes

4.9%	Are college professors
13.8%	Teach at any level
47.3%	Have post-graduate degrees
50.2%	Live in dual-income homes
91.2%	Are currently employed

See pages 134–135 for detailed explanations and definitions.

Alumni Activities During College

25.4% Community Service
34.4% Intramural Sports
41.1% Internships
10.2% Media Programs
14.7% Music Programs
54.0% Part-Time Jobs

Prepared Me for Career Success % Strongly Agree	Was A Good Value for the Money % Strongly Agree	Percent of Alumni Worth >$1MM
UC Davis 26.7% All College Grads 31.9%	UC Davis 50.0% All College Grads 46.1%	UC Davis 14.7% All College Grads 14.6%

Alumni Employment

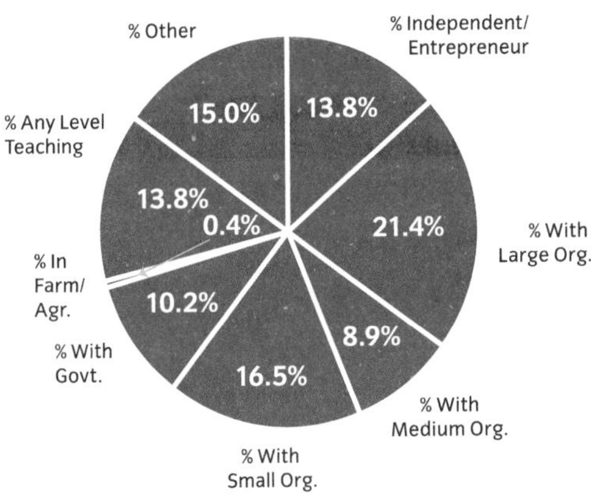

Income Distribution of Graduates

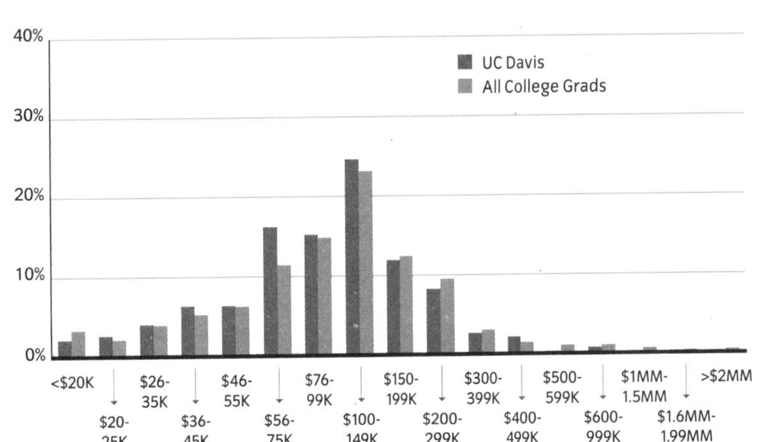

Current Selectivity & Demand Analysis for University of California, Davis

Attribute	% Accepted	% Accepted Who Enroll	Freshman Retention Rate	Graduation Rate	Demand Index	Reputation Index
Score	46.0%	22.0%	92.0%	82.0%	9.21	0.48
Rank	96	149	86	91	81	127

Where are the Graduates of University of California, Davis on the Political Spectrum?

Very Liberal	Liberal	Somewhat Liberal ↑	Somewhat Conservative	Conservative	Very Conservative

University of California, Irvine

Location: Irvine, CA
Campus Setting: City: Midsize
Total Expenses: $29,425
Estimated Average Discount: $16,208 (55%)
Estimated Net Price: $13,217

Type of Institution: National University
Number of Undergraduates: 21,976
SAT Score: Reading: 510–620, Math: 560–680
Student/Faculty Ratio: 19 to 1
Transfer Out Rate: 12%

Rank Among 104 National Universities	**72**
Overall Rank Among 177 *Alumni Factor* Schools	**139**

Overview

The fifth largest of the ten schools in the UC system, the University of California, Irvine is carving its own unique position as a strong player in California education. Correspondingly, its graduates are accomplishing the very same strong reputation in the marketplace. With a 31st ranking in Financial Success (2nd in the UC system behind only UCLA), it is clear that UCI is doing many things well – as are its graduates. It ranks 20th in Percentage of Households with Income >$150K and ranks 1st in this measure within the UC system. In fact, among the 33 schools in our Top 177 that have more than 20,000 undergraduates, UCI ranks 2nd in the Percentage of Households with Income >$150K, behind only the University of Michigan. UCI grads are also the happiest among the UC system schools, ranking 40th in Overall Happiness among national universities. Therefore, its strongest Ultimate Outcome is Financial Success and Happiness where it ranks 36th, and is 2nd in the UC system behind UCLA. UCI grads in general have centrist political views, making them the most conservative among the UC system schools.

Notable Alumni

While notable alumni are understandably few, given UCI's short tenure, standouts include Kleiner Perkins partner and Golden State Warriors owner Joe Lacob and Pulitzer Prize winner Michael Ramirez.

The Alumni Factor Rankings Summary

Attribute	University Rank	Overall Rank
College Experience	**88**	**161**
Intellectual Development	72	143
Social Development	83	152
Spiritual Development	46	112
Friendship Development	88	158
Preparation for Career Success	85	157
Immediate Job Opportunities	90	150
Overall Assessment	**68**	**125**
Would Personally Choose Again	101	171
Would Recommend to Student	68	124
Value for the Money	43	79
Financial Success	**31**	**57**
Income per Household	37	61
% Households with Income >$150K	20	40
Household Net Worth	44	78
% Households Net Worth >$1MM	36	66
Overall Happiness	**40**	**76**
Alumni Giving	**102**	**175**
Graduation Rate	**41**	**86**
Overall Rank	**72**	**139**

Other Key Alumni Outcomes

6.1% Are college professors
10.5% Teach at any level
54.1% Have post-graduate degrees
53.7% Live in dual-income homes
89.5% Are currently employed

See pages 134–135 for detailed explanations and definitions.

Alumni Activities During College

26.5% Community Service
25.4% Intramural Sports
25.4% Internships
11.1% Media Programs
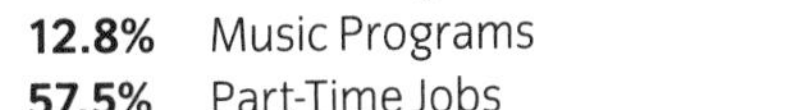
12.8% Music Programs
57.5% Part-Time Jobs

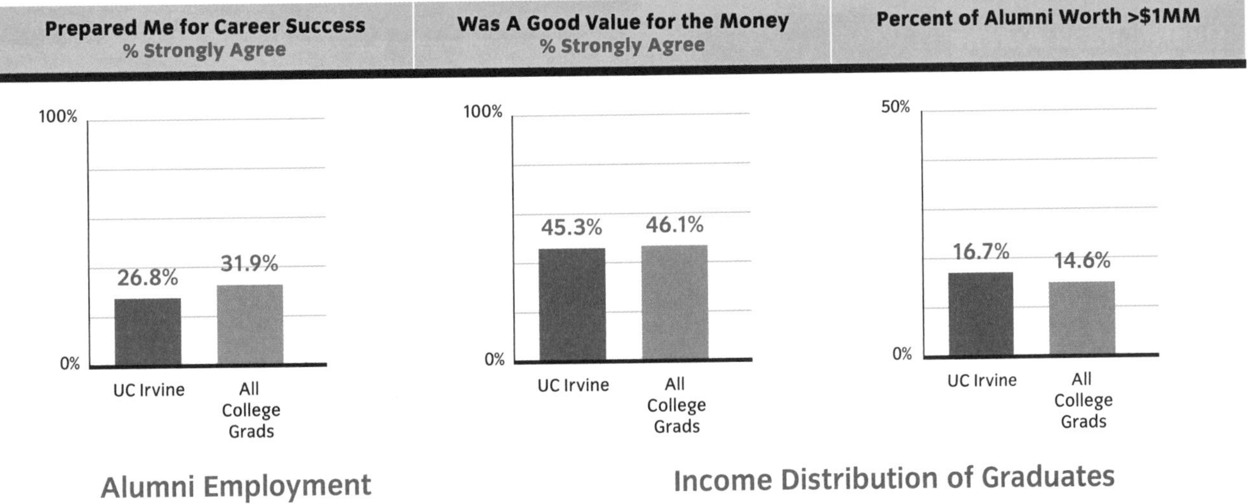

Alumni Employment

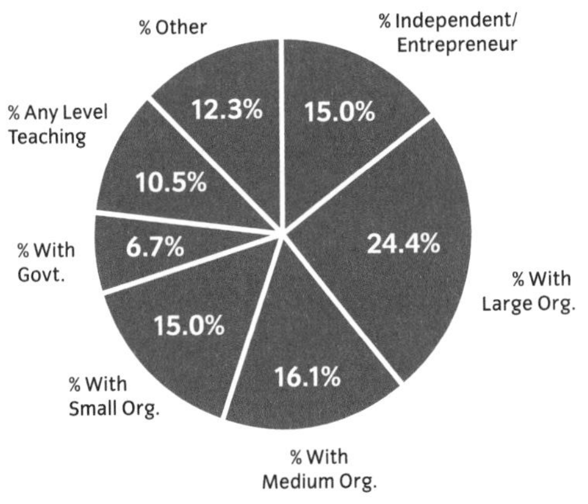

Income Distribution of Graduates

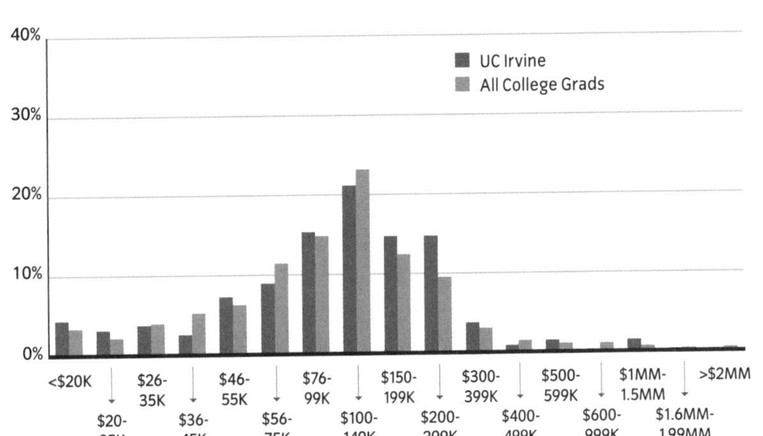

Current Selectivity & Demand Analysis for University of California, Irvine

Attribute	% Accepted	% Accepted Who Enroll	Freshman Retention Rate	Graduation Rate	Demand Index	Reputation Index
Score	45.0%	21.0%	95.0%	83.0%	8.94	0.47
Rank	91	156	47	86	85	130

Where are the Graduates of University of California, Irvine on the Political Spectrum?

Very Liberal	Liberal	Somewhat Liberal	Somewhat Conservative	Conservative	Very Conservative

University of California, Los Angeles

Location: Los Angeles, CA
Campus Setting: City: Large
Total Expenses: $31,556
Estimated Average Discount: $17,082 (54%)
Estimated Net Price: $14,474

Type of Institution: National University
Number of Undergraduates: 26,162
SAT Score: Reading: 570–680, Math: 610–740
Student/Faculty Ratio: 16 to 1
Transfer Out Rate: Not Reported

Rank Among 104 National Universities	**33**
Overall Rank Among 177 *Alumni Factor* Schools	**79**

Overview

The glamorous standout of the University of California system, UCLA has it all – stellar academics, storied athletics programs, and a prime location in upscale Westmont. Our data clearly indicate that UCLA generates high levels of graduate success. It earns the 33rd spot among all national universities; the 2nd highest rank in the UC System (behind Berkeley); and is ranked 10th among the 33 universities with more than 20,000 undergraduates that made our Top 177 list.

UCLA's Overall Assessment by grads is superb and receives a Top 20 ranking. Within that is a Top 10 ranking in Value for the Money. The College Experience at UCLA is ranked in the middle by its graduates (73rd), with its strongest score in Intellectual Development (31st). It is the Financial Success of UCLA grads that is the real differentiator. It ranks 21st among national universities in Financial Success overall, with a 17th ranking in Net Worth. However, among the 33 largest universities, UCLA is 1st in Percentage of Households with Net Worth above $1 million; is 2nd in average net worth; and is 3rd in average household income.

Notable Alumni

UCLA has had six Nobel Laureates since 1950, and can count numerous professional athletes, writers, lawyers, business leaders, government officials and Hollywood luminaries as famous alumni. Some of these include John Williams, Kareen Abdul Jabbar, Arthur Ashe, Tom Bradley, Carol Burnett, Francis Ford Coppola, Jimmy Connors, Mayim Bialik, Michael Ortiz, Steve Martin, Lisa Fernandez, Amy Pascal and Iva Teguri D'Aquino.

The Alumni Factor Rankings Summary

Attribute	University Rank	Overall Rank
College Experience	**73**	**144**
Intellectual Development	31	81
Social Development	52	111
Spiritual Development	67	139
Friendship Development	84	154
Preparation for Career Success	69	135
Immediate Job Opportunities	86	145
Overall Assessment	**19**	**35**
Would Personally Choose Again	17	41
Would Recommend to Student	28	62
Value for the Money	8	14
Financial Success	**21**	**39**
Income per Household	21	38
% Households with Income >$150K	35	60
Household Net Worth	17	35
% Households Net Worth >$1MM	19	37
Overall Happiness	**90**	**148**
Alumni Giving	**83**	**152**
Graduation Rate	**24**	**39**
Overall Rank	**33**	**79**

Other Key Alumni Outcomes

4.8% Are college professors
13.1% Teach at any level
56.1% Have post-graduate degrees
52.3% Live in dual-income homes
89.4% Are currently employed

See pages 134–135 for detailed explanations and definitions.

Alumni Activities During College

33.3% Community Service
20.1% Intramural Sports
19.7% Internships
10.9% Media Programs
12.9% Music Programs
50.0% Part-Time Jobs

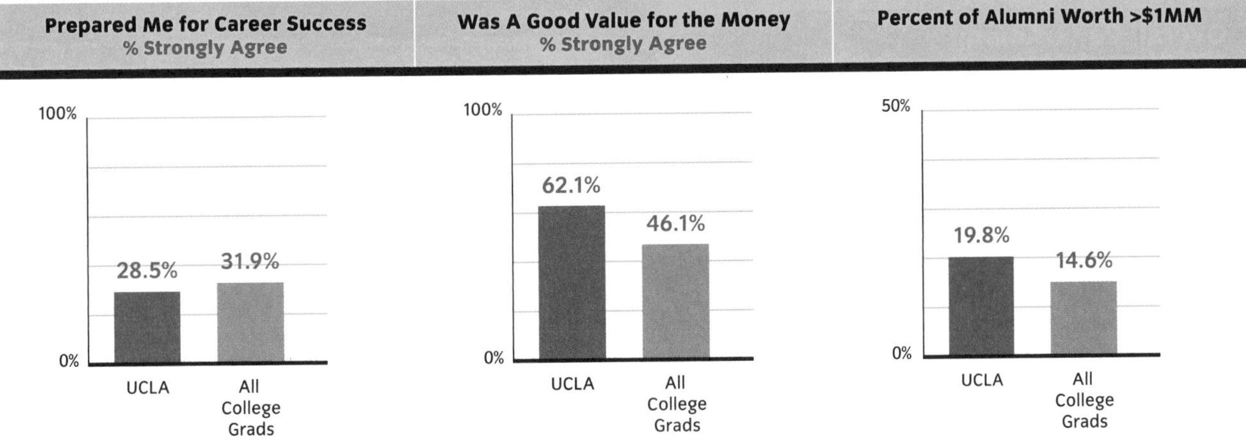

Alumni Employment

% Other 14.8%
% Independent/ Entrepreneur 18.7%
% With Large Org. 19.0%
% With Medium Org. 15.6%
% With Small Org. 10.4%
% With Govt. 8.4%
% Any Level Teaching 13.1%

Income Distribution of Graduates

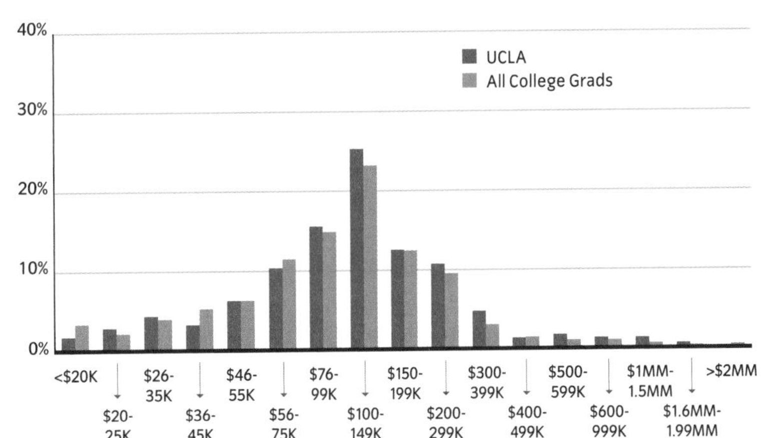

Current Selectivity & Demand Analysis for University of California, Los Angeles

Attribute	% Accepted	% Accepted Who Enroll	Freshman Retention Rate	Graduation Rate	Demand Index	Reputation Index
Score	26.0%	29.0%	97.0%	90.0%	10.57	1.12
Rank	42	107	13	39	62	55

Where are the Graduates of University of California, Los Angeles on the Political Spectrum?

Very Liberal	Liberal	Somewhat Liberal	Somewhat Conservative	Conservative	Very Conservative
		↑			

See pages 134–135 for detailed explanations and definitions.

University of California, Riverside

Location: Riverside, CA
Campus Setting: City: Large
Total Expenses: $30,335
Estimated Average Discount: $18,995 (63%)
Estimated Net Price: $11,340

Type of Institution: National University
Number of Undergraduates: 18,242
SAT Score: Reading: 450–560, Math: 480–610
Student/Faculty Ratio: 18 to 1
Transfer Out Rate: Not Reported

Rank Among 104 National Universities	**100**
Overall Rank Among 177 *Alumni Factor* Schools	**173**

Overview

One of the ten campuses in the University of California system, UC Riverside began as a citrus experimentation farm and, since the 1950s, has been home to a growing university. While UCR's reputation has been steadily building in California, it is still somewhat unknown outside the state, and is toward the bottom of the UC system, reputation-wise. That, however, does not mean that its alumni do not fare well post-graduation.

Alumni give UC Riverside average marks in the College Experience (ranked 102nd), with Intellectual Development its highest attribute (77th) of the actual experience. Like all schools in the UC system, UCR is considered a good value (56th) and grads do quite well financially after graduation (83rd in Financial Success). In fact, UCR ranks 48th in Percentage of Households with a Net Worth of $1 Million, and 90th in average Income per Household. UCR's strongest Ultimate Outcome is Financial Success & Happiness, where it is ranked 86th.

Given its relatively brief history, UCR's alumni list is not yet as deep as that of the many older colleges on this list. Ranking a strong 6th in percent of alums who are professors, its alumni list is populated with heads of departments and institutes at universities across the US. And while its grads may not be household names, they are nonetheless impressive.

Notable Alumni

Editorial cartoonist and two-time Pulitzer Prize winner Steve Breen; Nobel Prize winner in Chemistry, Richard Schork; and FAA chief and managing director of the 2002 Winter Olympic Games, Michael Huerta.

The Alumni Factor Rankings Summary

Attribute	University Rank	Overall Rank
College Experience	**102**	**175**
Intellectual Development	77	149
Social Development	91	162
Spiritual Development	94	166
Friendship Development	99	171
Preparation for Career Success	104	176
Immediate Job Opportunities	98	169
Overall Assessment	**88**	**156**
Would Personally Choose Again	99	168
Would Recommend to Student	98	170
Value for the Money	56	104
Financial Success	**83**	**135**
Income per Household	90	143
% Households with Income >$150K	103	169
Household Net Worth	75	123
% Households Net Worth >$1MM	48	84
Overall Happiness	**84**	**141**
Alumni Giving	**98**	**171**
Graduation Rate	**85**	**153**
Overall Rank	**100**	**173**

Other Key Alumni Outcomes

12.7% Are college professors
25.4% Teach at any level
59.7% Have post-graduate degrees
50.4% Live in dual-income homes
90.0% Are currently employed

See pages 134–135 for detailed explanations and definitions.

Alumni Activities During College

31.9% Community Service
24.1% Intramural Sports
25.9% Internships
13.0% Media Programs
14.6% Music Programs
50.9% Part-Time Jobs

Prepared Me for Career Success % Strongly Agree	Was A Good Value for the Money % Strongly Agree	Percent of Alumni Worth >$1MM
UC Riverside 25.6%; All College Grads 31.9%	UC Riverside 43.5%; All College Grads 46.1%	UC Riverside 14.8%; All College Grads 14.6%

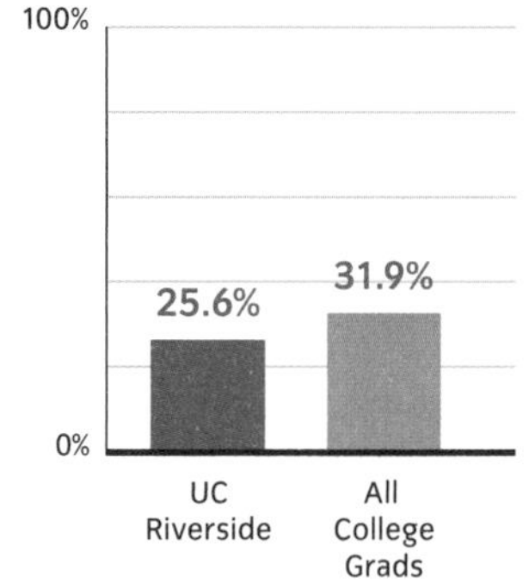

Alumni Employment

Category	%
% Independent/ Entrepreneur	8.5%
% With Large Org.	16.1%
% With Medium Org.	5.9%
% With Small Org.	12.7%
% With Govt.	9.3%
% In Farm/ Agr.	0.8%
% Any Level Teaching	25.4%
% Other	21.3%

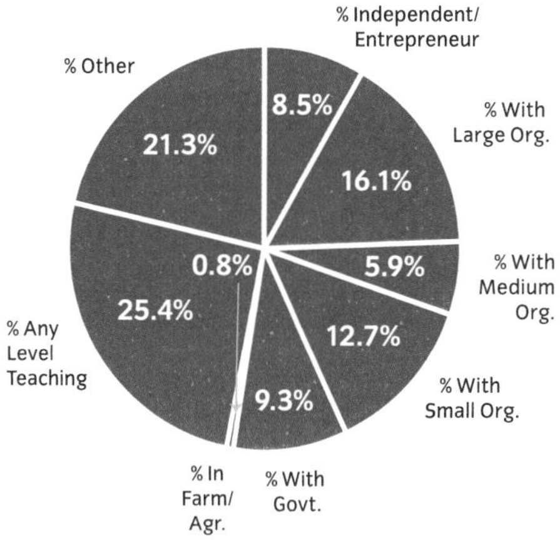

Income Distribution of Graduates

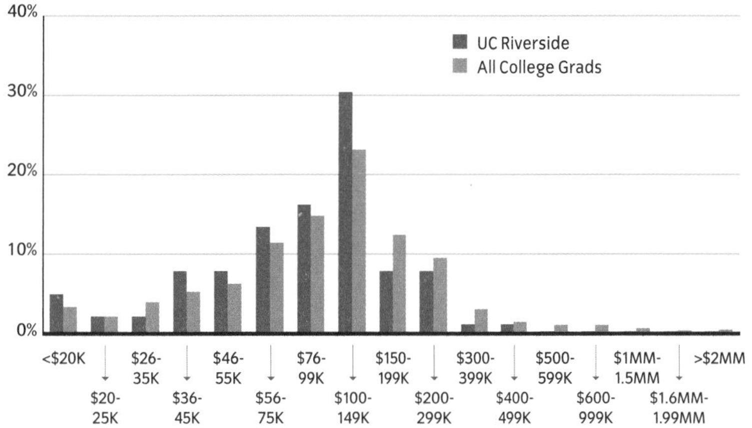

UC Riverside
All College Grads

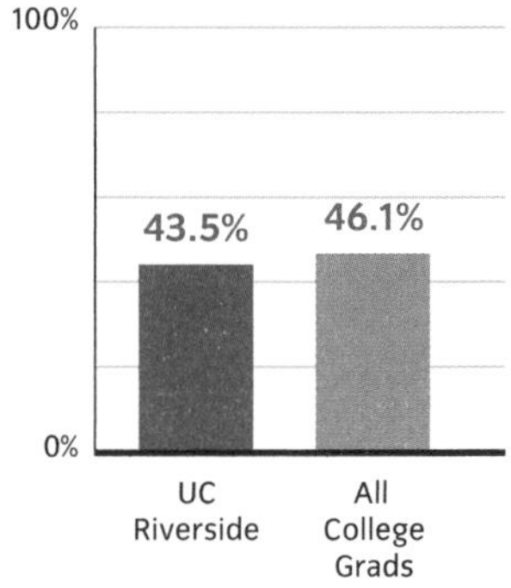

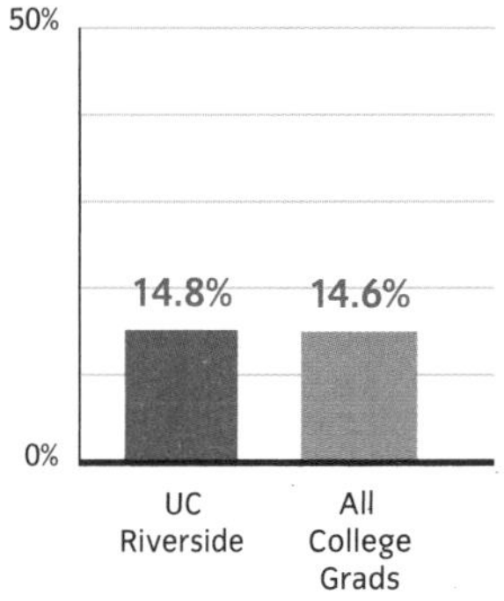

40%
30%
20%
10%
0%

<$20K, $20-25K, $26-35K, $36-45K, $46-55K, $56-75K, $76-99K, $100-149K, $150-199K, $200-299K, $300-399K, $400-499K, $500-599K, $600-999K, $1MM-1.5MM, $1.6MM-1.99MM, >$2MM

Current Selectivity & Demand Analysis for University of California, Riverside

Attribute	% Accepted	% Accepted Who Enroll	Freshman Retention Rate	Graduation Rate	Demand Index	Reputation Index
Score	76.0%	22.0%	87.0%	68.0%	7.23	0.29
Rank	162	149	140	153	112	169

Where are the Graduates of University of California, Riverside on the Political Spectrum?

Very Liberal	Liberal	Somewhat Liberal	Somewhat Conservative	Conservative	Very Conservative
		↑			

See pages 134–135 for detailed explanations and definitions.

University of California, San Diego

Location: La Jolla, CA
Campus Setting: City: Large
Total Expenses: $29,506
Estimated Average Discount: $16,885 (57%)
Estimated Net Price: $12,621

Type of Institution: National University
Number of Undergraduates: 23,663
SAT Score: Reading: 540–670, Math: 610–720
Student/Faculty Ratio: 19 to 1
Transfer Out Rate: Not Reported

Rank Among 104 National Universities	**69**
Overall Rank Among 177 *Alumni Factor* Schools	**135**

Overview

The biotech research hub of the University of California system, UC San Diego is growing in its importance to California and to the world. Intellectual Development is its strongest suit – ranked 26th among national universities and ranked 2nd (behind Berkeley) in the UC system. UCSD is a very large school (the 26th largest in our Top 177 schools), which brings challenges smaller schools do not face. Specifically, schools like UCSD, without a major unifying factor such as a strong athletic program or centuries of history, have a tougher time creating a campus environment that is special and transformational. That fact is apparent in the fairly lackluster rankings across the rest of the College Experience.

In terms of the Overall Assessment and Financial Success of alums, UCSD ranks quite high at 52nd and 54th, respectively. UCSD performs equally well across all the Ultimate Outcomes, showing a slight edge in Friendships & Intellectual Capability. Impressively, it ranks 7th among the 33 large schools (20,000 or more undergrads) on our list in percentage of millionaire households.

Notable Alumni

Groundbreaking biologist Craig Venter, first to sequence the human genome; Nobel Prize-winning geneticist Bruce Beutler; biotechnology pioneer David Goeddel; *Beavis and Butthead* creator Mike Judge; and many other leaders in their fields.

The Alumni Factor Rankings Summary

Attribute	University Rank	Overall Rank
College Experience	**79**	**151**
Intellectual Development	26	73
Social Development	93	164
Spiritual Development	69	141
Friendship Development	67	137
Preparation for Career Success	66	132
Immediate Job Opportunities	92	152
Overall Assessment	**52**	**101**
Would Personally Choose Again	68	122
Would Recommend to Student	64	119
Value for the Money	28	53
Financial Success	**54**	**91**
Income per Household	52	82
% Households with Income >$150K	64	110
Household Net Worth	69	119
% Households Net Worth >$1MM	40	72
Overall Happiness	**67**	**115**
Alumni Giving	**91**	**162**
Graduation Rate	**34**	**67**
Overall Rank	**69**	**135**

Other Key Alumni Outcomes

9.0% Are college professors
11.7% Teach at any level
49.1% Have post-graduate degrees
50.0% Live in dual-income homes
90.2% Are currently employed

See pages 134–135 for detailed explanations and definitions.

Alumni Activities During College

29.3% Community Service
31.5% Intramural Sports
29.7% Internships
10.8% Media Programs
7.8% Music Programs
50.0% Part-Time Jobs

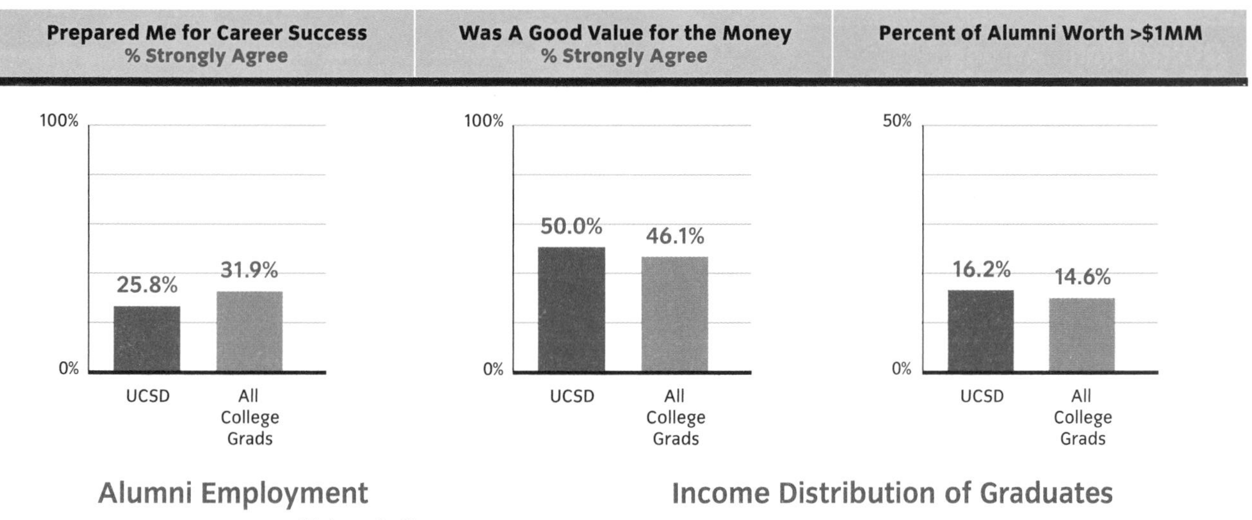

Alumni Employment

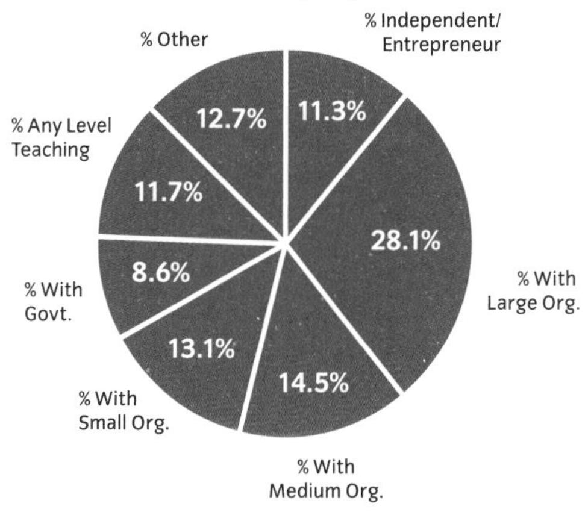

Income Distribution of Graduates

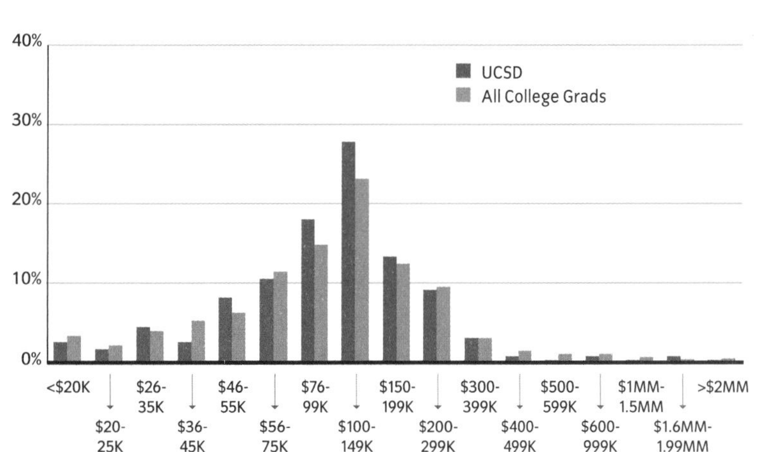

Current Selectivity & Demand Analysis for University of California, San Diego

Attribute	% Accepted	% Accepted Who Enroll	Freshman Retention Rate	Graduation Rate	Demand Index	Reputation Index
Score	38.0%	22.0%	96.0%	86.0%	7.96	0.58
Rank	73	149	27	67	91	107

Where are the Graduates of University of California, San Diego on the Political Spectrum?

Very Liberal	Liberal	Somewhat Liberal	Somewhat Conservative	Conservative	Very Conservative
		↑			

See pages 134–135 for detailed explanations and definitions.

University of California, Santa Barbara

Location: Santa Barbara, CA
Campus Setting: Suburb: Midsize
Total Expenses: $31,691
Estimated Average Discount: $16,801 (53%)
Estimated Net Price: $14,890

Type of Institution: National University
Number of Undergraduates: 19,186
SAT Score: Reading: 540–650, Math: 550–670
Student/Faculty Ratio: 17 to 1
Transfer Out Rate: 10%

Rank Among 104 National Universities	**58**
Overall Rank Among 177 *Alumni Factor* Schools	**123**

Overview

The hip, friendly, laid-back gem in the UC system, UC Santa Barbara has it all: a beautiful campus beside the Pacific in Santa Barbara; the 2nd happiest grads in the UC system and the 2nd best College Experience among them all (behind Berkeley). UCSB has the strongest Ultimate Outcome rank in the UC system (39th among national universities) and enjoys, by far, the strongest Social and Friendship Development among the ten UC system campuses. Like other UC schools, it is virtually impossible to gain entry from outside California – to the detriment of non-Californians.

For a well-rounded, comprehensive education, UCSB is very hard to beat. Among UC system schools, UCSB ranks 3rd in the overall *Alumni Factor* rankings behind Berkeley and UCLA. However, with its consistent strength across each of the graduate outcomes we measure, UCSB is an excellent all-around choice for the undergraduate years. It ranks 2nd (just behind UCLA) in average Household Net Worth. And among all national universities, it falls in the Top 30 on three attributes, including Value for the Money, making it hard to beat.

Notable Alumni

Michael Douglas and Benjamin Bratt; singer-songwriter Jack Johnson; Nobel Prize winner Carol Greider; and famed oceanographer Robert Ballard.

The Alumni Factor Rankings Summary

Attribute	University Rank	Overall Rank
College Experience	**49**	**113**
Intellectual Development	42	99
Social Development	19	59
Spiritual Development	31	92
Friendship Development	24	79
Preparation for Career Success	92	163
Immediate Job Opportunities	83	134
Overall Assessment	**47**	**93**
Would Personally Choose Again	65	119
Would Recommend to Student	46	94
Value for the Money	30	57
Financial Success	**60**	**100**
Income per Household	77	118
% Households with Income >$150K	74	124
Household Net Worth	35	60
% Households Net Worth >$1MM	56	97
Overall Happiness	**56**	**102**
Alumni Giving	**98**	**171**
Graduation Rate	**60**	**118**
Overall Rank	**58**	**123**

Other Key Alumni Outcomes

4.3%	Are college professors
13.5%	Teach at any level
52.1%	Have post-graduate degrees
51.8%	Live in dual-income homes
90.1%	Are currently employed

See pages 134–135 for detailed explanations and definitions.

Alumni Activities During College

31.4% Community Service
38.6% Intramural Sports
27.1% Internships
16.5% Media Programs
7.8% Music Programs
55.0% Part-Time Jobs

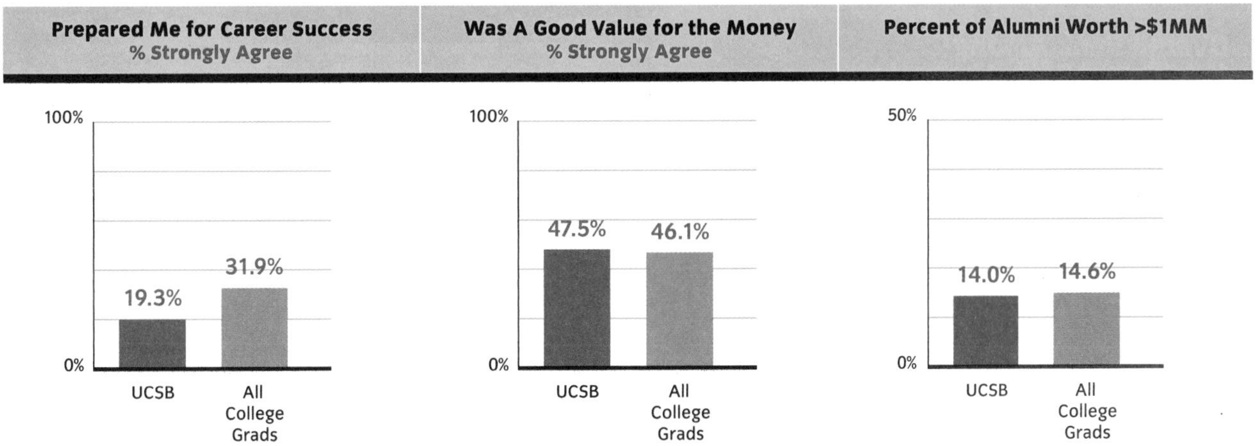

Prepared Me for Career Success % Strongly Agree	Was A Good Value for the Money % Strongly Agree	Percent of Alumni Worth >$1MM
UCSB 19.3%; All College Grads 31.9%	UCSB 47.5%; All College Grads 46.1%	UCSB 14.0%; All College Grads 14.6%

Alumni Employment

Category	%
% Independent/ Entrepreneur	16.3%
% With Large Org.	19.1%
% With Medium Org.	14.2%
% With Small Org.	12.1%
% With Govt.	7.0%
% Any Level Teaching	13.5%
% Other	17.8%

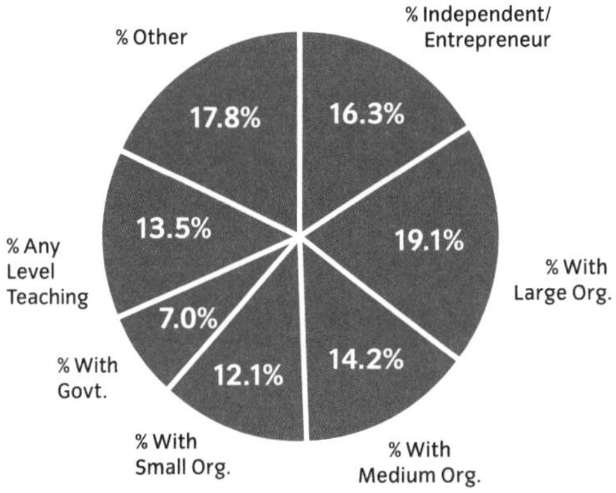

Income Distribution of Graduates

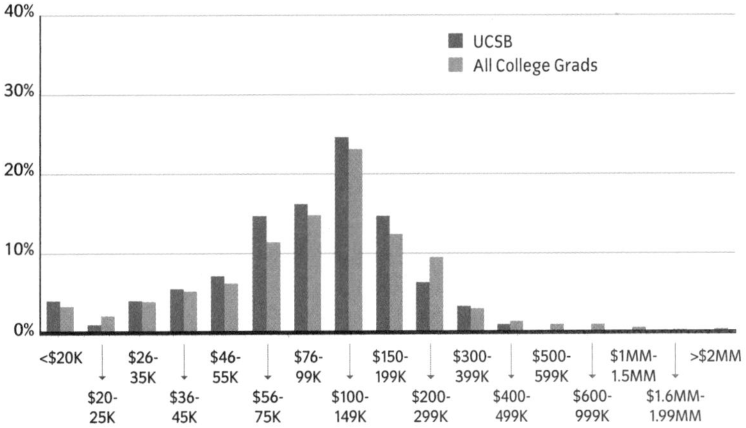

Current Selectivity & Demand Analysis for University of California, Santa Barbara

Attribute	% Accepted	% Accepted Who Enroll	Freshman Retention Rate	Graduation Rate	Demand Index	Reputation Index
Score	45.0%	18.0%	91.0%	79.0%	11.40	0.40
Rank	91	169	102	118	51	146

Where are the Graduates of University of California, Santa Barbara on the Political Spectrum?

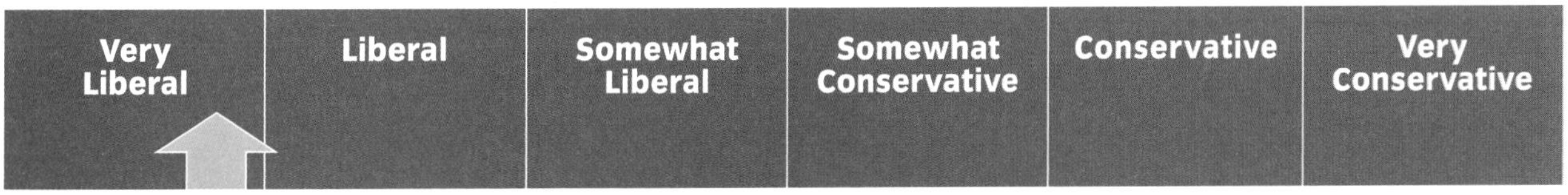

Very Liberal	Liberal	Somewhat Liberal	Somewhat Conservative	Conservative	Very Conservative
↑					

See pages 134–135 for detailed explanations and definitions.

University of Chicago

Location: Chicago, IL
Campus Setting: City: Large
Total Expenses: $59,950
Estimated Average Discount: $30,026 (50%)
Estimated Net Price: $29,924

Type of Institution: National University
Number of Undergraduates: 5,270
SAT Score: Reading: 700–790, Math: 700–780
Student/Faculty Ratio: 6 to 1
Transfer Out Rate: Not Reported

Rank Among 104 National Universities	**52**
Overall Rank Among 177 *Alumni Factor* Schools	**114**

Overview

America's Midwest home for deep and serious thinkers, the University of Chicago is an intellectual powerhouse – an eclectic academic culture where the mind rules. It is a school that challenges preconceptions and is extremely rigorous (the country's 11th toughest school in grading). It is also one of the schools among the 177 listed whose *Alumni Factor* ranking will be most surprising – it is ranked 52nd among national universities.

In line with its excellent reputation, grads give the school extremely high marks in Intellectual Development (1st among national universities, 4th among all schools), but they are less effusive about Social Development (101st), Friendship Development (61st) and Preparation for Career Success (66th). They are also less likely to Personally Choose Again (83rd) or Recommend to a Prospective Student (72nd). However, the Financial Success of UChicago grads is excellent (44th). Not surprisingly, its highest ranking Ultimate Outcome is Financial Success & Intellectual Capability (ranked 21st). Perhaps, in the end, this is why alums give back to the school at such a high rate, earning it the 12th spot in Alumni Giving.

Despite the market-oriented, conservative rep of the famed "Chicago School" economists, alums skew toward the liberal side overall, though graduates of both stripes populate its impressive alumni list.

Notable Alumni

Notable alumni, such as public servants David Axelrod, Robert Bork, John Paul Stevens and Eliott Ness; film director Philip Kaufman; business leaders Casey Cowell, Karen Katen and Thomas Ricketts; and numerous government leaders, academicians and Nobel Laureates are all proud UChicago grads.

The Alumni Factor Rankings Summary

Attribute	University Rank	Overall Rank
College Experience	**54**	**122**
Intellectual Development	1	4
Social Development	101	174
Spiritual Development	39	104
Friendship Development	61	130
Preparation for Career Success	66	132
Immediate Job Opportunities	88	147
Overall Assessment	**64**	**121**
Would Personally Choose Again	83	146
Would Recommend to Student	72	130
Value for the Money	40	72
Financial Success	**44**	**76**
Income per Household	31	49
% Households with Income >$150K	40	69
Household Net Worth	73	121
% Households Net Worth >$1MM	45	81
Overall Happiness	**99**	**171**
Alumni Giving	**12**	**57**
Graduation Rate	**12**	**16**
Overall Rank	**52**	**114**

Other Key Alumni Outcomes

7.4%	Are college professors
10.0%	Teach at any level
63.4%	Have post-graduate degrees
45.0%	Live in dual-income homes
91.1%	Are currently employed

See pages 134–135 for detailed explanations and definitions.

Alumni Activities During College

26.3% Community Service
35.3% Intramural Sports
16.3% Internships
22.6% Media Programs
20.9% Music Programs
40.5% Part-Time Jobs

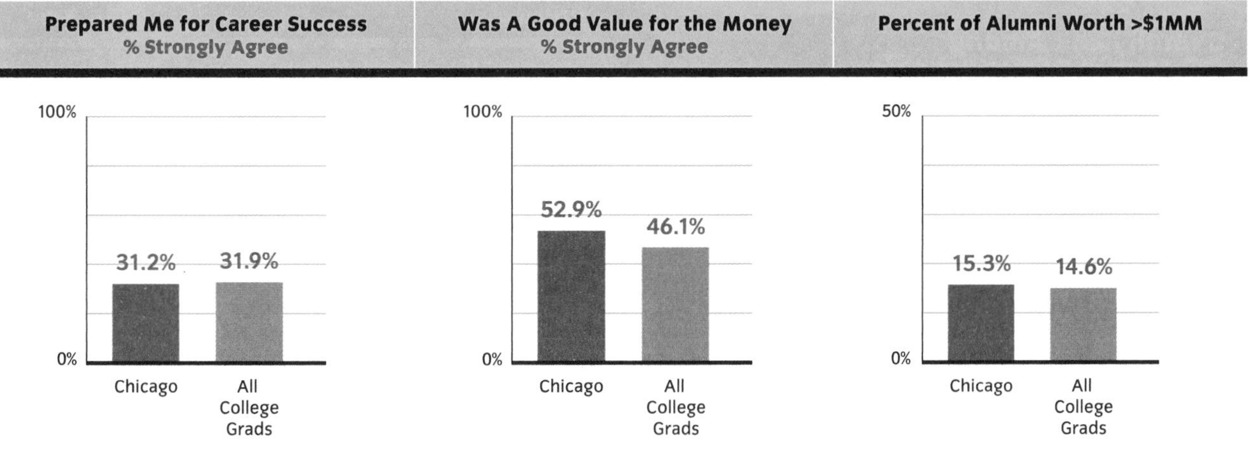

Alumni Employment

% Other 13.7%
% Independent/ Entrepreneur 15.8%
% With Large Org. 19.5%
% With Medium Org. 21.6%
% With Small Org. 14.7%
% With Govt. 4.7%
% Any Level Teaching 10.0%

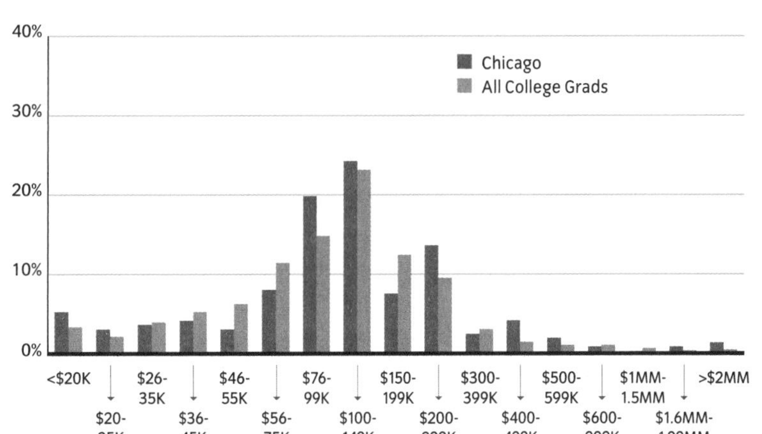

Current Selectivity & Demand Analysis for University of Chicago

Attribute	% Accepted	% Accepted Who Enroll	Freshman Retention Rate	Graduation Rate	Demand Index	Reputation Index
Score	16.0%	40.0%	98.0%	93.0%	15.42	2.50
Rank	18	42	4	16	19	21

Where are the Graduates of University of Chicago on the Political Spectrum?

Very Liberal	Liberal	Somewhat Liberal	Somewhat Conservative	Conservative	Very Conservative
	↑				

See pages 134–135 for detailed explanations and definitions.

University of Colorado Boulder

Location: Boulder, CO
Campus Setting: City: Small
Total Expenses: $27,236
Estimated Average Discount: $8,859 (33%)
Estimated Net Price: $18,377

Type of Institution: National University
Number of Undergraduates: 26,648
SAT Score: Reading: 520–630, Math: 540–650
Student/Faculty Ratio: 18 to 1
Transfer Out Rate: 18%

Rank Among 104 National Universities	**81**
Overall Rank Among 177 *Alumni Factor* Schools	**149**

Overview

If you are looking for a vibrant social life in a beautiful setting – with as much academic challenge as you desire – University of Colorado Boulder is a good choice. Boulder produces some of the happiest graduates in the nation (ranked 17th), and it is not difficult to figure out the reason – laid-back contentment is the goal for many Boulder students and grads. Well-known as a bohemian, relaxed, social school, Boulder develops a wide range of graduates, from the diligent and successful, to the outdoor lover, to the artistic dreamer. This kind of diversity is abundant at Boulder, and it is what gives the campus and community its appeal.

The biggest surprise is that grads don't give higher scores for the College Experience itself (95th) versus other schools. Social Development (54th) is its strongest developmental attribute. In fact, Boulder performs at or below the composite of all college graduates on virtually every measure, yet grads would repeat the experience at a higher rate than 75% of the schools in *The Alumni Factor* rankings. Accordingly, Would Personally Chose Again is its second highest attribute. That says something about the Boulder mystique.

Notable Alumni

Rick Reilly; co-founder of ad agency Wieden & Kennedy, David Kennedy; ESPN host Chris Fowler; and some of our country's finest astronauts.

The Alumni Factor Rankings Summary

Attribute	University Rank	Overall Rank
College Experience	**95**	**168**
Intellectual Development	85	157
Social Development	54	114
Spiritual Development	82	154
Friendship Development	77	147
Preparation for Career Success	96	168
Immediate Job Opportunities	96	165
Overall Assessment	**62**	**115**
Would Personally Choose Again	45	83
Would Recommend to Student	69	126
Value for the Money	68	124
Financial Success	**62**	**103**
Income per Household	55	88
% Households with Income >$150K	66	112
Household Net Worth	67	114
% Households Net Worth >$1MM	52	90
Overall Happiness	**17**	**38**
Alumni Giving	**91**	**162**
Graduation Rate	**85**	**153**
Overall Rank	**81**	**149**

Other Key Alumni Outcomes

5.5% Are college professors
13.8% Teach at any level
54.1% Have post-graduate degrees
52.0% Live in dual-income homes
91.0% Are currently employed

Alumni Activities During College

28.1% Community Service
25.3% Intramural Sports
22.9% Internships
10.7% Media Programs
10.4% Music Programs
54.5% Part-Time Jobs

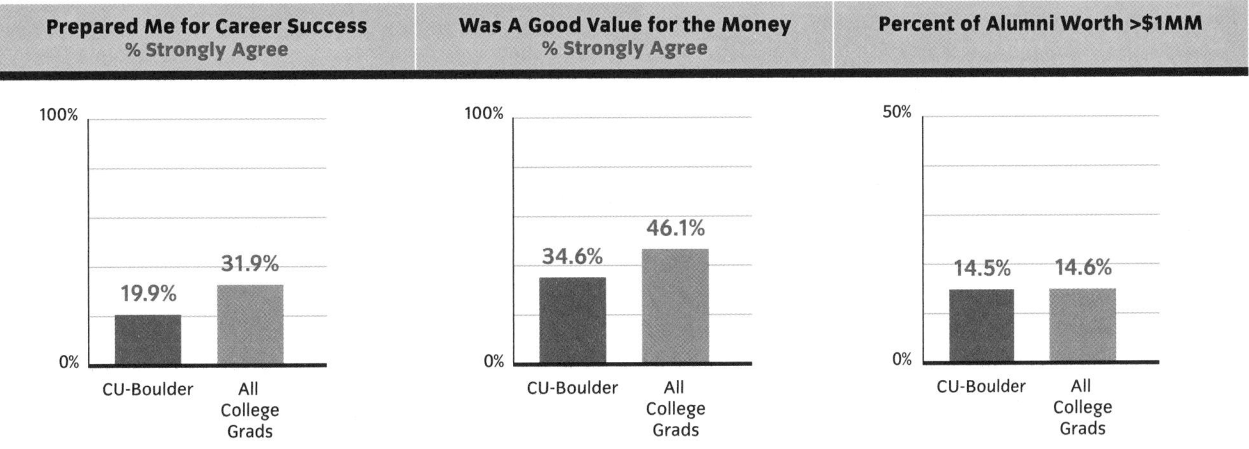

Alumni Employment

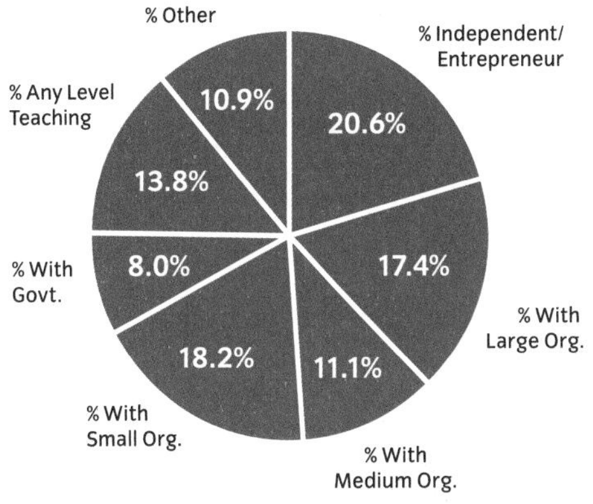

Income Distribution of Graduates

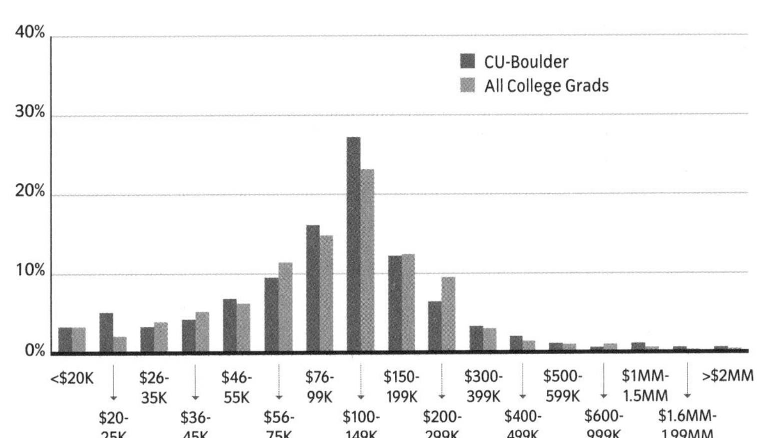

Current Selectivity & Demand Analysis for University of Colorado Boulder

Attribute	% Accepted	% Accepted Who Enroll	Freshman Retention Rate	Graduation Rate	Demand Index	Reputation Index
Score	87.0%	32.0%	85.0%	68.0%	3.60	0.37
Rank	173	92	151	153	162	154

Where are the Graduates of University of Colorado Boulder on the Political Spectrum?

Very Liberal	Liberal	Somewhat Liberal	Somewhat Conservative	Conservative	Very Conservative
		⇧			

See pages 134–135 for detailed explanations and definitions.

University of Connecticut

Location: Storrs, CT
Campus Setting: Town: Fringe
Total Expenses: $25,220
Estimated Average Discount: $10,343 (41%)
Estimated Net Price: $14,877

Type of Institution: National University
Number of Undergraduates: 17,345
SAT Score: Reading: 550–640, Math: 580–670
Student/Faculty Ratio: 18 to 1
Transfer Out Rate: 14%

Rank Among 104 National Universities	**82**
Overall Rank Among 177 *Alumni Factor* Schools	**151**

Overview

The University of Connecticut is a school whose reputation is deservedly on the rise – and our data suggest that this rise will continue. Schools such as UConn, with grads whose actual Financial Success (ranked 42nd) and Happiness (62nd) significantly outpace their school's overall ranking (82nd) tend to be larger schools where the College Experience suffers in comparison to alumni results. UConn is a case in point. Schools such as this need a catalytic strategy to ignite change and unify students and alumni around the future. Whether it is a redefined academic focus, a revitalized commitment to athletics, a major infrastructure improvement or, as in UConn's case, all three, heightened excellence typically follows. When these transformational events change the student experience, we expect to eventually see it in the school's *Alumni Factor* ranking. Larger schools without a strong athletic program or similar community unifier (Emory, Tufts, NYU, Johns Hopkins, Northeastern, Drexel) will have a more difficult task improving the College Experience. Fortunately for UConn, they are now in an excellent spot to leverage their position – and they have the campus and resources to do it.

Notable Alumni

Walmart US President Bill Simon; Juilliard School President Joseph Polisi; Tulane President Scott Cowen; and numerous men and women basketball players that have made the Huskies famous.

The Alumni Factor Rankings Summary

Attribute	University Rank	Overall Rank
College Experience	**103**	**176**
Intellectual Development	102	175
Social Development	86	156
Spiritual Development	99	171
Friendship Development	95	166
Preparation for Career Success	98	170
Immediate Job Opportunities	98	169
Overall Assessment	**77**	**139**
Would Personally Choose Again	90	156
Would Recommend to Student	72	130
Value for the Money	56	104
Financial Success	**42**	**73**
Income per Household	24	42
% Households with Income >$150K	28	52
Household Net Worth	43	77
% Households Net Worth >$1MM	75	126
Overall Happiness	**62**	**111**
Alumni Giving	**78**	**145**
Graduation Rate	**48**	**100**
Overall Rank	**82**	**151**

Other Key Alumni Outcomes

4.8%	Are college professors
16.7%	Teach at any level
52.6%	Have post-graduate degrees
59.2%	Live in dual-income homes
93.0%	Are currently employed

See pages 134–135 for detailed explanations and definitions.

Alumni Activities During College

22.0% Community Service
32.2% Intramural Sports
22.0% Internships
16.8% Media Programs
14.4% Music Programs
42.5% Part-Time Jobs

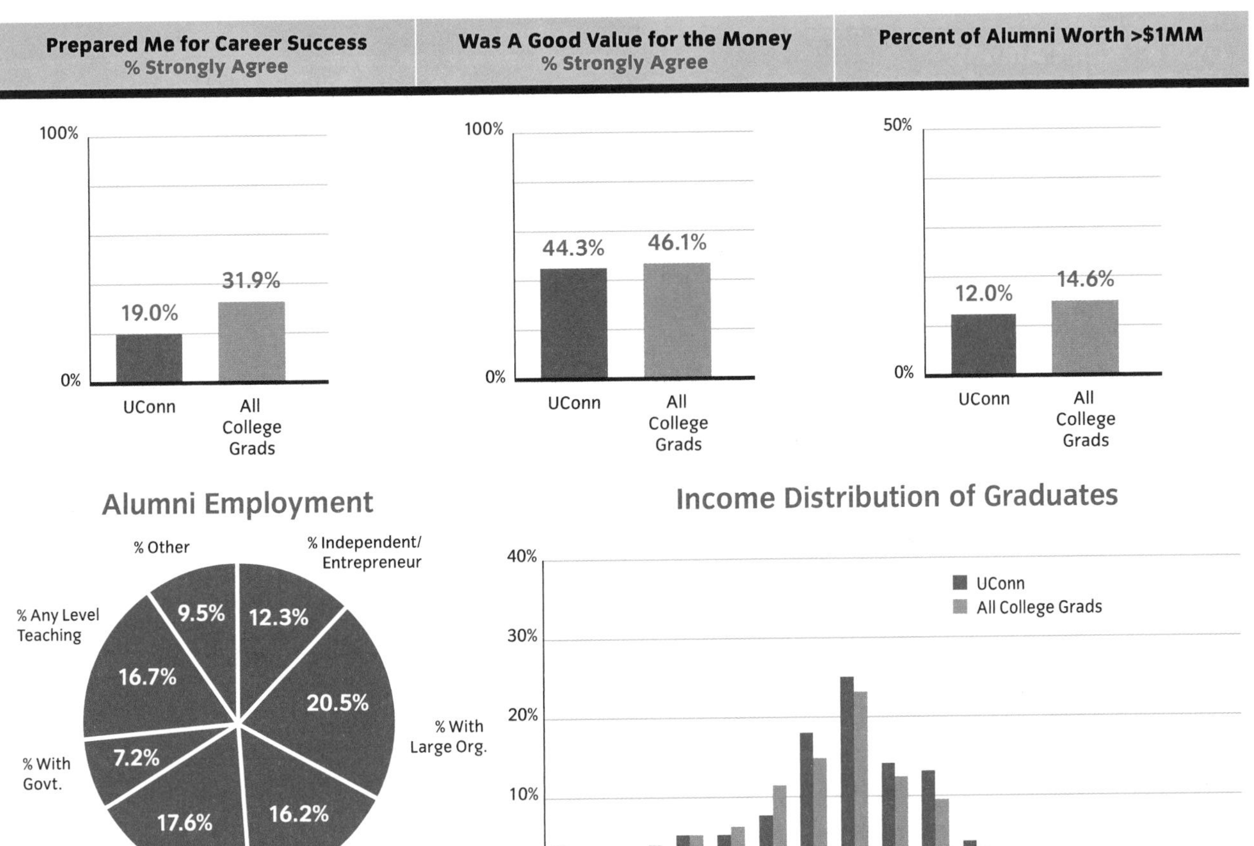

Current Selectivity & Demand Analysis for University of Connecticut

Attribute	% Accepted	% Accepted Who Enroll	Freshman Retention Rate	Graduation Rate	Demand Index	Reputation Index
Score	47.0%	26.0%	93.0%	81.0%	8.19	0.55
Rank	99	125	73	100	98	112

Where are the Graduates of University of Connecticut on the Political Spectrum?

Very Liberal	Liberal	Somewhat Liberal	Somewhat Conservative	Conservative	Very Conservative
			↑		

See pages 134–135 for detailed explanations and definitions.

University of Delaware

Location: Newark, DE
Campus Setting: Suburb: Large
Total Expenses: $23,688
Estimated Average Discount: $10,312 (44%)
Estimated Net Price: $13,376

Type of Institution: National University
Number of Undergraduates: 17,507
SAT Score: Reading: 540–650, Math: 560–660
Student/Faculty Ratio: 15 to 1
Transfer Out Rate: Not Reported

Rank Among 104 National Universities	**78**
Overall Rank Among 177 *Alumni Factor* Schools	**146**

Overview

While it has a relatively minor national profile, the University of Delaware is well known to the Northeast metro corridor as a provider of solid academics at a good value. Graduates concur with that reputation. With a strong Overall Assessment (55th) and its highest ranking in Would Recommend to a Student (42nd), it is clear that grads are pleased with UD. The College Experience is fairly strong (83rd) with Social Development (61st) and Immediate Job Opportunities (63rd) as its best attributes.

From a Financial Success standpoint, income measures are higher than net worth measures, indicating a hard-working group of alumni who were not particularly privileged (the opposite could indicate inherited wealth). UD's strongest Ultimate Outcome is Friendships & Intellectual Capability (52nd), but it performs consistently across all the Ultimate Outcomes. UD feels like a friendly, solid and slightly conservative Midwestern school that just happens to be on the East coast. The UD Blue Hens are quietly on the rise.

Notable Alumni

Vice President Joe Biden and his wife, Jill; pro quarterback Joe Flacco and former pro quarterback Rich Gannon; Chairman of EA Games Larry Probst; Sony Entertainment President Steve Mosko; and popular New Jersey Governor Chris Christie.

The Alumni Factor Rankings Summary

Attribute	University Rank	Overall Rank
College Experience	**83**	**155**
Intellectual Development	93	165
Social Development	61	122
Spiritual Development	80	152
Friendship Development	72	142
Preparation for Career Success	75	142
Immediate Job Opportunities	63	102
Overall Assessment	**55**	**105**
Would Personally Choose Again	56	106
Would Recommend to Student	42	85
Value for the Money	62	113
Financial Success	**69**	**112**
Income per Household	53	85
% Households with Income >$150K	56	97
Household Net Worth	78	126
% Households Net Worth >$1MM	76	127
Overall Happiness	**59**	**106**
Alumni Giving	**67**	**131**
Graduation Rate	**65**	**127**
Overall Rank	**78**	**146**

Other Key Alumni Outcomes

5.5% Are college professors
14.1% Teach at any level
54.2% Have post-graduate degrees
60.1% Live in dual-income homes
91.5% Are currently employed

See pages 134–135 for detailed explanations and definitions.

Alumni Activities During College

20.5% Community Service
32.3% Intramural Sports
24.1% Internships
12.8% Media Programs
20.9% Music Programs
44.1% Part-Time Jobs

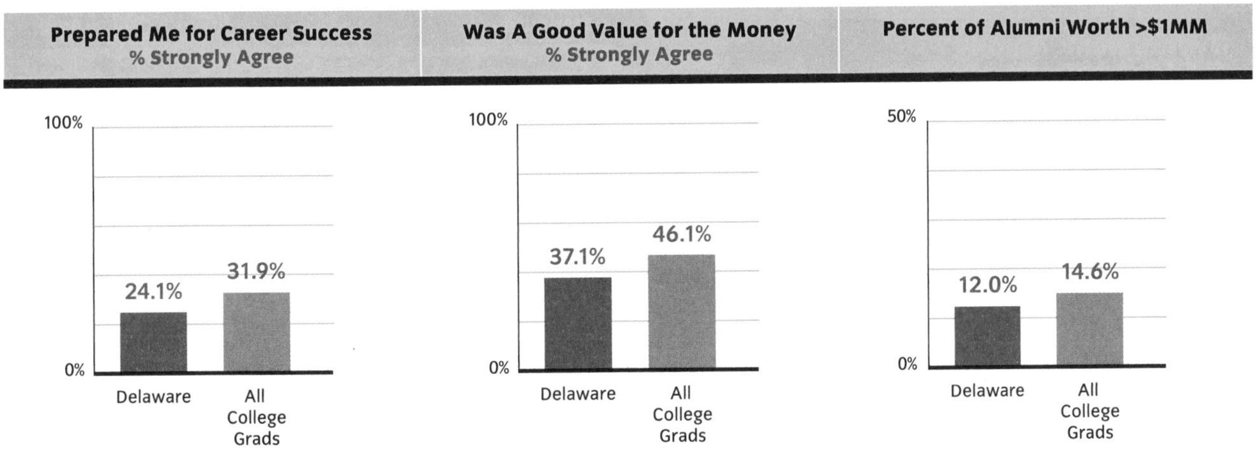

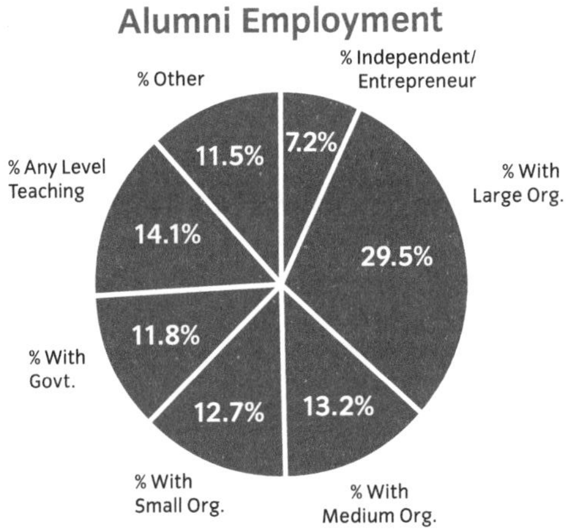

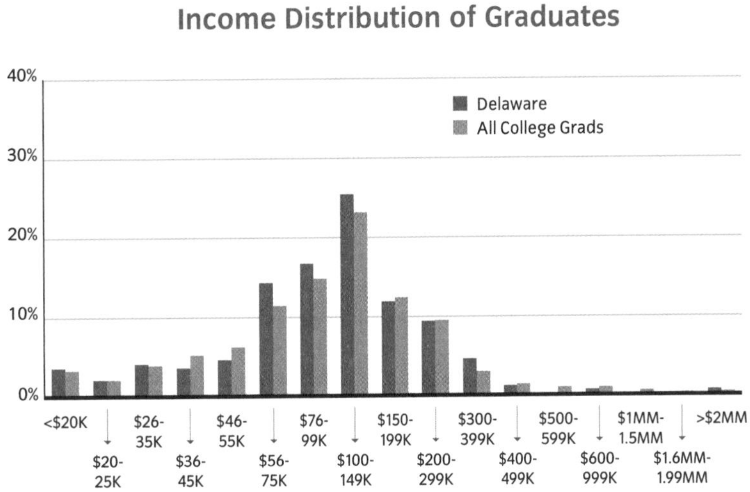

Prepared Me for Career Success (% Strongly Agree)

	Delaware	All College Grads
%	24.1%	31.9%

Was A Good Value for the Money (% Strongly Agree)

	Delaware	All College Grads
%	37.1%	46.1%

Percent of Alumni Worth >$1MM

	Delaware	All College Grads
%	12.0%	14.6%

Alumni Employment

Category	%
% Independent/ Entrepreneur	7.2%
% With Large Org.	29.5%
% With Medium Org.	13.2%
% With Small Org.	12.7%
% With Govt.	11.8%
% Any Level Teaching	14.1%
% Other	11.5%

Income Distribution of Graduates

Delaware
All College Grads

40%
30%
20%
10%
0%

<$20K, $20-25K, $26-35K, $36-45K, $46-55K, $56-75K, $76-99K, $100-149K, $150-199K, $200-299K, $300-399K, $400-499K, $500-599K, $600-999K, $1MM-1.5MM, $1.6MM-1.99MM, >$2MM

Current Selectivity & Demand Analysis for University of Delaware

Attribute	% Accepted	% Accepted Who Enroll	Freshman Retention Rate	Graduation Rate	Demand Index	Reputation Index
Score	61.0%	29.0%	92.0%	77.0%	5.57	0.48
Rank	130	107	86	127	134	127

Where are the Graduates of University of Delaware on the Political Spectrum?

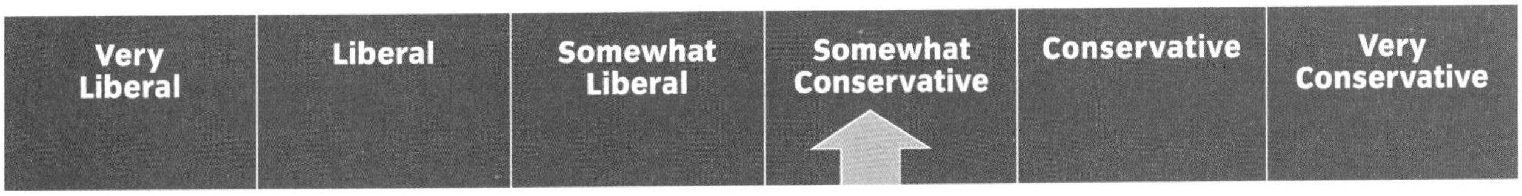

Very Liberal	Liberal	Somewhat Liberal	Somewhat Conservative	Conservative	Very Conservative
			↑		

See pages 134–135 for detailed explanations and definitions.

University of Florida

Location: Gainesville, FL
Campus Setting: City: Midsize
Total Expenses: $19,257
Estimated Average Discount: $7,678 (40%)
Estimated Net Price: $11,579

Type of Institution: National University
Number of Undergraduates: 32,660
SAT Score: Reading: 570–670, Math: 590–690
Student/Faculty Ratio: 21 to 1
Transfer Out Rate: 4%

Rank Among 104 National Universities	**36**
Overall Rank Among 177 *Alumni Factor* Schools	**81**

Overview

The state of Florida's highest ranked and second largest university, UF is not only tops in Florida – it ranks 12th among all universities with more than 20,000 undergraduates. The Gators rule the Sunshine State in *The Alumni Factor* rankings with the 36th spot among national universities. Florida grads also perform quite well in the market and have a lifetime love affair with the Gators.

Ranked 12th among national universities in the Overall Assessment (and in the Top 20 among all schools) Gator spirit is well founded. UF earns Top 25 rankings in six attributes. Its across-the-board strong scores in the College Experience show that the Gators have cracked the code for building a unified experience for its large student body, with its stellar athletic programs leading the way. UF ranks 9th in Would Recommend (3rd among large schools with more than 20,000 students) and is in the Top 20 in Value for the Money. Gator grads are also very happy (31st) and fare well financially (81st) – perhaps a reflection of their 21st spot in Preparation for Career Success.

Despite its national prominence, die-hard Gators will want to know how they fare versus their SEC competitors – and on that measure, they can be quite proud. They are 2nd in the SEC in Value for the Money, 3rd in the league in Preparation for Career Success, 2nd in Would Personally Choose Again, 4th in Would Recommend, and 2nd in grads who get a post-graduate degree. UF grads are known as power players in the Florida political scene and beyond.

Notable Alumni

Academy Award-winning filmmaker Jonathan Demme; author Rita Mae Brown; actress Faye Dunaway; *SNL* alum Darrell Hammond; Rite Aid founder Alexander Grass; Tim Tebow; Olympian Dara Torres; ESPN's Erin Andrews; and Senators Marco Rubio and Bob Graham.

The Alumni Factor Rankings Summary

Attribute	University Rank	Overall Rank
College Experience	**33**	**89**
Intellectual Development	51	117
Social Development	19	59
Spiritual Development	33	94
Friendship Development	53	119
Preparation for Career Success	21	49
Immediate Job Opportunities	45	74
Overall Assessment	**12**	**20**
Would Personally Choose Again	23	50
Would Recommend to Student	9	14
Value for the Money	17	32
Financial Success	**81**	**132**
Income per Household	61	96
% Households with Income >$150K	76	126
Household Net Worth	73	121
% Households Net Worth >$1MM	100	165
Overall Happiness	**31**	**57**
Alumni Giving	**45**	**108**
Graduation Rate	**38**	**81**
Overall Rank	**36**	**81**

Other Key Alumni Outcomes

5.2% Are college professors
13.1% Teach at any level
53.5% Have post-graduate degrees
48.0% Live in dual-income homes
92.7% Are currently employed

See pages 134–135 for detailed explanations and definitions.

Alumni Activities During College

28.8% Community Service
29.1% Intramural Sports
25.5% Internships
8.6% Media Programs
11.6% Music Programs
51.5% Part-Time Jobs

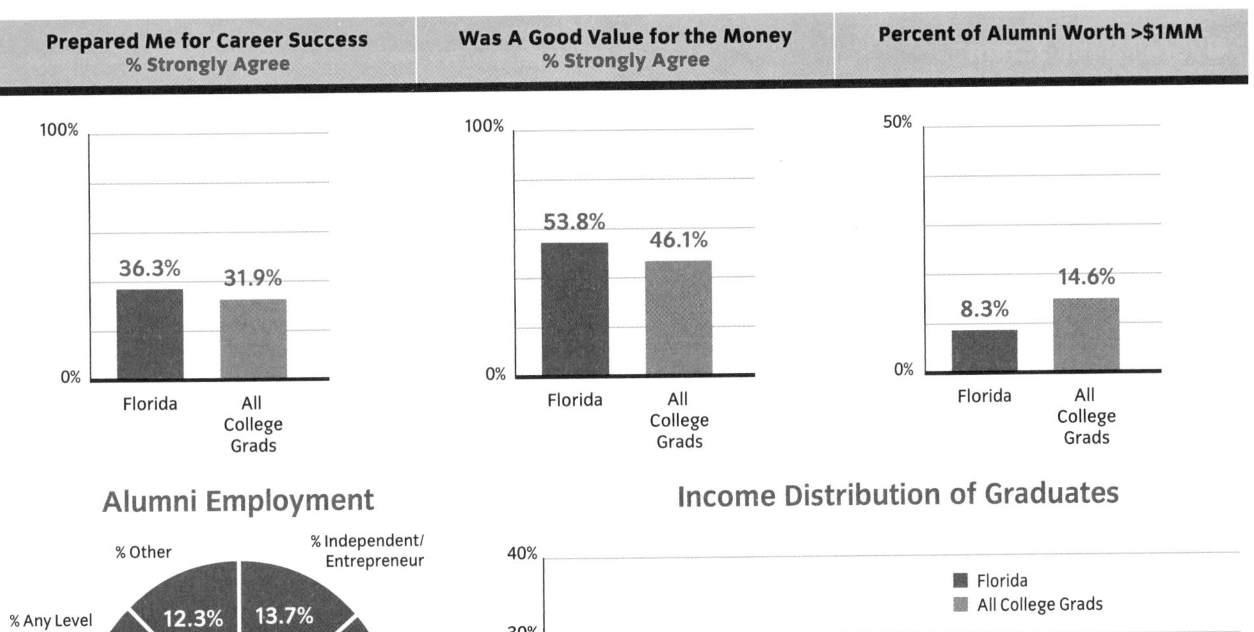

Alumni Employment

% Other 12.3%
% Independent/Entrepreneur 13.7%
% With Large Org. 25.2%
% With Medium Org. 12.2%
% With Small Org. 12.5%
% With Govt. 11.0%
% Any Level Teaching 13.1%

Income Distribution of Graduates

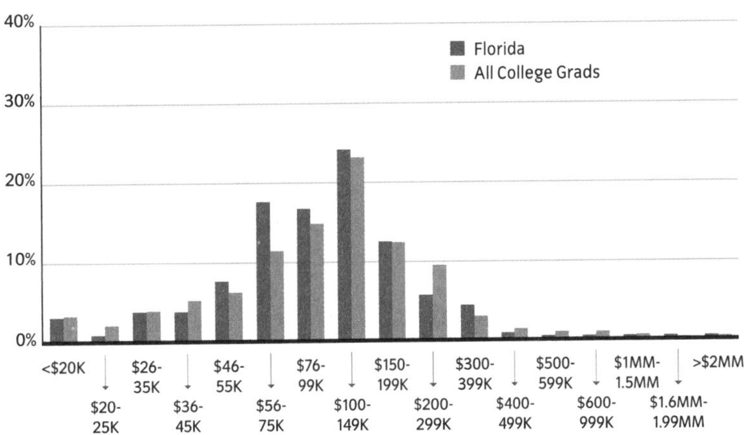

Current Selectivity & Demand Analysis for University of Florida

Attribute	% Accepted	% Accepted Who Enroll	Freshman Retention Rate	Graduation Rate	Demand Index	Reputation Index
Score	43.0%	55.0%	96.0%	84.0%	4.25	1.28
Rank	88	14	27	81	150	47

Where are the Graduates of University of Florida on the Political Spectrum?

Very Liberal	Liberal	Somewhat Liberal	Somewhat Conservative	Conservative	Very Conservative
				⇧	

See pages 134–135 for detailed explanations and definitions.

University of Georgia

Location: Athens, GA
Campus Setting: City: Midsize
Total Expenses: $20,820
Estimated Average Discount: $11,127 (53%)
Estimated Net Price: $9,693

Type of Institution: National University
Number of Undergraduates: 25,947
SAT Score: Reading: 560–660, Math: 560–670
Student/Faculty Ratio: 19 to 1
Transfer Out Rate: 7%

Rank Among 104 National Universities	**63**
Overall Rank Among 177 *Alumni Factor* Schools	**128**

Overview

There is nothing like a fall Saturday in Athens – a college town with classic collegiate architecture and winning football teams. Chartered in 1785, making it one of America's oldest public universities, the University of Georgia has spent the last decade climbing the ladder of respect among large, public universities for its excellence in research and undergraduate education. While its increasingly strong academic credentials may be a more recent occurrence, its fabulous campus experience and alumni loyalty have been evident for more than two centuries. With a rank of 18th in grad's Overall Assessment (4th in the SEC) and a 60th rank in the College Experience, UGA grads are committed and true. Georgia's strongest Ultimate Outcome is Friendships & Intellectual Capability (69th) – both of which are abundant among UGA alumni. No wonder the Bulldogs take the 7th spot in their willingness to recommend their school to prospective students today.

Notable Alumni

The B-52's, Lady Antebellum, REM and Sugarland all, in some way, had their start in Athens. The list of famous Georgia alumni is a long one and includes such notables as: former senator Phil Gramm; twenty Governors of the State of Georgia; athletes Fran Tarkenton, Terrell Davis, Herschel Walker, Dominque Wilkins, Jake Scott, Kim Black, Kara Braxton and Lisa Coole; Augusta National President Billy Payne; PGA tour pros Bubba Watson and Chip Beck. Lest one think its stars only shine in the field of athletics and politics, famous grads also include journalist Deborah Norville; the inventor of anesthesia, Crawford Long; personality Ryan Seacrest; and professional wrestler Glen Gilberti. The Bulldogs have produced twenty-one Rhodes Scholars throughout the school's history.

The Alumni Factor Rankings Summary

Attribute	University Rank	Overall Rank
College Experience	**60**	**129**
Intellectual Development	59	126
Social Development	56	117
Spiritual Development	70	142
Friendship Development	53	119
Preparation for Career Success	75	142
Immediate Job Opportunities	47	76
Overall Assessment	**18**	**34**
Would Personally Choose Again	38	72
Would Recommend to Student	7	11
Value for the Money	19	34
Financial Success	**92**	**156**
Income per Household	98	158
% Households with Income >$150K	88	144
Household Net Worth	75	123
% Households Net Worth >$1MM	96	159
Overall Happiness	**87**	**142**
Alumni Giving	**52**	**115**
Graduation Rate	**50**	**106**
Overall Rank	**63**	**128**

Other Key Alumni Outcomes

4.1% Are college professors
11.5% Teach at any level
50.4% Have post-graduate degrees
52.8% Live in dual-income homes
92.6% Are currently employed

See pages 134–135 for detailed explanations and definitions.

Alumni Activities During College

24.8% Community Service
28.9% Intramural Sports
19.8% Internships
10.8% Media Programs
14.9% Music Programs
57.0% Part-Time Jobs

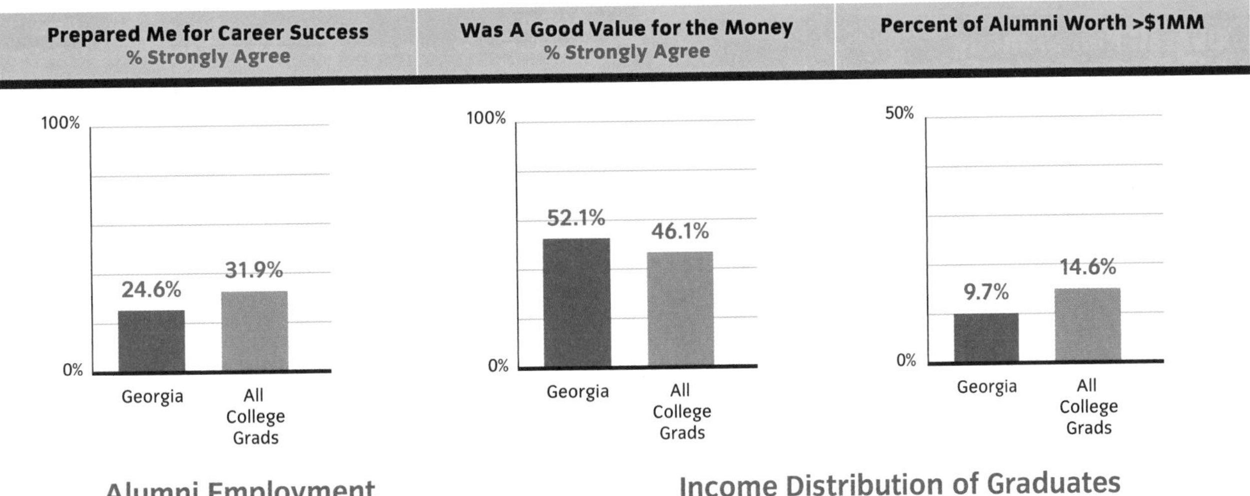

Alumni Employment

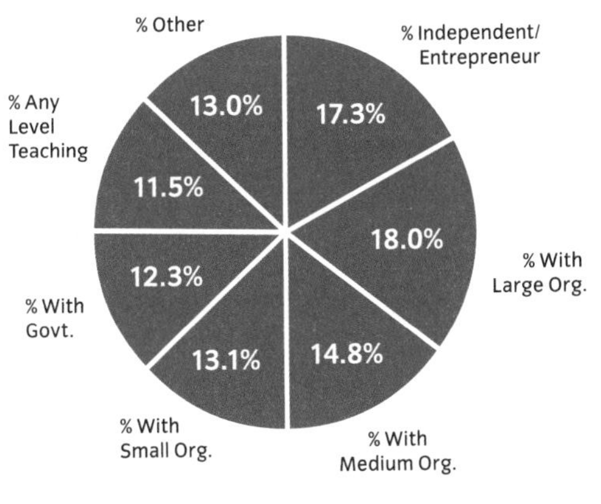

Income Distribution of Graduates

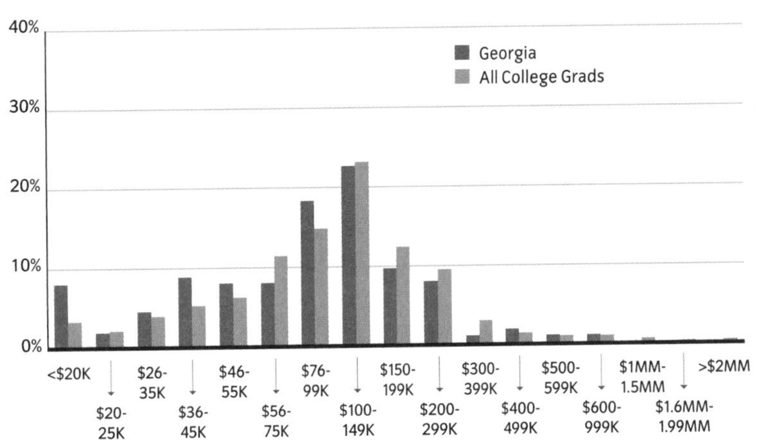

Current Selectivity & Demand Analysis for University of Georgia

Attribute	% Accepted	% Accepted Who Enroll	Freshman Retention Rate	Graduation Rate	Demand Index	Reputation Index
Score	59.0%	45.0%	94.0%	80.0%	3.16	0.76
Rank	127	25	58	106	168	78

Where are the Graduates of University of Georgia on the Political Spectrum?

Very Liberal	Liberal	Somewhat Liberal	Somewhat Conservative	Conservative	Very Conservative
					⇧

University of Illinois at Urbana-Champaign

Location: Champaign, IL
Campus Setting: City: Small
Total Expenses: $27,628
Estimated Average Discount: $12,018 (43%)
Estimated Net Price: $15,610

Type of Institution: National University
Number of Undergraduates: 31,540
SAT Score: Reading: 540–660, Math: 690–780
Student/Faculty Ratio: 19 to 1
Transfer Out Rate: Not Reported

Rank Among 104 National Universities	**39**
Overall Rank Among 177 *Alumni Factor* Schools	**86**

Overview

One of America's finest public universities, the University of Illinois has long been heralded for its excellence in engineering, science and business education. It is one of America's most elegantly designed large universities and sources a surprising 13% of its undergraduate student body from outside the US. The Fighting Illini are very successful graduates who not only cherish their College Experience (ranked 58th) and give it a very high Overall Assessment (27th), but are very successful financially (30th in Financial Success – with a 27th ranking in Household Net Worth). Impressively, U of I ranks 3rd among Big Ten schools in graduate households of high net worth; and 3rd in household income (behind only Michigan and Northwestern). With strengths across all key attributes, the Illini rank a very strong 42nd in the Ultimate Outcomes, with their strongest Ultimate Outcome being Financial Success & Happiness (26th). Illinois is collegiate excellence in a friendly, unpretentious middle America culture.

Notable Alumni

Former Goldman Sachs chairman & CEO Jon Corzine; Susan G. Komen Foundation founder and former US ambassador Nancy Brinker; Academy Award-winning director Ang Lee; Tesla Motors founder Martin Eberhard; former Kodak CEO George Fisher; BET founder Robert Johnson; Mosaic creator/Netscape founder and Silicon Valley luminary Marc Andreessen; and Oracle co-founder Robert Miner.

The Alumni Factor Rankings Summary

Attribute	University Rank	Overall Rank
College Experience	**58**	**126**
Intellectual Development	51	117
Social Development	63	124
Spiritual Development	74	146
Friendship Development	53	119
Preparation for Career Success	56	113
Immediate Job Opportunities	52	83
Overall Assessment	**27**	**57**
Would Personally Choose Again	30	62
Would Recommend to Student	33	67
Value for the Money	24	45
Financial Success	**30**	**54**
Income per Household	30	48
% Households with Income >$150K	30	54
Household Net Worth	27	51
% Households Net Worth >$1MM	51	88
Overall Happiness	**42**	**82**
Alumni Giving	**83**	**152**
Graduation Rate	**38**	**81**
Overall Rank	**39**	**86**

Other Key Alumni Outcomes

6.0% Are college professors
13.5% Teach at any level
61.4% Have post-graduate degrees
53.6% Live in dual-income homes
93.0% Are currently employed

See pages 134–135 for detailed explanations and definitions.

Alumni Activities During College

25.0% Community Service
29.3% Intramural Sports
17.9% Internships
14.3% Media Programs
13.2% Music Programs
48.6% Part-Time Jobs

Prepared Me for Career Success % Strongly Agree	Was A Good Value for the Money % Strongly Agree	Percent of Alumni Worth >$1MM
Illinois 27.9%; All College Grads 31.9%	Illinois 51.4%; All College Grads 46.1%	Illinois 14.7%; All College Grads 14.6%

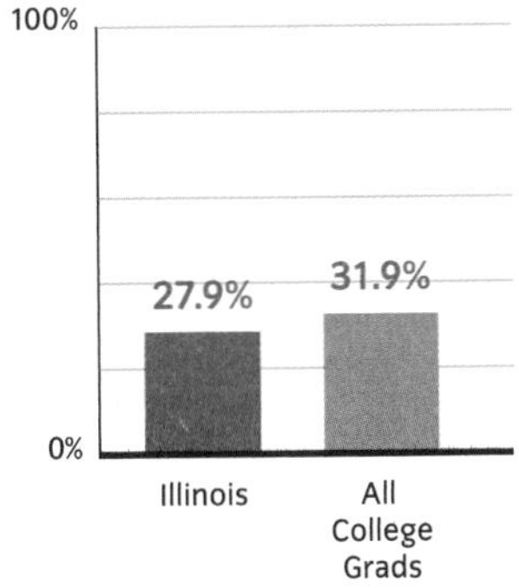

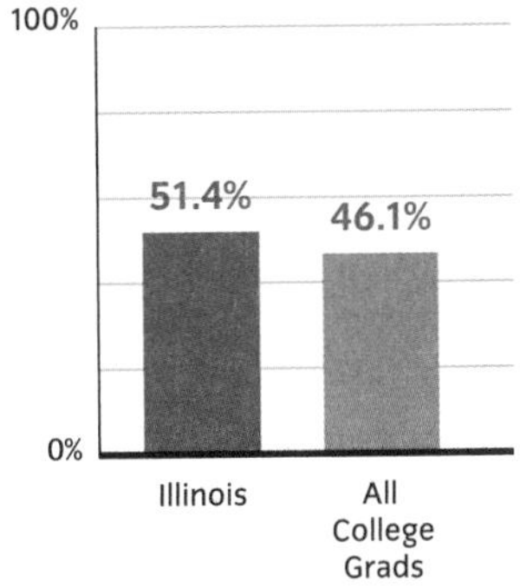

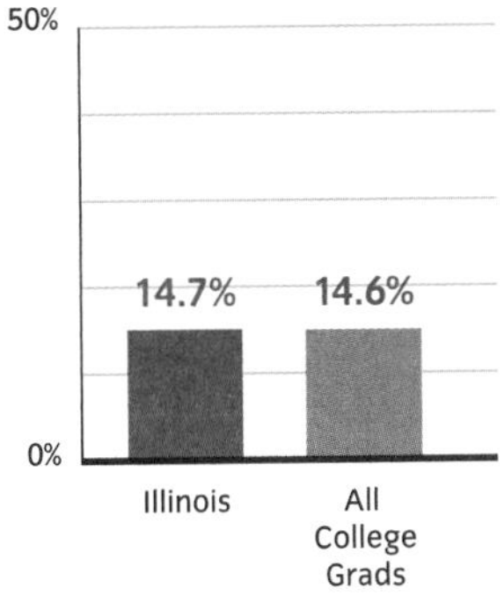

Alumni Employment

- % Other: 11.0%
- % Independent/ Entrepreneur: 12.8%
- % With Large Org.: 29.2%
- % With Medium Org.: 13.9%
- % With Small Org.: 13.9%
- % With Govt.: 5.7%
- % Any Level Teaching: 13.5%

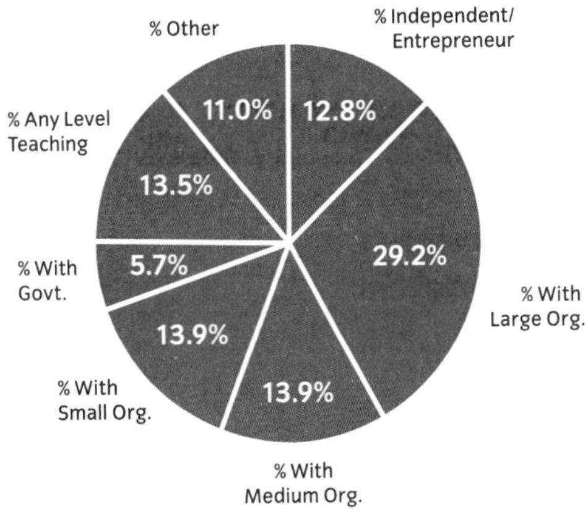

Income Distribution of Graduates

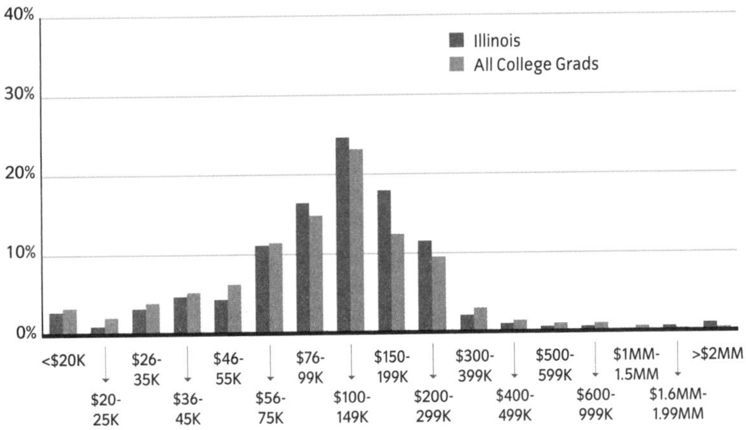

Current Selectivity & Demand Analysis for University of Illinois at Urbana-Champaign

Attribute	% Accepted	% Accepted Who Enroll	Freshman Retention Rate	Graduation Rate	Demand Index	Reputation Index
Score	68.0%	37.0%	94.0%	84.0%	3.96	0.54
Rank	145	60	58	81	155	115

Where are the Graduates of University of Illinois at Urbana-Champaign on the Political Spectrum?

Very Liberal	Liberal	Somewhat Liberal	Somewhat Conservative	Conservative	Very Conservative
			↑		

See pages 134–135 for detailed explanations and definitions.

University of Iowa

Location: Iowa City, IA
Campus Setting: City: Small
Total Expenses: $21,120
Estimated Average Discount: $6,875 (33%)
Estimated Net Price: $14,245

Type of Institution: National University
Number of Undergraduates: 21,176
SAT Score: Reading: 450–630, Math: 540–685
Student/Faculty Ratio: 16 to 1
Transfer Out Rate: 22%

Rank Among 104 National Universities	**60**
Overall Rank Among 177 *Alumni Factor* Schools	**126**

Overview

Often overshadowed by its more famous Big Ten competitors, the University of Iowa is a progressive academic and social force in the heart of the American Midwest. It was the first public university in the US to admit women and men on an equal basis (1855); the first to offer insurance benefits to the domestic partners of employees (1993); and the first state university to officially recognize the Gay, Lesbian, Bisexual, Transgender and Allied Union in 1970. It also offers a thriving social scene to its over 20,000 undergraduates (ranked 38th in Social Development – its highest ranked experiential attribute). Alumni really love this university, and most Would Personally Choose it Again (ranked 15th). With its strong focus on writing, teaching and communication, many grads become teachers and academicians – in fact, Iowa ranks 51st among all colleges and universities in grads who teach at any level. Hawkeyes are also quite happy (37th) and hard working, with the 38th best employment rate of any school.

Notable Alumni

Playwright Tennessee Williams; actor Gene Wilder; famous pollster George Gallup; President of the National Education Association Dennis Van Roekel; former Big Ten commissioner Wayne Duke; and Olympic Gold Medal wrestler Tom Brands, who now coaches Iowa's perennially powerful wrestling team.

The Alumni Factor Rankings Summary

Attribute	University Rank	Overall Rank
College Experience	**65**	**134**
Intellectual Development	60	128
Social Development	38	88
Spiritual Development	59	128
Friendship Development	61	132
Preparation for Career Success	65	130
Immediate Job Opportunities	77	124
Overall Assessment	**37**	**75**
Would Personally Choose Again	15	39
Would Recommend to Student	40	78
Value for the Money	56	104
Financial Success	**72**	**116**
Income per Household	43	69
% Households with Income >$150K	57	99
Household Net Worth	72	120
% Households Net Worth >$1MM	101	166
Overall Happiness	**37**	**66**
Alumni Giving	**62**	**125**
Graduation Rate	**77**	**143**
Overall Rank	**60**	**126**

Other Key Alumni Outcomes

8.0% Are college professors
16.4% Teach at any level
55.4% Have post-graduate degrees
59.3% Live in dual-income homes
94.8% Are currently employed

See pages 134–135 for detailed explanations and definitions.

Alumni Activities During College

22.5% Community Service
27.5% Intramural Sports
14.7% Internships
8.6% Media Programs
17.5% Music Programs
54.3% Part-Time Jobs

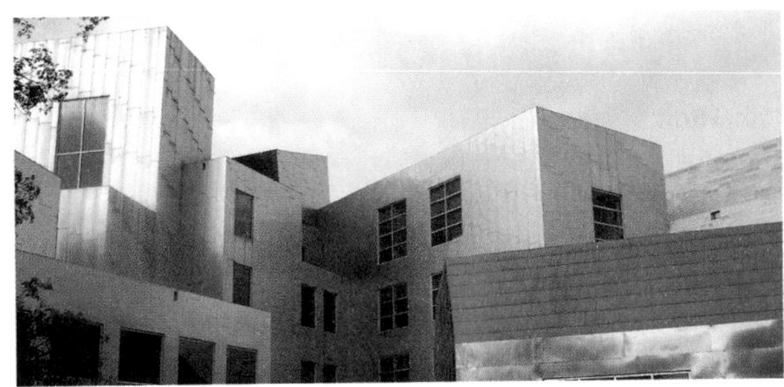

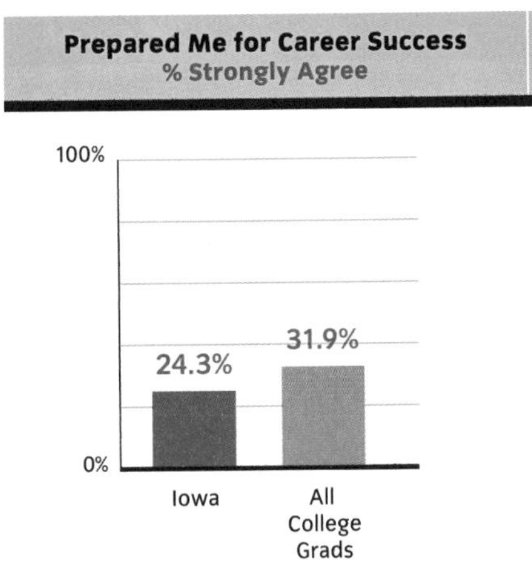
Prepared Me for Career Success
% Strongly Agree
100%
0%
24.3%
31.9%
Iowa
All College Grads

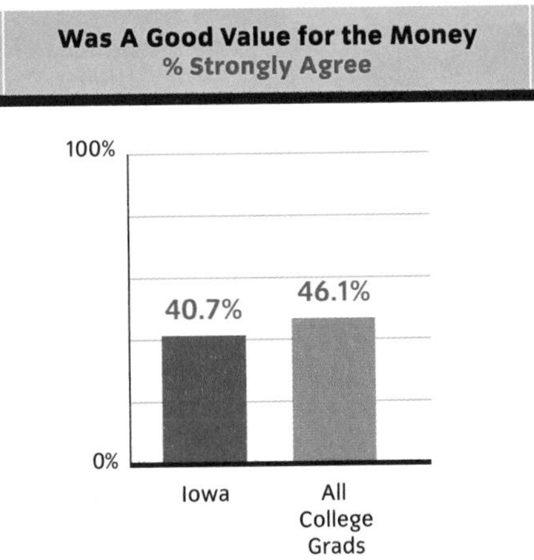
Was A Good Value for the Money
% Strongly Agree
100%
0%
40.7%
46.1%
Iowa
All College Grads

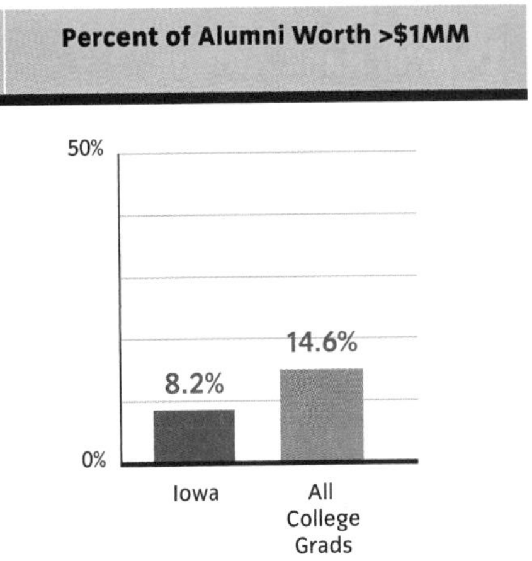
Percent of Alumni Worth >$1MM
50%
0%
8.2%
14.6%
Iowa
All College Grads

Alumni Employment

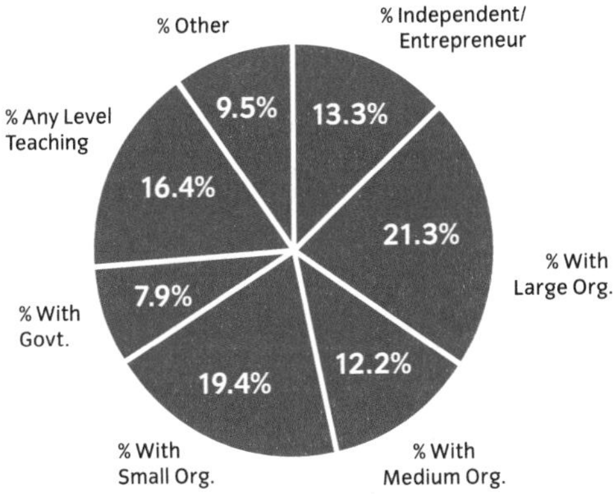
% Other
9.5%
% Independent/ Entrepreneur
13.3%
% With Large Org.
21.3%
% With Medium Org.
12.2%
% With Small Org.
19.4%
% With Govt.
7.9%
% Any Level Teaching
16.4%

Income Distribution of Graduates

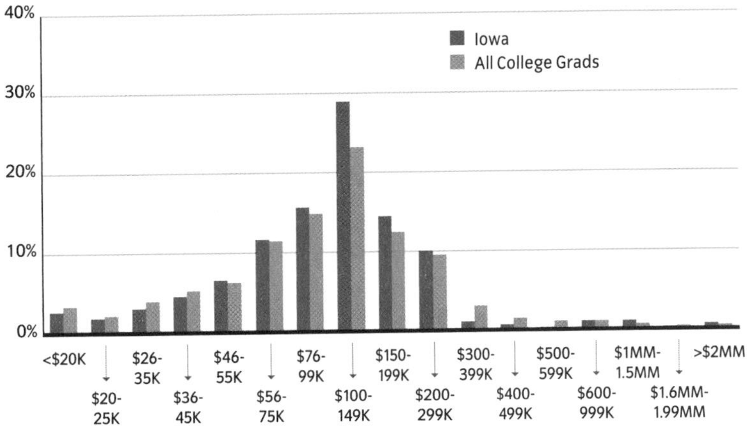
40%
30%
20%
10%
0%
Iowa
All College Grads
<$20K
$20-25K
$26-35K
$36-45K
$46-55K
$56-75K
$76-99K
$100-149K
$150-199K
$200-299K
$300-399K
$400-499K
$500-599K
$600-999K
$1MM-1.5MM
$1.6MM-1.99MM
>$2MM

Current Selectivity & Demand Analysis for University of Iowa

Attribute	% Accepted	% Accepted Who Enroll	Freshman Retention Rate	Graduation Rate	Demand Index	Reputation Index
Score	80.0%	30.0%	86.0%	70.0%	4.15	0.38
Rank	167	103	146	143	153	151

Where are the Graduates of University of Iowa on the Political Spectrum?

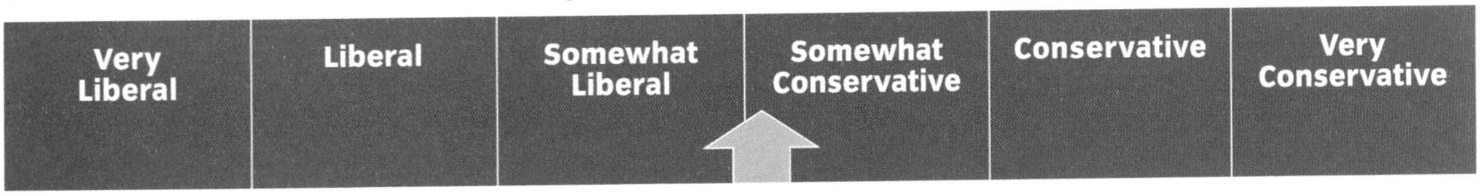
Very Liberal
Liberal
Somewhat Liberal
Somewhat Conservative
Conservative
Very Conservative

See pages 134–135 for detailed explanations and definitions.

University of Kansas

Location: Lawrence, KS
Campus Setting: City: Small
Total Expenses: $21,802
Estimated Average Discount: $7,034 (32%)
Estimated Net Price: $14,768

Type of Institution: National University
Number of Undergraduates: 20,343
SAT Score: Not Reported
Student/Faculty Ratio: 20 to 1
Transfer Out Rate: 34%

Rank Among 104 National Universities	**41**
Overall Rank Among 177 *Alumni Factor* Schools	**88**

Overview

Of the colleges and universities we've analyzed, the University of Kansas is certainly one of the most underrated. With an *Alumni Factor* ranking of 41 among national universities, the success of KU alumni far exceeds the reputation of the school – and the school already has a very good reputation. KU ranks 7th among national universities and 12th among all schools in graduate's Overall Assessment. It also has the 15th happiest grads in the country – 34th among all schools. Indeed, KU's strongest Ultimate Outcome is Happiness &Friendships, where it ranks 25th. In light of such strength, it is no surprise that Jayhawks are generous to their school, with a Top 40 Alumni Giving rank. Rock Chalk Jayhawk, KU!

Notable Alumni

The following current and former CEOs are all KU grads: Alan Mulally, Ford Motor Co.; Philip Anschutz, Quest; Dave Dillon, Kroger; Cynthia Carroll, Anglo American; Robert Eaton, Chrysler; Lou Montulli, Netscape engineering; Chris Sinclair, Pepsi; Robert Kaplan, Vice Chair Goldman Sachs. Plus, Tennessee Titans owner Bud Adams; NBA All-Star Danny Manning; UNC basketball coach Dean Smith; NFL Hall of Famer Gayle Sayers; Olympic Gold medalist Billy Mills; legendary miler Jim Ryun; and actors Paul Rudd and Mandy Patinkin are all KU graduates, as well.

The Alumni Factor Rankings Summary

Attribute	University Rank	Overall Rank
College Experience	**25**	**77**
Intellectual Development	44	102
Social Development	14	44
Spiritual Development	30	91
Friendship Development	27	83
Preparation for Career Success	27	63
Immediate Job Opportunities	44	73
Overall Assessment	**7**	**12**
Would Personally Choose Again	5	12
Would Recommend to Student	12	18
Value for the Money	20	35
Financial Success	**88**	**149**
Income per Household	89	141
% Households with Income >$150K	83	138
Household Net Worth	91	156
% Households Net Worth >$1MM	83	139
Overall Happiness	**15**	**34**
Alumni Giving	**32**	**90**
Graduation Rate	**95**	**166**
Overall Rank	**41**	**88**

Other Key Alumni Outcomes

7.1% Are college professors
12.7% Teach at any level
45.9% Have post-graduate degrees
49.0% Live in dual-income homes
91.9% Are currently employed

See pages 134–135 for detailed explanations and definitions.

Alumni Activities During College

26.7% Community Service
27.2% Intramural Sports
24.1% Internships
15.4% Media Programs
12.9% Music Programs
48.2% Part-Time Jobs

Prepared Me for Career Success % Strongly Agree	Was A Good Value for the Money % Strongly Agree	Percent of Alumni Worth >$1MM

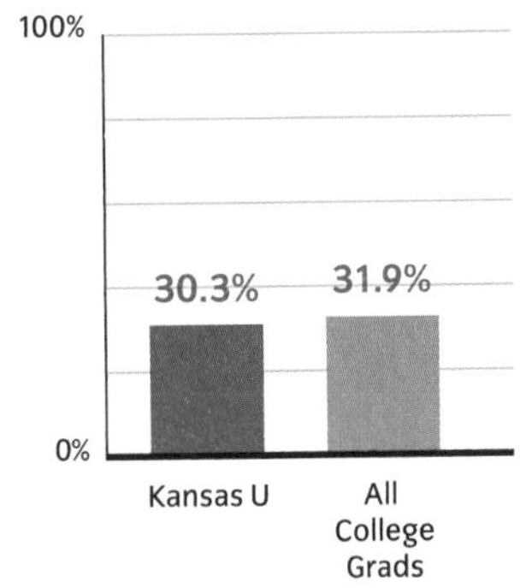
100%
0%
30.3%
31.9%
Kansas U
All College Grads

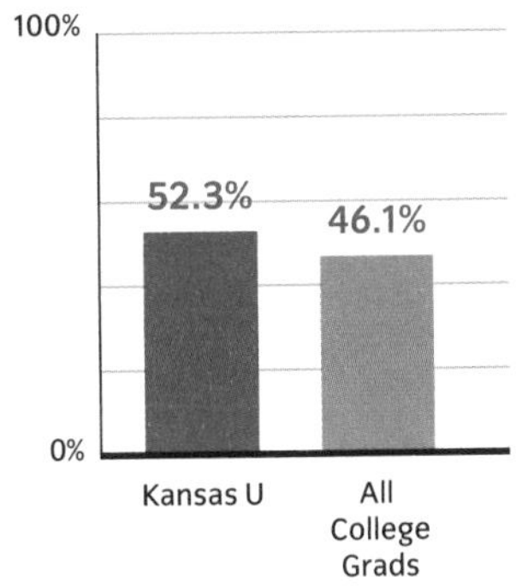
100%
0%
52.3%
46.1%
Kansas U
All College Grads

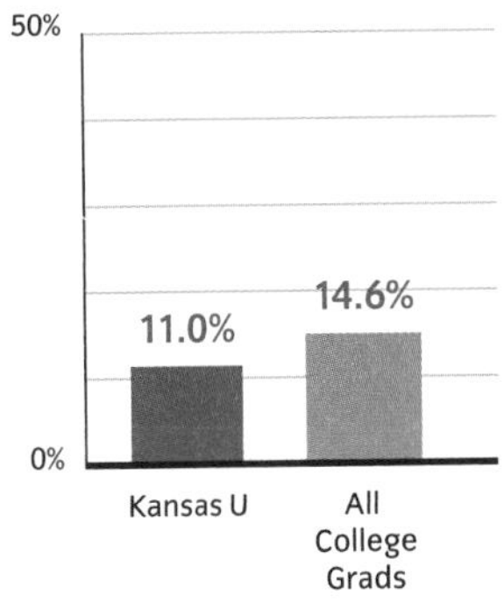
50%
0%
11.0%
14.6%
Kansas U
All College Grads

Alumni Employment

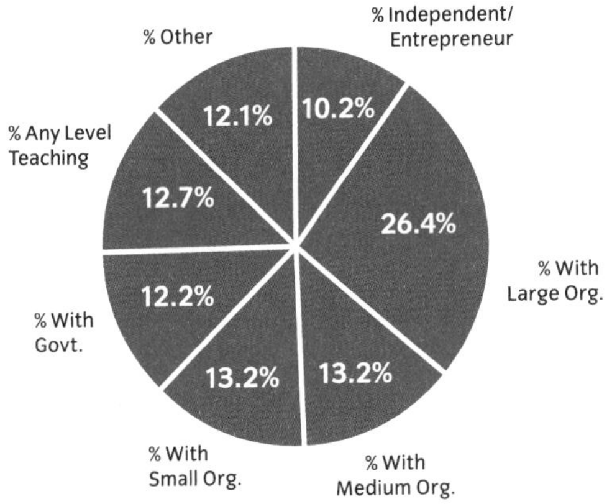
% Other
12.1%
% Independent/ Entrepreneur
10.2%
% With Large Org.
26.4%
% With Medium Org.
13.2%
% With Small Org.
13.2%
% With Govt.
12.2%
% Any Level Teaching
12.7%

Income Distribution of Graduates

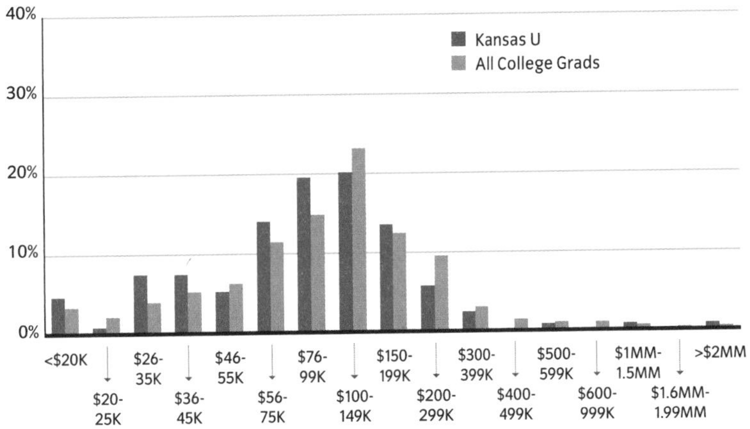
40%
30%
20%
10%
0%
Kansas U
All College Grads
<$20K
$20-25K
$26-35K
$36-45K
$46-55K
$56-75K
$76-99K
$100-149K
$150-199K
$200-299K
$300-399K
$400-499K
$500-599K
$600-999K
$1MM-1.5MM
$1.6MM-1.99MM
>$2MM

Current Selectivity & Demand Analysis for University of Kansas

Attribute	% Accepted	% Accepted Who Enroll	Freshman Retention Rate	Graduation Rate	Demand Index	Reputation Index
Score	93.0%	39.0%	79.0%	61.0%	2.84	0.42
Rank	175	46	175	166	173	145

Where are the Graduates of University of Kansas on the Political Spectrum?

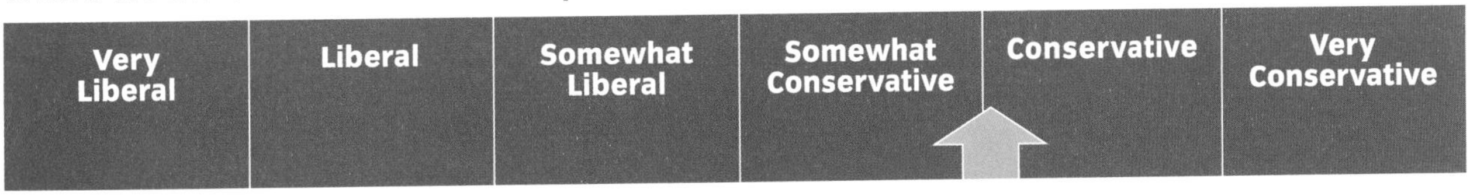
Very Liberal
Liberal
Somewhat Liberal
Somewhat Conservative
Conservative
Very Conservative

See pages 134–135 for detailed explanations and definitions.

University of Kentucky

Location: Lexington, KY
Campus Setting: City: Large
Total Expenses: $22,168
Estimated Average Discount: $9,252 (42%)
Estimated Net Price: $12,916

Type of Institution: National University
Number of Undergraduates: 19,927
SAT Score: Reading: 490–620, Math: 500–630
Student/Faculty Ratio: 18 to 1
Transfer Out Rate: Not Reported

Rank Among 104 National Universities **99**

Overall Rank Among 177 *Alumni Factor* Schools **172**

Overview

Known for basketball and its agricultural school, the University of Kentucky would not be expected by most to do much better than the 172nd position it achieves in our *Alumni Factor* ranking. In fact, some would not expect it to crack a list of top colleges at all. However, it does so on the strength of its graduates' Overall Assessment (ranked 152nd among all colleges and 85th among national universities), the Immediate Job Opportunities available to grads (76th) and the Overall Happiness of UK alumni (83rd). UK grads become teachers at a much higher rate than other colleges and rank 26th among all schools in the percent who become college professors. Its strongest Ultimate Outcome is Happiness & Friendships (81st) – not an easy task for a school with nearly 20,000 undergraduates.

With nearly 80 percent of the undergrads coming from in-state, it is not a surprise that most of its graduates go on to achieve their successes in and around Kentucky.

Notable Alumni

Actress and activist Ashley Judd; current Kentucky Governor Steve Beshear; American educator and Vassar's first female President, Sarah Gibson Blanding; and former Kentucky governor and Major League Baseball commissioner Happy Chandler.

The Alumni Factor Rankings Summary

Attribute	University Rank	Overall Rank
College Experience	**89**	**162**
Intellectual Development	101	173
Social Development	81	150
Spiritual Development	71	143
Friendship Development	78	148
Preparation for Career Success	84	154
Immediate Job Opportunities	76	122
Overall Assessment	**85**	**152**
Would Personally Choose Again	96	163
Would Recommend to Student	88	157
Value for the Money	67	123
Financial Success	**102**	**170**
Income per Household	99	161
% Households with Income >$150K	101	167
Household Net Worth	94	159
% Households Net Worth >$1MM	99	163
Overall Happiness	**83**	**140**
Alumni Giving	**41**	**99**
Graduation Rate	**102**	**173**
Overall Rank	**99**	**172**

Other Key Alumni Outcomes

9.6% Are college professors
17.7% Teach at any level
50.7% Have post-graduate degrees
48.1% Live in dual-income homes
90.5% Are currently employed

See pages 134–135 for detailed explanations and definitions.

Alumni Activities During College

17.5% Community Service
24.8% Intramural Sports
26.3% Internships
8.7% Media Programs
15.4% Music Programs
51.1% Part-Time Jobs

Prepared Me for Career Success % Strongly Agree	Was A Good Value for the Money % Strongly Agree	Percent of Alumni Worth >$1MM
Kentucky 26.3%; All College Grads 31.9%	Kentucky 43.0%; All College Grads 46.1%	Kentucky 8.9%; All College Grads 14.6%

Alumni Employment

% Independent/ Entrepreneur 14.0%
% With Large Org. 16.9%
% With Medium Org. 9.6%
% With Small Org. 11.8%
% With Govt. 9.6%
% Any Level Teaching 17.7%
% Other 20.4%

Income Distribution of Graduates

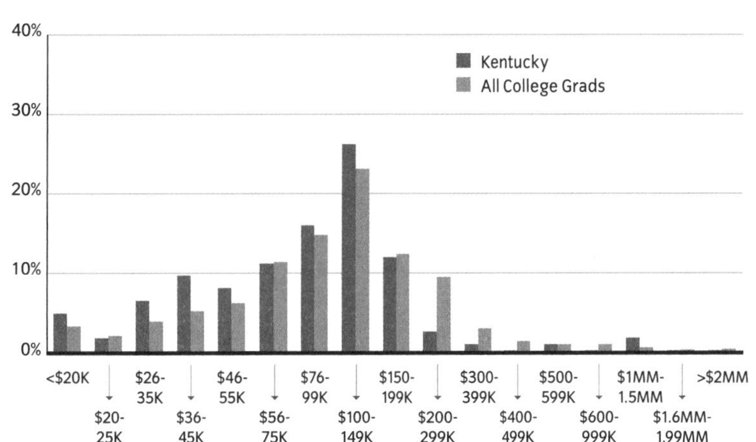

Current Selectivity & Demand Analysis for University of Kentucky

Attribute	% Accepted	% Accepted Who Enroll	Freshman Retention Rate	Graduation Rate	Demand Index	Reputation Index
Score	69.0%	47.0%	82.0%	58.0%	3.27	0.68
Rank	148	22	167	173	165	88

Where are the Graduates of University of Kentucky on the Political Spectrum?

Very Liberal	Liberal	Somewhat Liberal	Somewhat Conservative	Conservative	Very Conservative
				↑	

See pages 134–135 for detailed explanations and definitions.

University of Massachusetts Amherst

Location: Amherst, MA
Campus Setting: Town: Fringe
Total Expenses: $24,709
Estimated Average Discount: $8,564 (35%)
Estimated Net Price: $16,145

Type of Institution: National University
Number of Undergraduates: 21,373
SAT Score: Reading: 530–630, Math: 560–650
Student/Faculty Ratio: 19 to 1
Transfer Out Rate: Not Reported

Rank Among 104 National Universities	**91**
Overall Rank Among 177 *Alumni Factor* Schools	**163**

Overview

Surrounded by smaller and more elite New England schools, it would be easy for the Unversity of Massachusetts Amherst and its graduates to feel somewhat envious and inferior. But they do not – and they should not. UMass grads do quite well in the market, performing with remarkable consistency across all attributes. Their toughest ranking is Would Personally Choose Again (176th among all colleges and universities – 104th among the national universities), which is likely due, in large part, to the difficult comparisons to the schools around them.

The strongest UMass showing is in Overall Happiness, where it ranks 45th among national universities. Its 62nd ranking in high income households is also quite impressive, given its size and the breadth of the student population accepted. (UMass is the largest public university in New England with more than 20,000 undergrads). It is even more commendable when one realizes that UMass is 11th in production of teachers – an important but not necessarily highly remunerative occupation.

Notable Alumni

Legendary former GE CEO Jack Welch; singer Natalie Cole; the New York Giant's Victor Cruz; Vermont's 77th governor Madeleine Kunin; former General Motors CEO Jack Smith; basketball coach Rick Pitino; and *This Old House* star Norm Abram.

The Alumni Factor Rankings Summary

Attribute	University Rank	Overall Rank
College Experience	**94**	**167**
Intellectual Development	99	171
Social Development	71	136
Spiritual Development	81	153
Friendship Development	86	156
Preparation for Career Success	85	157
Immediate Job Opportunities	78	127
Overall Assessment	**86**	**153**
Would Personally Choose Again	104	176
Would Recommend to Student	94	163
Value for the Money	56	104
Financial Success	**80**	**129**
Income per Household	71	110
% Households with Income >$150K	62	107
Household Net Worth	78	126
% Households Net Worth >$1MM	92	155
Overall Happiness	**45**	**88**
Alumni Giving	**67**	**131**
Graduation Rate	**81**	**148**
Overall Rank	**91**	**163**

Other Key Alumni Outcomes

4.9% Are college professors
22.5% Teach at any level
58.9% Have post-graduate degrees
49.8% Live in dual-income homes
91.4% Are currently employed

See pages 134–135 for detailed explanations and definitions.

Alumni Activities During College

22.1% Community Service
24.0% Intramural Sports
25.0% Internships
22.6% Media Programs
18.2% Music Programs
38.5% Part-Time Jobs

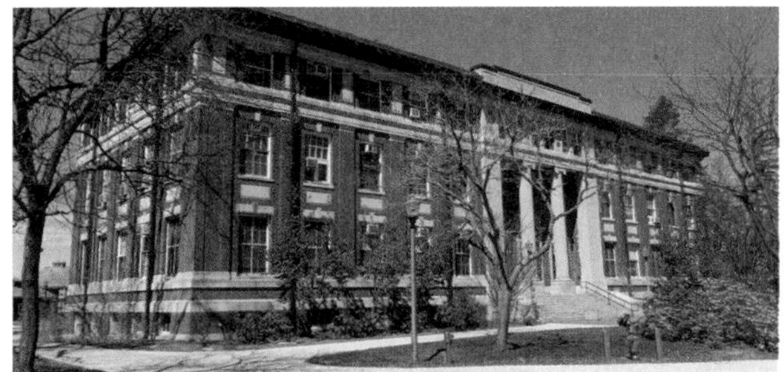

Prepared Me for Career Success
% Strongly Agree

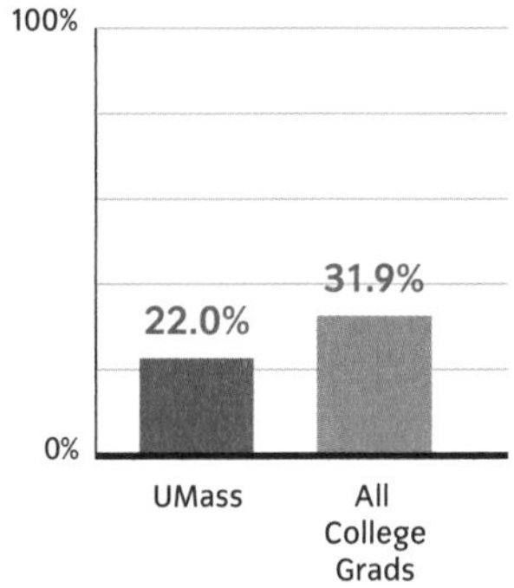
100%
0%
22.0%
31.9%
UMass
All College Grads

Was A Good Value for the Money
% Strongly Agree

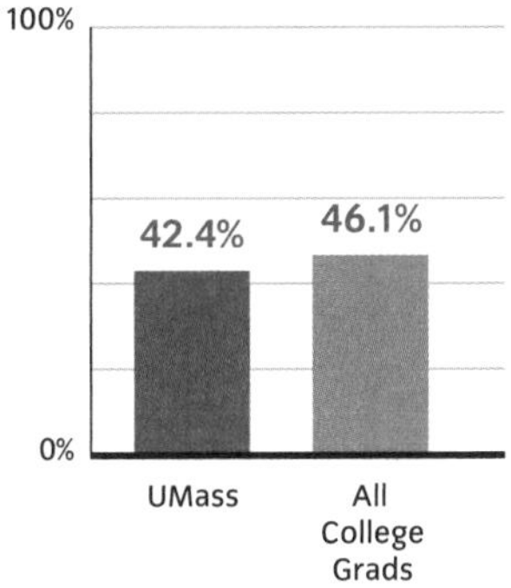
100%
0%
42.4%
46.1%
UMass
All College Grads

Percent of Alumni Worth >$1MM

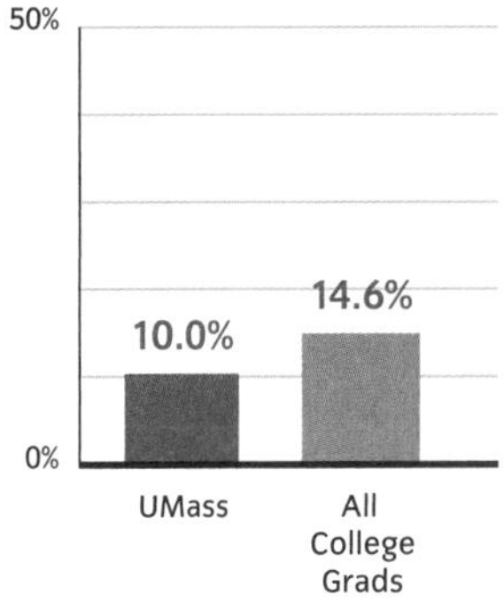
50%
0%
10.0%
14.6%
UMass
All College Grads

Alumni Employment

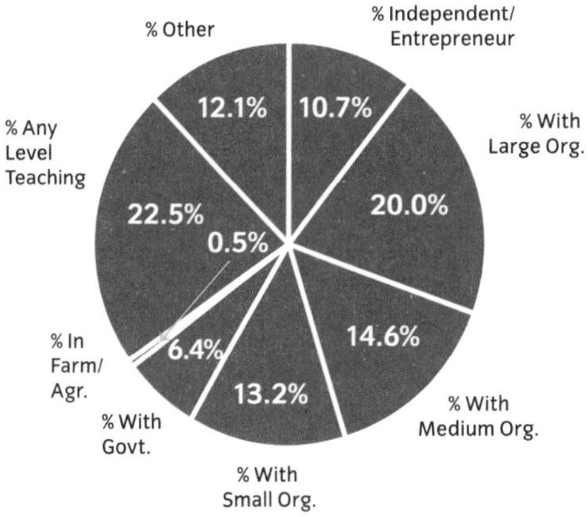
% Other
12.1%
% Independent/ Entrepreneur
10.7%
% With Large Org.
20.0%
% With Medium Org.
14.6%
% With Small Org.
13.2%
% With Govt.
6.4%
% In Farm/ Agr.
0.5%
% Any Level Teaching
22.5%

Income Distribution of Graduates

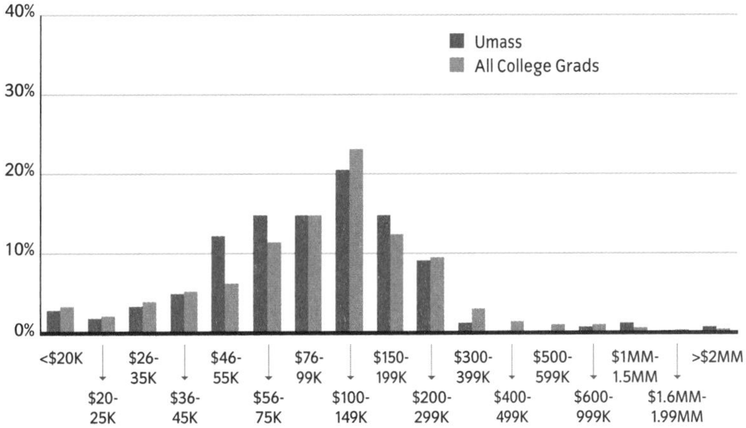
40%
30%
20%
10%
0%
Umass
All College Grads
<$20K
$20-25K
$26-35K
$36-45K
$46-55K
$56-75K
$76-99K
$100-149K
$150-199K
$200-299K
$300-399K
$400-499K
$500-599K
$600-999K
$1MM-1.5MM
$1.6MM-1.99MM
>$2MM

Current Selectivity & Demand Analysis for University of Massachusetts Amherst

Attribute	% Accepted	% Accepted Who Enroll	Freshman Retention Rate	Graduation Rate	Demand Index	Reputation Index
Score	66.0%	22.0%	89.0%	69.0%	6.82	0.33
Rank	142	149	124	148	116	162

Where are the Graduates of University of Massachusetts Amherst on the Political Spectrum?

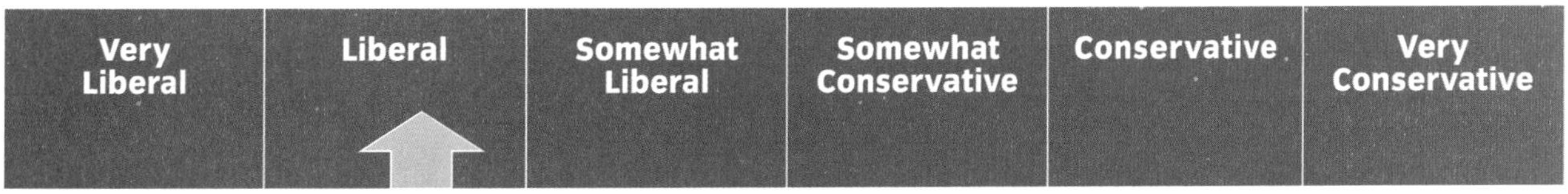
Very Liberal
Liberal
Somewhat Liberal
Somewhat Conservative
Conservative
Very Conservative

See pages 134–135 for detailed explanations and definitions.

University of Miami

Location: Coral Gables, FL
Campus Setting: Suburb: Large
Total Expenses: $56,512
Estimated Average Discount: $28,876 (51%)
Estimated Net Price: $27,636

Type of Institution: National University
Number of Undergraduates: 10,368
SAT Score: Reading: 600–690, Math: 630–710
Student/Faculty Ratio: 11 to 1
Transfer Out Rate: Not Reported

Rank Among 104 National Universities	**80**
Overall Rank Among 177 *Alumni Factor* Schools	**148**

Overview

The transformation of the University of Miami has been amazing to witness. Since Donna Shalala became President in 2001, the school has undergone a reputational shift from the notorious swagger of winning football to serious scholarship in the classroom. Some would say that the academic excellence has always been the standard but was simply overshadowed by athletic misdeeds – because renegade athletes get more press than devoted scholars. Regardless of your view of history, the present situation is clear. Now a highly selective, acclaimed university in one of the finest locations available for a college campus, U Miami ranks 80th among national universities overall, with significant strength in graduate Financial Success (56th) and loyalty (37th in Alumni Giving). Miami's strongest Ultimate Outcome is the one most colleges covet for their graduates – Financial Success & Intellectual Capability – in which it ranks 46th.

Notable Alumni

Grammy winners Gloria Estefan and Bruce Hornsby; actor Dwayne "The Rock" Johnson; Tony Award-winning playwright Mark Medoff; sports journalist Roy Firestone; prominent attorney Roy Black; former McDonald's president Ralph Alvarez; former Merrill Lynch CEO David Komansky; and more Miami Hurricane football players than can fit in this space.

The Alumni Factor Rankings Summary

Attribute	University Rank	Overall Rank
College Experience	**67**	**136**
Intellectual Development	91	163
Social Development	47	106
Spiritual Development	34	95
Friendship Development	89	159
Preparation for Career Success	52	108
Immediate Job Opportunities	66	107
Overall Assessment	**83**	**148**
Would Personally Choose Again	76	134
Would Recommend to Student	66	121
Value for the Money	100	172
Financial Success	**56**	**95**
Income per Household	58	92
% Households with Income >$150K	52	87
Household Net Worth	65	111
% Households Net Worth >$1MM	58	100
Overall Happiness	**72**	**125**
Alumni Giving	**37**	**93**
Graduation Rate	**50**	**106**
Overall Rank	**80**	**148**

Other Key Alumni Outcomes

3.8%	Are college professors
12.0%	Teach at any level
52.4%	Have post-graduate degrees
49.7%	Live in dual-income homes
91.5%	Are currently employed

See pages 134–135 for detailed explanations and definitions.

Alumni Activities During College

23.3% Community Service
23.6% Intramural Sports
27.5% Internships
13.9% Media Programs
19.1% Music Programs
40.5% Part-Time Jobs

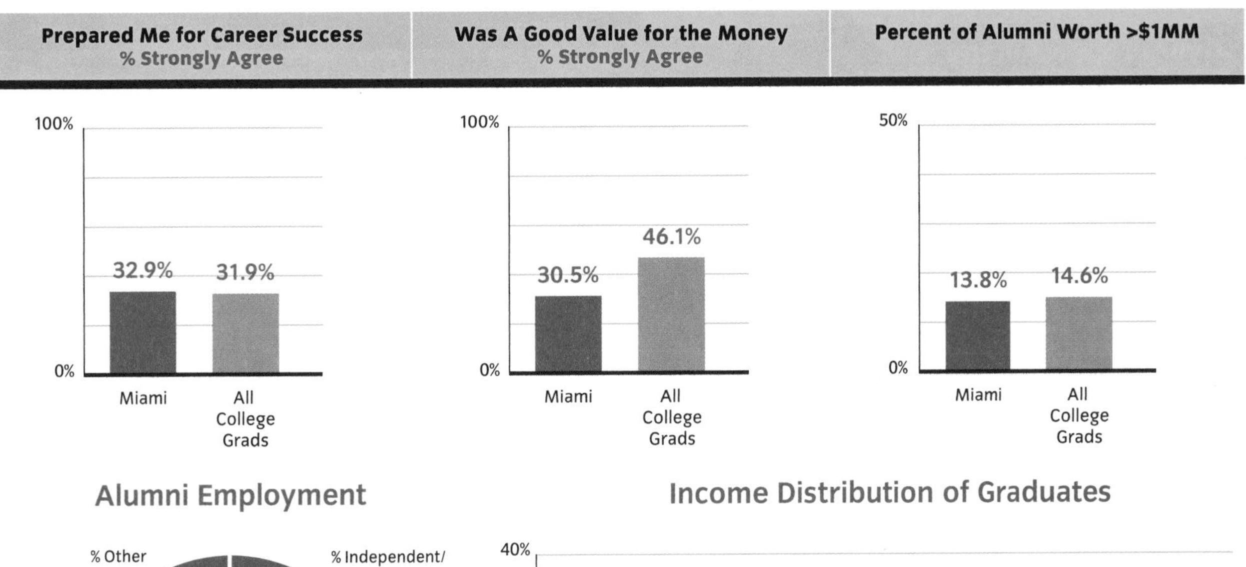

Alumni Employment

Category	%
% Independent/ Entrepreneur	18.8%
% With Large Org.	22.0%
% With Medium Org.	14.0%
% With Small Org.	9.2%
% With Govt.	7.6%
% Any Level Teaching	12.0%
% Other	16.4%

Income Distribution of Graduates

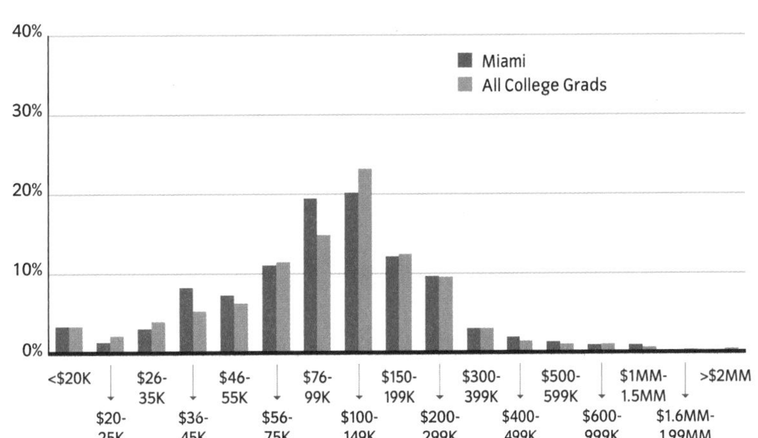

Current Selectivity & Demand Analysis for University of Miami

Attribute	% Accepted	% Accepted Who Enroll	Freshman Retention Rate	Graduation Rate	Demand Index	Reputation Index
Score	38.0%	20.0%	90.0%	80.0%	12.77	0.53
Rank	73	161	113	106	39	117

Where are the Graduates of University of Miami on the Political Spectrum?

Very Liberal	Liberal	Somewhat Liberal	Somewhat Conservative	Conservative	Very Conservative
				↑	

See pages 134–135 for detailed explanations and definitions.

University of Michigan

Location: Ann Arbor, MI
Campus Setting: City: Midsize
Total Expenses: $25,204
Estimated Average Discount: $11,130 (44%)
Estimated Net Price: $14,074

Type of Institution: National University
Number of Undergraduates: 27,027
SAT Score: Reading: 630–730, Math: 670–770
Student/Faculty Ratio: 12 to 1
Transfer Out Rate: Not Reported

Rank Among 104 National Universities	**17**
Overall Rank Among 177 *Alumni Factor* Schools	**34**

Overview

One of the world's finest all-around universities, the University of Michigan is simply stellar in every measurement of alumni outcomes we consider. Among national universities, it ranks in the Top 50 in every college experience attribute; ranks 9th in grads' Overall Assessment (with an astonishing 2nd spot in Would Personally Choose Again); is Top 25 in the Financial Success of its grads and ranks 26th in the Ultimate Outcomes. No other large university has done so well, for so many, for so long, across so many attributes. Among schools with more than 20,000 undergrads, Michigan is 1st in high income households; 1st in the percentage of grads pursuing a post-grad degree; 2nd in average household income; and 3rd in the percent of alumni in millionaire households. Somehow, U of M is able to offer the combination of a smaller school academic experience with the winning social and athletic scene of a major university. Hail, Hail to Michigan!

Notable Alumni

26 Rhodes Scholars; 116 Olympic Medalists; multiple billionaires, including Google co-founder Larry Page; Stephen Ross and Detroit Pistons owner Bill Davidson; former president Gerald Ford; H&R Block co-founder Henry Bloch; advertising icon Leo Burnett; actors Lucy Liu and Darren Criss; pro quarterback Tom Brady; and 4 Nobel Prize winners (among its undergrad alums only).

The Alumni Factor Rankings Summary

Attribute	University Rank	Overall Rank
College Experience	**26**	**79**
Intellectual Development	28	77
Social Development	31	76
Spiritual Development	44	110
Friendship Development	32	88
Preparation for Career Success	25	63
Immediate Job Opportunities	31	47
Overall Assessment	**9**	**14**
Would Personally Choose Again	2	5
Would Recommend to Student	16	26
Value for the Money	22	38
Financial Success	**23**	**41**
Income per Household	15	27
% Households with Income >$150K	16	31
Household Net Worth	29	53
% Households Net Worth >$1MM	32	60
Overall Happiness	**54**	**102**
Alumni Giving	**62**	**125**
Graduation Rate	**24**	**39**
Overall Rank	**17**	**34**

Other Key Alumni Outcomes

2.6% Are college professors
6.7% Teach at any level
64.1% Have post-graduate degrees
51.0% Live in dual-income homes
91.3% Are currently employed

See pages 134–135 for detailed explanations and definitions.

Alumni Activities During College

30.9% Community Service
35.7% Intramural Sports
24.1% Internships
11.5% Media Programs
15.2% Music Programs
53.1% Part-Time Jobs

Prepared Me for Career Success % Strongly Agree	Was A Good Value for the Money % Strongly Agree	Percent of Alumni Worth >$1MM
Michigan: 32.0%	Michigan: 52.9%	Michigan: 17.0%
All College Grads: 31.9%	All College Grads: 46.1%	All College Grads: 14.6%

Alumni Employment

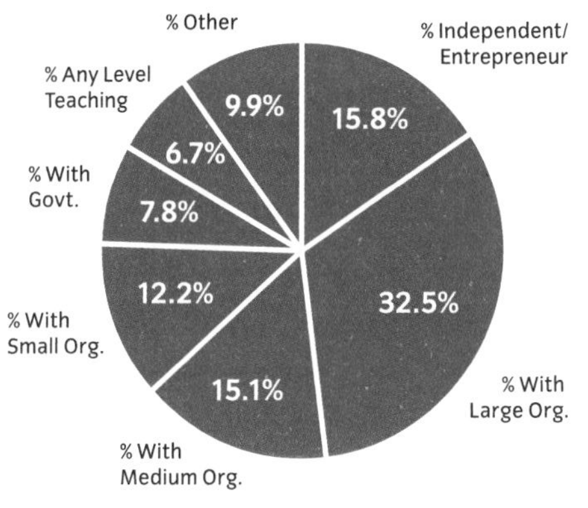

Income Distribution of Graduates

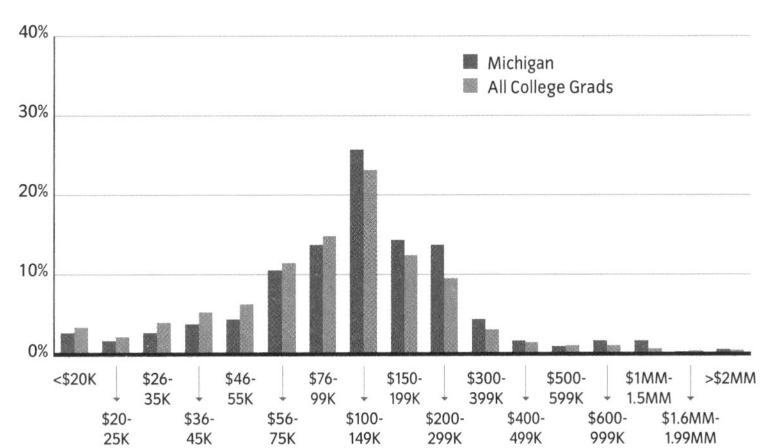

Current Selectivity & Demand Analysis for University of Michigan

Attribute	% Accepted	% Accepted Who Enroll	Freshman Retention Rate	Graduation Rate	Demand Index	Reputation Index
Score	41.0%	39.0%	96.0%	90.0%	6.33	0.95
Rank	84	46	27	39	124	63

Where are the Graduates of University of Michigan on the Political Spectrum?

Very Liberal	Liberal	Somewhat Liberal	Somewhat Conservative	Conservative	Very Conservative
			↑		

See pages 134–135 for detailed explanations and definitions.

University of Minnesota

Location: Minneapolis, MN
Campus Setting: City: Large
Total Expenses: $24,050
Estimated Average Discount: $8,031 (33%)
Estimated Net Price: $16,019

Type of Institution: National University
Number of Undergraduates: 33,607
SAT Score: Reading: 540–690, Math: 610–740
Student/Faculty Ratio: 21 to 1
Transfer Out Rate: Not Reported

Rank Among 104 National Universities	**103**
Overall Rank Among 177 *Alumni Factor* Schools	**176**

Overview

Spread across two cities, with the Mississippi River running through it, the University of Minnesota is the fourth largest college campus in the US. The dynamic city of Minneapolis is a fabulous location for this progressive university, and provides the backdrop for a plethora of academic, cultural and social opportunities for students. Given its massive size and dispersion, we would not expect it to create the close-knit environment of a smaller campus – and it does not (ranked 104th in College Experience). In fact, among the 177 colleges and universities we profile, the University of Minnesota falls in the lower echelon on most of the attributes we measure. However, there are three specific metrics where the Golden Gophers stand out, and it is these three that earn it a place on our list. They are its uniquely strong showing in Would Personally Choose Again (77th); the percentage of its graduates who become millionaires (71st); and its Alumni Giving (78th). All are quite impressive given the size and diversity of the undergraduate population. It is a credit to the school that despite some relative shortcomings on the College Experience, alumni believe in its Value for the Money, earning it the 79th spot.

Known for its smart student body (ranked 43rd in reported SAT scores by alumni), Minnesota has produced accomplished alumni for more than two centuries.

Notable Alumni

Former Supreme Court justice Warren Burger; former US vice presidents Hubert Humphrey and Walter Mondale; former congresswoman Patricia Schroeder; former chairman and CEO of Target Robert Ulrich; author Garrison Keillor and Pulitzer Prize-winning journalist Thomas Friedman.

The Alumni Factor Rankings Summary

Attribute	University Rank	Overall Rank
College Experience	**104**	**177**
Intellectual Development	95	167
Social Development	97	170
Spiritual Development	101	173
Friendship Development	100	172
Preparation for Career Success	100	172
Immediate Job Opportunities	95	163
Overall Assessment	**92**	**162**
Would Personally Choose Again	77	136
Would Recommend to Student	103	176
Value for the Money	79	142
Financial Success	**94**	**160**
Income per Household	102	172
% Households with Income >$150K	95	156
Household Net Worth	89	152
% Households Net Worth >$1MM	71	121
Overall Happiness	**92**	**148**
Alumni Giving	**78**	**145**
Graduation Rate	**77**	**143**
Overall Rank	**103**	**176**

Other Key Alumni Outcomes

6.4% Are college professors
11.5% Teach at any level
57.5% Have post-graduate degrees
49.4% Live in dual-income homes
83.5% Are currently employed

See pages 134–135 for detailed explanations and definitions.

Alumni Activities During College

30.8% Community Service
28.9% Intramural Sports
27.7% Internships
11.3% Media Programs
10.7% Music Programs
56.0% Part-Time Jobs

Current Selectivity & Demand Analysis for University of Minnesota

Attribute	% Accepted	% Accepted Who Enroll	Freshman Retention Rate	Graduation Rate	Demand Index	Reputation Index
Score	47.0%	29.0%	89.0%	70.0%	7.40	0.62
Rank	99	107	124	143	111	99

Where are the Graduates of University of Minnesota on the Political Spectrum?

Very Liberal	Liberal	Somewhat Liberal	Somewhat Conservative	Conservative	Very Conservative

University of Mississippi

Location: Oxford, MS
Campus Setting: Town: Remote
Total Expenses: $19,852
Estimated Average Discount: $7,336 (37%)
Estimated Net Price: $12,516

Type of Institution: National University
Number of Undergraduates: 14,159
SAT Score: Reading: 460–590, Math: 470–590
Student/Faculty Ratio: 18 to 1
Transfer Out Rate: Not Reported

Rank Among 104 National Universities	**51**
Overall Rank Among 177 *Alumni Factor* Schools	**113**

Overview

There is no better place to experience the social and intellectual charm of the Old South than at Ole Miss – particularly on a fall Saturday. Unabashedly conservative, with deep pride in its traditions and culture, the University of Mississippi is a refreshingly dynamic example of how large universities can achieve new excellence while maintaining the cultural, academic and social strengths of their past. Ole Miss produces happy (ranked 66th), loyal, successful graduates who have true appreciation for their College Experience (27th) and perform quite well in the market across a variety of careers (57th in Financial Success). Ole Miss' strongest attribute is the Social and Communication Skills (12th) graduates take away from their undergraduate years. Given its southern location, the Household Net Worth ranking (50th) and the percent of Households Worth >$1 million (53rd) are also particularly impressive. And its 14th rank in employment rate stands as a testament to the quality of Ole Miss graduates.

Importantly, Ole Miss stacks up quite well versus its Southeastern Conference competitors. Among the SEC, it ranks 3rd in percent of millionaire households; 4th in Preparation for Career Success; 5th in Friendship Development and 3rd in percent of households with a high income.

Notable Alumni

Former US senator Trent Lott and current senator Roger Wicker; Archie and Eli Manning, from the NFL's most famous family of quarterbacks; and former Netscape CEO Jim Barksdale.

The Alumni Factor Rankings Summary

Attribute	University Rank	Overall Rank
College Experience	**27**	**80**
Intellectual Development	62	131
Social Development	12	41
Spiritual Development	26	85
Friendship Development	36	98
Preparation for Career Success	22	58
Immediate Job Opportunities	37	56
Overall Assessment	**45**	**90**
Would Personally Choose Again	37	71
Would Recommend to Student	52	105
Value for the Money	47	85
Financial Success	**57**	**97**
Income per Household	69	106
% Households with Income >$150K	63	108
Household Net Worth	50	88
% Households Net Worth >$1MM	53	91
Overall Happiness	**66**	**115**
Alumni Giving	**78**	**145**
Graduation Rate	**100**	**171**
Overall Rank	**51**	**113**

Other Key Alumni Outcomes

6.1% Are college professors
11.7% Teach at any level
51.8% Have post-graduate degrees
50.9% Live in dual-income homes
95.8% Are currently employed

See pages 134–135 for detailed explanations and definitions.

Alumni Activities During College

27.0% Community Service
33.1% Intramural Sports
17.8% Internships
23.4% Media Programs
16.5% Music Programs
42.3% Part-Time Jobs

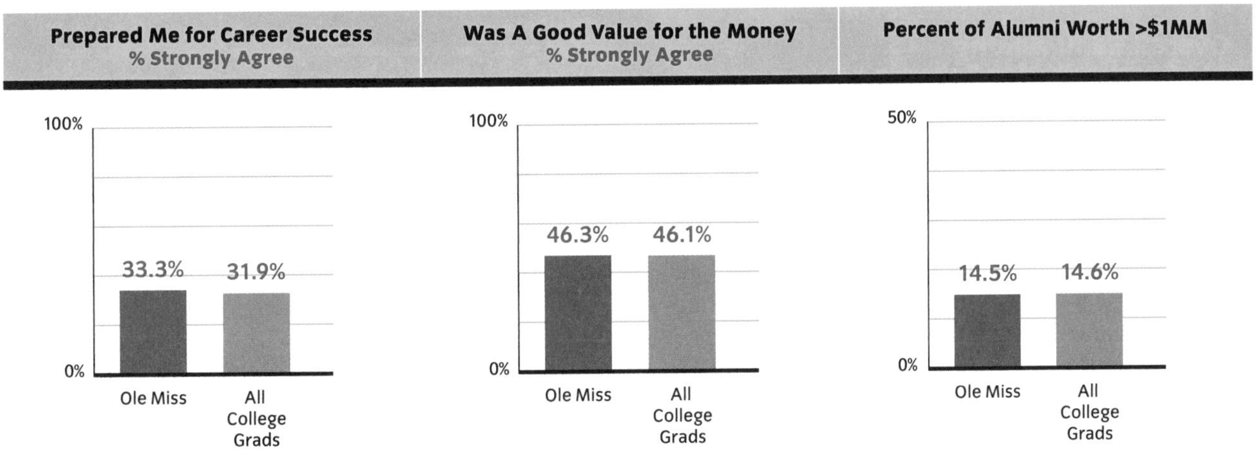

	Prepared Me for Career Success (% Strongly Agree)	Was A Good Value for the Money (% Strongly Agree)	Percent of Alumni Worth >$1MM
Ole Miss	33.3%	46.3%	14.5%
All College Grads	31.9%	46.1%	14.6%

Alumni Employment

Category	%
% Independent/ Entrepreneur	14.0%
% With Large Org.	27.4%
% With Medium Org.	15.9%
% With Small Org.	13.4%
% With Govt.	9.2%
% In Farm/ Agr.	0.6%
% Any Level Teaching	11.7%
% Other	7.8%

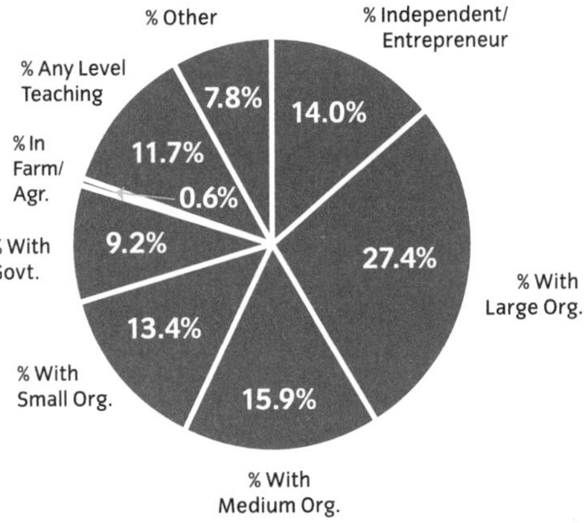

Income Distribution of Graduates

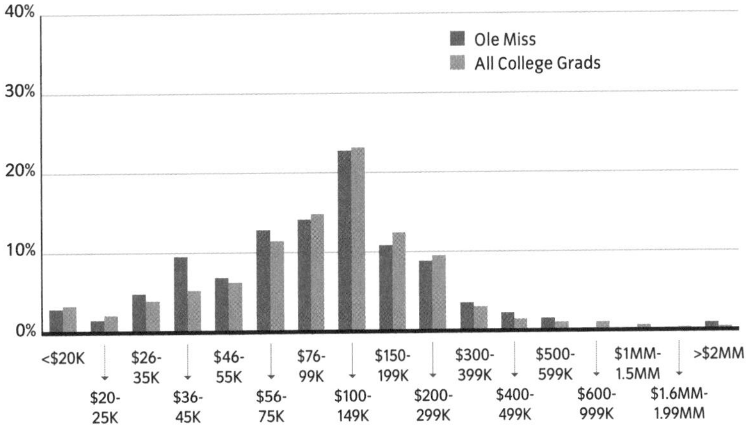

Current Selectivity & Demand Analysis for University of Mississippi

Attribute	% Accepted	% Accepted Who Enroll	Freshman Retention Rate	Graduation Rate	Demand Index	Reputation Index
Score	79.0%	34.0%	83.0%	59.0%	3.73	0.43
Rank	165	76	161	171	157	142

Where are the Graduates of University of Mississippi on the Political Spectrum?

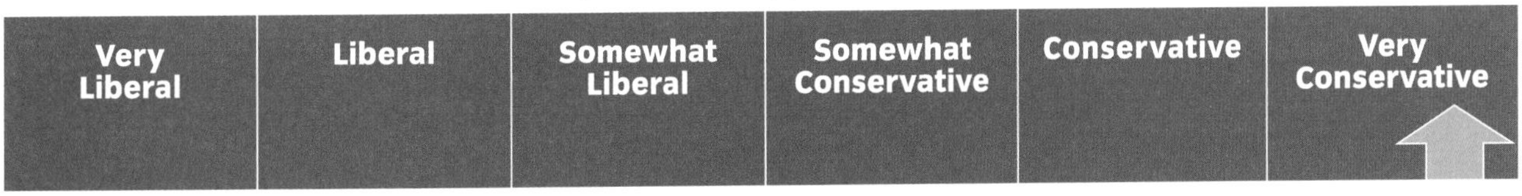

Very Liberal	Liberal	Somewhat Liberal	Somewhat Conservative	Conservative	Very Conservative
					↑

University of Nebraska-Lincoln

Location: Lincoln, NE
Campus Setting: City: Large
Total Expenses: $20,201
Estimated Average Discount: $7,093 (35%)
Estimated Net Price: $13,108

Type of Institution: National University
Number of Undergraduates: 19,383
SAT Score: Reading: 510–660, Math: 520–670
Student/Faculty Ratio: 20 to 1
Transfer Out Rate: Not Reported

Rank Among 104 National Universities	**94**
Overall Rank Among 177 *Alumni Factor* Schools	**166**

Overview

The state's oldest and largest university, the University of Nebraska has provided a solid, pragmatic education in the sciences and arts for more than 140 years. It was the first university west of the Mississippi to have a graduate school. It produces happy (ranked 58th) grads who are hard working (41st best employment rate). Nebraska's strongest Ultimate Outcome is Happiness & Friendships where it is ranked 82nd. It also has one of the most loyal fan bases for its beloved Cornhuskers to be found anywhere in the world. It has sold out every home football game for an amazing 50 years!

Readers should not necessarily be dismayed by Nebraska's relatively lower rankings on measures of Financial Success. Nebraska is one of the country's most prolific producers of teachers (ranked 29th in its percent of grads teaching at any level). This alone could skew alum's financial results and certainly comes into play in lower Ultimate Outcome rankings.

With Nebraska's transition into the Big Ten Conference, it is in a new league in many ways – athletically, academically and in comparisons of alumni outcomes. This is not an easy comparison for Nebraska, and the Cornhuskers will have to set new sights for future achievements. We are confident Nebraska will rise to the occasion.

Notable Alumni

Revered billionaire Warren Buffet; talk-show legend Johnny Carson; former Nebraska governor and senator Bob Kerrey and three Heisman trophy winners, Johnny Rogers, Mike Rozier, Eric Crouch; along with NFL star Roger Craig.

The Alumni Factor Rankings Summary

Attribute	University Rank	Overall Rank
College Experience	**81**	**153**
Intellectual Development	81	153
Social Development	68	133
Spiritual Development	77	149
Friendship Development	84	154
Preparation for Career Success	74	141
Immediate Job Opportunities	53	84
Overall Assessment	**75**	**136**
Would Personally Choose Again	69	124
Would Recommend to Student	77	140
Value for the Money	66	121
Financial Success	**103**	**172**
Income per Household	100	168
% Households with Income >$150K	102	168
Household Net Worth	98	166
% Households Net Worth >$1MM	98	162
Overall Happiness	**58**	**106**
Alumni Giving	**75**	**141**
Graduation Rate	**93**	**164**
Overall Rank	**94**	**166**

Other Key Alumni Outcomes

7.7% Are college professors
18.7% Teach at any level
55.5% Have post-graduate degrees
53.6% Live in dual-income homes
94.5% Are currently employed

See pages 134–135 for detailed explanations and definitions.

Alumni Activities During College

32.3% Community Service
35.3% Intramural Sports
20.0% Internships
11.5% Media Programs
21.3% Music Programs
55.3% Part-Time Jobs

Prepared Me for Career Success % Strongly Agree	Was A Good Value for the Money % Strongly Agree	Percent of Alumni Worth >$1MM
Nebraska 21.0%; All College Grads 31.9%	Nebraska 38.4%; All College Grads 46.1%	Nebraska 9.1%; All College Grads 14.6%

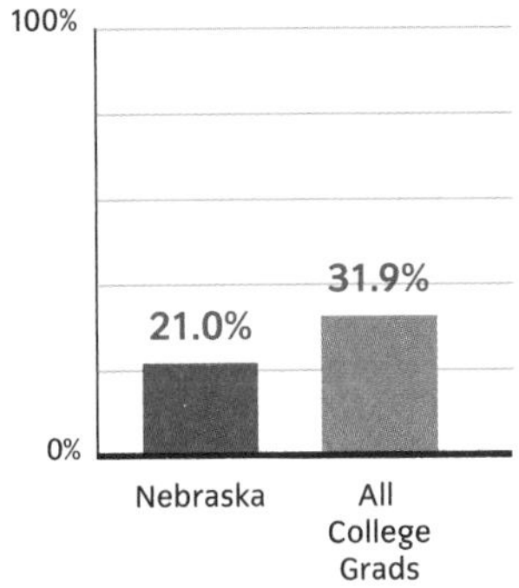

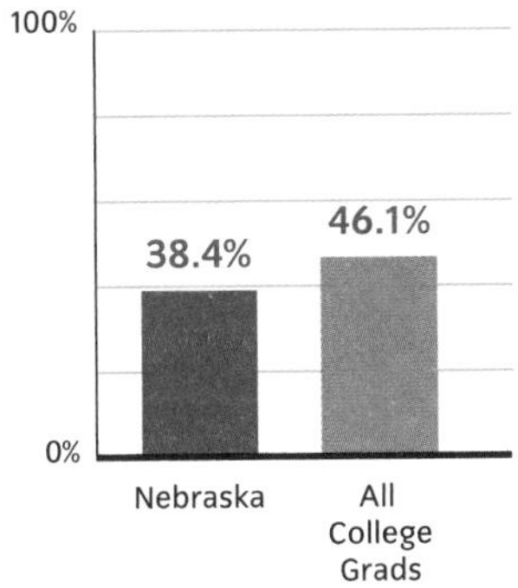

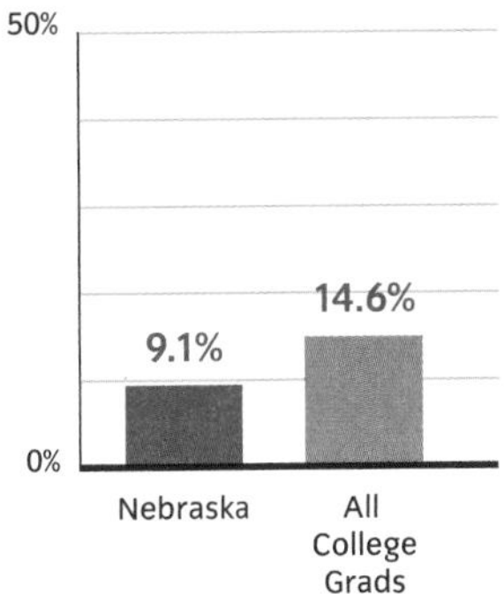

Alumni Employment

Category	%
% Other	9.9%
% Independent/ Entrepreneur	10.2%
% With Large Org.	19.1%
% With Medium Org.	13.2%
% With Small Org.	12.8%
% With Govt.	16.1%
% Any Level Teaching	18.7%

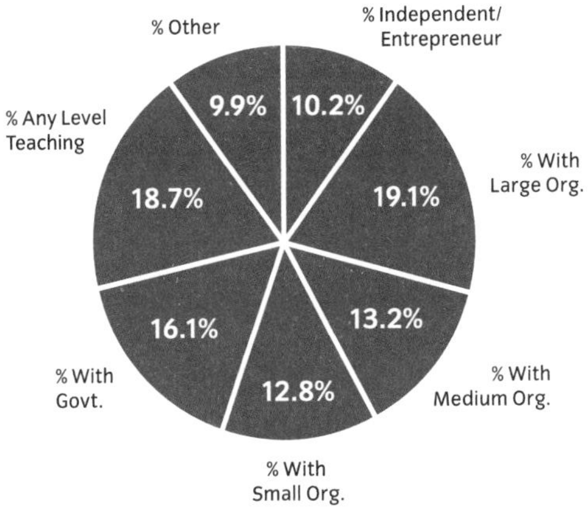

Income Distribution of Graduates

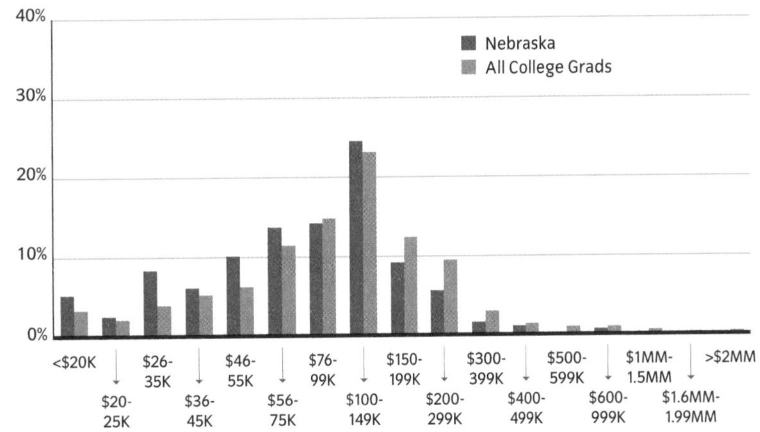

Nebraska / All College Grads

0% 10% 20% 30% 40%

<$20K, $20-25K, $26-35K, $36-45K, $46-55K, $56-75K, $76-99K, $100-149K, $150-199K, $200-299K, $300-399K, $400-499K, $500-599K, $600-999K, $1MM-1.5MM, $1.6MM-1.99MM, >$2MM

Current Selectivity & Demand Analysis for University of Nebraska-Lincoln

Attribute	% Accepted	% Accepted Who Enroll	Freshman Retention Rate	Graduation Rate	Demand Index	Reputation Index
Score	59.0%	69.0%	84.0%	64.0%	2.45	1.17
Rank	127	7	158	164	174	51

Where are the Graduates of University of Nebraska-Lincoln on the Political Spectrum?

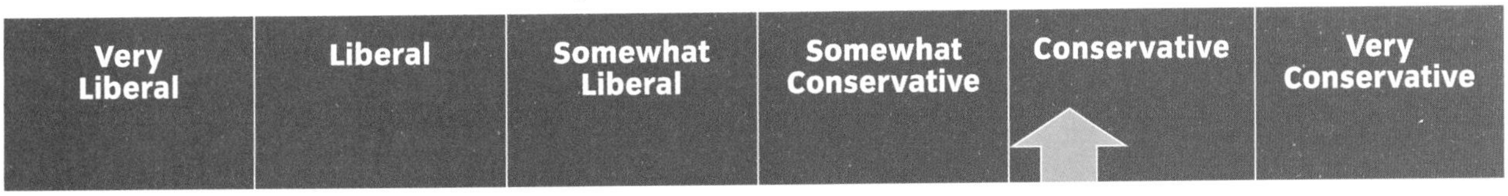

Very Liberal	Liberal	Somewhat Liberal	Somewhat Conservative	Conservative	Very Conservative
				↑	

See pages 134–135 for detailed explanations and definitions.

University of North Carolina at Chapel Hill

Location: Chapel Hill, NC
Campus Setting: City: Small
Total Expenses: $21,315
Estimated Average Discount: $10,287 (48%)
Estimated Net Price: $11,028

Type of Institution: National University
Number of Undergraduates: 18,579
SAT Score: Reading: 590–700, Math: 610–710
Student/Faculty Ratio: 14 to 1
Transfer Out Rate: 3%

Rank Among 104 National Universities	**12**
Overall Rank Among 177 *Alumni Factor* Schools	**30**

Overview

UNC-Chapel Hill receives the finest Overall Assessment from its graduates of any college or university in our study. Not only is it 1st among all schools in graduates' Overall Assessment, it ranks in the Top 5 among national universities in each of the three elements that constitute the Overall Assessment. Combine that passion for their school with an Overall Happiness rank of 6th, a College Experience ranking of 20th and a Financial Success ranking of 41st, and you can see why UNC-Chapel Hill is our 12th ranked national university.

Extraordinarily popular both in-state and across the country (it sources 84 percent of students from North Carolina), Chapel Hill has the social life, the athletics, the history and the academics to compete with any institution in the country as a place to spend the undergraduate years. While many view it as very liberal (relative to the local North Carolina poltical climate), graduates actually lean slightly conservative compared to other college graduates in their political and social views.

Notable Alumni

Former US president James Polk; former BB&T chairman John Allison; former Kidder Peabody CEO Max Chapman; former CEO of JP Morgan Chase William Harrison; founder of DLJ Rick Jenrette; former CEO of Bank of America Hugh McColl; and American favorite Andy Griffith.

The Alumni Factor Rankings Summary

Attribute	University Rank	Overall Rank
College Experience	**20**	**63**
Intellectual Development	21	67
Social Development	3	12
Spiritual Development	22	80
Friendship Development	34	94
Preparation for Career Success	29	70
Immediate Job Opportunities	50	81
Overall Assessment	**1**	**1**
Would Personally Choose Again	4	8
Would Recommend to Student	2	4
Value for the Money	5	8
Financial Success	**41**	**72**
Income per Household	36	59
% Households with Income >$150K	44	76
Household Net Worth	30	55
% Households Net Worth >$1MM	62	106
Overall Happiness	**6**	**17**
Alumni Giving	**22**	**72**
Graduation Rate	**32**	**52**
Overall Rank	**12**	**30**

Other Key Alumni Outcomes

7.3% Are college professors
16.6% Teach at any level
51.4% Have post-graduate degrees
57.7% Live in dual-income homes
95.6% Are currently employed

See pages 134–135 for detailed explanations and definitions.

Alumni Activities During College

30.4% Community Service
31.1% Intramural Sports
17.3% Internships
19.2% Media Programs
15.0% Music Programs
48.7% Part-Time Jobs

Prepared Me for Career Success % Strongly Agree	Was A Good Value for the Money % Strongly Agree	Percent of Alumni Worth >$1MM
UNC 31.7% / All College Grads 31.9%	UNC 63.3% / All College Grads 46.1%	UNC 13.5% / All College Grads 14.6%

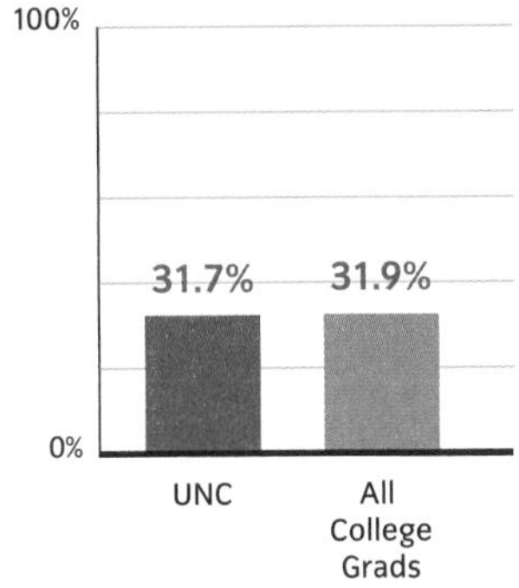

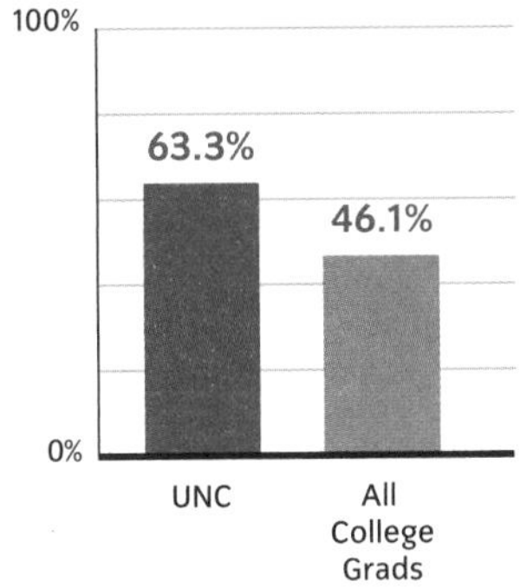

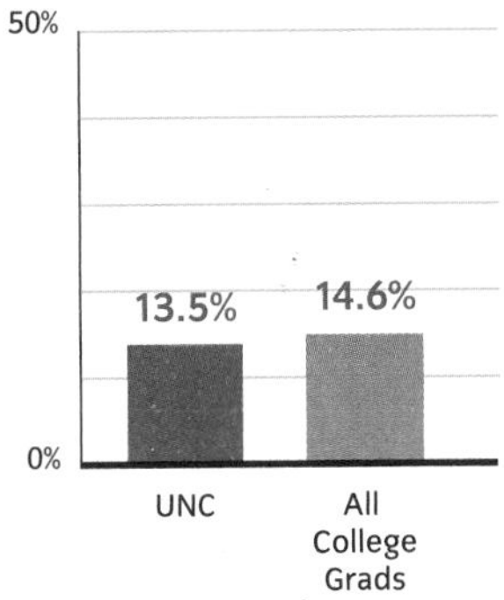

Alumni Employment

Category	%
% Independent/Entrepreneur	17.2%
% With Large Org.	18.8%
% With Medium Org.	11.8%
% With Small Org.	13.7%
% With Govt.	9.5%
% In Farm/Agr.	0.3%
% Any Level Teaching	16.6%
% Other	12.1%

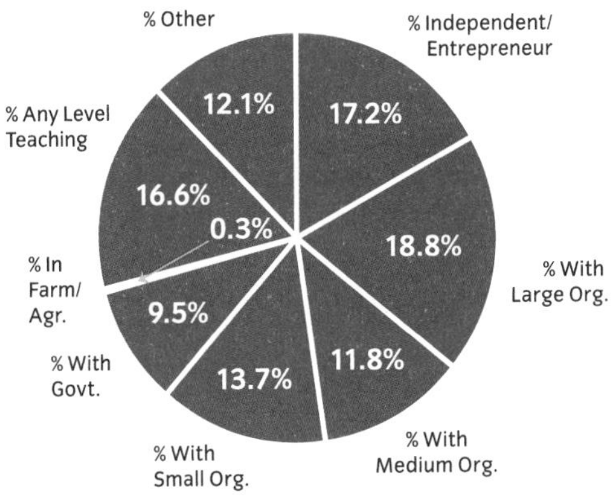

Income Distribution of Graduates

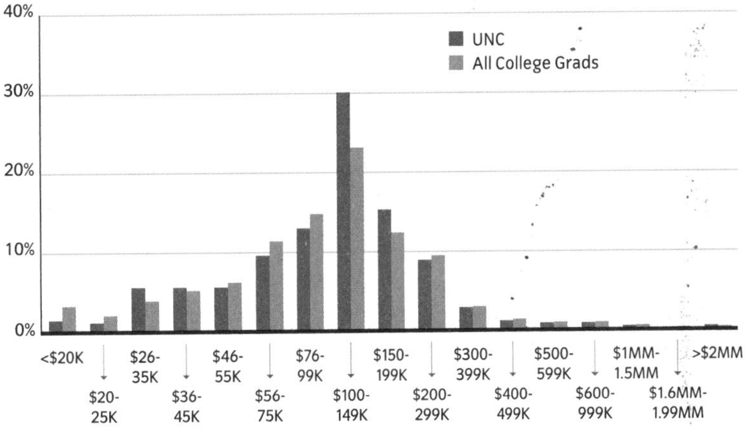

Current Selectivity & Demand Analysis for University of North Carolina at Chapel Hill

Attribute	% Accepted	% Accepted Who Enroll	Freshman Retention Rate	Graduation Rate	Demand Index	Reputation Index
Score	34.0%	52.0%	96.0%	88.0%	5.54	1.53
Rank	66	16	27	52	135	37

Where are the Graduates of University of North Carolina at Chapel Hill on the Political Spectrum?

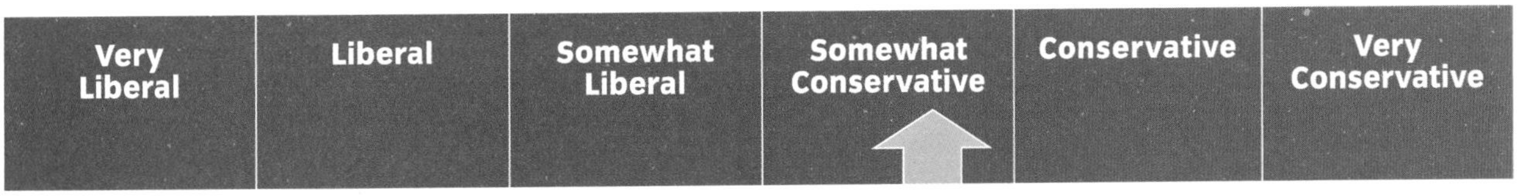

Very Liberal	Liberal	Somewhat Liberal	Somewhat Conservative	Conservative	Very Conservative
			↑		

See pages 134–135 for detailed explanations and definitions.

University of Notre Dame

Location: Notre Dame, IN
Campus Setting: Suburb: Large
Total Expenses: $55,257
Estimated Average Discount: $30,625 (55%)
Estimated Net Price: $24,632

Type of Institution: National University
Number of Undergraduates: 8,442
SAT Score: Reading: 660–750, Math: 680–770
Student/Faculty Ratio: 10 to 1
Transfer Out Rate: Not Reported

Rank Among 104 National Universities	**4**
Overall Rank Among 177 *Alumni Factor* Schools	**6**

Overview

This world-renowned university, with its storied reputation as a leader in values-based education and athletic excellence, has another strong tradition that is likely less well known – its history of developing some of country's most successful and accomplished alumni. Ranked 6th among all US colleges and universities and 4th among national universities, Notre Dame even exceeds its glowing reputation when it comes to developing happy, accomplished, loyal alumni who are extraordinarily successful across a wide range of fields.

Ranked 2nd in the College Experience and Graduation Rate, 3rd in Alumni Giving, and an amazing 4th in the Ultimate Outcomes, Notre Dame is a powerhouse in terms of graduate outcomes. It ranks in the Top 35 in every single attribute we measure – a feat of which only six other schools can boast. And it is an impressive 22nd in its percentage of grads who go on to earn graduate degrees. When it comes to Financial Success (ranked 17th), the Irish are again among the finest in the country, ranking 11th in percent of graduates with net worth above $1 million and 14th in high income households.

Notable Alumni

Condoleeza Rice; Edward DeBartolo (both Sr. and Jr.); Milwaukee Bucks owner and philanthropist Jim Fitzgerald; CEO of Sprint Dan Hesse; former CEO of Morgan Stanley Philip Purcell; CFO of GE Keith Sherin; Regis Philbin, Phil Donahue and Hannah Storm – and numerous football standouts such as Joe Montana and Joe Theisman.

The Alumni Factor Rankings Summary

Attribute	University Rank	Overall Rank
College Experience	**2**	**8**
Intellectual Development	11	45
Social Development	27	69
Spiritual Development	2	2
Friendship Development	1	15
Preparation for Career Success	6	18
Immediate Job Opportunities	8	12
Overall Assessment	**21**	**40**
Would Personally Choose Again	21	48
Would Recommend to Student	23	45
Value for the Money	20	35
Financial Success	**17**	**32**
Income per Household	34	54
% Households with Income >$150K	14	25
Household Net Worth	21	41
% Households Net Worth >$1MM	11	23
Overall Happiness	**12**	**29**
Alumni Giving	**3**	**18**
Graduation Rate	**2**	**2**
Overall Rank	**4**	**6**

Other Key Alumni Outcomes

5.8% Are college professors
13.7% Teach at any level
67.1% Have post-graduate degrees
54.6% Live in dual-income homes
90.9% Are currently employed

See pages 134–135 for detailed explanations and definitions.

Alumni Activities During College

46.2% Community Service
43.4% Intramural Sports
20.3% Internships
23.8% Media Programs
25.2% Music Programs
16.1% Part-Time Jobs

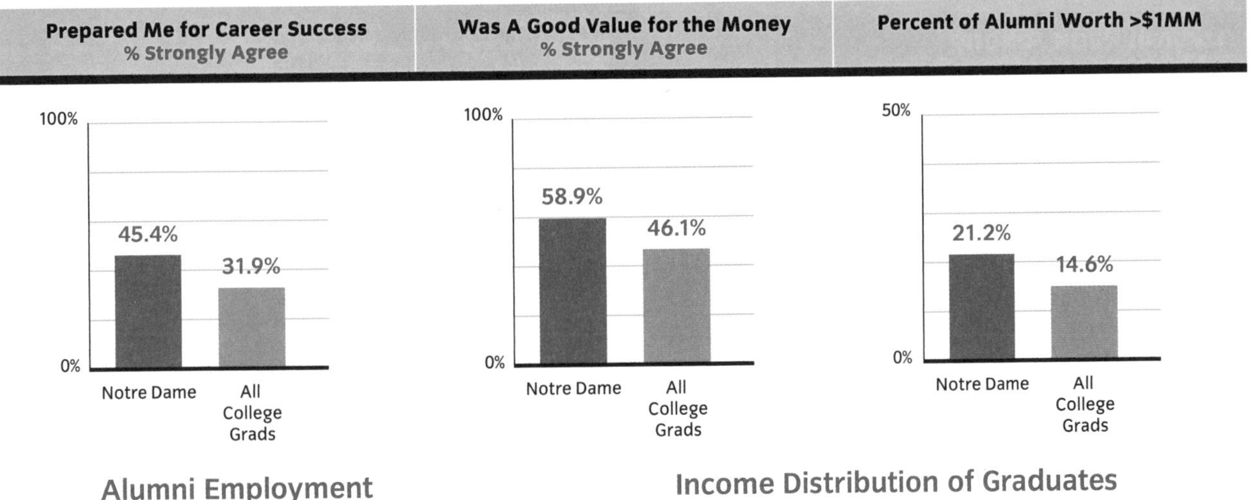

Alumni Employment

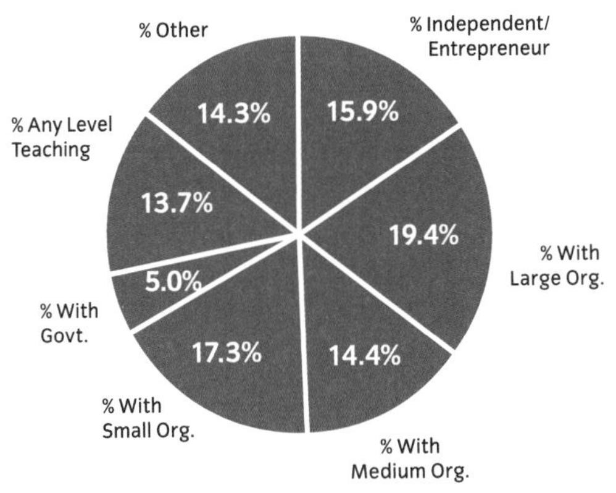

Income Distribution of Graduates

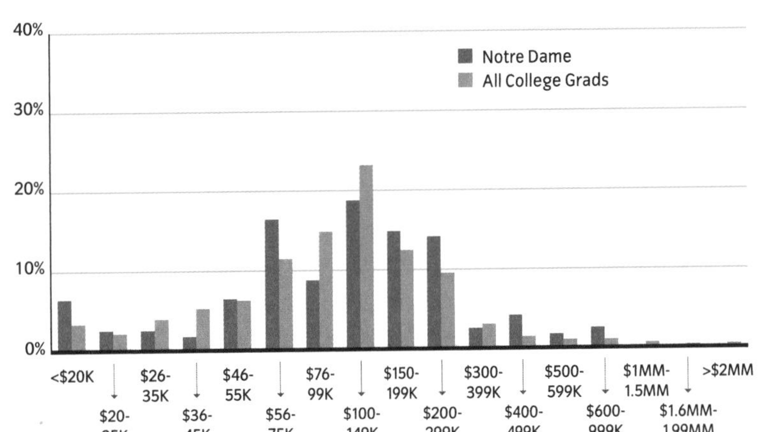

Current Selectivity & Demand Analysis for University of Notre Dame

Attribute	% Accepted	% Accepted Who Enroll	Freshman Retention Rate	Graduation Rate	Demand Index	Reputation Index
Score	24.0%	50.0%	98.0%	96.0%	8.19	2.08
Rank	37	19	4	2	97	27

Where are the Graduates of University of Notre Dame on the Political Spectrum?

Very Liberal	Liberal	Somewhat Liberal	Somewhat Conservative	Conservative	Very Conservative
			⇧		

University of Oregon

Location: Eugene, OR
Campus Setting: City: Midsize
Total Expenses: $22,052
Estimated Average Discount: $7,353 (33%)
Estimated Net Price: $14,699

Type of Institution: National University
Number of Undergraduates: 19,528
SAT Score: Reading: 492-607, Math: 499-611
Student/Faculty Ratio: 23 to 1
Transfer Out Rate: 6%

Rank Among 104 National Universities	**98**
Overall Rank Among 177 *Alumni Factor* Schools	**171**

Overview

The University of Oregon is as friendly and laid-back a campus community as can be found anywhere. Awash in college-town charm, the Eugene-based university has cultural room for everyone and takes great pride in its social and intellectual tolerance. Graduates are a reflection of the vast opportunities offered at UO, with many successful and accomplished alumni spread across politics, business, journalism, the arts, government, athletics, education, academia, science and medicine. UO ranks 98th among national universities and 171st among all colleges and universities in our outcomes-based analysis.

UO's strongest performance is in the Overall Assessment (65th), where it gets its best ranking in Would Personally Choose Again (59th). Oregon's strongest Ultimate Outcome is Friendships & Intellectual Capability where it ranks 64th among national universities. UO produces many college professors (ranked 52nd among all colleges and universities), and grads lean quite liberal on the political spectrum.

Notable Alumni

Nike co-founders Phil Knight and Bill Bowerman; Columbia University President Lee Bollinger; advertising luminary Dan Wieden; author Ken Kesey; former senators Paul Simon and Richard Neuberger; former P&G chairman Ed Artzt; and NFL quarterbacks Norm Van Brocklin, Dan Fouts and Joey Harrington. The Ducks can be mighty proud of their results.

The Alumni Factor Rankings Summary

Attribute	University Rank	Overall Rank
College Experience	**96**	**169**
Intellectual Development	72	143
Social Development	77	145
Spiritual Development	61	131
Friendship Development	79	149
Preparation for Career Success	95	166
Immediate Job Opportunities	101	172
Overall Assessment	**65**	**122**
Would Personally Choose Again	59	110
Would Recommend to Student	60	115
Value for the Money	69	126
Financial Success	**101**	**169**
Income per Household	103	175
% Households with Income >$150K	93	153
Household Net Worth	103	173
% Households Net Worth >$1MM	85	143
Overall Happiness	**101**	**173**
Alumni Giving	**67**	**131**
Graduation Rate	**85**	**153**
Overall Rank	**98**	**171**

Other Key Alumni Outcomes

7.7% Are college professors
13.3% Teach at any level
39.5% Have post-graduate degrees
46.7% Live in dual-income homes
88.9% Are currently employed

See pages 134–135 for detailed explanations and definitions.

Alumni Activities During College

27.5% Community Service
27.5% Intramural Sports
25.0% Internships
12.0% Media Programs
24.5% Music Programs
51.5% Part-Time Jobs

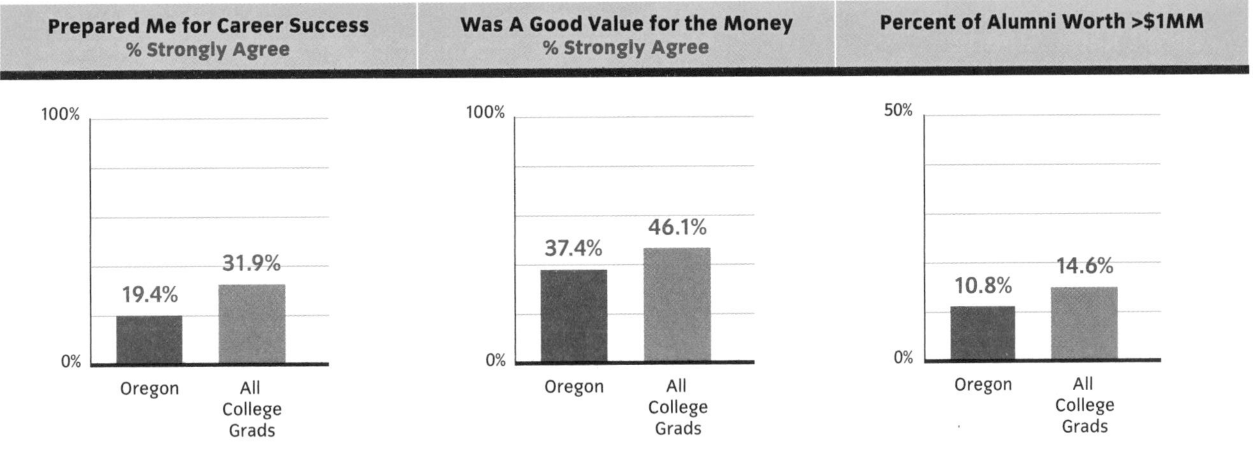

Alumni Employment

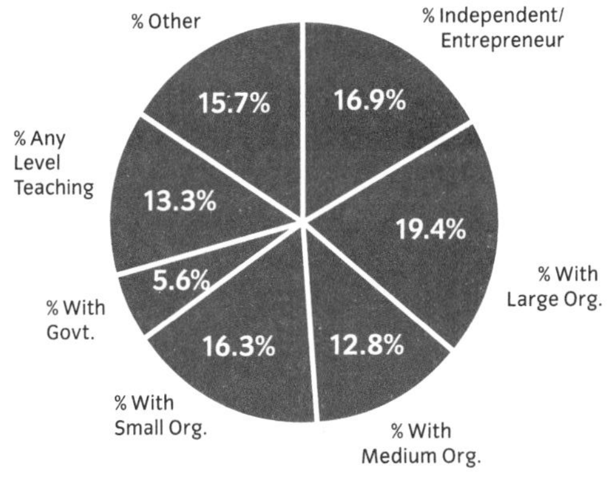

Income Distribution of Graduates

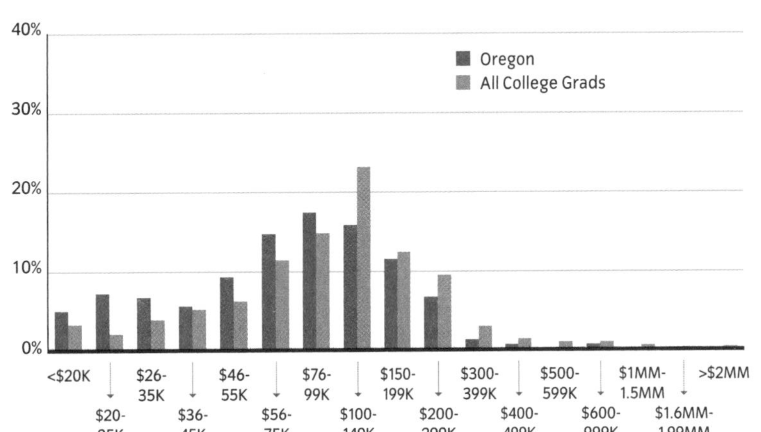

Current Selectivity & Demand Analysis for University of Oregon

Attribute	% Accepted	% Accepted Who Enroll	Freshman Retention Rate	Graduation Rate	Demand Index	Reputation Index
Score	79.0%	27.0%	86.0%	68.0%	4.44	0.34
Rank	165	119	146	153	146	160

Where are the Graduates of University of Oregon on the Political Spectrum?

Very Liberal	Liberal	Somewhat Liberal	Somewhat Conservative	Conservative	Very Conservative
	↑				

See pages 134–135 for detailed explanations and definitions.

University of Pennsylvania

Location: Philadelphia, PA
Campus Setting: City: Large
Total Expenses: $57,360
Estimated Average Discount: $36,768 (64%)
Estimated Net Price: $20,592

Type of Institution: National University
Number of Undergraduates: 11,940
SAT Score: Reading: 660–750, Math: 690–780
Student/Faculty Ratio: 6 to 1
Transfer Out Rate: 1%

Rank Among 104 National Universities	**25**
Overall Rank Among 177 *Alumni Factor* Schools	**51**

Overview

The financial and economic powerhouse of the Ivy League, Penn is to finance and economics what Cal Tech and MIT are to engineering and science. While Penn offers world-class excellence across a broad set of disciplines from medicine to the liberal arts, the business of Penn is business. If there is a global center for finance and business education, Penn's Wharton school is it.

Penn graduates are a reflection of that reknown. You won't find many of them teaching (ranked 176th in becoming a professor); and they won't rave about the campus life (63rd and 57th in Social Development and Friendships respectively), but few are better at becoming financially successful (3rd). Grads won't tell you it's a great value (imagine the grueling cost-benefit calculations implied in that 82nd rank) even though it clearly is. But, if you want Financial Success and Intellectual Development, there is hardly a better school in the world. Ranked third in Financial Success, Top 10 on every financial measurement, Top 10 on three Ultimate Outcomes and 23rd in SAT scores, Penn grads have sizzling intellects and use them to advance capitalism, their nation and their own good fortune. Pragmatic founder Ben Franklin would certainly be proud.

Notable Alumni

Former US president William Henry Harrison; 3 supreme court justices; 9 signers of the US Constitution; 8 signers of the Declaration of Independence; billionaire financier/philanthropist Ronald Perelman; H&R Block co-founder Richard Bloch; Warburg Pincus founder Lionel Pincus; former senator Arlen Specter and countless other accomplished leaders.

The Alumni Factor Rankings Summary

Attribute	University Rank	Overall Rank
College Experience	**48**	**112**
Intellectual Development	34	87
Social Development	63	124
Spiritual Development	84	156
Friendship Development	57	123
Preparation for Career Success	54	111
Immediate Job Opportunities	16	22
Overall Assessment	**66**	**123**
Would Personally Choose Again	62	114
Would Recommend to Student	49	98
Value for the Money	82	146
Financial Success	**3**	**8**
Income per Household	3	7
% Households with Income >$150K	2	6
Household Net Worth	4	12
% Households Net Worth >$1MM	9	19
Overall Happiness	**73**	**126**
Alumni Giving	**8**	**41**
Graduation Rate	**2**	**2**
Overall Rank	**25**	**51**

Other Key Alumni Outcomes

1.0% Are college professors
6.7% Teach at any level
71.5% Have post-graduate degrees
53.6% Live in dual-income homes
94.7% Are currently employed

See pages 134–135 for detailed explanations and definitions.

Alumni Activities During College

32.6% Community Service
23.7% Intramural Sports
18.9% Internships
20.1% Media Programs
23.2% Music Programs
33.2% Part-Time Jobs

Prepared Me for Career Success % Strongly Agree	Was A Good Value for the Money % Strongly Agree	Percent of Alumni Worth >$1MM
Penn 35.6%; All College Grads 31.9%	Penn 37.2%; All College Grads 46.1%	Penn 22.0%; All College Grads 14.6%

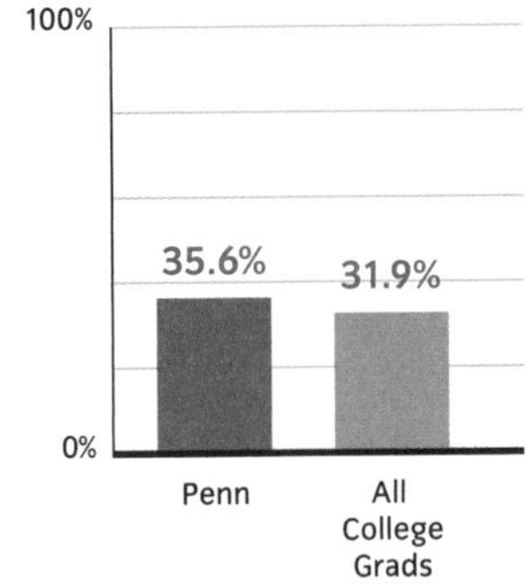

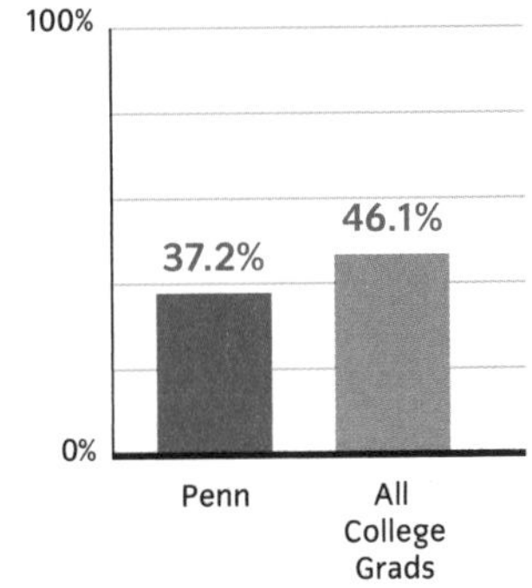

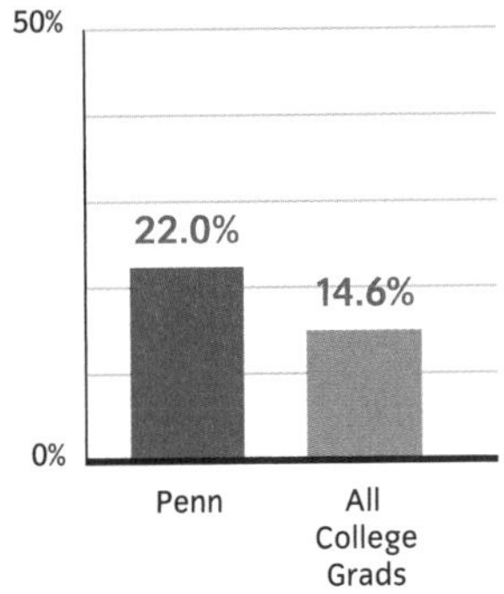

Alumni Employment

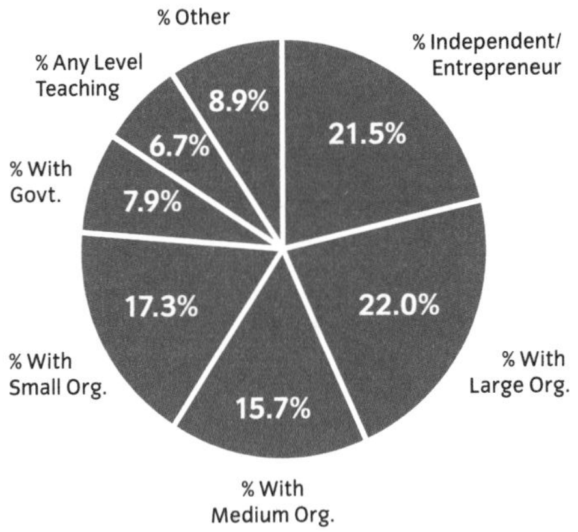

Income Distribution of Graduates

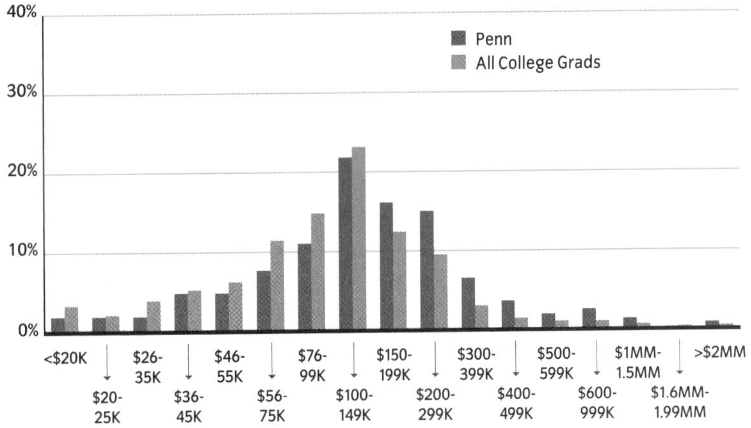

Current Selectivity & Demand Analysis for University of Pennsylvania

Attribute	% Accepted	% Accepted Who Enroll	Freshman Retention Rate	Graduation Rate	Demand Index	Reputation Index
Score	12.0%	62.0%	98.0%	96.0%	12.88	5.17
Rank	11	10	4	2	36	11

Where are the Graduates of University of Pennsylvania on the Political Spectrum?

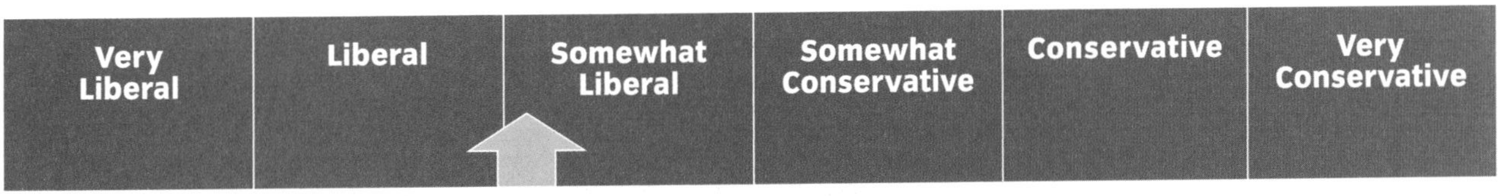

See pages 134–135 for detailed explanations and definitions.

University of Pittsburgh

Location: Pittsburgh, PA
Campus Setting: City: Large
Total Expenses: $29,732
Estimated Average Discount: $9,656 (32%)
Estimated Net Price: $20,076

Type of Institution: National University
Number of Undergraduates: 18,371
SAT Score: Reading: 570–680, Math: 600–690
Student/Faculty Ratio: 14 to 1
Transfer Out Rate: Not Reported

Rank Among 104 National Universities	**95**
Overall Rank Among 177 *Alumni Factor* Schools	**167**

Overview

The University of Pittsburgh has offered a well-rounded liberal arts curriculum in the humanities, arts and sciences to its undergraduates since its founding in 1787. As a large and prominent research university, it has been at the forefront of important medical and scientific advances in the last century. Dr. Jonas Salk and his team at Pitt created the polio vaccine in 1955, and Pitt is one of the world leaders in organ transplants.

In terms of alumni success upon graduation, Pitt makes it into our Top 177 (95th among national universities and 167th overall) based on its graduates' relatively strong Overall Assessment (79th). Pitt gets very consistent marks from its alumni across the key attributes of the College Experience (92nd), and grads perform well in both Financial Success (93rd) and in the Ultimate Outcomes (93rd). Overall Happiness (94th) gets similar marks. Pitt's strongest Ultimate Outcome is Happiness & Intellectual Capability, in which it is ranked 67th. Notably, Pitt is a Top 25 producer of teachers and professors.

Notable Alumni

Academy Award winner Gene Kelly; footballers Mike Ditka, Tony Dorsett, Dan Marino, Jimmy Johnson and Marty Schottenheimer; many members of the prominent Mellon family; hedge-fund manager David Tepper; former US Steel CEO Thomas Usher; former US congressman John Murtha; and many other accomplished leaders.

The Alumni Factor Rankings Summary

Attribute	University Rank	Overall Rank
College Experience	**92**	**165**
Intellectual Development	89	160
Social Development	67	130
Spiritual Development	91	163
Friendship Development	96	167
Preparation for Career Success	78	146
Immediate Job Opportunities	78	127
Overall Assessment	**79**	**143**
Would Personally Choose Again	91	157
Would Recommend to Student	58	113
Value for the Money	78	141
Financial Success	**93**	**157**
Income per Household	96	155
% Households with Income >$150K	92	149
Household Net Worth	81	132
% Households Net Worth >$1MM	93	156
Overall Happiness	**94**	**161**
Alumni Giving	**67**	**131**
Graduation Rate	**62**	**123**
Overall Rank	**95**	**167**

Other Key Alumni Outcomes

9.6% Are college professors
19.2% Teach at any level
54.8% Have post-graduate degrees
54.5% Live in dual-income homes
93.0% Are currently employed

See pages 134–135 for detailed explanations and definitions.

Alumni Activities During College

24.4% Community Service
15.4% Intramural Sports
24.4% Internships
19.9% Media Programs
11.5% Music Programs
48.1% Part-Time Jobs

	Pitt	All College Grads
Prepared Me for Career Success (% Strongly Agree)	22.1%	31.9%
Was A Good Value for the Money (% Strongly Agree)	32.5%	46.1%
Percent of Alumni Worth >$1MM	9.9%	14.6%

Alumni Employment

Category	%
% Independent/ Entrepreneur	12.1%
% With Large Org.	25.5%
% With Medium Org.	8.9%
% With Small Org.	11.5%
% With Govt.	7.0%
% Any Level Teaching	19.2%
% Other	15.8%

Income Distribution of Graduates

Current Selectivity & Demand Analysis for University of Pittsburgh

Attribute	% Accepted	% Accepted Who Enroll	Freshman Retention Rate	Graduation Rate	Demand Index	Reputation Index
Score	58.0%	29.0%	92.0%	78.0%	6.08	0.50
Rank	119	107	86	123	125	121

Where are the Graduates of University of Pittsburgh on the Political Spectrum?

Very Liberal	Liberal	Somewhat Liberal	Somewhat Conservative	Conservative	Very Conservative
			⇧		

See pages 134–135 for detailed explanations and definitions.

University of Richmond

Location: Richmond, VA
Campus Setting: City: Midsize
Total Expenses: $54,460
Estimated Average Discount: $35,031 (64%)
Estimated Net Price: $19,429

Type of Institution: Liberal Arts College
Number of Undergraduates: 3,457
SAT Score: Reading: 580–690, Math: 610–700
Student/Faculty Ratio: 9 to 1
Transfer Out Rate: Not Reported

Rank Among 53 Liberal Arts Colleges	**15**
Overall Rank Among 177 *Alumni Factor* Schools	**22**

Overview

Well-known and respected in the Northeast corridor and the Mid-Atlantic States, the University of Richmond should rightly gain national prominence for producing some of the most successful alumni in the country. In fact, the outcomes of Richmond alumni well exceed the school's current reputation. Ranked 15th among liberal arts colleges and 22nd among all colleges and universities, University of Richmond grads perform extraordinarily well in Financial Success (7th) and in the Ultimate Outcomes (16th). Richmond grads also give very high marks to the school in their Overall Assessment (19th) and in overall College Experience (34th). Of particular note is Richmond's strongest Ultimate Outcome, Financial Success & Intellectual Capability, where it ranks 5th among liberal arts colleges and in the Top 10 among all colleges and universities. This is quite impressive for a small school with limited national awareness. Add in the Spiders' 17th ranking in rate of employment, and soon the rest of the country will recognize Richmond's excellence. The Spiders are on the move.

Notable Alumni

Washington Redskins GM Bruce Allen; longtime congressman Watkins Abbitt; former CEO of Wachovia Bank Bud Baker; and actor Grant Shaud.

The Alumni Factor Rankings Summary

Attribute	Liberal Arts Rank	Overall Rank
College Experience	**34**	**64**
Intellectual Development	46	81
Social Development	31	53
Spiritual Development	46	100
Friendship Development	49	90
Preparation for Career Success	23	46
Immediate Job Opportunities	8	34
Overall Assessment	**19**	**47**
Would Personally Choose Again	17	35
Would Recommend to Student	14	42
Value for the Money	28	72
Financial Success	**7**	**13**
Income per Household	6	11
% Households with Income >$150K	5	10
Household Net Worth	6	10
% Households Net Worth >$1MM	14	30
Overall Happiness	**26**	**66**
Alumni Giving	**49**	**65**
Graduation Rate	**26**	**60**
Overall Rank	**15**	**22**

Other Key Alumni Outcomes

4.8% Are college professors
8.7% Teach at any level
45.3% Have post-graduate degrees
49.5% Live in dual-income homes
96.2% Are currently employed

See pages 134–135 for detailed explanations and definitions.

Alumni Activities During College

32.1% Community Service
45.3% Intramural Sports
21.7% Internships
11.4% Media Programs
11.3% Music Programs
29.2% Part-Time Jobs

Prepared Me for Career Success (% Strongly Agree)	Was A Good Value for the Money (% Strongly Agree)	Percent of Alumni Worth >$1MM
Richmond 31.4%; All College Grads 31.9%	Richmond 46.7%; All College Grads 46.1%	Richmond 20.2%; All College Grads 14.6%

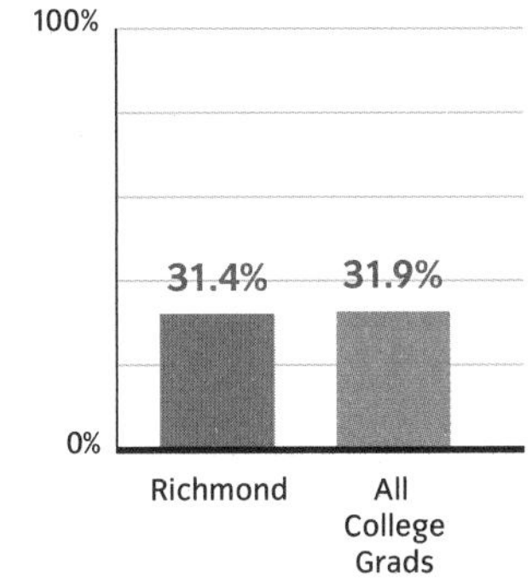

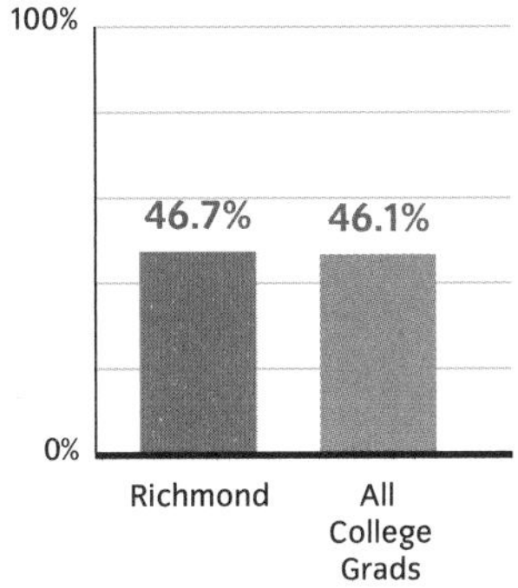

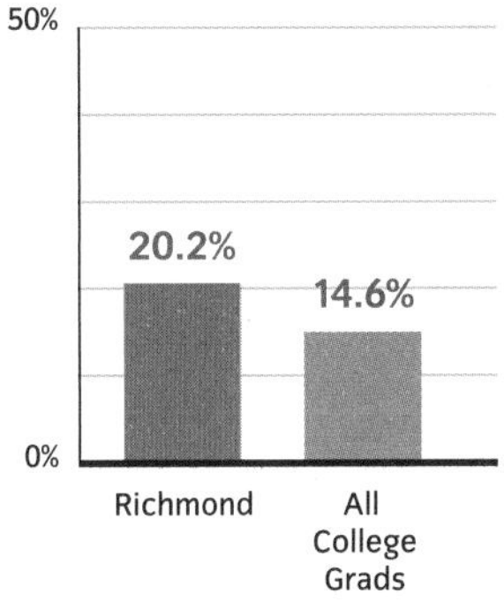

Alumni Employment

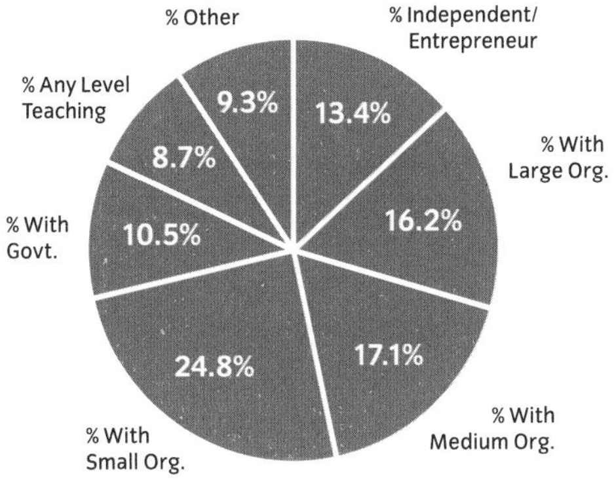

Income Distribution of Graduates

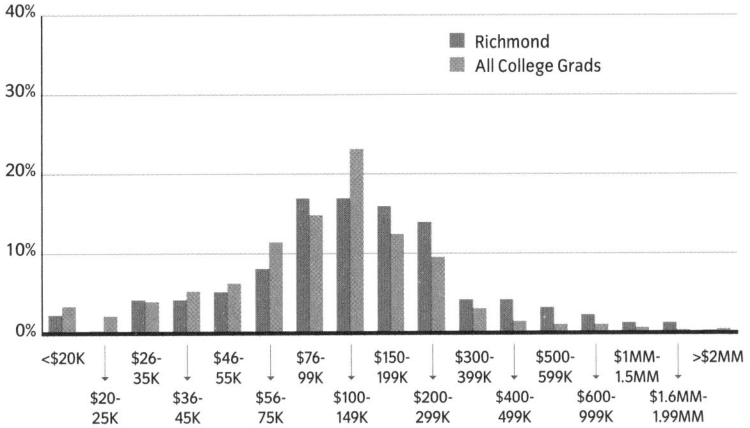

Current Selectivity & Demand Analysis for University of Richmond

Attribute	% Accepted	% Accepted Who Enroll	Freshman Retention Rate	Graduation Rate	Demand Index	Reputation Index
Score	33.0%	25.0%	93.0%	87.0%	12.06	0.76
Rank	61	130	73	60	44	78

Where are the Graduates of University of Richmond on the Political Spectrum?

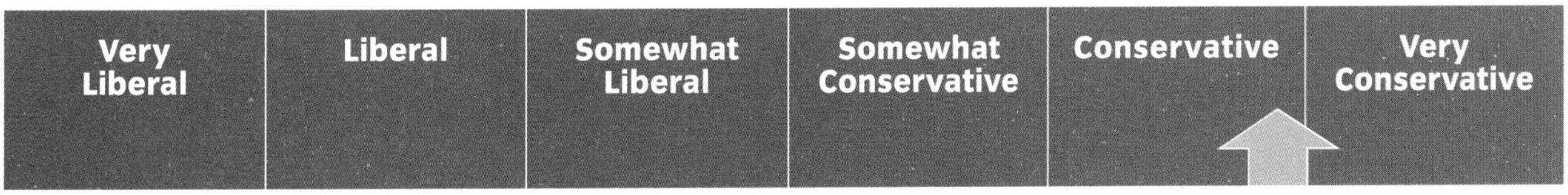

University of Rochester

Location: Rochester, NY
Campus Setting: City: Midsize
Total Expenses: $56,760
Estimated Average Discount: $26,652 (47%)
Estimated Net Price: $30,108

Type of Institution: National University
Number of Undergraduates: 5,601
SAT Score: Reading: 600–700, Math: 650–740
Student/Faculty Ratio: 11 to 1
Transfer Out Rate: Not Reported

Rank Among 104 National Universities	**67**
Overall Rank Among 177 *Alumni Factor* Schools	**132**

Overview

The University of Rochester faces challenges similar to those faced by other excellent, small-to-mid-sized universities which have neither a nationally recognized athletic program nor "brand awareness" on a national scale that would allow the school to be seen as a major player in the increasingly national competition for America's best and brightest undergrads. Undoubtedly, Rochester gets bright students – graduates rank 56th among all colleges and universities in their reported SAT scores. The strongest attribute of the school is Intellectual Development (42nd), which carries through to strength in the Ultimate Outcomes, where Intellectual Development is a component. Also, Rochester grads go on to significant success and accomplishment (33rd in Financial Success and 16th in getting a post-graduate degree). However, relative to the alums of other Top 177 colleges and universities, they hold only mediocre views of their College Experience (80th) and are middling in their Overall Assessment (89th).

Notable Alumni

US Energy Secretary and Nobel laureate Steven Chu; author, playwright, director and producer George Abbott; legal scholar Arthur Miller; actors Robert Forster and Debra Jo Rupp; former secretary of the Navy Donald Winter; and former Kodak chairman & CEO Gerald Zornow.

The Alumni Factor Rankings Summary

Attribute	University Rank	Overall Rank
College Experience	**80**	**152**
Intellectual Development	42	99
Social Development	80	149
Spiritual Development	88	160
Friendship Development	50	114
Preparation for Career Success	85	155
Immediate Job Opportunities	78	127
Overall Assessment	**89**	**158**
Would Personally Choose Again	73	131
Would Recommend to Student	84	153
Value for the Money	95	166
Financial Success	**33**	**61**
Income per Household	38	64
% Households with Income >$150K	31	55
Household Net Worth	38	69
% Households Net Worth >$1MM	41	73
Overall Happiness	**76**	**131**
Alumni Giving	**41**	**99**
Graduation Rate	**38**	**81**
Overall Rank	**67**	**132**

Other Key Alumni Outcomes

6.3% Are college professors
11.5% Teach at any level
68.4% Have post-graduate degrees
55.3% Live in dual-income homes
93.7% Are currently employed

See pages 134–135 for detailed explanations and definitions.

Alumni Activities During College

31.0% Community Service
36.4% Intramural Sports
24.1% Internships
24.0% Media Programs
26.7% Music Programs
34.2% Part-Time Jobs

Current Selectivity & Demand Analysis for University of Rochester

Attribute	% Accepted	% Accepted Who Enroll	Freshman Retention Rate	Graduation Rate	Demand Index	Reputation Index
Score	36.0%	24.0%	95.0%	84.0%	11.50	0.67
Rank	71	138	47	81	50	91

Where are the Graduates of University of Rochester on the Political Spectrum?

Very Liberal	Liberal	Somewhat Liberal	Somewhat Conservative	Conservative	Very Conservative
	↑				

See pages 134–135 for detailed explanations and definitions.

University of Southern California

Location: Los Angeles, CA
Campus Setting: City: Large
Total Expenses: $57,876
Estimated Average Discount: $30,335 (52%)
Estimated Net Price: $27,541

Type of Institution: National University
Number of Undergraduates: 17,380
SAT Score: Reading: 610–720, Math: 670–770
Student/Faculty Ratio: 9 to 1
Transfer Out Rate: 6%

Rank Among 104 National Universities	**24**
Overall Rank Among 177 *Alumni Factor* Schools	**48**

Overview

California's oldest and most famous private university is recognized globally for its excellence. In fact, like Hollywood and other famous Southern California originals, USC often acts as a global ambassador for American higher education. This distinctly American institution has the highest number of international students of any school in the country; has more Olympic medal winners than any other college (indeed outpacing all but 12 countries in medal count and preserving its edge in London with 24 medals to University of Florida's 21); and has one of the most successful sports programs in collegiate history. It produces truly happy (47th), loyal (4th in Alumni Giving) and financially successful (16th) alumni in a way that few other colleges can match.

The school motto, "Trojan for Life," plays out in the market as USC has one of the most staunchly loyal and supportive alumni groups in the country. Alums love to help each other along the way. It's what helps USC earn the 22nd spot in Immediate Job Opportunities in our ranking. USC's strongest Ultimate Outcome, Financial Success & Happiness (17th), best summarizes grads of this iconic university.

Notable Alumni

Just a few of the non-athlete, non-Olympian alumni: Salesforce.com founder Marc Benioff; co-founder of Intuit Scott Cook; E.F. Hutton CEO Robert Fomon; hotel scion Barron Hilton; former CEO of MGM Mirage Terrence Lanni; film producer extraordinaire Brian Grazer; venture capitalist Mark Stevens; the legendary George Lucas; singer Macy Gray; composer James Newton Howard; and the loveable Will Ferrell.

The Alumni Factor Rankings Summary

Attribute	University Rank	Overall Rank
College Experience	**32**	**88**
Intellectual Development	49	111
Social Development	22	63
Spiritual Development	37	102
Friendship Development	42	105
Preparation for Career Success	40	89
Immediate Job Opportunities	22	34
Overall Assessment	**53**	**103**
Would Personally Choose Again	48	88
Would Recommend to Student	28	62
Value for the Money	84	150
Financial Success	**16**	**27**
Income per Household	19	36
% Households with Income >$150K	17	35
Household Net Worth	11	23
% Households Net Worth >$1MM	16	33
Overall Happiness	**47**	**90**
Alumni Giving	**4**	**32**
Graduation Rate	**29**	**47**
Overall Rank	**24**	**48**

Other Key Alumni Outcomes

4.0% Are college professors
10.3% Teach at any level
46.1% Have post-graduate degrees
46.7% Live in dual-income homes
91.4% Are currently employed

See pages 134–135 for detailed explanations and definitions.

Alumni Activities During College

39.2% Community Service
18.6% Intramural Sports
33.6% Internships
11.8% Media Programs
12.7% Music Programs
43.1% Part-Time Jobs

	Prepared Me for Career Success % Strongly Agree	Was A Good Value for the Money % Strongly Agree	Percent of Alumni Worth >$1MM
USC	34.7%	36.0%	19.9%
All College Grads	31.9%	46.1%	14.6%

Alumni Employment

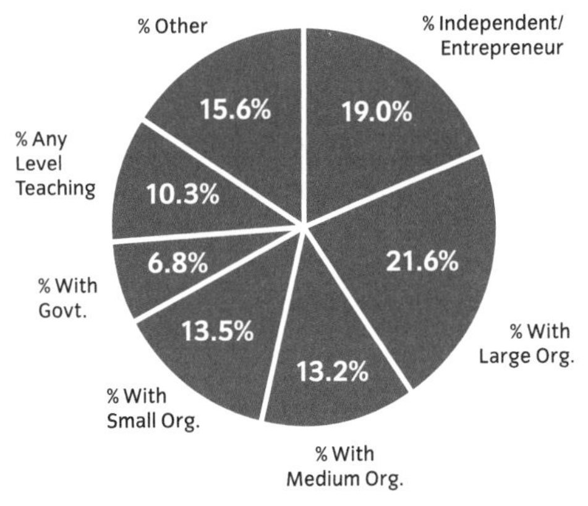

Income Distribution of Graduates

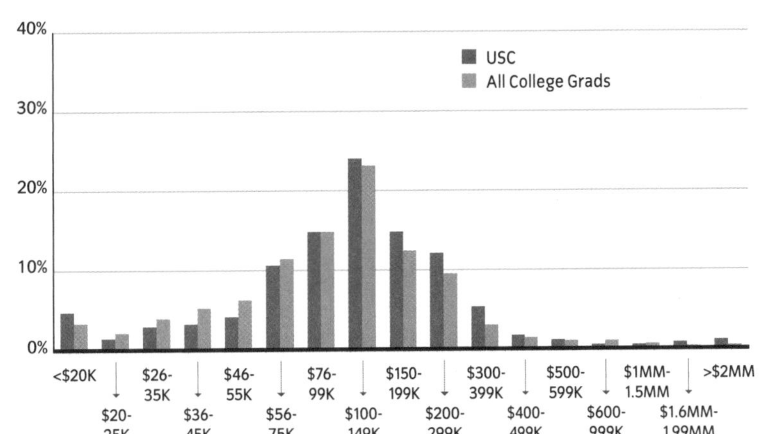

Current Selectivity & Demand Analysis for University of Southern California

Attribute	% Accepted	% Accepted Who Enroll	Freshman Retention Rate	Graduation Rate	Demand Index	Reputation Index
Score	23.0%	34.0%	97.0%	89.0%	12.70	1.48
Rank	34	76	13	47	40	40

Where are the Graduates of University of Southern California on the Political Spectrum?

Very Liberal	Liberal	Somewhat Liberal	Somewhat Conservative	Conservative	Very Conservative

University of Tennessee

Location: Knoxville, TN
Campus Setting: City: Midsize
Total Expenses: $23,571
Estimated Average Discount: $9,813 (42%)
Estimated Net Price: $13,758

Type of Institution: National University
Number of Undergraduates: 21,392
SAT Score: Reading: 520–640, Math: 530–640
Student/Faculty Ratio: 15 to 1
Transfer Out Rate: Not Reported

Rank Among 104 National Universities **57**

Overall Rank Among 177 *Alumni Factor* Schools **122**

Overview

There is much more than meets the eye at the University of Tennessee. Founded in 1794 and still the largest university in the state, UT is one of the most underrated universities in the country. The success of its alumni well outweighs its reputation in the college marketplace. While students and grads are crazy for all things orange, including UT football and Pat Summit's Vols, UT alumni are also some of the happiest graduates in the country (ranked 24th). They are financially successful (71st, with an impressive 45th ranking in Household Net Worth) and are quite high in their Overall Assessment of UT (36th). Grads tend towards the conservative side on political and social issues, and their strongest Ultimate Outcome is Financial Success & Happiness (45th). The fact that alums place it in the Top 30 for Value for the Money should come as no surprise.

Since Vanderbilt receives well-deserved credit for being the state's intellectual center, and Sewanee earns the award for liberal arts excellence, it is often difficult for Tennessee to earn its rightful spot in the state's academic hierarchy. But it certainly deserves a prominent position.

Notable Alumni

Former congressman Howard Baker, Sr.; Reagan White House counsel Arthur Culvahouse; former US Department of the Treasury secretary William McAdoo; QB-turned-Congressman Heath Shuler; actress Dixie Carter; financial guru Dave Ramsey; and one of the finest quarterbacks ever to play the game – Peyton Manning.

The Alumni Factor Rankings Summary

Attribute	University Rank	Overall Rank
College Experience	**66**	**135**
Intellectual Development	95	167
Social Development	41	96
Spiritual Development	100	172
Friendship Development	68	138
Preparation for Career Success	58	117
Immediate Job Opportunities	30	46
Overall Assessment	**36**	**74**
Would Personally Choose Again	33	65
Would Recommend to Student	53	107
Value for the Money	26	50
Financial Success	**71**	**114**
Income per Household	68	105
% Households with Income >$150K	65	111
Household Net Worth	45	81
% Households Net Worth >$1MM	90	153
Overall Happiness	**24**	**48**
Alumni Giving	**75**	**141**
Graduation Rate	**96**	**167**
Overall Rank	**57**	**122**

Other Key Alumni Outcomes

7.7% Are college professors
9.5% Teach at any level
50.9% Have post-graduate degrees
50.9% Live in dual-income homes
93.2% Are currently employed

See pages 134–135 for detailed explanations and definitions.

Alumni Activities During College

33.9% Community Service
39.1% Intramural Sports
31.3% Internships
13.9% Media Programs
18.2% Music Programs
43.5% Part-Time Jobs

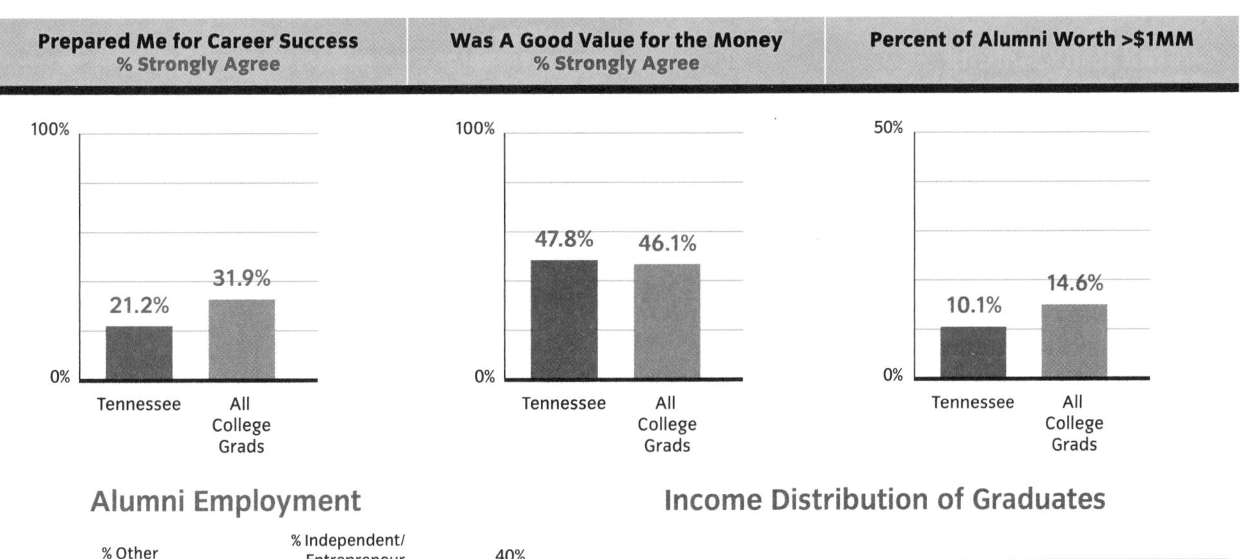

Alumni Employment

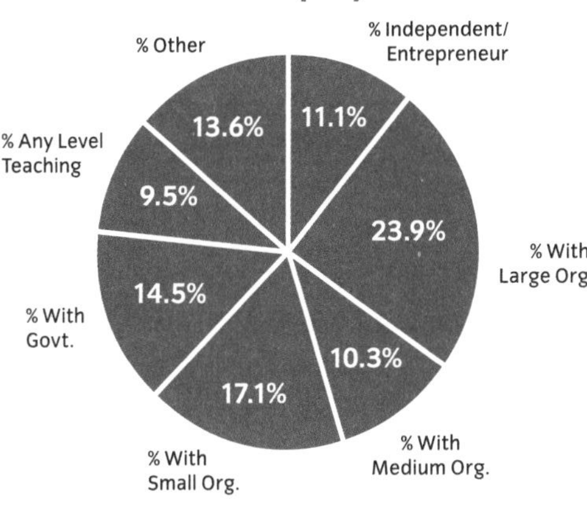

Income Distribution of Graduates

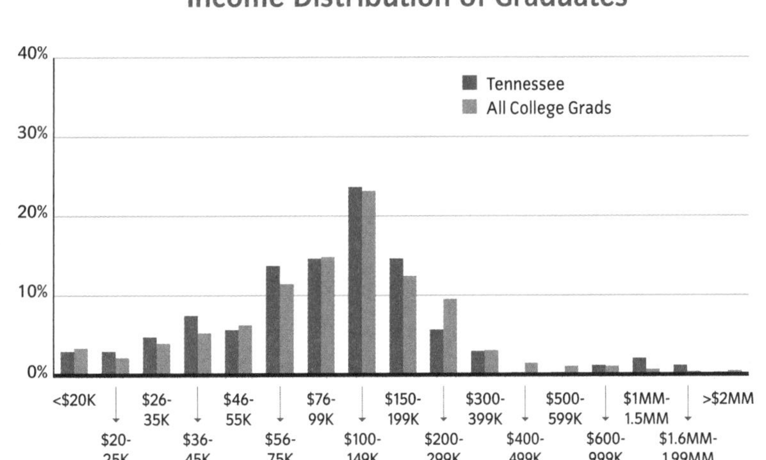

Current Selectivity & Demand Analysis for University of Tennessee

Attribute	% Accepted	% Accepted Who Enroll	Freshman Retention Rate	Graduation Rate	Demand Index	Reputation Index
Score	70.0%	44.0%	86.0%	60.0%	3.29	0.63
Rank	149	26	146	167	164	96

Where are the Graduates of University of Tennessee on the Political Spectrum?

Very Liberal	Liberal	Somewhat Liberal	Somewhat Conservative	Conservative	Very Conservative
					⇧

See pages 134–135 for detailed explanations and definitions.

University of Texas at Austin

Location: Austin, TX
Campus Setting: City: Large
Total Expenses: $24,714
Estimated Average Discount: $10,085 (41%)
Estimated Net Price: $14,629

Type of Institution: National University
Number of Undergraduates: 38,420
SAT Score: Reading: 540–670, Math: 580–710
Student/Faculty Ratio: 18 to 1
Transfer Out Rate: Not Reported

Rank Among 104 National Universities	**29**
Overall Rank Among 177 *Alumni Factor* Schools	**71**

Overview

Like everything in Texas, UT Austin is larger than life. UT is the biggest university in Texas and one of the five largest in the country. The university has shaped Austin and has made it one of the most progressive, dynamic cities in the country. Richly eclectic with a niche for all types, UT produces fiercely loyal "Texas Exes" who adore their school (ranked 8th in the Overall Assessment) and richly value their years spent there (41st in the College Experience). This great university gets very high marks from its graduates for Preparation for Career Success (36th) and for providing Immediate Job Opportunities (38th). Hence, UT grads do quite well financially (65th) and are quite loyal to their school (52nd in Alumni Giving). Ranked 19th in Overall Happiness, it will not surprise many that UT's strongest Ultimate Outcome is Financial Success & Happiness (51st).

Notable Alumni

CEO Michael Dell; former first lady Laura Bush; former senator Lloyd Benson; former Florida governor Jeb Bush; former US secretary of state James Baker; actors Renee Zellweger, Owen Wilson and Matthew McConaughey; Senator Kay Bailey Hutchison; former US attorney general Ramsey Clark; and many CEOs including James Mulva, Conoco Phillips; Rex Tillerson, Exxon Mobil and Gary Kelly, Southwest Airlines.

The Alumni Factor Rankings Summary

Attribute	University Rank	Overall Rank
College Experience	**41**	**101**
Intellectual Development	44	102
Social Development	27	69
Spiritual Development	50	116
Friendship Development	76	146
Preparation for Career Success	36	83
Immediate Job Opportunities	38	60
Overall Assessment	**8**	**13**
Would Personally Choose Again	7	15
Would Recommend to Student	16	26
Value for the Money	16	30
Financial Success	**65**	**106**
Income per Household	47	75
% Households with Income >$150K	50	84
Household Net Worth	80	129
% Households Net Worth >$1MM	78	129
Overall Happiness	**19**	**42**
Alumni Giving	**52**	**115**
Graduation Rate	**50**	**106**
Overall Rank	**29**	**71**

Other Key Alumni Outcomes

6.1% Are college professors
14.3% Teach at any level
50.9% Have post-graduate degrees
54.4% Live in dual-income homes
92.1% Are currently employed

See pages 134–135 for detailed explanations and definitions.

Alumni Activities During College

31.0% Community Service
30.0% Intramural Sports
24.0% Internships
12.2% Media Programs
11.5% Music Programs
54.1% Part-Time Jobs

Prepared Me for Career Success % Strongly Agree	Was A Good Value for the Money % Strongly Agree	Percent of Alumni Worth >$1MM
UT Austin: 33.2% All College Grads: 31.9%	UT Austin: 55.5% All College Grads: 46.1%	UT Austin: 11.8% All College Grads: 14.6%

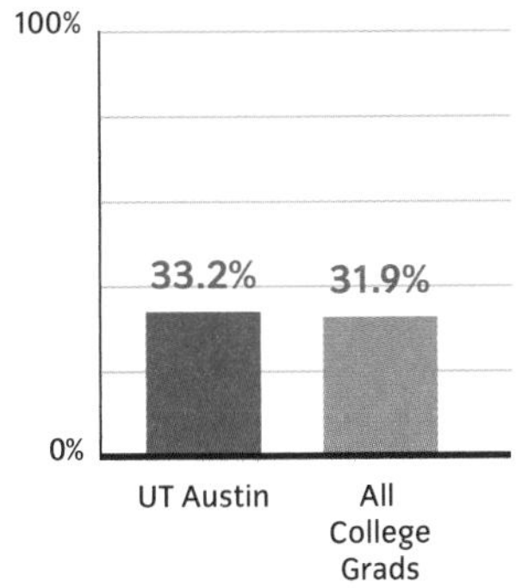

Alumni Employment

Category	%
% Independent/ Entrepreneur	13.2%
% With Large Org.	25.2%
% With Medium Org.	11.9%
% With Small Org.	13.5%
% With Govt.	8.3%
% Any Level Teaching	14.3%
% Other	13.6%

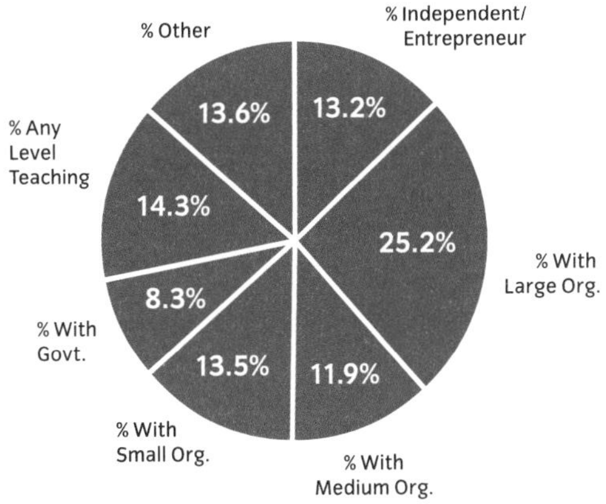

Income Distribution of Graduates

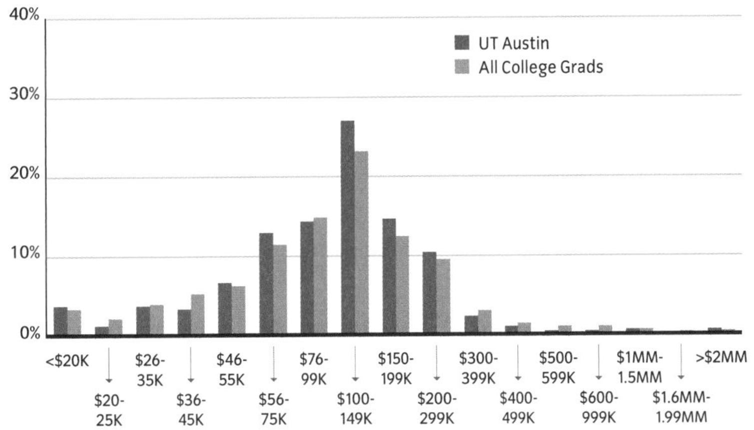

UT Austin / All College Grads

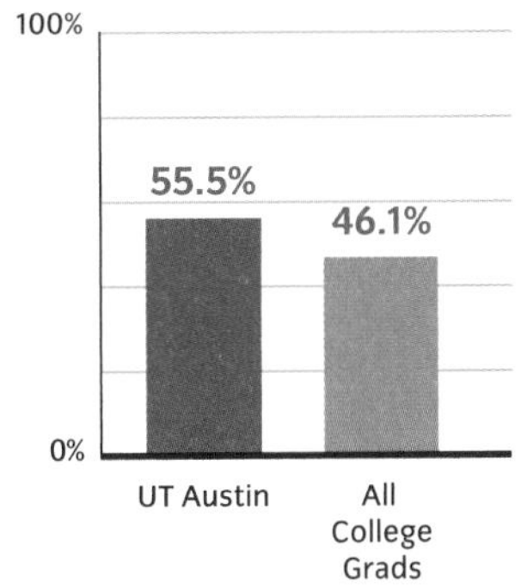

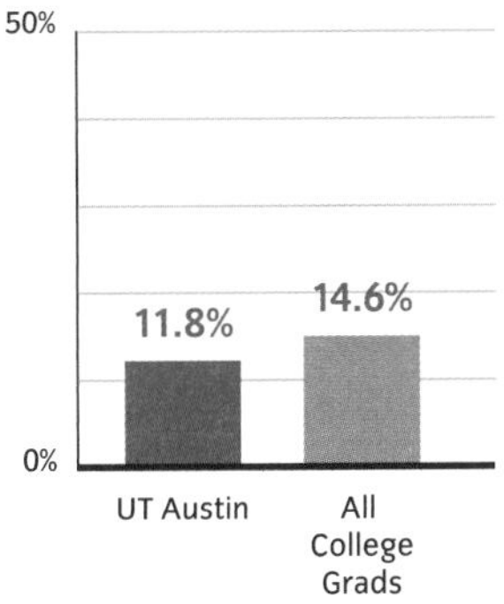

Income brackets: <$20K, $20-25K, $26-35K, $36-45K, $46-55K, $56-75K, $76-99K, $100-149K, $150-199K, $200-299K, $300-399K, $400-499K, $500-599K, $600-999K, $1MM-1.5MM, $1.6MM-1.99MM, >$2MM

Current Selectivity & Demand Analysis for University of Texas at Austin

Attribute	% Accepted	% Accepted Who Enroll	Freshman Retention Rate	Graduation Rate	Demand Index	Reputation Index
Score	47.0%	47.0%	92.0%	80.0%	4.56	1.00
Rank	99	22	86	106	145	60

Where are the Graduates of University of Texas at Austin on the Political Spectrum?

Very Liberal	Liberal	Somewhat Liberal	Somewhat Conservative	Conservative	Very Conservative
				↑	

See pages 134–135 for detailed explanations and definitions.

University of Utah

Location: Salt Lake City, UT
Campus Setting: City: Midsize
Total Expenses: $21,982
Estimated Average Discount: $13,209 (60%)
Estimated Net Price: $8,773

Type of Institution: National University
Number of Undergraduates: 23,371
SAT Score: Reading: 490–630, Math: 513-650
Student/Faculty Ratio: 15 to 1
Transfer Out Rate: Not Reported

Rank Among 104 National Universities	**92**
Overall Rank Among 177 *Alumni Factor* Schools	**164**

Overview

Located at the foot of the Wasatch Mountains on the outskirts of Salt Lake City, the University of Utah is in a perfect location for the outdoor enthusiast. Hiking, skiing and four seasons of outdoor activity await U of U students. A predominantly commuter campus, this is a large university with plenty of breadth in its academic and social offerings. This leads to wide variation in the type of alumni it produces. U of U graduates are extremely happy (ranked 13th), give a fairly high Overall Assessment of their school (69th) and give high marks to the school for Intellectual Development (56th), as well as Value for the Money (43rd). Not surprisingly, U of U graduates lean to the conservative side relative to other college graduates across the US. They are industrious and hard working (ranked 15th in employment rate) and do quite well financially. In fact, Utah grads rank 77th in households with high income and 84th in average household income.

Notable Alumni

Former US senators Bob Bennett, Frank Moss and Jake Garn; George W. Bush strategist Karl Rove; Gore-Tex founder Wilbert Gore; successful serial entrepreneur Jim Clark; former Cincinnati Bengal tight end Bob Trumpy; ESPN sideline reporter Holly Rowe; and best-selling author Stephen Covey.

The Alumni Factor Rankings Summary

Attribute	University Rank	Overall Rank
College Experience	**87**	**160**
Intellectual Development	56	122
Social Development	87	158
Spiritual Development	75	147
Friendship Development	103	176
Preparation for Career Success	82	151
Immediate Job Opportunities	72	115
Overall Assessment	**69**	**127**
Would Personally Choose Again	89	155
Would Recommend to Student	76	140
Value for the Money	43	79
Financial Success	**95**	**161**
Income per Household	84	126
% Households with Income >$150K	77	126
Household Net Worth	100	168
% Households Net Worth >$1MM	102	168
Overall Happiness	**13**	**31**
Alumni Giving	**98**	**171**
Graduation Rate	**103**	**176**
Overall Rank	**92**	**164**

Other Key Alumni Outcomes

3.7% Are college professors
10.5% Teach at any level
57.3% Have post-graduate degrees
46.3% Live in dual-income homes
96.3% Are currently employed

Alumni Activities During College

31.9% Community Service
21.3% Intramural Sports
19.4% Internships
10.6% Media Programs
11.3% Music Programs
54.4% Part-Time Jobs

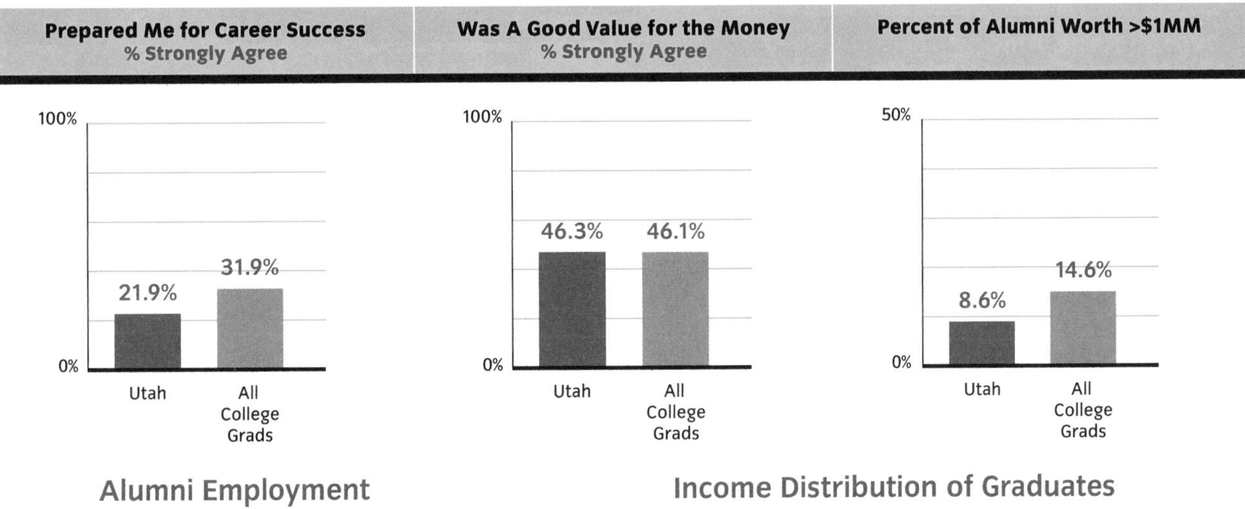

Alumni Employment

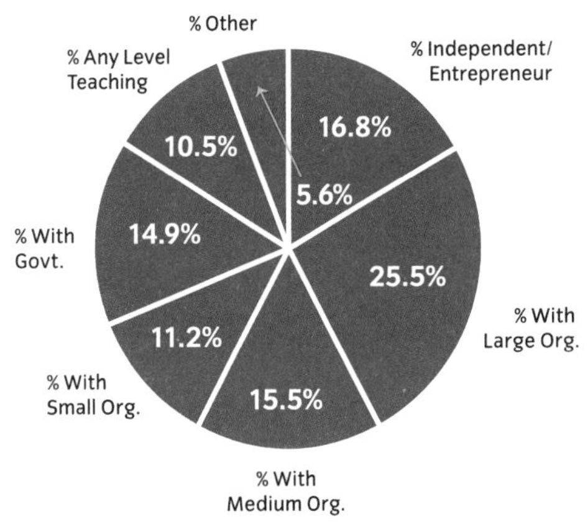

Income Distribution of Graduates

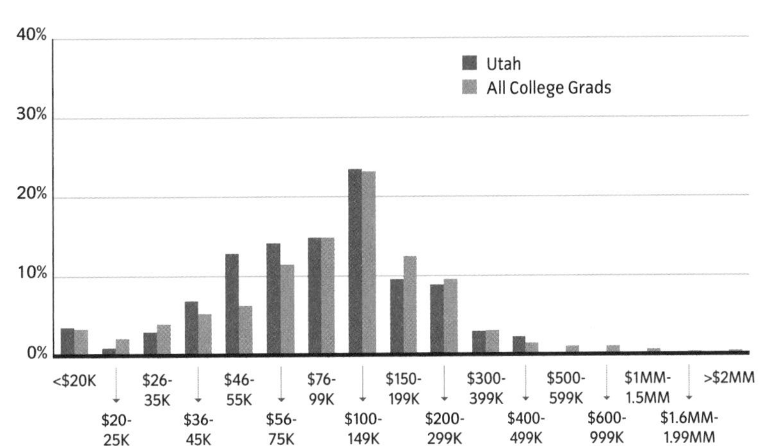

Current Selectivity & Demand Analysis for University of Utah

Attribute	% Accepted	% Accepted Who Enroll	Freshman Retention Rate	Graduation Rate	Demand Index	Reputation Index
Score	83.0%	41.0%	85.0%	56.0%	2.92	0.49
Rank	171	39	151	176	172	125

Where are the Graduates of University of Utah on the Political Spectrum?

Very Liberal	Liberal	Somewhat Liberal	Somewhat Conservative	Conservative	Very Conservative
					↑

See pages 134–135 for detailed explanations and definitions.

University of Vermont

Location: Burlington, VT
Campus Setting: City: Small
Total Expenses: $27,558
Estimated Average Discount: $13,694 (50%)
Estimated Net Price: $13,864

Type of Institution: National University
Number of Undergraduates: 11,593
SAT Score: Reading: 540–640, Math: 550–640
Student/Faculty Ratio: 17 to 1
Transfer Out Rate: Not Reported

Rank Among 104 National Universities	**96**
Overall Rank Among 177 *Alumni Factor* Schools	**169**

Overview

Founded in 1791 as the 5th college in New England (behind the original four Ivy League schools), making it the 23rd oldest college in the country, the University of Vermont sits in beautiful Burlington above Lake Champlain. The campus and community are decidedly laid-back, social-justice oriented and environmentally focused. Located in a state known for its progressive liberalism, it is not surprising that UVM and its graduates lean to the political left as well. UVM has long been known as a relaxed school for skiers and snowboarders or for those who simply love the outdoors. Its graduates, however, rank quite well in three important Ultimate Outcomes: Happiness & Intellectual Capability (52nd); Financial Success & Intellectual Capability (53rd) and Friendships & Intellectual Capability (53rd). Interestingly, UVM's highest ranking is in millionaire households where it ranks an impressive 31st. This is an especially surprising outcome given the high percentage of Vermont grads who go on to become teachers. When a college has graduates of high net worth, yet only average incomes, it can signal the school tends to attract and graduate privileged students (though there could be other factors at work, as well).

Notable Alumni

Former ABC executive Daniel Burke; former first lady Grace Coolidge; film director and screenwriter David Franzoni; basketball coach Rollie Massimino; and Nobel Peace Prize-winning teacher Jody Williams.

The Alumni Factor Rankings Summary

Attribute	University Rank	Overall Rank
College Experience	**99**	**172**
Intellectual Development	95	167
Social Development	92	163
Spiritual Development	52	119
Friendship Development	86	156
Preparation for Career Success	101	173
Immediate Job Opportunities	102	173
Overall Assessment	**98**	**169**
Would Personally Choose Again	92	158
Would Recommend to Student	81	150
Value for the Money	101	173
Financial Success	**68**	**111**
Income per Household	88	134
% Households with Income >$150K	82	137
Household Net Worth	60	103
% Households Net Worth >$1MM	31	59
Overall Happiness	**98**	**166**
Alumni Giving	**52**	**115**
Graduation Rate	**65**	**127**
Overall Rank	**96**	**169**

Other Key Alumni Outcomes

7.3% Are college professors
18.2% Teach at any level
47.7% Have post-graduate degrees
56.9% Live in dual-income homes
91.9% Are currently employed

See pages 134–135 for detailed explanations and definitions.

Alumni Activities During College

28.2% Community Service
31.8% Intramural Sports
22.7% Internships
9.9% Media Programs
10.9% Music Programs
41.8% Part-Time Jobs

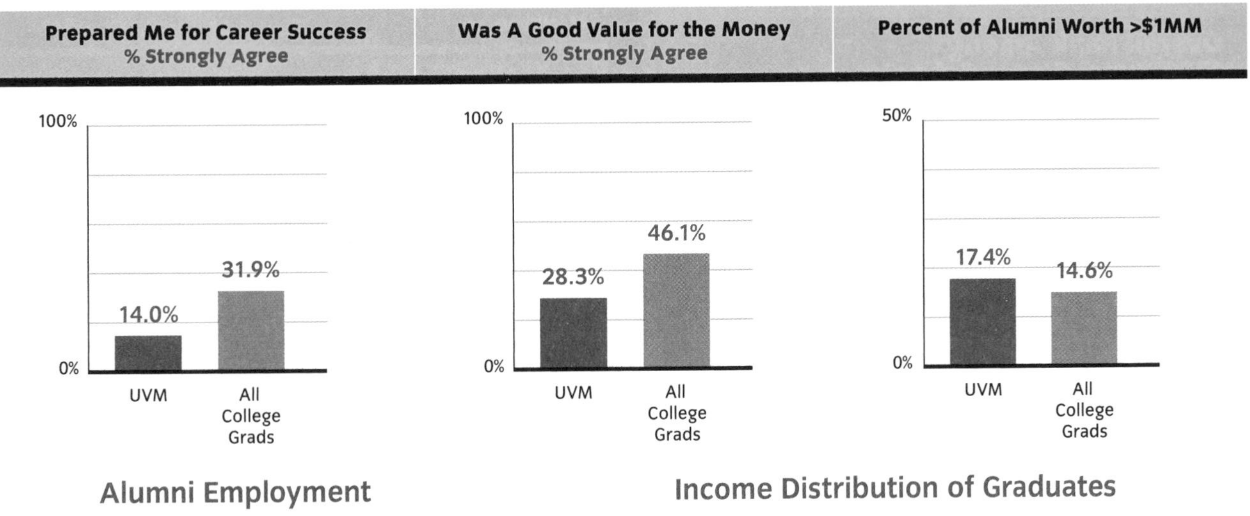

Alumni Employment

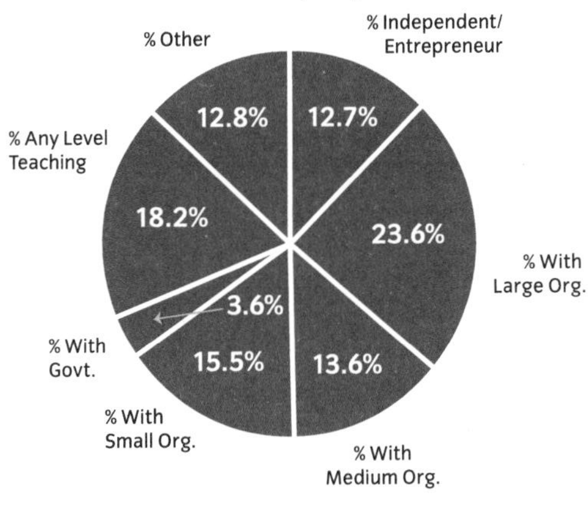

Income Distribution of Graduates

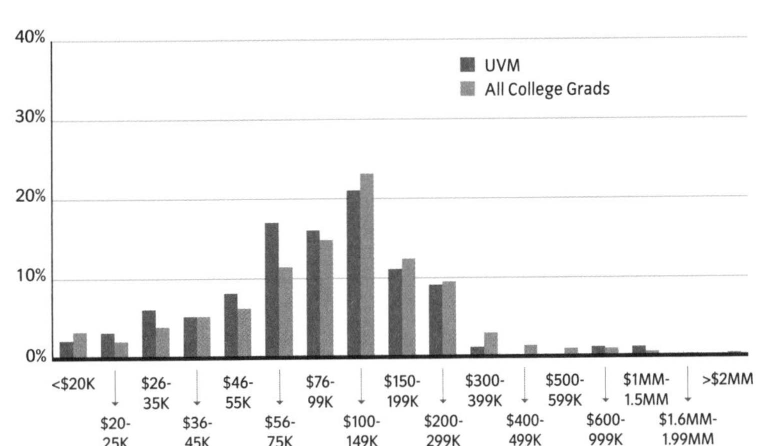

Current Selectivity & Demand Analysis for University of Vermont

Attribute	% Accepted	% Accepted Who Enroll	Freshman Retention Rate	Graduation Rate	Demand Index	Reputation Index
Score	75.0%	14.0%	87.0%	77.0%	9.22	0.19
Rank	160	174	140	127	80	176

Where are the Graduates of University of Vermont on the Political Spectrum?

Very Liberal	Liberal	Somewhat Liberal	Somewhat Conservative	Conservative	Very Conservative
	↑				

See pages 134–135 for detailed explanations and definitions.

University of Virginia

Location: Charlottesville, VA
Campus Setting: Suburb: Small
Total Expenses: $23,986
Estimated Average Discount: $12,396 (52%)
Estimated Net Price: $11,590

Type of Institution: National University
Number of Undergraduates: 15,595
SAT Score: Reading: 610–720, Math: 630–740
Student/Faculty Ratio: 16 to 1
Transfer Out Rate: 4%

Rank Among 104 National Universities	**6**
Overall Rank Among 177 *Alumni Factor* Schools	**12**

Overview

One of the country's finest universities, demonstrating excellence across every alumni success outcome we measure, the University of Virginia simply gets it right when it comes to producing happy, successful and comprehensively developed graduates. Ranked 3rd in the Overall Assessment by its graduates and 12th in the College Experience, UVA is clearly a university that has a transformational impact on its graduates. However, it is combining those facts with UVA's 19th ranking in Financial Success and its 21st ranking in the Ultimate Outcomes that propels UVA to the top echelon of schools in the country, earning it the 6th spot among all national universities. In fact, UVA is the top-ranked school among universities with more than 10,000 undergraduates. This stunningly successful track record of producing accomplished graduates means that UVA's results are even better than its already stellar reputation.

Notable Alumni

18th speaker of the house Robert Hunter; political analyst Larry Sabato; secretary of state under Roosevelt and Truman, Edward Stettinius; former premier of China Yan Huiqing; former president of NASDAQ Alfred Berkeley; Tudor Investments founder and billionaire Paul Tudor Jones; former CEO of Fannie Mae Daniel Mudd; legendary US Army physician Walter Reed; America's favorite Katie Couric; journalist Brit Hume; sportscaster Melissa Stark; and the hilarious Tina Fey.

The Alumni Factor Rankings Summary

Attribute	University Rank	Overall Rank
College Experience	**12**	**37**
Intellectual Development	14	52
Social Development	5	19
Spiritual Development	24	83
Friendship Development	27	83
Preparation for Career Success	16	39
Immediate Job Opportunities	23	37
Overall Assessment	**3**	**5**
Would Personally Choose Again	7	15
Would Recommend to Student	9	14
Value for the Money	4	7
Financial Success	**19**	**34**
Income per Household	23	41
% Households with Income >$150K	19	38
Household Net Worth	18	37
% Households Net Worth >$1MM	21	39
Overall Happiness	**23**	**42**
Alumni Giving	**29**	**81**
Graduation Rate	**12**	**16**
Overall Rank	**6**	**12**

Other Key Alumni Outcomes

7.1%	Are college professors
14.1%	Teach at any level
68.1%	Have post-graduate degrees
52.7%	Live in dual-income homes
95.3%	Are currently employed

See pages 134–135 for detailed explanations and definitions.

Alumni Activities During College

43.9% Community Service
32.9% Intramural Sports
22.3% Internships
17.7% Media Programs
16.3% Music Programs
40.5% Part-Time Jobs

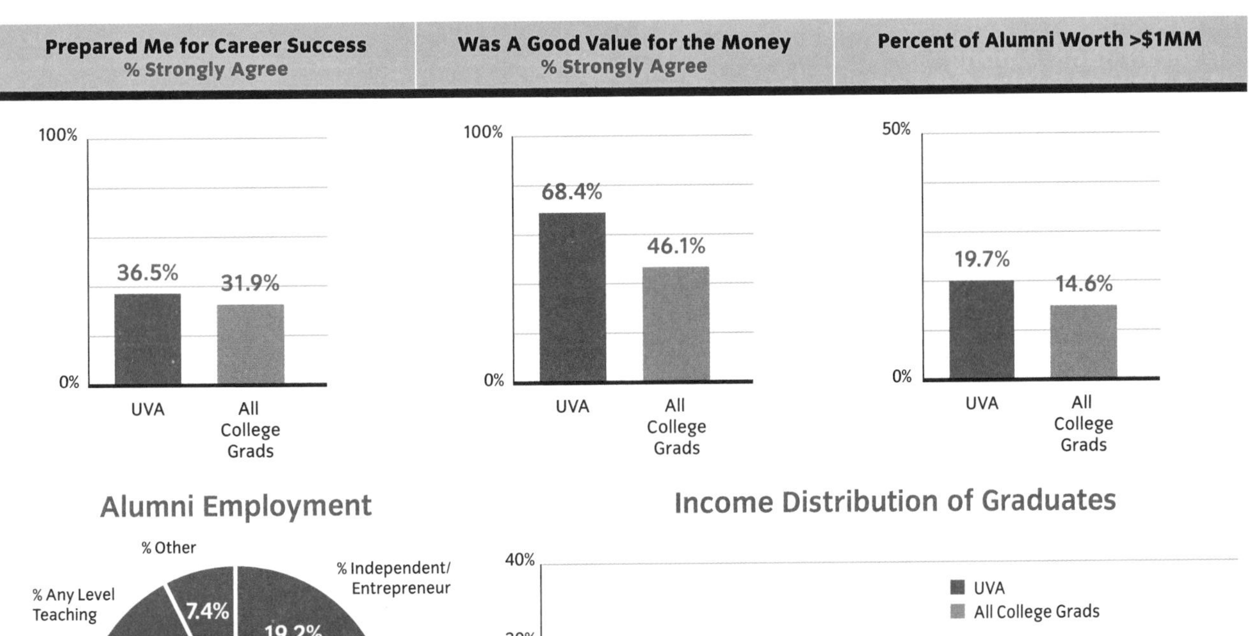

Alumni Employment

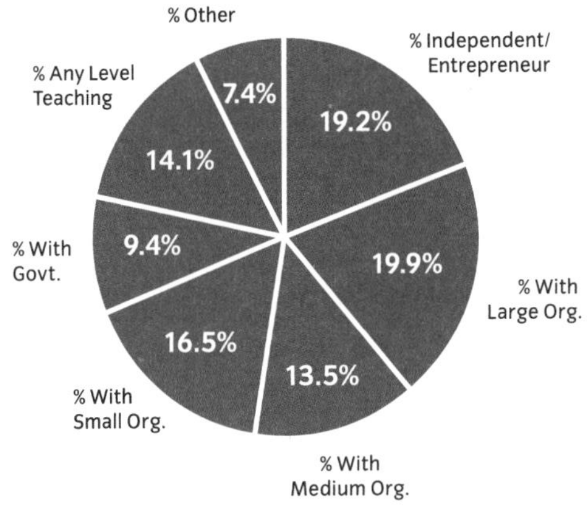

Income Distribution of Graduates

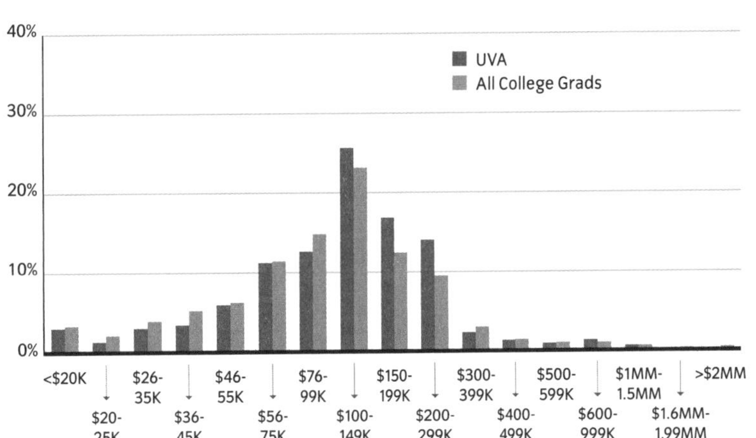

Current Selectivity & Demand Analysis for University of Virginia

Attribute	% Accepted	% Accepted Who Enroll	Freshman Retention Rate	Graduation Rate	Demand Index	Reputation Index
Score	33.0%	44.0%	96.0%	93.0%	6.87	1.33
Rank	61	26	27	16	115	45

Where are the Graduates of University of Virginia on the Political Spectrum?

Very Liberal	Liberal	Somewhat Liberal	Somewhat Conservative	Conservative	Very Conservative
		⇧			

University of Washington

Location: Seattle, WA
Campus Setting: City: Large
Total Expenses: $24,059
Estimated Average Discount: $15,320 (64%)
Estimated Net Price: $8,739

Type of Institution: National University
Number of Undergraduates: 29,307
SAT Score: Reading: 520–650, Math: 580–700
Student/Faculty Ratio: 12 to 1
Transfer Out Rate: Not Reported

Rank Among 104 National Universities	**90**
Overall Rank Among 177 *Alumni Factor* Schools	**161**

Overview

The University of Washington is the largest university in the Pacific Northwest, with more than 29,300 undergraduates. With that honor comes both the benefits and challenges of its largesse. To start with the benefits, its wide array of academic choices is staggering, and the ability to find your own unique niche, whether socially or academically, is quite high. But if you are looking for a defining undergraduate college experience that is personal and intimate, Washington may not be the best place for you. Ranked 98th in the College Experience (101st in Friendship Development) and 95th in Ultimate Outcomes, Washington does not distinguish itself when compared to the top universities, but it is hard to argue with the success of its graduates. It earns its highest rankings in the Overall Assessment (56th), its Alumni Giving rate (41st) and its graduation rate (50th) – all very impressive for a school with nearly 30,000 undergrads.

Notable Alumni

Chairman of Apple and former chairman of Genentech, Arthur Levinson; Irvine Company Chairman Donald Bren; founder of the Texas Pacific Group David Bonderman; former CEO and co-founder of MySpace, Chris DeWolfe; and saxophonist Kenny G.

The Alumni Factor Rankings Summary

Attribute	University Rank	Overall Rank
College Experience	**98**	**171**
Intellectual Development	66	137
Social Development	87	158
Spiritual Development	98	170
Friendship Development	101	173
Preparation for Career Success	89	160
Immediate Job Opportunities	84	137
Overall Assessment	**56**	**108**
Would Personally Choose Again	50	97
Would Recommend to Student	56	110
Value for the Money	55	101
Financial Success	**96**	**162**
Income per Household	93	151
% Households with Income >$150K	100	165
Household Net Worth	86	146
% Households Net Worth >$1MM	84	142
Overall Happiness	**68**	**115**
Alumni Giving	**41**	**99**
Graduation Rate	**50**	**106**
Overall Rank	**90**	**161**

Other Key Alumni Outcomes

3.7% Are college professors
7.9% Teach at any level
39.0% Have post-graduate degrees
45.6% Live in dual-income homes
90.6% Are currently employed

See pages 134–135 for detailed explanations and definitions.

Alumni Activities During College

24.6% Community Service
22.5% Intramural Sports
22.2% Internships
11.5% Media Programs
8.6% Music Programs
53.2% Part-Time Jobs

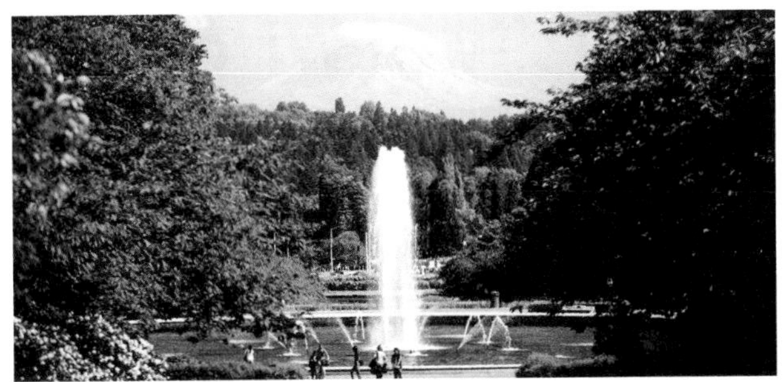

Prepared Me for Career Success % Strongly Agree	Was A Good Value for the Money % Strongly Agree	Percent of Alumni Worth >$1MM

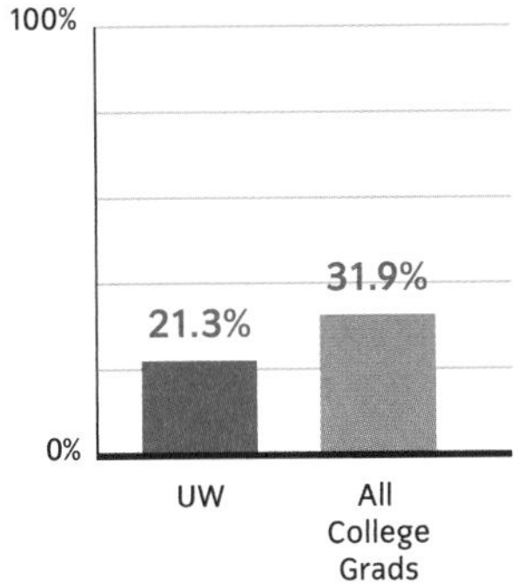

100%
0%
21.3%
31.9%
UW
All College Grads

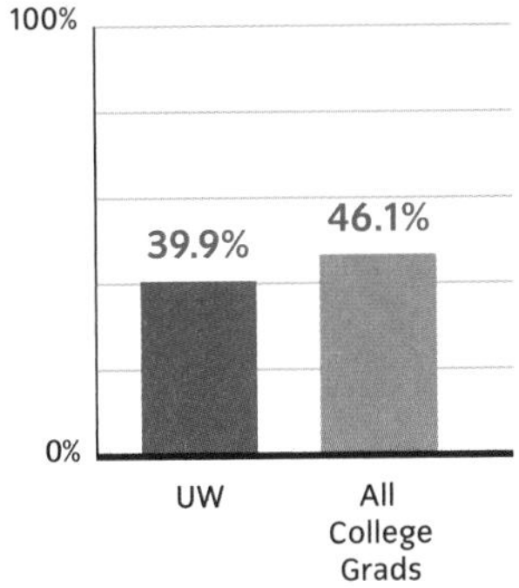

100%
0%
39.9%
46.1%
UW
All College Grads

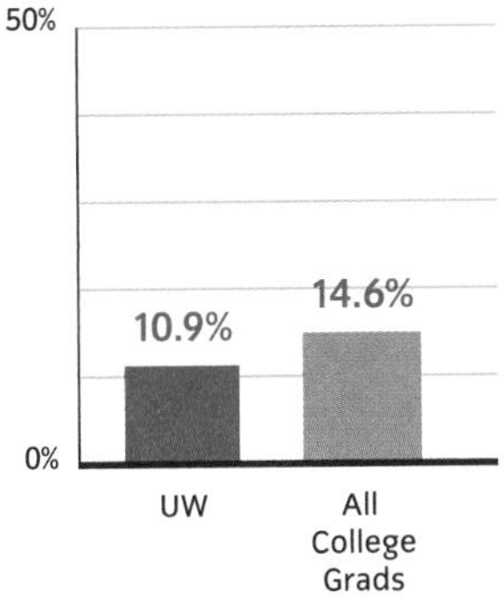

50%
0%
10.9%
14.6%
UW
All College Grads

Alumni Employment

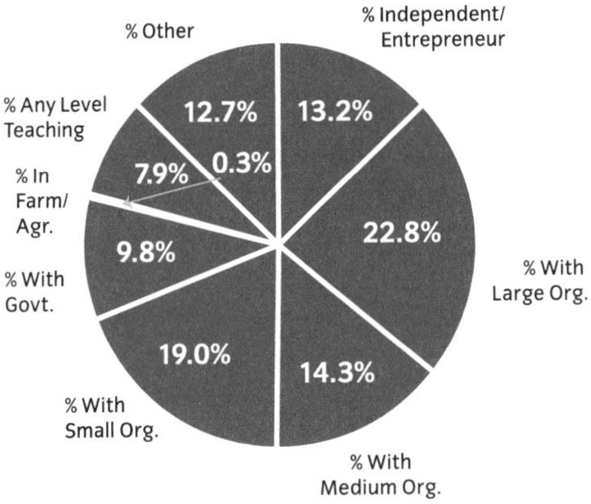

% Other
% Independent/ Entrepreneur
% Any Level Teaching
% In Farm/ Agr.
% With Govt.
% With Small Org.
% With Medium Org.
% With Large Org.
12.7%
13.2%
7.9%
0.3%
9.8%
22.8%
19.0%
14.3%

Income Distribution of Graduates

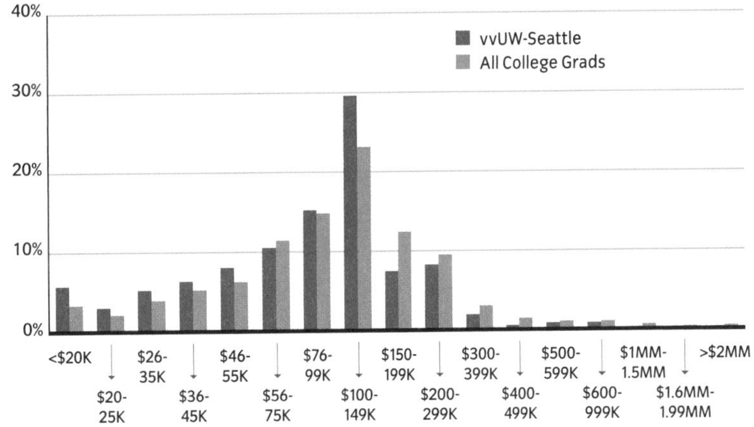

40%
30%
20%
10%
0%
vvUW-Seattle
All College Grads
<$20K
$20-25K
$26-35K
$36-45K
$46-55K
$56-75K
$76-99K
$100-149K
$150-199K
$200-299K
$300-399K
$400-499K
$500-599K
$600-999K
$1MM-1.5MM
$1.6MM-1.99MM
>$2MM

Current Selectivity & Demand Analysis for University of Washington

Attribute	% Accepted	% Accepted Who Enroll	Freshman Retention Rate	Graduation Rate	Demand Index	Reputation Index
Score	58.0%	40.0%	93.0%	80.0%	4.210	0.69
Rank	119	42	73	106	151	86

Where are the Graduates of University of Washington on the Political Spectrum?

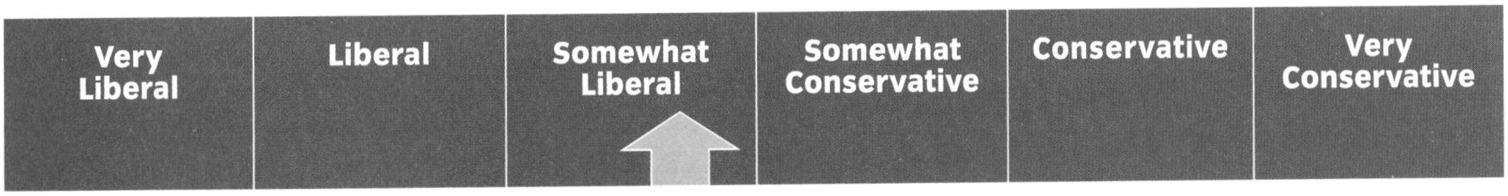

Very Liberal
Liberal
Somewhat Liberal
Somewhat Conservative
Conservative
Very Conservative

See pages 134–135 for detailed explanations and definitions.

University of Wisconsin-Madison

Location: Madison, WI
Campus Setting: City: Midsize
Total Expenses: $22,449
Estimated Average Discount: $7,509 (33%)
Estimated Net Price: $14,940

Type of Institution: National University
Number of Undergraduates: 30,170
SAT Score: Reading: 530–670, Math: 620–740
Student/Faculty Ratio: 22 to 1
Transfer Out Rate: 6%

Rank Among 104 National Universities	**23**
Overall Rank Among 177 *Alumni Factor* Schools	**46**

Overview

Wisconsin's cultural and academic epicenter, UW-Madison serves as the state's heart and soul. With its proud history of intellectual excellence, social progressivism and political activism, UW-Madison has long been at the forefront of modern thinking and action in politics, business, science and the arts. Earning *The Alumni Factor's* 2nd rank among Big Ten Conference schools (behind Michigan), Wisconsin is a very strong performer overall (ranked 23rd among national universities), with particular strength in the Overall Assessment (14th) and Financial Success (27th) of its alumni.

Impressively, Wisconsin is 1st in the Big Ten in the percent of households that are millionaires; 1st in Friendship Development; and 1st in Value for the Money. It is 2nd in the Big Ten in average Household Net Worth; 1st in Would Recommend and 1st in Social and Communication Skills Development. Indeed, with such a stellar track record, we find its 7th ranking in Alumni Giving lower than expected.

Notable Alumni

Actors Joan Cusack and Jane Kaczmarek; producers Jerry Zucker, Steve Levitan, Adam Horowitz and Tom Rosenberg; Harley Davidson founder William Harley; former president of Exxon-Mobil Lee Raymond; television journalist Jeff Greenfield; news analyst Greta Van Susteren; Major League Commissioner Bud Selig, and thousands more.

The Alumni Factor Rankings Summary

Attribute	University Rank	Overall Rank
College Experience	**28**	**82**
Intellectual Development	31	81
Social Development	19	59
Spiritual Development	38	103
Friendship Development	19	64
Preparation for Career Success	42	92
Immediate Job Opportunities	45	74
Overall Assessment	**14**	**23**
Would Personally Choose Again	30	62
Would Recommend to Student	12	18
Value for the Money	13	21
Financial Success	**27**	**48**
Income per Household	31	49
% Households with Income >$150K	39	68
Household Net Worth	24	45
% Households Net Worth >$1MM	25	48
Overall Happiness	**46**	**90**
Alumni Giving	**62**	**125**
Graduation Rate	**41**	**86**
Overall Rank	**23**	**46**

Other Key Alumni Outcomes

6.7% Are college professors
13.0% Teach at any level
53.0% Have post-graduate degrees
58.2% Live in dual-income homes
91.7% Are currently employed

See pages 134–135 for detailed explanations and definitions.

Alumni Activities During College

21.4% Community Service
24.7% Intramural Sports
21.7% Internships
14.4% Media Programs
13.4% Music Programs
59.2% Part-Time Jobs

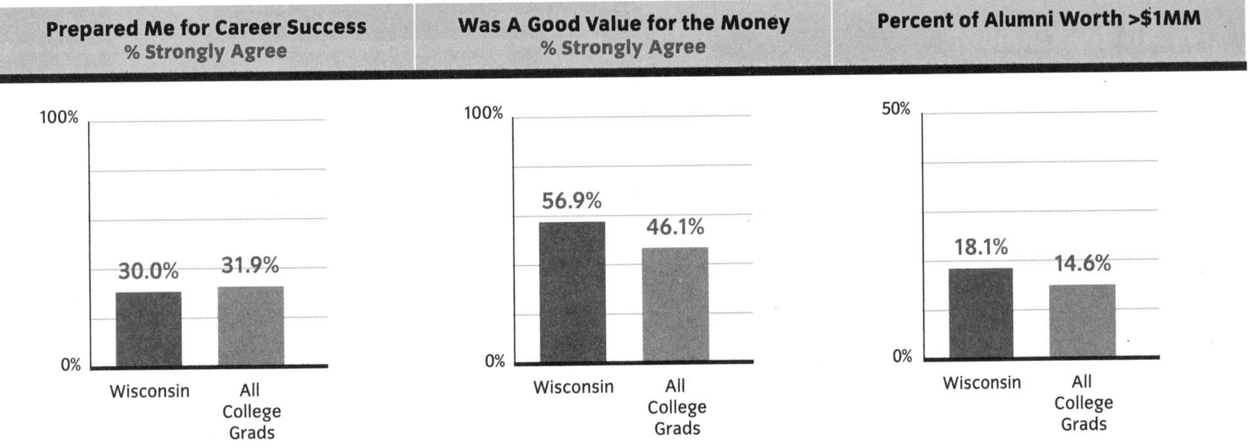

Alumni Employment

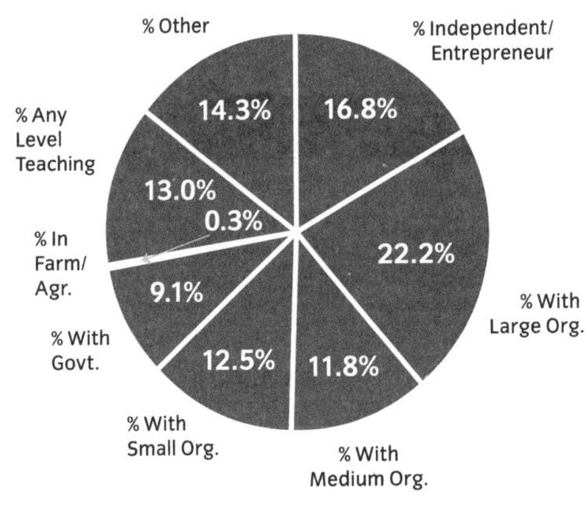

Income Distribution of Graduates

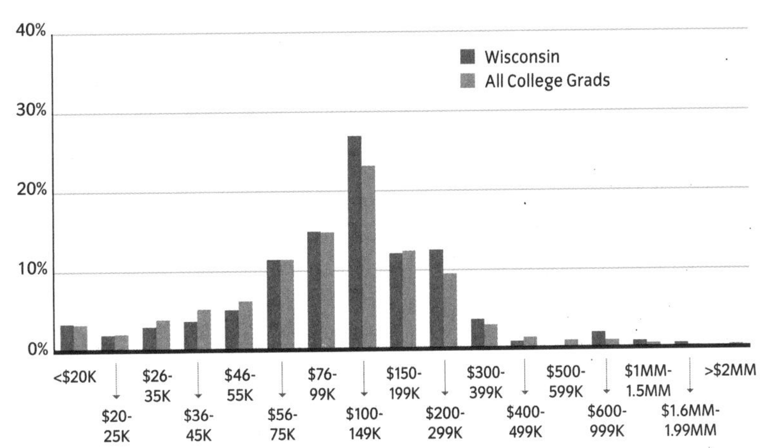

Current Selectivity & Demand Analysis for University of Wisconsin-Madison

Attribute	% Accepted	% Accepted Who Enroll	Freshman Retention Rate	Graduation Rate	Demand Index	Reputation Index
Score	66.0%	41.0%	95.0%	83.0%	3.72	0.62
Rank	142	39	47	86	158	99

Where are the Graduates of University of Wisconsin-Madison on the Political Spectrum?

Very Liberal	Liberal	Somewhat Liberal	Somewhat Conservative	Conservative	Very Conservative
		↑			

See pages 134–135 for detailed explanations and definitions.

University of Wyoming

Location: Laramie, WY
Campus Setting: Town: Remote
Total Expenses: $17,174
Estimated Average Discount: $6,398 (37%)
Estimated Net Price: $10,776

Type of Institution: National University
Number of Undergraduates: 10,079
SAT Score: Reading: 490–600, Math: 490–610
Student/Faculty Ratio: 14 to 1
Transfer Out Rate: 30%

Rank Among 104 National Universities	**48**
Overall Rank Among 177 *Alumni Factor* Schools	**106**

Overview

Not just for ranchers and wranglers, the University of Wyoming is a strong performer in producing hard-working, self-sufficient grads who are happy, successful and well prepared for their careers. Hewn from the raw prairie that was Laramie, the UW campus is uniquely beautiful, perched on a high plain between two mountain ranges. The college town of Laramie is about as progressive as it gets in the state of Wyoming, which is famously conservative and independent. While Laramie might be considered the "liberal" enclave of the state, the grads are very conservative relative to their peers across the country.

They are also well prepared for their careers (ranked 19th in Preparation for Career Success) and are well-developed intellectually (51st). At under $12,000, UW is one of the best values in the country (10th), contributing to a very strong Overall Assessment by its graduates (26th). What will surprise many (only because UW does not have a national reputation) is the strong Financial Success (ranked 59th) of its graduates. In fact, UW is ranked 32nd in average Household Net Worth, just behind Michigan, UNC-Chapel Hill and William & Mary.

Notable Alumni

LA Laker owner Jerry Buss; former US vice president Dick Cheney; quality guru Edward Deming; legendary sportscaster Curt Gowdy; Miami Dolphin great Jim Kiick; Wyoming Governor Matt Mead; NFL Pro-Bowler Jay Novacek; and former senator Alan Simpson.

The Alumni Factor Rankings Summary

Attribute	University Rank	Overall Rank
College Experience	**42**	**103**
Intellectual Development	51	117
Social Development	44	101
Spiritual Development	68	140
Friendship Development	80	150
Preparation for Career Success	19	45
Immediate Job Opportunities	20	28
Overall Assessment	**26**	**55**
Would Personally Choose Again	25	54
Would Recommend to Student	51	101
Value for the Money	10	17
Financial Success	**59**	**99**
Income per Household	61	96
% Households with Income >$150K	89	145
Household Net Worth	32	57
% Households Net Worth >$1MM	57	98
Overall Happiness	**51**	**97**
Alumni Giving	**78**	**145**
Graduation Rate	**104**	**177**
Overall Rank	**48**	**106**

Other Key Alumni Outcomes

3.8% Are college professors
14.3% Teach at any level
36.5% Have post-graduate degrees
58.7% Live in dual-income homes
94.3% Are currently employed

See pages 134–135 for detailed explanations and definitions.

Alumni Activities During College

29.8% Community Service
32.7% Intramural Sports
19.2% Internships
21.2% Media Programs
21.1% Music Programs
48.1% Part-Time Jobs

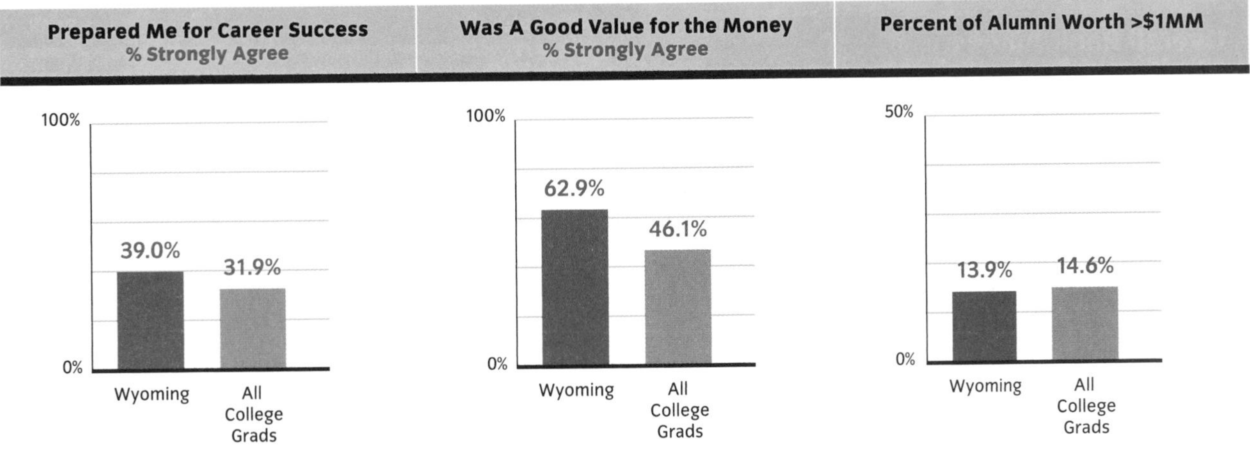

Alumni Employment

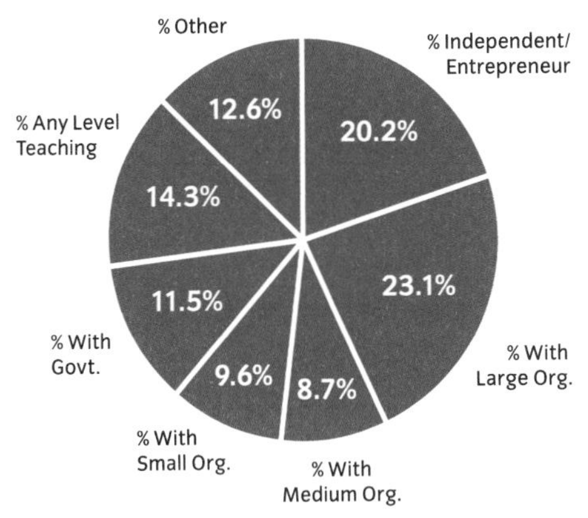

Income Distribution of Graduates

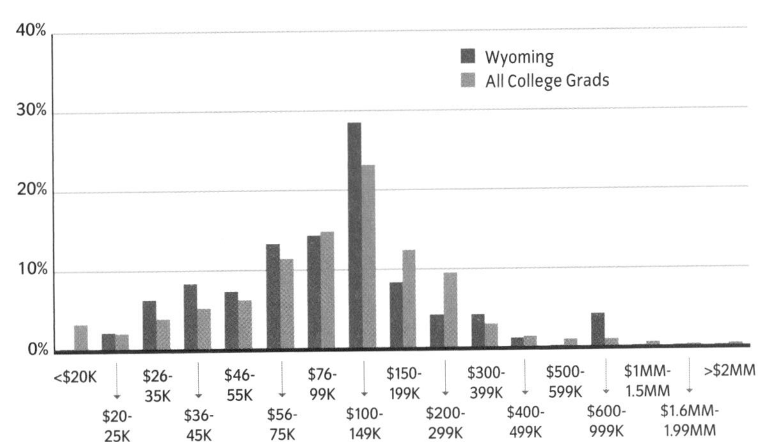

Current Selectivity & Demand Analysis for University of Wyoming

Attribute	% Accepted	% Accepted Who Enroll	Freshman Retention Rate	Graduation Rate	Demand Index	Reputation Index
Score	95.0%	42.0%	74.0%	53.0%	2.41	0.44
Rank	176	33	177	177	175	138

Where are the Graduates of University of Wyoming on the Political Spectrum?

Very Liberal	Liberal	Somewhat Liberal	Somewhat Conservative	Conservative	Very Conservative
					↑

See pages 134–135 for detailed explanations and definitions.

Valparaiso University

Location: Valparaiso, IN
Campus Setting: Suburb: Large
Total Expenses: $42,636
Estimated Average Discount: $21,407 (50%)
Estimated Net Price: $21,229

Type of Institution: Regional University
Number of Undergraduates: 2,872
SAT Score: Reading: 49 610, Math: 490–610
Student/Faculty Ratio: 13 to 1
Transfer Out Rate: Not Reported

Rank Among 20 Regional Universities	**14**
Overall Rank Among 177 *Alumni Factor* Schools	**121**

Overview

Valparaiso sits on the flat expanse of northern Indiana, about 15 miles south of Lake Michigan and less than 60 miles from Chicago. Firmly established in the Lutheran heritage, Valpo instills faith (ranked 14th in Spiritual Development) and friendship (52nd in Friendship Development) in its graduates – these are its two strongest attributes.

As the country's largest independent Lutheran university, Valpo takes seriously its mission of educational excellence "grounded in the Lutheran tradition of scholarship, freedom and faith." It excels at integrating scholarship with professional preparation, and produces large numbers of nurses, teachers and engineers. The overall College Experience is highly rated by graduates (62nd among all colleges and universities) and grads are quite happy in life (81st). Valpo's strongest Ultimate Outcome is Happiness & Friendships (63rd) and 82 percent of grads either *Strongly Agree* or *Agree* they would recommend Valpo to a prospective student today.

Notable Alumni

Former congressman Thurman Crook; former chairman and CEO of Caterpillar Donald Fites; and Chairman and founder of the Thatcher Technology Group, Jay Christopher.

The Alumni Factor Rankings Summary

Attribute	Overall Rank
College Experience	**62**
Intellectual Development	67
Social Development	76
Spiritual Development	14
Friendship Development	51
Preparation for Career Success	97
Immediate Job Opportunities	104
Overall Assessment	**94**
Would Personally Choose Again	47
Would Recommend to Student	105
Value for the Money	120
Financial Success	**158**
Income per Household	143
% Households with Income >$150K	174
Household Net Worth	129
% Households Net Worth >$1MM	144
Overall Happiness	**82**
Alumni Giving	**81**
Graduation Rate	**143**
Overall Rank	**121**

Other Key Alumni Outcomes

6.9% Are college professors
13.8% Teach at any level
46.9% Have post-graduate degrees
54.9% Live in dual-income homes
94.3% Are currently employed

See pages 134–135 for detailed explanations and definitions.

Alumni Activities During College

32.6% Community Service
37.7% Intramural Sports
29.7% Internships
29.1% Media Programs
40.6% Music Programs
34.3% Part-Time Jobs

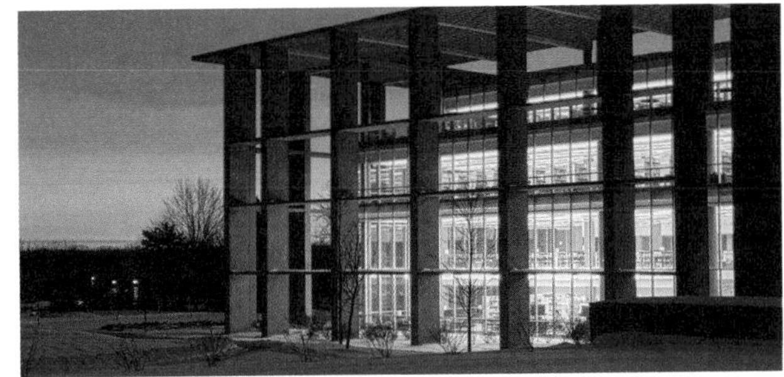

Photo courtesy of Valparaiso University

Prepared Me for Career Success
% Strongly Agree

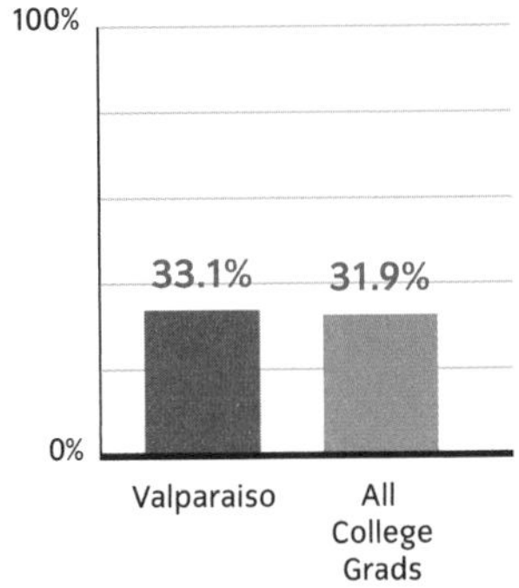
100%
0%
33.1%
31.9%
Valparaiso
All College Grads

Was A Good Value for the Money
% Strongly Agree

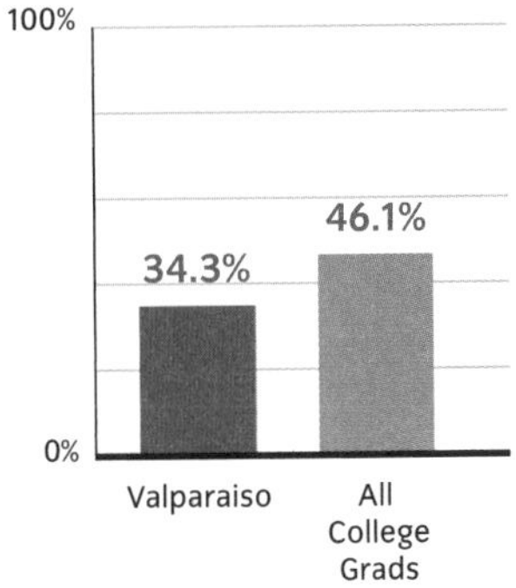
100%
0%
34.3%
46.1%
Valparaiso
All College Grads

Percent of Alumni Worth >$1MM

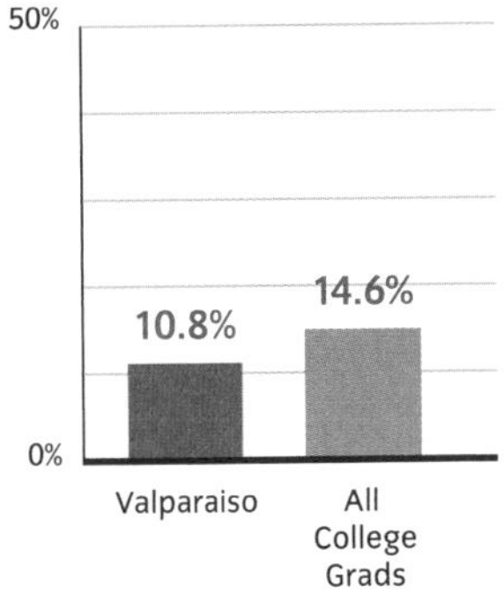
50%
0%
10.8%
14.6%
Valparaiso
All College Grads

Alumni Employment

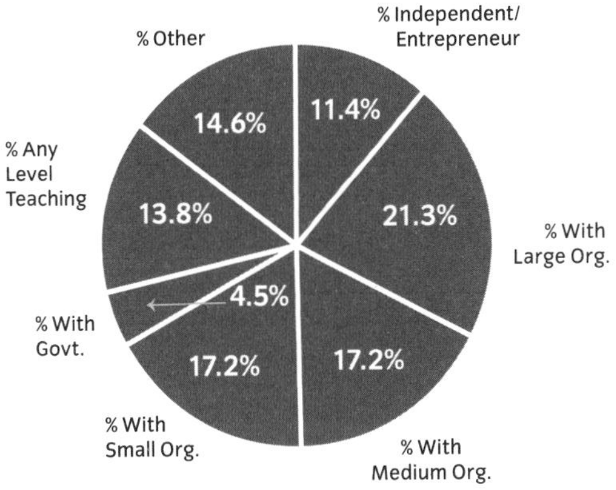
% Other
% Independent/ Entrepreneur
14.6%
11.4%
% Any Level Teaching
13.8%
21.3%
% With Large Org.
4.5%
% With Govt.
17.2%
17.2%
% With Small Org.
% With Medium Org.

Income Distribution of Graduates

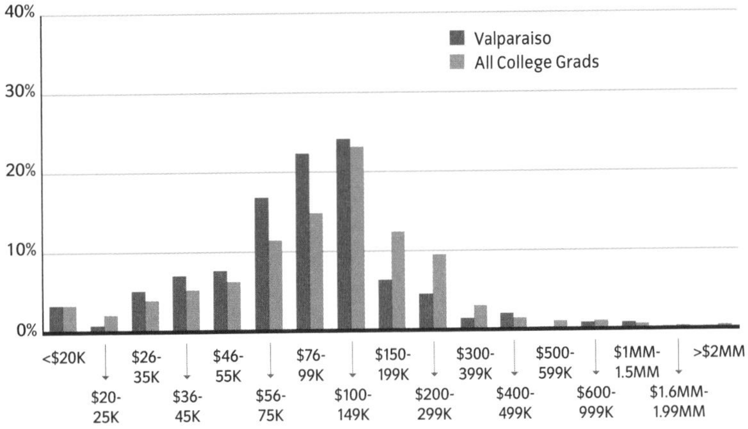
40%
30%
20%
10%
0%
Valparaiso
All College Grads
<$20K
$20-25K
$26-35K
$36-45K
$46-55K
$56-75K
$76-99K
$100-149K
$150-199K
$200-299K
$300-399K
$400-499K
$500-599K
$600-999K
$1MM-1.5MM
$1.6MM-1.99MM
>$2MM

Current Selectivity & Demand Analysis for Valparaiso University

Attribute	% Accepted	% Accepted Who Enroll	Freshman Retention Rate	Graduation Rate	Demand Index	Reputation Index
Score	74.0%	17.0%	82.0%	70.0%	7.76	0.23
Rank	158	170	167	143	102	173

Where are the Graduates of Valparaiso University on the Political Spectrum?

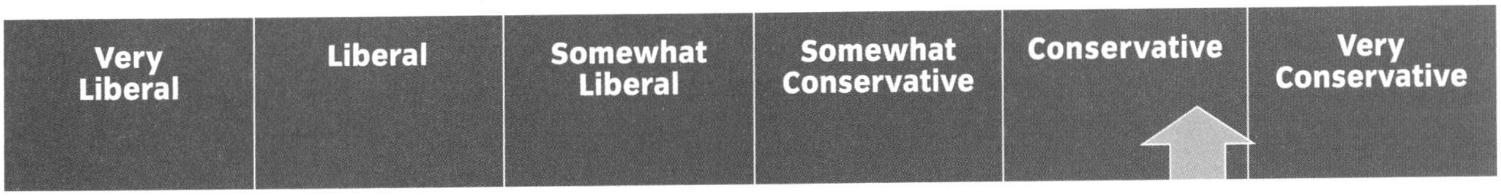
Very Liberal
Liberal
Somewhat Liberal
Somewhat Conservative
Conservative
Very Conservative

See pages 134–135 for detailed explanations and definitions.

Vanderbilt University

Location: Nashville, TN
Campus Setting: City: Large
Total Expenses: $58,554
Estimated Average Discount: $39,561 (68%)
Estimated Net Price: $18,993

Type of Institution: National University
Number of Undergraduates: 6,879
SAT Score: Reading: 680–770, Math: 700–780
Student/Faculty Ratio: 8 to 1
Transfer Out Rate: Not Reported

Rank Among 104 National Universities	**19**
Overall Rank Among 177 *Alumni Factor* Schools	**38**

Overview

Founded in 1873 with an initial endowment from Cornelius Vanderbilt, Vanderbilt University has become one of the finest universities in the country and among the best in the world. It is ranked 19th among national universities based on consistently strong performance by alumni across every attribute we measure. Vanderbilt ranks 1st overall among its Southeastern Conference competitors and ranks in the Top 20 in every Ultimate Outcome – one of only nine national universities with such breadth of excellence. While Vandy is highly ranked across each element of the College Experience (21st), it is particularly strong in Friendship Development (17th) and in Intellectual Development (21st). Graduates are very happy (33rd) and loyal (25th in Alumni Giving), but it is in Financial Success (15th) that Vandy grads truly excel.

Vandy ranks 8th among national universities (15th among all schools) in its percent of millionaire households (23 percent of alums are millionaires), 10th in average household net worth and 13th in high income households. This astonishing success is particularly impressive, given the geographic location of many grads (not necessarily in typically high income areas).

Notable Alumni

Writers James Dickey, Tom Schulman and Robert Penn Warren; founders of consulting groups Bain, Bill Bain and Boston Consulting Group, Bruce Henderson; and former chairman and CEO of Time, Inc., Ann Moore.

The Alumni Factor Rankings Summary

Attribute	University Rank	Overall Rank
College Experience	**21**	**67**
Intellectual Development	21	67
Social Development	27	69
Spiritual Development	40	105
Friendship Development	17	60
Preparation for Career Success	24	61
Immediate Job Opportunities	31	47
Overall Assessment	**58**	**111**
Would Personally Choose Again	42	78
Would Recommend to Student	53	107
Value for the Money	74	136
Financial Success	**15**	**26**
Income per Household	33	52
% Households with Income >$150K	13	24
Household Net Worth	10	22
% Households Net Worth >$1MM	8	15
Overall Happiness	**33**	**66**
Alumni Giving	**25**	**75**
Graduation Rate	**19**	**32**
Overall Rank	**19**	**38**

Other Key Alumni Outcomes

5.7% Are college professors
8.4% Teach at any level
55.0% Have post-graduate degrees
49.1% Live in dual-income homes
93.3% Are currently employed

See pages 134–135 for detailed explanations and definitions.

Alumni Activities During College

39.9% Community Service
32.1% Intramural Sports
26.5% Internships
21.7% Media Programs
26.5% Music Programs
30.2% Part-Time Jobs

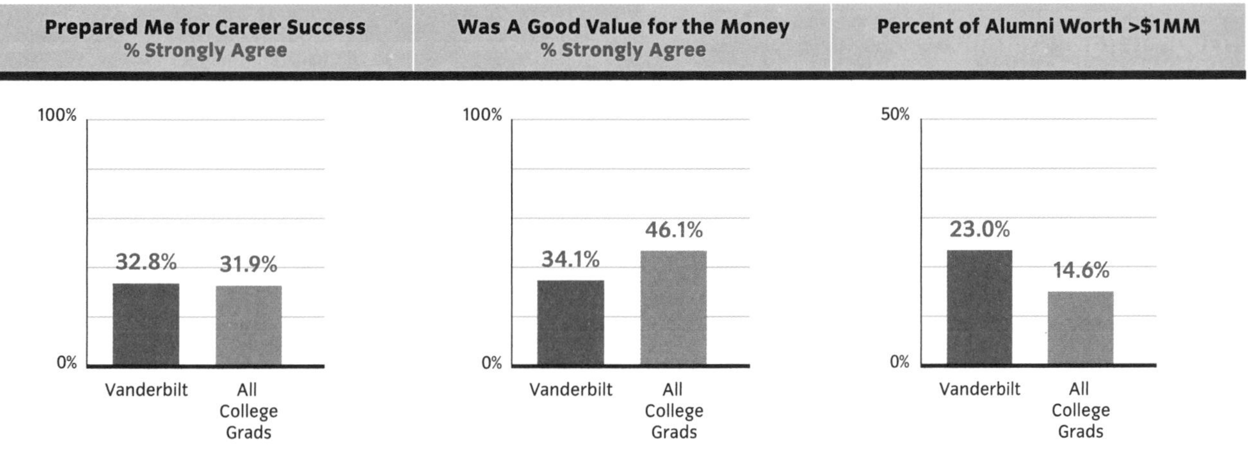

Alumni Employment

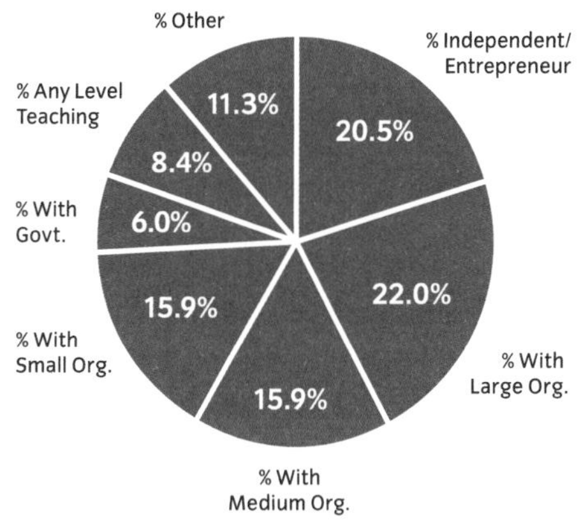

Income Distribution of Graduates

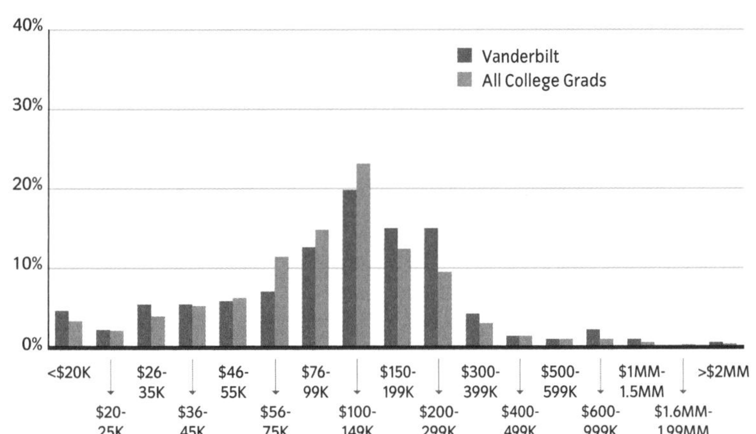

Current Selectivity & Demand Analysis for Vanderbilt University

Attribute	% Accepted	% Accepted Who Enroll	Freshman Retention Rate	Graduation Rate	Demand Index	Reputation Index
Score	16.0%	39.0%	97.0%	91.0%	15.51	2.44
Rank	18	46	13	32	17	23

Where are the Graduates of Vanderbilt University on the Political Spectrum?

Very Liberal	Liberal	Somewhat Liberal	Somewhat Conservative	Conservative	Very Conservative
				↑	

See pages 134–135 for detailed explanations and definitions.

Vassar College

Location: Poughkeepsie, NY
Campus Setting: Suburb: Large
Total Expenses: $57,385
Estimated Average Discount: $38,947 (68%)
Estimated Net Price: $18,438

Rank Among 53 Liberal Arts Colleges	**29**
Overall Rank Among 177 *Alumni Factor* Schools	**58**

Overview

Gracefully situated on one thousand of the Hudson Valley's most beautifully landscaped acres, Vassar is truly an intellectual, cultural and architectural jewel of the US collegiate system. Historically viewed as a college for the social and intellectual elite (originally Yale's sibling as one of the Seven Sister schools), Vassar today is a bold leader in fully developing distinctive individuals through a "well-proportioned and liberal education."

Resolutely committed to the liberal arts, Vassar creates an intense intellectual atmosphere (ranked 16th in Intellectual Development) that develops deep friendships (33rd) amidst individually tailored learning. Vassar ranks 21st in its alumni Willingness to Recommend the School to a Prospective Student and 5th in Graduation Rate. Vassar's strongest Ultimate Outcomes are Happiness & Intellectual Capability (11th) and Friendships & Intellectual Capability (17th).

Many Vassar grads pursue post-graduate degrees (28th), and nearly 18% of graduates teach at some level (35th among all colleges and universities).

Notable Alumni

Poet Edna St. Vincent Millay; founder of Oxygen Media Geraldine Laybourne; president of MSNBC Phil Griffin; founder of Flickr Caterina Fake; Academy Award winner Meryl Streep; *Friends* star Lisa Kudrow; George W. Bush speechwriter Marc Thiessen; and Cooper Union President Jamshed Bharucha.

Type of Institution: Liberal Arts College
Number of Undergraduates: 2,446
SAT Score: Reading: 670–740, Math: 650–730
Student/Faculty Ratio: 8 to 1
Transfer Out Rate: Not Reported

The Alumni Factor Rankings Summary

Attribute	Liberal Arts Rank	Overall Rank
College Experience	**29**	**53**
Intellectual Development	16	18
Social Development	30	49
Spiritual Development	30	56
Friendship Development	33	51
Preparation for Career Success	35	83
Immediate Job Opportunities	27	119
Overall Assessment	**33**	**83**
Would Personally Choose Again	35	93
Would Recommend to Student	21	55
Value for the Money	36	98
Financial Success	**30**	**90**
Income per Household	28	103
% Households with Income >$150K	30	90
Household Net Worth	36	109
% Households Net Worth >$1MM	31	78
Overall Happiness	**33**	**94**
Alumni Giving	**44**	**55**
Graduation Rate	**5**	**16**
Overall Rank	**29**	**58**

Other Key Alumni Outcomes

7.0% Are college professors
17.5% Teach at any level
69.4% Have post-graduate degrees
52.8% Live in dual-income homes
91.5% Are currently employed

See pages 134–135 for detailed explanations and definitions.

Alumni Activities During College

31.9% Community Service
21.7% Intramural Sports
26.4% Internships
22.5% Media Programs
23.0% Music Programs
21.3% Part-Time Jobs

Alumni Employment

Income Distribution of Graduates

Current Selectivity & Demand Analysis for Vassar College

Attribute	% Accepted	% Accepted Who Enroll	Freshman Retention Rate	Graduation Rate	Demand Index	Reputation Index
Score	23.0%	37.0%	96.0%	93.0%	11.92	1.61
Rank	34	60	27	16	45	33

Where are the Graduates of Vassar College on the Political Spectrum?

Very Liberal	Liberal	Somewhat Liberal	Somewhat Conservative	Conservative	Very Conservative
↑					

See pages 134–135 for detailed explanations and definitions.

Villanova University

Location: Villanova, PA
Campus Setting: Suburb: Large
Total Expenses: $54,520
Estimated Average Discount: $25,685 (47%)
Estimated Net Price: $28,835

Type of Institution: Regional University
Number of Undergraduates: 7,116
SAT Score: Reading: 590–680, Math: 620–710
Student/Faculty Ratio: 11 to 1
Transfer Out Rate: Not Reported

Rank Among 20 Regional Universities	**3**
Overall Rank Among 177 *Alumni Factor* Schools	**49**

Overview

As Pennsylvania's oldest and most prominent Catholic University, Villanova's motto, "Veritas, Unitas, Caritas" (Truth, Unity, Charity), stands as a distinctive mission among colleges and universities today. Unabashedly conservative and Catholic in its views and its culture, Villanova strives to create an environment where students "learn to think critically, act compassionately, and succeed while serving others." And succeed they do.

Villanova ranks an amazing 11th among all colleges and universities in Financial Success and 37th in Overall Happiness. This makes it the 5th ranked overall school in the Ultimate Outcome of Financial Success & Happiness. Driving its Financial Success ranking is Villanova's stunning 2nd ranking among all colleges and universities in the average Household Net Worth of graduates. It also ranks a strong 25th in the Ultimate Outcome of Financial Success & Friendships. With all that said, it is somewhat surprising that its Alumni Giving percentage is not higher than its 81st ranking.

Notable Alumni

Stanford University President John Hennessy; music legend Jim Croce; Golden Globe winner Maria Bello; Manhattan Transfer founder Tim Hauser; former vice chairman and CFO of J&J Robert Darretta; Chairman & CEO of Sunoco John Drosdick; founder of TD Waterhouse Lawrence Waterhouse; former Chase Manhattan CEO Thomas Labrecque; retired four-star general George Crist; Howie Long; and former US congressmen James Quigley and Stanley Prokop.

The Alumni Factor Rankings Summary

Attribute	Overall Rank
College Experience	**78**
Intellectual Development	106
Social Development	84
Spiritual Development	17
Friendship Development	114
Preparation for Career Success	97
Immediate Job Opportunities	38
Overall Assessment	**120**
Would Personally Choose Again	152
Would Recommend to Student	101
Value for the Money	94
Financial Success	**11**
Income per Household	18
% Households with Income >$150K	9
Household Net Worth	2
% Households Net Worth >$1MM	27
Overall Happiness	**39**
Alumni Giving	**81**
Graduation Rate	**39**
Overall Rank	**49**

Other Key Alumni Outcomes

5.7% Are college professors
17.0% Teach at any level
47.1% Have post-graduate degrees
48.1% Live in dual-income homes
93.2% Are currently employed

See pages 134–135 for detailed explanations and definitions.

Alumni Activities During College

35.6% Community Service
30.8% Intramural Sports
13.5% Internships
13.4% Media Programs
12.5% Music Programs
46.2% Part-Time Jobs

Current Selectivity & Demand Analysis for Villanova University

Attribute	% Accepted	% Accepted Who Enroll	Freshman Retention Rate	Graduation Rate	Demand Index	Reputation Index
Score	44.0%	24.0%	95.0%	90.0%	9.36	0.55
Rank	89	138	47	39	77	112

Where are the Graduates of Villanova University on the Political Spectrum?

Very Liberal	Liberal	Somewhat Liberal	Somewhat Conservative	Conservative	Very Conservative
					⇧

See pages 134–135 for detailed explanations and definitions.

Virginia Polytechnic Institute and State University

Location: Blacksburg, VA
Campus Setting: City: Small
Total Expenses: $23,869
Estimated Average Discount: $6,238 (26%)
Estimated Net Price: $17,631

Type of Institution: National University
Number of Undergraduates: 23,690
SAT Score: Reading: 540–640, Math: 570–670
Student/Faculty Ratio: 17 to 1
Transfer Out Rate: Not Reported

Rank Among 104 National Universities	**8**
Overall Rank Among 177 *Alumni Factor* Schools	**24**

Overview

It is very difficult to find a group of alumni more enthusiastic about their alma mater than those from Virginia Tech, and for good reason. Ranked 4th in the Overall Assessment by alumni and 1st in Would Personally Choose Again, Virginia Tech is perhaps the most underrated school in the country – where graduate outcomes, real-life performance and alumni assessments far exceed the school's perceived "reputation."

Make no mistake, if you are looking for Financial Success & Happiness, this is one of the Top 10 universities in the country where you can find it. Ranked 17th in the College Experience and 4th in the Overall Assessment, alumni are effusive about this world-class technical gem in Blacksburg. The hands-on learning from VT gets applied brilliantly by its grads, and it generates a Financial Success ranking of 18th among national universities. Impressively, VT ranks 9th in average Household Net Worth and ranks 15th in the important Ultimate Outcome of Financial Success & Friendships.

Notable Alumni

Nielsen CEO Dave Calhoun; 7 Medal of Honor recipients; Craigslist CEO Jim Buckmaster; former Georgia-Pacific CEO Robert Pamplin; former Exxon CEO Cifton Garvin; retired chairman & CEO of Raytheon, Thomas Phillips; former Iowa governor Chet Culver; *Today* co-host Hoda Kotb; Virginia Congressman Rob Wittman; Victoria's Secret Direct CEO Bridget Ryan-Berman; and many more.

The Alumni Factor Rankings Summary

Attribute	University Rank	Overall Rank
College Experience	**17**	**56**
Intellectual Development	39	97
Social Development	15	49
Spiritual Development	42	107
Friendship Development	25	81
Preparation for Career Success	11	29
Immediate Job Opportunities	9	13
Overall Assessment	**4**	**6**
Would Personally Choose Again	1	4
Would Recommend to Student	4	6
Value for the Money	15	27
Financial Success	**18**	**33**
Income per Household	12	22
% Households with Income >$150K	27	49
Household Net Worth	9	21
% Households Net Worth >$1MM	34	62
Overall Happiness	**16**	**37**
Alumni Giving	**59**	**122**
Graduation Rate	**50**	**106**
Overall Rank	**8**	**24**

Other Key Alumni Outcomes

5.5% Are college professors
14.5% Teach at any level
52.2% Have post-graduate degrees
59.9% Live in dual-income homes
93.4% Are currently employed

See pages 134–135 for detailed explanations and definitions.

Alumni Activities During College

26.5% Community Service
39.6% Intramural Sports
22.3% Internships
9.1% Media Programs
15.9% Music Programs
36.0% Part-Time Jobs

Prepared Me for Career Success % Strongly Agree	Was A Good Value for the Money % Strongly Agree	Percent of Alumni Worth >$1MM
Virginia Tech: 37.1% All College Grads: 31.9%	Virginia Tech: 54.9% All College Grads: 46.1%	Virginia Tech: 16.9% All College Grads: 14.6%

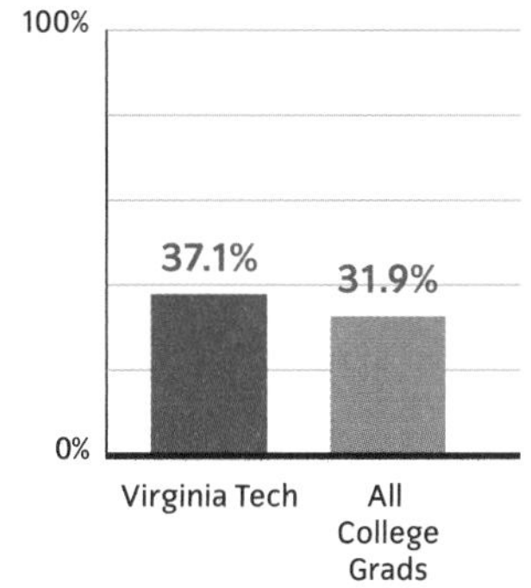

Alumni Employment

Category	%
% Other	11.0%
% Independent/Entrepreneur	12.1%
% With Large Org.	23.2%
% With Medium Org.	15.2%
% With Small Org.	14.9%
% With Govt.	9.1%
% Any Level Teaching	14.5%

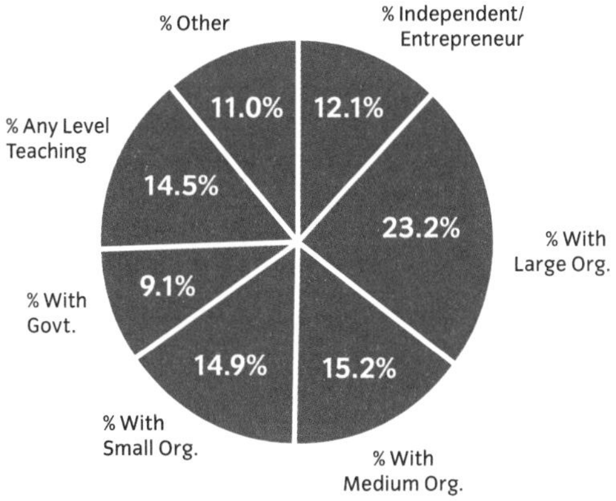

Income Distribution of Graduates

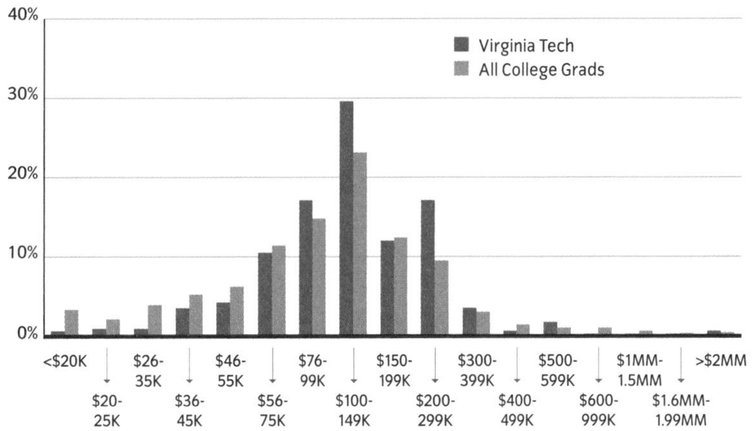

Virginia Tech / All College Grads

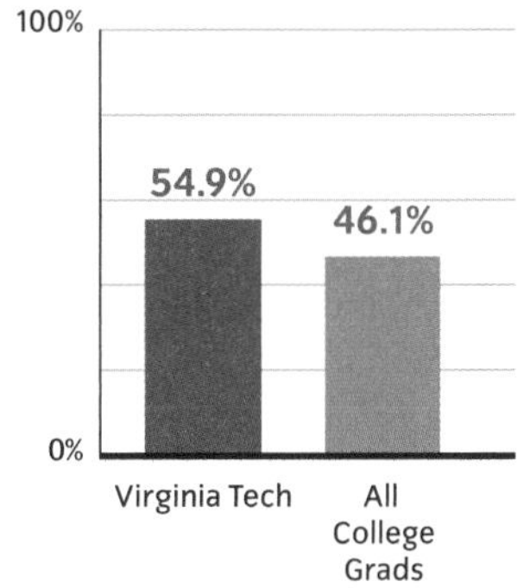

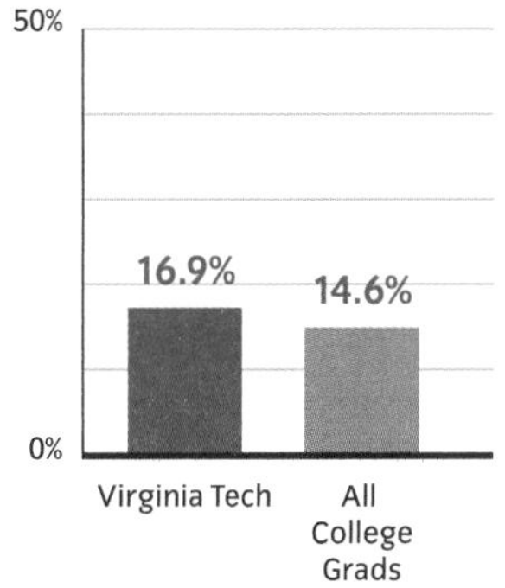

0% 10% 20% 30% 40%

<$20K, $20-25K, $26-35K, $36-45K, $46-55K, $56-75K, $76-99K, $100-149K, $150-199K, $200-299K, $300-399K, $400-499K, $500-599K, $600-999K, $1MM-1.5MM, $1.6MM-1.99MM, >$2MM

Current Selectivity & Demand Analysis for School Name

Attribute	% Accepted	% Accepted Who Enroll	Freshman Retention Rate	Graduation Rate	Demand Index	Reputation Index
Score	67.0%	38.0%	92.0%	80.0%	3.99	0.57
Rank	144	55	86	106	154	109

Where are the Graduates of Virginia Polytechnic Institute and State University on the Political Spectrum?

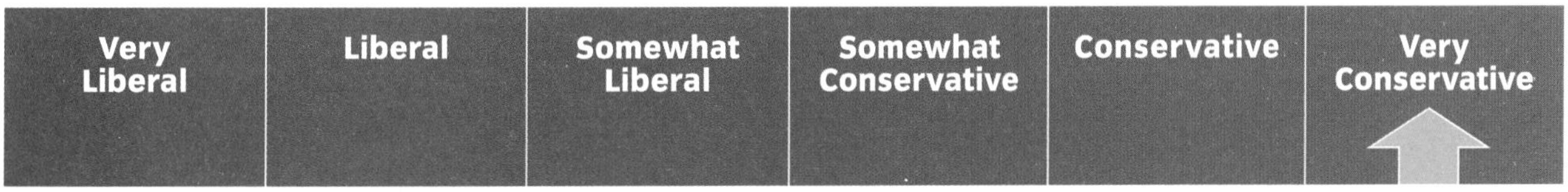

Very Liberal	Liberal	Somewhat Liberal	Somewhat Conservative	Conservative	Very Conservative
					↑

See pages 134–135 for detailed explanations and definitions.

Wake Forest University

Location: Winston Salem, NC
Campus Setting: Citiy: Midsize
Total Expenses: $56,236
Estimated Average Discount: $25,051 (45%)
Estimated Net Price: $31,185

Type of Institution: National University
Number of Undergraduates: 4,657
SAT Score: Not Reported
Student/Faculty Ratio: 11 to 1
Transfer Out Rate: Not Reported

Rank Among 104 National Universities	**21**
Overall Rank Among 177 *Alumni Factor* Schools	**42**

Overview

Wake Forest University, with its expansive lawns, exceptionally bright students, quintessentially collegiate architecture and friendly campus community is, quite simply, among the finest places to spend one's undergraduate years. With its 6th ranking in the College Experience (1st in Social Development) and its 5th ranking in Overall Happiness, it is no wonder that Wake's acceptance letter is quickly becoming one of the nation's most desired.

It has earned its stellar reputation through results. Wake graduates succeed in a wide range of endeavors because they are thoroughly developed intellectually (10th), prepared for their career success (15th) and experience the power of lasting friendships (8th). Wake graduates enjoy strong Financial Success (45th) and are extremely loyal to the school (12th in Alumni Giving). It is 3rd among all national universities in the Ultimate Outcome of Happiness & Friendships. Most impressively, it is ranked in the Top 35 in every Ultimate Outcome – with four of the six pairs in the Top 20.

Notable Alumni

Former congressman David Funderburk; former ambassador James Cain; Smithfield Foods CEO Joseph Luter III; actors Marc Blucas and Lee Norris; NBA superstar Tim Duncan; Brian Piccolo; and perhaps the finest group of golfers ever produced by one school: Arnold Palmer, Curtis Strange, Lanny Wadkins, Jay and Bill Haas, Billy Andrade, Gary Hallberg, Scott Hoch, Len Mattiace, Leonard Thompson, and Robert Wrenn.

The Alumni Factor Rankings Summary

Attribute	University Rank	Overall Rank
College Experience	**6**	**20**
Intellectual Development	10	42
Social Development	1	7
Spiritual Development	11	50
Friendship Development	8	43
Preparation for Career Success	15	36
Immediate Job Opportunities	39	63
Overall Assessment	**54**	**104**
Would Personally Choose Again	71	126
Would Recommend to Student	36	72
Value for the Money	56	104
Financial Success	**45**	**78**
Income per Household	49	79
% Households with Income >$150K	26	47
Household Net Worth	52	91
% Households Net Worth >$1MM	67	113
Overall Happiness	**5**	**17**
Alumni Giving	**12**	**57**
Graduation Rate	**29**	**47**
Overall Rank	**21**	**42**

Other Key Alumni Outcomes

7.9% Are college professors
12.4% Teach at any level
57.5% Have post-graduate degrees
49.3% Live in dual-income homes
92.8% Are currently employed

See pages 134–135 for detailed explanations and definitions.

Alumni Activities During College

39.1% Community Service
48.8% Intramural Sports
24.6% Internships
17.4% Media Programs
31.4% Music Programs
29.5% Part-Time Jobs

Prepared Me for Career Success % Strongly Agree	Was A Good Value for the Money % Strongly Agree	Percent of Alumni Worth >$1MM
Wake Forest: 38.0%	Wake Forest: 41.8%	Wake Forest: 13.2 %
All College Grads: 31.9%	All College Grads: 46.1%	All College Grads: 14.6%

Alumni Employment

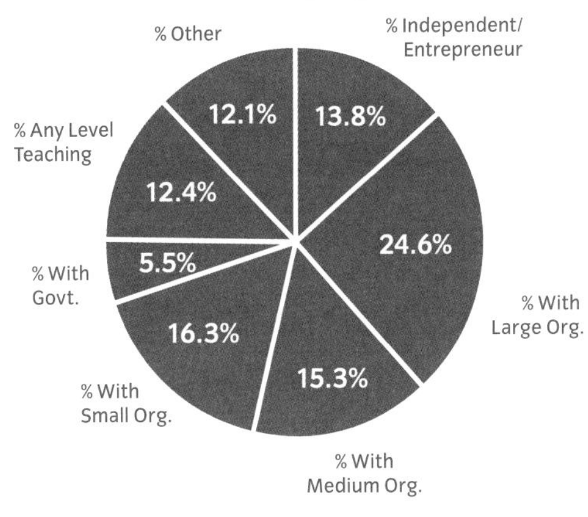

Income Distribution of Graduates

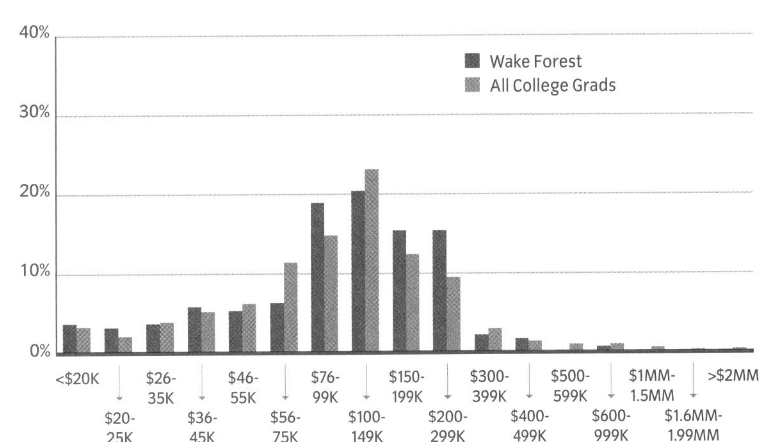

Current Selectivity & Demand Analysis for Wake Forest University

Attribute	% Accepted	% Accepted Who Enroll	Freshman Retention Rate	Graduation Rate	Demand Index	Reputation Index
Score	40.0%	32.0%	94.0%	89.0%	7.98	0.80
Rank	77	92	58	47	99	74

Where are the Graduates of Wake Forest University on the Political Spectrum?

Very Liberal	Liberal	Somewhat Liberal	Somewhat Conservative	Conservative	Very Conservative
				↑	

See pages 134–135 for detailed explanations and definitions.

Washington and Lee University

Location: Lexington, VA
Campus Setting: Town: Distant
Total Expenses: $54,843
Estimated Average Discount: $34,258 (62%)
Estimated Net Price: $20,585

Type of Institution: Liberal Arts College
Number of Undergraduates: 1,759
SAT Score: Reading: 650–740, Math: 660–740
Student/Faculty Ratio: 7 to 1
Transfer Out Rate: 4%

Rank Among 53 Liberal Arts Colleges	**1**
Overall Rank Among 177 *Alumni Factor* Schools	**1**

Overview

The Alumni Factor's #1 ranked liberal arts college in the country, and the #1 school overall, Washington & Lee is an academic and post-graduate performance powerhouse. Founded through a grant from George Washington as the 9th oldest college in the country, W&L has been producing seriously accomplished graduates in each of the last four centuries. Undeniably selective (roughly 18 percent of applicants are admitted) and thoroughly rigorous, W&L and Yale are the only 2 colleges in the country to rank in the Top 60 of all 177 schools on all 26 measures ranked by *The Alumni Factor*. It also ranks in the Top 30 among the liberal arts colleges for every single measure. Ranked 1st in the Ultimate Outcomes, 2nd in Financial Success and 6th in the College Experience, W&L is ranked among the Top 20 liberal arts colleges in an astonishing 24 of 26 attributes. There simply is not a better liberal arts college anywhere in terms of overall graduate performance.

While W&L already has a strong reputation, the results of its alumni far exceed that reputation, therefore, its stature will expand even further. W&L grads are superbly prepared for a life of success, happiness, friendships and intellectual accomplishment.

Notable Alumni

Nobel Prize winner Joseph Goldstein; billionaires Rupert Johnson and Gerry Lenfest; author Tom Wolfe; Legg Mason CEO Bill Miller; CBS veteran Roger Mudd; and former secretary of commerce Robert Mosbacher.

The Alumni Factor Rankings Summary

Attribute	Liberal Arts Rank	Overall Rank
College Experience	**6**	**6**
Intellectual Development	30	39
Social Development	3	3
Spiritual Development	17	37
Friendship Development	6	6
Preparation for Career Success	7	9
Immediate Job Opportunities	6	30
Overall Assessment	**8**	**19**
Would Personally Choose Again	9	19
Would Recommend to Student	22	58
Value for the Money	6	15
Financial Success	**2**	**3**
Income per Household	2	2
% Households with Income >$150K	4	5
Household Net Worth	8	13
% Households Net Worth >$1MM	4	5
Overall Happiness	**8**	**12**
Alumni Giving	**10**	**11**
Graduation Rate	**5**	**16**
Overall Rank	**1**	**1**

Other Key Alumni Outcomes

3.3%	Are college professors
6.5%	Teach at any level
62.7%	Have post-graduate degrees
48.8%	Live in dual-income homes
95.2%	Are currently employed

See pages 134–135 for detailed explanations and definitions.

Alumni Activities During College

29.1% Community Service
43.3% Intramural Sports
15.7% Internships
48.8% Media Programs
22.9% Music Programs
18.1% Part-Time Jobs

Prepared Me for Career Success % Strongly Agree	Was A Good Value for the Money % Strongly Agree	Percent of Alumni Worth >$1MM
Washington and Lee: 48.8%	Washington and Lee: 56.8%	Washington and Lee: 25.4%
All College Grads: 31.9%	All College Grads: 46.1%	All College Grads: 14.6%

Alumni Employment

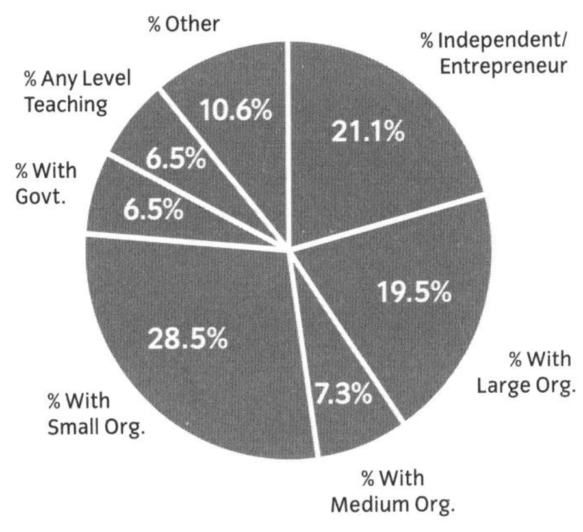

Income Distribution of Graduates

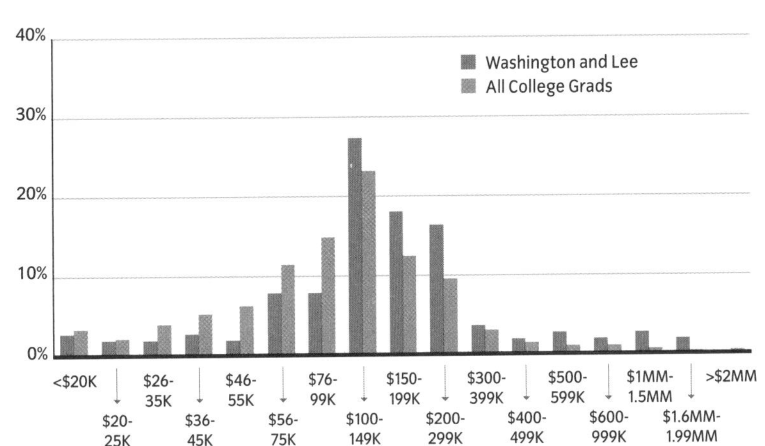

Current Selectivity & Demand Analysis for Washington and Lee University

Attribute	% Accepted	% Accepted Who Enroll	Freshman Retention Rate	Graduation Rate	Demand Index	Reputation Index
Score	18.0%	42.0%	94.0%	93.0%	13.13	2.33
Rank	24	33	58	16	33	24

Where are the Graduates of Washington and Lee University on the Political Spectrum?

Very Liberal	Liberal	Somewhat Liberal	Somewhat Conservative	Conservative	Very Conservative
					↑

See pages 134–135 for detailed explanations and definitions.

Washington State University

Location: Pullman, WA
Campus Setting: Town: Distant
Total Expenses: $24,939
Estimated Average Discount: $9,454 (38%)
Estimated Net Price: $15,485

Type of Institution: National University
Number of Undergraduates: 21,816
SAT Score: Reading: 470–580, Math: 480–600
Student/Faculty Ratio: 15 to 1
Transfer Out Rate: Not Reported

Rank Among 104 National Universities	**64**
Overall Rank Among 177 *Alumni Factor* Schools	**130**

Overview

Tucked away in the rolling wheat fields of southeastern Washington along the Idaho border sits Washington State University – home of the Cougars. While typically seen as "inferior" in reputation to its cross-state rival University of Washington, you might be interested to know that WSU beats University of Washington in 19 of the 26 metrics in our analysis. With a 39th ranking in the College Experience (UW is 98th), WSU grads give very high marks to their school for every developmental attribute, including Preparation for Career Success (36th) – the most important indicator of overall success. WSU also slightly outperforms University of Washington in Financial Success (90th versus 96th); in Overall Happiness (22nd versus 68th) and in the Ultimate Outcomes (73rd versus 95th). Both are excellent schools and serve different purposes, but it is time to give WSU the respect it deserves. To be fair, University of Washington is significantly larger than WSU, and we know that can dramatically impact (negatively) the College Experience for graduates. Regardless, WSU has earned the right to hold its head high for its continued excellence in producing happy, successful, loyal graduates.

Notable Alumni

Legendary sportscaster Keith Jackson; famed economist and college president Howard Bowen; president of the Ford Foundation Henry Heald; broadcaster Edward Murrow; physicist Phillip Abelson; and countless NFL stars.

The Alumni Factor Rankings Summary

Attribute	University Rank	Overall Rank
College Experience	**39**	**99**
Intellectual Development	56	122
Social Development	36	84
Spiritual Development	54	122
Friendship Development	40	103
Preparation for Career Success	36	83
Immediate Job Opportunities	35	53
Overall Assessment	**63**	**118**
Would Personally Choose Again	80	142
Would Recommend to Student	57	111
Value for the Money	50	91
Financial Success	**90**	**151**
Income per Household	101	170
% Households with Income >$150K	98	162
Household Net Worth	89	152
% Households Net Worth >$1MM	55	95
Overall Happiness	**22**	**42**
Alumni Giving	**37**	**93**
Graduation Rate	**81**	**148**
Overall Rank	**64**	**130**

Other Key Alumni Outcomes

5.1% Are college professors
19.4% Teach at any level
47.9% Have post-graduate degrees
44.4% Live in dual-income homes
92.4% Are currently employed

See pages 134–135 for detailed explanations and definitions.

Alumni Activities During College

30.2% Community Service
40.5% Intramural Sports
22.4% Internships
10.3% Media Programs
6.9% Music Programs
34.5% Part-Time Jobs

	Washington State	All College Grads
Prepared Me for Career Success (% Strongly Agree)	31.0%	31.9%
Was A Good Value for the Money (% Strongly Agree)	44.0%	46.1%
Percent of Alumni Worth >$1MM	14.2%	14.6%

Alumni Employment

Category	%
% Independent/ Entrepreneur	15.3%
% With Large Org.	19.5%
% With Medium Org.	11.9%
% With Small Org.	12.7%
% With Govt.	9.3%
% Any Level Teaching	19.4%
% Other	11.9%

Income Distribution of Graduates

Current Selectivity & Demand Analysis for Washington State University

Attribute	% Accepted	% Accepted Who Enroll	Freshman Retention Rate	Graduation Rate	Demand Index	Reputation Index
Score	84.0%	38.0%	82.0%	69.0%	2.93	0.45
Rank	172	55	167	148	171	136

Where are the Graduates of Washington State University on the Political Spectrum?

Very Liberal	Liberal	Somewhat Liberal	Somewhat Conservative	Conservative	Very Conservative
				↑	

See pages 134–135 for detailed explanations and definitions.

Washington University in St. Louis

Location: St. Louis, MO
Campus Setting: Suburb: Large
Total Expenses: $58,901
Estimated Average Discount: $26,031 (44%)
Estimated Net Price: $32,870

Type of Institution: National University
Number of Undergraduates: 7,138
SAT Score: Reading: 690–760, Math: 710–780
Student/Faculty Ratio: 7 to 1
Transfer Out Rate: Not Reported

Rank Among 104 National Universities	**30**
Overall Rank Among 177 *Alumni Factor* Schools	**74**

Overview

Washington University is among the finest universities in the country, but it is a well-kept secret from many. Wash U is in the Top 10 in Graduation Rate; Top 25 in Alumni Giving; Top 20 in the Ultimate Outcomes; Top 40 in both Happiness & Financial Success; and Top 50 in both the Overall Assessment and College Experience. With these graduate outcomes and alumni loyalty you might think that the world would be singing its praises from the rooftops. But Wash U has two challenges: first, St. Louis is not exactly an epicenter for the cognoscenti of post-secondary education. Second, its name can be easily confused with many others. Those hurdles are easy to clear once one sees the results. Wash U grads are exceptionally bright (27th in reported SAT scores); do very well financially (37th); are very happy (36th) and do very well across all the Ultimate Outcomes (ranked 18th). Their strongest Ultimate Outcome is Happiness & Intellectual Capability (3rd).

Notable Alumni

Lions Gate Entertainment CEO Jon Feltheimer; TV Producer Caryn Mandabach ; actor, director and writer Harold Ramis; writer Allen Rucker; actor Peter Sarsgaard; Chairman and CEO of Zapata, Avi Glazer; former CEO of P&G Howard Morgens; and many other luminaries.

The Alumni Factor Rankings Summary

Attribute	University Rank	Overall Rank
College Experience	**47**	**109**
Intellectual Development	28	77
Social Development	68	133
Spiritual Development	32	93
Friendship Development	36	98
Preparation for Career Success	47	97
Immediate Job Opportunities	69	111
Overall Assessment	**49**	**96**
Would Personally Choose Again	36	69
Would Recommend to Student	36	72
Value for the Money	74	136
Financial Success	**37**	**66**
Income per Household	35	57
% Households with Income >$150K	21	41
Household Net Worth	56	96
% Households Net Worth >$1MM	47	83
Overall Happiness	**36**	**66**
Alumni Giving	**22**	**72**
Graduation Rate	**9**	**11**
Overall Rank	**30**	**74**

Other Key Alumni Outcomes

6.7% Are college professors
9.7% Teach at any level
65.2% Have post-graduate degrees
49.8% Live in dual-income homes
94.2% Are currently employed

See pages 134–135 for detailed explanations and definitions.

Alumni Activities During College

40.7% Community Service
31.9% Intramural Sports
24.2% Internships
22.0% Media Programs
16.9% Music Programs
39.6% Part-Time Jobs

Prepared Me for Career Success % Strongly Agree	Was A Good Value for the Money % Strongly Agree	Percent of Alumni Worth >$1MM
WashU 31.5%; All College Grads 31.9%	WashU 38.2%; All College Grads 46.1%	WashU 15.0%; All College Grads 14.6%

Alumni Employment

Category	%
% Independent/ Entrepreneur	16.4%
% With Large Org.	28.4%
% With Medium Org.	14.6%
% With Small Org.	17.2%
% With Govt.	5.2%
% Any Level Teaching	9.7%
% Other	8.5%

Income Distribution of Graduates

WashU
All College Grads

0% 10% 20% 30% 40%

<$20K, $20-25K, $26-35K, $36-45K, $46-55K, $56-75K, $76-99K, $100-149K, $150-199K, $200-299K, $300-399K, $400-499K, $500-599K, $600-999K, $1MM-1.5MM, $1.6MM-1.99MM, >$2MM

Current Selectivity & Demand Analysis for Washington University in St. Louis

Attribute	% Accepted	% Accepted Who Enroll	Freshman Retention Rate	Graduation Rate	Demand Index	Reputation Index
Score	17.0%	31.0%	97.0%	94.0%	19.37	1.82
Rank	22	96	13	11	7	30

Where are the Graduates of Washington University in St. Louis on the Political Spectrum?

Very Liberal	Liberal	Somewhat Liberal	Somewhat Conservative	Conservative	Very Conservative
	↑				

See pages 134–135 for detailed explanations and definitions.

Wellesley College

Location: Wellesley, MA
Campus Setting: Suburb: Large
Total Expenses: $55,300
Estimated Average Discount: $36,900 (67%)
Estimated Net Price: $18,400

Type of Institution: Liberal Arts College
Number of Undergraduates: 2,546
SAT Score: Reading: 650–740, Math: 640–750
Student/Faculty Ratio: 7 to 1
Transfer Out Rate: 4%

Rank Among 53 Liberal Arts Colleges	**8**
Overall Rank Among 177 *Alumni Factor* Schools	**15**

Overview

America's most consequential women have often been Wellesley graduates. Whether in politics, the media, journalism, Hollywood, science, law or business, Wellesley women are present and accounted for as they lead and shape the future. Wellesley is the #1 women's college in our *Alumni Factor* rankings, ranks 8th among all liberal arts colleges and 15th among all colleges and universities in our analysis.

Wellesley women are super smart (25th in reported SAT scores) and have a passion to learn and grow (15th in their pursuit of a post-graduate degree). They are also extraordinarily successful, as indicated by their Financial Success ranking (12th) and their excellent performance in the Ultimate Outcomes (6th).

The undergraduate years at Wellesley are a transformative experience for those women fortunate enough to experience them. Wellesley ranks 12th in the College Experience, led by strong Preparation for Career Success (10th), and ranks 8th in Would Recommend. Wellesley graduates are also ranked 2nd among all schools in their percentage of millionaire households. When you add its 12th ranking in Alumni Giving to the other facts, the esteem Wellesley women have for their college becomes perfectly clear.

Notable Alumni

Madeleine Albright, Diane Sawyer, Nora Ephron, Hilary Clinton, Lulu Wang, Susan Estrich, Cynthia Glassman, Anne Patterson, Cokie Roberts, and Susan Sheehan.

The Alumni Factor Rankings Summary

Attribute	Liberal Arts Rank	Overall Rank
College Experience	**12**	**17**
Intellectual Development	21	24
Social Development	31	53
Spiritual Development	25	51
Friendship Development	15	17
Preparation for Career Success	10	14
Immediate Job Opportunities	16	67
Overall Assessment	**18**	**43**
Would Personally Choose Again	34	91
Would Recommend to Student	8	25
Value for the Money	7	17
Financial Success	**12**	**29**
Income per Household	21	62
% Households with Income >$150K	20	48
Household Net Worth	13	26
% Households Net Worth >$1MM	2	2
Overall Happiness	**35**	**97**
Alumni Giving	**12**	**14**
Graduation Rate	**16**	**39**
Overall Rank	**8**	**15**

Other Key Alumni Outcomes

8.2% Are college professors
13.6% Teach at any level
70.9% Have post-graduate degrees
51.0% Live in dual-income homes
89.9% Are currently employed

See pages 134–135 for detailed explanations and definitions.

Alumni Activities During College

35.1% Community Service
11.5% Intramural Sports
28.4% Internships
30.4% Media Programs
19.6% Music Programs
41.9% Part-Time Jobs

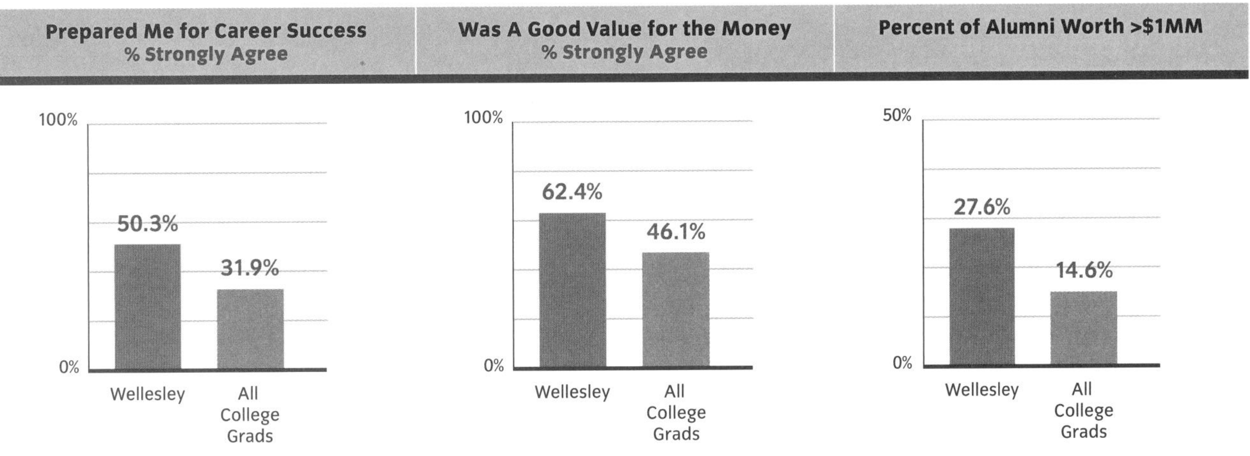

Alumni Employment

% Other 18.4%
% Independent/ Entrepreneur 17.6%
% With Large Org. 19.7%
% With Medium Org. 10.9%
% With Small Org. 13.6%
% With Govt. 6.2%
% Any Level Teaching 13.6%

Income Distribution of Graduates

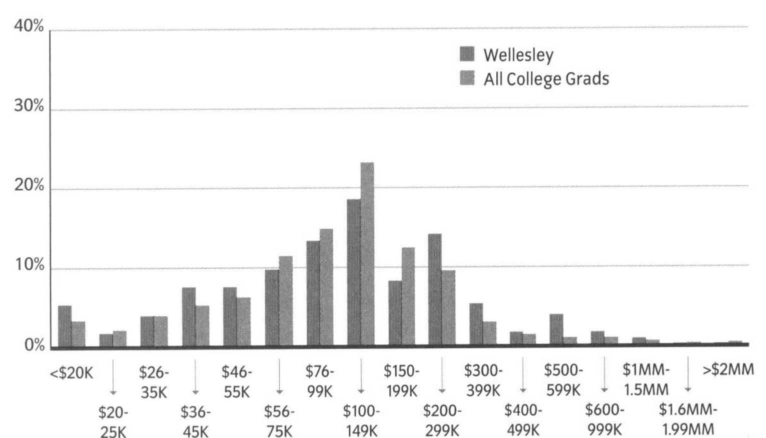

Current Selectivity & Demand Analysis for Wellesley College

Attribute	% Accepted	% Accepted Who Enroll	Freshman Retention Rate	Graduation Rate	Demand Index	Reputation Index
Score	31.0%	42.0%	96.0%	90.0%	7.75	1.35
Rank	55	33	27	39	104	44

Where are the Graduates of Wellesley College on the Political Spectrum?

Very Liberal	Liberal	Somewhat Liberal	Somewhat Conservative	Conservative	Very Conservative
↑					

Wesleyan University

Location: Middletown, CT
Campus Setting: City: Small
Total Expenses: $58,371
Estimated Average Discount: $36,517 (63%)
Estimated Net Price: $21,854

Type of Institution: Liberal Arts College
Number of Undergraduates: 2,854
SAT Score: Reading: 635-740, Math: 660–740
Student/Faculty Ratio: 9 to 1
Transfer Out Rate: Not Reported

Rank Among 53 Liberal Arts Colleges	**12**
Overall Rank Among 177 *Alumni Factor* Schools	**19**

Overview

Long considered to be one of the finest liberal arts schools in the country, Wesleyan fully lives up to its sterling reputation in terms of graduate success. Wesleyan produces a highly loyal (8th in Alumni Giving), extremely successful (14th in Financial Success) graduate who has a strong appreciation for their undergraduate years (15th in the College Experience). With Top 20 rankings in each element of Financial Success and a very strong showing in the Ultimate Outcomes (ranked 18th), Wesleyan grads are in the Top 10 in Would Personally Choose Again and Would Recommend to a Prospective Student. This school is the real deal when it comes to the full development of its graduates – it has one of the broadest success profiles of any college we have analyzed. Its alumni are extremely successful across a diversity of fields.

Wesleyan's strongest Ultimate Outcome is Financial Success & Friendships (ranked 18th among all schools) but performs well across all of the Ultimate Outcomes. It is very hard to find any weakness in the Wesleyan proposition, except perhaps the slightly lower ranking of Overall Happiness of its grads (50th), where still 73% of grads consider themselves happy or very happy.

Notable Alumni

Herb Kelleher; Jonathan Schwartz; Amy Bloom; Robert Ludlum; Ron Bloom; famous professor and historian August Seher; numerous screenwriters, politicians, and journalists; and many other highly successful leaders in their fields.

The Alumni Factor Rankings Summary

Attribute	Liberal Arts Rank	Overall Rank
College Experience	**15**	**26**
Intellectual Development	4	4
Social Development	17	24
Spiritual Development	12	32
Friendship Development	18	20
Preparation for Career Success	24	54
Immediate Job Opportunities	29	123
Overall Assessment	**12**	**30**
Would Personally Choose Again	10	20
Would Recommend to Student	6	22
Value for the Money	24	66
Financial Success	**14**	**31**
Income per Household	15	38
% Households with Income >$150K	17	34
Household Net Worth	17	38
% Households Net Worth >$1MM	15	32
Overall Happiness	**50**	**167**
Alumni Giving	**8**	**9**
Graduation Rate	**3**	**11**
Overall Rank	**12**	**19**

Other Key Alumni Outcomes

8.3% Are college professors
14.2% Teach at any level
68.8% Have post-graduate degrees
57.8% Live in dual-income homes
90.7% Are currently employed

See pages 134–135 for detailed explanations and definitions.

Alumni Activities During College

36.6% Community Service
33.2% Intramural Sports
22.4% Internships
37.1% Media Programs
30.3% Music Programs
29.8% Part-Time Jobs

Prepared Me for Career Success % Strongly Agree	Was A Good Value for the Money % Strongly Agree	Percent of Alumni Worth >$1MM

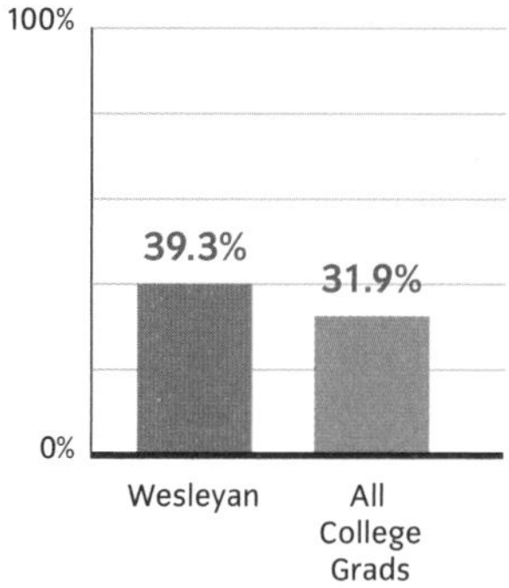

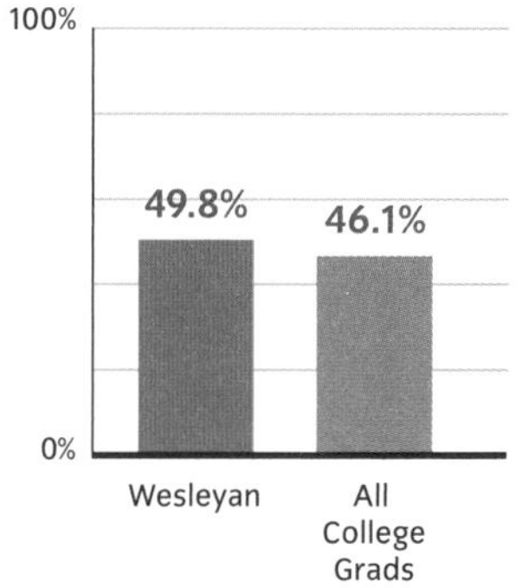

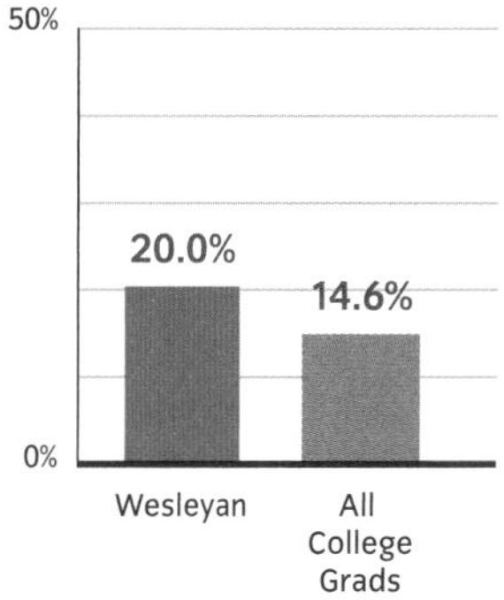

100%
39.3% 31.9%
0%
Wesleyan
All College Grads

100%
49.8% 46.1%
0%
Wesleyan
All College Grads

50%
20.0% 14.6%
0%
Wesleyan
All College Grads

Alumni Employment

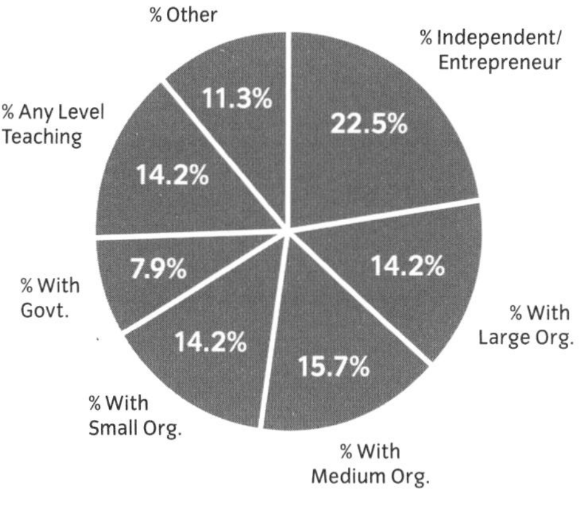

Income Distribution of Graduates

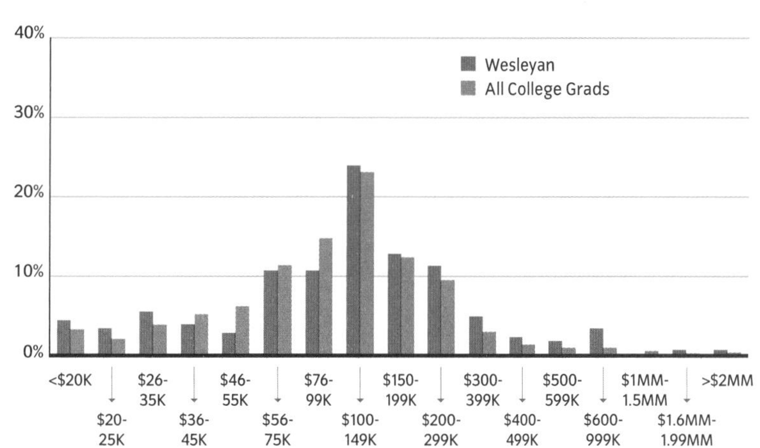

Current Selectivity & Demand Analysis for Wesleyan University

Attribute	% Accepted	% Accepted Who Enroll	Freshman Retention Rate	Graduation Rate	Demand Index	Reputation Index
Score	21.0%	34.0%	98.0%	94.0%	13.19	1.62
Rank	30	76	4	11	32	32

Where are the Graduates of Wesleyan University on the Political Spectrum?

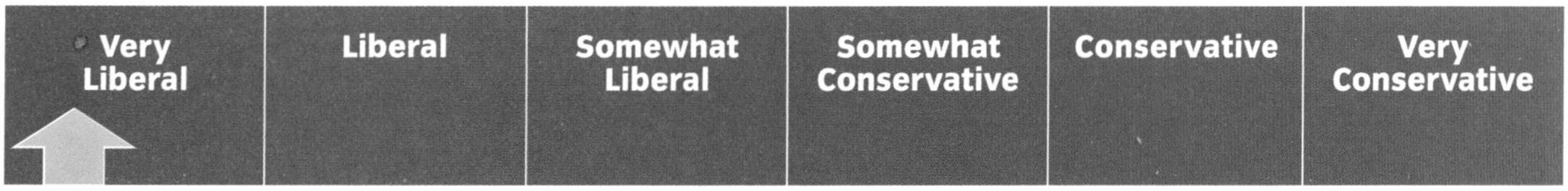

Very Liberal	Liberal	Somewhat Liberal	Somewhat Conservative	Conservative	Very Conservative

See pages 134–135 for detailed explanations and definitions.

Whitman College

Location: Walla Walla, WA
Campus Setting: Town: Remote
Total Expenses: $52,856
Estimated Average Discount: $23,563 (45%)
Estimated Net Price: $29,293

Type of Institution: Liberal Arts College
Number of Undergraduates: 1,555
SAT Score: Reading: 630–730, Math: 620–710
Student/Faculty Ratio: 10 to 1
Transfer Out Rate: Not Reported

Rank Among 53 Liberal Arts Colleges	**30**
Overall Rank Among 177 *Alumni Factor* Schools	**60**

Overview

The gold rush of the 1850's gave Walla Walla, Washington enough population to make a town, which in turn grew enough to support Whitman College, which opened its doors to four-year students in 1883. Since then, Whitman has prided itself on providing an intense academic experience without the elitism and perceived snobbery of the Eastern liberal arts establishment. It has succeeded famously on both fronts. With the 30th highest reported SAT scores among colleges and universities, a rank of 4th in Intellectual Development and its strong 10th rank in the Ultimate Outcome of Happiness & Intellectual Capability, Whitman certainly creates a rigorous academic environment for its students. Add to that its 21st Happiness rank and a 27th rank in the College Experience, and it is clear that grads love the laid-back, Northwest liberal arts environment that is Whitman. Whitman grads are also quite successful from a financial standpoint, with a 34th ranking in Financial Success.

Notable Alumni

Former Supreme Court justice William O. Douglas; former General Electric chairman and CEO Ralph Cordiner; actor Adam West (Batman); Nobel Prize winner Walter Brattain; former 24-year Oregon congressman Al Ullman; former Idaho congressman Walt Minnick and Western Wireless founder and former CEO John Stanton.

The Alumni Factor Rankings Summary

Attribute	Liberal Arts Rank	Overall Rank
College Experience	**27**	**49**
Intellectual Development	4	4
Social Development	25	41
Spiritual Development	28	54
Friendship Development	31	40
Preparation for Career Success	30	68
Immediate Job Opportunities	46	160
Overall Assessment	**35**	**91**
Would Personally Choose Again	33	88
Would Recommend to Student	38	98
Value for the Money	29	76
Financial Success	**34**	**101**
Income per Household	47	150
% Households with Income >$150K	37	114
Household Net Worth	25	66
% Households Net Worth >$1MM	29	71
Overall Happiness	**21**	**51**
Alumni Giving	**21**	**24**
Graduation Rate	**32**	**67**
Overall Rank	**30**	**60**

Other Key Alumni Outcomes

5.6% Are college professors
14.4% Teach at any level
56.0% Have post-graduate degrees
50.4% Live in dual-income homes
93.5% Are currently employed

See pages 134–135 for detailed explanations and definitions.

Alumni Activities During College

35.5% Community Service
50.8% Intramural Sports
15.3% Internships
42.7% Media Programs
37.1% Music Programs
29.0% Part-Time Jobs

Current Selectivity & Demand Analysis for Whitman College

Attribute	% Accepted	% Accepted Who Enroll	Freshman Retention Rate	Graduation Rate	Demand Index	Reputation Index
Score	53.0%	24.0%	92.0%	86.0%	7.76	0.45
Rank	107	138	86	67	103	136

Where are the Graduates of Whitman College on the Political Spectrum?

Very Liberal	Liberal	Somewhat Liberal	Somewhat Conservative	Conservative	Very Conservative

See pages 134–135 for detailed explanations and definitions.

Williams College

Location: Williamstown, MA
Campus Setting: Town: Distant
Total Expenses: $57,141
Estimated Average Discount: $40,648 (71%)
Estimated Net Price: $16,493

Type of Institution: Liberal Arts College
Number of Undergraduates: 2,048
SAT Score: Reading: 660–770, Math: 650–760
Student/Faculty Ratio: 7 to 1
Transfer Out Rate: Not Reported

Rank Among 53 Liberal Arts Colleges	**22**
Overall Rank Among 177 *Alumni Factor* Schools	**47**

Overview

When it comes to college reputation, Williams College is at the very pinnacle of the liberal arts world. It is the rare ranking that does not have Williams ranked either 1st or 2nd among liberal arts colleges (Amherst is typically the other). So, one of our biggest surprises was finding Williams in the 22nd spot among liberal arts colleges.

The simple fact is that Williams, as expected, is stellar in Financial Success (18th – despite an alumni base that has a 50% higher likelihood of being a teacher than the total population of schools), the Ultimate Outcomes (15th), Alumni Giving (3rd) and Graduation Rate (1st). However, it does not do as well in the College Experience (ranked 35th versus Amherst's 13th), the Overall Assessment (ranked 39th versus Amherst's 6th) or in reported Overall Happiness (ranked 42nd versus Amherst's 26th).

With that said, Williams, at 22nd overall, ranks in our Top 25 and has had an illustrious history of producing some of the most accomplished graduates of any school in the country. For a small school to produce such a large and prestigious list is as impressive as the Williams reputation itself – and likely its cause.

Notable Alumni

Former president James Garfield; Lester Thurow, Stephen Sondheim, investor Herbert Allen; Edgar Bronfman; founder of AOL, Steve Case; Walter Shipley; George Steinbrenner; Jamie Tarses; Joe Rice of Clayton, Dubilier & Rice; Susan Schwab; and former CIA director Richard Helms.

The Alumni Factor Rankings Summary

Attribute	Liberal Arts Rank	Overall Rank
College Experience	**35**	**65**
Intellectual Development	39	55
Social Development	46	101
Spiritual Development	43	82
Friendship Development	33	42
Preparation for Career Success	29	63
Immediate Job Opportunities	14	59
Overall Assessment	**39**	**109**
Would Personally Choose Again	44	141
Would Recommend to Student	34	88
Value for the Money	31	82
Financial Success	**18**	**45**
Income per Household	23	69
% Households with Income >$150K	13	29
Household Net Worth	19	49
% Households Net Worth >$1MM	22	54
Overall Happiness	**42**	**142**
Alumni Giving	**3**	**4**
Graduation Rate	**1**	**7**
Overall Rank	**22**	**47**

Other Key Alumni Outcomes

14.3% Are college professors
23.0% Teach at any level
76.0% Have post-graduate degrees
45.3% Live in dual-income homes
93.7% Are currently employed

See pages 134–135 for detailed explanations and definitions.

Alumni Activities During College

32.8% Community Service
37.5% Intramural Sports
15.6% Internships
32.0% Media Programs
40.7% Music Programs
17.2% Part-Time Jobs

Prepared Me for Career Success % Strongly Agree	Was A Good Value for the Money % Strongly Agree	Percent of Alumni Worth >$1MM
Williams 39.7% All College Grads 31.9%	Williams 54.3% All College Grads 46.1%	Williams 17.5% All College Grads 14.6%

Alumni Employment

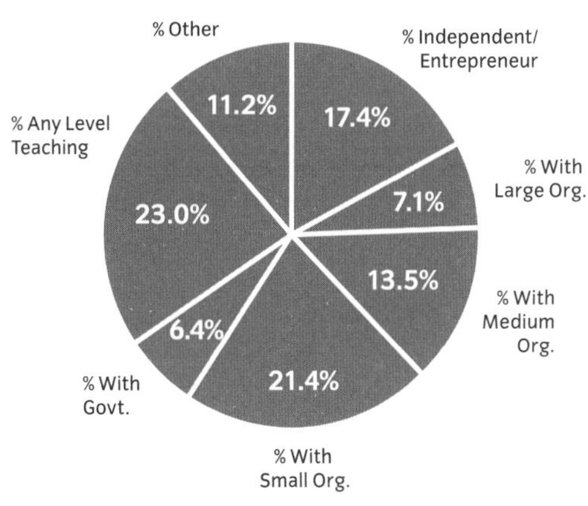

Income Distribution of Graduates

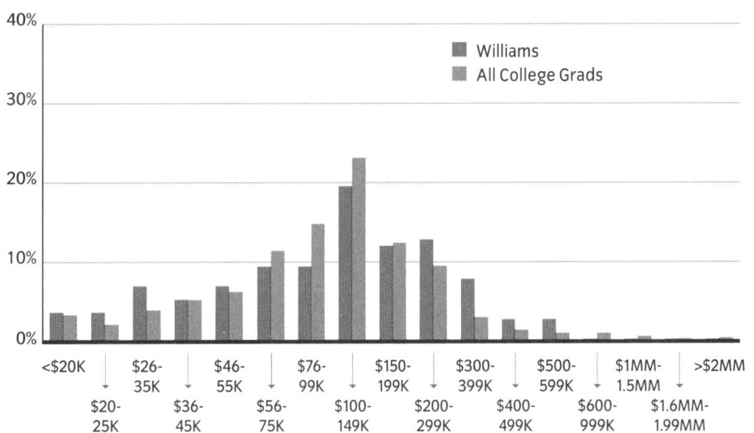

Current Selectivity & Demand Analysis for Williams College

Attribute	% Accepted	% Accepted Who Enroll	Freshman Retention Rate	Graduation Rate	Demand Index	Reputation Index
Score	19.0%	44.0%	97.0%	95.0%	12.17	2.32
Rank	26	26	13	7	42	25

Where are the Graduates of Williams College on the Political Spectrum?

Very Liberal ↑	Liberal	Somewhat Liberal	Somewhat Conservative	Conservative	Very Conservative

See pages 134–135 for detailed explanations and definitions.

Worcester Polytechnic Institute

Location: Worcester, MA
Campus Setting: City: Midsize
Total Expenses: $54,164
Estimated Average Discount: $19,826 (37%)
Estimated Net Price: $34,338

Type of Institution: National University
Number of Undergraduates: 3,649
SAT Score: Not Reported
Student/Faculty Ratio: 14 to 1
Transfer Out Rate: Not Reported

Rank Among 104 National Universities **55**

Overall Rank Among 177 *Alumni Factor* Schools **118**

Overview

Often seen as a high-class back-up school to MIT, Caltech or some other ultra-selective technical school, WPI offers extremely strong programs to a very bright student body (55th in reported SAT scores). This is a school whose actual graduate results well exceed its reputation in the college market. WPI graduates are exceptionally hard workers (ranked 2nd among schools in employment rate), are well-prepared to succeed in their careers (10th) and have plenty of job opportunities upon graduation (9th). But here is what makes WPI so unique – it is a rigorous technical school where strong friendships develop (ranked 21st in Friendship Development) and graduates go on to lead happy lives (20th in Overall Happiness). These are highly capable engineers who can interact with others and enjoy it. WPI's strongest Ultimate Outcome is Happiness and Friendships, where it ranks 18th.

This biotech leader brings a practical, hands-on bent to academics and is a leader in fields such as nanotechnology, Six Sigma quality and fuel cells.

Notable Alumni

Liquid-fueled rocket inventor Robert Goddard; former chairman and CEO of GM, Robert Stempel; brilliant inventor Dean Kamen; previous Xerox CEO Paul Allaire; Missouri Congressman Todd Akin; and noted American geologist William Hobbs.

The Alumni Factor Rankings Summary

Attribute	University Rank	Overall Rank
College Experience	**40**	**100**
Intellectual Development	74	146
Social Development	95	166
Spiritual Development	87	159
Friendship Development	21	70
Preparation for Career Success	10	26
Immediate Job Opportunities	9	13
Overall Assessment	**70**	**128**
Would Personally Choose Again	58	108
Would Recommend to Student	72	130
Value for the Money	72	132
Financial Success	**78**	**125**
Income per Household	45	72
% Households with Income >$150K	80	131
Household Net Worth	101	169
% Households Net Worth >$1MM	72	122
Overall Happiness	**20**	**42**
Alumni Giving	**45**	**108**
Graduation Rate	**50**	**106**
Overall Rank	**55**	**118**

Other Key Alumni Outcomes

5.5% Are college professors
8.3% Teach at any level
53.2% Have post-graduate degrees
47.3% Live in dual-income homes
98.2% Are currently employed

See pages 134–135 for detailed explanations and definitions.

Alumni Activities During College

22.9% Community Service
29.4% Intramural Sports
14.7% Internships
17.5% Media Programs
19.3% Music Programs
38.5% Part-Time Jobs

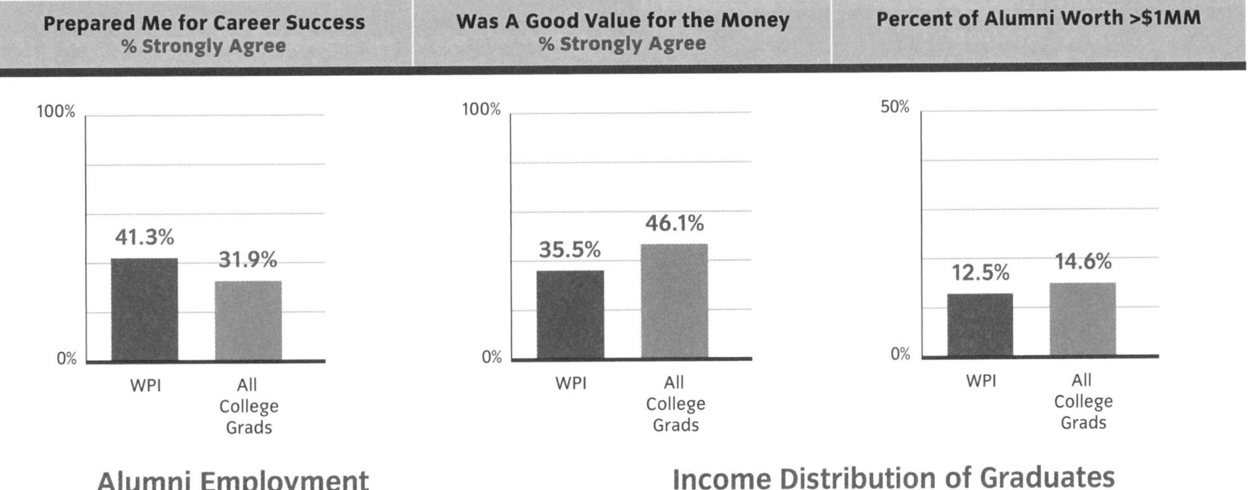

Alumni Employment

% Independent/Entrepreneur 5.5%
% With Large Org. 37.6%
% With Medium Org. 11.9%
% With Small Org. 22.9%
% Any Level Teaching 5.5%
% With Govt. 8.3%
8.3%

Income Distribution of Graduates

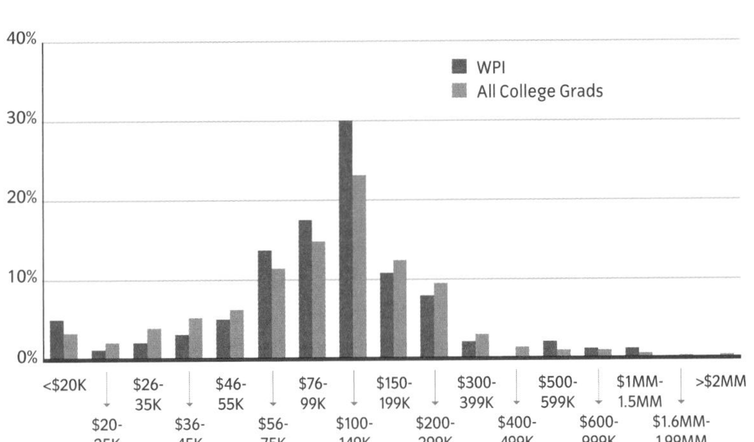

Current Selectivity & Demand Analysis for Worcester Polytechnic Institute

Attribute	% Accepted	% Accepted Who Enroll	Freshman Retention Rate	Graduation Rate	Demand Index	Reputation Index
Score	57.0%	25.0%	95.0%	80.0%	7.01	0.44
Rank	116	130	47	106	114	138

Where are the Graduates of Worcester Polytechnic Institute on the Political Spectrum?

Very Liberal	Liberal	Somewhat Liberal	Somewhat Conservative	Conservative	Very Conservative
			↑		

See pages 134–135 for detailed explanations and definitions.

Xavier University

Location: Cincinnati, OH
Campus Setting: City: Large
Total Expenses: $43,880
Estimated Average Discount: $18,151 (41%)
Estimated Net Price: $25,729

Type of Institution: Regional University
Number of Undergraduates: 4,368
SAT Score: Reading: 480–600, Math: 500–610
Student/Faculty Ratio: 12 to 1
Transfer Out Rate: Not Reported

Rank Among 20 Regional Universities	**7**
Overall Rank Among 177 *Alumni Factor* Schools	**90**

Overview

A top-notch Jesuit University just northeast of Cincinnati, Xavier is ranked 7th among the Top 20 regional universities and 90th among all colleges and universities. This is an excellent school whose star is rising – and that elevation is well-deserved. Ranked an impressive 18th among all colleges and universities in the College Experience, Xavier grads are well developed on all fronts. Ranked 22nd in Preparation for Career Success and 29th in Immediate Job Opportunities, Xavier well prepares its graduates to succeed in a wide variety of fields. Couple that with strong social & communication skills (24th) and an intense academic experience (61st in Intellectual Development) laced with Jesuit values (9th in Spiritual Development), and the result is a happy (57th in Overall Happiness) and successful graduate.

Financial Success for Xavier graduates (ranked 167th) is somewhat low because of the high percentage of teachers in the alumni population. In fact, Xavier grads are nearly three times as likely to become a high school or elementary school teacher as all college graduates.

Notable Alumni

US Speaker of the House John Boehner; former US senator and baseball Hall of Famer Jim Bunning; surgeon and inventor of the embolectomy catheter Thomas Fogarty; founder of Adobe Systems Charles Geschke; and former US ambassador to Singapore, Patricia Herbold.

The Alumni Factor Rankings Summary

Attribute	Overall Rank
College Experience	**18**
Intellectual Development	61
Social Development	24
Spiritual Development	9
Friendship Development	93
Preparation for Career Success	22
Immediate Job Opportunities	29
Overall Assessment	**48**
Would Personally Choose Again	33
Would Recommend to Student	22
Value for the Money	101
Financial Success	**167**
Income per Household	156
% Households with Income >$150K	172
Household Net Worth	129
% Households Net Worth >$1MM	172
Overall Happiness	**57**
Alumni Giving	**131**
Graduation Rate	**118**
Overall Rank	**90**

Other Key Alumni Outcomes

6.9% Are college professors
15.8% Teach at any level
52.4% Have post-graduate degrees
48.9% Live in dual-income homes
93.1% Are currently employed

See pages 134–135 for detailed explanations and definitions.

Alumni Activities During College

39.6% Community Service
39.6% Intramural Sports
21.5% Internships
18.1% Media Programs
13.2% Music Programs
49.3% Part-Time Jobs

Alumni Employment

% Other: 12.4%
% Independent/ Entrepreneur: 12.4%
% With Large Org.: 21.4%
% With Medium Org.: 16.6%
% With Small Org.: 15.2%
% With Govt.: 6.2%
% Any Level Teaching: 15.8%

Income Distribution of Graduates

■ Xavier
■ All College Grads

40%, 30%, 20%, 10%, 0%

<$20K, $20-25K, $26-35K, $36-45K, $46-55K, $56-75K, $76-99K, $100-149K, $150-199K, $200-299K, $300-399K, $400-499K, $500-599K, $600-999K, $1MM-1.5MM, $1.6MM-1.99MM, >$2MM

Current Selectivity & Demand Analysis for Xavier University

Attribute	% Accepted	% Accepted Who Enroll	Freshman Retention Rate	Graduation Rate	Demand Index	Reputation Index
Score	70.0%	16.0%	85.0%	79.0%	8.71	0.23
Rank	149	172	151	118	90	173

Where are the Graduates of Xavier University on the Political Spectrum?

Very Liberal	Liberal	Somewhat Liberal	Somewhat Conservative	Conservative	Very Conservative
				↑	

See pages 134–135 for detailed explanations and definitions.

Yale University

Location: New Haven, CT
Campus Setting: City: Midsize
Total Expenses: $58,250
Estimated Average Discount: $39,316 (67%)
Estimated Net Price: $18,934

Type of Institution: National University
Number of Undergraduates: 5,310
SAT Score: Reading: 700–800, Math: 710–790
Student/Faculty Ratio: 6 to 1
Transfer Out Rate: Not Reported

Rank Among 104 National Universities	**1**
Overall Rank Among 177 *Alumni Factor* Schools	**2**

Overview

Yale's legendary reputation as one of the world's finest universities is corroborated by the extraordinary outcomes of its graduates. Yale earns *The Alumni Factor's* #1 rank among national universities in the US for its stellar performance in producing happy, successful and fully developed alumni who succeed at astonishing rates across virtually all fields. Every ranking for Yale is in the Top 25 among national universities and in the Top 50 among all schools – the only college among the 177 we include here that can make that claim. In addition, the fact that Yale ranks in the Top 5 in every Ultimate Outcome is illustrative of the long-term impact of a Yale education. It is the top-ranked College Experience in the country among national universities; it ranks 2nd in the Overall Assessment by its demanding graduates, and ranks 3rd in Overall Happiness. Not surprisingly, Yale graduates also do very well financially (ranked 11th). In the toughest comparison of them all, versus its Ivy League competitors, Yale ranks 1st overall and 1st in 11 of the attributes we rank.

Notable Alumni

Four former US presidents, ten Nobel Laureates (counting undergrads only); Benjamin Spock; Eli Whitney; Samuel Morse; Robert Bass; mulitple members of the world-shaping Shriver family; Donna Dubinsky; former Coca-Cola CEO Roberto Goizueta; Pulitzer Prize winners Wendy Wasserstein, Samantha Power, and John Hersey; Grace Hopper, inventor of the COBOL programming language; Eero Saarinen; and actors Angela Bassett, Jodie Foster, David Alan Grier and Paul Giamatti.

The Alumni Factor Rankings Summary

Attribute	University Rank	Overall Rank
College Experience	**1**	**7**
Intellectual Development	3	18
Social Development	1	7
Spiritual Development	8	38
Friendship Development	5	29
Preparation for Career Success	4	15
Immediate Job Opportunities	17	23
Overall Assessment	**2**	**4**
Would Personally Choose Again	3	6
Would Recommend to Student	2	4
Value for the Money	13	21
Financial Success	**11**	**20**
Income per Household	5	10
% Households with Income >$150K	7	16
Household Net Worth	25	47
% Households Net Worth >$1MM	13	25
Overall Happiness	**3**	**13**
Alumni Giving	**12**	**57**
Graduation Rate	**2**	**2**
Overall Rank	**1**	**2**

Other Key Alumni Outcomes

6.4% Are college professors
11.9% Teach at any level
67.5% Have post-graduate degrees
52.5% Live in dual-income homes
91.7% Are currently employed

See pages 134–135 for detailed explanations and definitions.

Alumni Activities During College

41.9% Community Service
30.5% Intramural Sports
18.7% Internships
29.1% Media Programs
37.9% Music Programs
35.5% Part-Time Jobs

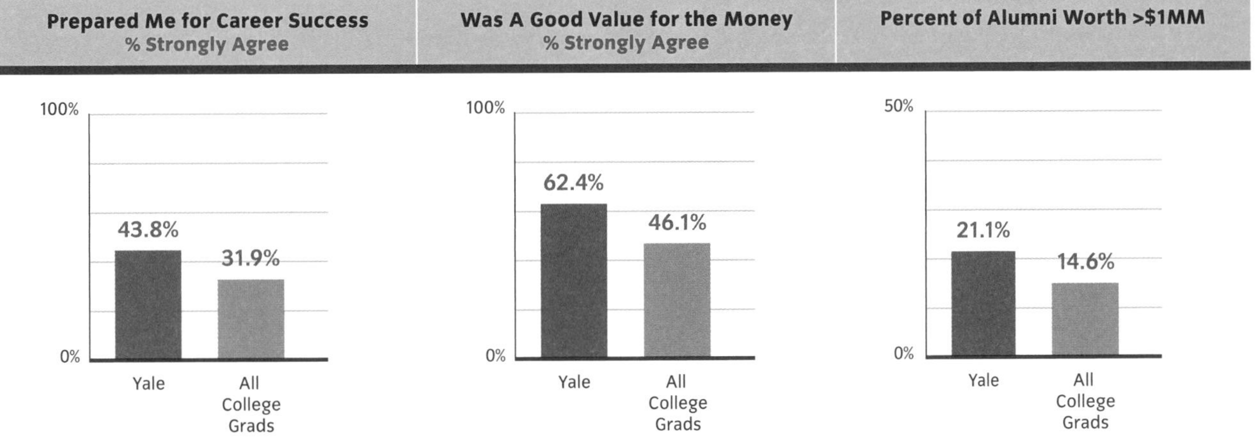

Alumni Employment

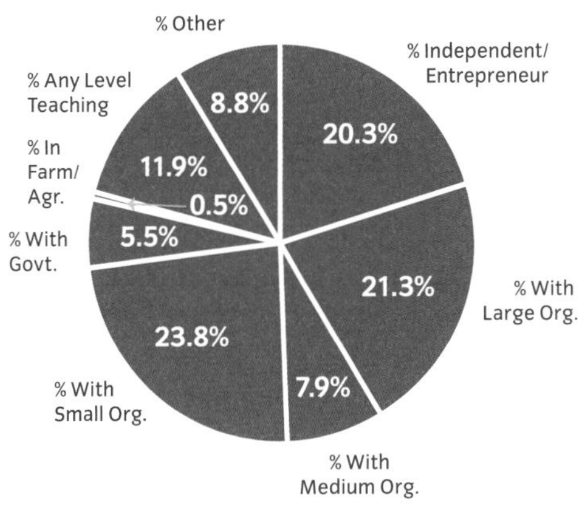

Income Distribution of Graduates

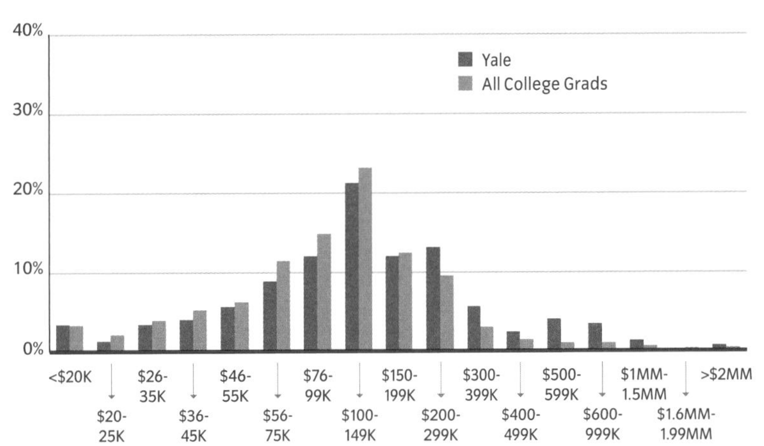

Current Selectivity & Demand Analysis for Yale University

Attribute	% Accepted	% Accepted Who Enroll	Freshman Retention Rate	Graduation Rate	Demand Index	Reputation Index
Score	8.0%	66.0%	99.0%	96.0%	19.18	8.25
Rank	4	8	1	2	8	4

Where are the Graduates of Yale University on the Political Spectrum?

Very Liberal	Liberal	Somewhat Liberal	Somewhat Conservative	Conservative	Very Conservative

Photo Attributes

American University
This photo is in the public domain
Amherst College
This photo is in the public domain
Arizona State University
ASU Photo by Scott Troyanos
Auburn University
Photo courtesy of Wikipedia (user Organizedchaos02)
Bard College
This photo is in the public domain
Bates College
Photo courtesy of Wikipedia (user Arthur)
Baylor University
This photo is in the public domain
Boston College
Photo courtesy of Harvey D. Egan
Boston University
Photo courtesy of Wikipedia (user Shorelander)
Bowdoin College
Photo courtesy of Wikipedia (user Ilove2run)
Bradley University
Photo courtesy of Wikipedia (user AscendedAnathema)
Brandeis University
Photo courtesy of Mike Lovett
Brigham Young University
Photo courtesy of Ken Lund
Brown University
Photo courtesy of Wikipedia (user chensiyuan)
Bryn Mawr College
This photo is in the public domain
Bucknell University
Photo courtesy of Bill Cardoni
California Institute of Technology
Photo courtesy of Wikipedia (user Canon.vs.nikon)
Carleton College
This photo is in the public domain
Carnegie Mellon University
Photo courtesy of Wikipedia (user Youchen)
Case Western Reserve University
Photo courtesy of Wikipedia (user Soundoftoday)
Centre College
This photo is in the public domain
Claremont McKenna College
Photo courtesy of Claremont McKenna College
Clark University
This photo is in the public domain
Clemson University
Photo courtesy of Wikipedia (user blahedo)
Colby College
Photo courtesy of Colby College
Colgate University
This photo is in the public domain
College of Charleston
Photo courtesy of College of Charleston
The College of New Jersey
This photo is in the public domain
College of the Holy Cross
Photo courtesy of Paul Keleher
The College of William and Mary
This photo is in the public domain
Colorado College
Photo courtesy of Timothy Hursley
Colorado State University
Photo courtesy of CSU Photography
Columbia University
Photo courtesy of Wikipedia (user Nowhereman86)
Connecticut College
Photo courtesy of Vickers and Bleechler
Cornell University
Photo courtesy of Alex Sergeev
Creighton University
Photo courtesy of Troy Johnson
Dartmouth College
Photo courtesy of Wikipedia (user Kane5187)
Davidson College
This photo is in the public domain
Denison University
Photo courtesy of Wikipedia (user Pbass1956)
DePaul University
Photo courtesy of Wikipedia (user Chameleon131)
DePauw University
Photo courtesy of DePauw University
Dickinson College
This photo is in the public domain
Drexel University
Photo courtesy of Wikipedia (user ImmortalGoddezz)
Duke University
Photo courtesy of Wikipedia (user Bluedog423)
Elon University
Photo courtesy of Elon University

Emory University
Photo courtesy of Wikipedia (user Mpspqr)
Florida State University
This photo is in the public domain
Franklin and Marshall College
Photo courtesy of Eric Forberger
Furman University
Photo courtesy of Nathan Guinn
George Washington University
Photo courtesy of Jessica McConnell Burt, The George Washington University
Georgetown University
Photo courtesy of Wikipedia (user Patrickneil)
Georgia Institute of Technology
Photo courtesy of Brooke Novak
Gettysburg College
This photo is in the public domain
Gonzaga University
Photo courtesy of Matthew Hendricks
Grinnell College
Photo courtesy of Wikipedia (user Aureliusxv)
Hamilton College
Photo courtesy of Wikipedia (user DanielPenfield)
Harvard University
Photo courtesy of Wikipedia (user chensiyuan)
Harvey Mudd College
Photo courtesy of Wikipedia
Haverford College
Photo courtesy of Wikipedia (user Jackbauerinvc)
Howard University
This photo is in the public domain
Indiana University Bloomington
Photo courtesy of Wikipedia (user McAnt)
Iowa State University
Photo courtesy of Wikipedia (user Cburnett)
James Madison University
Photo courtesy of Ben Schumin
Johns Hopkins University
This photo is in the public domain
Kansas State University
This photo is in the public domain
Kenyon College
Photo courtesy of Wikipedia (user .curt.)
Lafayette College
Photo courtesy of Benjamin D. Esham
Lehigh University
Photo courtesy of Wikipedia (user IR393DEME)
Loyola Marymount University
This photo is in the public domain
Loyola University Chicago
Photo courtesy of Wikipedia (user Amerique)
Loyola University Maryland
This photo is in the public domain
Loyola University New Orleans
This photo is in the public domain
Macalester College
Photo courtesy of Wikipedia (user Evenjk)
Marquette University
Photo courtesy of Matthew Hendricks
Massachusetts Institute of Technology
Photo courtesy of Wikipedia (user madcoverboy)
Miami University
This photo is in the public domain
Michigan State University
This photo is in the public domain
Middlebury College
This photo is in the public domain
Morehouse College
Photo courtesy of Adam Hughes
Mount Holyoke College
Photo courtesy of Wikipedia (user BenFrantzDale)
New York University
Photo courtesy of Wikipedia (user jim.henderson)
North Carolina State University
Photo courtesy of Wikipedia (user SMaloney)
Northeastern University
Photo courtesy of Wikipedia (user Aleyx1234)
Northwestern University
Photo courtesy of Wikipedia (user madcoverboy)
Oberlin College
This photo is in the public domain
Occidental College
Photo courtesy of B. Kelley
Ohio Northern University
This photo is in the public domain
Ohio State University
Photo courtesy of Robert Chriss
Oregon State University
Photo courtesy of Wikipedia (user saml123)
Pennsylvania State University
Photo courtesy of George Chriss

Pepperdine University
This photo is in the public domain
Pitzer College
Photo courtesy of Pitzer College
Pomona College
Photo courtesy of Pomona College
Princeton University
Photo courtesy of Geir Thorarinsson
Purdue University
Photo courtesy of Huw Williams
Reed College
Photo courtesy of Kelvin Kay
Rensselaer Polytechnic Institute
Photo courtesy of Wikipedia (user UpstateNYer)
Rice University
Photo courtesy of Wikipedia
Rollins College
This photo is in the public domain
Rutgers University
Photo courtesy of Wikipedia (user Lacwal12)
San Diego State University
Photo courtesy of Wikipedia (user Nehrams2020)
Santa Clara University
Photo courtesy of Matthew Hendricks
Scripps College
Photo courtesy of Scripps College
Sewanee: The University of the South
Photo courtesy of Sewanee
Skidmore College
Photo courtesy of Sam Brook
Smith College
Photo courtesy of Smith College
Southern Methodist University
Photo courtesy of Wikipedia (user Spencerjc1)
Spelman College
Photo courtesy of Spelman College
St. Olaf College
Photo courtesy of Daniel Edwins
Stanford University
Photo courtesy of Wikipedia (user King of Hearts)
Swarthmore College
Photo courtesy of Wikipedia (user Kungming2)
Syracuse University
Photo courtesy of Wikipedia (user Elstad Ranch)
Texas A & M University
Photo courtesy of Wikipedia (user eschipul)
Trinity College
This photo is in the public domain
Trinity University
Photo courtesy of Trinity University
Tufts University
Photo courtesy of Wikipedia (user HereToHelp)
Tulane University
Photo courtesy of Wikipedia (user Infrogmation)
United States Air Force Academy
Photo courtesy of Mike Kaplan, US Air Force Public Affairs
United States Military Academy
Photo courtesy of USMA Directorate of Communication Press Kit, Current Photos
United States Naval Academy
Photo courtesy of Michael Slonecker
University of Alabama
This photo is in the public domain
University of Arizona
Photo courtesy of Wikipedia (user Huperphuff)
University of California, Berkeley
Photo courtesy of Wikipedia (user brainchildvn)
University of California, Davis
Photo courtesy of Wikipedia (user Veritas117)
University of California, Irvine
This photo is in the public domain
University of California, Los Angeles
Photo courtesy of Wikipedia (user b r e n t)
University of California, Riverside
Photo courtesy of Wikipedia (user Amerique)
University of California, San Diego
Photo courtesy of Wikipedia (user Alex Hansen)
University of California, Santa Barbara
Photo courtesy of Wikipedia (user Carl Jantzen)
University of Chicago
Photo courtesy of Bryce Lanham
University of Colorado Boulder
This photo is in the public domain
University of Connecticut
Photo courtesy of The University of Connecticut
University of Delaware
Photo courtesy of University of Delaware
University of Florida
Photo courtesy of Wikipedia (user WillMcC)
University of Georgia
Photo courtesy of Wikipedia (user Chuck)

University of Illinois at Urbana-Champaign
This photo is in the public domain
University of Iowa
Photo courtesy of Wikipedia (user Cbenning)
University of Kansas
Photo courtesy of Wikipedia (user InaMaka)
University of Kentucky
Photo courtesy of Wikipedia (user J654567)
University of Massachusetts Amherst
Photo courtesy of John Phelan
University of Miami
This photo is in the public domain
University of Michigan
Photo courtesy of Wikipedia (user AndrewHorne)
University of Minnesota
Photo courtesy of Wikipedia (user Bsstu)
University of Mississippi
Photo courtesy of Wikipedia (user Matthiasb)
University of Nebraska-Lincoln
Photo courtesy of Wikipedia (user ensign_beedrill)
University of North Carolina at Chapel Hill
Photo courtesy of Caroline Culler
University of Notre Dame
Photo courtesy of Michael Fernandes
University of Oregon
This photo is in the public domain
University of Pennsylvania
Photo courtesy of Bryan Y.W. Shin
University of Pittsburgh
Photo courtesy of Michael G White
University of Richmond
This photo is in the public domain
University of Rochester
Photo courtesy of J. Adam Fenster, University of Rochester
University of Southern California
Photo courtesy of Wikipedia (user Padsquad)
University of Utah
Photo courtesy of Brian Davis
University of Tennessee
Photo courtesy of Jake Sumner, Creative Communications, University of Tennessee
University of Texas at Austin
This photo is in the public domain
University of Utah
Photo courtesy of Brian Davis
University of Vermont
Photo courtesy of Jared C. Benedict
University of Virginia
Photo courtesy of Wikipedia (user Patrickneil)
University of Washington
Photo courtesy of Dennis Wise
University of Wisconsin-Madison
This photo is in the public domain
University of Wyoming
Photo courtesy of Wikipedia (user Cqfx)
Valparaiso University
Photo courtesy of Valparaiso University
Vanderbilt University
This photo is in the public domain
Vassar College
Photo courtesy of Wikipedia (user Noteremote)
Villanova University
Photo courtesy of Wikipedia
Virginia Polytechnic Institute and State University
Photo courtesy of Wikipedia (user CBGator87)
Wake Forest University
This photo is in the public domain
Washington and Lee University
Photo courtesy of Wikipedia
Washington State University
Photo courtesy of Wikipedia (user Iidxplus)
Washington University in St Louis
This photo is in the public domain
Wellesley College
Photo courtesy of Wikipedia (user Jared and Corin)
Wesleyan University
Photo courtesy of Wikipedia (user Smartalic34)
Whitman College
Photo courtesy of Wikipedia (user Poecilia)
Williams College
Photo courtesy of Wikipedia (user SERSeanCrane)
Worcester Polytechnic Institute
This photo is in the public domain
Xavier University
Photo courtesy of Greg Rust, Xavier University
Yale University
Photo courtesy of Wikipedia

CHAPTER 12

Statistical Reliability of Our Methodology

Remarks on Our Statistical Methodology

The results in *The Alumni Factor* are almost all based on surveys taken by graduates of some of the finest colleges and universities across the country. Ideally, every single alumnus from every single school in the US would be included in our survey, but this is simply not possible – at least not yet. Fortunately, we can instead appeal to standard statistical methods to take a *sample* of alumni from the nation's best schools, and then make valid statistical conclusions based on that sample. In fact, over 42,000 alumni (a very significant sample size) answered our questionnaire, and they responded to a wide variety of interesting questions – on topics ranging from the strength of their friendships to current earning power to certain political leanings. A total sample of 42,000 is a very good start, and as we accumulate more and more data, we will be able to draw stronger conclusions involving more schools and more topical areas of interest.

Meanwhile, what do 42,000 observations buy in terms of the ability to assess alumni opinions of their schools? A great deal, it turns out. We designed our survey sampling scheme to obtain approximately 200 respondents from each school, spread out over a variety of majors and graduation years. In any sampling survey in which you wish to make statistically valid conclusions, the general rule is, the more observations, the better. For instance, it's a lot easier to determine whether or not a coin is fair if you flip it 1000 times instead of just two times. In any case, the sample sizes that we are dealing with in *The Alumni Factor* (42,000 in total and between 100 to 500 from each school) allow us to answer all of the interesting questions we pose with a reasonably high level of statistical confidence.

Let's look at a couple of typical examples. First of all, if we go to Figure 1.0, we find that 49.6% of the 42,000 sample respondents were in strong agreement with the statement "My College Developed Me Intellectually." Besides noting that about half of this particular sample put forth strong agreement to the statement, does the 49.6% figure tell us anything else? Yes – the beautiful thing about using statistics is that such a sample size allows us to generalize these findings to the *entire population* of college students (subject to some caveats we discuss below). In fact, using elementary statistics, we can also state with 95% confidence that the true proportion p of the alumni population that is in strong agreement with the statement is in the range:

$$0.496 - 1.96\,[0.496\,(1 - 0.496) / 42000]^{1/2} < p < 0.496 + 1.96\,[\,0.496\,(1 - 0.496) / 42000]^{1/2}$$

Put more simply, the true proportion is 49.6% +/– 0.5% upon simplification. The 0.5% is known as *sampling error*, and it informally represents our uncertainty with the results – 0.5% is not bad at all.

The reason we get such a small sampling error in the previous example is because we used a large sample size of 42,000 to formulate our confidence statement – the more observations, the better. But what happens if we use a smaller sample size, say a sample based on 200 respondents from a single school? For example, let's suppose that 57.0% of the 200 respondents from a certain school expressed strong agreement with the statement "My College Developed Me Intellectually." In this case, we can state with 95% confidence that the proportion *p* of the alumni population from College X that is in strong agreement with the statement is in the range:

$$0.57 - 1.96\,[0.57\,(1 - 0.57) / 200]^{1/2} < p < 0.57 + 1.96\,[0.57\,(1 - 0.57) / 200]^{1/2}$$

Or stated simply, 57.0% +/– 6.9%. This is a broader confidence range than before, a result of the fact that the sample size for this particular school (200) is much lower than the sample size for the entire survey (42,000). After all, having 42,000 observations at our disposal allows us to make much stronger conclusions than the case in which we have just 200 observations. Yet 200 observations are clearly enough to give a *reasonable* idea of where people at any school stand with respect to the statement in play. Every element of *The Alumni Factor* rankings has been subjected to this sort of rigorous statistical validation. Hence, readers can read with confidence, knowing *The Alumni Factor* data are sound.

David M. Goldsman, Ph.D.
Independent Advisor to The Alumni Factor
Statistician
Professor of Industrial & Systems Engineering
Stewart School of Industrial and Systems Engineering
Georgia Institute of Technology

The Alumni Factor
Index

A
Air Force Academy, United States *370, 371*
Alabama, University of *376, 377*
American University *136, 137*
Amherst College *138, 139*
Annapolis, United States Naval Academy *374, 375*
Arizona State University *140, 141*
Arizona, University of *378, 379*
Auburn University *142, 143*

B
Bard College *144, 145*
Bates College *146, 147*
Baylor University *148, 149*
Berkeley, University of California *380, 381*
Boston College *150, 151*
Boston University *152, 153*
Bowdoin College *154, 155*
Bradley University *156, 157*
Brandeis University *158, 159*
Brigham Young University *160, 161*
Brown University *162, 163*
Bryn Mawr College *164, 165*
Bucknell University *166, 167*

C
California, Berkeley, University of *380, 381*
California, Davis, University of *382, 383*
California Institute of Technology (Caltech) *168, 169*
California, Irvine, University of *384, 385*
California, Los Angeles, University of *386, 387*
California, Riverside, University of *388, 389*
California, San Diego, University of *390, 391*
California, Santa Barbara, University of *392, 393*
Carleton College *170, 171*
Carnegie Mellon University *172, 173*
Case Western Reserve University *174, 175*
Centre College *176, 177*
Chicago, University of *394, 395*
Claremont McKenna College *178, 179*
Clark University *180, 181*
Clemson University *182, 183*
Colby College *184, 185*
Colgate University *186, 187*
College of Charleston *188, 189*
College of New Jersey *190, 191*
College of the Holy Cross *192, 193*
College of William & Mary *194, 195*
Colorado Boulder, University of *396, 397*
Colorado College *196, 197*
Colorado State University *198, 199*
Columbia University *200, 201*
Connecticut College *202, 203*
Connecticut, University of *398, 399*
Cornell University *204, 205*
Creighton University *206, 207*

D
Dartmouth College *208, 209*
Davidson College *210, 211*
Davis, University of California *382, 383*
Delaware, University of *400, 401*
Denison University *212, 213*
DePaul University *214, 215*
DePauw University *216, 217*
Dickinson College *218, 219*
Drexel University *220, 221*
Duke University *222, 223*

E
Elon University *224, 225*
Emory University *226, 227*

F
Florida State University *228, 229*
Florida, University of *402, 403*
Franklin & Marshall College *230, 231*
Furman University *232, 233*

G
George Washington University *234, 235*
Georgetown University *236, 237*
Georgia Institute of Technology (Georgia Tech) *238, 239*
Georgia, University of *404, 405*
Gettysburg College *240, 241*
Gonzaga University *242, 243*
Grinnell College *244, 245*

H

Hamilton College *246, 247*
Harvard University *248, 249*
Harvey Mudd College *250, 251*
Haverford College *252, 253*
Holy Cross, College of the *192, 193*
Howard University *254, 255*

I

Illinois, University of *406, 407*
Indiana University Bloomington *256, 257*
Iowa State University *258, 259*
Iowa, University of *408, 409*
Irvine, University of California *384, 385*

J

James Madison University *260, 261*
Johns Hopkins University *262, 263*

K

Kansas State University *264, 265*
Kansas, University of *410, 411*
Kenyon College *266, 267*
Kentucky, University of *412, 413*

L

Lafayette College *268, 269*
Lehigh University *270, 271*
Los Angeles, University of California *386, 387*
Loyola Marymount University *272, 273*
Loyola University Chicago *274, 275*
Loyola University Maryland *276, 277*
Loyola University New Orleans *278, 279*

M

Macalester College *280, 281*
Marquette University *282, 283*
Massachusetts Institute of Technology *284, 285*
Massachusetts Amherst, University of *414, 415*
Miami University (OH) *286, 287*
Miami, University of (FL) *416, 417*
Michigan State University *288, 289*
Michigan, University of *418, 419*
Middlebury College *290, 291*
Military Academy, United States *372, 373*
Minnesota, University of *420, 421*
Mississippi, University of *422, 423*
MIT (Massachusetts Institute of Technology) *284, 285*
Morehouse College *292, 293*
Mount Holyoke College *294, 295*

N

Naval Academy, United States *374, 375*
Nebraska-Lincoln, University of *424, 425*
New Jersey, College of *190, 191*
New York University *296, 297*
North Carolina State University *298, 299*
North Carolina at Chapel Hill, University of *426, 427*
Northeastern University *300, 301*
Northwestern University *302, 303*
Notre Dame, University of *428, 429*

O

Oberlin College *304, 305*
Occidental College *306, 307*
Ohio Northern University *308, 309*
Ohio State University *310, 311*
Oregon State University *312, 313*
Oregon, University of *430, 431*

P

Pennsylvania State University *314, 315*
Pennsylvania, University of *432, 433*
Pepperdine University *316, 317*
Pittsburgh, University of *434, 435*
Pitzer College *318, 319*
Pomona College *320, 321*
Princeton University *322, 323*
Purdue University *324, 325*

R

Reed College *326, 327*
Rensselaer Polytechnic Institute *328, 329*
Rice University *330, 331*
Richmond, University of *436, 437*
Riverside, University of California *388, 389*
Rochester, University of *438, 439*
Rollins College *332, 333*
Rutgers University *334, 335*
RPI (Rensselaer Polytechnic Institute) *328, 329*

S

St. Olaf College *352, 353*
San Diego State University *336, 337*
San Diego, University of California *390, 391*
Santa Barbara, University of California *392, 393*
Santa Clara University *338, 339*
Scripps College *340, 341*
Sewanee: The University of the South *342, 343*
Skidmore College *344, 345*
Smith College *346, 347*
Southern California, University of *440, 441*

Southern Methodist University *348, 349*
Spelman College *350, 351*
Stanford University *354, 355*
Swarthmore College *356, 357*
Syracuse University *358, 359*

T

Tennessee, University of *442, 443*
Texas A&M University *360, 361*
Texas at Austin, University of *444, 445*
The College of New Jersey *190, 191*
The College of William & Mary *194, 195*
Trinity College *362, 363*
Trinity University *364, 365*
Tufts University *366, 367*
Tulane University *368, 369*

U

United States Air Force Academy *370, 371*
United States Military Academy (West Point) *372, 373*
United States Naval Academy (Annapolis) *374, 375*
University of Alabama *376, 377*
University of Arizona *378, 379*
University of California, Berkeley *380, 381*
University of California, Davis *382, 383*
University of California, Irvine *384, 385*
University of California, Los Angeles *386, 387*
University of California, Riverside *388, 389*
University of California, San Diego *390, 391*
University of California, Santa Barbara *392, 393*
University of Chicago *394, 395*
University of Colorado Boulder *396, 397*
University of Connecticut *398, 399*
University of Delaware *400, 401*
University of Florida *402, 403*
University of Georgia *404, 405*
University of Illinois at Urbana-Champaign *406, 407*
University of Iowa *408, 409*
University of Kansas *410, 411*
University of Kentucky *412, 413*
University of Massachusetts Amherst *414, 415*
University of Miami *416, 417*
University of Michigan *418, 419*
University of Minnesota *420, 421*
University of Mississippi *422, 423*
University of Nebraska-Lincoln *424, 425*
University of North Carolina at Chapel Hill *426, 427*
University of Notre Dame *428, 429*
University of Oregon *430, 431*
University of Pennsylvania *432, 433*
University of Pittsburgh *434, 435*
University of Richmond *436, 437*
University of Rochester *438, 439*
University of Southern California *440, 441*
University of Tennessee *442, 443*
University of Texas at Austin *444, 445*
University of Utah *446, 447*
University of Vermont *448, 449*
University of Virginia *450, 451*
University of Washington *452, 453*
University of Wisconsin-Madison *454, 455*
University of Wyoming *456, 457*
Utah, University of *446, 447*

V

Valparaiso University *458, 459*
Vanderbilt University *460, 461*
Vassar College *462, 463*
Vermont, University of *448, 449*
Villanova University *464, 465*
Virginia Polytechnic Institute and State University (VA Tech) *466, 467*
Virginia, University of *450, 451*

W

Wake Forest University *468, 469*
Washington and Lee University *470, 471*
Washington State University *472, 473*
Washington University in St. Louis *474, 475*
Washington, University of *452, 453*
Wellesley College *476, 477*
Wesleyan University *478, 479*
West Point, United States Military Academy *372, 373*
Whitman College *480, 481*
William & Mary, College of *194, 195*
Williams College *482, 483*
Wisconsin-Madison, University of *454, 455*
Worcester Polytechnic Institute (WPI) *484, 485*
Wyoming, University of *456, 457*

X

Xavier University *486, 487*

Y

Yale University *488, 489*